Father and Child

Father and Child

Developmental and Clinical Perspectives

Edited by

Stanley H. Cath, M.D.

Associate Clinical Professor of Psychiatry, Tufts University School of Medicine; Member, Boston Psychoanalytic Society; Medical Director, Family Advisory Service and Treatment Center; Founding Member, Boston Society for Gerontologic Psychiatry, Boston

Alan R. Gurwitt, M.D.

Associate Clinical Professor, Child Study Center, Yale University School of Medicine, New Haven, Connecticut; Member, Western New England Institute for Psychoanalysis, New Haven, Connecticut; Faculty, Hartford Child Psychiatry Consortium, Hartford, Connecticut

John Munder Ross, Ph.D.

Clinical Associate Professor of Psychiatry, State University of New York Downstate Medical Center College of Medicine, Brooklyn, New York; Adjunct Assistant Professor of Psychology in Psychiatry, Cornell University Medical College, New York City; Affiliate Member, American Psychoanalytic Association; Member, American Psychological Association, New York City

Little, Brown and Company
Boston

To our wives and children and parents, from whom we have learned the meanings of fatherhood

Contents

Contributing Authors

Richard N. Atkins, M.D.

Assistant Professor of Psychiatry, State University of New York, Downstate Medical Center College of Medicine, Brooklyn, New York; Clinical Assistant Professor of Social Work, Smith College, Northampton, Massachusetts; Fellow, American Academy of Psychoanalysis, New York City; Director of Training and Attending Psychiatrist, Division of Child and Adolescent Psychiatry, Kings County Hospital Center, Brooklyn, New York
Chapter 8

Sylvia Brody, Ph.D.

Visiting Adjunct Professor, Postdoctoral Program in Psychoanalysis and Psychotherapy, New York University; Associate, Center for Social Research, Graduate Center, City University of New York, New York City
Chapter 25

Claire Cath, M.Ed.

Tufts Family Support Program, New England Medical Center Hospital, Boston
Chapter 35

Stanley H. Cath, M.D.

Associate Clinical Professor of Psychiatry, Tufts University School of Medicine; Member, Boston Psychoanalytic Society; Medical Director, Family Advisory Service and Treatment Center; Founding Member, Boston Society for Gerontologic Psychiatry, Boston
Editor; Chapters 21, 22, 29

Calvin A. Colarusso, M.D.

Director of Child Psychiatry Fellowship, Associate Clinical Professor of Psychiatry, University of California, San Diego, School of Medicine, La Jolla, California; Training and Supervising Analyst in Child and Adult Analysis, and Director, San Diego Psychoanalytic Institute, San Diego, California
Chapter 20

John Demos

Professor of History, Brandeis University, Boston
Chapter 27

Aaron H. Esman, M.D.

Professor of Clinical Psychiatry, Cornell University Medical College; Member, New York Psychoanalytic Institute; Attending Psychiatrist, Payne Whitney Clinic, The New York Hospital, New York City

Chapter 17

Julian B. Ferholt, M.D.

Associate Clinical Professor of Pediatrics and Psychiatry, Yale University School of Medicine; Attending Physician, Pediatrics, Yale–New Haven Hospital, New Haven, Connecticut

Chapter 36

Eleanor Galenson, M.D.

Clinical Professor of Psychiatry, Mount Sinai School of Medicine of the City University of New York; Member, American Psychoanalytic Association; Attending Psychiatrist, The Mount Sinai Hospital, New York City

Chapter 9

Martin Greenberg, M.D.

Consulting Psychiatrist, Adolescent Unit, Kellogg Psychiatric Hospital, Corona, California; Private Practice, San Diego

Chapter 5

Stanley I. Greenspan, M.D.

Associate Clinical Professor of Psychiatry and Behavioral Science and Child Health, George Washington University School of Medicine and Health Sciences, Washington, D.C.; Chief, Mental Health Study Center, National Institute of Mental Health, Adelphi, Maryland

Chapter 7

Linda Gunsberg, Ph.D.

Private Practice; Member, American Psychological Association, New York City

Chapter 4

Alan R. Gurwitt, M.D.

Associate Clinical Professor, Child Study Center, Yale University School of Medicine, New Haven, Connecticut; Member, Western New England Institute for Psychoanalysis, New Haven, Connecticut; Faculty, Hartford Child Psychiatry Consortium, Hartford, Connecticut

Editor; Chapters 18, 36

James M. Herzog, M.D.

Assistant Professor of Psychiatry, Harvard Medical School; Member, American Psychoanalytic Association, New York City; Attending Psychiatrist and Director, Clinic for the Development of Young Children and Parents, The Children's Hospital Medical Center, Boston

Chapters 10, 19, 22

Sudhir Kakar, Ph.D.

Member, International Psychoanalytic Association; Senior Fellow, Center for the Study of Developing Societies, Delhi, India
Chapter 26

Irving Kaufman, M.D.

Clinical Instructor of Psychiatry, Harvard Medical School; Supervisor of Residents, Child Psychiatry, Gaebler Children's Hospital, McLean Hospital, Boston
Chapter 31

Joan B. Kelly, Ph.D.

Director, Northern California Mediation Center, Greenbrae, California
Chapter 28

Judith S. Kestenberg, M.D.

Clinical Professor of Psychiatry, New York University School of Medicine, New York City; Member, American Psychoanalytic Association, New York City; Attending Physician, Pediatric Psychiatry, Hillside–Long Island Jewish Hospital, New Hyde Park, New York; Co-Director, Center for Parents and Children, Child Development Research Center, Sands Point, New York
Chapter 13

Frank M. Lachmann, Ph.D.

Training Analyst, Senior Supervisor, Faculty Member, Postgraduate Center for Mental Health, New York City
Chapter 34

George F. Mahl, Ph.D.

Professor of Psychology, Departments of Psychology and Psychiatry, Yale University, New Haven, Connecticut
Chapter 3

Hershey Marcus, M.D.

Director, Fathers' Project, Child Development Research Center, Sands Point, New York
Chapter 13

Norman Morris, Ph.D.

Professor and Chairman, Department of Obstetrics and Gynaecology, Charing Cross Hospital and Medical School, London
Chapter 5

Robert A. Nemiroff, M.D.

Associate Clinical Professor of Psychiatry, University of California, San Diego, School of Medicine, La Jolla, California; Training and Supervising Analyst, San Diego Psychoanalytic Institute; Director, Residency Training Program, Department of Psychiatry, University of California Medical Center, San Diego, California
Chapter 20

Ana-Maria Rizzuto, M.D.

Clinical Professor of Psychiatry, Tufts University School of Medicine; Faculty Member, Psychoanalytic Institute of New England, East, Boston
Chapter 23

Herman Roiphe, M.D.

Associate Professor of Psychiatry, Mount Sinai School of Medicine of the City University of New York; Associate Attending Psychiatrist, The Mount Sinai Hospital, New York City
Chapter 9

John Munder Ross, Ph.D.

Clinical Associate Professor of Psychiatry, State University of New York Downstate Medical Center College of Medicine, Brooklyn, New York; Adjunct Assistant Professor of Psychology in Psychiatry, Cornell University Medical College, New York City; Affiliate Member, American Psychoanalytic Association; Member, American Psychological Association, New York City
Editor; Chapters 1, 2, 12, 15

Nathaniel Ross, M.D.

Clinical Professor Emeritus of Psychiatry, State University of New York Downstate Medical Center College of Medicine, Brooklyn, New York; Life Member, American Psychoanalytic Association, New York City
Chapter 33

Shera Samaraweera, M.D., D.P.M.

Associate Clinical Professor of Psychiatry, Tufts University School of Medicine; Staff Psychiatrist and Director, Tufts Family Support Program, New England Medical Center Hospital, Boston
Chapter 35

Charles A. Sarnoff, M.D.

Lecturer, Department of Psychiatry, Columbia University College of Physicians and Surgeons; Psychoanalyst, Psychoanalytic Institute of Columbia University College of Physicians and Surgeons, New York City
Chapter 16

Paul Schwaber, Ph.D.

Associate Professor of Letters, Wesleyan University, Middletown, Connecticut; Instructor and Clinical Associate, Western New England Institute for Psychoanalysis, New Haven, Connecticut
Chapter 24

Charles W. Socarides, M.D.

Clinical Professor of Psychiatry, Albert Einstein College of Medicine of Yeshiva University; Member, American Psychoanalytic Association; Attending Psychiatrist, Bronx Municipal Hospital Center, New York City
Chapter 32

K. Mark Sossin

*Doctoral Candidate in Clinical Psychology, Yeshiva University, New York City;
Early Childhood Therapist, Bronx-Lebanon Hospital Center, Bronx, New York;
Researcher, Child Development Research Center, Sands Point, New York*
Chapter 13

Brandt F. Steele, M.D.

*Professor Emeritus of Psychiatry, University of Colorado School of Medicine;
Member, American Psychoanalytic Association, New York City; Acting Director,
National Center for Prevention and Treatment of Child Abuse and Neglect,
University of Colorado Health Sciences Center, Denver, Colorado*
Chapter 30

Richard Stevenson, Jr.

*Doctoral Candidate in Clinical Psychology, Yeshiva University, New York City;
Psychology Extern, Roosevelt Hospital, New York City; Staff Member, Child
Development Research Center, Sands Point, New York*
Chapter 13

Robert D. Stolorow, Ph.D.

*Professor of Psychology, Ferkauf Graduate School, Yeshiva University; Visiting
Professor, Postdoctoral Program in Psychoanalysis, New York University, New
York City*
Chapter 34

Lora Heims Tessman, Ph.D.

*Clinical Psychologist, Psychiatric Service, Massachusetts Institute of Technology,
Cambridge, Massachusetts; Private Practice of Psychotherapy and Consultation,
Newton, Massachusetts*
Chapter 14

Phyllis Tyson, Ph.D.

*Candidate, San Diego Psychoanalytic Institute; Psychologist, Regional Center for
the Developmentally Disabled, Children's Hospital and Health Center, San
Diego, California*
Chapter 11

Judith S. Wallerstein, Ph.D.

*Senior Lecturer, School of Social Welfare, University of California at Berkeley,
Berkeley, California; Member, Association for Child Psychoanalysis; Executive
Director, Center for the Family in Transition, Corte Madera, California*
Chapter 28

Michael W. Yogman, M.D.

*Assistant Professor, Department of Pediatrics, Harvard Medical School; Associate
Chief, Child Development Unit, The Children's Hospital Medical Center, Boston*
Chapter 6

Preface

Some Recent History

A decade ago the psychological literature contained few pieces on fathers and fathering. The father was "the forgotten parent." Since then, the focus on fatherhood has intensified, with a proliferation of research studies on the subject. This newfound interest in a man's importance to his children can be attributed to a variety of recent, far-reaching developments.

Many social forces, including the women's movement, have stimulated a serious reevaluation of our existing notions about the gender roles of men and women. And not only has feminism entered into the *Zeitgeist* as an ideological influence on our thinking; it has had a concrete impact on many families, altering the distribution of occupational and domestic responsibilities. The work and family roles of men and women have been reconsidered and reorganized as more and more mothers turn to pursuits outside the home, thus inviting and requiring their husbands to become more active in childrearing, sometimes as coequal or even primary caretakers, as James Levine demonstrated in 1976.

The statistics for the late 1970s, for example, testify to dramatic shifts in what are so often taken for granted as traditional patterns in family life. Only 25 percent of families now conform to the stereotype of the working husband and housewife. The statistic that roughly one million children under 5 live with their fathers represents a significant increase over the findings of a decade ago. Divorce rates are also increasing, with more and more instances of joint or paternal custody of children.

For many men, then, fathering has come to entail far more than material provision and occasional superficial encounters with children. Being a father now is seen to carry with it a fuller, more profound, if also more everyday commitment to parenting, to fatherhood per se.

And yet the roles and functions specific to the male parent and those that can be reasonably shared with the mother are matters about which the experts in development know or at least have said relatively little. Lacking a basis for pinpointing a father's functions in the so-called traditional nuclear family, we are hard put to assess his place and impact in the new family structures that are now emerging.

Another set of influences derives from the intense and increasingly painstaking observations of infancy on the part of developmental and psychoanalytic investigators over the past 35 years (Spitz, Escalona, Provence, Murphy, Kestenberg, Mahler, along with Pine and Bergman, Bowlby, Brazelton, Stern, Lewis, and many others). Giving shape to a whole new clinical discipline, "infant psychiatry," these studies have brought into relief the subtle, complex, and dynamic emotional and cognitive transactions that take place between parents and child from the very beginning of life. For the most part, the practicalities and biases inherent in the research have precluded a systematic or long-term scrutiny of the male parent's interaction with his baby. One constraint, for example, is the fact that it is difficult to get men into the labs on a regular daily basis. For other reasons, too, many of them less tangible, fathers tend to be excluded from study (see Chap. 36). And thus most of this work has highlighted the need for the establishment of mother-infant attachment and the deep, powerful, and seemingly exclusive bond that can be cemented between mother and child. But even such an emphasis as this—on the "maternal dialogue," to borrow from Rene Spitz (1965), and the vital necessity of what Winnicott has called "good enough mothering"—has established a base for an examination of the father-child relationship. Our sensitivities and instruments have been honed, attuned to the role a man comes to play during the early years in modulating the intensity of the mother-child tie, inviting that child to become a separate individual in an ever-widening world (Chaps. 7, 10). Researchers have become more aware of the subtle exchanges of identity taking place and of the mother's *and* father's part in facilitating development, even as he or she as an adult parent also changes in response to the maturing child.

This last point touches on yet another source of the recent attention to the father. A general belief in and careful consideration of the continuous adult developmental process have recently led to a more specific appreciation of the evolution and dynamics of parenthood. In their 1970 pioneering volume *Parenthood*, editors Anthony and Benedek demonstrated convincingly that mothers and fathers grow with their children. How the parent negotiates the difficult tasks of procreation and child care will shape both the adult's sense of identity and the child's ability to contend with the powerful forces that impel him or her along the pathways of development. Parents bring their individual and collective pasts to their children, who in and of themselves lack a history yet find themselves quickly enough embedded in the parental universe (Chaps. 5, 18, 35). Once again, however, studying the "effects of the infant on its caretaker" has meant for the most part exploring the regressive preparations for motherhood and the impact of infants on the *women* who bear and rear them.

Finally, family theorists have begun to pay heed to the complex, interwoven relations that entwine parents and children. Although the father has been included in these studies, it is interesting that the problems isolated for deliberation have typically centered on his absence or ineffectuality rather than the nature and impact of his presence. Perhaps this and the other omissions noted arise through psychological and historical trends, some of which we will consider in this introduction and in later chapters of the work. The resistances to considering fathers and the health care professions' complicity in excluding them from family life are quite remarkable, their impact disturbing, and their causes as yet uncertain (Chap. 36).

And so within the last 10 years, developmental psychologists, pediatricians, and clinicians have been moved to begin studying fathers and babies (Chaps. 4, 6). For the most part, investigators have used the laboratory as their field of observation, quantifying behavior and, in this way, demonstrating the existence and intensity of an early "paternal dialogue" (e.g., the work of Lamb, Pedersen, Lewis, Kotelchuck, Parke, Sawin, and others). Convincing, provocative, and necessary, studies such as these are not sufficient, however. In our view, their accent on behavior alone has led these researchers to ignore at times the intricate inner worlds of parent and child.

This "representational world," as the analysts call it, is fraught with the ghosts of the past, images and apparitions that are all too real in their influence on everyday life, projected as they are onto living people who, especially as children, find their actions and emotions greeted in predetermined ways. This elusive inner life remains the particular contribution as well as the subject matter of the dynamic psychiatrist and psychologist. In our view, an understanding of a man's and a child's half-hidden imagery and experience will illuminate the more observable, behavioral aspects of fatherhood.

And this is where we, the psychoanalytically oriented clinicians, theorists, and researchers, may offer something new and different to the social science disciplines and the health care professions. We believe that the rich data available through psychoanalysis may provide a unique window on the evolution and vicissitudes throughout life of fatherhood and fathering from the perspectives of both parent and child. Our field, more than others, is sensitive to the emotional upheavals attending any developmental journey. That our particular school of thought (with rare exceptions) has not thus far systematically looked at fathers is astounding, betraying our own vulnerability to the unconscious forces of resistance (Chaps. 1, 2). This relative dearth of reflection on paternity is an old void crying to be filled.

Broader Perspectives and the Limits of Theory

At this point we should pause. The history just sketched is indeed a "recent history," and it, too, has its context. Talk of "traditional families and fathering" must be taken with a grain of salt. A man's dealings with his offspring have revealed great variations through the centuries. Family historians, beginning with Aries in his classic *Centuries of Childhood*, have for some time now noted the only recent sensitivity to the vulnerabilities of children as children and to the parent's more-or-less benevolent role in their sons' and daughters' passage to adulthood. At certain times in the past, Laius, Oedipus' cruelly absent and murderous father, may best have served as a paradigm of paternity. At other historical moments, fathers have been both more present and more benevolent (the two qualities seem bound together) as forces in their children's lives.

To construct a whole theory of fathers as instrumental patriarchs within traditional families, as some psychoanalysts and sociologists tend to do (Parsons, 1955), not only ignores the rapid changes in family life attending our current technological revolution; it further overlooks the broad historical and cultural context in which our own society is embedded (Chap. 27). Perhaps by recognizing the limited nature of the evidence from which our "ideal types" of families, fathers, and children are derived and by attempting at least to encompass a fuller range of individual development, we will better approximate the variety of relations between fathers and their progeny. At the very least we may be dissuaded from pat generalizations about what we take for granted as the inevitable and eternal.

When our authors speak of "the" man or "the" child, then, theirs is a heuristic conceit, a fiction, and should be understood in this vein. Historically, our theory is time-bound as well, reflecting both the realities and the value-laden impositions of the theorists' *Zeitgeist*. The danger exists that these unreal generalizations will be mistaken for norms or, worse still, for prescriptions and proscriptions. This would indeed be a grave error, doing violence to individual differences and historical relativity. Yet constructing theories requires yardsticks of some sort, whatever the disservice done to the infinite variety of a complex, dynamic, and continually evolving reality.

The Goal

At any rate, there is more to our fathers than the so-called oedipal father of Freud's primal horde, the figure who now pervades the current dynamic psychology. Freud himself sensed this when he singled out the death of a father as the most poignant event in a man's life (Chaps. 3, 22) and later underlined the need for a father's protection as the central childhood imperative, though he himself did not explore the nurturing and generative dimensions of fatherhood. We simply hope to make good some of these longstanding omissions by turning our authors' and readers' attention to the long dance that takes place between fathers and children throughout their lives, extending even beyond death.

In this spirit, then, out of our shared enthusiasm about the contributions of analytically oriented research, theory, and practice to an understanding of fathers and fathering, we have collected some of the leading thinkers in the field of child, adolescent, and adult development, both inside and outside psychoanalysis. We have invited them to engage in a series of reflections, anchored in the data of both empirical research and clinical practice, on the meaning of the father to his children, and the children to their father. We have further attempted to encompass the entire life cycle, isolating its critical eras, with subsequent attention to some of the sociocultural applications and variations of which we must remain cognizant, and, finally, to the implications of clinical intervention and prevention (Cath, 1962).

Some Personal Words

Before proceeding with our analytic enterprise, we would like to pause for a final moment to consider briefly John Irving's *The World According to Garp*. A book with an avid following, *Garp* has been heralded as a minor modern-day *Magic Mountain*, with its panoply of terminating lives and poignant deaths, and its sustained irony. Its self-conscious outrageousness, however, places it in a genre along with other new American fiction such as Doctorow's *Ragtime*. It is very much a book of our time— elegant, fresh, urgent, chaotic, and breathtaking.

Whatever the critical verdict, what is most significant about the novel for our purposes is its consistent and insistent focus on the hero's (Garp's) parenthood. There is, first of all, the parenting of him. His mother Jenny, hating men, copulates with a brain-damaged gunner, his functions reduced to erections, masturbation, and rapidly receding syllabification. The last erotic gasp of this erstwhile man leaves the son fatherless, entrusted to the sole tutorship of his mother, just as she planned it.

Then there is Garp the father. It is striking that Garp as a grown-up writer and "house husband" should himself parent his two sons with a vengeance, a protective zeal that borders on a special insanity and that leaves everybody vulnerable. The second "event" of the book, following a middle section which dwells on Garp's anxieties about his sons, is a bizarre and hideous automobile crash that kills one of the boys and maims the other. For this tragedy, Garp is not without responsibility and certainly not without guilt. The concluding pages chronicle the vicissitudes of Garp's now unspoken penance (at one point he finds himself robed as a transvestite) until he returns home to meet, at last, his own death.

And so there it is at last: the absent father; the exclusion of men from procreation and childrearing; the embracing of a maternal role in order to reinstate and relish the paternal prerogative; the silent and unwitting destruction of one's own children; and, one of the real-life tragedies that haunts us all, the death of a child. In this novel, as in other fictional accounts and memoirs (there is a growing number of autobiographical accounts by sons and daughters of their fathers—great and ordinary, wonderful and terrible), the critical themes of fatherhood seem to be more and more fully represented. The popular reception of a book and the resonance of its apparent whimsy with its readership are telling and do not owe themselves, we believe, to the author's artistry alone.

In the book, Garp the father chases down reckless drivers who endanger his neighborhood and his children (only later to kill and cripple them with his own car). One of this book's editors (the youngest of them and then the father of a 3-year-old boy) had found himself similarly violently indignant in guarding his family's territory. When he shared this fact with his coeditors, whose children had grown into adolescence and young adulthood (we are, interestingly, of three generations), they too recalled their own rage and fierceness in protecting their young from marauding automobiles—reactions that had subsided as their children became able to "watch out for themselves."

There is something elemental and instinctive in our fathering, then, which may challenge our powers of further analysis, transcending the specifics of an individual's development. In this instance, it is the territorial male's protectiveness that comes to our attention. Yet there is also the specter of Laius, and the grown man's fear of being supplanted and depleted by his own legacy, soon enough his rivals. Our colleagues in ethology inform us repeatedly of the male animal's inherent aggression toward his own offspring. It is to tensions such as these, that, in human experience, are not settled in predetermined ways at prescribed times—to the poignant and compelling paradoxes of fatherhood—that the ensuing volume is dedicated.

John Munder Ross
Alan R. Gurwitt
Stanley H. Cath

Acknowledgments

We wish to express our gratitude to the many people who have assisted in the preparation of this book: to Dr. Judith Kestenberg, who brought the three of us together and helped launch our cooperative efforts; to Dr. Arnold Cooper and Miss Ellen Fertig of the American Psychoanalytic Association, who made possible the establishment of an ongoing discussion group on Issues in Paternity that has been an important source and forum; to Martha Stuart, Claire and Sandra Cath, Nissa Simon, Katherine Ball Ross, and Natalie Altman, who in a variety of ways helped shape the book's form and substance; to the Family Advisory Service of Belmont, the Children's Clinic of The Institute of Living, especially its director, Dr. Paul N. Graffagnino, and the Division of Child and Adolescent Psychiatry at Downstate Medical Center, especially its training director, Dr. Richard Atkins, for the time and encouragement they and their staffs offered when carrying out our tasks; and to Dr. Albert J. Solnit of the Yale Child Study Center for his continued interest in this endeavor.

Ingrid Baumgartner assisted us greatly by typing and retyping much of the manuscript, as well as managing the complex task of keeping track of multiple people and materials, with patience and steadiness. Her husband, David Baumgartner, provided extremely helpful editing and suggestions.

Jean Brown, Joan Collins, Jean Detiere, Lois Golliher, and Nancy Hickey provided valuable secretarial assistance.

Fred Belliveau, Elizabeth Welch, and Joyce Connell of Little, Brown and Company have been wonderfully tactful and patient in guiding us through the various stages of creating and preparing this book.

Our families have had to spend many weekends and some vacation time without us, to the point of our personal concern about the effects of absent fathers, but have always understood, helped, and encouraged.

S. H. C.
A. R. G.
J. M. R.

Father and Child

I

History and Review

We turn first to a survey of the professional literature on fathers. The first two chapters by John Munder Ross, one of the volume's editors, chronicle existing psychoanalytic and related efforts to unearth the ontogenetic roots of psychological fatherhood and to consider the impact of fathering. Next, George Mahl's analysis of Freud's dreams serves to reveal the more personal origins of psychoanalysis as a father-son psychology. Linda Gunsberg then surveys the psychological literature on fathers and children in a review that is condensed yet, we hope, representative.

These introductory chapters are fairly straightforward in their content and intent. Only a few editorial emphases seem to be in order. The exclusion of the father from the procreative process by analytic theorists, as noted by Ross, may require further editorial underscoring. It also needs to be emphasized that Linda Gunsberg's has been a Herculean labor, which she has distilled into a selective rather than exhaustive review of the so-called empirical literature. George Mahl's disciplined and scrupulous analysis of early Freud is very much his own. His assertion about the lack of fear of the father in the manifest content of and associations to the dreams may meet with skepticism on the part of certain analysts. Nonetheless, the facts, no matter how they are considered, do speak for themselves.

1

The Roots of Fatherhood:
Excursions into a Lost Literature

John Munder Ross

In phantasy he was a mother and wanted children with whom he could repeat the endearments that he had experienced himself.
Sigmund Freud (1909a, p. 93)

Psychoanalysts have recently reevaluated their notions about the development of female sexual identity. Within the feminine *Zeitgeist*, both their newer efforts and the early foreshadowing of these (the work of Karen Horney, for example) have been highlighted.

They have been slower to reconsider the parallel progression in boys. Such contributions as do exist on the more problematic aspects of male sexual identity have receded all too quickly into the shadows of the past. For reasons of resistance perhaps, the analytic community has continued to embrace Freud's first hypotheses about a boy's progress toward manhood, all but forgetting the alternative views of many of his disciples and contemporaries.

Yet boys share with girls the prototypical life task of disengaging from their mother while assimilating many of her mediating functions. And their senses of sexuality and selfhood are therefore inevitably equally complex. The ambiguities and ambivalences that comprise a male's sexual identity, which are interwoven with the theme of an emergent parenthood, have been and must continue to be addressed.

In the first of two review chapters I shall survey psychoanalytic contributions on the childbearing and childrearing fantasies and attitudes in boys and men (cf. Jaffe, 1968) and on the precursors of paternal identity. Against this backdrop, I will later turn to the theory's more scattered offerings regarding a real-life father's role in his children's development.

This chapter is a revised and abridged version of a previous contribution, The development of paternal identity: A critical review of the literature on nurturance and generativity in boys and men, *J. Am. Psychoanal. Assoc.* 23:783–817, 1975.

The work for this chapter was in part funded by the U.S. Department of Health and Human Services, Grant No. MH 05816, sponsored by the Department of Psychiatry, Downstate Medical Center, Brooklyn, New York.

Oedipal Reversal and Regression: Freud's Contributions

Freud's sporadic discussions of procreative and caretaking aspirations in boys and men generally reflect the early preoccupation of psychoanalysis with the libido theory and the oedipal complex. In retrospect, however, many of his speculations seem prophetic, well in advance of his own general theory.

In his major treatise on sexuality, *Three Essays* (1905b), Freud scrutinized the efforts of all children to solve "the Riddle of the Sphinx." He conjectured that, distorted though they may be, childish birth theories nonetheless contain at least "a germ of truth," attributable to their "origin in the components of the sexual instinct already active in the childish organism." Instinctual urges provide a basis for intuitive knowledge.

Freud (1908, pp. 219–220) suggested that children's so-called cloacal theories of birth, equating genital and excretory organs and functions, spring from anal urges, the boy's myth of the universal penis, and, implicitly, his envy of maternal power:

> It was only logical that the child should refuse to grant women the *painful prerogative of giving birth to children*. If babies are born through the anus, then a man might give birth just as well as a woman . . . a boy can therefore imagine that he, too, has children of his own, without there being any need to accuse him . . . of feminine inclinations. He is merely giving evidence . . . of the anal eroticism which is still alive within him (emphasis added).

Freud's first explicit discussion of reproductive *wishes* (in contrast to theories) on the part of little boys occurs in his first and only case history of a little boy—the analysis by paternal proxy of 5-year-old Little Hans (1909a). Hans came to imagine that he, a boy, could bear and care for babies; he theorized, plausibly enough, that little babies were born like *lumf*, thus dissolving distinctions of gender. Freud ascribed all of this essentially to the young boy's typical ignorance of the female genitals, and to his convoluted oedipal ambitions.

He highlighted the ambivalence with which Hans entertained his wish for a child. Freud discerned in the child's young mind a contradiction which "was one between fantasy and reality, between wishing and having. Hans knew that in reality he was a child and that other children would only be in his way; but in phantasy he was a mother and wanted children with whom he could repeat the endearments that he had himself experienced" (p. 93).

Freud depicted a transformation in Hans's phobia. At first the boy was afraid of being bitten by horses. Subsequently he dreaded their falling down and making a "row with their feet," just as he did when seated on the potty to deliver *lumf*. Freud interpreted the falling horse as representing not only Hans's dying rival father, killed by him, but also his mother in childbirth. Stimulated by the great riddle as to the origin of babies, the boy could refer only to his own bodily, sensorimotor experience to solve the problem. Thus, he discovered in the sensation of pleasure that accompanied evacuation an analogue to "the pleasure of giving birth to babies and the pleasure (compensatory, as it were) of looking after them" (p. 133). From what Hans had seen of it, however, sex seemed a kind of violence and the father's role a sadistic one; therefore, he also wondered "whether the mother liked having babies or was compelled to."

The boy's fantasy of having a baby came to entail impregnation and penetration by an adult male. He fantasized being bored open by a plumber while seated in his bath. This "material . . . far outstripped our powers of understanding. . . . It was not until later that it was interpreted as a remoulding of a *phantasy of procreation* distorted by anxiety" (pp. 127–128). And thus Freud remarked on every little boy's erotic interest in the father, which would later be deemed the "negative Oedipus complex" (Freud, 1923a).

Indeed, despite the child's, and Freud's, protestations, his parents kept him ignorant of the mechanics of reproduction and in this way forced him to submit to consensual denial. At the close of his analysis, Hans thus turned to powers other than his own. Here, as with the child's sexual researches, Freud's own "inquiry broke off," leaving the threads of his analysis hanging. At times he verged on later analytic concepts, such as the negative Oedipus complex, the transitional object, the transmuting internalizations of the mother's soothing function, and envy of her power. Without a theory of the preoedipal relation of mother and child, however, Freud could not pursue these ideas. Besides, in 1909 he had enough of a task before him in illustrating his new-found negative oedipal complex.

Two years later, in his study of Schreber's memoirs, Freud (1911) did try to explain at length the dynamics of one man's wish to bear children. This time, however, his focus on the etiology of paranoia in general, compounded by the bizarre character of the subject's psychosis in particular, may have led him to underplay the "positive," age-appropriate aspects of such wishes when evident in younger subjects like Hans or their inevitability as unconscious wishes in more normal adults.

Schreber was convinced that he was being transformed into a woman in order to become God's wife and give birth to a whole new race of men. "Homosexual libido," Freud inferred, constituted "the exciting cause of the illness" (p. 43). God was none other than Schreber's own godlike father, whom he both loved and hated. The father's death intensified

Schreber's castration anxiety, which in turn fostered the idea of becoming a woman. Schreber's fear of attack reflected a desire to be penetrated, a secret wish that fed a full-blown delusion of grandeur, serving to justify his suspicions and to express as well as compensate for his underlying sense of emasculation.

The delusion further offered an "escape from childlessness." It was not the barrenness in itself, but rather the fact that Schreber had "no son to drain off his homosexual libido" that Freud saw as most disquieting, touching for a moment on the potentially pathogenic aspects of adult development and on the adaptive functions of fatherhood. Recoiling from a fruitless marriage, Schreber secretly, narcissistically, unconsciously took on as lovers his father, his brother, his physician, and finally himself, all of them men possessed of a penis. Thus, Schreber's procreative ambitions bespoke a supreme if unsublimated secondary narcissism (Freud, 1914, 1923a) and a defensive maneuver against the fear of castration.

In 1916 Freud generalized his views about childbearing fantasies in children, summarizing what he saw as the differences between the sexes. The girl's discovery of the penis, he theorized, results in envy of it, which is then transformed into desire for a man as the owner of a penis; whereas in boys, the equation is made when (p. 133):

The boy's sexual researches lead him to the discovery of the absence of the penis in women. He concludes that the penis must be a detachable part of the body, something analogous to feces, the first piece of bodily substance the child has to part with. Thus the old anal defiance enters into the composition of the castration complex . . . . When a baby appears on the scene he regards it as "lumf" . . . . The function of the penis (in making it) is not usually discovered.

Thus Freud underscores "bisexual" elements on the part of both sexes in their yearning for a baby (Brunswick, 1940) and their initial ignorance of the man's procreative role. For the "passive" girl, the fantasy fulfills essentially phallic strivings; for the more "active" boy, having a baby harkens back to feces "given up" passively during his anal phase.

In 1918, in the case of the Wolf Man (1918a), Freud linked a boy's wish for a child to a self-emasculation that invited the father's love and not his retribution. He touched briefly on a boy's aspiration to his mother's maternal power per se, although the development of his envy of and identification with her once again escaped consideration.

Freud did not substantially amend his notions until Ruth Mack Brunswick's paper on the preoedipal era (1940), which, avowedly written in collaboration with him, may possibly be taken as an extension of his own ideas. The author(s) postulated a progression from "activity" and "passivity" to "phallic" and "castrated," and finally to "masculine" and "feminine," taking a more traditional perspective than that of many of their contemporaries. However, they also posited an age-appropriate wish for a baby on the part of young boys, a desire that is initially "asexual" and stems from their normal, virtually universal identification with the mother. Like a girl, a boy wants to emulate his mother in having a baby; indeed he hopes to get an infant *from* her. At first, his wish is passive, a longing to "be given to," but during the phallic phase this yearning gives way to an active striving to present the mother with a child. A boy now suppresses his passivity in consolidating his identification with the father in the service of his "masculine" ambitions (Lampl-de-Groot, 1947). Rather different from the early notions just sketched, these ideas presaged those of subsequent analysts on the childhood sources of a man's wish to become a father.

Many analysts followed in Freud's footsteps, emphasizing, among other phenomena, the male's myth of the "universal penis" and its manifestations in perversions (Lorand, 1939; Greenacre, 1955; Socarides, 1960, 1970; Bak, 1968); birth fantasies and rivalry (Ross, 1960); unconscious pregnancy fantasies (Eisler, 1921; Aronson, 1952); the etiological role of such fantasies in pathology other than homosexuality or transvestitism (Deutsch, 1929; Blos, 1957); pregnancy wishes in treatment (Rose, 1962, 1969); their resurgence in myths about the father's reproductive role or tribal customs such as couvade (Reik, 1946; Röheim, 1950); and the sublimation of thwarted urges to inseminate oneself in creativity (e.g., Kris, 1952).

Envy of the Power of Mother: A Growing Recognition

In *Thalassa* (1924), Freud's closest disciple, Sandor Ferenczi, discerned in intercourse an "amphimixis" whereby many pregenital aims coalesced and were satisfied simultaneously. This was, he asserted, especially true for the man, who might "return to the womb" of his ontogenetic origins, and indeed to the great seas of the distant phylogenetic past. In the absence of clinical or developmental anchorage, these trains of thought could be regarded only as unscientific, and Freud did indeed dismiss even his beloved Ferenczi's conjectures as so much "paleo-biological speculation" (Freud, 1918a), flights of fantasy reminiscent of his more rebellious erstwhile adherents Jung and Rank.

Yet, by the 1920s other analysts had begun to question the primacy of both the libidinal drive and the oedipal complex. These authors had not speculated beyond the clinical evidence within their purview, and so their notions could not be so easily discarded. Moreover, their search for other

7

moving forces and increasing interest in earlier developmental crises led them to consider birth and childrearing wishes in both men and women. Karl Abraham (1925), for example, also a close colleague of Freud's, described a male patient who believed that either spittle passes from the father's mouth into the mother's to make a baby, or else the infant is somehow osmosed from his breast to hers. Abraham inferred the presence of "breast envy," which in its turn made for an unconscious equation in his patient's mind between breast and penis and for the myth that women were possessed of an especially large phallus. Decrying the "phallocentric bias" of psychoanalysis, Freud's official biographer, Ernest Jones (1927, 1933), pointed to many dimensions in the male's reactions to parturition, among them the fear of castration so evident in Little Hans (indeed of loss in general) and an envy of the mother's creative power.

Of all the analysts of this era (Groddeck, 1924), however, it was Karen Horney (1924, 1932, 1933) who laid the greatest stress on a son's awe of his mother. Horney found clinical merit in Ferenczi's amphimixis and derived for both sexes the implications of Abraham's ideas (1920) about penis envy in the girl.

Horney underscored a boy's "dread of woman." It is not, however, his fear for his penis that is so disturbing, but rather his "wishes to be a woman," strong and succoring, just like his mother. Only with the phallic phase are "feminine" or "maternal" urges labeled as such, equated with castration, and repressed, if only to resurface in other guises. Among these is that ominous reversal, men's degradation of women, a misogyny that buttresses a "whole sociology of male superiority." Behind men's subjugation of women there lies, then, their intense longing to be with and to be like mother, to share her power, both to be and to have her child.

A focus on destructive aggression led Melanie Klein (1921, 1923, 1927, 1933, 1957; Klein and Riviere, 1937) to underline a child's envy of "the giving mother." Klein noted that a man may attempt to satisfy unfulfilled womanly cravings by obtaining for himself a good relationship with a woman. Fathering her child and identifying himself with child and mother at once, he can assuage his archaic desire to possess his mother's breast and the magical powers exclusive to women, thus "completing himself" (Kubie, 1974).

In 1930, Felix Boehm described the "femininity complex in men." Like Horney, Boehm (p. 456) held that

Distaste by many men for everything feminine arises out of the wish to be a woman . . . . The impression conveyed by parturition is one of the activity—*the expulsion of the child from the body seems a stronger evidence of potency than erection.* All men find it overwhelming when they see for the first time the baby's head appearing from the vagina. Envy of the woman's capacity to bear children is a considerable incentive for the capacity for production in men (emphasis added).

Boehm continued, "The male is first of all a little girl, then, when little by little he has mastered his castration anxiety, he becomes a man" (p. 466). This notion, which parallels those of Freud's regarding the little girl, stands in contrast to more recent studies of the early unfolding of core gender identity (Stoller, 1968, 1975). Nonetheless, Boehm's ideas were revolutionary. Like Horney, he challenged Freud's "male chauvinism" when he suggested that older boys may regress to the "feminine phase" but, in terror of emasculation, hide their desire for woman's maternal resources, womb and breasts, behind a facade of misogyny.

Ego Psychology and the Mother in Every Man

Boehm did not emphasize aggression, envy, urges to power, and domination to the extent that Horney and Klein did in the sort of conceptualizations that eventually led both away from traditional psychoanalysis to general theories of their own. However, like those of Horney and Klein, Boehm's paper does reflect the theoretical limitations of its time. For one thing, analysts did not yet appreciate fully a child's efforts at mastery, at a reversal of voice in relation to his or her parents. Authors of this period might possibly underscore a boy's admiration of childbearing as a single maternal act, but they would tend not to highlight this ongoing experience of the mother's active childrearing and his consequent efforts to take care of himself. For another, even if they did recognize a child's emulation of maternal nurturance, these theorists tended to exaggerate the aggressive dimensions of urges to have at one's own disposal the mother's ability to give or withhold at will.

What was required was the broader perspective offered by a "developmental ego psychology." From this vantage point, a child's tendencies toward activity in general and his progressive incorporation and internalization of love objects—the images of his caretakers—would be singled out as guiding and organizing principles crucial to a little boy's emerging attempts to master and to take care of himself. Desires to have and tend babies of one's own could then be seen in light of the processes of identification, as expressions not only of instinctual urges but also of more general, purposeful, age-specific, and adaptive *goals* (Hartmann, 1939).

With these shifts of focus, psychoanalysts also questioned the societal stereotypes plaguing their theory of sexual identity. Indeed, the germs of the revision may be discovered as early as 1923, in Freud's own reassessment of the oedipal complex within the context of his nascent structural id, ego, superego theory (1923a). He described how lost and abandoned parental objects continue to be replaced by identifications which accrue to build ego "character," or "identity" (Erikson, 1950). Thus, Freud came to consider not only the constitutional but also the experiential underpinnings of "bisexuality." Describing the formation of the "ego ideal" at the close of the oedipal era, he concluded that "the broad general outcome of the sexual phase dominated by the Oedipus complex may . . . be taken to be the forming of a precipitate in the ego, consisting of these two identifications [with father and mother] *in some way united with each other*" (p. 34, emphasis added).

The exact nature of such a "union" at a stage when so much of the ego's "character" has already been structured (as is now recognized), and when "core gender identity" has been clearly consolidated (Stoller, 1968, 1973), appears subtle and problematic, and its manifestations not transparent (Erikson, 1950, pp. 258–259; 1964).

But, in the meantime, Freud's new overview at least helped spur critical reexaminations of male sexual identity (Bryan, 1930; Rado, 1940). By the 1940s, Erich Fromm (1943) and Gregory Zilboorg (1944) had become eloquently skeptical of the lines presumed to run from activity to masculinity and from passivity to femininity. Fromm highlighted "the fact that woman has the capacity of natural reproduction which man is lacking. . . . Somewhere in man exists an awe of woman for this capacity. . . . He is envious and fearful of it. . . . [Also present] in woman [is] a feeling of superiority over him" (1943, p. 29). Zilboorg decried Freud's "androcentric bias" and the cliché, prevalent in Western culture and propagated by psychoanalysis, that woman is somehow inferior. Such notions serve to obscure man's envy of woman, which lies at the heart of his depreciation of her. Like other products of social institutions and myths that legitimize them, the psychoanalytic idea of a basically "masculine libido" (Freud, 1905b) defies nature's facts. Yet these truths will surface, for "despite all his economic and sadistic and phallic superiority, man could not fail to discover that the woman . . . still possessed a unique power over mankind. She could produce children who always clung to her, who loved her without stint" (Zilboorg, 1944, p. 288).

No doubt many of these authors, notably Klein, Horney, and Fromm, were mavericks who became peripheral to classical psychoanalysis and its later ego psychology; however, their influence was destined to be felt within the field, with many of their assertions later vindicated by responsible research on sexual identity (A. Bell, 1968; Stoller, 1968, 1973; Clower, 1970). In fact, their indirect impact was evident in

1950, in pioneer ego psychologist Edith Jacobson's groundbreaking paper, "Development of the Wish for a Child in Boys."

Jacobson had charted the maternal progression of girls as early as 1939. A girl's fantasies of orally incorporating the mother and of being reborn arise earlier than her wish for a penis: The "breast baby" predates the "penis baby." Subsequently, during the phallic phase, a girl's maternal urges intensify, whereas a boy's identification with his father triumphs over his "homosexual" desires for him. A girl's longings for a penis and a boy's for a baby must both be sacrificed in the service of solidifying gender identity.

Nevertheless, for a boy, the wish for a child, accompanied by identification with the mother, may become revivified if at the height of his castration anxiety during the phallic phase a younger sibling is born. Indeed, this circumstance characterizes the life history of many creative men, implying that one motive for productivity is the desire to make children (Kris, 1952; Nelson, 1956).

Jacobson (1950) conjectured about generativity in adult men: "The absence of longing for children in men until they approach marriage is also due to firm defenses against their envy of women's reproductive function" (p. 144). She went on to suggest that psychoanalysts' persistent failure to exhume and illumine the maternal elements in men may intimate some bona fide resistance to similar unconscious fantasies on the part of male analysts themselves.

Fear of death and a sense of life's shortness militate against commitment and intimacy, even though a man may anticipate his "narcissistic" survival and the embodiment of his own self-ideal in the children he hopes to father. In reality, however, the actual birth of his babies tends to temper these competing infantile needs. Fatherhood may evoke a paternal love on a man's part which resonates with a productive identification with his own father, who now replaces his mother as the nurturing and creative figure to whom he can liken himself. Thus, an assumption of the father's role in reproduction and relation to caretaking helps an adult man come to terms with his hitherto repressed and disquieting "maternal" desires.

A number of related articles followed Jacobson's (Evans, 1951; Heimann, 1952; Simenauer, 1954; Kleeman, 1966). The most far-reaching were psychohistorian Erik Erikson's discussions of productivity and ego identity. Despite his beginnings as a child analyst, Erikson, who first opened up the entire life cycle to psychoanalytic reflection, said rather little about foreshadowings of mature desires to produce children, reserving most of his remarks for a sense of "generativity" and "care" age-specific to young and middle adulthood (1950, 1964). Nevertheless, in the opening pages of *Childhood and Society* (1950), he did relate the case of Peter, a boy bloated with retained feces because of an unconscious pregnancy fantasy. Erikson pointed to the importance of identification as a means of retaining or recovering a lost caretaker. The child in question, he wrote, "identified with both partners of a lost relationship. He is like the nurse (a now-absent mother surrogate) who is now with child, and he is the baby whom she likes to tend. Identifications which result from losses are like that" (p. 58).

Although he has not dwelled on fantasies such as these, the entire import of Erikson's early work relates to the very issues they express. For example, the thrust toward industry that Erikson deems central to middle childhood is at least partly fueled by frustrated strivings to assume generative and generational authority. "Before the child, psychologically already a rudimentary parent, can become a biological parent, he must begin to be a worker and potential provider. With the oncoming latency period, the normally advanced child . . . sublimates the necessity to 'make' people . . . or to become mama and papa . . . he now learns to win recognition by producing things" (1950b, pp. 258–259; see also Freud, 1923a). Manifestations of the union that Freud hypothesized in 1923 thus become clearer. Parental ambitions and sexual dualities move a child to assume his generational authority, further transforming his psychosexual and, more broadly, psychosocial identity.

Twenty years later, Erikson (1969) described at length the maternal man of power par excellence, India's Gandhi, within whom resided simultaneously "autocratic malehood and enveloping maternalism." Erikson discerned in him an augury of men to come, the ultimate devaluation of the "martial model of masculinity." Stripped of weaponry yet authoritative beyond compare, Gandhi revealed sublimely just how a "sublimated motherhood" might become integral to "the positive identity of a whole man."

Other anthropologists and analysts began to focus on the universality of maternal undercurrents in the psychosocial identity of boys and men everywhere (Reik, 1946; Mead, 1949; Wolff, 1950; Rangell, 1953a). Following these leads, Bruno Bettelheim (1954), famed for his treatment of deeply disturbed children, surveyed initiation rites in preliterate societies. He argued that Freud (1912) had too hastily ascribed mutilation of the initiates' genitals to a castration threat by a culture's collective fatherhood. Psychoanalysts had been "too engrossed with what seems to be destruction . . . and . . . overlooked the more hidden fascination with pregnancy and birth. . . . Certain initiation rites originate in the adolescent's attempts to integrate his envy of the other sex or (conversely) to adjust to the social role prescribed for his sex and give up pregnancy wishes, and childhood gratifications" (p. 25).

Among the most aboriginal groups, a boy's penis may be subincised, rather than circumcised, so that he must thereafter urinate in a squatting position, in which case it may then be referred to as a "vulva" or "penis womb." Or male genitals may be lacerated in imitation of menstrual bleeding. In contrast, circumcision is an excision of skin like the labia, an eradication of emblems of feminine trends acceptable only during childhood (Nunberg, 1947; Bird, 1958).

Important, too, are the ceremonial reenactments of childbirth in initiation rites. The envious older men claim that the initiated boys are reborn by them. Women are excluded to delude them into believing that males possess procreative powers *greater* than theirs.

For peoples who do not recognize the connection between intercourse and reproduction, the man's inability to give birth remains a cruel fact of life. Women are adored as the divine and exclusive agents of creation, and men take pains, as it were, to persuade themselves that they too possess the wherewithal to foster new life. In societies cognizant of the man's procreative role, manhood may become aggrandized beyond measure; penis and semen become objects of adulation.

Other analysts underscored the significance of what might be called both self-generative and "ambisexual" strivings. However, in emphasizing exclusively the urges or drives involved, such efforts paid little heed to the significance of those internalizations whereby representations of love objects are transmuted into multifaceted identifications that foster autonomy (Freud, 1923a; Hartmann, 1939). Nevertheless, wild as some of these later speculations may have been (Fodor, 1948), like those of Rank or Ferenczi, they did indeed contain truths which, unheralded, may have inspired more conceptually and experientially grounded hypotheses about sexual identity during the later 1950s and 1960s.

The reanalysis of Schreber by MacAlpine and Hunter (1954, 1955) was more convincing than most (Kubie, 1974). The authors agreed with Freud that Schreber's childlessness precipitated his psychosis. Rather than emphasizing homosexual urges, however, they viewed the judge's delusional "parthenogenesis" and vision of himself as the "sole survivor to renew mankind" as a struggle to transcend mortality. MacAlpine and Hunter then extravagantly declared that parthenogenetic fantasies underlie all severe psychopathology.

Developmental Contributions

Once again a more solid conceptual and empirical platform was needed from which to oversee these yearnings. Such was the impact of these major theoretical advances, tied as they were to careful observations of babies and toddlers. These contributions served to concretize Freud's hitherto abstract conjectures about two transmuting processes: (1) the transformation of beloved objects into identifications subsequently loved and valued as part of the self; and (2) the but gradual demarcation of self and object.

René Spitz, studying normal and institutionalized infants, demonstrated the vital necessity of "mother love" and of the anaclitic or dependent relationship with mother (1945, 1946). Subsequently he pinpointed the signs of recognition, attachment, and gradual differentiation whereby the child takes from the mother the emotional sustenance with which to organize his own autonomous self (Spitz, 1965).

Donald Winnicott (1953, 1957, 1958), the great English pediatrician and psychoanalyst, pointed to the virtual universality of what he called transitional objects and transitional phenomena. In the so-called security blanket and related self-soothing objects and activities, he discerned the infant's and later the toddler's efforts to detach himself from the mother by representing himself in relation to her. In so doing, the child also begins to differentiate reality from fantasy—retaining the illusion of his mother's presence while realizing, in his compensatory or crudely defensive activity, his separateness and difference from her.

Margaret Mahler, with her concepts of symbiosis and separation-individuation (Mahler and Furer, 1968; Mahler, Pine, and Bergman, 1975) implicitly integrated these findings with Jacobson's conceptions of self- and object representations (1964) and Erikson's formulations of the early stages of ego-identity formation (1950, 1959, 1964). It is significant that in 1975 Mahler came to dub the evolution she described, a progression central to preoedipal development as a whole, the "psychological birth of the human infant." Moved by such an aphorism, one might search for the rudimentary symbolic acts by which a child externalizes and represents *to* the self the mysterious changes taking place *within* the self.

Stages in Parental Identity

During the 1950s, 1960s, and 1970s, Judith Kestenberg attempted to do just that. Underlining the ramifications of somatic sensation and movement, she set forth an overview of *successive* childbearing and childrearing urges and aspirations in children.

Kestenberg pursued the implications of the psychosexual modalities inherent in inner and outer anatomical space (1956a,b, 1968; Erikson, 1950, 1968). Both sexes, she hypothesized, pass through a prephallic "inner genital stage." They may reveal a psychic equation: woman equals inside equals vagina equals uterus equals baby equals doll. Eventually a male will project this reproductive constellation and the representations of self associated with it onto a woman as a love object. Partly to compensate for his own insufficiency in this regard (Kubie, 1974), he will then seek after her. Male and female alike retain the fantasy of making babies, until, in a boy, "the phase of identification with the preoedipal mother is terminated by denial of femininity, renunciation of the wish for a live baby, and repudiation of the inside as babyish and feminine" (Kestenberg, 1968, pp. 505–506).

In 1971, Kestenberg discussed disturbances in sexual identity that may arise out of conflicts during the inner genital phase. These conflicts may lead in adult life to splitting off of reproductive and coital urges and a renunciation of parenthood. Certain individuals, men especially, apathetic in barrenness, may fabricate a mere "pseudosexual identity."

The concept of the inner genital phase and the attendant upsurge of maternal feelings that flood the psychological life of boys and girls alike, postulated by Kestenberg, may be seen both to parallel and to dethrone phallic primacy and penis envy. If girls have no penis, one learns from Kestenberg, boys lack a womb and may be destined to feel empty in this respect all their lives. The "male" phallic phase of girls finds its complement in the feminine inner genital stage through which boys also pass. Therefore, boys may seek various ways of filling or fleeing from their less capacious inner space, just as their sisters try to find a phallus and then to veil their quest for it. Kestenberg has thus moved from Freud's position to one like the view espoused by Horney, if a good deal more complex and balanced.

A number of analysts have examined related issues and arrived at somewhat similar conclusions (Brenner, 1951; Bradley, 1961; Barnett, 1966). For example, Peter Blos noted in his treatise on adolescence (1962) the greater ease with which girls express their masculinity than boys their femininity. A pubescent girl's search for completion takes the form of heterosexual love, and this helps resolve her bisexuality. But the preadolescent boy must once again, more secretively, confront his wishes for passivity, the breast, and a child of his own; only then can he master residual tasks from the oedipal period. The last of these desires, for a baby, may be fulfilled in creative work. Alternatively, a fixation may result at this transitional stage because of inordinate castration anxiety and an irrepressible identification with the "phallic mother," the woman endowed with a penis.

In a somewhat similar vein, John Nelson (1956) observed and described boys' efforts to assume a mother's productive power. Pressures to produce originate in a boy's awe of feminine functions, especially childbirth. Later derivatives of womb envy may be manifested in preoc-cupations with growing, breeding, and the like, which express not so much negative oedipal or homosexual solutions as a deep-seated identification with the producing mother. Nelson underlined the "early envy of the mother's power and magic of productivity linked in part to her femininity and therefore to her womb, an organ which may not be recognized in name until years later" (1956, p. 372; see also Van Leeu-wen, 1966).

Toward a Paternity of Self

Whatever their pretenses to adult power, young children remain largely helpless, and uncertain in their distinctions between self and other, real-ity and illusion. Even older boys and girls may be overwhelmed by their sexuality, a source of both pleasure and confusion which is fueled, gratified, and frustrated by all-powerful parents on the periphery of their own being. Such is the stance of those analysts who stress the sense of weakness and futility to which a child's preemptive sensuality subjects him. These authors see pregnancy fantasies as attempts to counter or bind the anxiety that ensues upon erotic impulses and their frustration (Niederland, 1957; Sperling, 1964).

In 1958, P. J. Van der Leeuw, a Dutch analyst, discussed the com-plex interrelation of childish helplessness and would-be procreativity. He argued that the prototypes for activity are not to be found in a boy's phal-lic phase, but rather are discovered in his preoedipal experiences of parental power. For Van der Leeuw, so-called passivity—traditionally, in-sidiously equated with "femininity"—is more properly the problem of in-fancy. A boy's wishes to bear or rear children as his mother does are less problematic than his acquiescence to the futility of this ambition. "Childbearing is experienced as achievement, power, and competition with the mother. It represents being *active* like mother. It is an *identifica-tion with the active producing mother*" (p. 373, emphasis added). A boy's imitation of mother is an early form of that activity, which elsewhere promotes the use of transitional objects (Winnicott, 1953, 1957, 1958). Such activity is prevalent in both sexes and predates penis or even womb envy, although a boy must eventually give up or at least repress his pri-mary maternal identification.

A boy's dilemma is this: To avoid being castrated he may attempt to become womanly and symbolically part with his penis. In so doing, how-ever, he is confronted again with his archaic aspirations to motherhood, having never completely conceded his wish to have children. Con-sequently, he may be led to identify with the mother's powerful and later phallic person as well as with her passive relation to the oedipal father. At all levels he risks a deepened sense of narcissistic injury. Van der Leeuw concludes that to be "active, productive and creative in spite of feeling helpless and having aggressive impulses . . . is the 'problem' dominating our whole life from the cradle to the grave, but it is . . . particularly pressing in this earliest phase of a young ego organization" (1958, pp. 368–369).

Contributions from Other Disciplines on the Theme of Birth

Psychologists of different persuasions have criticized analytic views of birth theories, sexual identity, and so forth. Although many of these objections seem like caviling, the cry for evidential substantiation and a broader perspective may have merit.

Most serious is the psychoanalysts' underestimation of cognitive development. Empirically minded researchers decry a lack of data (Kreitler and Kreitler, 1966) for the theories set forth, failures to clarify evidence on which inferences are based, or the fallacy of generalizing from single cases.

The trouble is, the large-scale research posed as an alternative has proved inescapably superficial. Researchers who would disprove analytic formulations (e.g., Conn, 1947; Kreitler and Kreitler, 1966) have ignored splits within consciousness and states of "dynamic disequilibrium" (Inhelder and Piaget, 1958) whereby a young child may believe one thing one minute and something quite different the next. Even more sympathetic investigators have encountered similar pitfalls in trying to infer abiding, latent meanings from manifest behavior or momentary utterances. Their hypotheses more grounded in theory, such researchers, although gleaning rich and suggestive data, nonetheless find themselves constrained by brevity of contact with subjects and the strictures of quantitative proof, forced to render conclusions that are often meager, tentative, self-evident, or contradictory (Nagy, 1953; Ross, 1974).

None of the analytic authors, a cognitive or developmental psychologist laments, pays much more than lip service to changes in reasoning processes and information available to the child and to the impact of these on his fantasy life. Indeed, significant complements to psychoanalytic induction from case history have come from the cognitive psychologists Jean Piaget and, later, Laurence Kohlberg. Both proved alert to the elusive, emotionally laden quality of their subject matter.

Jean Piaget, the great Swiss psychologist and philosopher, related a child's theories of birth to unfolding epistemological structures and modes of explanation (1929). Although he did cite the observations of others, Piaget himself retreated from the sort of queries that were his hallmark, but which in this case he believed might disturb the sensibilities of young subjects. For "ethical" and "pedagogical" reasons, he contented himself with speculation. The end product of this was his assertion that human scientific endeavor, all attempts to explain the universe and its causal relationships, could be traced to a young child's struggle to solve the problem of where babies come from.

Children's notions of birth cannot be attributed to what they are taught, but rather to their "liberated convictions," which reveal the primitive belief that everything must have its *raison d'être* (Piaget, 1929). *Artificialism* (the notion that the things of the world have been manmade), and *animism* shape a child's questions and conceptions about babies and birth. Lacking a causal sense of how things happen, very young children assume that a baby exists before birth and appears on the scene because parents have willed its arrival. They wonder where the infant came from and contrive various preartificialist notions of birth.

Older children focus on the evident bond between parent and child. They see birth as an artificial process of production in which matter, either initially independent of the parents or else the fruit of their bodies, is purposefully endowed by them with life. For example, "meat on ladies" may be shaped in a butcher shop and fashioned into a fetus. Indeed, children between 3 and 7 years old generalize from this to infer that such is the means by which all things are created. Only by age 6 or 7 do they begin to look beyond people, beyond human intention, for some further "primal cause." (Ross [1974], in contrast, found an earlier timetable.) The child's developing mind inquires into the beginnings not only of the individual but of the race as well, and ultimately of the whole universe.

Thus, "nature becomes the depository of the productive activity of man." All phenomena share the artificial yet animistic characteristics of the baby: They are, paradoxically, both "made" and "living." Thus, following a different route, Piaget agreed with Freud (1905b) that the Riddle of the Sphinx, the mystery of childbirth, spurs all later thinking, all attempts to understand causality.

Influenced by Piaget, researcher Laurence Kohlberg (1966, 1967) more recently examined the acquisition of "sex role identity" (cf. Stoller, 1968) and of "sex constancy." The process is influenced by the moral development described by Piaget: Along with an experience of his or her genitals, a child singles out the social attributes these signify, equating being his (or her) particular sex with being "good." More specifically, Kohlberg tried to demonstrate that 3- and 4-year-olds lack an invariant concept of gender and may believe that a change of clothes makes for a transformation of sex. By 6 years, however, boys have assimilated their

18

culture's consignment of power to their fathers—to males. They have developed a rigid notion of themselves as boys, and, in fact, are ardent male chauvinists. Especially among brighter children, adolescence erodes such stereotypes, permitting inclinations not wedded to a child's particular sex. Thus liberated, a teenage boy may even rekindle in another form the long-lost hope of certain 3- and 4-year-olds that one day they may become, not a pilot or firefighter, but a "mommy."

In Retrospect: A Summary

One of Freud's objectives had been to dethrone the idealizations of his age and in their place substitute a realistic view of humankind's instinctual, most often unconscious, motives. The "infernal regions" rumbled, and motherhood, cherished so in an epoch that confined woman's sexuality to the brothel, fell before an icy analytic eye. Freud detected in that most virtuous of womanly pursuits the wish to possess a man's penis as her own. In boys, such desires derived from pathological efforts that again related to the penis: to safeguarding one's own and receiving love from the father's. Revolutionary in so many respects, inevitably Freud's ideas betrayed the ideological limitations of the Victorianism they had toppled—that is, a sexual *Zeitgeist* that granted woman little of her own and certainly nothing very enviable. At best, in the eyes of the man, her exclusive capacity for childbirth was a "painful prerogative."

In the 1920s and 1930s, with the war behind them, feminism in the air, and increasing numbers of women joining the field, psychoanalysts began to recognize, perhaps even to defer to a mother's power. Some saw objects of awe and envy in birth and succoring, maternal capacities that many boys would seize on as their own or, thwarted, thereafter dismiss in postures of violent indifference and superiority. Only subsequently in a boy's development did "womb envy" come to imply a homosexual, passive regression from an active, phallic masculinity.

Ego psychology enabled analysts to remove the once necessary blinders imposed by an exclusive focus on libido and then aggression, restoring to theoretical legitimacy the "higher planes" of mental life. They considered man in all his social vicissitudes and extraordinary self-consciousness. In his urge to bear and nurture babies they now discerned a boy's or even an adult man's history of dependent relationships and his efforts to draw from these "strengths and virtues" (Erikson, 1950, 1964) of his own.

One's "ego identity" is a long time in developing, it was discovered from infant observation. Many transitions might be pinpointed in the ongoing labor to give birth to the "self." Birth fantasies and nurturant behavior might be seen to express age-specific if often inchoate aims in this vein. Subsequently, these wishes and the attitudes, affects, and conflicts accompanying them, it was recognized, develop throughout childhood in a progression involving loss and restitution and the transfiguration of one set of age-appropriate interests, goals, tasks, and impulses into another. The process might come to fruition much later in an adult's actual and psychological fatherhood, and ideally, in an old man's "paternity of self" (Erikson, 1950).

Even in the end, however, the parental ambitions of the boy and man, their urges to create life, have generally remained linked to maternal, womanly ambitions and prerogatives. Psychoanalytic theorists have allowed little place for fatherhood in the developmental scheme of things. It is almost, one senses, as if to be a parent one must be a woman. Like everyone else, psychoanalysts have tended to defy nature's facts and to exclude men from the creation and care of children.

2

In Search of Fathering: A Review

John Munder Ross

In the previous chapter, I reviewed the existing psychoanalytic contributions on the parental elements of a boy's and a man's identity, uncovering an extensive if lost literature on this subject matter. Psychoanalytic references to fathers in their paternal role, however, are much sparser, indeed, surprisingly so. At times it seems that the professional community has succumbed to the kind of primitive myths described by Bettelheim (1954), whereby procreation and parenthood are relegated to the realm of women alone. The father has for years remained the "forgotten parent" (Ross, 1979) in the psychoanalytic literature, treated in passing perhaps as some austere and remote overlord uninvolved in the direct care of his children and in their emotional growth.

A scrutiny of recent writings suggests at least the glimmers of dawning change, indicating that the psychoanalytic community may have begun at last to cast off many of the male stereotypes and silent myths of the culture as a whole and, with this, to attend to the matter of fathering. Within the past decade, then, the psychoanalytic literature has begun to reveal a slowly growing appreciation of a father's active, positive part in his children's development, as well as of the influence of his own paternal needs and strivings with regard to his sons and daughters. The intention here is to survey the early foreshadowings and recent burgeoning of this new consciousness of the father.

Freud's Father

When he published *The Interpretation of Dreams* (1900), Freud ferreted from Sophocles' tragedy *Oedipus* a universal truth. Killing father and lying with mother, Oedipus accomplished what all men had once and secretly still wanted, only to suffer the fate they so abhorred: furious remorse, self-inflicted blindness (in part a substitute for castration), exile, and lonely death. There were other ingredients in the legend that Freud

This is an abridged and revised version of Fathering: A review of some psychoanalytic contributions on paternity, *Int. J. Psychoanal*. 60:317–328, 1979.

The work for this chapter was in part funded by the U.S. Department of Health and Human Services, Grant No. MH 05816, sponsored by the Department of Psychiatry, Downstate Medical Center, Brooklyn, New York.

pretty much ignored at the time, but to which he would return later, such as the theme of adoption and the family romance (1909b); still others he never explicated. Notable among the latter are Laius's terror of his infant son, Oedipus, because of the prophecy that he would one day usurp his place; the neglect and cruelty the father inflicted on the child as a result; and the boy's abandonment by a father *unknown* to him. I shall return to these aspects of the Oedipus complex and to the father's role within the drama later.

Perhaps it was the discrepancy between the oedipal father of his and his patients' dreams and his own father in reality—apparently gentle, frail, and disappointingly meek—that moved Freud to search for the "primal father" in prehistory. Then, too, Freud had become habituated to reconstructing ontogeny. So why not venture speculations about the phylogenetic origins of those dreads suffered by modern man without apparent cause?

In the beginning was the deed. In *Totem and Taboo* (1912), *Civilization and Its Discontents* (1930), *Moses and Monotheism* (1939), spanning almost three decades, Freud repeatedly put forward his own conjectures about Charles Darwin's "primal horde." In primeval times, a savage tribe was dominated by an older, all-powerful male, who reserved the females for himself, emasculating or putting to death those transgressing sons who challenged his authority and sexual prerogative. Eventually the sons banded together to slay and eat their terrible overlord. The violence of their cannibalism, repeated ritualistically thereafter, engraved itself on the memory of their sons and of the children they sired, as did the prototype of the authoritarian father so consumed. Thus, Freud speculated, the psychic reality of modern man's horror of losing his genitals at the hands of a vengeful father and his guilt with respect to him had their genesis in the actual rebellion and real remorse of primeval times. Oddly enough, though he sees the sons' defiance as reactive to frustrated sexual strivings, Freud rarely refers to a love for the females for whom they fought. His apparent accent on filial aggression is all the more surprising, given Freud's belated introduction of the destructive drives (1920), and then in the form of primary masochism.

Here and there Freud did modulate his view of the violence inherent in the relationship between sons and fathers. Significantly, he wrote that early man and "the primitives of today," namely children, "not only hated and feared their father but also honored him as a model, and wished to take his place in reality. . . . We can, if so, understand the cannibalistic act as an attempt to ensure identification with him by incorporating a piece of him" (1939, p. 82). The father thus emerges for a moment not only as an opponent and a tyrant, but as a figure revered for his power.

We might remind ourselves in passing that, since Oedipus did not know Laius, the father was unavailable to be taken in in this way. This poignant omission, a metaphor for a failure in internalization, entered into Oedipus's predicament and fall. The confrontation on the road eluded the son's recollection. Moreover, tenacious and curious to a fault, he brought about his own downfall by eschewing the "fatherly" advice of the old shepherd and of aging Tiresias that he leave the truth well enough alone, enshrouded in the past. Fatherless, Sophocles' Oedipus would know no mentor other than himself. And, indeed, he proved a bona fide parent to his people, sacrificing his well-being for the sake of theirs. For his pains he was repaid in his helpless old age by the good faith of his own daughters. Apparently, aspiration and silent fantasy can fill the voids and repair some of the damage occasioned by a less than adequate reality.

The awesomeness attributed by Freud to the father might be understood in a psychobiographical context. For example, one might see in it Freud's projective identification with his father and thus his attempt to endow the man with powers greater than those he possessed and to make of Jakob a worthy opponent and model, a Hannibal's Hamilcar, the worthy father of a great Semitic avenger and conqueror.

Freud's idealization of Wilhelm Fliess during the 1890s, the decade of "splendid isolation" when he conceived his psychoanalysis, certainly bespeaks a search for powers other, and perhaps greater, than his own, from which to derive sustenance and strength: a quest for a "grandiose or self-object." This era saw the efflorescence of Freud's genius as well as the demise of his many father figures; fathers both real and intellectual, lost by death, desertion, and combinations thereof. His erstwhile mentors, Brücke, Charcot, Meynert, and Freuer fell away, intellectually senescent or actually dead, earthbound all of them in the presence of Freud's soaring discoveries and ideas. And his father, always old, never had comprehended the mind of a son whom he claimed to discipline but whom he patently revered. When Jakob Freud died in 1896, his son was left behind, left not only guilty but inwardly alone.

In death, then, his father may have found greater substance than in life. It is possible to speculate from the famous *non vixit* dream (Freud, 1900) that Freud's Jakob not only no longer lived but, in a certain sense for Freud, never had. Jakob's ghost, inhabiting seemingly worthier men than he, *revenants* all of them, appeared more awesome than the man himself. On his deathbed, another of Freud's dreams reveals, Jakob became a Garibaldi. Clearly, then, a family romance was at work, one that not only counteracted oedipal conflicts but also enhanced Freud's narcissistic but no less necessary conviction of his capacity for conquest. No wonder, then, he bypassed the first half of the oedipal myth; Freud was himself an orphan of sorts, casting about for a science, an ego ideal, and an identity of his own making (see Chap. 3).

One can also sense Freud's rebellion against the platitudes of his moralistically oppressive, mystifying culture and his struggle to exhume knowledge buried by consensual and authoritative denial. Oedipal motifs, in the typical sense of the word, cannot be dismissed, even though rivalry and defiance per se do not emerge as the organizing themes in Freud's inner and intellectual experience.

At any rate, granted their limitations, the truth of Freud's notions about fathers remains undeniable. At some level and in some measure, sons did then and do now hate their fathers and do wish to take their place, notwithstanding their love and filial duty. And however beneficent and well meaning they may be, fathers in their turn must nonetheless discipline and deny their sons the full enjoyment of their pleasures and ambitions; for such are the requirements of childhood and the obligations of paternity. What Freud presented was the inevitable dynamic dualism of a son's grateful affection for a nurturant and giving father on the one hand, and the enraged, defiant son's battle against a depriving and constraining overlord on the other.

Perhaps nowhere is this dialectic of opposing paternal representations clearer than in Freud's first case study of a child, the analysis by paternal proxy of 5-year-old Little Hans (1909a; Chap. 1). However dubious an analysis by a parent may be in the eyes of current practitioners, whatever the potential violations of a developmentally imperative privacy, still the very real care proffered by Hans's father in the guise of therapist must have done much to undo the boy's image of him as a dangerous aggressor. The father's tolerant concern must further have attested to his durability in withstanding the son's unconscious aggressions against him. More than his many elaborate interpretations, often couched in a form that seems linguistically and conceptually beyond the ken of a boy Hans's age, the man's attentive presence may very well have been the curative factor. One would be tempted to speak of a "transference cure" were it not for the fact that the analyst in this instance was none other than the real object, the parent himself.

Indeed, Freud's other case histories of men (e.g., Rat Man [1909b], Schreber [1911], Wolf Man [1918a]) and of women as well (Dora [1905a]) might all be reexamined in terms of failures on the part of each patient's father to provide his child with a generous, appropriately detached, and facilitating parental love and of these sons' and daughters' desperate and contorted appeals to his elusive paternity, cries that were most often eroticized and therefore repressed. Even Oedipus' ultimately damning act—his search for the truth buried in the past—may be reinterpreted, at least in part, as his quest to rediscover the father.

This is speculation. Whatever its validity, I shall now leave Freud behind. In so doing, I would allude to his own ideas about the developments that he speculated took place after the debacle of the primal patricide. Patriarchy, Freud conjectured, gave way to matriarchy, only later to resume its preeminent place. Disputable as this sort of formulation might be on the part of historians and anthropologists, nonetheless its irony is that it may apply to the history of psychoanalysis itself. After Freud and the oedipal father, there came the preoedipal mother of symbiosis and separation-individuation—the mother, most of all, of Margaret Mahler (Mahler, Pine, and Bergman, 1975).

But here and there in her work (Mahler and Gosliner, 1955; Mahler, 1966) and that of other theorists to whom I will turn shortly, there were glimmers of a different sort of father. He is a father who is just now beginning to assume his rightful role in our analytic understanding of his child's experience, offsetting (in theory at least) and to fill the void left by what the empirical researchers have described as "paternal deprivation" (Biller, 1974; Biller and Meredith, 1974; Lamb, 1975).

Developmental Ego Psychology: Mother and Father

In introducing his tripartite structure of personality in 1923, Freud also realigned other perspectives within psychoanalysis. For example, he began to concentrate not only on conflicts between so-called instinctual impulses or drive derivatives and the internalized injunctions of social reality, but also on the identifications that accrue to build the "ego's character." This new emphasis then allowed psychoanalysis to plumb the mysterious "prehistory," as Freud put it, of the oedipal period—a primeval era in ontogeny when the personality is not sufficiently structured nor the individual's sense of selfhood adequately delineated from the world of objects to permit of intrapsychic conflict in the strict sense of the term. Rather one must speak of self-consciousness and object awareness, libidinal aims and identifications in concert with one another. Ego psychology, an emphasis on identifications in conjunction with instinctual strivings, thus arose interdependently with an exploration of the preoedipal phase.

A child has as a prototypical life task to take from mother what he needs to negotiate reality and thereafter to individuate as an entity distinct from her and other objects. As Mahler, Pine, and Bergman (1975), Spitz (1965), and Jacobson (1964) have underlined, it is by way of increasingly *selective* identifications with mother that a child is able to internalize features of her executive functions, of her ego as it were, as his own.

But, as Robert Stoller has pointed out so dramatically in his pioneer studies of transsexualism and core gender identity (1968, 1975), this process leaves in its wake a further problem, one that a father's presence is necessary to help resolve. "Imprinted" to mother, a child has her as a primary object of love as well as of identification. Freud long ago speculated on a little girl's difficulties and convoluted maneuverings in turning from mother to father as her would-be lover (1924a, 1925, 1931, 1933). Other authors have stressed the equally problematic transformations that take place as a boy endeavors to "disidentify," in Ralph Greenson's felicitous words (1968), from his mother and to identify himself as both individual and male (Horney, 1924, 1926, 1932, 1933; Boehm, 1930; Kestenberg, 1956a,b, 1968, 1975a; Van der Leeuw, 1958; Stoller, 1968; Ross, 1974, 1975, 1976, 1979; Kubie, 1974; Gurwitt, 1976).

Rarely, if ever, can fathers rival early on the encompassing presence of the mother. And yet, notwithstanding his seemingly diminished developmental importance, this perspective on earliest individuation and the power of identification also implied a new "positive" notion of the father. No longer is his sole impact on children that of an inhibitor; now he is seen to invite self-articulation and independent expression. It is father who first offers ways out of a child's potentially arresting entanglement with the mother.

During the preoedipal phase, a father has come to be viewed as the first representative of masculinity and, more fundamentally, as the first significant other, apart from siblings perhaps, outside the orbit of mother and child. His importance is as a purveyor of triangulation and the Oedipus complex, which in turn structure the child's personality in ways that consolidate gender identity and object choice and make of him a complex little person with inner wishes, fantasies, restraints, and outer actions that are his own. A father's absence or unavailability robs children of necessary counterpoints to the mother and makes for uncertain sexual identifications (Socarides, 1968). Thus, in many ways, a father serves as mediator between mother and child, preparing the way for further independent development, as indeed Mahler and her co-workers have indicated (Mahler and Gosliner, 1955; Mahler, et al., 1975; Abelin, 1971, 1975).

Developed in several relatively brief papers by Loewald (1951), Greenacre (1966), and Abelin (1971, 1975, 1977), these ideas were presaged by some remarks of Freud's in one of his seminal essays on ego psychology. In *Group Psychology and the Analysis of the Ego* (1921), Freud spoke of what Loewald would later call a "positive nonhostile" relationship on the boy's part with his father, which provided an identificatory basis for the later oedipal position. Freud wrote (p. 105):

A little boy will exhibit a special interest in his father; he would like to grow like him and be like him, and take his place everywhere. . . . This behaviour has nothing to do with a passive or feminine attitude towards his father (and towards males in general); it is on the contrary typically masculine. It fits in very well with the Oedipus complex, for which it helps to prepare the way. . . . The boy then exhibits, therefore, two psychologically distinct ties: a straightforward sexual object-cathexis towards his mother and an identification with his father which takes him as his model.

Using Freud's remarks as his springboard, Hans Loewald (1951) explored the father's role in an essay devoted to the general problem of acquiring a sense of reality during the first years of life. Loewald (p. 16) noted that "in psychoanalysis, notwithstanding other observations, the predominant emphasis was laid on the secondary, threatening character of the father image." But, as Freud's remarks suggest, initially the father does not loom as "*primarily* hostile, representing the threat of castration with which the boy copes by submission and/or rebellion." Rather, the boy first makes an active, productive identification with his "positive stature," one that is "essential to the development of ego (and reality)."

Loewald hypothesized two pairs of relationships with the parental figures: (1) a positive libidinal relationship to the mother, growing out of the primary narcissistic position and a defensive, negative dread of the womb, of sinking back into an unstructured state of identity with her; and (2) a positive identification with the father, "which lends powerful support against the danger of the womb, and a defensive relationship concerning the paternal castration threat" (p. 16). The two relationships with the father, positive and negative, facilitate a boy's differentiation and disengagement from the mother, both moving him to escape reengulfment by her. The "paternal force" is thus crucial in preventing him from sinking back into the structureless unity from which the ego emerged. Loewald touched briefly on what he believed to be a developmental sequence: Preoedipally a boy emulates an idyllic father, while postoedipally he retreats from his retaliatory power. But he did not dwell at length on the successive transformations taking place in a boy's images of his father. Nor did he ponder the impact of a father on a little girl's early identity formation. Such considerations would have to await further efforts, one of these again a fragment of an article concentrating on other matters.

In a paper on the "overidealization of the analyst," Phyllis Greenacre (1966, pp. 747–749), an analyst renowned for her reconstructions of early development, concluded that "the role of the father in the first two years of the child's life has been rather neglected," perhaps, she added, because the research settings in which mother and child have been studied had excluded fathers. Greenacre's conviction was that a father is indeed important in the early months, not only as his "influence is mediated through the mother but by his own (direct) contribution to the special magic and the omnipotent qualities in the child's life."

To be sure, the father is not so constant a presence as the mother, but rather he emerges as a "twilight figure" who takes shape mostly in the morning and evening, who is "exposed to daylight" over weekends and holidays, and who may loom mysteriously as a "midnight marauder or ogre." A father's presence, then, facilitates the baby's slowly developing sense of time. His relative distance from his child as well as his place (adjunctive or interfering) in relation to the mother-child pair are individual matters.

In most cases, however, fathers play with children in typical ways (romping, roughhousing, tossing them up in the air), especially during the end of the first or the beginning of the second year, when the baby has just learned to toddle. These behaviors, which resonate with the toddler's inherent thrust toward muscular activity, intensify body eroticism, enhance the child's "sense of body self," and encourage the exploration of space. The child may identify with the father's movements with "great exhilaration" while he is also fascinated by a presence who serves to enhance what Greenacre referred to elsewhere (1957) as the child's "love affair with the world." (Sometimes, however, overstimulation may foster submission rather than delight in novelty and conquest, with consequences for later psychosexual development.) Gradually, a father becomes delineated as a character whose "activity is generally more powerful, mysterious and glamorous than the everyday familiar concerns of the mother" (p. 749). By 2 years or so, the good parents coalesce as "the all-giving mother" and "the more than life-sized heroic father," while the bad emerge as punishing or absent, or both.

Prophetic and eloquent as they are, Greenacre's remarks again merely hint at a developmental line and fail to mention sex differences in boys' and girls' experiences of father. Direct child observation rather than reconstruction or anecdote would be required to flesh out the former and elucidate the latter. It was this methodology that provided the basis for a series of papers by Swiss psychiatrist Ernst Abelin (1971, 1975, 1977) on the father's positive role in separation-individuation, papers that grew out of the author's collaboration with Margaret Mahler.

Interactions of babies with their fathers and with various male researchers led Abelin to the following initial hypotheses. Specific recognition of the father starts during symbiosis, somewhat later than recognition of the mother. Stranger reactions to father gradually subside until, with differentiation at roughly 6 months, the father becomes irreplaceable and interesting. With the "practicing subphase," the father comes to figure as the exciting, the "different, the other parent" for the toddler. He stands for "nonmother space," while the mother constitutes a "home base" for "refueling."

Girls attach themselves to their fathers earlier than boys do, Abelin asserted in 1971, although they are warier at first of strange men. By the second year, girls seek and invite physical affection with other men as well. The father is not immediately cast as a rival by his son, generally remaining "an uncontaminated parent" who does not suffer the ambivalence leveled at mother during rapprochement.

Distinguishing between representations of and earlier actual relations with parents, Abelin noted that the initial rapprochement struggle centers on the dyad of maternal and self-representation and on the interplay of their fusion and differentiation. Gradually, however, the father appears in fantasy as the more powerful parent, an image crucial to the resolution of a toddler's "rapprochement crisis" around 17 or 18 months. With this, the child can begin to identify with him rather than with mother alone and to represent in his mind a relationship between two distinct, delimited objects: mother and father and, by extension, self and other. This development constitutes a pre-stage of triangulation proper: "The simultaneous representation of the three images of the self and both parents would constitute an even more elaborate step—perhaps representing the formal element of the oedipus complex" (p. 248). In any event, the "nuclear image" of the father buttresses the constancy of a nascent self-representation and enables the young child to become a psychologically separate individual.

Thus, intrapsychic separation and, most important, individuation require both parents. Babies gravitate away from mothers toward fathers. The father is, furthermore, aligned with reality and the growing toddler's exuberant would-be conquest of it. Rivalry with him is basically a later development, which implies empathy with a now-envied competitor.

In 1975, Abelin expanded on his earlier impressions in an observational history of a little boy. The parents, he asserted, provide a "double mirror," reflecting a child's quests for specific objects, quests that lead to a "discovery of the self." Their attitudes and observable interactions as a couple are also important. The father in particular figures as a distinct person toward whom the child will turn more and more for "specific refueling" and with whom he or she builds a distinct relationship. Subsequently, the father's presence promotes a child's dawning sense of generational as well as gender identity. Abelin further alluded to various researchers who had highlighted the impairments in intellectual and overall ego functioning associated with paternal absence during critical periods.

Abelin then revised many of his complex formulations (1977), elaborating on sex differences in the early development of identity. He emphasized what he called the little girl's "madonna complex," her early attempts to enact a maternal, generational identity, to become a mommy and be mothered. These strivings contrast with a boy's emulation of fatherly activities associated quite specifically with a male gender identity. Perhaps most important and most controversial are Abelin's latest ideas about early triangulation at 18 months. Perceiving himself in the "double mirror" provided by the parents and responding to their relationship as a couple, a toddler passes beyond the stage of sensed symbiotic yearnings to an articulation of a wish in identification and potential rivalry with the one parent for the other—all participants being represented as delimited objects in his mind's eye. The words, "I" (perhaps like daddy) "want mommy," betray the emergence of a representational triad, especially for the boy, whose sense of self becomes more clearly defined than that of the girl.

The import of Abelin's findings is, it seems, that the father's is a vital presence from which the child draws, especially during transitional phases, to articulate a sense of self-identity, ideally one charged with joy and confident mastery. At the height of the rapprochement crisis in particular, he helps consolidate self-constancy. The father's presence during the second year is thus essential.

Whether the toddler can maintain simultaneous and stable images of a self and two others in his mind's eye is a moot question. His capacity for representation and hence object constancy remains rather tenuous. Thus, the assertion that early triangulation is a major developmental organizer requires further exposition and evidential support. At the very least, individual differences in the achievement of triangulation must be taken into account.

Sex differences figure in Abelin's thinking as he has pursued the implications of selectively identifying with the father as a means of disidentifying with mother for the primary self (body) identity of girls in contrast to that of boys. Significantly, however, Abelin fails to elaborate on an individual father's character qua father, that is, as a male *parent*.

And here is a central omission in much of the ego-psychological literature on fathering. A father's age-specific and individual contributions during the preoedipal and other developmental phases and their behavioral consequences have been underplayed. The dynamically evolving father-child dyad is not considered as such.

Other analysts have made fleeting circumscribed attempts at discussing paternal attitudes and behavior. Phillip Weissman (1963), for example, offered examples of the nature and influence of "pathologic" play between fathers and sons during the preoedipal phase, but he did not explicitly consider normal development. Marjorie Leonard (1966) described various types of fathers in relation to adolescent daughters (absent, nonparticipatory, seductive, possessive, projectively identifiable). She further emphasized the crucial impact of his "counteroedipal orientation" to his daughter, declaring that "desexualized relation to the father" and "affection without seduction" during latency are what enable a girl to assume "a feminine role without guilt or anxiety." Dorothy Burlingham (1973), a longtime collaborator of Anna Freud at the Hampstead Clinic, wrote of the preoedipal currents between fathers and children, emphasizing the difference in a father's reactions to sons and daughters, his quest to embody his ego ideal in a boy and receive "loving feelings" from a girl. She noted that fathers can "mother," that their recollections of their own fathers influence their parenting, and that very often they "need" smiles from their children in order to feel secure in caring for them. Fathers, she felt, stimulate their babies more than mothers do and may at times be the "preferred," "the much loved parent." Significantly, Burlingham noted that later in development babies take over the active role in initiating play with fathers.

Most recently, drawing from analytical data, Alan Gurwitt (1976, Chap. 18) has scrutinized the multifaceted conflicts aroused in a man in becoming a father. His is one of the first efforts to explicate fatherhood as a dynamic psychological state affected by the child's gestation, birth, and growth.

All these contributions are interesting and poignant. With the exception of Gurwitt, however, these authors fail to consider simultaneously the maternal orbit, and thus they seem to lack a context. Nor have they attempted to study the dynamic psychology of the father, his inner life and its reciprocity with the phenomenology of the child. Furthermore, by isolating segments along lines of development, they do not provide an epigenetic overview. It remains to place fatherhood and fathering in the context of the whole life cycle.

Conclusions

Surveying the existing analytical literature, one finds that certain dimensions of the father-child relationship are in need of further clarification and elaboration.

First, the lines of the developing relationship between father and children running from the preoedipal through the oedipal, postoedipal, and latency periods and on into adolescence and adulthood need to be drawn systematically, with reference to gender identity, generative development, self and object differentiation, and so on. For instance, the second year is vital in cementing self and gender identity, and the father plays a central part in these processes. Further, the father's invitation to both sons and daughters that they assume their sexual identity—communications that become most inescapable during the third year of life, though they begin much earlier—must be scrutinized and set within a developmental progression. In so doing, one must consider differences in a father's relationships with sons and daughters. Not only the family triangle but also the dyad of father and child, admittedly less preemptive and primary than the maternal "dual unity," must be dealt with explicitly. To do so requires that the father's character, his fantasies, and the tacit paternal demands he makes on his growing children be scrutinized. Attention must be paid to phenomena such as the *Laius complex* (i.e., the father's rivalry with and hostility toward the child), selective identifications the father makes with mother, his mental representations of mother, his representations of and identification with his own father as a "good father," and his capacity for new representations of his children and modes of representing them (visual, tactile, even proprioceptive) in order to reveal the resonances between a father's and child's dynamic identities. To these as well as to other problems the authors of the following chapters turn their attention.

3

Father-Son Themes in Freud's Self-Analysis

George F. Mahl

Sigmund Freud turned 40 in May 1896. His aged father (then 81) died the following October, after having been seriously ill for several months.

His father's death affected Freud profoundly. His letters to his most intimate friend, Wilhelm Fliess, indicate his immediate personal reaction. The day after the funeral, he wrote, "The old man died on the night of the 23rd, and we buried him yesterday. He bore himself bravely up to the end, like the remarkable man he was" (Letter 49, Freud, 1887–1902, p. 170).*

In a week, he wrote to Fliess (Letter 50, p. 170):

I find it so difficult to put pen to paper at the moment that I have even put off writing to you to thank you for the moving things you said in your letter. By one of the obscure routes behind the official consciousness the *old man's death affected me deeply. I valued him highly* and understood him very well indeed, and with his peculiar mixture of deep wisdom and imaginative light-heartedness *he meant a great deal in my life*. By the time he died his life had long been over, *but at a death the whole past stirs within one.*

I feel now as if I had been torn up by the roots (emphasis added).

By the middle of the following summer, July 1897, Freud had already started his systematic self-analysis. His primary method was the analysis of his own dreams. The first edition of *The Interpretation of Dreams*, which appeared in the fall of 1899, constitutes the major public record of

This is a condensed version of a paper first presented to the Western New England Psychoanalytic Society, New Haven, Connecticut, June 5, 1976. I dedicate this paper to Neal E. Miller, esteemed teacher and colleague, in celebration of his retirement in 1980. I am very grateful to Carmel Lepore for her dedicated assistance.
*Freud's letters to Fliess have been published in two versions. The original and more complete one appeared as an independent volume (Freud, 1887–1902). The second version, Extracts from the Fliess papers (1892–1899), appears in *The Standard Edition of the Complete Psychological Works of Sigmund Freud*, transl. and ed. by J. Strachey with others. London: Hogarth and Institute of Psycho-Analysis, 1966. Vol. 1. It contains selections and excerpts from the first version. References in this chapter to the Letters are to the first version, which will simply be called *Origins*, except where otherwise indicated.

what is referred to by the term, "Freud's self-analysis." Many of the dreams and associations in it were his. The Fliess Letters also include dreams and associations that supplement the material in the dream book.

Freud's beginning his systematic self-analysis was, in part at least, a delayed reaction to his father's death. He explicitly acknowledged this cause, and further revealed the personal significance of his father's death in 1908 in the preface to the second edition of *The Interpretation of Dreams*. There, he wrote that he was not revising his dream theory stated in the first edition, because it had stood the test of time. Then he continued (Freud, 1900, p. xxvi):

An equal durability and power to withstand any far-reaching alterations . . . has been shown by the *material* of the book, consisting as it does of dreams of my own. . . . For this book has a further subjective significance for me personally—a significance which I only grasped after I had completed it. It was, I found, a portion of my own self-analysis, my reaction to my father's death—that is to say, to the most important event, the most poignant loss, of a man's life. Having discovered that this was so, I felt unable to obliterate the traces of the experience.

Freud was not expressing transitory sentiments in that preface. Twelve years later, he wrote to Ernest Jones when his father died in 1920, "You will soon find out what it means to you. I was about your age when my father died . . . and it revolutionized my soul" (Schur, 1972, p. 318). His father's death also revolutionized psychoanalysis, through his self-analysis, as I shall show.

Goals of the Study

My interest in this study began when I was preparing a review of the evolution of Freud's empirical observations and ideas about the father-son relationship. I realized that I had to start the survey with the observations and ideas arising from his self-analysis that were presented in the first edition of *The Interpretation of Dreams*, and in the Fliess Letters. He was his own most significant subject in this regard in the early years of psychoanalysis, and he remained his only significant publicly-reported-on subject in this regard until 1909, when the case reports about Little Hans and the Rat Man appeared (Freud, 1909a,b).

Because Freud never publicly systematized the father-son data in his self-analysis or explicitly related his oedipal theory presented in *The Interpretation of Dreams* to *his* specific data, it was necessary to institute such a study. Moreover, I had come to believe that Freud's earliest self-observations and related thoughts went far beyond those concerning his oedipal complex. Material in *The Interpretation of Dreams* shows that Freud had made observations about many aspects of his relationship to his own father, and also some about his relationship to his sons. All of this material seemed to deserve study.

The specific goals of this study were (1) to determine what Freud discovered in his self-analysis about his relationship to his father, and to his sons; and (2) to compare those discoveries with certain aspects of his evolving theory about the father-son relationship.

Procedure
Selection of Materials

While Freud started his systematic, purposeful self-analysis in the summer of 1897 (Jones, 1953; Kris, 1954), he had begun the activity of self-analysis at least as early as July 24, 1895, when he analyzed his dream of Irma's injection.* He presented a detailed account of that analysis in *The Interpretation of Dreams* (1900). According to Jones (1953, p. 327), Freud continued self-analysis after 1897 on a regular basis, for the rest of his life.

Consonant with its goals, this contribution deals with that portion of Freud's self-analysis, accomplished through associations to his dreams, that started with his analysis of the dream, Irma's injection, and ended with his completion of the manuscript for the first edition of *The Interpretation of Dreams*. The latter happened in September 1899.† Most of the material available for study, however, is from the years 1897 and 1898.

The first procedural step was to locate in the first edition of the dream book and in the Fliess Letters Freud's dreams, their associations, and related discussions for the time period designated. In the case of the dream book, identifying the relevant material required a close reading of the text of *The Standard Edition* (guided primarily, but not exclusively, by the use of the Index of Dreams Dreamt by Freud) combined with

---

*The dream titles used in this paper are, for those dreams reported in *The Interpretation of Dreams*, the same as the titles used in that volume's Index of Dreams. For the few dreams that were either reported in *The Interpretation of Dreams* but not indexed or were reported only in the Fliess Letters, I have devised original titles that seem to me similar to those in that index.

†In thus dating Freud's self-analysis, I am in agreement with Schur's perspective, and, indeed, with Jones' (1953) general view. Schur (1972) considers Freud to have started *systematic* self-analysis sometime in the spring of 1897, with a preceding introductory phase. Although giving no date for the onset of this introductory phase, Schur seems to regard it as extending at least back to July 1895, the time of the dream of Irma's injection. He describes Freud's self-analysis as being periodically dormant between then and the spring of 1897.

Freud wrote in a footnote in *Studies on Hysteria* that he was, for a period, recording and analyzing his dreams (Breuer and Freud, 1895, p. 69). Strachey (Freud, 1900, p. xv) dates that period as probably being sometime between June 1894 and March 1895.

Trosman (1969, 1978) makes a strong case for the likelihood that Freud deliberately engaged in free association in his adolescence and early adulthood. This being the case, it could be said that Freud started his self-analysis in adolescence, probably interrupted it in his 20s, and resumed it in his late 30s, continuing it for the rest of his life.

editor James Strachey's annotations in the text identifying those parts of the book added after 1900. In the case of the Fliess Letters, this step required merely a close reading for the identification of the relevant items, which yielded two types of material: (1) supplementary material about particular dreams and associations cited in the dream book (with the aid of Strachey's cross-references to the Fliess Letters); and (2) a small number of dreams that Freud did not use in the dream book. These "new" dreams are identified in the footnotes of Table 1.

Dating the Dreams

In the text of the dream book Freud dated only a few of his dreams. In attempting to determine the dates of other dreams, I used Strachey's cross-references to the Fliess Letters where available and followed up additional clues detectable in the letters and the text. The dating done by Grinstein (1968) for a sample of the dreams also was utilized.

Determining the People Who Appeared in
Freud's Dreams and Associations

I listed for all dreams and related material each specifically named person (e.g., Father, Mother, Brücke, Irma) and specified classes of people (e.g., "my children," "my teachers"). Then I determined the frequency with which the members of Freud's family of origin and of his own nuclear family, as well as certain intimates, appeared in the dreams and related associations. These frequency counts included both specific naming and mention by class. Thus, if a son was named once and "my children" was mentioned once, the count for that son would be 2.

Figure 1 diagrams the families concerned, as well as others intimately involved. Except where otherwise indicated, the dates given are birth dates. Fliess and Old Nurse are included in the frequency counts because of their very special positions in Freud's life. The principal characters in this study are indicated by the squares with heavy outlines: Freud, his father, and his three sons.

Freud's family of origin was both large and complex. The age and the multiple marriages of Freud's father, Jakob, introduced unusual features. Each of Freud's half-brothers, Philipp and Emmanuel, was old enough to be his father; Emmanuel's son, John, was slightly older than Freud, yet Freud was his uncle.

In earliest childhood, Sigmund and John were very close playmates, almost like brothers—intimate friends, companions in crime, and at times intense rivals. The two families lived very near each other in the village of Freiberg, in what is now Czechoslovakia, until Sigmund was 3

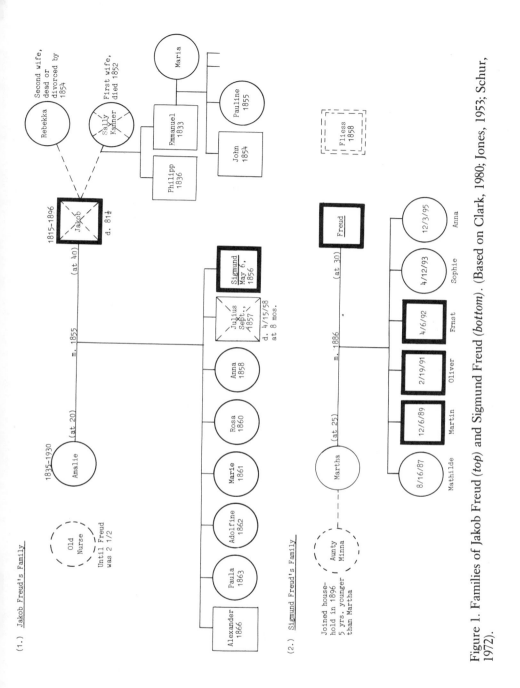

(1.) Jakob Freud's Family

(2.) Sigmund Freud's Family

Figure 1. Families of Jakob Freud (*top*) and Sigmund Freud (*bottom*). (Based on Clark, 1980; Jones, 1953; Schur, 1972).

37

Table 1. Chronology of Freud's Dreams (Dreamt Before 1900)
I. Datable Dreams (N = 32)

Year	Date	Dream	Father-Son Dreams[a]	Basis for Dating (ID, Letters, or AG)
1863 or 64		Bird-beaked figures	Father	ID
"Youth"		Dream of standing at washstand[b]		ID
1895	July 23–24	Irma's injection		ID
Father dies on October 23, 1896.				
1896	Oct. 25–26	'Close the eyes'[c]	Father	ID, L50
1897	By Jan. 24	Primitive devil religion[d,e]		L57
	Feb. 8–Mar. 15	Uncle with the yellow beard[c]	Father	ID, L58, 85
	Before Apr. 18	Rome in a mist, view of (Rome series)	Father	ID
	Before Apr. 18	Tiber, view of the (Rome series)	Father	ID
	Before Apr. 18	Rome, asking Herr Zucker the way to (Rome series)[c]	Father	L77
	Before Apr. 18	Rome, a street corner in (Rome series)[c]	Father	L77
	Apr. 27–28	Villa Secerno[c]		L60
	Before May 31	Overaffection for Mathilde[d]		L64
	Before May 31	Undressed, running upstairs[c]		L64
	Oct. 3–4	"Bad treatment" by Old Nurse[b,c]		L70
	Oct. 4–15	One-eyed doctor and schoolmaster[c]		L71

Freud abandons seduction theory and announces his discovery of Oedipal Complex in Letters 69, 70, 71 dated September 21, October 3–4, and October 15, 1897.

Year	Date	Event	Role	Reference
1898	After Dec. 29, 1897	'Myops, my son the'	Son	AG
	About Feb. 9	"Unpublishable" dream[d,e]		L83
	Mar. 8 or 9	Botanical monograph[c]	Father	L84
	About Apr. 27	Goethe's attack on Herr M.		AG
	Early May	Hall with machines		ID
	Early May	Castle by the sea[c]	Son	ID and L88
	July or early Aug.	Closet, open-air[c]	Father, son	L90, 91
	July 18–19	'Hollthurn'	Father	AG
	Early Aug.	Count Thun	Father	AG
	Early fall	Three Fates		AG
	About Oct. 16	'Non vixit'	Father, son	ID
	October	Riding on a horse (Boil)		ID
	Dec. 6–7	Frau Doni and the three children	Son	AG
1899	Late Feb.–early Mar.	Father on his deathbed like Garibaldi	Father, son	AG
	June 27	Being in sixth form[d]		L109
After father's death		1851 and 1856 (communication from town council)	Father	ID
After father's death and summer of 1897		Dissecting my own pelvis	Son	ID

39

Table 1 (Continued)

Year	Date	Dream	Father-Son Dreams[a]	Basis for Dating (ID, Letters, or AG)
		II. Nondatable dreams (N = 13)		
		1. 'Autodidasker' (Son)		
		2. Otto was looking ill (Son)		
		Briefly noted dreams[e]		
		3. Cliff in Böcklin style		
		4. Etruscan cinerary urn		
		5. Famous speakers (Dr. Lecher)		
		6. Funeral oration by young doctor		
		7. 'Hearsing'		
		8. Keeping a woman waiting		
		9. Mother and daughter		
		10. Norekdal[f]		
		11. Periodical for 20 florins		
		12. Phantasies during sleep		
		13. Social Democrats, communication from		

[a] "Father" refers to Freud's father in dream thoughts; "son" refers to sons (including "children") in dream thoughts.
[b] Mentioned, but not indexed, in ID.
[c] Direct or indirect reference is made to these 11 dreams in the Letters.
[d] In *Origins* only.
[e] The primitive devil religion dream and the "unpublishable" dream, listed with the datable dreams, and also "briefly noted dreams."
[f] Misindexed under "Dreamt by Others" in ID.
N = number; ID = *The Interpretation of Dreams*; L = Letters to Fliess (*Origins*); AG = Grinstein (1968).

years old. Then an economic recession forced the families to leave Freiberg and to separate. Emmanuel and Philipp and their families went to England; Jacob took his family first to Leipzig, and a year later to Vienna.

Extraction of Father-Son Themes

I identified and assembled all the father-son references in the material. These references included (1) autobiographical items, such as memories, feelings, wishes specific to Freud and his father, or to Freud and his sons, and (2) general comments about the father-son relationship that Freud made as he discussed specific dreams.

I then studied these assembled father-son references and extracted themes from them. In most instances these themes were explicitly stated by Freud. Then I categorized these themes. The themes and categories developed during analysis of the material.

My goal was to systematize what Freud more or less explicitly stated about the father-son relationship, his own specifically as well as the relationship in general. I made no attempt to interpret things about Freud's unconscious that he himself did not assert. Even if that had been my interest, it would have been very difficult, if not impossible, to do, because Freud censored his dreams and associations in both the dream book and in the Fliess Letters. He explicitly admitted this several times, at one point asserting he did so in the case of every personal dream analysis in the dream book (Freud, 1900, p. 121).

The fact of Freud's conscious censorship limits the validity of even the present study, which will at best produce partial, not complete knowledge. One can form an impression about the targets of Freud's conscious censorship by noting the points in the dream book at which he informs us of censoring and by comparing dream material in the Letters with that in the dream book. These methods suggest that most of his omissions involved heterosexuality. The examination for censorship did reveal, however, one striking omission involving hostility toward males in his life. He failed to mention in the dream book his sibling rivalry with his short-lived brother, Julius, despite opportunities for such mention. He did report that rivalry to Fliess as one discovery of his self-analysis (Letter 70), but the results suggest that this particular form of censorship did not distort the father-son material.

Results and Discussion

The Sample

The search yielded a sample of 45 dreams (listed in Table 1) from the following sources:

38 dreams are from the first edition of *The Interpretation of Dreams*, and are listed in the Index of Dreams Dreamt by Freud in *The Standard Edition*. (That index also lists eight other of Freud's dreams, which he added to later editions.) Direct or indirect reference to 11 of these 38 dreams appears in the Letters (see footnotes to Table 1).

3 other dreams also come from *The Interpretation of Dreams*, where they are erroneously indexed (see footnotes to Table 1).

4 dreams were mentioned only in the Letters (see footnotes to Table 1).

45 dreams, total sample.

The amount of material about the individual dreams varies widely, ranging from four printed lines (Cliff in Böcklin style) to about twenty printed pages (Irma's injection). Nevertheless, in obtaining the quantitative results to be presented, each dream was given equal weight.

Chronology of the Dreams

It was possible to obtain at least approximate dates for 32 of the dreams (see Table 1). The large majority of the nondatable dreams, none of which contributed significant data to this study, are ones very briefly noted in the dream book. Strachey's cross-references from *The Interpretation of Dreams* to the Letters and Grinstein's independent scholarship accounted for most of the chronology contained in Table 1. The following observations are based on that chronology.

Prevalence and Distribution of Father and Son Dreams. Dreams that led Freud to thoughts about his father and sons are indicated in Table 1. Of these 20 dreams, 18 are datable, only 2 undatable.

It is very striking to see that Freud did not report any datable son dreams during the early months of his self-analysis. Father dreams, however, are evenly distributed throughout 1897 and 1898. If these frequencies based on *reported* dreams are representative of his unreported dreams as well, it is possible that they reflect an early primary concern with his relationship to his father in reaction to his father's death.

Father's Death as Impetus for Father Dreams. All of Freud's 14 Father dreams are approximately datable. All but one of them followed his father's death. (The sole exception, Bird-beaked figures, was analyzed "some 30 years" after it occurred, probably only after his father's death.) The associations to these dreams make up a large part of the personal material included in the first edition of the dream book. This information

42

is consistent with his description of the "material" of the book as a portion of his self-analysis, his reaction to his father's death.

Childhood Seduction Replaced by Oedipus Complex. The chronology and its preparation illuminate certain aspects of the early development of Freud's thinking about the Oedipus complex. Before discussing those matters, I will provide their historic context in brief.

Freud started to study and treat neurotic patients as soon as he opened his private practice of neurology in 1886. Over the next 10 years his method of treatment and his theories about the etiology of neuroses changed rapidly. (For a detailed review of this tumultuous period, see Jones's 1953 survey of these events.) For the present it is sufficient to realize that his treatment turned from physical to psychological methods and that he gradually became convinced that sexual experiences were the ultimate causes of neuroses.

In the early part of 1896, Freud (1896) published his seduction theory of the neuroses, which he privately called his *neurotica*. This was a theory about the specific etiologies of hysteria and of the obsessive-compulsive neurosis. According to this theory, the ultimate source of conversion hysteria was the traumatic experience in childhood of being the passive victim of a sexual seduction by an older person, usually an adult. The future obsessional had suffered the same experience, this theory held, but then, a bit later in childhood, had turned the tables by actively seducing a younger child, usually a younger sibling.

The following circumstances gave rise to this seduction theory. Freud's treatment increasingly took the form of orienting, and urging, the patient to recall traumatic experiences of the distant past that might have included a feeling, thought, or action that persisted now under the guise of the symptom. In the beginning Freud relied heavily on the use of hypnosis to facilitate this recall; he later turned to various active techniques for facilitating this recall in the waking state. His patients often responded by recalling traumatic experiences; those that appeared to be the ultimate source of their symptoms were of a sexual nature, of the specific types just mentioned.

Often the adult recalled by patients as the seducer in these traumatic experiences was the father, especially in the case of female hysterical patients. In his publications at that time, Freud avoided isolating either parent, let alone the father, for special mention among the seducing adults. Over the following year, however, he developed his theory into one of *paternal seduction*, according to which the father was always the perpetrator of the childhood seduction, regardless of whether the child was a girl or a boy. Freud never published this theoretical development, however;

we know about it only from the Fliess Letters (Letters 52, 60, 64, 69, 70). He did not exempt his own father from this theory (Freud, 1892–1899; Letter 69). Jones (1953, p. 322) states that Freud believed then that his father's seduction had created neurotic symptoms in his brother, Alexander, and in several of his sisters.

Freud stood firm in his private belief in the paternal seduction theory in the spring of 1897, when he accelerated his self-analysis. That activity increasingly engrossed him over that summer and the following fall. The first fruit of it was his (initial) abandonment of his neurotica, as reported to Fliess on September 21, 1897 (Letter 69). His stated reasons for this step consisted of reconsiderations and realizations that were probably the result of personal discoveries in his self-analysis, although he was not explicit on this point. The former included "surprise at the fact that in every case [of hysteria] the father, *not excluding my own*, had to be blamed as a pervert . . . though such a widespread extent of perversity towards children is, after all, not very probable" (Freud, 1892–1899, p. 259, emphasis added). The former also included the realizations that his patients' memories of seductions in their childhood may have been unconscious sexual fantasies, and, if so, they would have been experienced as real experiences, since there is no distinction in the unconscious between truth and affect-laden fiction. The realizations of his seduction theory's flaws and of the power of unconscious fantasy were major events that had both personal and scientific repercussions for Freud. It is understandable that he went to Berlin in a few days, where he and Fliess met in what was apparently an uncharacteristically hastily arranged meeting.

In the next few weeks, the intensity of his self-analysis increased, proceeding apace in dreams and their analyses, to which Freud apparently devoted a great deal of time. A temporary reduction in the size of his practice facilitated this activity. He reconstructed, bit by bit, several important events and processes of his childhood, the most important being his Oedipus complex. This work culminated in the announcement to Fliess in a letter dated October 15, 1897, "My self-analysis is the most important thing I have in hand. . . . I have found love of the mother and jealousy of the father in my own case too, and now believe it to be a general phenomenon of early childhood, even if it does not always occur so early as in children who have been made hysterics" (Letter 71, pp. 221–223).

Freud continued to work intensively on his self-analysis for the next several months, and in the course of doing so he unraveled further important aspects of his early family relationships. By the following February, it appears, the intensity and pace of his self-analysis had gradually decreased and he became increasingly involved in writing the dream book, as reported in the Letters (Letter 83). Both activities continued, of course, and he completed the dream book in the fall of 1899, as mentioned before.

I have already qualified Freud's abandonment of his seduction theory in September 1897 as *initial*. The reason for this qualification is that he apparently then retracted that abandonment temporarily, starting in November (Letter 75) soon after he had announced it in September, and continuing into the following spring (Letter 84). In Letter 75 he speculated that memories of pregenital (seduction?) *experiences* produced symptoms later. In Letter 84 he speculated that psychoneuroses resulted from *experiences*, while dreams and fantasies resulted only from sights and sounds of primal sexual scenes. Throughout these months the Letters show him struggling with the issue of the relationship between memories and fantasies of childhood. Evidently he felt uncertain about his earlier conclusion that the seduction memories were in fact fantasies.

Final, complete abandonment of the seduction theory came over a year after the initial doubts. In January 1899, Freud wrote his final judgment about the nature of the childhood sexual life of his patients, and indeed of every child. "The answer to the question of what happened in infancy is: Nothing, but the germ of a sexual impulse was there" (Letter 101, p. 271). He explained to Fliess that he based his conclusions on finding in his self-analysis that what had seemed to be a veridical memory of his childhood was a defensive fantasy he unconsciously created in his young adulthood and projected backward to his childhood.* This resolved the lingering doubts he had had since September 1897 that the seduction "memories" were fantasies.

Returning to the discussion of those aspects of Freud's early thinking about the Oedipus complex that the chronology illuminates, let us consider three points. First, our survey shows that Freud's discovery of the Oedipus complex contributed to his abandonment of the seduction theory, but was not the sufficient cause of it. Rather, his initial abandonment preceded that discovery, and the discovery did not forestall his reversion to the seduction theory. Complete conviction as to the validity of the screen memory phenomenon was the cause of his final abandonment of that theory.

The second point concerns the role of Freud's self-analysis in the discovery of *the* Oedipus complex as a general feature of development, in

---

*Freud presents anonymously in his paper, Screen Memories (Freud, 1899), a detailed account of the childhood "memory" and his analysis of it.

contrast to the discovery of *his* Oedipus complex. It is commonly believed that Freud discovered the Oedipus complex in his self-analysis. Strachey, the usually reliable guide to the reading of Freud, illustrates the prevalence of this belief when he asserts the following in the editor's note to *Three Essays on the Theory of Sexuality* (Freud, 1905b): "He announced the event [i.e., the abandonment of the seduction theory] in a letter to Fliess of September 21 . . . and his almost simultaneous discovery of *the* Oedipus complex in his self-analysis . . . led inevitably to the realization that sexual impulses operated normally in the youngest children without any need for outside stimulation" (p. 128, emphasis added).

The previously quoted passage from Letter 71 clarifies this matter. There Freud says he found the Oedipus complex *"in my own case too"* (emphasis added). Clearly he had previously discovered an Oedipus complex in one or more of his patients before discovering his own. Having thus found it in both a "normal" person and one or more with a severe neurosis, he was prepared to generalize it to the childhood of all people.* His self-analysis was crucial in postulating the generality of the Oedipus complex, but it was not the occasion for his discovery of the complex.

Freud never specified the patient or patients in whom he had first discovered Oedipus complexes. In his first published discussion of the complex, in the first edition of *The Interpretation of Dreams* (Freud, 1900, pp. 248–266), he refers to the Oedipus complexes of three patients, two women and one man. (He does not mention his own complex.) In all likelihood, one or all of these patients were meritorious, for the unfolding of the total discussion in that section of the dream book closely resembles the sequence of steps in the emergence and discussion of the complex in the Letters.

The male patient may have been the first one in whom Freud observed an Oedipus complex. And he may have been the one Freud had in mind when he wrote "in my own case too." Consider the following. Freud refers to this patient twice in the dream book (pp. 260, 457–458). This patient's intense oedipal hostility had erupted in the conscious wish, when he was 7 years old, to push his father off a cliff to his death. His father died 24 years later, whereupon the patient developed a severe neurosis featuring an extreme obsessional fear that he might accidentally kill people on the street. Just such a patient is mentioned in Letter 33,

---

*Freud used the same kind of data base—himself and one or more patients—in another instance, where he concluded that aspects of guilt over the nursing and death of parents were universal (Letter 125). His *The Psychopathology of Everyday Life* (1901) also has the same kind of data base. His heavy reliance on such a data base in his early years of momentous discoveries seems obvious.

October 31, 1895. "Another man (who dares not go out into the street because of homicidal tendencies) has got to help me solve another riddle" (p. 131). This is very probably the patient mentioned in the dream book. If so, Freud was treating him 2 years before he announced what he found "in my own case too." Furthermore, in associating to his most openly acknowledged oedipal dream, Freud realized he had identified with this patient and was thus "seeking to confess to something analogous" to that patient's "hostile impulses against his father, dating from childhood and involving a sexual situation" (Freud, 1900, p. 458). Freud did not specify the nature of "the riddle" that this patient was to help him solve. That enigmatic comment stands as significantly prophetic.

The third point concerning Freud's early thinking about the Oedipus complex illuminated by the chronology concerns the raw clinical material in which Freud discovered his own Oedipus complex. The unearthing of this material would be comparable to excavating the site of man's first fire or finding the first wheel. Unfortunately that hope is doomed for the present. The chronology clearly reveals that Freud left posterity ignorant of the raw data. The clinical material most likely was a dream (or several) that occurred during the 3 weeks between September 21 and October 15, 1897—that is, between Freud's initial abandonment of his seduction theory and his announcement of the discovery of his oedipal complex. The dream chronology shows that the *datable* dreams during that period (Bad treatment by Old Nurse and One-eyed doctor and schoolmaster) and their published associations contained no reference to his father, nor did they refer to the Oedipus complex in general. Moreover, the "most oedipal" of Freud's published dreams ('Hollthurn,' Count Thun, and Three Fates) are datable and occurred subsequent to his discovery of his complex.

There remain three possibilities. One is that "*the* dream" is one of the undatable ones. Another is that it is one of the datable dreams occurring before October 3, to which Freud returned for further analysis in the interval between September 21 and October 15, 1897. He often did return to former dreams for further analysis (Freud, 1900, pp. 521–522) during his writing of the dream book. Perhaps he did this as early as the fall of 1897. The third possibility is that Freud deliberately decided to avoid *any written record* of "the dream(s)." No such dream appears in the published Letters. It is inconceivable that the editors of the Letters censored such material, since their purpose in screening the Letters for publication was to make available those relevant to Freud's scientific progress. There is ample evidence in the case of the Oedipus complex that they adhered to their purpose. Thus one must conclude that he did not *write* to Fliess about the details of this dream. He probably discussed the dream with Fleiss during one of their meetings.* In any event he did not inform posterity about the specific raw data for his discovery of his Oedipus complex.

The chronology suggests that the occurrence and the analysis in the year 1898 of some very important dreams may have also played a part in convincing Freud absolutely of the validity of his belief in childhood sexuality. The Closet, open-air; 'Hollthurn'; Count Thun; Three Fates; Riding on a horse (Boil); and *'Non vixit'* dreams could have been especially effective in this regard. In the analysis of these he realized the intensity of his unconscious childhood megalomania, vengefulness against his father, sibling rivalry, erotic love for his mother, and thoughts of sexual punishment.

Frequency of Appearance of Family Members

Freud thought of a large variety and number of people in his dreams and associations: members of his family of origin and of procreation; many teachers and colleagues; a fair number of his patients; numerous literary characters; many historical figures including rulers, generals, political leaders, writers, and poets. Most frequently, however, he thought about the members of his families and Fliess, who are identified in Figure 1. Table 2 indicates how many of the 45 dreams involved the various people of Figure 1, either in the manifest dream or in the associations. In nearly all cases the people appear in the associations, rather than in the manifest dreams.

The family members are listed in this table in the rank order with which they were mentioned as specific people. "Specific mention," as of nephew John, for example, refers to mention of him *specifically* rather than a "general mention" of "my brother's family." Likewise, "specific mention" of son Martin refers to mention of "oldest son," or "my sons," rather than the more "general mention" of "my children."

Freud's father ranks first in the numerical tabulation. My definite,

---

*Twice in the Letters Freud refers to dreams he cannot make public. One of these can be eliminated as a reference to *the* oedipal dream, for he dreamt it early in February 1898. About it he said, "it is unpublishable, because its background, its deeper meaning, shuttles to and fro between my nurse (my mother) and my wife" (Letter 83, p. 245). The following August he refers to the results of analyzing the momentary forgetting of the surname of a poet, Julius Mosen. He said, "The analysis resolved the thing completely; unfortunately, I cannot make it public any more than *my big dream*" (Letter 94, p. 262, emphasis added). Is he here referring to the missing oedipal dream, or to the one just mentioned?

Freud's only other use in the Letters of the expression "big dream" is in a letter written a year later, August 1, 1899. Referring to some editorial suggestions Fliess had sent about the manuscript for part of the dream book, Freud said, "The gap made by *the big dream* which you took out is to be filled by a small collection of dreams" (Letter 113, p. 288, emphasis added). Are these "big dreams" one and the same? Did Freud decide to publish his "big dream" only to have Fliess censor it?

Table 2. Frequency of Appearance of Family Members
(and Fliess) in the 45 Dreams or Association Sets

Family of Origin	Family of Procreation	Fliess or Minna	Specific Mention	General Mention*
Father			14	
	Wife		12	3
		Fliess	11	
John			8	4
Mother			9	3
Emmanuel			5	3
	Anna		3	7
	Martin		3	5
Alexander			3	1
	Mathilde		2	8
	Ollie		2	7
Pauline			2	3
Old Nurse			3	
Anna			2	
	Ernst		1	7
	Sophie		1	7
Philipp			1	3
		Minna	1	
Emmanuel's wife			1	4
Julius			0	
Other sisters			0	

*Mention by "class," as in "my children," "my brother's family."

distinct impression is that he also stands far ahead of the others in variety and intensity of the affects Freud referred to in the dream associations. Again, these observations are consistent with Freud's reference to the material of the dream book as a reaction to his father's death.

Father-Son Themes

As stated earlier, the search yielded 45 dreams. Table 1 identifies 13 of these as "briefly noted dreams." That designation means that Freud did not report enough of the dream or associations to it to allow any meaningful attempt to identify any themes. Freud mentioned most of these dreams in a few sentences to illustrate some detail of his dream theory, such as the existence of day residues in the manifest dream. Thus the number of dreams offering the potential for themes was 32. We shall refer to this as the "theme sample."

Fatherhood Themes

The fatherhood themes pertain to Freud's relationship as father to his sons. Material was extracted and used for this purpose when Freud spoke of "my children," "my sons," or a specific son.

Ten dreams, about one-third of the theme sample, led Freud to fatherhood themes. Six distinct categories of themes emerged readily from the material. These categories are shown in Table 3, together with the number of dream-association sets in which they occurred.

The following discussion of the themes and specific comments pertains to these six categories. (Titles of the dreams that led Freud to the theme-related thoughts are given in parentheses.)

1. *Concern for his children's future.* His concerns included both hopes and worries.
   a. He expressed these hopes.
      (1) He hopes that he has saved his children from falling ill with neurosis by having discovered the infantile etiology of neurosis. (Closet, open-air)
      (2) He hopes that his eldest son will have good intellectual development: that he will not be shortsighted, nor one-sided. ('Myops, my son the')
   b. Freud worried about these things.
      (1) He is concerned about his children's future suffering from anti-Semitism, his children to whom he cannot give a country to reduce such suffering.

      He wishes enviously that he could take his children to another country, as relatives had done, where there was less anti-Semitism.

      He is concerned about educating his children so that they will be able to move freely across frontiers. ('Myops, my son the')
      (2) He unconsciously worries about the future development of his children, despite his conscious belief in their good upbringing, about which he reassures his wife.

      He especially worries about the danger of his sons coming to grief over women, for example, over sexuality, syphilis, dying in a duel, or a woman-related neurosis. ('*Autodidasker*')
      (3) He worries about the possibility of his premature death and the consequences of that for his children.

Table 3. Fatherhood Themes in Freud's Dreams

Categories	Frequency (Total = 10)*
1. Concern for his children's future	5
2. Pride-satisfaction in having children	4
3. Achievement of immortality, fulfillment of one's wishes and unfinished work through one's children	3
4. Wishes for esteem of his children, after death	1
5. Children as *revenants* of significant people	1
6. Longing to be with his children	1

*The number of dream-association sets in which the theme category appears, out of a total of 10 sets concerning sons.

    (a) Who will care for them after his death? ('Myops, my son the')

    (b) What will their future be, in that case? (Castle by the sea)

    (c) Who will be their substitute guide? He is unconsciously concerned that Otto won't do it, despite his promise to do so. (Otto was looking ill)

    (d) Freud wishes to live long enough to guide his sons himself through puberty with sexual education. (Otto was looking ill)

2. Freud's *pride and satisfaction in his children* were expressed in the following dream thoughts.*

    a. "It is absurd to be proud of one's ancestry; it is better to be an ancestor oneself" (p. 434). (Count Thun)

    b. "[My children are] my pride and my treasure" (p. 301). ('Autodidasker')

    c. Having children is satisfying; for example, the poetic gifts of his eldest son bring satisfaction.

        The satisfaction of having children is greater than that brought by social and material success. (Frau Doni and the three children)

    d. He is satisfied that he had a second son. (Father on his deathbed like Garibaldi)

3. About *his children as a source of immortality, fulfillment of his unfulfilled wishes, and unfinished work*, Freud's associations included the following thoughts.

    a. A son can fulfil a father's suppressed megalomania (as Oliver can by

*The page numbers refer to *The Interpretation of Dreams* (Freud, 1900).

having the name of Cromwell). (Father on his deathbed like Garibaldi)

And Freud said further, "It is easy to see how the suppressed megalomania of fathers is transferred in their thoughts on to their children, and it seems quite probable that this is one of the ways in which the suppression of that feeling, which becomes necessary in actual life, is carried out" (p. 448).

b. Freud feels old and fearful that he will not live long enough to finish *The Interpretation of Dreams*, which will bring him immortality. He unconsciously wishes that his children will finish it, if he dies beforehand. (Dissecting my own pelvis)

c. A person's identity may be retained through a series of generations. (Dissecting my own pelvis)

d. Having children is "our only path to immortality" (p. 487). ('Non vixit')

4. Freud's *wish for the esteem of his children, after his death* was expressed as follows: "To stand before one's children's eyes, after one's death, great and unsullied—who would not desire this" (p. 429). (Father on his deathbed like Garibaldi)

5. Freud believed that he had made his children into *revenants* of people important to him by naming his children after people of whom he was fond. ('Non vixit')

6. Freud's *longing for his children* was expressed in the form of longing to be off from work and with his vacationing children. (Closet, open-air)

Freud's fatherhood categories fall into two superordinate groups: (1) paternal caretaking and (2) the fulfilment of his emotional needs by his sons.

Was the degree of Freud's dream preoccupation with his children influenced by the recency of his father's death? There is no way to answer this question completely satisfactorily, but the following comment by Jones (1957) indicates that this was a lasting, not a situational characteristic of Freud. "During their voyage to America in 1909 Freud used to relate his dreams to his companions, Jung and Ferenczi, as they did to him, and they told me shortly after that the predominant theme running through them was care and anxiety about the future of his children and of psychoanalysis" (p. 44).

I shall make one exception at this point and cite material added to later editions of *The Interpretation of Dreams*. In 1911, at 55, he added the acknowledgment that some of his dreams (recurrent laboratory dreams, which are not indexed in the dream book) were caused by "one of the constantly [unconscious] gnawing wishes of a man who is growing older

. . . the . . . deeply-rooted wish for youth" (p. 476). In 1919, at 63, Freud realized that this wish of an aging father could add a new dimension to his relationship with his sons. About a dream that one of his sons was alive, but wounded, in The War (News from son at the front), Freud wrote, "Deeper analysis . . . enabled me to discover . . . the concealed impulse . . . which might have found satisfaction in the dreaded accident to my son: it was the envy which is felt for the young by those who have grown old, but which they believe they have completely stifled" (p. 560).

The material of the dream book from the early phase of his self-analysis did not contain a single reference to negative feelings about his sons. In this later material, containing such a reference, Freud shows that he realizes that a father's feelings about his son may change as both their lives progress.

Sonhood Themes

Arriving at the themes pertaining to Freud's relationship to his father (sonhood) was more complicated than arriving at those pertaining to his relationship to his sons (fatherhood), because his sonhood material is more complex than his fatherhood material. It includes more themes, a greater variety in the type of material reported (e.g., in current thoughts and affects, memories of the past), and frequent contradictions.

Of the 32 dreams of the theme sample, 14, or 44 percent, led Freud to thoughts about his relationship with his father. We shall call these the 14 "father dreams."

I arrived at the following categories of themes concerning Freud's relationship with his father:

1. Formative experiences involving his father
2. Roles (real or fantasied) his father played in his life
3. Wishes concerning his father
4. Affects about his father

Since these categories overlap, our presentation of them will involve some repetition. This repetition, however, should mutually elucidate the material involved.

Formative Experiences Involving His Father

Table 4 lists Freud's formative experiences with his father, as well as his various ages and the titles of the dreams whose associations led Freud to mention or recall the experience. It should be noted that these are the significant formative experiences involving his father that Freud reported in *The Interpretation of Dreams*. There is no reason to assume that these comprise the total of such experiences in his life with his father. He may

Table 4. Formative Experiences of Freud Involving His Father

Item	Age	Experience and Outcome to Which it Contributed	Relevant Dream-Association Sets
1	Childhood to adulthood	Freud's general experience of father's assistance and support and authority. → Filial piety	Count Thun 1851 and 1856 (communication from town council) Ancillary texts
2*	2 years old	Father reproaches Freud for wetting bed. Freud "consoles" father and promises to buy him new bed. → Lifelong wish to "repay" father	Count Thun
3	5 years old	Father gives Freud and sister Anna a book with colored illustrations for them to destroy page by page. → Freud's love of books and later conflict with father at 17 years over size of book bills	Botanical monograph
4	7 or 8 years old	Freud dreams about primal scene.	Bird-beaked figures
5	"Early in childhood" (possibly when 7)	Freud intrudes into parents' bedroom to satisfy oedipal curiosity. Father frustrates him. → Oedipal murderous hostility and guilt	'Hollthurn'
6	7 or 8 years old	Freud enters parents' bedroom and urinates in chamber pot in front of them. Father's reproaches include, "This boy will come to nothing." This was a great blow to Freud's self-esteem and ambition. → Lifelong wish to prove self to father, and urethral megalomania, megalomania in general, rebelliousness, vengefulness, and murderous hostility	Closet, open-air Count Thun Father on his deathbed like Garibaldi
7	10 to 12 years old	Freud is disillusioned by father's account of lack of heroism in face of anti-Semitism. → Militaristic wishes to combat anti-Semitism and long-standing conflict over going to Rome.	Rome series
8	11 or 12 years old	Father honors cabinet members of "Bürger Ministry," who include some Jews. → Freud's ambition to succeed, to succeed as a Jew, and an early interest in study of law.	Uncle with the yellow beard
9	At 40½ years	Father's terminal illness and death. → Great sense of loss, revival of hostility conflicts, guilt of survivor, self-analysis, revolutionizing of his soul and of psychoanalysis	'Close the eyes' Ancillary texts

*See also item 6.

54

have become aware of others in his self-analysis that he did not report; still others he may have come to appreciate later. In order to formulate the first and last items in the table, I have gone beyond the dream-association sets mentioned, incorporating obviously related discussions or comments made elsewhere by Freud.

Although these experiences are not discussed here, the table should be sufficiently explicit and detailed. The reader can refer to Freud's full descriptions in his discussions of the relevant dreams. Moreover, later discussions of some of the roles, wishes, and affects will relate to some of these experiences. In the table, the arrow represents "contributed to" rather than simply "caused." One implication of this usage is the assumption that multiple experiences, rather than the single ones mentioned, contributed to the various outcomes mentioned in the table.

Roles (Real or Fantasied) His Father Played in His Life

Table 5 presents the roles in which Freud's associations cast his father, and in certain instances "the father" in general. The number of the 14 father dreams whose associations dealt with these roles is noted in the table.

I have placed the oedipal role of his father at the top of the list: Freud saw his father as the sexual partner of his mother, as the frustrator of his oedipal wishes, and as the hated oedipal rival whom he wanted to kill.

But it is obvious that Freud appreciated the variegated roles of his father and "the father." A large proportion of his dreams led him to associations dealing with nonoedipal roles. Thus he refers to the caretaking and instrumental roles of his father: as a source of support and security and as a teacher about the world. He also appreciated the role of his father as an ideal esteemed figure in his life, as a source of his self-esteem, and as a promoter of his goals and ego ideals. He was keenly aware of the role of his father as a general authority figure in his life, with whom he was in a perpetual ambivalent struggle.

In a remarkable footnote in the dream book to his discussion of the Count Thun dream in which he had ruthlessly savaged his father, Freud referred to the father as the "oldest, first, and, for children the only authority" (p. 217). Then he asserted that the father was the source of societal institutions, especially those representing the social authorities of civilized society. Earlier in this footnote he generalized from his father to the father-gods.

Wishes Concerning His Father

Table 6 lists these wishes and shows the number of the 14 father dreams that led Freud to them. All of the wishes are presumed to have been

Table 5. Real or Fantasied Roles His Father Played in Freud's Life

Role	Number[a]
Sexual partner of mother	2
Sexual pervert[b]	2
Frustrator of son's oedipal wishes	1
Hated oedipal rival	1
Source of support and security for son	2
Son's companion and teacher	6
Son's hero, and fallen hero	4
An exemplary person	2
Promoter of son's goals, ideals	8
In 'positive' manner	2
In 'negative' manner	6
Father as source of son's self-esteem	2
Father as authority figure	8
To be revered	2
To be rebelled against	3
To be reviled	3
To be killed	2
A judge, arbiter	2
A source of societal institutions[c]	1
Father-god	
Social authorities of civilized society	
Who is involved in displacements of authority conflicts	1
Father as helpless, childlike in dying days	1
A compassionate brother	1

[a]Number of the 14 father dream-association sets involving the role.
[b]Here Freud is explicitly generalizing from his dreams to "some fathers." Ancillary material shows he privately included his own father, for a short period.
[c]Here Freud is generalizing about "the father."

active at the time of dreaming. Some had originated in childhood, others were of recent origin. Reference to Table 4, dealing with formative experiences, will bring to light more specific content of most of these wishes and experiences contributing to their creation. Previous discussions have touched on other wishes, such as the wish to blame the father as a pervert.

The only wish I will discuss here is the wish that his father were braver and more belligerent in the face of anti-Semitism. This wish arose during formative experience 7 noted in Table 4, and it was the source of Freud's openly avowed militaristic wish to combat anti-Semitism and his derivative longstanding, conflicted wish to go to Rome. I am singling out this wish complex for special discussion partly because of the inherent interest of the material, but primarily because the material should illus-

Table 6. Freud's Wishes About His Father

Wish	Number*
Wishes Originating in Childhood	
To console father, for having wet his bed	1
To amount to something	2
To satisfy sexual curiosity about father and mother	1
That father were braver and more belligerent regarding anti-Semitism	4
To rebel against father	3
To take revenge on father for wounded pride	3
To kill his father	2
Wishes of Recent Origin	
That father would stand "unsullied and great" after death	1
To show respect for dead father	1
To respect father's wishes for a simple funeral	1
To blame father as pervert and cause of neurosis	2
For a more successful father	1

*Number of the 14 father dreams leading Freud to the wish.

trate for the general reader the powerful, valid role the material of Freud's self-analysis played in his life.

Freud encountered this wish complex as he analyzed the Rome series of dreams. In part, these dreams, which occurred in the spring of 1897, expressed his conscious, unfulfilled wish to visit Rome. (The obstacle resided in his inner conflicts.) In his first reported associations to these dreams he referred to his confrontation with anti-Semitism at school and his identification (in his wish to go to Rome) with various Semitic heroes including Hannibal, who inspired him to take a courageous stand in the face of anti-Semitism. Then Freud (1900, pp. 196–197) said:

Thus the wish to go to Rome had become in my dream-life a cloak and symbol for a number of other passionate wishes. Their realization was to be pursued with all the perseverance and single-mindedness of the Carthaginian, though their fulfilment seemed at the moment just as little favoured by destiny as was Hannibal's lifelong wish to enter Rome.

At that point [in the associations] I was brought up against the event in my youth whose power was still being shown in all these emotions and dreams. I may have been ten or twelve years old, when my father began to take me with him on his walks and reveal to me in his talk his views upon things in the world we live in. Thus it was, on one such occasion, that he told me a story to show me how much better things were now than they had been in his days. "When I was a young man," he said, "I went for a walk one Saturday in the streets of your birthplace; I was well dressed, and had a new fur cap on my head. A Christian came up to me and with a single blow knocked off my cap into the mud and shouted: 'Jew! get off the pavement!'" "And what did you do?" I asked. "I went into the roadway and picked up my cap," was his quiet reply. This struck me as unheroic conduct on the part of the big, strong man who was holding the little boy by the hand. I contrasted this situation with another which fitted my feelings better: the scene in which Hannibal's father, Hamilcar Barca, made his boy swear before the household altar to take vengeance on the Romans. Ever since that time Hannibal had had a place in my phantasies.

Martin Freud (1958) gives us the following interesting sequel to Freud's comments, without, however, making any reference to Freud's experience with *his* father. In the following, Martin Freud (1958, pp. 70–71) describes an episode that occurred in the summer of 1901 when Freud and his family were vacationing at the Alpine village of Thumsee. Martin was 13 years old at the time. Freud was a little over 45.

Unhappily, towards the end of our holiday there was an ugly and depressing incident which remains strongly marked in my memory. My brother Oliver and I were fishing one morning on the opposite side of the lake a few yards from the high-road which ran somewhat above the lake's level. A number of men had been watching us from the road, something which meant little to us, because fishermen are often watched by passers-by. We were shocked and considerably surprised when the men began abusing us, shouting that we were Israelites—which was true—that we were stealing fish—which was untrue—and being very offensive indeed.

We ignored them, refusing to reply; and we went on with our fishing. After a time, the men were met by other people with whom they marched off. Nevertheless, the joy in our fishing had gone and we returned home earlier than usual with less fish caught. We told father about it all, and he became very serious for a few moments, remarking that kind of thing could happen to us again, and that we should be prepared for it.

That same afternoon father had to go to Reichenhall and, as usual, Oliver and I rowed him across the lake to the highway to save him part of the walk. The men who had abused Oliver and me that morning were now reinforced by a number of other people, including women, and stood on the road near the primitive landing-place, apparently prepared to block the way to Reichenhall. As we moored the boat, they began shouting anti-Semitic abuse.

Father, without the slightest hesitation, jumped out of the boat and, keeping to the middle of the road, marched towards the hostile crowd. When he saw me following him, he commanded me in so angry a voice to stay where I was that I dared not disobey. My mild-mannered father had never spoken to me in anything but kindly tones. This display of anger, as I thought it, upset me more than all the abuse of the strangers. Nevertheless, I took an oar from the boat, swung it over my shoulder and stood by, ready to join any battle that might develop. It is unlikely that this armed reserve of one boy with an oar impressed the enemy very much. They numbered about ten men, and all were armed with sticks and umbrellas. The women remained in the background, but cheered on their men-folk with shouts and gestures.

In the meantime, father, swinging his stick, charged the hostile crowd, which gave way before him and promptly dispersed, allowing him a free passage. This was the last we saw of these unpleasant strangers. We never found out from where they came nor what their object had been in waylaying father.

This unpleasant incident made a deep impression on me; the impression was so deep that after more than fifty-five years I can still recall the faces of these crusaders in racial hatred. Time has, undoubtedly, distorted their outline but without blurring them; they remain fiendishly ugly. But there is no evidence that father was affected in the least. He never recalled the incident at home, and I am not aware that he ever mentioned it in any of his letters to our family or friends.

. . .

    Father duly left us at Thumsee and went with his brother to Rome, the fulfilment of a long and cherished wish and, as he wrote, a high spot in his life.

What the son of 10 or 12 experienced with his father must have contributed very significantly to his later actions that were experienced by his sons. One can only speculate about the exact nature of the links between the two episodes. It is clear, however, that Freud fulfilled his ideals concerning anti-Semitism and the proper behavior of a father, ideals inadvertently fostered by his father. It could not have been an accident that Freud resolved his conflict and went to Rome for the first time soon afterward.

Affects About His Father

Table 7 lists the feelings about his father that emerged in Freud's associations to the 14 father dreams. The table shows the variety of affects involved. Freud mentioned the outright positive, loving affects of "filial piety," that is, loving devotion, deep affection, and admiration. Other affects were unpleasant ones that arise because of an underlying loving relationship: compassion, grief, guilt, hurt feelings, and disillusionment. And there were the outright negative affects of rebelliousness, vengefulness, and murderous anger. The megalomania seems to involve both positive and negative features. Freud referred to childhood versions or sources of most of these affects. The list of formative experiences in Table 4 refers to the childhood sources he mentioned. His grief and his guilt for hostile feelings about his father arose in reaction to his father's death.

    Table 7 depicts a balance between positive and negative feelings. Freud found that his love (filial piety) was a dominant conscious feeling for his father, but that his unconscious feelings (expressed indirectly in his dreams) included intensely hostile ones such as vengefulness and murderous anger. Thus, one of the fundamental emotional themes that emerged in his particular relation to his father was the *ambivalence of love and hate*.

    Freud mentions four major sources of his hostility toward his father. Three of them, the basic ones, arose in childhood.

His father's frustration of his oedipal wishes
His father's more general, seemingly restrictive, authority
Wounded pride: narcissistic blows dealt by his beloved, idealized father in
    the form of belittling verbal reproaches

Table 7. Freud's Affects About His Father

Affect	Number*
Filial piety	2
Admiration	7
Compassion	3
Grief	1
Guilt (hostility)	2
Hurt	2
Disappointment	1
Disillusionment	4
Megalomania	2
Rebelliousness	3
Vengefulness	3
Murderous anger	2

*Number of 14 dream-association sets in which affect appears.

His father's terminal illness and death became ancillary sources of his adult hostility, because they rekindled his unconscious hostility dating from childhood. His father's symptoms (e.g., his incontinence) and death provided him with unconscious pleasure. This was expressed indirectly in dreams (e.g., Closet, open-air; Count Thun; 'Hollthurn'). And it resulted in his 'guilt of the survivor,' which he first mentioned in writing to Fliess about his dream, 'Close the eyes,' which occurred the night after his father's funeral.

Fear does not appear in Table 7. Freud never mentioned fear of his father in all the associative material in the dream book and Letters. Was this due to his conscious censorship? Or did fear of his father play a minimal role in his life? While we cannot answer this question definitively, there are two reasons for concluding that the latter possibility is the more probable one.

First, Freud did not censor the fact that his father and such an authority figure as Brücke, his most influential university teacher, had strong "negative" emotional impacts on him. We have seen in Table 4 his report that his father's reproach in childhood severely wounded his self-esteem. And when his associations to one of his dreams ('Non vixit') led him to it, Freud did not hesitate to report that Brücke had overwhelmed him in his youth with an angry reproach when Freud was late for the performance of duties in Brücke's laboratory. Revealing such reactions is not consistent with conscious, wholesale censorship of fear of his father.

Second, Freud's father does not seem to have been a frightening father. Freud's sister, Anna, emphasized how gentle and loving their father was (Bernays, 1940). Her description is directly consistent with the absence of fear of his father in Freud's dream associations. Freud, too, was a very gentle father, according to his son, Martin. The way he related to his sons must have been strongly influenced by the way his father related to him. Martin's report and this surmise are indirectly consistent with the absence of filial fear in Freud's self-analysis. It is possible that Freud's self-analysis simply failed to delve into his fear of his father, but that we cannot determine. Or perhaps Freud displaced *very early* fear of his father onto his half-brother Philipp, as Jones (1953, p. 11) suggests he did in childhood with his then-conscious oedipal hostility. Neither can we determine this.

The filial piety of Table 7 encapsulates Freud's love and affection for his father. In the original published hypotheses about the Oedipus complex, which appeared in *The Interpretation of Dreams*, the attitude and affect of filial piety played a crucial role. At that time Freud theorized that filial piety, not fear of the father, led to the repression of the oedipal hostility (Freud, 1900, pp. 256–257).

Conclusions

At the end of his life, Freud (1938) wrote, "I venture to say that if psychoanalysis could boast of no other achievement than the discovery of the repressed Oedipus complex, that alone would give it a claim to be included among the precious new acquisitions of mankind" (pp. 192–193). We have seen how he discovered this phenomenon and the early effects of that discovery on psychoanalysis.

Contrary to common belief, Freud discovered *the* Oedipus complex neither originally, nor solely, in his self-analysis. He did find that he had an Oedipus complex, just as did one or more of his neurotic patients. (The patient, crucial in this regard, may have been the one with whom he identified in the 'Hollthurn' dream.) This discovery emboldened him to posit the generality of the Oedipus complex. There is an identity between what he reported about his conflict over his oedipal hostility and what he proposed to be generally the case in his first published discussion about the Oedipus complex.

This study revealed two other findings about Freud's discovery of the Oedipus complex. The first is that he deprived posterity of *the* dream(s) leading to the discovery of *his* complex.* The second is that, contrary to

---

*As was shown, the dream most probably occurred in late September or early October 1897. The 'Hollthurn' dream would seem to be the most likely candidate for being 'the big dream,' for a set of interlocking reasons for which there is no space here to discuss. The arguments against that being the case, however, include Freud's dating of the dream as occurring during a certain July 18–19 night, Grinstein's (1968) reasonable dating of the dream to 1898,

another common belief, the discovery of the Oedipus complex did not lead Freud directly to abandon his seduction theory of neurosis. In fact, he reverted to his seduction theory after that discovery. It was not until some 15 months later that he finally disclaimed his seduction theory. The discovery of the screen memory phenomenon at that point in his self-analysis combined with his earlier discovery of the Oedipus complex to constitute the necessary and sufficient conditions for that revolutionary step.

Freud's discoveries about *his* father-son relationships, however, went far beyond the discovery of his Oedipus complex.

1. He encountered some important dimensions of a father's relationship to his sons. This fact is never mentioned about his self-analysis. He was, however, made keenly aware of the intense involvement of a father with his sons. He seems to have become keenly aware of the role children can have for the father as narcissistic extensions of himself through which he hopes to fulfil himself and the caretaking and (instrumental) concerns of the father for his children. Freud's associations also underscored his love for his children, but there is little likelihood he needed his self-analysis for that.

2. Freud became aware of many more influences of his father in his life than are encompassed by the concept of the Oedipus complex. For example, he became fully aware of the positive emotional bond of love a son may have to his father, as well as the oedipal rivalry. Thus he became aware of the ambivalent nature of the son's relationship to his father. And he became aware of the role of his father as an ideal, as a shaper of his own ideals, and as a complicated authority figure. Freud discovered his "father-complex," as well as his Oedipus complex. (He eventually used that term, *father-complex*, in *Totem and Taboo* [Freud, 1913, p. 157].)

The developmental family psychology that Freud elaborated subsequent to *The Interpretation of Dreams* was predominantly a "son psychology," and to a large extent a father-son psychology.* Many of the

---

the lack of any evidence that Freud made in 1897 the trip during which he had that dream, and the suggestion that he never published 'the big dream.' No one of these arguments is conclusive in itself. Thus he could have had the dream in July 1897 but analyzed it in September–October 1897. Yet the combination of all the arguments is quite persuasive.
*Indications of Freud's great interest in the psychology of the father-son relationship are that (1) the major case histories he wrote after 1901 were all about sons (Little Hans, the Rat Man, and Schreber [Freud, 1909a,b; 1911]), and (2) in those case histories the treatment of the father-son relationship greatly overshadowed that of the mother-son relationship.

ideas we have reported as arising from his self-analysis became central ideas in his later father-son psychology. Prominent examples include the following:

1. In *On Narcissism* (1914), Freud wrote about parents making their children repositories of some of their narcissism and sources of vicarious fulfilment.
2. The importance of the son's love as the source and means of repression of his hatred of his father anticipated the central role Freud assigned to this love-hate conflict in the life of Little Hans (Freud, 1909a) and of the Rat Man (Freud, 1909b). It also anticipated the significance he assigned to love-based remorse over the hypothesized parricide in *Totem and Taboo* (Freud, 1913), which significance he applied much later to the development of the individual's super-ego in *Civilization and Its Discontents* (Freud, 1930, p. 132).
3. Thus the seeds of his later ideas of the importance of the father-son relationship in the development of religion, other social institutions, and morality were clearly present in the material of his self-analysis.

However, not all of his subsequent thoughts about the father-son relationship in general were foreshadowed in his self-analysis, at least so far as he revealed it.

1. Especially noticeable in this regard is the lack of any material about the son's fear of the father, especially castration anxiety, and the role this might play in conflicts over his hostility toward his father and in the development of his ideals (super-ego).* Later, Freud proposed such fear is a prominent repressive force of the entire Oedipus complex (Freud 1918a, 1924a, 1926).
2. It is also very noticeable that Freud's later awareness of the general importance of homosexual ties to the father (Freud, 1923a) is absent

---

*Freud's emphasis on the role of filial piety and "neglect" of the role of castration anxiety must have been the result of a quite definite "theoretic set" produced by his conviction concerning the former. It was not due to a lack of available evidence that could have suggested a significant role of castration anxiety in this context. He referred in the dream book to that part of the Greek myths in which sons castrated their fathers (p. 256); he had a competitive sexual dream while suffering from a large, torturously painful scrotal boil (Riding on a horse [Boil]); and one of his frankly admitted oedipal sexual dreams (Three Fates) led him to "restraining thoughts of every kind and even threats of the most revolting sexual punishments" (p. 208). He repeated this tipping of the balance in favor of filial love at the expense of castration anxiety in his original formulations about the oedipal conflicts of Little Hans and the Rat Man (1909a, b).

from the material. Perhaps Freud could not become aware of this in the first 2 years or so of his systematic self-analysis; perhaps it didn't apply.* Perhaps it found distorted expression in his theory of the paternal etiology of the neuroses. Or perhaps he did become aware of it but censored it. By 1912 Freud indicated his awareness that he shared with all other people some degree of unconscious homosexual feelings (Jones, 1953, p. 317; 1955, p. 420). We do not know what he discovered about their childhood origin.

*Since this chapter went into press, I have become acquainted with Anzieu's (1975) comprehensive study of Freud's self-analysis. I have not yet assimilated the details of his work, but I do want to refer the reader to it. As a small part of his investigation, Anzieu compiled a chronology of discrete steps in Freud's self-analysis up to 1902. Part of his chronology deals with Freud's dreams during the period with which I have been concerned. I have compared that part of his chronology with my chronology of Freud's dreams. Strikingly, there are only minor discrepancies between our independently compiled chronologies. None of the discrepancies bear significantly on the substantive statements or conclusions in the present chapter.

4

Selected Critical Review of Psychological Investigations of the Early Father-Infant Relationship

Linda Gunsberg

Proverbs and folklore often speak to the essential role of the father. In India (Samaraweera, 1979) there is a tale about the father who takes the baby to the mountaintop and says, "This is the world; I will introduce you." The mother holds the baby and says, "I will comfort you." A Mayan Indian proverb (Collins, 1979) reads, "For in the baby lies the future of the world. Mother must hold the baby close so that the baby knows that it is his world. Father must take him to the highest hill so that he can see what his world is like." These two quotations imply the father's role is powerful only in its complementarity with the mother's. The father introduces the infant to the exciting and large outer world, the mother offers the baby a safe home from which to explore.

The first father-infant interaction research focused on the similarities and differences between mothers and fathers and their babies, the infants' responses to their parents, and the differences between attachment and affiliation with each parent (Clarke-Stewart, 1977; Lamb, 1978). Until recently, it was believed that the father's relationship with the infant became important only late in infancy and onward (Parke et al., 1979). The revolutionary study with regard to the father's importance to the young infant was that of Schaffer and Emerson (1964), who showed infant attachments to fathers and others who were not their regular caretakers and who perhaps never participated in caretaking activities. Now, a whole body of infant research points to the father's becoming important earlier and earlier (Yogman et al., 1976a, b; Yogman, 1977; Brazelton et al., 1978; Sullivan and McDonald, 1979).

In presenting this overview of the directions being pursued, I shall be stressing methodological aspects in the hope that certain pitfalls encountered in psychological research can be avoided.

Father-Infant Interaction Studies

Psychological studies have often obtained information about the father by interviewing the infant's mother and asking how her husband is involved with the infant (Mahler, Pine, and Bergman, 1975). These maternal reports about the father have been regarded as objective data when they more than likely reflect the mother's own perceptions, attitudes, and fantasies. Research has shown that mothers are not reliable informants or interpreters of the father's behavior (Eron et al., 1961). Another method of obtaining information about the father-infant relationship has been to ask the father about events retrospectively, even though the father's memory may be less than exact and may be colored by experiences since that time (Rendina and Dickerscheid, 1976).

When researchers study the father-infant interaction directly, they observe, organize, and interpret what they see in a particular way, depending on their theoretical orientation (Earls, 1977). However, all researchers must adhere to the reciprocal nature of dyadic interactions (R. Q. Bell, 1968, 1979). Infants are known to initiate a good proportion of interactive behaviors (R. Q. Bell, 1971; Schoggen, 1963; M. F. Wright, 1967). In interaction studies it is often hard to discriminate not only each person's contribution at the moment but also what elements of the behavior observed have to do with the interaction taking place at that moment as against the cumulative effect of previous events between those who are interacting (Schaffer, 1977). Sophisticated methodologies such as microanalysis are increasingly being employed in order not to lose this important data. Microanalysis allows the researcher to observe behavioral sequences at a slower speed so that subtle shifts in interactions can be observed and analyzed. Yet, many researchers still use rather simple categories to chart father-infant interaction. It is not only important to pick the appropriate level of analysis for the interaction data under investigation, but also to use different levels of analysis to compare and contrast the findings (Parke, 1978b).

Father-infant relationships are multidimensional. For this reason the approach of Brazelton's group seems most viable. This approach addresses the issue of clustering of behaviors that cannot be isolated into segments without losing the meaning of the overall sequence and combination of elements (Brazelton, Koslowski, and Main, 1974).

The researcher thus far has indicated some findings regarding the father-infant interaction that remain consistent over time, and other findings that seem to depend on the infant's age and developmental level. Unless infants are carefully matched on important variables, questions regarding the interpretation of the findings arise. For example, studies mix first- and second-born babies as if they had equal parenting experience, and infants are not carefully matched in terms of age and sex.

In order to assess shifts and development over time in the father-infant dyad, Parke (1979) urges researchers to complement the father-infant observations with independent assessments of the infant's changes and competencies as well as independent measures of the father's shifts and development. In addition, Parke recommends that behavioral observations be complemented by data regarding the father's attitudes and perceptions regarding his infant.

The father-infant dyad must also be viewed within the context of the family as a triad. This raises even further complications regarding the organization of data.

The question of where to observe father-infant interactions also must be taken into account. The context for father-infant interaction studies varies greatly from hospital observations of parents and newborn to observations at home or in the laboratory. Laboratory studies may yield greater control over the independent variable, making it easier to isolate cause-effect relationships. However, Parke (1978a) and Sroufe and associates (1974) point out that parents and infants tend to alter their behavior in unfamiliar settings, which significantly affects the authenticity of the behaviors in the interactions, as well as the ability to generalize the findings. Moreover, in laboratory studies, the parents are most likely to be restricted in their initiation of social interactions with their babies in order to reduce parental variance. However, parents feel unnatural being restricted, and the child is bewildered by the parents' holding back.

The context, whether it is a laboratory or a home, can also vary in terms of the degree of stress introduced. Laboratory studies have tended to introduce the most stress. Stress is introduced in order to assess the child's attachment to his father and mother. This is achieved by manipulating parent departures and reunions, and through the introduction of a stranger.

In that laboratory and naturalistic studies often complement each other, both kinds are needed. The naturalistic study is more global and exploratory and the laboratory study is more specifically designed to look at particular aspects of the interaction in a more isolated and controlled way (Parke, 1978a).

The Direct and Indirect Influence of the Father in the Father-Mother-Infant Triad

Although the father-infant relationship has been mentioned throughout this chapter, it should be emphasized that to talk about the father and infant in isolation is only to make a point. The father-infant relationship exists within the family, and not to view it within the context of an active triad is to simplify our subject matter (Hartup, 1979).

Boss (1977) questions the assumption that father's presence implies healthy family functioning and that father's absence implies family dysfunction. A father's presence must be considered in terms of physical presence and also psychological presence. Many fathers can be physically present and psychologically absent, or psychologically present and physically absent (Boss, 1977; Prall, 1978).

Father-infant studies (Kotelchuck, 1975) suggest that some amount of physical availability to the infant and emotional presence is the ideal combination. The quality of the father's psychological presence or absence is important to investigate, yet more difficult to explore. The father's influence has been investigated in terms of direct and indirect effects (Herzog and Sudia, 1973; Bronfenbrenner, 1974; Lewis and Weinraub, 1976; Lamb, 1978; Lewis and Feiring, 1978; Parke, 1979). Direct effect refers to the interaction between father and infant, whereas indirect effect refers to the father's influence on the infant through the mother.

To date, more research has investigated the father's indirect effects on the mother-infant interaction, and less is known about the equally powerful influence of the mother on father-infant interactions. Pedersen and associates (1977) have explored both the father's and mother's indirect effects within the father-mother-infant triad. In addition, the marital relationship can affect both the father and father-infant interaction as well as the mother and mother-infant interaction (Schaefer, 1974).

The effects of pathological mother-father relationships on children have been investigated in several studies (Gordon and Gordon, 1959; Glass et al., 1971; Rutter, 1971; Gunsberg, in progress). Poor marital relationships can create a more pathological atmosphere than the father leaving the home (Lamb, 1976d). It is also possible for children to have direct and indirect effects within the family. Lerner and Spanier (1978) have indicated that the influence that children exert on parents and their marriage is relatively unknown.

In summary, the father-infant research of the 1960s and 1970s was ushered in with great excitement and promise. To date, studies are still exploratory, and often are faulted for their attempt to look at father-infant interaction by employing the same categories of observation as mother-infant studies (Lamb, 1976d). There is not enough agreement yet about what the units of study should be in father-infant interaction studies or how to organize the data. At this point, however, agreement among researchers regarding the units of study may not be such a positive indication, since the area of father-infant interaction research is so new that the creative eye of each researcher is needed to broaden the observations rather than limit them by refinement. The work of Abelin (1971, 1975) and Yogman (Yogman et al., 1976a, b; Yogman, 1977) is unique in that they initially viewed in detail (Yogman with microanalysis) parent-infant interaction without predetermined categories.

To date we have had no longitudinal study of the father and infant from pregnancy through the first 3 years of life. Nor have studies to date carefully considered father intactness or psychopathology as a variable; they therefore fail to investigate the influence of the father's personality organization of the father-infant interaction. Finally, few studies look with equal emphasis at the role of the father in emotional and cognitive development as does Clarke-Stewart (1977). The father and his interaction with a physically or emotionally high-risk child has just begun to be explored (Gunsberg, in progress; Schwartzman, in progress). We also have not looked at the later effects of early father-infant interaction on the child's development, specifically in the areas of emotional, social, and cognitive development (Earls and Yogman, 1979).

In addition, with more data on the phenomenology of the father-infant relationship within a developmental context, researchers will be able to offer clinicians important information about the particular stresses in the transition to fatherhood and in the father-infant interaction.

Father-Infant Interaction from 6 Months to 3 Years: Attachment, Affiliation, and Social Interaction

Many of the psychological investigations that focus on father-infant interaction within the period from 6 months through 3 years are influenced by attachment theory (Ainsworth, 1969; Bowlby, 1969). These theorists believe that the role of the father is secondary to that of the mother. However, the father-infant research that has evolved from this theoretical position attempts to show, by measures similar to those used in assessing mother-infant relations, that father is important too. In terms of infant attachment to mother, Bowlby claims that infants begin to form attachments to their mothers in the second half of the first year of life. In order for the infant to be attached, he or she must cognitively understand that mother is an independent, separate entity, and that her existence remains permanent whether or not she is in the infant's view. Lamb (1977a) states that attachment behaviors probably peak at 12 to 13 months of age.

It seems arbitrary to look at attachment relations from 6 months onward as these studies do, since the precursors to attachment have been developing since birth. It would therefore make more sense to study attachment relations from the very beginning. Here, a distinction must be made between the practical inability of researchers to study attachment relations during the first 9 months of life as a result of inadequate experimental measures, as was the case with Kotelchuck (1972), and the theoretical issue of attachment relations developing over time. The question that still remains to be empirically investigated is whether infants form attachments to mothers earlier than to their fathers or whether they form attachments to fathers at the same time but show initial preferences for mothers that disappear over time.

Lamb (1978) concludes that the conditions for attachment are the same for both parents. He stresses the specific quality of the interaction between parent and infant and the parent's sensitivity to the infant's cues. He does not emphasize either the caretaking involvement with the infant (Kotelchuck and Shaw, 1976) or the amount of time the parent spends with the infant.

Still unresolved is the question of the appropriate measures to study the nature of the infant's attachment to the father. Separation and reunion-greeting behaviors are the focus of some studies (Pedersen and Robson, 1969); others use separation protest (Schaffer and Emerson, 1964). Inasmuch as differences exist in measures of attachment and the conditions under which behaviors occur, it is difficult to generalize the findings. Furthermore, as the infant develops, attachment to the father may be expressed in different ways, and measures must be sensitive to such shifts. For example, as the infant begins to crawl and locomote, he or she will indicate attachment through distal behaviors. It would be an error to view this change as a disappearance of attachment, or detachment, when, in fact, the attachment is still strong, although it is being expressed in new ways that are more appropriate to the infant's developmental level. Lewis and associates (1973) have referred to this shift in the expression of attachment as the *transformational hypothesis*.

Schaffer and Emerson (1964) were the first researchers to focus on the father-infant relationship, albeit through the eyes of the mother. The measure of attachment they used was the expression of separation protest in response to the everyday departures of either parent. Infants were attached to both mother and father by 9 months of age, and only 65 percent of these infants were reported to have an exclusive first attachment to their mothers. A small number of infants showed attachment first to their fathers. By 18 months, 80 percent of the infants were attached to both mother and father, and only 50 percent of the infants preferred their mothers to their fathers. Schaffer and Emerson found that infants were attached to people like their fathers, who did not necessarily play a role in their physical care. Despite this exciting discovery, however, they have been criticized for using separation protest as an index of attachment relations (Cohen and Campos, 1974; Lamb, 1975) and for collecting data from mothers rather than through direct observations.

Pedersen and Robson (1969), investigating the infant's response to separation from and reunion with the father, also used data gathered from maternal reports rather than direct observation. They found in their study of infants at 8 and 9½ months that fathers are very involved with their firstborn babies and show a stronger interest in their boy babies than their girl babies. In addition, most boy and girl babies were attached to their fathers. In terms of the relationship between paternal behavior and boy babies' attachments to their fathers, three positive correlations exist: (1) caretaking, (2) emotional investment, and (3) the level of stimulation in play. In addition, one negative correlation was significant: the father's irritability level. The relationship between paternal behavior and girl babies' attachments to their fathers is far less clear, with no positive correlations evident, and only one negative correlation, which was the father's apprehension over his baby's well-being. Availability of the father and amount of time spent in play did not significantly correlate with either the boy or girl baby's attachment to the father. Pedersen and Robson have also been criticized for not comparing the reunion behaviors of the infants with various people such as father, mother, and perhaps a stranger (Lamb, 1978). As the study stands, it is hard to know if these correlations between paternal behavior and the infant's attachments to the father are characteristic of the father-infant interaction specifically or are also shared in the interactions between the baby and other people as well.

Lamb (1976c, 1977a, b) conducted a series of studies that investigated the attachment, affiliative, separation, and reunion behaviors of infants toward their fathers and mothers. Twenty sets of mothers, fathers, and infants were observed at home. A friendly female stranger was introduced at various points while the parents were present. Attachment behaviors were defined as behaviors that reflect desire for security (such as wanting to be held), whereas affiliative behaviors reflect a desire to approach and communicate with friendly adults.

Although Lamb's studies contained some methodological flaws, they reveal some very important findings that point to the father's significance to the infant. The major finding is that at both 7 to 8 months and 12 to 13 months, there was no significant attachment preference for fathers or mothers, but both parents were preferred to a friendly female stranger. Affiliative behaviors showed different results. Here, at both ages, there was a clear preference for the father over the mother. Lamb points out that affiliative behaviors are influenced by the level of sociability and activity of the adult and that, as a result, attachment behaviors are more relevant in determining with whom the infant relates over time.

In terms of play, Lamb also found that the infant responded more positively to the father's than to the mother's play. Fathers play with their babies in a more physically stimulating manner, and their play is more unpredictable and idiosyncratic. Mothers play in a more conventional fashion, using toys and games such as peek-a-boo. In addition, fathers hold their infants as part of play and also because their infants want to be held. Mothers hold their babies less for play and more for caretaking purposes, and as a way to restrain babies from engaging in unsafe activities (Lamb, 1976c, 1977a). Fathers initiate more in play with their infants. Both fathers and mothers used toys more in their play with older infants, and physical stimulation was less important in their play with older infants.

In addition, Lamb (1976c, 1977a, b; Lamb and Lamb, 1976) found that fathers have significantly different reactions to their boy and girl babies by one year of age. Fathers are twice as active in their interactions with boy babies than with girl babies through the second year, whereas mothers are equally active with girl and boy babies.

In a further follow-up, Lamb (1977b) observed the same sample at 3-month periods from 15 to 24 months. He found an increase in both attachment and affiliative behaviors toward fathers as compared to mothers. Boys manifested a significant preference for father in attachment behaviors. Girls varied more, some showing preferences for mother, others for father, and some no preferences at all. The boy infant's preference for father as an attachment figure fits well with the father's own preference for the boy baby.

Lamb concludes that infants do not show the maternal preferences in the first year as indicated by Bowlby (1969) and Ainsworth (1969). Infants are attached to both parents in the first year of life, and in the second year of life boy infants have paternal attachments that they prefer over attachments to their mothers. Lamb also concludes from his observations that infants become attached to mothers and fathers at the same time. However, without looking at the first 6 to 7 months of infancy, it is not possible to state which attachment relationship develops first or whether they develop at the same time.

Clarke-Stewart (1977) studied the social play patterns of 14 sets of fathers, mothers, and infants at home in both unstructured and semi-structured play contexts. The results indicate that at 15 months mother is the primary playmate, at 20 months mother and father are equally involved in play, and at 30 months father becomes the primary playmate. Father was more physical and arousing in his play, and his play periods were briefer in duration. Father's play was less likely to be mediated by toys, involving more social interaction than mother's. Mother's play was primarily mediated through objects, more intellectual, and she offered the infant instruction. Mothers played more with infants in terms of actual time. Mothers were, however, the preferred partner when neither father nor mother initiated play with the infant. Father became the preferred partner when he initiated play with his infant. Fathers rewarded infants more during play, were successful in involving the infant in play, and enjoyed the play themselves with their infants.

Attachment Studies: Laboratory Studies on Separation Protest

The incentive for a whole body of research in the 1970s came from Schaffer and Emerson's (1964) finding that 80 percent of infants exhibited separation protest to fathers and mothers by the age of 18 months. Separation protest refers to the infant's reactions to the departure of a parent. Indices of this include crying, the disruption of play activity, and proximity-seeking behavior. These expressions of separation protest discriminate the infant's attachment responses to three adults: mother, father, and female stranger. The separation protest studies are difficult to compare because different measures are used, infant subjects are of different ages, and the experimental conditions and degree of stress introduced vary.

Kotelchuck (1972) observed 144 infants with their parents. Infants were observed at 3-month intervals from 6 to 21 months in the laboratory, and they underwent 13 different experimental conditions, each 3 minutes in duration. The purpose of the study was to observe the infant's reactions to the comings and goings of mother, father, and the female stranger.

Kotelchuck found that infants expressed separation protest when either mother or father left, but not when the stranger left. When either parent left the infant, the infant's play decreased. However, when the stranger left, the infant's play increased. From 6 to 9 months, no separation protest behavior was revealed toward any adult. At 12 months, infant play decreased when the mother left, but not after the father left. There was greater decrease in play on mother's departure than on the stranger's departure. At 15 months, play diminished after the father's departure for the first time. There was less play after the father left than after the stranger left. At 18 months, there was the greatest decrease in play on the departure of both mother and father. This response diminished at 21 months. Kotelchuck did not find differences in separation protest behaviors of girl and boy infants. Departures and returns of either parent caused stress for the infant, which was manifested in decrease in play when the parent left and an inability to return to play immediately when the parent returned. When the stranger left, the infant did resume play activity. The major distress was experienced when the infants were left alone with the stranger.

Spelke and associates (1973) pursued the Kotelchuck (1972) finding that among one-year-old infants, those whose fathers had greater care-taking involvement with them at home experienced less separation protest than those whose fathers had minimal caretaking involvement with them at home. They studied one-year-old infants with their mothers and fathers in the laboratory, using 13 experimental conditions including the introduction of a female stranger. The findings indicated that so long as one parent remained with the infant there was little separation protest behavior. Infants of fathers who were high in their caretaking involvement at home showed little distress when left alone with the stranger. Their separation protest began later and ended earlier. Infants of fathers who were intermediate in their caretaking involvement at home experienced some distress when left with the stranger alone. Infants of fathers with minimal caretaking involvement at home showed the greatest amount of distress when left alone with the stranger. Babies who have more than one caretaker are therefore less susceptible to distress at separations. However, the infant's ability to relate to the father as a second attachment object does not necessarily lead to positive experiences with strangers (Kotelchuck, 1975).

Cohen and Campos (1974) found that although the father was a stronger attachment figure than the stranger in terms of proximity-seeking behaviors, the father was second to mother on all proximity-seeking behaviors except one (latency to locomote). The differentiation remained stable across the 10- to 16-month age span studied. In addition, the infant at 13 months was at the height of a positive response to the stranger when in close proximity to mother, and also cried less when the mother departed since it was a time of most positive response to father. A few infants showed a greater attachment to father than to mother, but within this age range this number did not increase over time. Although proximity-seeking measures revealed a preference for mothers over fathers, the separation protest measures did not reveal preferences since they failed to discriminate mother and father as attachment objects.

Lamb (1976b) found that 18-month-old infants interacted more with parents in dyadic situations than in triadic situations. In stress-free situations, infants show a slight preference for fathers in attachment behaviors. In affiliative behaviors, infants show a considerable preference for father in the stress-free and minimal-stress situations. Fewer affiliative behaviors were directed toward father when the stranger was present than when the stranger was absent. The stranger also inhibited the infant's interaction with mother. In fact, it was found that the stranger had a more significant effect on the infant's interaction with mother than the infant's interaction with the father. Under stress, infants preferred mothers for attachment behaviors but continued to favor fathers for affiliative behaviors. However, fathers were also attachment figures under stressful conditions.

Lamb concludes that the stress conditions did not have as significant an impact on the infant at 18 months as was the case at 12 months (Lamb, 1976e). Mothers were not as overwhelmingly preferred under stress as they were at 12 months. At 18 months, infants still preferred mothers as attachment figures, but now this preference was only under stressful conditions, whereas at 12 months mother was the preferred attachment figure under stress and in stress-free conditions.

Lamb (1977b, 1977c) observed 20 infants with mother, father, and stranger in the home at 15, 18, and 21 months and in the laboratory at 24 months. In this study, Lamb found that by the second year, the infant's relationship to the father had consolidated and, as a result, infants turned to both fathers and mothers for their attachment and affiliative needs. At 24 months, parental preference in stress and stress-free conditions disappeared.

The Role of the Father in Cognitive Development:
The First 3 Years of Life

Since the mid-1950s a vast literature has developed that emphasizes the infant's early capacities for attention, sensory response, sensorimotor development, and perception (Stone, Smith, and Murphy, 1973). The impact of the father on the infant's cognitive development, however, has just begun to be investigated. Most of the research to date has been with preschool children and older children (Baumrind, 1971; Radin, 1972, 1973, 1976).

The research attempting to examine the relation between the father and the infant's cognitive development is primarily correlational (Pedersen, Rubenstein, and Yarrow, 1973; Clarke-Stewart, 1977). Also, the father's role in the infant's cognitive development must be inferred from most of the research on attachment and social interaction, since this is not studied directly. Longitudinal observation of the father's stimulation of or interference with the infant's cognitive development has not yet been undertaken. However, one outstanding study does consider the relationship between social labeling, cognition, and the father (Brooks-Gunn and Lewis, 1975).

One important problem is how to tease out the mother's impact from the impact of the father on the infant's cognitive development. This is particularly difficult since mothers and fathers overlap in their functions and relationships with their babies.

Pedersen and associates (1973) studied infants 5 to 6 months of age. They found when assessing scores on intellectual tests and exploratory and problem-solving behavior, that father presence made a significant impact on boys but not on girls. No significant findings were reported for comparisons between infants and mothers of father-present and father-absent groups.

Sigel (1970) and Brooks-Gunn and Lewis (1975) are interested in the father's contribution to the development of representational thought. Sigel elaborates this idea in his distancing hypothesis. That is, since the father usually leaves the home to go to work, the infant creates a label or cognitive representation for the absent parent in order to maintain a relationship with him. This may be more of an issue in the early relationship betweeen infant and father since the father, unlike the mother, is away a good deal of the time.

Brooks-Gunn and Lewis offer another hypothesis to explain the complex mental processes that are necessary in order to know an absent social object, which they call the transitivity hypothesis. That is, the infant can form a relationship with a second person through the mother, regardless of how much direct social contact the infant has with this person. For our purposes, this hypothesis requires the structure of a triad that includes the infant, mother, and father.

The Brooks-Gunn and Lewis study is exciting with regard to the roles played by father and mother in the development of representational thinking. They studied infants between 9 and 36 months of age. In general, the cognitive activity of labeling increased with age. More specifically, at 15 months, 25 percent of the infants labeled the picture of their fathers and labeled it correctly. By 18 months, 100 percent of the infants labeled the pictures of their fathers without errors. At 18 months, infants began to generalize the father label to the picture of the male adult.

Mothers were not labeled at all until the infants were 18 months old. However, the mother label was not used correctly all the time until 24 months of age. The infants did not generalize the mother label as frequently as they generalized the father label and, when they did so, made more errors. Thus, the label for mother remained more specifically attached to mother herself and generalization, when it occurred, took place later than the generalization of the father label. In addition, infants looked at the pictures of fathers for a longer time than the pictures of mothers. Mothers also reported that "daddy" preceded "mommy" in their infants' speech development.

Brooks-Gunn and Lewis interpret these findings in light of the two hypotheses of distancing and transitivity. The infant's labeling of the father is facilitated by the mother who, during the course of the day, may refer to the father (*transitivity*). Also, the representation of an object, in this case the father, is acquired when a certain amount of distance lies between the child and the object (*distancing*). The question still to be answered is what combination of object absence and object presence and interaction is optimal for representation of social objects (father) to occur. In addition, it would be interesting to see if sex differences regarding the labeling process occur, and if so, at what point in the infant's development. Brooks-Gunn and Lewis do not report sex differences in their data.

Lewis and associates (1973) and Clarke-Stewart (1977) attempted to look at the relationship between cognition and attachment. The relationship between intelligence, as measured by the Bayley, and proximal and distal attachment behaviors was explored by Lewis and associates (1973). Studying infants at 12 and 24 months, they found that distal behaviors characterized the interactions of the more intelligent boy infant with both mother and father. For the more intelligent girl infant, interactions with father were characterized by distal behaviors more than proximal behaviors. However, with mother, the more intelligent girl infant expressed both proximal and distal behaviors. In general, boy and girl infants who were more intelligent increased their use of distal behaviors in their interactions (looking and vocalization) and decreased their use of proximal behaviors in attachment. This transition offers support for a transformational hypothesis regarding attachment behaviors. That is, proximal attachment behaviors are more fundamental; distal behaviors are more advanced; and a further step may include the transformation of distal behaviors into symbolic behaviors such as thinking about parents without seeing them (*representational thinking*).

Clarke-Stewart (1977) studied 15- to 30-month-old infants. She was interested in the contributions of mother and father to the cognitive development of boy and girl infants. The findings indicated that the father's physical play with his son was the best predictor of cognitive development for the boy infant, and the father's verbal interaction (talking, positive emotional reaction, and praise) was a good predictor of the girl infant's cognitive development. Also, the mother's verbal stimulation of the girl infant positively affected cognitive development. These correlations suggest the presence of a same-sex influence between father and son and mother and daughter.

Lewis and Weinraub (1976) introduce the concept of tension intro-duction in the separation-protest-attachment studies. Since mother and father relate to their infant in similar but slightly different ways, the infant learns to discriminate between the two parents and has to cope with the frustration that arises when learning these subtle differences between parents and establishing different sets of expectations for mother and father. If the infant can resolve the issues of difference and similarity between mother and father, then he is more prepared to deal with the introduction of a total stranger into the situation. The ability to discrimi-nate the parents can be regarded as an important cognitive achievement, which then paves the way to a smoother response to the adult stranger. This idea implies that a certain amount of tension is necessary for the stimulation of cognitive development.

Two psychoanalysts, Galenson and Roiphe (1980), have conducted research on the preoedipal development of infants. They offer some new and exciting findings regarding the symbolic play of girl and boy infants in the second year of life. A boy at this age, when he perceives the genital difference between the sexes, denies the difference, a denial supported by the boy's turning to the father in identification with him. This need to deny the sexual difference has an effect on the symbolic capacities of the little boy. The boys are less likely to use fantasy as a symbolic elaboration, and their formation of an image of their own body is also affected. Their play is repetitive. Boys must remain distant from mother because she re-minds them of castration. Along the same lines, Galenson and Roiphe report that some words could not be learned by boys from the mother but could be learned from the father. The father's contributions to the boy infant in terms of identification and learning are emphasized here.

Girls do not deny the genital difference between the sexes and thus their symbolic activities flourish. They are extremely flexible in their play and are interested in trying new things. Galenson and Roiphe do not address the issue of the father's contributions to the little girl's symbolic play and interest in novelty. However, it is clear from their work that girls can turn toward both mother and father since they do not need to deny sex differences.

Abelin (1971, 1975) suggests that as a result of the extended need for a real relationship with father in order to separate from the preoedipal mother in the rapprochement subphase, the mental representation of the father lags behind the mental representation of the mother (see also Chap. 2). However, the Brooks-Gunn and Lewis (1975) social-labeling study showed that the father's pictures were accurately identified earlier than pictures of the mother. This suggests that abstract cognitive processes are at work in relation to the father since he is absent a great deal, requiring recognitory and evocative memory capacities to develop and aid in the steps necessary for an internal object representation of the father to occur.

The Father's Contribution to the
Development of the Infant's Gender Identity

The infant's gender identity is largely determined in the first 2 to 3 years of life (Money and Ehrhardt, 1972). Thus it is very important to look at the parents' contributions to the sexual identity of their infants. Their attitudes and fantasies about boys and girls as well as their feelings about their own sexuality influence mothers and fathers in their interactions with their infants and contribute greatly to their conscious and unconscious expectations for their infants (Parke, 1978b; Parke et al., 1979).

Parents, especially fathers, prefer male to female children (Hoffman, 1977; Parke, 1979). The psychological research (Rendina and Dickerscheid, 1976; Kotelchuck, 1976) indicates paternal preferences from the very beginning. Parke and O'Leary (1976) found that fathers touch and talk to firstborn boy infants more than firstborn girl infants. Parke and Sawin (1977) found that mothers and fathers differ in their play interactions with boy and girl infants. Fathers held their daughters closely and for longer duration during their play than sons, and mothers held sons more closely than daughters. Fathers also favored boy infants in terms of stimulation and visual attention. Within the feeding context, fathers stimulated their boy infants more by moving the bottle more for boys than for girls.

Attachment studies offer slightly different findings. Pedersen and Robson (1969) found no sex-of-infant differences in the father's social interactions and caretaking at 8 to 9 months. Lamb (1977b, c) found no differences between mother and father with boy and girl infants from 7 to 13 months. However, differences were observed with infants 15 to 24 months of age. Both parents talked to girl infants equally, but fathers talked to boy infants more than mothers and were more actively engaged with boy infants than girl infants at this age.

By the second year of life, it becomes clear that the infant responds to these clues from the parents, particularly the father's preference for his boy infant. Fathers discourage feminine behavior in their sons. They are concerned with a lack of aggressiveness and an inability to defend oneself in their little boys, yet such behavior is totally acceptable for their little girls (Tasch, 1952). Mothers are less concerned with the differentiation of infants along gender lines (Sears, Maccoby, and Levin, 1957; Bee et al., 1969; Lewis and Weinraub, 1976). One very important way in which mothers foster masculine identifications in their sons is if the mother feels positively toward the father and men in general (Weinraub, 1978).

Both psychoanalytic theory and observations regarding children under 3 years of age have made important contributions to understanding the role of the father in the infant's sexual development. At this point, more is known about the father's role in the son's than in the daughter's preoedipal development (see Chaps. 2, 14). Of interest are little boys' as well as little girls' preferences for sameness in sexual selection and consequent identifications, leading to gender-identity formation. This process also seems to be influenced by the same-sex preference on the part of the parent toward the child. Lamb's (1977b) research suggests that the father may foster the girl's attachment to the mother by his greater interest in the boy child in the family. As a result of his withdrawal from the girl infant, he may push her away from him and toward the mother. The birth order of the infant is significant here. That is, if the girl infant is firstborn and without siblings, her relationship with her father may be different and potentially more involving than if she is the second child with an older male sibling or the firstborn with a younger male sibling. Thus, it is possible that the father's active presence for his son fosters early gender identity in the boy infant, whereas the father's withdrawal from the girl infant and the mother's active presence for the girl infant fosters gender identity in the girl infant.

Psychological studies have identified several characteristics of the father that are related to the development of masculine core identity in boys. There is no simple relationship between the masculinity of the son and the masculinity of the father. Rather, masculinity of the boy child is related to the warmth, nurturance, encouragement, and availability of the father (Biller and Borstelmann, 1967; Bigner, 1970; Young and Hamilton, 1978). Also, the paternal characteristics of warmth and nurturance have been correlated with masculinity in boys and femininity in girls (Weinraub, 1978). These characteristics appear to be more crucial for development of gender identity than the father's disciplinary behavior and limit-setting role (Biller and Borstelmann, 1967). These findings, however, are not based on actual father-child interaction studies.

It has also been shown that fathers are more concerned with the sexual development of their children, especially with boy infants (Lynn, 1974), than are mothers. Yet the father's specific behaviors that are influential in this regard are still rather unclear (Weinraub, 1978). Only detailed longitudinal observations can gather this information in a meaningful way. Although many studies show sex-of-parent/sex-of-infant differences, there are no studies to date that directly focus on the role of the father and mother in the development of the infant's gender identity.

The psychological research (Biller, 1970) also suggests the need for further exploration of the relationship between father and daughter, particularly the influence of the father on the girl infant's development of gender identity.

Suggestions for Future Research

A great need exists for a longitudinal study that investigates the nature of the father-infant relationship during the first 3 years of life (see Chap. 35). Such a study would provide important information regarding the actual interactions that take place within the family triad and, in particular, between father and infant. But it would be incomplete without an investigation of the father's intrapsychic attachment to the infant. How the father feels about being a parent, what is communicated to him about his fathering abilities by his wife, his experiences with his own parents, and the particular conflicts he had as a child, which may still remain unresolved, are all factors contributing largely to how and in what ways a father can be available to his infant (Rohrer and Edmonson, 1960; Landis, 1965; Barry, 1970). Observations of what the father actually does directly and indirectly with the infant, as well as his internal experience of being a father will then provide the necessary data for theoretical formulations about the father's impact on the infant.

Several important hypotheses and questions could be explored within such an observational context. First, the capacity of both the mother and father to deal with the change from a dyadic to a triadic family structure will directly affect the father's ability to interact with the infant and develop his paternal role.

A second set of questions pertains to the father's contribution to the infant's emotional development. The father is from the very beginning experienced by the infant as more separate and distant. The father teaches his baby more about gross affective states such as real highs (being thrown up in the air) and real lows (being let down abruptly). He wishes, for a variety of reasons, that his infant would grow up and be older. Thus, the father promotes differentiation and individuation.

Third, the father probably facilitates the infant's capacity to deal with transitions and brief separations. With the father leaving the home for work in the morning and returning at night, the infant develops a sense of comings and goings. He learns to develop over time a mental image of the father. The infant also develops a sense of longing for the father, and he anticipates the return of the father with pleasure. However, since the infant has always felt more differentiated from the father, there is less emotional stress related to the father's departure and the separation experienced by the infant. This may actually enhance the building of libidinal object constancy.

Fourth, the father and the mother offer different and complementary cognitive and emotional organizations of the world to the infant. The father's cognitive organization, in Piagetian terms, is in the direction of the pole of accommodation. That is, there is stimulation for the child to adapt by taking in new information. In both the cognitive and affective spheres, the infant has to react to the father by adapting to him. The father initiates the new and unknown. The father offers the infant greater variety along the stimulus continuum.

Finally, the infant utilizes his father to fulfil specific developmental functions. First, the infant turns to his father to help him in his relationship with his mother. The infant may need the father's help in becoming closer to the mother. Also, the infant turns to the father when he needs help to differentiate and separate from mother. He turns to the father when there is something wrong in the mother-infant dialogue. With a normal infant-mother pair, this may be for brief and occasional moments, until things are back to normal. With disturbed mother-infant communications in which the disturbance is primarily due to the mother, the baby may turn to the father for help more as a general, frequent pattern. The infant turns to the father when he experiences separation anxiety vis-à-vis the mother.

In addition, the infant turns to the father to fulfil certain direct paternal functions. The infant experiences less separation anxiety with father and more separateness. This allows the infant to explore in a more autonomous manner, both emotionally and cognitively. Thus, the infant turns to the father out of his specific attachment to his father and with the desire for the kind of interaction the father offers him. Also, the infant turns to the father for novelty. And finally, the infant turns to the father as a protector in the home, and later outside the home.

II

Developmental Perspectives: The Early Phases

Against the backdrop of the foregoing perspective, the volume now turns to an exploration of the father's role in early development. The chapters that follow represent a broad spectrum in terms of theoretical preferences, disciplinary and research backgrounds, conceptual styles, and the nature and use of evidence. We have attempted to retain the integrity of each contribution and to present each one fairly intact. With this in mind, however, the diversity and controversial nature of some of the assertions that follow require some prefatory remarks.

The first chapter, by researcher-clinicians Greenberg and Morris, has become something of a classic in the field of father research. Their evidence, statistical and clinical, is presented simply and factually; the authors make few pretenses at thoroughgoing dynamic explanation. In two later chapters, Gurwitt and Herzog focus on the man's complex and intense inner upheavals and transformations during pregnancy and on the longstanding childhood motifs revivified in response to this adult developmental crisis.

In the second chapter, Michael Yogman, a pediatrician and developmentalist in the Brazelton tradition, reviews the growing body of research on father-infant interaction. He then details his own seminal research in this area. His is a careful quantitative approach with a shared data bank of videotapes and tabulations, and this contrasts with some of the subsequent offerings, whose evidential underpinnings are less explicit. One controversial issue in Yogman's work has to do with the nature of the young infant's representation of its father. Is the infant responding to some recognized form? Or is it the father's high-keyedness and intrusive style which fuel the apparent intensity of their encounter? Indeed, in all infant research the correspondences between the behavioral and the intrapsychic remain moot, matters for disciplined conjecture.

Stanley Greenspan is both an analyst and an empirical researcher. Because his conceptualizing bridges the two disciplines and because he reviews key issues in infant development, his chapter has been chosen to

follow Yogman's. In a sense, however, his contribution actually consti-
tutes two chapters in one. In the second half of the paper he presents a view
of triadic relations (involving mother, father, and child) which only begin
to crystallize during the third year of life. And, in this sense, the chapter is
somewhat out of sequence.

Richard Atkins, a child psychiatrist, in general describes material that
pertains to earlier development than that scrutinized by Greenspan. But,
like Greenspan, he also concentrates on early tendencies toward so-called
triangulation, emphasizing the mother's role in presenting and portraying
the father for the very young child. His references to Winnicott's "envi-
ronment" and "object" mothers are particularly intriguing and might in a
restricted sense be applied to fathers as well.

Galenson and Roiphe, psychoanalytic infant observers, are noted for
their work on the "early genital phase" and on what they believe to be the
preoedipal origins of castration anxiety. In this chapter they view the little
girl's interaction with her father in terms of these issues. The accent on the
mother's part in shaping the father-daughter relationship is quite striking,
as is the authors' reliance on the mother's reporting of events. Inevitably,
the father's complex motivations remain, for these and other reasons, out-
side their purview, reflecting some of the general difficulties besetting all
systematic child observation to date.

The current tendency to focus on the mother-child dyad tends to con-
trast with analyst and child psychiatrist James Herzog's account of the
child's craving for the modulating influence of a father. Herzog's delinea-
tion of sex differences and other hypotheses may require further systematic
confirmation. But still the clinical material is evocative and provocative.

The concluding three chapters, by Tyson, a psychologist, Ross, psy-
chologist and theorist, and Kestenberg, a pioneer in child analytic observa-
tion, represent forays into a relatively dark continent: the father's role in
the early inner unfolding of masculine and ultimately paternal identity of
little boys. Each author has postulated a developmental line for male pa-
rental and sexual identity, with emphases on the early oneness of mother
and son and on the father's function in offering alternatives that facilitate
disengagement from her. The evidence for their hypotheses derives from
various sources: clinical analytic work, child observation, and (in Ross's
case) the additional use of projective techniques. There are variations in
the sequences postulated as well as in what these authors see as critical
periods in masculine development. Thus, for example, Tyson lays great
stress on the era of urethral erotism in males, the boy's learning of upright
urination and the father's role in this regard. As a teacher and model, the
father helps consolidate male gender identity. Judith Kestenberg, in her
turn, stresses the abiding impact of what she believes to be an "inner geni-

84

tal phase," a specifically maternal phase in the development of both boys and girls. According to Kestenberg, this is rooted in psychosexual and anatomical structures and is signaled by certain telltale movement patterns. Both the indices of its existence and "inner genitality," the developmental concept itself, have been subjects of some controversy within the field. John Ross, whose first work in the field of fatherhood was based on an initial study of 60 boys between 3 and 10 years of age, utilizing specially designed projective procedures, finds a climax in a 5-year-old's assumption of a would-be fatherhood. Here he differs somewhat with Judith Kestenberg, who believes that such procreative ambitions come to the fore earlier, before full-fledged oedipal development, during the phase of so-called phallic narcissism. But, like her, more than Tyson, Ross lays stress on a boy's dawning awareness of a father's specifically procreative function.

Finally in this section, Lora Tessman turns to the father's part in melding sexual excitability with what she terms the "endeavor excitement" of little girls. Her focus is on the oedipal phase and its residua in adult life. Her presentation is enlivened and substantiated by an exemplary reporting of actual exchanges between patient and therapist. And where so many clinicians would seek out pathology, Tessman tends to find the seeds of health in the father-daughter relationship.

5

Engrossment: The Newborn's Impact upon the Father

Martin Greenberg and Norman Morris

This study is an attempt to understand the impact of the first newborn upon the father. In clinical interviews, specific aspects of the father's developing bond to his newborn were noted, and the development of this bond was observed to have a discernible influence upon the father. Further, the normal reflex activity and behavior of the newborn was observed to enhance this bond.

The senior author (M.G.) first became interested in the father-child relationship as a by-product of his study of the early mother-infant relationship and the various influences upon this relationship. The father, as a significant other person, was thought to have a considerable impact on the mother-infant relationship. Yet in perusing the literature it was noted that there was little mention of the father's influence. This has been commented upon by Nash (1965) and by Howells (1969), who noted the relative scarcity of literature and objective studies dealing with the father-child relationship. This scarcity of clinical studies is even more glaring in the area of the early father-newborn relationship, particularly in the first week.

In attempting to understand father relations to newborns, particularly in the first week, this researcher (Greenberg, 1972) surveyed the subject in three sources: animal literature, transcultural literature, and contemporary literature on obstetric and nursery practices.

The animal literature indicated that newborns have a strong impact upon males among many species. Considerable evidence of male involvement with the care of newborns was noted throughout the vertebrate animal world (Alvederdes, 1927; Tinbergen, 1953; Itani, 1959; Devore, 1963; Mason, 1965; Howells, 1969).

Studies of different cultures also indicate that the newborn infant has

This chapter is a reprint from the *American Journal of Orthopsychiatry* 44(4):520–531, July, 1974. Copyright © 1974 by the American Orthopsychiatric Association, Inc. Reproduced by permission.

powerful early impact on the father, and there is strong evidence of father involvement with their newborns. Many primitive cultures directly stress the father's role in childbearing. In some cultures, the father is required to remain in bed during the period of delivery and for some days thereafter. At the time of birth he mimics the labor and goes through the motions of having a birth. In many primitive cultures men hold and caress infants and show considerable interest and enjoyment of babies (Mead, 1934; Ford, 1945, 1964; Fock, 1967; Tyler, 1967).

In contemporary Western society, in hospitals where fathers had early contact with their newborns in the first week (through participation in rooming-in units), fathers were observed to have enthusiastic responses to, and intense involvement with, their newborns (Jackson, 1948; McBryde, 1951; Montgomery, 1952). Numerous obstetricians (Morris, 1960; Vellay, 1960; Bradley, 1962, 1965; Miller, 1964; Pawson and Morris, 1971) have also noted the powerful impact that the newborn has upon the father and the intense involvement that fathers have in their child's birth and in their newborn baby (Stender, 1968).

Thus, the animal, anthropological, and contemporary literature on obstetrical and nursery practices point out the strong impact of the newborn upon the father and give indication of early father involvement with newborns.

In our attempt to describe this involvement of the father with his newborn, we will employ the term *engrossment*, by which we refer to a sense of absorption, preoccupation, and interest in the infant. The potential for engrossment in one's newborn is considered an innate potential, and it is hypothesized that it is by early contact with the infant that this potential for involvement is released. Engrossment thus refers to the link-up of father to newborn from the point of reference of the father. It is the purpose of this chapter to attempt to delineate the characteristics of engrossment and to thereby determine if the concept has validity.

Method

Two groups of *first* fathers were studied: (1) a group whose first contact with their newborn occurred at the birth (in the delivery room), and (2) a group whose first contact with the newborn occurred after the birth, when it was shown to them by nursing personnel.

The study was carried out in London, England, at three maternity hospitals with similar demographic characteristics. All of the fathers were married. Only first fathers whose wives had normal pregnancies and vaginal deliveries without instrumentation (any kind of forceps) were included in the sample. Furthermore, only fathers whose infants were normal were included in the study. All of these problem situations were eliminated in an attempt to study the father-infant bond without interference from other extraneous factors.

Fifteen fathers in each group were given a written questionnaire dealing with their feelings toward their newborns between 48 and 72 hours after the child's birth (with the exception of one father not at his child's birth who received the questionnaire 24 hours after his child's birth). The multiple-choice questionnaire was organized from our previous experience in a pilot study at one of the hospitals and from previous analogous research upon mother-infant relationships (Levy, 1954; Greenberg, 1973). All answers were subsequently analyzed by the Chi-square test with the Yates correction. In addition, fathers from two of the hospitals were interviewed in an open ended session after the completion of their questionnaire. This included eight of the fifteen fathers who witnessed their child's birth and seven of the fifteen who had not witnessed the birth.

The two groups were similar in age, socioeconomic characteristics, amount of previous experience they had had with children, and in the age, occupation and education of the mothers. The majority of babies in both groups were planned. The average birth weights of the babies were similar, as was the length of time that the wives were in labor and the number of wives in each group attending classes on pregnancy.

Questionnaire Data

On the questionnaire, both groups of fathers showed evidence of strong paternal feelings and of involvement with their newborn. Ninety-seven percent (29 of 30) of the fathers rated their paternal feelings as average to very high. In response to the question, "When did you first get the feeling the baby was all yours?," 10 fathers in each group (20 of 30, or 67%) indicated this occurred immediately after the birth. The majority of the fathers were very glad both immediately after the delivery (24 of 28, or 85%) and on the day they completed the questionnaire (29 of 30, or 97%). In addition, the majority of the fathers were happy with the sex of their baby (29 of 30, or 97%).

Both groups of fathers judged themselves able to distinguish their own newborn from other babies by the way he looked (27 of 30, or 90%); however, the fathers who had been present at their child's birth thought they could do this all the time while the fathers who were not present thought they could do this only some of the time (0.1 significance level). Both groups of fathers had considerable difficulty in distinguishing their baby all or some of the time by his cry (7 of 30, or 23%). The majority of fathers in both groups were unable to attribute any meaning to their baby's cry (17 of 29, or 59%); however, a few fathers (4 of 29, or 14%) thought that they could tell from their baby's cry when he was hungry. The majority of fathers indicated that they wanted to share with their wives the responsibility of raising the baby (27 of 30, or 90%). The majority of fathers in both groups judged themselves as picking up the baby often or sometimes (23 of 30, 77%). There was a trend that fathers who were present at their infant's birth felt more comfortable in holding their baby.

The two groups were significantly different in the following respects. The fathers who were present at their child's birth had attended more classes dealing with labor and delivery as opposed to the other group ($p = 025$), judged themselves as having more knowledge of labor and delivery ($p = 025$), and spent more time in the labor room prior to the birth ($p = 025$).

Clinical Interview Data

The following interview data were applicable to both groups of fathers unless otherwise stated. Specific comments of the fathers are presented as examples.

Characteristics of Engrossment

Visual Awareness of the Newborn. The fathers enjoy looking at their own baby as opposed to other babies and perceive the newborn to be attractive, pretty, or beautiful. Mr. C., a first father, who saw the birth, stated:

I couldn't get over it. I suppose what it was, in the afternoon, I walked up and down and looked at all the babies in that room up there and they all looked a bit ugly, a bit rubbery and then when she came out she looked so beautiful, really, a little gem, so beautiful.

There is in addition a powerful impact made by the newborn's face, which is not only seen as beautiful but also makes the father aware of the baby as an individual. Mr. J., a father who did not witness his child's birth, stated:

There was much more character in the child than I ever thought there was going to be at that stage *in the face*. I mean it didn't remind me of anybody, but it seemed to have a personality immediately. . . . It was absolutely incredible, the sight itself.

Tactile Awareness of the Newborn. There is a desire for and pleasure in tactile contact with the newborn. The fathers have the desire to touch, pick up, move, hold, and play with the newborn and they find it extremely pleasurable to carry this out. Mr. C. stated that when he picks up his baby, "I feel great, just great; can't stop picking her up—really a strong feeling of pleasure. She wriggles in your hands, she wriggles when she's against your chest and in your arms."

The nature of the baby's skin had great impact on some of the fathers. Mr. J., for example, was impressed by the smoothness of his baby's skin. When asked how it felt to touch it he stated: "Oh, incredibly soft; one hears the expression as soft as a baby's backside, I suppose, but then, on the other hand, when I touched it, it seemed incredibly soft, like velvet."

Awareness of Distinct Characteristics of the Newborn. The fathers were aware of the unique features and characteristics of their newborn to such an extent that they often felt that they could distinguish their own baby from others. Some of the fathers could also describe their infants in great detail, and felt strongly that the infants looked like them. The resemblance to the father is often more emphasized by them than any resemblance to the wife. Mr. K., a father who did not see his baby born, commented with respect to his feeling for the baby: "It's a marvelous feeling, especially as he looks like me." When I asked how the baby looked like him, he stated:

He's got a longish body already although he's very light in weight. He's got large hands like me, he's got long feet, he's got large ears, he's got a broad nose like me, he's got a little chin with a cleft I think. He's got my wife's hair, long black silky hair, and her eyes—at the moment—which are brown. I definitely would be able to recognize him *by his face* and if I wasn't sure about the face, I could definitely go by the hands and the feet. I think I could pick him out of a crowd.

Many of the fathers who witnessed their infant's birth viewed this as important in giving them a feeling of certainty that the baby was really theirs. This was something not commented upon by the fathers who did not see their infant born. Mr. M., who witnessed his child's birth, commented:

The fact that you actually see it born—you *know* that it's yours. I'm not suggesting that if you don't go into the delivery room that they swap them then. But, you can see your wife actually giving birth. And you know that this is something that the two of you have produced.

Father Perceives Infant as Perfect. In spite of some so-called unsightly aspects and awkwardness of the baby, the infant is seen by many of the fathers as the epitome of perfection. For example, Mr. C. stated:

The little nervous system seems to be in its first stages. It seems to be not completely coordinated yet. . . . The legs seem to be shaking about as if they're a bit uncoordinated. But it all seems just right. It seems as though all these little systems are going into action, the eyes, the ears, the neck, the nervous system. Everything seems to be going into action and everything seems to be *just right, just right.*

Father Feels a Strong Feeling of Attraction to the Newborn Which Leads to a Focusing of His Attention on the Infant. This focusing of attention is illustrated by Mr. S., who stated that when he visits the hospital, "I just sit and stare at it and talk to the wife and comfort her a bit. But the main thing is the baby. I just want to hold the baby."

The fathers describe themselves as feeling drawn in toward the newborn. For example, Mr. C. stated:

When I come up to see my wife and I say, "Hi! How's things, everything all right, you need anything?" And then I go look at the kid and then I pick her up and then I put her down and then I say, "Hi! is everything all right?" And then I go back to the kid. I keep going back to the kid. It's like a magnet. That's what I can't get over, the fact that I feel like that.

This focusing on the baby can even make it seem larger. For example, Mr. C. commented: "Hey, she looked a bit bigger that night than she does tonight. I suppose, the birth, things are perhaps exaggerated or magnified a bit."

Father Experiences Extreme Elation. Almost all of the fathers experience a sensation often described as a "high" associated with the birth of their child, regardless of whether they actually saw the child born or had it brought to them by a nurse after the delivery had occurred. This high is variously described as feeling: "stunned, stoned, drunk, dazed, off-the-ground, full of energy, feeling ten feet tall, feeling different, abnormal, taken away, taken out of yourself." Almost all of the fathers developed this feeling in response to the birth, and those that developed this feeling initially still had it two to three days after the birth. The sensation of the high for many of the fathers seems partially related to the feeling of relief that the baby is healthy, and then that the baby is even more than that—that it is beautiful, perfect. Mr. J., who did not see his child born, stated:

One certainly felt somewhat high, you felt high, yeah, there's no doubt about it! I'm sure this was a combination of the birth and the relief that things were over. . . . The fact that everything, the hands and so on were so perfect at that stage, I think, it was in one piece and everything else. It was so gratifying. All the sense, all the fears that one had in one was suddenly released. I think that, combined in the fact that it was more than just all right, which is the first worry, I suppose. It was more than all right—it was beautiful! You went through that stage. You got the relief and then you got even more than that in the fact that it was even better than you could ever hope to think.

The newborn's face is a particularly powerful stimulus, which can trigger the father's experience of a high. Mr. C., a father who was present at his child's birth, stated, "I took a look at it and I took a look *at the face* and I left the ground—just left the ground! I thought, 'Oh! Jesus Christ! This is marvelous.'"

Father Feels an Increased Sense of Self-Esteem. The new fathers describe themselves as feeling proud, bigger, more mature and older after seeing their baby for the first time. Mr. S., a 23-year-old first father, who did not see his child born, commented:

It's a lovely little thing. I don't really want to leave. . . . I just feel a bit older now, I'm a father, a father at last. I feel I've got something of my own. I look at it and I say, "I done that—I done that, it's mine." I think it's just realizing that I'm a father and the baby's there and letting that sink in.

They often feel an increased sense of satisfaction when others see the baby. Mr. J., a first father, who was not present at his infant's birth, commented:

One looks forward to seeing it to begin with. One waits to come back in to see it. I think it's a sense of satisfaction. Here, again, the belief that one is seeing something that to you is perfect and coupled with relief that everything, the birth, is over. I can just feel very, very proud every time I see it. . . . I'm delighted when people look at it. I have a great deal of satisfaction from their reaction.

Father's Response to His Feelings of Involvement with the Newborn
Many fathers experience surprise at the degree of impact the baby has upon them, particularly when they are uninvolved during their wife's pregnancy:

Well, up to now, I didn't really feel all that involved, I suppose. I didn't really have much strong feeling one way or another. It was just my wife was pregnant and I was happy for her and that's just about as far as it went. But the little something was born, and—I did . . . a complete switch, just a complete switch! just felt tremendous about it. And I was surprised because I thought I wouldn't take too much interest in it until it was old enough to be a small human being. But it already is a human being.

One of the fathers indicated that he had some specific notions as to when he might become involved with his newborn. These, he thought, appeared to change after his child, a girl, was born. He stated:

I thought if it was going to be a boy and everything were going to be great, we could go out and jump around together and play about together. I was thinking about eighteen months, two years, two-and-one-half years, then we'd start to have a relationship. And I thought for the first eighteen months, it would be for the wife and everything would be fine for her and I'd just take it easy. But it wasn't like that at all. It was completely different. The kid was born—and I really had a strong feeling toward her.

The Impact of Normal Reflex Activity and Behavior of the Newborn Enhances Engrossment of the Father in the Newborn

The infant's movements have a strong impact upon the father; the liveliness and movements of the infant are a source of wonder and amazement to many fathers. They are even impressed that it appears alive. Mr. M., a father who saw his child's birth, commented that when he first saw his child he was: "Surprised at how lively it was . . . the way it wriggles about. Maybe it didn't, maybe it's my imagination! It looks so alive, so human, I expected it to be more wrinkled." One of the fathers described being "drawn" in to pick up the baby by its movements: "When she starts moving I go and pick her up and she starts moving in your hands and your arms and you can feel her moving up against you. It's like a magnet."

Some of the fathers see the infants opening its eyes in their presence as a communication, and Mr. C. stated that he felt his three-day-old infant had responded to him. He elaborated:

He was sleeping yesterday and his eyes were closed, and as I looked over he opened his eyes and I moved away and he closed them and I moved back again— and he opened them. Now, I don't know what that is, maybe some kind of telepathy or something, but I just think that he knew I was standing over him and he opened his eyes . . . it felt wonderful. This is the closeness that you have with a child knowing that he feels his father standing over him and opens his little eyes although he can't see anything.

Many of the fathers were very impressed by the infant's grasp reflex. For example, Mr. K. stated: "I put my finger into his little hand and he clasps hold of my finger and squeezes it. That's very encouraging." He described this as "some form of communication."

All of these normal aspects of infant behavior, taken together, have a powerful impact upon the father. They are rarely observed in isolation. For example, Mr. J., a father who didn't see the birth, commented when he first saw the child:

I was so surprised to find that it was already, even at this age, doing certain things like moving itself around. I thought it was going to be an object that just was going to be there. And it was looking around and it was gripping. At least I think it was gripping. You put your finger in its hand, and it was holding on . . . and when they just wrapped it up and put it in the cot by the side, it immediately took on somebody . . . somebody that one could look at and touch; and it was moving immediately. I felt suddenly I had a daughter! I didn't just have a baby. This was very satisfying.

Another father was particularly impressed by what he thought to be the infant's responsiveness to him, his movements and his voice. For example, he stated:

And when you talk to her, she seems to try and seek out the sound. And when you wave yourself at her, wave your hand, she seems to try and follow you with her eyes. . . . And once she looks at you, I don't know if she sees or not, but once she looks at you, and she's got really dark blue eyes, really dark, and beautiful, really beautiful.

Discussion

The results of this study suggest that fathers begin developing a bond to their newborn by the first three days after the birth and often earlier. Furthermore, there are certain describable characteristics of this bond which we call *engrossment*, which we observed in clinical interviews. Our findings suggest that the fathers develop a feeling of preoccupation, absorption, and interest in their newborn. The father is gripped and held by this particular feeling and has a desire to look at, hold, and touch the infant. It is as if he has been "hooked" by something that has transpired in the father-infant relationship.

The term *engrossment* is meant to mean more than involvement. The derivation of the word *engross* means *to make large*. When the father is engrossed in his individual infant, the infant has assumed larger proportions for him. In addition, it is suggested that the father feels bigger, and that he feels an increased sense of self-esteem and worth when he is engrossed in his infant.

There are indications in this research that the early contact by the father with the newborn seems to be significant in releasing engrossment. The father, by his presence, is able to observe his child. The newborn's face, activity, and eye movements were noted to be of tremendous significance for the father. Furthermore, any infant activity (grasp reflex, opening and closing eyes) occurring in the presence of the father was often perceived by the father as a response to him. The father's presence further enhanced the father's sensation of engrossment.

There were no highly significant differences in observations of engrossment among fathers who saw their newborn's birth as opposed to those who did not. However, it was noted on the questionnaire that fathers who were present at their infant's birth thought that they could distinguish their baby from other babies better than fathers who were not at the birth. There was also a trend suggesting that fathers who were present at the birth were more comfortable in holding the baby than were fathers who were not present. Furthermore, fathers who saw their child's birth repeatedly and spontaneously commented that "when you see your child born, you know it's yours." This "knowing it's yours" concept was not spontaneously mentioned by fathers who did not see their infant's birth. It is likely that the feeling is related to a sensation the father has of being hooked up or connected with his newborn. These observations suggest that there may be a qualitative difference in the degree of engrossment in the two groups of fathers based on the degree of contact with the newborn. Further studies would, however, be necessary, employing larger numbers of fathers to determine how the contact with the newborn is important and whether the presence at the birth is a highly significant contact in the development of engrossment.

It is likely that the greater the early physical contact with the infant, the more likely it is that engrossment will occur. Barnett and coworkers (1970) have alluded to this correlation with mothers of premature babies, noting increased attachment of mothers to their infants when tactile contact was permitted.

The first hour after birth may be a significant period and it would be an important time for the father (as well as the mother) to have contact with the newborn. In a previous investigation, it was observed that the infant tends to have its eyes open, is gazing around, has stronger sucking reflexes, cries more, and shows much more physical activity in the first hour after birth than it does in subsequent hours (Greenberg et al., 1967). The high incidence of the above infant behavior would be likely to reinforce and enhance the father's engrossment in his newborn.

It is hypothesized that engrossment is a basic, innate potential among all fathers. It is likely that there is an interaction between this innate potential and the cultural arena. Newton and Mead (1967) comment that cultures pattern not only the amount of emotional commitment but also who may show the greatest emotional commitment. In American society, attitudes toward the expression of fatherly behavior in the early weeks are becoming increasingly vague and ill-defined. Thus, in some instances, these cultural influences may result in an increased likelihood that the father will not make sufficient contact with his infant to result in the establishment of engrossment. Of particular interest are those fathers who appear to be ambivalent in their attitude toward the newborn; it is likely that the early contact with the newborn may be sufficient to push these fathers over the threshold, resulting in the release of engrossment. This was noted with several fathers in our study.

It is also likely that a father may feel engrossed in his infant, but afraid to give expression to his feelings. Some men think it is unmanly to express tender and affectionate feelings toward small babies. They may feel that the baby is just for the wife, a notion mentioned by one of the fathers in this study. Thus, when he experiences feelings toward the newborn that are counter to what he thinks is appropriate, the father may feel confused. Likewise, although most wives are pleased and surprised to see the extent of their husbands' involvement, some wives may feel threatened by the father becoming involved with the newborn, an area that she had considered her own staked-out territory. For example, Caplan (1960) and Leidenberg and Slap (1967) noted problems and competition between husband and wife in the care of the infant. These couples can greatly benefit from brief counseling from their physician or from psychiatric personnel in cooperation with their physician. The "permission" to be involved and the support of their physician may thus release the father's dammed-up expression of engrossment.

Hospital procedures may also be important in hindering or enhancing the father's engrossment in his newborn. Frequently, after the baby is born it is given to the mother and then returned to the nursery without the father having an opportunity to hold it. As a non-medical person, he may be afraid to assert himself, thinking that the staff have medical reasons for not inviting him to hold the baby. It is our impression that the infant should be offered to the father, as well as to the mother. In this way he would also be sharing in the immediate contact with the newborn, which most fathers find very enjoyable.

Many of the fathers have reported themselves to be so moved by the impact of the newborn that they feel drawn in toward the baby as if it were a magnet. Their attraction to the newborn is very powerful, and it appears to be something over which they have no control. They do not will it to happen; it just does. These feelings of intense involvement may be so great that the father may forget or be unaware of the need to express normal amenities to his wife. One of the wives became angered because her husband seemed to ignore her on his visits to the hospital, spending all of his time looking at the child. It is suggested that those fathers who are most surprised and unprepared for the development of engrossment are more likely to be totally overwhelmed by these feelings in the above fashion. We would advise physicians to explain briefly to this new father the general nature of engrossment so that he would have some insight into what he is experiencing. Hopefully, his greater awareness of his feelings to his newborn would allow him to respond more appropriately to his wife.

Fathers are at times absent from their newborns due to sickness, military, educational, or occupational obligations. It would be important to determine if there is a "sensitive period" in the development of the father's engrossment in his newborn. Is there any absolute time beyond which it is unlikely that engrossment will occur? In relation to this, Nash (1965) comments that the observations of Stolz (1954) suggest that there is a "critical period" in relation to the father's entry into the psychological development of the child. Brazelton (1970) observed that fathers absent from their newborns in the early months of their child's development had difficulty showing affection for their offspring. The time interval during which engrossment can occur has important consequences for the potential adoptive father. Further elucidation of the phenomenon of engrossment would be of great importance in helping both adopting fathers, as well as fathers separated from their newborns for long periods of time, to hook up with their newborns, that is, become *engrossed*.

The phenomenon of engrossment of the father in the newborn has important ramifications for the family triad. An engrossed father is unlikely to feel excluded and pushed out by the infant, for he too is involved and concerned with the care and welfare of the newborn. This concern is something he shares with his wife. In our study, many of the fathers commented that a feeling of closeness to their wives was often associated with the infant's presence. Fathers who were present at the birth particularly commented upon this in the clinical interviews.

The father's development of engrossment in his newborn infant may have important ramifications in the subsequent development and mental health of the child. Numerous investigators have noted increased anxiety, juvenile delinquency, and emotional disturbance among father-deprived children (Stolz, 1954; Holmes, 1959; Ostrovsky, 1959; Andry, 1960). A father who is engrossed early on in his newborn is likely to continue to be involved and maintain his contact with his developing child.

We believe that the study of the father's engrossment in his newborn infant is an important area of investigation because of its ramifications for the father, in addition to his wife and child. Our study suggests that the engrossed father has an increased sense of self-esteem and worth within the family. There is a tremendous emphasis on success and achievement placed upon men in Western society. The father's increased feelings of self-esteem, adequacy, and worth, which seem to occur with his engrossment in his child, would seem to be protective factors in his own mental hygiene. Engrossment of the father in his newborn is thus a significant issue for the father, with far-ranging consequences for the child and the family.

Conclusions

Thirty first fathers were given a questionnaire, and fifteen of them were interviewed 48 to 72 hours after their child's birth. Almost all of the fathers (97%) rated their paternal feelings as average to very high on the questionnaire. In clinical interviews it was observed that there were specific aspects of the father's developing bond to his newborn infant of note. The development of this bond was observed to have a discernible influence upon the father. This bond of the father to his newborn is described as *engrossment*; it consists of the following:

1. Visual awareness of the newborn—perceived as attractive, pretty, and beautiful.
2. Tactile awareness of the newborn—manifested by a desire to touch and hold the baby, which was perceived as very pleasurable.
3. Awareness of distinct features of the newborn.
4. Perception of the newborn as "perfect."
5. A strong attraction to the newborn, which leads the father to a focusing of his attention upon the infant.
6. Extreme elation, experienced by almost all fathers and often described as a high, following the birth of his child.
7. An increased sense of self-esteem experienced by fathers upon seeing their newborn for the first time.

Many of the fathers were extremely surprised at the extent of their feelings of involvement with the newborn. Furthermore, it was observed that the normal reflex activity and behavior of the newborn enhanced the father's engrossment in his newborn.

6

Observations on the Father-Infant Relationship

Michael W. Yogman

Recent observational studies suggest that the father's role with young infants is far less biologically constrained than was once thought. Wide variability in the behavior and roles of the two parents challenges, I believe, many of the stereotypes of the father as incompetent or not involved with the infant. Research I have conducted on patterns of father-infant interaction in the infant's first 6 months of life reveals that fathers can and often do form a significant relationship with their infants, one that is in some respects similar to and in other respects different from the mother-infant relationship. Indeed, the infant's capacity to elicit and engage in different patterns of interaction with father and mother, as well as with strangers, requires some revision of our previous ideas of the infant as passive, reactive, incapable of delay, and lacking any ego functions.

Observations of Fathers and Infants

In the past 10 years, empirical studies based on direct observations of father-infant interaction and interviews with fathers have allowed us to begin to outline the simultaneous development of the infant and his parents within a broader social world that also includes grandparents, friends, siblings, peers, and strangers. Previous conceptualizations of infant social development focused almost exclusively on the mother-infant

This is an abbreviated version of another chapter by the author, Development of the Father-Infant Relationship, in H. Fitzgerald, B. Lester, and M. W. Yogman (Eds.), *Theory and Research in Behavioral Pediatrics*, Vol. 1. New York: Plenum. 1982.

I wish to express my appreciation to the families who participated in these studies and shared a special time in their lives with me. Much of the research on which this chapter was based was done in collaboration with Dr. Suzanne Dixon and with the encouragement and assistance of Edward Tronick, Ph.D., Lauren Adamson, Ph.D., and T. Berry Brazelton, M.D. The generous support of The Robert Wood Johnson Foundation, The Carnegie Corporation, and the National Institutes of Mental Health is gratefully acknowledged. Part of this research was conducted at the Mental Retardation Research Center, Children's Hospital Medical Center, Boston, Massachusetts.

relationship, whether the importance of the mother was tied to her gratification of instinctual drives in psychoanalytic theory or her association with the feeding experience in social learning theory. While *attachment theory* conceptualized the infant as active rather than passive in seeking the caregiving and love necessary for survival, this theory also tended to minimize the role of the father in the infant's first year of life (Bowlby, 1969; Ainsworth, 1973). No theory acknowledged a meaningful direct role for fathers until the child entered the oedipal period and began to identify with the father (Freud, 1923d, 1925) or until the father could play a clear instrumental role in the family such as teaching his child to throw a ball (Parsons and Bales, 1955).

Sociocultural shifts that have occurred in the last 10 years have legitimized the study of the father-infant relationship, and a number of comprehensive reviews of studies of the father-infant relationship have appeared (Nash, 1965; Lynn, 1974; Lamb, 1975, 1976d, 1979; Lewis and Weinraub, 1976; Earls and Yogman, 1979; Parke, 1979; Yogman, 1982).

First, secular changes in infant care, documented by Bronfenbrenner (1961, 1976), have led fathers to play a more active role. These secular changes include an increase in the number of families in which both parents work and caretaking is shared (Howells, 1973) and, while rare in absolute terms, an increase in single-parent families in which the father is the primary caretaker (Mendes, 1976). They also include a shift in the father's role in the traditional family from a more hierarchical authoritarian one, to a more individualized and flexible one in which the father is encouraged to have more direct contact with his infant (Benedek, 1970a).

Second, our understanding of the mother-infant relationship has been modified by findings that the feeding experience is not as critical as was once thought (Harlow, 1958), that social responsiveness and stimulation are key dimensions contributing to psychological development (Rheingold, 1956), that infants could be attached to fathers who were not primary caretakers (Schaffer and Emerson, 1964), and by suggestions that studies of maternal deprivation were, more accurately, studies of parental deprivation (Green and Beall, 1962).

Interest in the father-infant relationship has come at a time when the field of infancy research has enormously expanded. Studies have demonstrated a wide range of perceptual, cognitive, and social competencies that are either present at birth or acquired by infants in the first few weeks (Wolff, 1963; Kessen, 1970; Brazelton, 1973; Bruner, 1973; Stone et al., 1973; Appleton et al., 1975; Lewis and Brooks, 1975; Bower, 1977).

Many of these competencies represent biological preadaptations of the infant that function to elicit caregiving from adults and ensure the infant's survival. Thus not only does the infant help the adult to develop appropriate responses (R. Q. Bell, 1968; Lewis and Rosenblum, 1974), but the processes of mutual recognition and regulation by both infant (Cassell and Sander, 1975) and parent (Klaus and Kennell, 1976) begin much earlier than attachment theory suggests. This shift in thinking about infants as capable of influencing caregivers means that any theory of the father-infant relationship must account for bidirectional influences of both the infant on the father and the father on the infant. A theory of the father-infant relationship must also recognize that these reciprocal influences can be direct as well as indirect (mediated through the mother or another family member), so the family is often the meaningful unit of analysis. In many ways the development of the father-infant relationship is similar to the mother-infant relationship in that infants can elicit competent loving caregiving from both male and female adults. Furthermore, there are similarities in the developmental transitions of adulthood that mothers and fathers experience in becoming parents. In other ways, however, it seems that the father-infant relationship is unique and complementary to the mother-infant relationship.

Perinatal Period

Fathers are now increasingly encouraged by obstetric services to accompany their wives during labor and delivery. In fact, Anderson and Standley (1976) have shown that husband support lessens the degree of maternal distress during this time. A recent interview study done in London of fathers' reactions to labor and delivery documented the powerful impact on the father of seeing and holding the newborn immediately after birth, whether or not he was present at delivery (see Chap. 5). Fathers seemed particularly impressed by the liveliness, reflex activity, and movements of the baby: "When she starts moving I go and pick her up, and she starts moving in your hands and your arms and you can feel her moving up against you. It's like a magnet."

While these descriptions may be particularly characteristic of father, other descriptions appear characteristic of either parent: feelings of extreme elation, relief that the baby is healthy, feelings of pride and increased self-esteem, and feelings of closeness when the baby opens his eyes (Robson and Moss, 1970). Fathers' descriptions of their newborns have also been reported to be more sex-typed than mothers' as evidenced by postpartum interviews on day one in which fathers rated sons as firmer, more alert, stronger, and hardier and daughters as softer, finer featured, and more delicate (Rubin et al., 1974).

Debate goes on about the existence of a sensitive period for maternal contact with newborns (Klaus et al., 1972), but in one recent study, early contact between father and baby was also associated with increased en face play in the early weeks of life (Keller et al.,1981). Moreover, in one study of a small sample of five fathers, the sequence in which fathers touch their newborn over the first 3 days of life has been shown to be the same as with mothers: first with fingertips and then with full palms and first on the extremities and later on the trunk (Klaus et al., 1970; Abbott, 1975); although fathers took longer than mothers before they displayed this progression. Even fathers whose babies were delivered by cesarean section displayed the same progression with increased eye-to-eye contact (Rodholm and Larsson, 1979). Whether this sequence is specific to parents or characteristic of all human adults in general has yet to be determined.

Studies by Parke and Sawin (1975, 1977) of father-newborn interaction in the postpartum period suggest that fathers and mothers are equally active and sensitive to newborn cues during the postpartum period. In general, these conclusions hold for middle-class as well as lower-class families and in both the dyadic (father-infant) and triadic (mother-father-infant) situations. These studies also suggest differences between father- and mother-newborn interaction: Fathers held, rocked, and provided more auditory and physical stimulation to their infants.

Moreover, fathers of newborns reported that their babies needed more stimulation and affection and were more perceptually competent than mothers did. Pedersen (1975), studying 4-week-old babies, has shown that fathers had an indirect influence on their babies as well, mediated through support of mother, that resulted in a more effective mother-infant relationship. While these studies describe how fathers and mothers interact with their newborn babies, little is known about the baby's influence on the father during the newborn period. It seems reasonable to assume that a father's sleep rhythms are modified by the new baby's schedule of night waking. Considering Sander's (1975) studies on the entrainment of biorhythms for mothers and infants, one wonders about similarities and differences in this process for fathers and infants as family schedules and periodicities become reorganized during the early weeks of postnatal life.

Early Infancy

During the first 6 months of life, infants become increasingly social as they begin to smile and vocalize. One might suspect that these socially responsive infants are good elicitors of social interaction with fathers as well as mothers. Together with colleagues at Boston Children's Hospital,

I began in 1974 to study the social interactions of fathers with their healthy full-term infants during the first 6 months of life. In contrast to functional tasks such as feeding and diapering, I studied unstructured face-to-face interaction because it placed maximal demands on the social capabilities of the participants. Although face-to-face communication may occupy only a small proportion of an infant's day at home, video-taped interactions in the laboratory allowed us to elicit and study in a detailed way exchanges of expressive communication that may underlie the developing father-infant relationship. This method of studying early social interaction was developed by Brazelton and associates (1975) and has been used to characterize mother-infant interaction as a mutually regulated reciprocal process.

I compared the face-to-face interaction of infants with fathers to their interaction with mothers and with strangers in order to study how infants differ in their patterns of expressive behavior during interaction with fathers as compared with mothers and strangers.

Subjects

The subjects were six firstborn infants (three females and three males) recruited in the newborn period as part of an ongoing study of social interaction, their mothers and fathers, and several adult strangers. Mothers were the primary caretakers in all families. The strangers were both male and female adults and varied in previous experience with infants.

Infants were all full-term, weighed more than 2,900 grams (approximately 6⅓ pounds) at birth, and were delivered vaginally after uncomplicated pregnancies. Apgars were all higher than seven and all were healthy neonates.

Observations

Each infant was studied during interaction with each parent and a stranger and seen weekly in a laboratory. A schematic representation of the laboratory can be seen in Figure 2. Two-minute face-to-face interactions were videotaped. The infant when alert and calm was seated in an infant seat placed on a table surrounded by curtains. The adult entered from behind the curtain, sat in front of the infant, and was instructed to "play without using toys and without removing the infant from the seat." One video camera focused on the infant, the other on the adult. The two images appeared simultaneously on the split-screen monitor (Fig. 3), which showed a single frontal view of adult and infant along with a digital time display. Sound was simultaneously recorded.

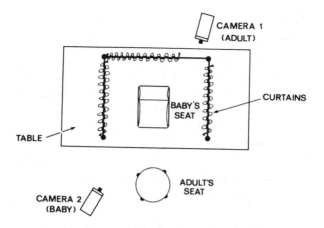

Figure 2. Schema of laboratory during observations of adult-infant interaction. (From T. Brazelton et al., Early Mother-Infant Reciprocity. In R. Hinde [Ed.], *Parent-Infant Interaction* [Ciba Foundation Symposium, no. 33]. Amsterdam: Elsevier, 1975. Reprinted with permission.)

Figure 3. Picture of monitor screen during father-infant session.

Each session consisted of a total of 7 minutes' recording: 2-minute periods of play with mother, father, and a stranger, separated by 30 seconds of infant alone to assure that she or he was alert and comfortable.

Analysis of Data

We used the videotapes to answer several different questions:

1. Could infants 3 months of age in an interactive situation discriminate familiar adults, mother, and father from each other and from unfamiliar strangers?
2. What are the similarities in mutual regulation and reciprocity between mother-infant and father-infant interaction?
3. What are the differences both in the quality of regulation and in the structure and content of games parents play with their infants?

Each of these questions required a different method of data analysis. The analysis of discrete behaviors will be discussed first, followed by analysis of more structural characteristics of social interaction, monadic phases, and social games.

Differential Interaction: Analyses of Discrete Behavior

First, we set out to determine whether the 3-month-old infants in our study interacted differently with mothers, fathers, and strangers. For this question, the videotapes were analyzed by using a microbehavioral scoring system to describe the behaviors each participant displayed second by second. The system consists of four categories of infant behavior (gaze patterns, limb movements, facial expressions, and vocalization), each with three mutually exclusive subdivisions; and five categories of adult behavior (gaze patterns, body positions, facial expressions, vocalizations, and touching patterns), each with four mutually exclusive subdivisions.

These analyses of discrete behaviors showed that infants by 80 days of age displayed different patterns of interaction with fathers as compared with mothers and strangers. They differentiated unfamiliar adults from their familiar parents as evidenced by less frequent displays of negative facial expressions with both mothers and fathers than with strangers. Infant differentiation of mother from father was more subtle and was evidenced only by the fact that they remained still more with their fathers than with their mothers (Yogman, 1982). Infant looking and vocalizations were not different with mothers, fathers, and strangers during the sessions. Analysis of data from sessions with infants as young as 6 weeks of age has shown similar findings (Yogman et al., 1976a, b; Dixon et al., 1981).

Not only does the infant interact differently with father, mother, and stranger, but the adults also behave differently (Yogman et al., 1976a, b). Our data indicate that within the ongoing context of an interaction, the infant rapidly adapts his behaviors to the familiarity and action of his partner even within a 2-minute period.

Similarities in Mutual Regulation: Analyses of Monadic Phases
Because we believed that the interactive messages and communicative meaning were carried not in discrete behaviors but rather in sequences of clusters of substitutable behaviors, we adapted a method of data analysis developed by Tronick (1977) and clustered the discrete behaviors into more meaningful units of analysis called monadic phases. For both the infant and the adult, a priori decision rules were created to translate each second-by-second display into one of the following monadic phases: talk, play, set, elicit, monitor, avert, and protest-avoid. Talk represents the most affectively positive phase while protest-avoid represents the least positive phase. Each of the monadic phases is made up of a set of substitutable second-by-second displays and is not defined by a single behavior. The choice of phases and rules for clustering were guided by the expectation that each phase would convey an affective message from one partner to the other.

The monadic phase analysis enabled us to look at both similarities and differences in the structural characteristics of mother-infant and father-infant interaction. This analysis derived from one of the sessions is depicted graphically in Figure 4. For each second of interaction, infant and adult behavior has been translated into monadic phases, and the sequence of phases with adult and infant superimposed is shown graphically (infant with a solid line, adult with a broken line).

Looking first at the father-infant graph, the figure shows that both father and infant cycle through similar phases shifting from set up to play and talk and then back to set again. Both father and infant spend more than 90 percent of the interaction in phases set, play, and talk, the three most affectively positive phases.

Furthermore, the graph allows one to focus on the transitions between phases and to see that these transitions are jointly regulated. The lower-case letters *a* through *j* below the graph mark transitions in which both partners move in the same direction within one to two seconds of each other. One can see that father and infant often change phases simultaneously during face-to-face interaction.

Comparing father-infant interaction on the top of Figure 3 with mother-infant interaction on the bottom, the similarities are striking. Mother and infant also cycle through similar affectively positive phases

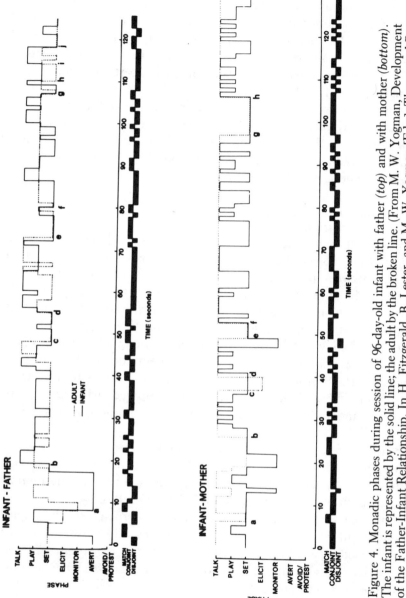

Figure 4. Monadic phases during session of 96-day-old infant with father (*top*) and with mother (*bottom*). The infant is represented by the solid line; the adult by the broken line. (From M. W. Yogman, Development of the Father-Infant Relationship. In H. Fitzgerald, B. Lester, and M. W. Yogman [Eds.], *Theory and Research in Behavioral Pediatrics*, Vol. 1. New York: Plenum, 1982. Reprinted with permission.)

109

and on several occasions also change phases simultaneously, as indicated by the lower-case letters *a* through *h* directly below the graph. With both parents, the cycling between phases limits the duration of time spent in any one phase. With both mothers and fathers, this cycling appears to maintain the level of affective involvement of each partner within certain limits in a homeostatic fashion.

These data suggest similarities in joint regulation and reciprocity displayed during dyadic interactions of infants with mothers and fathers. Similarities exist in the levels of affective involvement of the partners and the almost simultaneous timing of transitions between phases present during interactions with both parents.

Differences in Quality of Regulation:
Analyses of Transitions and Games
Differences between father-infant and mother-infant interaction are also evident in the graphs of Figure 4. These differences exist in the kinds of transitions between phases that occur. Using the graphs to analyze transitions from the phase infant talk, these data suggest that after infants talk with fathers, they are more likely to shift through lower phases and remain there for a longer time; while with mothers they are more likely to return immediately to talk. This difference in the quality of transitions between phases is characteristic of the more accentuated shifts from peaks of maximal attention to valleys of minimal attention that occur during father-infant interaction. This can be compared with the more gradual and modulated shifts that occur during mother-infant interaction.

Further differences are evident in the temporal structure and specific behavioral content of the games played by parents and infants. An "interactive game" is defined as "a series of episodes of mutual attention in which the adult uses a repeating set of behaviors with only minor variations during each episode of mutual attention" (Stern, 1974b). Examples of the father-infant games included such activities as exercising an infant in a "pull-to-sit" game (Fig. 5), repeatedly tapping the infant at three places (under the nose and at both corners of the mouth) while accompanying the taps with clicks of varying pitch, repeatedly buttoning the baby's lips, and bicycling the baby's legs (Yogman, 1977). These games resulted in a very aroused, attentive infant and were seen with both male and female infants as young as 23 days of age.

We chose to look at verbal games and motor games in more detail. In order to accurately describe the components of these games, we reviewed the videotapes from all six babies in the initial study and described in detailed narrative form episodes that met Stern's definition. The sample

110

Figure 5. Game between father and 45-day-old infant. (From M. W. Yogman, Development of the Father-Infant Relationship. In H. Fitzgerald, B. Lester, and M. W. Yogman [Eds.], *Theory and Research in Behavioral Pediatrics*, Vol. 1. New York: Plenum, 1982. Reprinted with permission.)

for this analysis consists of nine sessions recorded for each infant with mother and father at 4, 6, 8, 10, 12, 14, 16, 20, and 24 weeks of age. Descriptions of the games that occurred during these 54 sessions were then categorized according to a system devised by Crawley and coworkers (1978) for motor games, which we then modified by adding verbal games, combinations of games, and omitting gross-body-movement games since our setting precluded their occurrence. The categories we used and the results can be seen in Table 8.

First of all, while games occurred during most sessions, they were more likely to occur during sessions with fathers than with mothers. Mothers and infants played games during 75 percent of the 54 sessions, while fathers and infants played games during 87 percent of the sessions. Parents usually played more than one game per session (mean for mothers = 1.7 games per session; mean for fathers = 1.65 games per session). Of the games that did occur, pure tactile and pure verbal games and combinations of the two were quite common with both parents. Visual games in which the parent displayed distal motor movements that may be observed by the infant and appeared to be attempts to maintain

Table 8. Types of Games Played by Parent and Infant

	Games (%)		Sessions (%)		Sessions Any Games Occurred (%)	
	Mother-Infant	Father-Infant	Mother-Infant	Father-Infant	Mother-Infant	Father-Infant
Tactile	26.0	27.0	37.0	31.4	48.7 *	36.1
Limb movement	4.3 *	21.3	7.4 *	31.4	9.7 *	36.1
Conventional limb movement	8.6 *	2.2	14.8 *	3.7	19.5 *	4.2
Visual	35.8 *	20.2	46.2	31.4	60.9 *	36.1
Conventional visual	2.1	3.3	3.7	1.8	4.8	2.1
Pure verbal	14.1	20.2	22.2	29.6	29.2	34.0
Combination	8.6	5.6	9.2	7.4	12.2	8.5

*$p \leq 0.05$ (t-test [Bruning and Kintz, 1968]).
Source: From M. W. Yogman, Development of the Father-Infant Relationship. In H. Fitzgerald, B. Lester, and M. W. Yogman (Eds.), *Theory and Research in Behavioral Pediatrics*, Vol. 1. New York: Plenum, 1982.

the visual attention of the infant were also quite common, whether or not accompanied by verbal games. These visual games were more common with mothers than with fathers. They represented the most common mother-infant games (36 percent of all games played) and occurred during 46 percent of all mother-infant sessions (61 percent of sessions in which any games occurred). With fathers, these games represented only 20 percent of all games played, significantly lower than with mothers. The most common types of father-infant games were tactile games, representing 27 percent of all father-infant games. In contrast to mothers, fathers more often engaged in limb-movement games in which their behavior attempted to arouse the infant. These limb-movement games (whether or not accompanied by verbal games) occurred in 31 percent of all father-infant sessions (36 percent of sessions in which any games occurred) and represented 21 percent of all father-infant games, while they occurred in only 7 percent of all mother-infant sessions and represented only 4 percent of mother-infant games. All of these differences were significant (*t*-test, Bruning and Kintz, 1968). Mothers also played frequent limb-movement games but they were a different category in which the infant assumed a conventional motoric role such as pat-a-cake, peek-a-boo, or waving.

The visual games more often played by mothers may represent a more distal attention-maintaining form of interactive play than the more proximal idiosyncratic limb-movement games played more often by fathers. Studies of the games parents play with 8-month-old infants have shown similar findings: Mothers played more distal games while fathers engaged in more physical games (Power and Parke, 1979). Stern (1974b) has suggested that the goal of such games is to facilitate an optimal level of arousal in the infant in order to foster attention to social signals. The more proximal games of infants and fathers may serve to modulate the infant's attention and arousal in a more accentuated fashion than occurs during the more distal games of infants and mothers. Since accentuated temporal shifts may also increase the infant's arousal (Stern, 1977), further attention to the temporal structure of these games and their burst-pause patterns may provide additonal evidence of differences between mother- and father-infant interaction.

Developmental Changes

Finally, I also used the monadic-phase analysis and the description of games to look in more detail at the ontogenesis of these patterns of father-infant interaction. The data suggest that, as the infant's age increases, the range of the infant's affective displays with father expands, the infant spends a greater proportion of time in more affectively positive phases, and affective expressions become more differentiated.

In sum, while the data described in this section are based on a few selected families, they support the hypothesis that fathers are capable of skilled and sensitive social interaction with young infants. These studies suggest that both similarities and differences exist between these mother-infant and father-infant interactions. Dyadic interaction of infants with both mothers and fathers appears mutually regulated and in both cases, partners build to a peak of attentional involvement and come down in an orderly and cyclic fashion. Furthermore, infants exhibit well-organized expressive displays that are affectively positive with both parents and that become more differentiated in a similar, orderly, developmental progression of modulated social exchanges. Through these mutually regulated reciprocal exchanges, both parents provide a responsive, protective environment that matches the infant's developmental capacities.

Along with these structural similarities, we have illustrated differences in the quality and content of play that we believe provide the *anlage* for different functional tracks of development. Both types of play offer the infant the opportunity to participate in "turn-taking" activities, through which the infant develops early notions of sharing control in an interactive situation. Through play, the infant learns the rules of culture and of family (Bruner et al., 1976). At least for the six families studied in this manner, interaction with fathers can be characterized as heightened and playful while the interactions with mothers appeared more smoothly modulated and contained.

Each of these differential tracks may serve a unique function in the infant's development. Together, they foster the development of a wider range of social skills than if only one pattern were available. Both of these tracks seem available to infants as early as one month of age and both depend on the parents' relationship with their infant. This relationship allows both parents to be aware of the physiological and psychological capacities of their infant and, in turn, to support as well as to test the limits of those capabilities.

One possible explanation of the differences between mother- and father-infant interaction found in these studies and others (Lamb, 1976d; Clarke-Stewart, 1978) is that in families where the father is out of the home at work all day, the infant may show a more excited response to his father when he returns because he is a novel stimulus. In an effort to assess the contribution of the familiarity of the parents to the quality of their interaction with babies, I began to study families in which traditional caregiving roles were reversed: Mothers returned to work in the first few weeks and fathers remained at home as primary caregivers. For this study our data consists of naturalistic home observations as well as face-to-face interactions in the laboratory. While this study is still in progress, our observations of the quality of father-infant interaction during the caretaking tasks suggests that the qualitative difference between mothers and fathers observed in the earlier studies are not based purely on the infant's familiarity with the parent. The primary caretaker fathers I have observed while bathing, diapering, and feeding their babies carry out these tasks with great skill and sensitivity but with the same vigorous, exciting quality seen in face-to-face play with secondary caretaker fathers. One infant's response to the father's vigorous rubdown after the bath was to chortle, cycle his legs, and engage the father in a limb-movement game identical in structure to that seen in the earlier study.

Similar findings have been shown in another study of 4-month-old infants in a laboratory face-to-face interaction with primary and secondary caretaker fathers and with primary caretaker mothers, namely, increased game playing and poking by both groups of fathers (Field, 1978). In Field's study, primary caregivers (mothers and fathers) engage in more smiling and baby talk with their infants. Similarly, home observations of 3-month-old infants in Sweden suggested that differences in parental behavior were related more closely to gender than to the degree of involvement in child care (Lamb et al., in press). Perhaps a more important influence on the father's behavior is the nature of the marital relationship. Pedersen and associates (1977) have done home observations with infants aged 5 months and find that the father's behavior with his infant is closely related to the quality of his relationship with his wife even though maternal and paternal perceptions of the baby's temperament may differ widely. Marital tension and conflict were associated with less competent maternal feeding and with the display of negative affect during mother-infant interaction (Pedersen et al., 1977). Given Pedersen's earlier findings (1975) that the baby's alertness and motor maturity at 4 weeks of age are associated with the husband's support of his wife, it appears that the baby's behavior may have a continuing influence at 5 months.

Later Infancy: Further Studies

The study of the father-infant relationship with infants aged 6 to 24 months focuses primarily on the development of attachment as Bowlby (1968) and Ainsworth (1973) have defined it. These studies have asked: Do infants greet, seek proximity with, and protest on separation from fathers as well as mothers? Such studies provide conclusive evidence that infants are attached to fathers as well as mothers.

Clinically important and yet not well studied are the influences on father-infant attachment. Pedersen and Robson (1969) report that father's investment in caretaking as well as the level of stimulation and play he provides are positively correlated with the attachment greeting behaviors in 8- to 9-month-old babies. Infants whose fathers participate highly in caregiving show less separation protest and cry less with a stranger than infants whose fathers are less involved (Kotelchuck, 1975; Spelke, Zelazo, Kagan, and Kotelchuck, 1973). Qualitative aspects of infant attachment to mothers and fathers studied using Ainsworth's "strange situation" suggested that infants could develop a secure attachment with father in spite of an insecure attachment with mother (Lamb, 1978b).

Given that infants are attached to both mothers and fathers, how are their relationships different? First, mothers and fathers interact differently: Fathers engage more in play than in caretaking activities with 6-month-olds (Rendina and Dickerscheid, 1976) and more often pick up their infants (8 months) to play physical, idiosyncratic, rough-and-tumble games, while mothers are more likely to hold infants, engage in caregiving tasks, and either play with toys or use conventional games such as peek-a-boo (Lamb, 1975). When parents were asked to engage the 2½-year-old child in specific play activities, fathers were better able to engage the child in play. Father's play was more likely to be proximal (as was described for younger infants), social, physical, arousing, and briefer in duration, and fathers reported that they enjoyed it more than mothers (Clarke-Stewart, 1978, 1980). Infants at 8 months responded more positively to play with fathers than with mothers (Lamb, 1975) and, by age 2½ years, not only preferred to play with fathers but were judged to be more involved and excited with them (Clarke-Stewart, 1978). It is fascinating to note that fathers' physical play with their infants correlates most highly with mothers' verbal stimulation ($r = .89$) and toy play ($r = .96$) (Clarke-Stewart, 1980). These maternal behaviors are found in other studies to be part of a pattern of "optimal maternal care" (Clarke-Stewart, 1973). Although there may be qualitative differences in the relationship of mothers and fathers with their infants, parents of 9-month-olds were equally sensitive to infant smiles and cries (Frodi et al., 1978).

In summary, these studies suggest that infants seem to be attached to both parents, although when stressed prefer their mother. Fathers engage in more physical play, and their infants, particularly males, respond more positively to play with their fathers.

Influences on Later Development

The influence of the father-infant relationship on later cognitive, social, and emotional development of the infant has not been well studied. In a prenatal and postpartum interview study of the influence of maternal and paternal expectations and roles, Fein (1976) suggests that the most effective male postpartum adjustment was related not simply to high or low paternal involvement but rather to a coherent role that met the needs of the father himself, as well as those of the mother and the baby.

The influence of the father-infant relationship on the infant during these early months is suggested by the report that, at least in males, increased father involvement at home is associated with greater infant social responsiveness at 5 months of age during a Bayley test (Pedersen, Rubenstein, and Yarrow, 1978). Concurrent predictions of infant Bayley scores at 16 and 22 months were related to father's positive perceptions of the child and to his abilities to engage the child in play and anticipate independence on the part of the child. Predictions of concurrent social competence were related to father's verbal and playful behavior and, for girls, his expectation of independence (Clarke-Stewart, 1978, 1980). Boys in particular have been found to be more autonomous when both parents are warm and affectionate (Baumrind and Black, 1967). The use of cross-lagged correlations led Clarke-Stewart (1980) to suggest that mother's warmth, verbal stimulation, and play with toys with infants at 15 months of age was related to higher infant Bayley scores at 30 months, which, in turn, influenced fathers to engage in play more often, to expect more independence, and to perceive their children more positively.

In summary, these studies of the normal adaptation of infants and their fathers during the first 2 years have supported the idea that parent and infant development proceed in parallel. After birth, both the father and infant are available for meaningful social interaction, although there appear to be qualitative differences between mother-infant and father-infant interaction. Communication between the parents also appears to have a major influence on the parents' relationship with their baby. By the end of the first year, an enduring attachment exists between fathers and infants, even though fathers may spend less time interacting with their infants than mothers do. Finally, interactions between fathers and infants commonly involve physical play. These studies have barely begun to unravel the complexity of the influence of the father-infant relationship on the child's later cognitive and social development.

Theories on the Father's Role During Infancy

These studies of fathers and infants are beginning to form the basis for theorizing about the nature of the father-infant relationship and about the influences of paternal involvement on infant personality development. I should like to suggest that fathers may play both an indirect and a direct role with young infants. First, the importance of the indirect role played by fathers may only be apparent and certainly becomes more important during periods of high stress, when the father may indirectly influence the infant by serving as a readily available source of emotional and physical (helping with caregiving tasks) support. Such support can offer the mother both the help and leisure that an extended family may have offered in the past. As families have grown smaller and women either need or want to work, it seems easier for a mother to have a partner in caretaking responsibilities. During periods of stress, such as illness in the infant (prematurity) or in the mother, this support function becomes critical. If paternal feelings of competition with the mother displace this support function, they may adversely influence the infant.

Secondly, the studies suggest that fathers can have a meaningful direct relationship with their infants right from birth. Mediated through social interaction, particularly play, fathers may have a direct influence on their infants by offering more physically arousing, playful experiences for the infant. If appropriately and sensitively timed to the infant's needs, these paternal interactions may facilitate the infant's development of exploration and independence during the second year. The fact that both parents can have a direct, sensitive, and responsive relationship with their infant suggests that highly invested adults are capable of forming a consistent, loving relationship sensitive to an infant's emotional state and immature attentional capacities.

The fact that either parent can learn to perform certain caretaking tasks may be a reflection of both the infant's eliciting capabilities and the adult's capability to learn. As Rossi (1977) points out, however, while what men and women do is not entirely genetically determined, the biological contributions shape what is learned, and there are differences in the ease with which the different sexes can learn certain things.

Therefore, it seems unlikely that the relationships of fathers and mothers with their infants are identical or redundant. The biological fact of pregnancy sets the stage for an intimacy between mother and baby from birth and a facilitated process of entrainment that a father can only develop over a period of time. In our studies, fathers were able to achieve mutually regulated, reciprocal interactions with their infants by 3 months of age, but the fathers offered the infant a qualitatively different experience from that with mother.

In spite of different research strategies and samples, the studies have shown considerable consistency in describing the nature of father-infant interaction. In the newborn period fathers held and rocked their babies more than mothers and were more stimulating (Parke and Sawin, 1975). By 3 months of age in our studies, fathers and infants engaged in more proximal, arousing idiosyncratic games, whereas mothers and infants were more likely to engage in smoothly modulated, soothing distal games, especially verbal ones. Fathers provided a more novel and complex environment (Pedersen, 1979) and were more likely to play physical, arousing idiosyncratic games with their infants at one and two years of age while mothers were more likely to play conventional games (Lamb, 1977; Clarke-Stewart, 1980). Furthermore, infants responded to their fathers with more excitement. While fathers have been shown to be sensitive to infant cues (Parke and Sawin, 1975, 1977) and skilled interactants with young infants (Yogman, 1977), consistent and fairly stable differences in the quality of behavioral regulation have been demonstrated between father- and mother-infant interaction. Fathers are more likely to develop a heightened, arousing, and playful relationship with their infants (Yogman, 1977; Parke, 1979; Clarke-Stewart, 1980).

While it is clear that cultural and social influences and the amount of time spent with the infant influence these interactions, it may also be true that these qualitative differences in the way fathers and infants interact are based on sex-linked biological predispositions. When reinforced by cultural stereotypes, both parents can be viewed as playing direct but complementary roles with their infants in which attempts by either to entirely substitute for the other require prolonged periods of learning. The interaction of biological predispositions and cultural influences could be elucidated by studying the influences on the father's role in several modern societies: For example, a comparison of fathers' roles with infants in France, Germany, Japan, and the Soviet Union might help us understand the influences of political and economic forces on the transmission of values within a culture.

Keeping in mind the impact of the differences in parent behavior, it is also important to consider the influence of the infant on the father. For example, Rosenblatt's (1969) studies of rats showed that maternal behavior was under the control of both a short-term hormonal system surrounding parturition and a second longer term postpartum system that relies on the presence of the infant to elicit maternal behavior. Given our understanding of the competencies of the human newborn, it is likely that the infant's capabilities to elicit and shape parenting are longer lasting than either biological or hormonal influences in parents. Perhaps future research will more clearly delineate the infant's role in shaping his parents to play different but complementary roles, roles that are both stable and expectable from each parent.

It also seems useful, given the differences between mother- and father-infant interaction, to consider the influences of paternal involvement on infant personality development. One wonders whether the father's more stimulating and arousing pattern of interaction with his infant is related to the acquisition and differentiation of new skills by the infant or to the development of independence, exploration, and autonomy. One also wonders whether an infant who is securely attached to both father and mother is in some way less vulnerable to stress since the relationship with one parent could compensate for difficulties in the relationship with the other.

The developmental process for both parents and infant may be conceptualized in terms of Werner's developmental theory as one of increasing differentiation and integration of skills (Langer, 1970) and in terms of Sander and associates' (1975) theory of systems regulation. Shortly after birth, the infant's biorhythms become entrained with those of the caregiver (Sander et al., 1975), and the infant becomes more stable physiologically. These accomplishments are shaped by social interactions, often with mother, which are modulated and contained in keeping with the infant's physiological immaturity; and by other interactions, characterized by more intense, arousing stimulation, which commonly occur with fathers. In these early months, interactions with mother may prolong the concurrent state of the infant, often resulting in prolonged periods of quiet alertness, while interactions with father may elicit repeated changes of state and may be associated with greater proprioceptive and kinesthetic stimulation. These social interactions become a way of learning, not only about basic trust in the external world engendered by synchronous interaction, but also learning about one's own mechanisms for internal control and homeostasis when stressed (Brazelton et al., 1974).

Interactive games during this period also provide differential experiences for the infant. One can speculate about the developmental significance of these games. Conventional games, more common with mothers, may allow the establishment and consolidation of rules of interchange that provide the foundation for later language development, while more arousing physical games, more common with fathers, may differentiate into alternative forms of social play, eventually incorporating objects and later leading into further instrumental activities (Yogman, 1977; Tronick, 1977).

By the end of the first year, the infant is beginning to explore his surroundings while maintaining focused attachment relationships with both mother and father. Although we know that many infants show comparable attachment behaviors toward both parents, we know much less about the way either parent encourages the child's exploration during physical play. Finally, by around 18 months, infants' interactions with parents provide differential experiences, including the opportunity to be closer to their mothers (*rapprochement*) (Mahler et al., 1975) as well as to use their fathers as the third member of the family triangle to facilitate their separation and individuation: "There must be an I, like him, wanting her" (*intrapsychic triangulation*) (Abelin, 1971, 1975). Autonomy seem to appear as a gradually evolving phenomenon, following the progression of competence in the infant and the infant's feelings of mastery and control in an increasingly novel and stressful situation.

At various stages of development, the father-infant relationship may complement the infant's relationship with mother and facilitate the development of autonomy by providing a range of novel, arousing, and playful experiences with the father. As yet, we know little about the salience of specific aspects of the infant's experience with fathers as compared to that with mothers (differences in kinds of stimulation, quality of voice, or of handling) or about how early perceptions are influenced by repeated experiences with various caretakers. It is interesting to speculate about the relationship between the recent trend for fathers to be increasingly involved with their infants and the evolving cultural objectives of childrearing to prepare children for more complex roles in society. The greater social emphasis on individualism and self-sufficiency in personal growth is demanding that children be capable of autonomy at increasingly earlier ages (as an example, consider the growth of day care and preschool education in Western societies). It is to be hoped that future studies may elucidate the influences of paternal involvement with infants on personality development.

The triadic model of mother and father playing complementary roles in rearing their baby provides one model for a nuclear family. The fact that single parents and in particular, single women, also raise autonomous children means that parents can and do play dual roles with their children, but in no way does it imply that playing dual roles is an easy task.

Conclusions

In spite of all that has recently been written, our knowledge of the nature of the father's relationship with and influence on young infants is still quite limited.

While cultural changes have permitted mothers and fathers to play similar roles if they wish, biologically based predispositions to adult sex differences may shape the quality of parental behavior. These sex differences appear to start in infancy. Males are more active and more sensitive to physical stimuli while females are more verbally productive. These differences are then supported by cultural expectations (Maccoby and Jacklin, 1974). Fathers in the studies described here interacted with their babies with a more arousing, physical style than did mothers.

The studies reviewed in this chapter not only call for more differentiated theories of adult male and female social development, but also imply the need for revisions in our prior theories of infant development. Classic theories of object relationship that do not acknowledge a meaningful, active, social role for the infant before the end of the first year are no longer adequate. Similarly, theories that exclude everyone except the mother from the infant's social world must now be seen as too limited.

Increasing paternal involvement with young infants may have important influences on the father himself and may provide critical support for the mother, particularly if she is stressed. Influences on the infant are less well understood. If the infant and caregiver together are viewed as part of a biological system, then increased paternal involvement may influence the regulation of that system and alter the structure of the infant's social experiences. Fathers seem to provide infants with more intense, arousing, differentiating experiences, and such experiences, combined with others, may shape the infant's temperament. It is tempting to speculate that infants may also be predisposed to seek an appropriate balance of both arousing and well-modulated, contained stimulation from the caregiving system. Both the expectations and goals of adult caregivers and the needs of the infant may interact to maintain the regulation of the system even as social and cultural expectations are shifting.

Finally, given our limited knowledge, any efforts to change clinical care and social policy toward fathers should aim at increasing the options available to fathers as well as mothers rather than promoting specific alternative prescriptions. At the same time, any renegotiation of caregiving tasks with regard to adult equality should remain sensitive to the implications for infants and their needs. The emotional rewards of fatherhood— the sense of delight, renewal, and creativity from observing one's infant grow up—are now publicly acclaimed in the popular press, but even Charles Darwin, late in his life, wrote to one of his children: "When you were very young it was my delight to play with you all, and I think with a sigh that such days can never return" (Schwartz, 1967).

"The Second Other": The Role of the Father in Early Personality Formation and the Dyadic-Phallic Phase of Development

Stanley I. Greenspan

A particularly useful way to understand the role of the father in early personality development is in the context of the specific stages and tasks of the child's development. After describing substages of early personality formation from a developmental structuralist approach (Greenspan, 1979), I will discuss the father's role in facilitating early personality formation, with special focus on the "dyadic-phallic" stage of early childhood (Greenspan, 1980). During this stage, the father's role is especially unique in helping the child to stabilize basic ego functions such as reality testing, impulse regulation, mood stabilization, delineation of self from others, and focused concentration.

The developmental structuralist approach observes the way in which the infant, toddler, or young child organizes his unique emotional as well as cognitive experience (Greenspan, 1979). According to their range, depth, stability, and personal uniqueness, the characteristics that define the experiential organization at each developmental stage may be viewed as a structure (Piaget, 1962, 1968).

The degree to which an individual experiences the full range of stage- and age-appropriate experience in stable, stress-resilient personal configurations may indicate involvement in a particular stage of development and readiness to move into the next developmental stage. The more optimal the child's structural capacity at each developmental stage, the more he or she facilitates further development. For example, the baby who organizes experiences of physical closeness and interpersonal affection is more likely to be available to learn the later forms of such intimate exchanges than is the infant who wards off intimacy. This is not to suggest that "catch-up" learning does not occur; it does. Such learning, however, may have a different developmental sequence and final configuration.

Before we enter into a fairly comprehensive discussion of the special role of the father during the dyadic-phallic stage of development, we shall briefly review the earlier stages and the role the father plays in each.

Stage 1: Homeostasis

During the stage of homeostasis, where the major goals are helping the infant to balance appropriate comfort and internal regulation with engagement and interest in the world, the role of the father is crucial as a complement to the mother. One of the major adaptive features of the environment during this stage, for example, is determination of the special characteristics of the infant. Is the infant withdrawn, requiring more interesting stimulation, or is this infant hyperlabile and excitable, requiring greater soothing? Does the infant have a special sensorihypersensitivity and require soothing and protection around particular sensorimodes? It is in such instances, with the infant who requires special patterns of care, that the father can complement the mother, each one helping the other to overcome "blind spots" and limitations in their understanding of their baby's special characteristics. Together, they can provide those special patterns of care that will maximize the infant's comfort regulation and interest in the world. The father, as an added interesting human stimulus, also increases the range and depth of the youngster's experience in the world.

Stage 2: Forming a Human Attachment

Once the infant has achieved increasing central nervous system (CNS) maturation (between 2 and 4 months), he or she clearly begins to demonstrate a unique interest in the animate world. The infant becomes more attuned to social and interpersonal interactions, more capable of responding to the external environment and forming a special relationship with the significant primary caregivers. Thus, as evidenced by the social smile (Spitz, 1965), a second, very closely related stage can be formulated: the process of forming a human attachment.

In terms of the range of this new stage with its evolving stage-specific "structural" capacity for attachment, the father may also complement the mother. Here again, parents need to understand the individual characteristics of the infant and to use this understanding to create an environment that not only comforts, regulates, and stimulates, but also fosters that especially human tie, a loving relationship. Ideally, father becomes available as another very important love object, without causing jealous or artificial triangles that would distract mother from what, under optimal

124

circumstances, would be her time for "falling in love with her infant." While the infant may not as yet clearly differentiate between mother and father, the infant does show the capacity to recognize at some level differences between the two, as evidenced through differential reactions and preferences. The availability of more love objects (such as extended family members or siblings) increases the infant's opportunity for forming especially affectionate human ties. With the infant who presents a challenge and needs to be wooed into a relationship, or the irritable infant who needs to be comforted into a loving relationship, the father, once again, through his unique and special characteristics, may become a complementary loving object who provides an important flexibility to the nurturing environment. The father's availability may enhance not only the depth and range of affect in the early attachment patterns (e.g., variety of positive affects, tolerance of negative affects) but also the ability of the environment to maintain stability, even in the face of stress (e.g., an illness to mother, the infant being fussy). Also the father will relate to his infant somewhat differently than mother and provide an additional and beneficial set of experiences through which the infant comes to know him- or herself, others, and a world of loving relationships (see Chap. 6).

If the infant forms an affective and relatively pleasurable attachment (an investment in the human, animate world), then with growing maturational abilities he develops complex patterns of communication within this primary human relationship. This development in the infant's capability in complicated human communications (Charlesworth, 1969; Brazelton et al., 1970; Tennes et al., 1972; Stern, 1974a) parallels development of basic schemes of causality in the infant's relationship to the inanimate world (means to ends relationships [Piaget, 1962]).

Stage 3: Somatopsychological Differentiation

As means to ends (causal) relationships are established between the infant and the primary caregiver, the infant manifests a growing ability to discriminate significant primary caregivers from others as well as to differentiate his own actions from their consequences affectively, somatically, behaviorally, and interpersonally. A process of differentiation begins to occur along a number of developmental lines (e.g., with sensorimotor integration, affects, relationships). A third stage, therefore, centers on differentiation and may formally be termed *somatopsychological differentiation* to indicate processes occurring at the somatic (e.g., sensorimotor) and emerging psychological levels.* It should be emphasized

---

*In this context, *psychological* refers to higher-level mental processes characterized by the capacity to form internal representations or symbols as a way to register experience.

that while the infant establishes schemes of causality in relationship to the interpersonal world, it is not at all clear that these schemes exist at an organized representational or symbolic level. Rather, they appear to exist for the most part at a somatic level (Greenspan, 1979), some perhaps even prenatally determined (Lourie, 1971), even though we do observe the precursors of representational capacities.

In the stage of somatopsychological differentiation, even more than in the stage of attachment, the role of the father becomes important for broadening the range of appropriate responses to complement the mother's loving, stabilizing, comforting, interesting, and nurturing responses. The father has a special role: to increase the range of reciprocal communication in the affective as well as impersonal cognitive sphere of experience. It is rare, for example, that mother alone will encompass the full range of affects: love, assertiveness, protest, and even anger. Most healthy adults have some limitations in terms of the empathic range in which they can engage a growing infant. The father, as a complementary figure to the mother, should be able to increase the range of contingent responses. Again, as with attachment, the availability of the second loving figure can enhance the stability and personal uniqueness of the emerging infant's organization.

With appropriate reading of cues and systematic differential responses, the infant or toddler develops a more complicated behavioral repertoire and his or her communications take on more organized, meaningful configurations. By 12 months the infant, for example, is able to begin connecting behavioral units into larger organizations as he or she manifests complex emotional responses such as affiliation, wariness, and fear (Bowlby, 1970; Ainsworth et al., 1974; Sroufe and Waters, 1977). As the toddler moves further into the second year of life in the practicing subphase of development of individuation (Mahler et al., 1975), formation of original behavior schemes (Piaget, 1962) is begun, and imitative activity and intentionality increase.

Stage 4: Behavioral Organization, Initiative, and Internalization

A type of learning through imitation that the infant evidenced in earlier development now seems to take on a more dominant role. As his imitations assume a more integrated personal form, the toddler appears to "take on" or internalize attributes of his caretakers. A fourth stage, which centers on complex organized emotional and behavioral patterns delineated as *behavioral organization, initiative,* and *internalization,* is useful to describe these new capacities.

As the toddler reaches the stage of behavioral organization, initiative, and internalization, the role of the father becomes more specialized. Here, in addition to increasing the range and depth, stability, and personal uniqueness of the experiential organizations available to the growing toddler, the father begins to have a special role as the "significant other." Although before this stage, the infant, through differential responses, clearly shows recognition of the father as different from others, such distinction does not necessarily imply a mental representation. From the perspective of the infant, this preliminary differential responsiveness to mother and father may be less important than the complementary or additive aspects of a mother-father availability. In other words, while different, father and mother can still spell each other, and both essentially enhance the overall nurturing and early communication patterns. At this next stage, however, father becomes used now as a *distinct* significant other. Typically beginning with the "stranger anxiety" characteristic at 8 months, and continuing during the next few months with even stronger separation anxieties and more organized emotional and behavioral systems, the toddler comes to perceive the father more clearly as a significant other with distinct features.

The father becomes important in a number of ways, three of which will be mentioned briefly. First, as the toddler progresses through the practicing subphase in the early separation and individuation process (Mahler et al., 1975), the knowledge that there is also another adult available, a significant other, fosters considerably the youngster's sense of security in moving out independently from, and returning periodically to, his or her base of security. The availability of a second significant other is especially important for the youngster's ability to deal with aggressive stirrings. Since the youngster is still not able to differentiate self from nonself fully, personal aggressive feelings and those of others are frightening. The availability of a second adult, particularly when the youngster is angry at the first, is extraordinarily helpful in maintaining internal harmony and progress in the individuation process. It is common, for example, to see the youngster split the mother and father into good and bad objects and achieve some degree of safety and security from the fantasized good object after being angry at the bad one. It is not uncommon for the youngster, when hurt through his or her own action, to protest angrily to mother, blaming the fantasized omnipotent mother for the hurt, and running to father for comforting. The reverse may also occur if father happens to be closer to the youngster. Interestingly, when assigning blame for a hurt or pain, the youngster is more likely to choose the more primary love object, usually mother.

I would speculate that the ability to run to the significant second other for comforting at these times enhances the flexibility of the youngster in maintaining the separation and individuation process and increasing the youngster's capacity for initiative and further behavioral and emotional organization. Thus, the presence of the second significant other also helps the youngster to integrate and deal with aggressive feelings, particularly toward the primary object.

Second, the role of the father is also important at this stage to help the child gain the ability to integrate affective and behavioral polarities. If these goals are not achieved, we see a youngster who is chronically negativistic, or chronically passive and compliant, or chronically impulsive and aggressive. In optimal development we see rich behavioral and emotional patterns that reflect integration of assertiveness and intimacy, passivity and aggressiveness, and so forth.

Third, the presence of the father facilitates an emerging sense of self as a "gender self." Toward the middle or end of the second year many toddlers begin to inquire overtly, through gesture and sometimes through the use of words, about sexual differences. They become interested in their own genitals and in those of their siblings and parents. While this process is obviously gradual, it does appear to be manifested more overtly toward the middle and end of the second year of life. Implications of the availability of a father as well as a mother for both comparisons and identifications are apparent.

Stage 5: Forming Mental Representations

As the toddler approaches the end of the second year, with further maturation of the CNS, we notice an increased capacity to form and organize mental representations. What were once perhaps internal sensations and unstable images are now organized in a somewhat stable representational form, which the child evokes almost at will (Piaget, 1962; Gouin-Décarie, 1965; S. Bell, 1970). While this capacity is initially fragile (i.e., between 16 and 24 months), it soon appears to become a dominant mode in organizing the child's behavior, leading to a fifth stage, formation of mental representations. To clarify a related concept, it should be pointed out that the capacity for "object permanence," which is relative and goes through a series of stages (Gouin-Décarie, 1965), refers to the toddler's ability to search for "hidden" inanimate objects. Representational capacity refers to the ability to organize and evoke internal multisensory organized experiences of the animate object. These are obviously related capacities that depend on both myelinization of the CNS and appropriate experiences. The process of internalization may be thought of as an intermediary process, leading to the stage in which internalized experiences eventually become organized enough to be considered representations.

During this stage of representational capacity, the availability of the father is again especially important. Here we can postulate that the toddler readily perceives the differences between mother and father, relates to the parents quite uniquely and individually, and internalizes different and unique self-object representations based on these experiences. It is important to emphasize the value to the growing toddler of having a number of individually different and not easily substituted self-object representations to build richness, flexibility, and further integration of the polarities of affective and behavioral life. The variety of internalized experiences also minimizes the expected concerns with aggression, merging, and regressive dedifferentiation. The availability of a number of dyadic systems that contain the dimensions of ongoing rich relationships affording more love than pain, and leading to vivid delineated internal representations, therefore, facilitates the toddler's development.

While the discussion presented here thus far may naturally lead to the impression, the "more the merrier" (the more dyadic objects available, the better the youngster's homeostatic potential, attachment, differentiation potential, representational capacities, and so forth), this is not the case. While the presence of loving adults in certain extended families may, in fact, provide a more secure environment for the youngster, obviously the individual characteristics of each dyadic relationship, primarily the main one or ones, will prove pivotal. The extreme, however, of the more the merrier concept should also be discussed in its maladaptive potential. The youngster who is presented with too many dyadic objects may be "spread too thin," thereby compromising richness and intensity with any one object. What the optimal number is for a youngster obviously depends on the youngster's own internal zest and the way in which the adults react to each other and the youngster. The important issue is that the intensity of relatedness to one or two adults not be compromised by the availability of others. It certainly seems that the extended family members present should not be allowed to compromise the intensity of affective involvement found in the nuclear family unit.

One could imagine a father, who instead of facilitating a youngster's ability to work through certain ambivalences toward mother, would always offer himself as a substitute. Such interference could undermine the youngster's capacity to deal with ambivalence and to integrate the feeling states toward the mother (integrating images of the good and bad mother perhaps). Again, this is characteristic not primarily of the availability of a number of objects but more of the relationship of the objects both to the youngster and to each other. At this point, it is mentioned only to point out that there is no absolute in considering these issues.

At a representational level the child again develops his capacities for elaboration, integration, and differentiation. Just as earlier, causal schemes were developed at a somatic and behavioral level, now causal schemes are developed at a representational level. The child begins to elaborate and eventually differentiate between those feelings, thoughts, and events that emanate from the self and those that emanate from others. He or she begins to differentiate experiences and actions from their impact on the world. This process is the basis for the differentiation of "self" representations from those representations that embody the external world, animate and inanimate.

Gradually the capacity for differentiating internal representations becomes consolidated (e.g., object constancy [Mahler et al., 1975]). Subsequently, in middle childhood, representational capacity becomes reinforced with the ability of the child to develop derivative representational systems. These new representational systems are tied to the original representations and transform them in accord with adaptive and defensive goals. This permits greater flexibility in dealing with experiences such as perceptions, feelings, thoughts, and emerging ideals.

The task in representational differentiation and consolidation is to foster a balance between representational elaboration and reality orientation, to encourage symbolic elaboration and fantasy as well as reality testing capacities. The availability of the father strongly supports the child's ability both to deal with ambivalence, limit-setting, and frustration, and to experience sadness and mourning. At this time, a sexual identity is also becoming more differentiated, and, as mentioned earlier, the availability of both sexes to the youngster is of obvious importance for comparison and identification (Chap. 11).

During this stage of representational differentiation and consolidation we also observe, in a structural sense, the beginning of the dyadic-phallic stage of development. This stage occurs toward the end of representational differentiation (ages 2½ through 4) and at the beginning of the early phallic stage of psychosexual organization. Because the role of the father can be so essential at this time, the remainder of this chapter will concern itself with this special phase of development. The principles elaborated here regarding the special role of the father will also be true during later stages of development.

We shall introduce this phase of development by describing first what is going on from the perspective of both drives and ego structure.

The Dyadic-Phallic Stage of Development

The early phallic stage of development is important as a transition point for a number of developmental processes and may be much more important in the development of various psychopathologies and adaptive functions than has heretofore been recognized. During this stage object relationships switch from dyadic to triangular patterns, the increased flexibility of which has significant implications for structure formation, including the development of the infantile neurosis as an organizing entity for the personality. In addition, the shift from dyadic to triangular patterns solidifies the relatively full attainment of object constancy (Mahler et al., 1975). The stable, delineated internal representation of self and object also stabilizes a number of core ego functions including the capacity for distinguishing internal from external, testing reality, regulating impulse, organizing emotions, and integrating thought and affect. Movement into triangular patterns also coincides maturationally with new cognitive abilities that permit higher-level defensive organizations to protect the ego and provide it with greater flexibility. Secondary elaborations of defenses and higher-level compromise formations permit greater flexibility in dealing with wishes, fears, and internalized prohibitions (Greenspan, 1979).

Aspects of the early phallic stage have been described as the phallic-narcissistic stage (Edgcumbe and Burgner, 1975). Edgcumbe and Burgner go beyond earlier conceptualizations (Freud, 1923b, 1924a, 1931; Lampl-de-Groot, 1928; Deutsch, 1930) and point out that in Freud's classic paper, "Three Essays on the Theory of Sexuality" (1905b), he did not differentiate the phallic and oedipal phases. However, in this most important paper they limit their discussion of the implications of this early phallic stage solely to the development of sexual identity, exhibitionism, and scoptophilia and suggest that it is a pivotal point for regression in the hysteric character. They do point out briefly that in the phallic-narcissistic phase, object relationships are dyadic and lack the complexity and personal intimacy of the oedipal phase; however, because their focus is on the vicissitudes of the drives, they do not fully consider the implications of this stage for either the internalization of object relationships or the development of basic ego functions and the flexibility of the ego.

Since there are multiple transitions occurring in the early phallic phase, it may be appropriate to consider a term for this stage of development that suggests its importance as a pivotal point not only in the level of drive organization but also in the development of object relations and new ego functions. Perhaps a more appropriate term is the *dyadic-phallic stage* (Greenspan, 1980), because this term connotes the importance of the relationship between drive organization, level of ego functioning, and level of object relationships in both interpersonal and internalized dimensions.

In this regard, it is important to consider the relationship between drive development, object relationship, internalized object relationship, and ego structure at this stage of development. During the early phallic phase, the hypothesized dyadic-phallic stage, there are both phallic wishes toward the dyadic object and emerging phallic oedipal wishes toward objects in triangular configuration (the latter still unstable). At the same time, important changes occur in yet another dimension of object relationships, their internalization into internalized self and object representations. This line of development relates to the formation of ego structure and basic ego functions (e.g., reality testing), in that the internalization of early experience with human objects under favorable circumstances leads to the formation of organized self and object representations that are differentiated from each other and stabilized in the face of drive-affect pressure and the experience of separation. In somewhat different terms, the favorable accomplishment in this line of development is described as the relative achievement of object constancy (Mahler et al., 1975). Because the stable differentiated organization of self and object representations is the foundation not only for related ego functions but also for differentiating an organized sense of self from nonself, internal from external, and real from unreal, its achievement is a crucial modal point in development.

Because the child in the dyadic-phallic stage has not yet fully achieved the level of organization of internalized object relationships, the basic ego functions are still vulnerable. Therefore, maintaining the stability and differentiation of self and object organization and preventing even mild trends toward differentiation become the child's foremost developmental tasks. Yet at the same time, the emerging early phallic drive organization and related interest in objects propel the growing child into a more complicated configuration of wishes, feelings, and relationships.

Under favorable circumstances this dilemma is resolved through the progression of development wherein the child further secures object constancy (strengthens ego functions) and confidently pursues movement into a full phallic-oedipal configuration.

Under less favorable circumstances, the individual does not progress into a full oedipal configuration, often because of the underlying fear that to do so would disrupt his already fragile or tenuous capacity for object constancy and related ego functioning. Modifications in the very structure of the ego (character distortions) serve to consolidate the personality at the early phallic level where relationships are predominantly still dyadic (even though triangular interests are emerging). Such modifications, in a sense, protect the ego from those types of experiences (e.g., anger, assertion, competition, integrated nonsplitting love experiences)

132

that could threaten its level of organization. Rigid characterologic distortions and primitive defenses, therefore, protect a cohesive but inflexible personality organization. Under these circumstances, the child may never experience developmentally more advanced affects such as balanced empathy, "integrated" love, sadness, and assertive anger and competition.

Studying this pivotal point in development offers a unique opportunity for understanding, as a foundation for ego structure and functioning, the relationship between drive development (including the relationship with, and interest in, the object of the drives) and the process of internalizing object relationships.

It is interesting to speculate that because the phase-specific drive organization leads the child to increased focus on the genital area and the body as representative of the new phallic organization while, at the same time, object constancy is now nearing full consolidation, investment in the representation of the self in an overly intense way may therefore serve the developmental need for differentiation. In a sense, the focus on the representation of the self is necessary in part to fight off the regressive pulls into less differentiated states. The self-focus becomes the alternative to an undifferentiated self-object focus. Perhaps this is why we observe increased narcissism in the early phallic phase in almost all normal, healthy children.

Also of special interest in this phase of development is the confluence of fears that are operating. The superego is not yet fully internalized or formed. There are beginning concerns with castration anxiety. At the same time, because this is a transitional phase, the child has not yet repressed or structuralized (in terms of the superego) earlier fears. Therefore, the child fears simultaneously general bodily injury, damage to the emerging sexual identity, loss of love, loss of the object, annihilation, inundation by the instincts, and fusion with the dyadic object. All these fears can exist together, more or less, in various configurations. There are also particularly intense stage-specific fears having to do with the phallic exhibitionistic drive components relating to envy and humiliation. There is a great deal of envy, the desire to conceal it, and the fear that, should it be exposed, one would feel humiliated. These fears are transitional between higher and lower ones on the developmental continuum (i.e., castration anxiety at the higher oedipal level; fears of loss of approval, loss of the object, fragmentation, and other preoedipal concerns at the lower level). The youngster is struggling to move ahead in development, but is frightened of moving into a real oedipal triangle because he or she may not yet have achieved full separation from the dyadic partner and may not be ready to take on a libidinal triangular object. At the same time the child is frightened of regressing into a less differentiated state where earlier aggressive and libidinal concerns may be overwhelming. The child may have major concerns about even limited regressions because regression along libidinal or aggressive lines to preoedipal fixation points brings with it fears of ego regressions and loss of already attained differentiations.

The Role of the Father in Traversing the Dyadic-Phallic Stage of Development

The role of the father during the dyadic-phallic stage of development may, in part, be self-evident from the preceding discussion. As mentioned earlier, there are three chief tasks for the youngster: (1) to consolidate object constancy, (2) to stabilize the differentiation of self from nonself, thus consolidating basic ego functions, and (3) to prepare for stable movement into triangular relationship patterns characteristic of the phallic-oedipal phase of development.

It is clear that in order to do this a youngster must be able to pull away from the intense relationship with the primary significant other in his or her life. In the traditional family where this other would be the mother, the significant second other, the father, plays a unique role. His availability at this stage permits the youngster to begin experimenting with being angry at the significant other, that is, mother. It is hard to pull away from the intense dyadic relationship unless one is comfortable with one's anger. Often the child accomplishes greater internalization and object constancy of the representational mother only through a "lover's quarrel" of sorts. Here, the availability of father as the secure other figure is pivotal. If there is no father available and mother is the only significant other, the risk of being angry at her and destroying her may be so overwhelming as to leave the youngster in an even more regressive and chaotic symbiotic mode of relating. Such a youngster, for example, may vacillate between anger, fear, and regression to a clinging intimacy, only to have the cycle begin again. We see these patterns not only in our borderline patients, but in many primitive character disorders in which a full resolution of object constancy has not occurred. Therefore, when the father is available as another adult, he can help the youngster both to deal with angry feelings that are part of the "lover's quarrel" and to pull away somewhat from the real relationship with mother at least in terms of certain affective themes and tones.

It is not enough to speak of the father's "help" unless we define it as an available warm relationship between father and child. This is fundamental. In addition, the relationship with father must be characterized by trust and security. The child must not see father as a person who is too supportive of the youngster's own aggressive drives. Or, if he views the father as too supportive of the mother, the child once again fears the combined opposition, feeling overwhelmed by a sense of abandonment and lack of support. Therefore, the ideal father during this phase of development sides neither with the youngster too much, nor with the mother. He is able to maintain his primary family relationships and place himself in a position to further the youngster's development. In optimally healthy family circles this happens quite intuitively and empathically as the father senses at various times the young child's need for security and reaches out to help and at other times effectively sets limits when the youngster is provocative. The youngster gets a picture of father as an objective figure who is available for warmth and security, yet does not align himself to excess with the youngster's own drives or fears or the feared external reality figure (e.g., the malevolent phallic mother figure).

In addition to the father's availability, involvement, warmth, and restraint with regard to alignment, there is another equally important dimension to his role. Father, from his balanced position in an empathic response to the child's need, does ally himself with the youngster temporarily when mother seems too overwhelming and frightening. Thus, father lends himself, almost in a preliminary sense, to a triangular pattern, prior to the more libidinized oedipal relationship. Father is an ally in the phallic-aggressive drama but not in the libidinal drama to take place shortly. This distinction is important, since phallic-aggressive triangles are seen in the thematic and affective life of patients and these triangles are confused with full oedipal-level development. Here again, father needs to be comfortable in moving from his middle-of-the-road position to ally himself temporarily with the youngster, returning to the more balanced position when the crisis is over. In this way the youngster develops further confidence in taking on or taking leave of the imagined phallic-aggressive mother. The father's intervention becomes relatively more important if mother is overinvested in intense or symbiotic trends, or has difficulty with the youngster's growing assertiveness and sense of sexual identity. Thus, optimally, father is temporarily available as an ally to help the youngster pull out of the dyadic drama. One may imagine the father's offering his hand to the youngster who is trying to swim to shore, while fighting off the malevolent phallic dragons that wish once again to submerge the child in the dangerous undifferentiated waters (even though the "phallic dragons" may be in part products of the youngster's own imagination). The picture of the secure second other on the shoreline is a tremendous boost in helping the youngster to climb out of the water.

Another way in which father is quite important to the youngster who is consolidating object constancy and resolving the dyadic-phallic phase is in his availability as a defined gender object. Here, as discussed earlier in this section, youngsters use their investment in themselves, and particularly their sexual differentiation, as a way of further defining their self-representation and differentiating it from the object representation. At this early phallic stage, the girl focuses on the body phallus and the boy on the penis phallus to provide a center of interest for self-organization and self-delineation. This focus fosters sexual differentiation and stabilizes differentiation between the self and the object, setting the foundation for the separateness between internal and external that is at the foundation of all basic ego functions. Here the identification, or the transient fantasy of being like father even without full-fledged organized identification, helps the youngster consolidate, either transiently (as in little girls) or more permanently (as in boys), the early phallic self-organization.

Yet another way that father's role is very important to the resolution of this phase of development is in the facilitation of a mourning process. In order to let go of the symbiotic partner and internalize the partner in terms of a solid, differentiated, object representation (object constancy), the child must let go of the real object. For successful letting go, the youngster must be able to experience some sadness. Youngsters who never achieve this mourning often evidence character problems in which "symbiotic-type" battles are always occurring, in which "others" must be held on to in the real sense because they cannot be internalized and felt as alive inside the person. Father facilitates the mourning process by his availability as another secure adult, someone to mourn with, a supportive person to use as a base of security. At this stage, father may be seen intermittently as second best to the primary object the youngster is relinquishing; yet to have second best available to modify the intensity of the mourning may make mourning possible at this age level.

In essence, the youngster knows, at some intuitive level, that to grow up, he or she must permit some letting go and experience some loss. Children have already experienced, at prerepresentation stages, the fact that each new achievement and development must involve giving up an earlier type and style of relationship. It is no different here. Earlier, walking meant not being held. Now, to move into the excitement and richness of the triangular oedipal phase means parting with mother as a dyadic object and consolidating basic ego functions. Father, optimally, is a sympathetic and concerned other who is equitable and just, does not side too strongly with either the drives of the child or the retaliatory fearful maternal object, and acts as a partner and a facilitator for the mourning and letting-go experience.

Together with all of the above, father also continually plays a role as a confirmer of reality. During this phase of development the youngster has some reality orientation but is vulnerable to regression. Put another way, the youngster has some stabilization of the differential self and the differentiated other, but is vulnerable to dedifferentiation, where self and other boundaries merge. Father, as a less ambivalently held significant other, serves as a base of reality.

We have described several important ways in which the father's role helps the youngster to resolve the dyadic-phallic phase of development from regression to reality orientation. These are pivotal, not only for stabilization of the youngster's basic ego functions, but for the delineation of his or her appropriate sexual identity.

Oedipal and Postoedipal Phases:
Some General Comments on the Father's Role

Neither the role of the father nor the basic issues just discussed are ever entirely resolved: They reverberate throughout the remaining stages of development. It is especially important that the father's role in resolving these issues be kept in mind as one considers the oedipal and latency stages. We know that besides being available to the youngster during all developmental stages as a figure of identification, a basis for the ego ideal, a facilitator of superego consolidation, a model for friendship patterns with peers, as well as an ongoing friend during latency, the father is important to many latency children in helping them maintain differentiation. Some brief examples are the youngster whose mother has trouble accepting his assertiveness, or whose mother may be enticing the youngster back into more dependent modes; or the youngster who because of unsolved oedipal issues is fearful of the independence and assertiveness required of latency and may be easily tempted into more regressive styles and modes. The availability of the father to help maintain differentiation, to always lend a hand to pull one out of the relatively undifferentiated (at a representational level) waters, so to speak, is of vital importance. Regardless of the stage-specific issues of latency, offering friendship, warmth, and support and being a source of identificatory patterns are the pivotal important (often intuitive) roles of the father. This helping hand helps the youngster pull himself out of regressive episodes or to hold on when the regressive pressures become too intense.

The same is also true during adolescence when we see the second separation-individuation phase and the tendency, again, toward differentiation. In essence, throughout the course of life the availability of a relationship with a secure reality oriented empathic father figure provides a continuing boost, a support against the regressive pulls and the dedifferentiated patterns.

The issues of the earlier developmental stages are always a backdrop to the new developmental tasks of adolescence and early adulthood, regardless of how competently these new tasks are pursued. As is well known, each developmental challenge provides an opportunity for progression, but also for regression into dedifferentiated and often overidealized patterns of nurturance. To be sure, other individuals may substitute for the original father, but no matter who takes the part, the basic patterns of relatedness and the ability to be used as the significant second other in the ways described play a key role in providing lifelong, dependable coping strategies for each new developmental task.

8

Discovering Daddy: The Mother's Role

Richard N. Atkins

Young Andrew, pugnacious and verbally precocious at only 5 years of age, sat on my office floor setting up opposing ranks of toy soldiers. Another battle was about to begin.

Andrew's father had recently brought the youngster for a consultation following a divorce and custody settlement 6 months previously. The boy's mother had, since his birth, been the frequent victim of psychotic episodes. During the periodic depths of her psychic turmoil, mother clung tenaciously to her son as a tiny, redheaded island of stability in her world gone mad. Mother and son were, hence, inseparably close. When the court awarded custody of the child to the father, Andrew's unquestionable "best interests" were quickly drowned in his long periods of tense detachment. Frequent, nearly unmanagable temper tantrums frightened his frankly obsessional father, and Andrew was referred by his nursery school for psychotherapy.

Consequently, on the battlefield of shag carpet, the "good boys" and the "bad girls" were about to exchange yet another volley. As he picked up his little all-green "Lootenerant," Andrew heard his father come into the waiting room, in anticipation of the end of the youngster's session. Andrew reflected for an instant, little green man in his hand. "Daddy," he noted, pointing to the door of the consulting room. I nodded. Pushing the soldier into his mouth, he gave one long minute of suck, then snorted and sighed, "I don't know Daddy so good. Children spend a long time with their mommies, I think. I used to, too. Mommy and I were home all day together. And then, after such a lon-n-ng day," he held his arms at their full span, "Daddy came home from work. So you see, you don't know daddy so good. Not like mommy." With another suck on the soldier, he looked quizzically at me, "How *do* you get to know your daddy good?"

Andrew's manifest question has always been an interesting one for psychoanalysts to ponder. For decades, we assumed that a child's endur-

This chapter was prepared in part through Grant MH05816, funded by the U.S. Department of Health and Human Services, National Institute of Mental Health, Office of Psychiatric Education.

ing and meaningful relationship to his or her father reached significance only at the onset of the oedipal phase. During the last 10 years or so, we have begun to understand the vital relatedness between child and father in preoedipal life as well. The rich experiences shared between a father and his offspring from birth onward have been elaborated in the important psychoanalytic contributions of many authors, including Abelin (1971, 1975) and J. M. Ross (1975, 1977, 1979). In fact, psychoanalytic perspectives on the early father-child relationship have been paralleled by similar recent explorations in academic and empirical developmental psychology (Lynn, 1974; Lamb, 1976a).

Present Theoretical Approaches

While these and other contributors have taught us a good deal about children and their fathers, their shared investigative methodologies merit some scrutiny. Kernberg (1976) points out that our current psychoanalytic object-relations theory stresses the simultaneous "building" of dyadic or bipolar intrapsychic self and object representations as reflections of the original infant-mother relationship. This "original" relationship is mirrored in the development of other dyadic, or later "triangular and multiple internal and external interpersonal relationships" (p. 57). Schaffer and Emerson (1964) suggest that by 18 months children have formed multiple one-to-one relationships, including one to the father. Our tendency, in psychoanalytic object-relations theory, is to assume that, at least in their early ascendancy, the intrapsychic representations relative to each dyad derive from experiences unique to it. In other words, a child "gets to know" his father representationally through experiences generated out of transactions, from birth on, between a father and his child.

As Bronfenbrenner (1979) puts it, this paradigm simply substitutes father for mother in the investigative technique. Such a substitution does, I believe, limit what we can know about a child's early relationship to his or her father. Early father representations do derive from sources beyond the specific father-child dyad, particularly from mediations by the mother and her attitude and relationship to her husband.

Emergence of Human Relatedness: Parents' Roles

To provide a clearer understanding of this assumption, let me begin by outlining our psychoanalytic sense of how a child gets to know, or develops attachments to, each parent early in life. We assume that there is a complex series of transactions between an infant and its environment right from the beginning of life. We further suppose that these transactions generate a wealth of potential experiences for the infant. At the beginning of life, the mother, as traditional principal caretaker, is the cardinal mediator of environmentally based experience. The mother's role additionally extends to her infant's constitutional experiences, insofar as she helps to mollify his or her drives, maintains and supports a state of quiet alert inactivity (Wolff, 1966; Weil, 1970; Brazelton and Als, 1979) that facilitates the infant's "other" or "outward" directedness, and aids in the "drawing" of her infant toward herself as an object of interest, gratification, and progressive reality mediation. As Jacobson (1964, p. 37) so aptly put it,

In fact, when a mother turns the infant on his belly, takes him out of his crib, diapers him, sits him up in her arms and on her lap, rocks him, strokes him, kisses him, feeds him, smiles at him, talks and sings to him, she offers him not only all kinds of libidinal gratifications but simultaneously stimulates and prepares the child's sitting, standing, crawling, walking, talking, and so on, i.e., the development of functional ego activity.

We have recently begun to explore what, on the surface of it, seems to be a simultaneous and parallel relationship to the father (Abelin, 1971, 1975; Lynn, 1974; Ross, 1975, 1977, 1979; Lamb, 1976a).

Distinction Between Self and Others

This potential psychological wealth, deriving from objectively internal and external events, gains inner meaning for the child through the epigenetic capacity to represent experience mentally. At the beginning of life, we consider an infant's psychic matrix to be relatively undifferentiated and incapable of distinguishing self from other, or mental phenomena related to internal states from those related to actual ministrations or occurrences in the environment. Psychically, representational boundaries that are at first fluid and indeterminate gradually coalesce into more discrete distinctions reflecting increasing sophistication, clarity, and complexity as development proceeds. Beginning at the level of body-boundedness, the infant first achieves the capacity to distinguish inside from outside stimulations, then gradually sharpens a clarity of external ministrations belonging to a progressively differentiated and objectified mother, and finally distinguishes the self and other as psychically different and separate, although dynamically related to one another in a relatively constant or invariant way. We can say that, at the apex of their functioning, mental representations are a coherent organization of images, ideas, fantasies, and their associated affects, psychically defining the relationship between self and others (e.g., mother and father).

Although perhaps somewhat overschematized, the foregoing describes the emergence of a child's human relatedness and representational capacities in a caretaking matrix where both parents are vital and available participants. However, what if the father becomes dynamically unavailable to the young child through untimely death, separation, or other conditions of relative or total deprivation?

Effects of Father Deprivation

The now classic observations of Freud and Burlingham (1947) shows us that oedipal-phase children in wartime London, when deprived of father's actual presence, compensated representationally by constructing a father in fantasy. Whether there was a preexisting relationship with father, or a meager series of transactions with a father substitute, or the entire absence of a "father experience," these children seemed "compelled to create in fantasy what [did] not exist in fact" (Neubauer, 1960). We find similar fantasy compensations among children whose fathers die early in their lives (Furman, 1974) and among children whose fathers live away from home through parental divorce or separation (Hetherington, 1979).

Positive and Negative Idealizations
Such fantasies frequently result in an extremely idealized or extremely punitive father representation, the ideal "good" or the ideal "bad" relationship (Schecter, 1974). While the circumstances surrounding the deprivation of the father certainly contribute to the "shape" of the fantasy of him, psychoanalysis traditionally views such fantasies as the product of the timing of the loss, the child's phase-specific intrapsychic wishes, and the phase-specific developmental imperatives of the child's cultural reality (Neubauer, 1960; Schecter, 1974; Chap. 29). As Fenichel (1931) put it, "When the parent of the child's own sex dies, this is perceived as a fulfillment of the oedipal wish with strong feelings of guilt [the ideal bad relationship]. If the other parent dies, the oedipal longing which remains unsatisfied leads to the fantastic idealization of the dead parent, and to an increase of the longing [the ideal good relationship]." Later, Isaacs (1943, 1945) suggested positive idealization of the same-sex absent parent as a furthering of inverted oedipal aims. Lewin (1937) reported on the idealization of the lost parent of the same sex as a protection against the resurgence of incestuous conflicts in adolescence.

These and other dynamic issues are unquestionably important to positive and negative idealizations of the father when the father is lost. Unfortunately, however, we often rely on such dynamic labeling without also investigating other important contributions to the formation of such fantasy representations. During World War II, Bach (1946), in an impeccable study, elicited through play the father fantasies of father-separated children, aged 6 to 10 years. This study group was equally divided into boys and girls, and all the fathers had been called into military service when the children were between 1 and 3 years old. A group of matched controls with fathers at home was similarly studied. In comparison to the control group, the children with absent fathers did indeed idealize them, both positively and negatively. According to predictable developmental considerations, the boys, on the whole, showed significantly more aggressive fantasies and the girls, on the whole, remained ideally affectionately attached to their fathers.

Mother's Role

Bach also coupled interviews with the mothers to the research study. He identified two subgroupings of mothers' attitudes to the absent father, those whose attitudes were unambiguously deprecating and unfavorable (the four mothers of two boys and two girls in the study) and those whose attitudes were unquestionably favorable and positively idealizing (a similar grouping of four mothers). The mother's attitude toward the father was a significant variable. Those children, both boys and girls, whose mothers bore ill feelings toward the father tended to negatively idealize the father to a much greater degree than all other children.

Quantity Versus Quality of Father's Presence

A child's identification with his or her mother's attitude toward the father is, to my mind, a significant variable extending not only to father-absent families but to intact nuclear families as well. While the epigenesis of father representations is certainly tied to actual transactions in the father-child dyad, the number of transactions may be more theoretical speculation than developmental fact. Our research findings, derived from Lewis and Weinraub (1976), tell us that, in contrast to mothers, fathers spend very little time in dyadic interaction with their children. Pedersen and Robson (1969) note that fathers play with their 9-month-old infants for approximately only 8 hours every week, slightly more than an hour a day, including weekends. Rebelsky and Hanks (1971) suggest that, although there is a range, fathers spend an average of 37½ seconds a day verbally interacting with their 3-month-old or younger infants. Ban and Lewis (1974), in interviews with middle-class fathers, found that playtime with their 1-year-old children amounted to an average of only 15 minutes a day. Despite this rather limited amount of time together, Pedersen and Robson (1969) found that the amount of time a father interacts with his child does not correlate with measures of the child's attachment to the father. This lack of correlation represents, with the exception of the father-absence literature, a rather consistent finding in developmental studies. One of our frequent homilies to such findings is that the quality of dyadic interaction, not the quantity of time together, governs both attachment to the father and the vicissitudes in the representational world. Yet, quantity and quality must clearly intersect in the lower range. If children can develop manifest attachment to their fathers in the face of such statistics, both the attachment and the governing representations must arise from or receive contributions from sources beyond the father-child dyad.

Impact of Triangular Family Constellation on the Child

Abelin's (1971, 1975) seminal psychoanalytic contributions to the field of early father-child relatedness suggest that a particular transformation occurs in the representational world of children in the middle of the second year of life. With the emergence of evocative memory (Fraiberg, 1969), youngsters at this time, in addition to apprehending a separate dyadic relationship to each parent, also apprehend a relatedness between father and mother. This "early triangulation" serves especially to consolidate both the self-representation and the parental representations. Such a child is then well on the road toward an oedipal constellation. Yet, this concept suggests that triangulation is truly present only when the child can cognitively assimilate its presence. I postulate that a "triangular" family constellation has a developmental impact on a child from birth on, even though these complex relationships are neither objectified nor differentiated in the child's early experience.

Mother's Role

In the infant's early development, the mother fosters an interest in herself as an object as well as interests in other persons or objects in the child's environment, especially the father. During the first year of her child's development, the manner in which a mother brings her youngster into contact with the father can catalyze or discolor the child's affective attachment to him. During the normal autistic and symbiotic phases, the mother can facilitate or retard the sustaining of periods of quiet alert inactive other-directedness in her child in her husband's presence. She can aid or inhibit her husband's capacity to do the same with their child, if he is willing or interested. She can foster phase-appropriate cathectic shifts (Jacobson, 1964) toward the father, or cull singular narcissistic investments in herself. An infant in the symbiotic phase, for example, propped over the mother's shoulder, can be grossly or subtly stimulated to engage another, frequently the father, in periods of mutual responsiveness and reciprocal dialogue (Spitz, 1965). The mother can hold her infant out toward the father, promote smiling, vocal cuing, reaching and grabbing, staring, and so forth. She can promote the foregoing in an affectively loving way or in a withdrawing, impeding fashion. It is important to stress the affective underpinnings of the mother's relationship to father, whether his presence induces love, caring, and happiness or anger, depression, and hatred. These more subtle nuances can be equally communicative to the infant about his or her father.

In an infrequently cited paper, Winnicott (1963, pp. 182–183) says, "The infant develops two kinds of relationships at the same time—that to the *environment-mother* and that to the object, which becomes the *object-mother*. The environment-mother is human, and the object-mother is a thing, although it is also the mother or part of her" (emphasis added).

In another stimulating contribution, Lichtenberg (1979, pp. 378–379) suggests that, as the environment mother:

She [the mother] constitutes the whole background world in which the infant exists: the air he breathes, the force of gravity that holds him to his crib, *the emotional climate in which he feels*. As the "object" mother, she is the mother with whom the infant interacts in response to all of his drive urgencies, the mother who feeds, the mother he cries to have come, the mother whose face he explores, the mother against whom his rage is directed. . . . Experiencing the mother as "environment" is the paradigm of the tendency to generalize, experiencing the mother as "object" . . . is the paradigm of the tendency to particularize. Particularizing establishes the sense of borders and boundaries; *generalizing crosses boundaries within the sense of self and between self and object* (emphasis added).

Particularizing and Generalizing

Lichtenberg suggests that when we emphasize developmental trends toward reality testing and objectivity, such as the prevailing object-relations theory which suggests that a child's sense of the other shifts epigenetically only from an "environmental" to an "object" one, we miss the fluidity with which children experience the object at one and the same time.

Consider some examples of the fluidity between particularizing and generalizing. Lichtenberg cites the infant-toddler's insistence on his or her transitional object as an example of particularizing. The use of the transitional object, its shifting back and forth from comfort-giving aspects of self and of mother, is an example of generalizing. The 6-month-old infant's delight at the awareness of *his* or *her* mother, is a further example of particularizing. That same infant's awareness of the primitive interaction of drive state and anticipation of gratification, or of other primordial internal or exteroceptive signs (Fraiberg, 1969) of the mother's (or gratifying object's) imminent appearance, is an example of generalizing.

An infant's generalizing experience with the environment mother may involve fluid shifts with other individuals beyond the object mother. The fluid relationship between the environment mother and the object father, evident in the following clinical example, is particularly important.

Don is a wide-eyed, active little boy just past his first half year. He likes to sit face to face with his mother, supported in her lap.

During this observation, mother was verbally playing with her son. She would coo "nice boy" or "handsome boy" to Don, pausing after each pair of utterances. While she was talking, Don would stare at his mother's face with eyes and mouth agape. During each pause, he would burst into a smile, then, seemingly delighted, simultaneously squeal and kick.

When father entered the room, mother, maintaining eye contact with Don, cooed, "There's your daddy!," in the same warm, even pitch. Don squealed right back at mother. She then turned him toward father at the instant that father approached. Don's eyes and father's eyes met. Father cackled. Don smiled wide and squealed and kicked. Meanwhile, mother, now silent, gently continued to move Don's body toward the father.

Just at that moment a telephone in the room rang. Father reached to answer it, and, in so doing, broke eye contact with his son. As father began the phone conversation, Don's face sobered. After a short pause, however, the infant again smiled widely at his preoccupied father, squealed, and kicked. After a few seconds, the boy sobered again. Staring steadily at his father, he again seemingly tried to reengage the man on the telephone with smiling, squealing, and kicking. The father was not paying attention, and, after one more brief attempt, Don turned his head back toward mother's face.

In this example, it is the father who ultimately loses the opportunity for sustained interaction with his infant son. Mother, by contrast, has generously fertilized the field between father and son, through gentle and reciprocal attentiveness to her infant and through facilitating the child's other-directedness, both to herself and, noncompetitively, to her husband. We could alternatively construe other examples (see below) where the father is ignored as much as he is ignoring, potentiating a pernicious setting for the emergence of the child's representational world.

Hence, the way mother "prepares" her child may well affect the separate, yet related, relationship that the child develops with the father. As the environment mother stimulates, frustrates, gratifies, vitalizes, or (Lichtenstein, 1977) negates her child's experience with the object father, she can infer in that child affective dispositions that color the more ideational father representations. The rest of the story is contained in how the father reaps what the mother sows.

Development of Evocative Memory in the Infant

Fraiberg (1969), in a remarkably comprehensive paper, discusses the developmental progression of representational functioning. Her considerations may help to heighten a sense of the close relationship between the mother's (and child's) affective disposition toward and the ultimate cognitive image of the father.

Mental registration, as relatively undifferentiated experience early in life, does have a particular meaning. Objects, including persons, are psychically enduring only to the extent that they remain perceived. We think that such perception is significantly related to and undifferentiated from: (1) the action performed by or performed upon the object, and (2) the capacity of the infant to assimilate or accommodate to the exteroceptive or internal stimulus surrounding the perception.

The capacity to differentiate and sustain the image of the object as autonomous from its actions, from the presenting stimulus, and ultimately as independent of perception (imaging the absent object) is what Fraiberg (1969), borrowing from Piaget, refers to as evocative memory. It is this capacity that consolidates in the middle of the second year of life and places us, in our psychoanalytic sense, firmly on the road to libidinal object constancy.

Yet, the child at the end of the first year of life, although his or her perceptions remain relatively bound to stimuli and action schema, may lay down particular representational patterns of the father through the following mechanism. We know that children in the last trimester of the first year of life can recover objects hidden by a single screen. As Fraiberg (1969) suggests, this mental image of the object is linked to the visual stimulus of the screen and to the action of recovery of the object. The stability of the image is sustained, so long as the object is conceived of as "belonging to the hiding place." Once the object is moved behind a second screen it cannot be mentally followed. Hence the object is recognized in, or as part of, the context in which it appears.

The context acts as a primitive sign for the object. In Piaget's experiments, the screen signs the object that is to materialize from behind it, in the sense that the screen and the object now belong together. If the desired object is not with the screen, the screen loses its sign value and the mental image of the object in its context wanes.

Mother's Role

In the nuclear mother-father-infant constellation, the mother can either help to establish an affectively vital position for the father or quite literally and negatively put him "in his place" as a hostile intruder. She can sign, through her affective valence, her attitude toward the father's holding and caring for their child or her attitude toward the father's comings and goings. Her relative pleasures and unpleasures may manifest either as open expressions or be mediated through subtle changes in body contact while holding her infant. These shifts in her affective "body language" may register in her infant both as primitive affectomotor representations (Jacobson, 1964), and as signs communicating an anticipation either of father or the "father context." Such may well be the origins of the child's enduring positively or negatively charged father representations. This transaction may also provide a tableau for, or source of, idealizations or denigrations of the other.

As the child develops evocative representational capacities, fantasies or mental images of father may remain linked to the mother's capacity to vitalize her husband even in his absence. The following observations illustrate this point:

Pete

A rambunctious 2-year-old, Pete loved to engage his mother in many playful activities. One of his special games at the time involved chattering away to his mother in simple sentences; she would chatter back. Often Pete or his mother would invoke "Daddy" as a subject of conversation. If, for example, Pete looked inquisitively at Mommy and asked, "Daddy at work?," Mother would construct an elaborate playful escapade around "Daddy at work." She would pick up a crayon and paper, start drawing, and say, "Daddy writes at work." She would run a wooden car across the floor, explaining, "Daddy drives to work, and then he drives home to see Pete!" Pete would join in, captivated with the activity. One morning in the nursery, while Pete's mother was talking with the other mothers, Pete initiated the play himself. He began to scribble with crayon and paper, saying, "Pete working!," looking playfully at Mother. Mother, having caught sight of the activity in midstage, clapped her hands with a delighted chuckle and beamed back at her son. Pete laughed. As the play continued in other contexts, Pete became more engaged in driving the cars around himself and in carrying a little doctor's kit, seemingly qua briefcase, around with him. Pete's father representations appeared to blossom, even in the absence of Father.

Charlotte

Charlotte, 23 months old, was grossly overweight, as was her mother. The mother, again pregnant and seemingly depressed about it, would come to the nursery because it afforded her a social outlet among other things. Charlotte would be plopped onto the floor when they arrived, whereupon Mother would pour herself a cup of coffee and pursue a kaffeeklatsch with the other mothers. If during the nursery time, any of the other mothers would initiate play with their children, Charlotte's mother would join in. She was rarely generative in this regard, however. Charlotte enjoyed rattling a chain of plastic keys and frequently poked, prodded, and entreated Mother for the rings of house and car keys she carried in her purse. She would pick a key on one or the other ring and twist it on some solid object near Mother. This was frequently accompanied by a somewhat vacuous "Daddy?" and a stare at mother. If Mother was paying attention, she would respond with a very perfunctory, "Daddy is at work," and return to her adult conversation. Mother frequently ignored her daughter and refused to provide an answer. Charlotte repeated the question many times during the nursery sessions. Sometimes, when no response was forthcoming, Charlotte would sit and stare for many seconds at the keys she was holding. Although it was impossible to ascertain their exact significance, the keys seemed to have something to do with Daddy coming home or Daddy going away. Within a short period of time, this particular play disappeared from the child's repertoire. During my brief tenure in the nursery, I saw no additional play about Daddy, certainly not to the extent that it could be seen with Pete.

The father's inherent capacity to establish himself as a new object (Loewald, 1960) and, during separation-individuation, as a parent who effectively cleaves the child's symbiosis with the mother, can help to reshape and reform the child's representations of him. Representational triangulation, in the sense that Abelin (1971, 1975) intended it, can further enhance the process.

Conclusions

We may do well to remember that psychological birth can never appropriately be equated to the birth of evocative representations, although our current tendency in psychoanalysis seems to force this representational world to become a system of psychic microorganizations that, motivationally, are also microdynamisms (Schafer, 1968). As Jacobson (1964, pp. 34–35) has so appropriately stated:

We do not know precisely at what time the psychic apparatus becomes capable of retaining memory traces of pleasure-unpleasure experiences; but there is no doubt that long before the infant becomes aware of the mother as a person and of his own self, engrams are laid down of experiences which reflect his responses to maternal care in the realm of his entire mental and body self.

Clinically, we are more frequently attending to earlier periods in developments as "critical" to the way a person thinks and feels about the self and the significant people in his or her history and current life. The subtle nuances in human relatedness may ultimately find their developmental origins in that vast and relatively unexplored territory of human life before ideas take hold, when the warmth of a mother and her alliance with the father create a milieu in which all subsequent representations are based.

9

The Preoedipal Relationship of a Father, Mother, and Daughter

Eleanor Galenson
Herman Roiphe

One of the most illuminating experiences in the course of psychoanalytic treatment is the opportunity to work with a patient's early childhood experiences as they emerge to either the patient or the patient's spouse under the impact of the birth of a baby. Under these circumstances, the patient's early life events assume a new sense of intimacy and veracity. In regard to the new infant's own developmental realities, however, they remain screened from the analyst in that they are viewed through the distorted prism created by patients' perceptions of their own children.

Another type of distortion characterizes most direct studies involving infant observation, since these provide a superficial view of infant and parental interactions without illuminating the underlying dynamic trends. The uniqueness of Mahler's research design (1975a) lay in the opportunity it offered for studying mother-infant interaction over the course of some time, and at intervals frequent enough so that in-depth observations and conclusions could be made and significant relationships between the mothers and participant observers in the study could develop. Our own research design (Galenson and Roiphe, 1976), modeled after Mahler's, shared these same advantages. Although the data obtained cannot be fully equated with the material of the analytic treatment situation, they do provide the analytically trained researcher with reflections of unconscious dynamic constellations in both parents, particularly in the mother, as these are stimulated once again by the infant's emerging individuality.

Issues of confidentiality usually interfere with the publication of more than vignettes from the voluminous records of the families studied. However, in this instance, the lapse of time and the permission granted by the family have enabled us to share the detailed complexities of the relationship of Mary and her parents as they evolved over a period of almost a year. Although there were many features unique to this triad we

151

shall report on, our experience with the 69 other families we studied in the course of our 10-year research project leads us to conclude that there were many commonalities shared by Mary's family and those of the other 34 girls and their parents.

Role of the Father During the Early Years as Reported by Others

Rather than attempt to review the literature on this subject, we will summarize the contributions that are most pertinent to our own study. Mahler and Gosliner (1955), Mahler and associates (1975), and Greenacre (1957) discussed the role of the father during the practicing subphases of the separation-individuation process in the development of the child's exploratory and early phallic attitudes, as well as his subsequent role in the rapprochement subphase, when he aided the infant's resistance against the regressive pull back into the maternal symbiotic attachment. Abelin (1975) summarized his own research findings verifying the data already alluded to: (1) There is a special relationship with the father during the symbiotic phase, a definite turning to the father at the beginning of the practicing subphase when there is a special quality of excitement linked with him; and (2) male adults in general represent the most fascinating kind of object, initially provoking a more violent reaction and eventually preferred over women. Abelin also found that girls attach themselves to fathers earlier than do boys, but are also more wary of strange men. The early triangulation proposed by Abelin, although not explicitly present in the overt material of his research, could apparently be inferred as occurring at the onset of the rapprochement subphase. Peers, rather than fathers, however, seemed to represent the first rivals in the typical triangular situation.

Finally, Abelin thought that the paternal relationship shared in the symbiotic quality of the maternal relationship, in spite of the differences described.

Nature of Research Data

Although our research sample was composed largely of middle-class intact families, there were wide variations both in the amount of time the fathers spent with their children and in the quality of the relationship. There seemed to be no simple correlation between the actual amount of time they spent together and the intensity of the child-father relationship. Somewhat unexpectedly, another factor proved to be more pertinent here, namely, the mother's largely unconscious expectations as to the role the father was to play in the infant's life, expectations that only gradually came to be reflected in the mother's behavior during the year or more of our contact with her. Yet this should have come as no surprise to us as psychoanalysts, since the marriages had been based on unconscious constellations of needs and wishes in both partners that had brought them together in the first place. As it turned out, the infant's relationship to the father could be understood only within the context of the relationship to the mother as well.

Mary and Her Parents: Background Data
Mary was the firstborn daughter of parents in their mid-20s. Her father, although deeply involved in preparation for his career, was very devoted to his child. Her mother wanted to have a career of her own eventually, but was now devoting herself primarily to rearing her family. Both parents had wished for a girl and had chosen only a female name in advance of the delivery. Pregnancy and delivery were uneventful, except that Mary was noted to have an extraordinary facial resemblance to her mother from the earliest days. There had been considerable postprandial colic following each nursing during the first 3 months, and although the father enjoyed bathing and diapering Mary even at that time, he never participated in the rocking required to comfort her after each nursing. The mother recalled his unavailability in this regard with considerable resentment 12 months later, when we first came to know the family.

Once the colic had subsided, Mary was a sunny, easygoing child with whom her mother established excellent rapport. The household was a fairly busy one; there were many visitors who often remained for several days, sharing Mary's bedroom. Mary seemed to accommodate to them just as easily as she had to several baby-sitters who came regularly twice each week while her mother went off on personal errands. Yet in spite of the generally lively home atmosphere, Mary's mother said she had felt housebound and burdened—a complaint that she reiterated throughout the first 2 years of Mary's life. Although the mother enjoyed her baby, there was clearly something lacking for her in this dual relationship.

Mary's Preference for Men
Although there was no definite stranger anxiety described by the parents retrospectively, a variant of stranger anxiety seemed to have emerged at about 5 to 6 months of age. Beginning in response to all adults except the mother, and soon becoming specific for men only, Mary had a "coy" or "flirtatious" look with which she greeted new people. Her partially lowered eyelids allowed her to peer up at strangers without a direct visual

confrontation. The "look" was experienced as attractive and appealing by the various men with whom she had contact, as well as by her own father.

When we first came to know Mary at 15 months, she was a dainty, charming child who was not yet walking alone, but cruised freely about our nursery while maintaining visual contact with her mother. During this first session, Mary sought out the senior male staff person and spontaneously settled in his lap, where she remained for some time. She also flirted with other male staff members but paid little attention to the females in the nursery. Mary was well within average expectations in regard to other aspects of her development, but there was no doubt about the special role that men already played in Mary's life. Her mother attributed this to her husband's very busy schedule, which kept him away from home most evenings until after Mary's bedtime. The mother seemed to be less aware of her own sadness over this absence than of Mary's need for him.

Separation from the Parents at 15 Months

Immediately after their initial visit to our nursery, the parents left for a 2-week vacation and professional trip. Mary remained with her grandparents, whom she knew well, in their house in another city. This separation coincided with the first news that the mother was pregnant, apparently a planned-for and desired event.

The many changes noted in Mary on her return to the nursery indicated that a marked spurt in the separation-individuation process had taken place during her absence; such an experience is not unexpected in the children we have studied. Mary had begun to walk independently, now selectively indicated her soiled diapers, had acquired a word for her bowel movements, and had developed semisymbolic play with dolls for the first time. She also now gesturally compared her own facial features with those of her mother and her dolls, and used the new word *ma-ma* to designate her mother. The new level of differentiation of self from maternal object elicited a host of new reciprocal games that she and her mother now played together, all of which involved some form of mutual tickling and touching.

The firmer definition of self (e.g., the upright locomotion, the awareness of anal functioning, and the advance in symbolic functioning) was clearly matched by a firmer definition of the maternal object (e.g., naming her mother, identifying her features). Of particular interest to us was Mary's new identification with the more active aspect of her mother's role with her. Mary now took care of her dolls very much as her mother had taken care of her, a step in developing autonomy that appears to be crucially important for the quality of the developing self-concept.

Relationship with Father

In contrast to the shift in relationship with her mother, Mary's relationship with her father had not changed perceptibly. As she had behaved at least as early as her fifth or sixth month, Mary was always delighted to see him; she would awaken spontaneously whenever he arrived home, and would then engage in a half-hour or so of exciting and joyful games that they played only with each other. The mother said she objected to having Mary awake at this time although she never tried to interfere; indeed, it was our impression that the mother enjoyed these interludes a great deal herself, for it was in connection with her description of Mary's play with her father that she described her childhood disappointment in her own father. Her mother was a warm and loving person, but her father seemed cold and aloof from all three children, did not participate in their rearing, and acted "like another baby in the house." However, even as the mother described her disappointment in her father, she mentioned that she had showered with him until her mid-latency, when she herself had withdrawn from this intimacy. We have construed from this and from additional material offered by the mother that the older father-daughter relationship seemed to be repeated now in certain of its aspects between Mary and her father. There were periods of intense stimulation and excitement interspersed with the letdown of total absence.

Here we see the influence of maternal unconscious attitudes in shaping the new daughter-father relationship. The mother's low-keyed, depressively tinged tie with her child was relieved by the zest, excitement, and probably erotic quality of reunion with the returning father. It is of interest that this is precisely the special paternal quality postulated by Greenacre and Mahler, and later verified by Abelin's observations.

Onset of the Early Genital Phase (15–17 Months)

Some weeks after Mary's early anal awareness at 15 months, she began to follow her mother into the bathroom and paid close attention to the sound of her mother's urinary stream in the toilet. Next came her selective awareness of her own wet diapers, and then her curiosity about her father's urination. This pattern of schematization of the anal and then the urinary function in self and parents emerged in the majority of children in our study during the early months of the second year, and was soon followed by the emergence of a new type of genital awareness, regardless of the specific degree of body exposure practiced by the parents. Mary's father, as it happened, was a rather modest man who had rarely been naked in Mary's presence before. But now she insisted on following him into the bathroom, where she was fascinated by the sight of his urinary stream and tried to touch it repeatedly.

Mary's interest in her own genitals was now of a different quality than her earlier casual touching during diapering, which had first appeared at about 11 months. During her diapering, she would now clutch and squeeze the small area between her labia with both hands, often for as long as 10 to 15 seconds, as she smiled and giggled. Her gaze was "inner-directed" at times, but she also smiled at her mother, who patiently waited until Mary was finished. Mary also now sought out the rocking horse and straddled her parents' leg in obvious nonmanual genital self-stimulation.

Mary showed a tendency to imitate her father's activities during the initial phase of her discovery of his urination and penis. She preferred wearing his shoes, pretended to listen to his watch (as he so often did himself), and appropriated his pens and pocket flashlight. It seems that this new level of her own genital cathexis led to a different quality of cathexis, not only in regard to the father's genitals, but also in the quality of their object relationship in general. We have described this as the advent of the early genital phase. Whereas their mutual play had always been exciting and probably somewhat erotically tinged, Mary now wanted a more intimate connection with her father. Both parents participated in and clearly enjoyed Mary's new interest in her own body and in theirs as well during Mary's incipient early genital phase.

Reaction to the Sexual Anatomical Difference (17–19 Months)

Mary's next 2 months were characterized by her very rapidly shifting attitudes and moods. This was a trying period with which her mother coped most empathetically and flexibly. The mother had from the beginning of our contact with her shown great ingenuity in avoiding direct confrontations with Mary, waiting patiently or offering substitutes whenever Mary balked at her mother's requests. Her ingenuity was now taxed to its fullest as Mary's reaction to the genital anatomical difference mounted.

Mary's masturbation became more and more inhibited and her anxiety in regard to anal loss increased. (The regressive revival of fears of anal loss as well as object loss in the face of the preoedipal castration problem has been found to be ubiquitous in the girls in our study; this has been described in detail elsewhere [Galenson and Roiphe, 1976].) There were bouts of stool retention, refusal to have her soiled diapers removed, and constant play with the toilet flushing mechanism; all these responses were means of coping with Mary's anxiety over anal loss. The issue of urinary control also soon became enmeshed in this anxiety over loss; Mary appeared acutely embarrassed and ashamed one morning as a stream of urine trickled down beside her diaper and pooled on the floor beneath her.

For a time, Mary actively compared her own genital area with those of her parents, looking back and forth first at herself and then at them. But gradually she began to avoid these genital visual confrontations altogether, and focused instead on the ubiquitous umbilicus and on the buttocks, particularly on her mother's body. It is probable that this shift also allowed her to deny her mother's increasingly prominent pregnancy —a matter in which she was aided and abetted by her mother's conviction that Mary had not yet noticed her clearly visible pregnant abdomen.

Mary's avoidance of the genital area itself was associated with a remarkable shift in her attitude toward her parents and other adults. Only her mother was accepted now for nighttime comforting, and women nursery staff members became of interest to her for the first time, as she avoided her former male favorites. With this shift in her preference toward women, her doll play became far more elaborate, one doll being singled out for special attention, probably because it produced a *ma-ma* sound as its string was pulled.

Mary's mother reacted to her daughter's increasing wish for closeness and her anxiety about separation with further dampening of her own mood. This period, typically the time of the rapprochement crisis in most children, was a stressful period for Mary and her mother on this account as well. However, it was Mary's sense of genital loss that revived her earlier fears of object and anal loss, so all three types of anxiety were now present as major threats to Mary's psychological state.

Reemergence of Genitality and the Developing Symbolic Function (19 and 20 Months)

Although Mary's ambivalence to her mother and her concomitant separation anxiety persisted, her interest in the genital area and in males began to reemerge. She now began to be intensely curious about her mother's pubic area as well as the pubic area in her peers and in dolls. Although she did not follow her father into the bathroom, apparently still avoiding direct confrontation with his genitals, she was happy to be with him and once again sought out the male staff observer whom she had identified with her father from the very start of her nursery experience.

A new and most interesting defensive development now made its appearance; whereas Mary had previously been interested in her father's pens and those of male observers, she now became passionately insistent on collecting these items, as well as crayons, toy cars, and small dolls. She hid many of them in her small hands and tried to take them with her as she left the nursery or other places she visited. We (Galenson, Miller, and Roiphe, 1976) have described this behavior as an early form of kleptomania. However, in addition to merely collecting these things, Mary used the crayons in her earliest attempts at graphic representations; she built tall towers with blocks (a favorite game which she played with her father); and she became far more elaborate and complex in her semisymbolic doll play.

We believe that Mary's impressive capacity for symbolization contributed significantly to this early precursor of sublimation and to her capacity to deal with her anxiety connected with genital, anal, and object loss. It was through this device that partial identification with both parents seemed to have been achieved, a development that allowed her to establish a harmonious relationship with them once again. Mother and daughter got along so well together now that her mother expressed to us for the first time her sense of deep satisfaction at being able to teach and guide her child, who was now interested in drawing and in books, as well as in sharing her mother's activities in caring for a neighbor's infant.

Regression During Mother's Final Months of Pregnancy (21–23 Months)

It is probable that the mother's advancing pregnancy was the important dynamic determinant of her increasing complaints about her husband's absorption in his work and his neglect of his family. These complaints were, of course, quite similar to her older complaints about her father's neglect of his children, although she herself did not consciously associate the two sets of dissatisfactions.

We believe it was the mother's own discontent which led her to suggest that Mary bathe with her father, a practice that was only now carried out regularly; also, Mary again habitually watched her father's urination. Soon after this renewed physical intimacy between father and daughter, Mary's excitement and flirtatiousness toward the male members of our staff reappeared. She also began to have a "love affair," as her mother called it, with an elderly male relative who was now visiting her more frequently and showering her with small gifts. On several occasions, Mary called these men "daddy," as if inadvertently, and also often gazed out the window, murmuring "daddy" to herself.

Mary's genital self-exploration and self-stimulation also gradually returned, and she explored her other body orifices, including her anus. Yet she continued to avoid viewing the anterior aspect of her mother's body entirely, exploring only the buttocks area. Mary thus apparently avoided the anxiety of acknowledging both her mother's genitals and her pregnancy, a denial with which her mother collaborated to an astonishing degree. It is likely that this denial interfered with Mary's ability to clarify sexual differences more effectively: She continued to confuse pictures of boys and girls, alluded to her mother's unshaven axillary hair as "like daddy's," and continued to resist soiled diaper changes with great vehemence.

The mother's encouragement of Mary's renewed closeness with her father undoubtedly had a number of determinants, only one of which was her conscious wish that Mary would be protected from missing her mother too much when she left to have the new baby. Again, we suspect that the mother was reliving her own past experience of having turned to her father under just such circumstances. Yet in spite of the mother's pressure to bring father and daughter together, Mary would now spend much time cuddling in her mother's lap and playing with dolls (which she interestingly enough labeled "daddy" and "baby"); she had also become neat and tidy and very tender with the two neighbors' babies whom her mother cared for on occasion, in a growing identification with her pregnant mother. And on several occasions she even arched her back, sticking out her abdomen in a comical yet most affectionate imitation of her mother.

An additional shift in Mary's object relations appeared only a few weeks before the birth of her new sibling. Mary had played with the other children in the nursery, but her interest in them had never approached the intensity of her involvement with adults. Now for the first time she sought out several boys with whom she played excited hide-and-seek and other games. She also favored a fire engine with an expandable ladder and a car with lights, although crayons remained her delight. As for her doll play, it remained intermittent and tender, but was still a solitary affair.

Reaction to Sister's Birth (24½ Months)
During her mother's 3-day absence from home, Mary was irritable and angry with the female relative who took care of her. She tried to urinate standing up like a boy on several occasions, and deliberately wet the carpet the first time she saw her mother nursing the new baby after their return home. There was little doubt about her anger at her mother, and at least one source of it seemed to be quite evident.

But just as she had earlier turned to her father (partially at her mother's instigation), once again she became very close to him, and he responded by taking time off from his work to be with her. Again her capacity for symbolic substitution came into play as she attempted to assuage her anger at her mother: A toy umbrella became her favorite plaything, and a small toy flute and her mother's nursing shield were placed at her pubic area at various times. On several occasions she was found asleep in her crib with these objects lying beneath her pelvis.

Apparently the anxiety about the genital difference was still considerably troublesome to Mary: All her former efforts at urinary control were now entirely abandoned and she avoided looking at the genital area of all family members, including her new sister and herself. Only the buttocks were of any interest to her.

Follow-Up (27 Months, 4 Years, and 7½ Years)

While her mother described Mary as "a little mother to her sister" at 27 months, it seemed to us that there was a stronger identification with her father at this time. She said she wanted to grow up to be like him; she was interested in books, as he was, and her favorite activity was building intricate structures with blocks, something she had shared with her father from the early part of her second year. Her major conflict with her mother remained confined to the area of bowel training, urinary control having been largely established by now.

Our next contact with the family was just before Mary's fourth birthday. She had begun nursery school at 34 months, and had achieved bowel control within 3 weeks of starting school, under the gentle prodding of her teacher. Her favorite activities were drawing and painting, but her mother thought her attention span was rather short.

We last met with the whole family when Mary was 7½ years old. She seemed rather shy and subdued, personality traits that her mother told us were now characteristic of her. She had rather few friends, although recently she had begun to seek out some girls, and her favorite activities were reading, doing crossword puzzles, and playing checkers and card games with her father. She had no interest at all in dolls, never having returned to the flurry of semisymbolic doll play that occurred during the period just preceding her mother's delivery. Until recently, she had wanted to follow her father in his profession, but now she wanted to be a teacher. The only real reminder of the lively, curious, and active little girl we had first encountered at 15 months was the flirtatious look, which occasionally returned during the course of our visit. We had the opportunity of discussing Mary with her current teacher at school, a woman of whom Mary was very fond. Her teacher considered Mary to be a most gifted child; her written stories showed a vivid and rich inner fantasy life that the teacher thought would one day enable Mary to become a writer of considerable ability.

Discussion

As we have traced the strands of a little girl's growing identification with both of her parents, we have attempted to take into account the effects of some aspects of the mother's unconscious wishes and attitudes, to which we had access because of the special conditions of our research design. We learned of the mother's early experiences with her parents as they were revived by the impact on her of her own infant's development, and it became evident to us that the mother was inexorably led, in her deep identification with her daughter, to repeat with her child her early experience of erotic attachment to her own father. This attachment had unfortunately ended in deep disappointment for her.

There were subtle kinds of communication by means of which Mary's relationship with her mother and the father's own needs collaborated to create the peculiarly erotic quality of Mary's early attachment to her father. This erotism was heightened considerably with the advent of Mary's early genital phase at 18 months of age. The intensity of this erotic attachment appears to have interfered to some extent with Mary's capacity for maternal identification, particularly in regard to her mother's role as a caretaker and nurturing person. The evolution of Mary's peer relationship during her second year also suffered because of this special attachment to males, and this seems to have had lasting repercussions.

The quality of excitement and joy experienced with the father was absent in Mary's otherwise close and warm relationship with her mother, probably in consequence of the mother's underlying depression of many years' duration. As stated above, we assume that it was this special excitement her mother had sought from her own father that she hoped to achieve for herself by way of identification with Mary and participation in Mary's relationship with her father.

The mother's pregnancy disrupted the greater closeness between mother and child that had been developing toward the end of Mary's second year. Mary had begun to identify more deeply with her mother as a feminine caretaking person. Here again, our knowledge of the mother's history and revived childhood feelings indicates that the mother was repeating her own earlier experience of turning to her father out of disappointment with her mother. We speculate that this disappointment had been connected with the issue of the discovery of the sexual anatomical difference, as well as the resulting heightened ambivalence to the mother that virtually all the girls in our research group experienced at that time.

As for Mary herself, she struggled valiantly with the problem of the sexual differences, first through direct genital exploration and comparisons, then by denial of the genital difference, and finally by use of her considerable capacity for symbolic expression, which allowed her to attack the problem on a higher conceptual level.

It is our impression that both mother and daughter suffered from the lack of resolution of this same issue, that is, their confrontation with the sexual difference and the consequent revival of the more regressive fears of anal and object loss. The mother sought to achieve a belated partial resolution by means of establishing a more satisfactory relationship with her husband than she had had with her father, as well as through identification with her female child through whom she might regain the lost father of her childhood. These attempts were, of course, doomed to at least partial failure. Although the relationship with her husband could at times, both directly and indirectly through identification with the child, alleviate her sense of personal inadequacy and low self-esteem, these feelings could never be eliminated altogether.

The mother's attitude effectively conveyed the message that only the father (the male) could provide the missing element. This missing element was not simply his phallus; it was in great part the excitement and erotic nature of their relationship, which had earlier been attached to the father in toto and now was identified as emanating from his phallus in particular.

Prediction is always a dangerous sport, but perhaps we may forecast a more optimistic future for Mary than our latency follow-up might indicate. Her early capacity for symbolic expression had indeed provided her with a partial solution of her earlier conflict about the genital difference and the other anxieties revived in its wake. Having known at first hand the delightfully vibrant child she was at 15 months, we hope her teacher's description of the richness and exciting quality of her latency-age inner life forecasts a reemergence at some future time of the joyous and zestful child we knew.

10

On Father Hunger: The Father's Role in the Modulation of Aggressive Drive and Fantasy

James M. Herzog

Psychoanalysts and others are increasingly turning their attention to the study of the father's role in a child's development. Initial studies emphasizing equality of caretaking potential are now giving way to more careful examinations of those purposes, roles, and functions specifically served by the male parent.

This chapter attempts to contribute to our knowledge of the father's specific role in the psychological development of the child by examining the fantasy, play, and dreams of children at different developmental stages when their fathers are absent, either completely or partially, because of divorce. A striking feature of these children's productions at all developmental stages is the predominance of aggressive themes and content. A second striking feature is the predominance of aggressive motives in boys thus bereft between the ages of 18 and 60 months. Later on (between 60 and 84 months of age), little girls begin to be represented in equal numbers. These observations lead to the hypothesis that a specific role is played by the male parent in the modulation of aggressive-drive fantasy in the young child, and that the father's absence at this time may have specific and long-range consequences.

A second hypothesis to be presented is that little boys are more vulnerable or at least feel more vulnerable to disruptions in the control of aggressive drives and fantasy than are their female counterparts, at least until the age of 5 years. Little boys therefore suffer more when family disruption leads to father loss.

Finally, the notion of "father hunger" is introduced to describe the affective state and longing experienced by father-deprived children. Fear of the loss of control of aggressive impulses, a significant component in this complex affective state, is explored.

Clinical Examples

In the Clinic for the Development of Young Children and Parents, I have been attempting to look simultaneously at the development of children and of their caretakers. One of our projects has been to examine the effects of divorce on children at various developmental stages. Simultaneously, we have had the opportunity to learn something about the parallel circumstances, both internal and external, that operate in the children's parents. More than 70 children have now been seen whose parents are divorced or divorcing. Some of these children have been seen in the clinic; a substantial number have been seen in a school setting. As the number of children has increased, three quite consistent groupings or syndromes have emerged. These appear to arise in a variety of different familial circumstances and, as such, may provide insight into the specific effects of father loss. By extrapolation we can learn something of the specific intrapsychic import of father presence.

Ira

Ira was 28 months old when his mother, a physician, brought him to the clinic. He was the youngest of three children. Four months earlier, his father, also a physician, had announced that he was in love with a female colleague and moved out of the home. Both parents were "working on the situation" in couples' treatment, and Ira saw his father on weekends. Ira's previous development had been unremarkable. Because both parents worked, however, he had been cared for by a devoted housekeeper from the time he was 3 months old until the present. His two older brothers, almost 5 and almost 7 years old, were functioning quite well. The mother attributed the continuing smooth functioning of the family to the steadying influence of the housekeeper who accompanied them to the clinic. The chief complaint was that Ira had been awakening every night for the past 2 weeks, screaming and tearful. He had his own room and would come darting out as though being chased. Neither the mother nor the housekeeper could comfort him at these times, and the situation was deteriorating rapidly. Ira had begun to refuse to go to bed and for the previous 3 nights had not fallen asleep until well after midnight. On the weekend following his first symptomatic week, Ira had been with his father. He had awakened screaming as usual. His father had come to him, held the screaming child, and said, "It's a dream Ira, do not be afraid." The little boy had sobbed, "daddy, daddy," and clung to his father with all his might. "They are after me. Please don't let them hurt me," he cried. The following week, in his mother's home, the nightmares continued. "Daddy said it's a dream," the little boy would say before going to sleep, as if to give himself courage. When he awoke in the night, he would scream for his father and could not be comforted by his mother. The housekeeper informed me that she had spoken to the boy's father and told him that he needed to come home; if not for his wife's sake, then he must for his son's.

Ira was a very tired-looking boy with big sad eyes. He separated from his mother and baby-sitter with great ease, taking my hand and saying, "You will help me. Are you a daddy?" We began to play, and before long a scenario evolved with a little boy puppet. I took out my pen, called it a dream machine, and placed it on the little boy puppet's head, saying, "Let's look into his head and see if we can see what he is dreaming." Ira said, "This little boy is having a bad dream. I have them too. He is dreaming Big Bird. He eats the boy's head. The boy is scared." "What can we do to help the boy?," I asked. "Get the daddy," Ira cried. The little boy was literally in tears. "Why the daddy, how can he help?," I asked. "He is like the boy. He can because he knows the boy. He is not a mommy," Ira cried. Ira's father did come back, and his nightmares abated. I have continued to see Ira in psychotherapy. He is greatly concerned about a number of Big Bird's blatantly aggressive proclivities and continues to employ phobic displacement as his principal defensive maneuver. He is not, however, seriously symptomatic.

Ira's parents had been married for 10 years. His mother appeared to be a sad but competent woman who felt that her husband was "sowing his wild oats." They had met and married in medical school and he had "never really had a chance to fool around." Ira's father seemed to fit the part. He was delighted initially with his new liaison and the fact that the new lady in his life was 10 years his junior and a beautiful blonde. Ira's daddy, however, was deeply disturbed by the effect that his escapade had had on his youngest son. When he returned to the family, he also embarked on psychoanalysis. The parents had not been able to serve as totally adequate monitors and receptacles for each other's sexual and aggressive drives. Yet it must be said that neither was severely disordered and the children had not been exposed to unbridled passion or other excessive stimulation.

Joey

Joey was 58 months old when his parents separated. His younger brother Anthony was 36 months old. Joey's mother contacted me with the chief complaint that her son was completely uncontrollable. "He hits and hurts Anthony at every opportunity," she explained. "He always says that Anthony needs to be spanked and punished. I tell you, he is downright strap-happy."

Joey's previous developmental history was unremarkable. He was a product of a planned pregnancy and was born when his mother was 27 and his father 31 years old. He was described as an active, outgoing child by both parents and had not been symptomatic in any way according to his history. His response to Anthony's birth when he was 18 months old had been to become more clinging and to want a baby bottle like his brother's; however, this lasted only a short time and then he wanted to be a big boy and use the "toidy" (toilet) just like his dad did, according to mom. Joey had gone to a preschool from the age of 2½ years and was now in a nursery school setting. Recent reports from the school suggested that Joey's anger and "aggression" were interfering with the smooth functioning of the classroom. One mother had angrily protested when Joey hit her son quite hard with a table tennis–like paddle, proclaiming, "He needs a good spanking right here and now."

The parents were involved in a bitter custody fight when I saw Joey, and they could barely tolerate each other's presence. Neither acknowledged the physical violence in their relationship with each other, but they stated that they had occasionally spanked both Joey and Anthony for misbehavior.

Joey separated easily from his mother and joined me in the playroom. He told me he liked to draw and produced a picture of a man. The man had very large hands, which I inquired about. "Oh, he needs them to spank with," Joey told me. "How come?" I asked. "Because a boy can be very naughty and has to be spanked," Joey told me. "A boy needs his dad for that. A mom won't do. I spank Anthony. He likes me to do it because our dad isn't around. I'm like my dad."

Before our next meeting, Joey's mother told me that Joey was continuously ordering her around. "He says, 'Do this, do that.' I find it maddening. He is worse than Vitorio [her husband] ever was. Boy, he is going to give some woman a hard time some day." We played in the dollhouse that day, and Joey played out a family drama in which the father spanked everyone in sight and ordered everyone around. "They like it," Joey maintained. I took the roles of the subservient members of the household and suggested that each might have experienced resentments about being beaten and regimented. "Oh, no," said Joey. "Well, maybe the mother doesn't like it and will get divorced; but the little boy needs it. Otherwise, who knows what might happen?" This interested me, so I tried to find out what might happen without the strict punitive control. "He could hurt someone," Joey said softly. "He could hurt the mommy or maybe the daddy. Oh, no, not the daddy. The daddy would whip him." With that comment, the anxiety that had briefly stirred in him seemed to quiet.

In another meeting, the little boy in the doll family was going to sleep. I produced my dream machine so that Joey and I could investigate what he was dreaming. The boy was dreaming of a volcano, "like on television," Joey told me. He was very close to it and wished that somone had made him stay further away. A big fireman appeared. He was very angry with the boy for going so close to the fire. "I will punish you," he said. Joey's voice showed great excitement. "No, no," the boy said. "I have a father." "Is it a happy dream?," I inquired. "Yes," said Joey. "That boy has a father."

Over the next several months, Joey's behavior toward Anthony and toward his mother and in nursery school continued to be hyperaggressive. In the play, the daddy spanked and spanked, and the little boy felt warmed and safe. He wouldn't dare get out of line, Joey said. Then the inevitable occurred in the play. The mommy and daddy separated. The little boy was frantic. He was terrified that the fireman of the dream would reappear or not appear. He was very naughty with his mother, but she didn't know what to do. Finally, a new baby appeared in the doll family, and the little boy started spanking him. According to Joey, he felt better now because someone was keeping things in line. "A boy needs someone around to do the spanking. The big brother can do that. He has the biggest hands," Joey reported.

Joey's psychotherapy was prolonged, and involved his anger and despair at losing his father and his understanding that controlling himself did not necessarily mean tormenting Anthony. By the time he entered kindergarten, he was no longer a menace at school; it took another year of work, however, before he stopped punishing Anthony. "I still think about spanking, though," he told me, "especially before I go to sleep at night. It gives me a good feeling to think about it."

Joey's parents, Angela and Vitorio, were quite different from Ira's parents and from each other. Their marriage had been shaky for some time. Each accused the other of terrible transgressions, and each felt compelled in some way to act out these accusations. Both parents had trouble with impulse control, but tended to act out outside of the family rather than inside it. Angela went into psychotherapy during the time I was seeing Joey. Her therapist saw her as a primitive hysteric whose caretaking abilities were only partially intact. She could nurture but had grave difficulties with limit setting. Vitorio was also seen by a therapist. He, too, could be very giving to the children, although some of this was in the service of winning the children to his side. He was the product of a restrictive, extremely religious family, and he felt very uncomfortable with his sexuality. He frequently visited prostitutes and felt that only they should be "fucked." His therapy focused on the relationship of his feelings about sex to his own marital situation and the notion of excluding marital relations from the marriage. Both parents did well in treatment. Both decided to seek new adult partners.

Brenda

Brenda was 6½ years (78 months) old when she first came to my attention. I had been asked by her first-grade teacher to consult with regard to this "obviously bright" girl who seemed to have slowed down and become disinterested in the classroom. On the day of my visit she was sitting in her seat and playing with her long blond hair, a sad, distant expression on her face. She looked very tired. When we met together after class, she shook hands with me quite mechanically and then looked away. I said that she looked tired; she yawned and said she didn't sleep very well. She had terrible dreams. I wondered what she dreamed about and she just looked away. I asked her what she would like to do. "Not much anymore," she replied. I picked up on the "anymore," and asked her if it used to be different. "Yes," said Brenda, "when we were all together as a family." Then very quickly she blurted out that mommy and daddy didn't love each other anymore and were divorced. "My dad's gone," she said. I learned that they had been apart for almost a year.

Brenda then started talking about school. It just did not seem interesting to her. I took out a book and asked her if she would like to read. She shook her head and then gave me the book. "You read," she said. I noticed that she began to play with her hair again and looked off into the distance. As I read to Brenda, she nestled her body against mine and seemed to doze off. After a few moments I stopped reading and she opened her eyes. "You must be very tired," I said. She agreed.

At our next meeting, Brenda began playing in the dollhouse. I noticed that she kept placing the little girl doll all by itself. I wondered why this happened. "That's the way it is," Brenda replied. As a scenario developed, the daddy had to go to work. The little girl wanted him to stay home but he wouldn't. "Who cares what she wants. Daddies just go away," Brenda had the little girl say. "Now the mommy and the daughter can be together," I suggested. Brenda looked at me quizzically. "No," she said. "The mommy is too busy. Besides, she doesn't want to be with the girl; she wants to be with daddy, but she can't; he doesn't love her anymore." She halted a minute and then said, "I mean he has to go to work."

In another session, Brenda put the little girl doll to bed. "Who will read her a bedtime story?," I inquired. Brenda looked blank, then smiled a little and said, "Maybe the daddy, but he is not there; or perhaps you, you read stories." Soon the little girl was asleep and I got out my dream machine, held it up to the doll's head, and asked Brenda to look through it and describe what she saw the little girl dreaming. Brenda looked up and said, "Let's do something else. Will you read to me?" I said yes and read, this time from Sendak's *Where the Wild Things Are* (1963). Brenda did not drift off as before, but listened intently. At the end of our time she gave me a little smile.

At our next meeting, she again put the little girl to bed. I again offered her the dream machine and she looked in. "They're all sick," she said, "the whole family. Oh, the daddy just died. He's gone. Now the mommy. Poor little girl, she died too." "You mean the little girl is dreaming the whole family is dying?," I asked. "She is even dying herself?" "Yes," said Brenda. "But what kind of disease is it?," I asked. "Why are they dying? What has happened? Who caused it?" "She did," said Brenda. "Now will you read? Without the daddy being there, she did. She killed them all. Please read to me again."

As she left my office that day, Brenda said, "I'm like the little girl, not like Max. At night, I die too."

Following this session, I met with Brenda's mother and strongly urged that she make arrangements for Brenda to continue psychotherapy. Her mother told me that Brenda had talked about meeting with me at school, that I had read to her, and that we talked about sleeping and dreams. The mother confessed to me that she had been very worried about Brenda, who seemed slowed down and not there. "It's not surprising, though," said the mother. "I've been so upset and so busy since the divorce that I haven't had any time for her. Since Brad [her husband] left, I have been afraid to do anything, really anything—why, last night Brenda asked me if I would read to her before she went to bed, and I realized that I haven't done that for over 2 years."

Susan, Brenda's mother, was 28 at the time I saw her daughter. She was clearly depressed. She was in her sixth year of graduate study: "A project which was old as Brenda," she told me. She had been in psychotherapy for about a year, but could not yet overcome or integrate what had happened to her marriage. Her husband had received his doctorate degree 5 years earlier and was teaching at another institution. According to Susan, their marriage had been good until she got her master's degree, which was when Brenda was 4 years old; since then, however, it had just not worked. "I couldn't handle everything," she said. "I couldn't sort out my priorities. I lost Brad; now I feel as if I have lost Brenda too." Susan's therapist told me that themes of loss, worthiness, and worries about "having enough to manage" had plagued this woman for many years. Brenda's father came to see me only twice. He was an attractive, composed man who discussed the difficulty of putting a bad marriage behind him without abandoning his daughter too. "I found someone new," he said. "We can give to each other and take from each other.

Susan and I used to be able to do that, then we couldn't. Now that I have someone new, I hope I can be a better father to Brenda. Poor Susan, however, will have to fend for herself."

Discussion

The 3 cases presented are drawn from some 70 similar ones. In each case the separation and disunion of those things previously closely united (Webster's definition of divorce) has resulted in demonstrable symptomatology and suffering on the part of the involved children. As previously mentioned, this sampling is particularly noteworthy in that in the two younger groupings (i.e., 18 to 28 months of age and 36 to 60 months of age) the vast majority of children seen were male. In fact, in the younger grouping of 12 children, all were male. In the second grouping of 30 children, 28 were boys. My third grouping of 30 children between 60 and 84 months of age consisted of 16 boys and 14 girls.

Children react to loss in many ways. Other investigators have demonstrated a number of behavioral changes of varying duration. By focusing on the child's affect, fantasy, play, and dreams, I hoped to be able to learn something of how divorce and father loss felt to a child and what the intrapsychic ramifications of such an experience might be. Ira's case is drawn from another article (Herzog, 1978). In this age group, children develop nightmares and their play reveals a precocious utilization of phobic processes. I understand the Big Bird dream and comparable material from other children to be manifestations of displaced aggression. There are, of course, other meanings as well. The absence of the father was perceived simultaneously as the child's own doing and as depriving him of necessary protection. The father's return was considered a treatment of choice.

Joey's case is drawn from yet another article (Herzog, unpublished). Here again, the drive that is experienced as unleashed, frightening, and out of control, is the aggressive drive. The need for a fireman is most compelling. That the fires to be quenched are both libidinal and aggressive seems more probable with Joey than with Ira. The spanking motive appears to be progressing toward an eroticized masturbatory status, and the possibility of a negative oedipal resolution seems apparent. There is also an inability to see the father as both nurturing and disciplining. (Compare this finding to Mussen and Distler's [1960] report that masculine boys have fathers who are both nurturing and disciplining.) It seems that Joey and his "29 siblings" are employing a manic defense and splitting, a kind of hyperidentification with the aggressor. To be the limit setter in a kind of grotesque caricature of male discipline emerges as a

170

common way of dealing with the loss of the father, the disruption of that which had previously been experienced as intact. Tooley (1976) and others have commented on this phenomenon, which I think is well-known to all who work with preschoolers who come from father-absent families.

Brenda manifested all the symptoms of childhood depression. Here, too, we see a mixture of libidinal longings and aggressive concerns, yet, from my viewpoint, it is the aggressive fantasies and fixations that are pathogenic. Brenda's aggression is turned against herself. She is the cause of the family disease and is struck down by it. The child in her play dies in her dream as well. In my experience, as well as that of others (Lucas, 1977), such a finding is pathognomonic of childhood depression. Other researchers as well as myself have also found the incidence of childhood depression to be quite substantial among latency-aged children of both sexes whose parents are divorced.

What is suggested here is that the modulation of aggressive drive and fantasy is a leading concern, perhaps an omnipresent one, in children of divorce. It would appear that the material presented by the children substantiates this formulation in a number of ways. The separation of what was previously united seriously discombobulates the inner world of the developing child: This alone might produce extreme distress. In each case, however (and this is true of all 72 cases), the father through his absence is linked in the child's mind with the emergence of aggressive material, and his return is seen as being restitutive. That mothers are often bereft and thoroughly overtaxed in the postdivorce situation must clearly be critically important. It is noteworthy, however, that even in situations where the mother is competent and proficient and is ostensibly pleased by the dissolution of the marriage, one finds the same kind of symptomatology and material similar to that described in the 3 cases.

Why the great predominance of boys in the first two groupings? The answer may well lie in a number of contributing areas. Boys probably have a greater aggressive endowment from birth (Maccoby, 1966) and a greater subsequent need for mentorship in its management. Every study of postdivorce adjustment acknowledges the greater morbidity in preschool-aged boys. "I'm hot," a 4-year-old said to me. "Daddy's hot, too. That's how we guys are." This sentiment has been voiced in more or less direct form by a large number of boys I have seen. The recognition of sameness with the father, the need to manage a mutual concern, and the need to be shown how is common. I have come to consider this need to be "shown how" a hallmark of the preoedipal boy's relationship with his father. Of course, girls need their fathers too. It may be, however, that either they need them more when they reach oedipal age, or they can make out better without them before that time. Certainly large amounts of cognitive research support this interpretation, as does Abelin's postulation (1975) of earlier generational triangulation in the girl and a critical need by her for her father in the oedipal period.

Why is aggression turned against the self in 60- to 84-month-old children? Is this a commentary on superego formation in children of divorce who have been protected less from certain harsh realities than luckier children growing up in an intact family? Perhaps. Alternatively, could it be an identification with a predominant affective state in some or many one-parent families? Again, perhaps. I am inclined to think that the situation with the older children gives us a strong clue as to the principal effect on all children of the departure of the father. It is true that aggressive drives and fantasies, and perhaps libidinal ones as well, are experienced as less controllable. However, there is also apparently a sense of disharmony or "discontrol" of a more passive nature. Spouses monitor and absorb, cultivate and discharge all sorts of affects, impulses, and derivatives of previous conflict and conflict resolution to and for each other. Such a field of two psyches contains and even neutralizes much of what is potentially deleterious in the adult-child interaction. Adult-adult interaction can thus be seen as a protective shield that permits caretaking to emerge and to be practiced by both sexes. When the father leaves, the mother may experience a breakdown of this protective shield. Libidinal and aggressive impulses or derivatives are more likely to be focused on the children. Perhaps male children receive more of these attentions from their mothers, at least preoedipally. Perhaps they feel less protected in their father's absence than do little girls. Certainly, defenses involving idealization are impaired, and a confrontation with innumerable aspects of reality may occur earlier than is optimal. Whatever the case, the evidence points to the identification of the father as a modulator of aggressive drive and fantasy in the material from all of the children, and suggests that his absence produces an unmodulated state of affairs. That the child experiences the father's loss as occasioning his aggressive discontrol does not prove actual causation, but it does establish intrapsychic association, a form of causality with which analysts deal constantly.

The material presented has briefly covered the character structure, marital relationship, and intrapsychic organization of the parents. Some attempt has been made to convey a "flavor" of who they are. Clearly, divorce never occurs in a smoothly functioning, mutually satisfying marriage. All of the marital relationships studied had by definition serious, even irreconcilable failings. Therefore, because the adult-adult interaction was impaired, the adult-child interaction was probably also affected. Nevertheless, the most compelling finding is that similar concerns and pain occurred, albeit in different guises, in a large number of the children; even though the parental personalities, conflicts, and modes of separation and divorce were quite diverse. To paraphrase Tolstoy, unhappy families may be very different, but certain effects of divorce and father loss may be the same. So far in this chapter, a great deal has been said about aggression, but it has not yet been defined. Freud (1933) stated: "The theory of instincts is, so to say, our methodology. Instincts are mythical entities, magnificent in their indefiniteness. In our work we cannot for a moment disregard them; yet we are never sure that we are seeing them clearly." Rather than defining aggression, much less the impulses and fantasies that derive from it, I have chosen the rather circular route of presenting clinical material that deals with harm, fright, and the infliction of pain, and labeled said material as a manifestation of aggression and aggressive drive. Of course, many objections can be voiced to this rather cavalier approach. Parens (1979), in his definitive volume, *The Development of Aggression in Early Childhood*, has accepted the challenge of more clearly defining the etiology and development of the aggression. His nomenclature, which involves the division of aggression into unpleasure-related discharges of destruction, the nonaffective discharge of destructiveness, the nondestructive discharge of aggression, and the pleasure-related discharge of destructiveness, seems to be a definitive way of conceptualizing the aggressive drive. When I use the term *aggression*, I am referring to all four types but with specific reference to discharges of destructiveness with an accompanying affective load.

The father fulfills many roles. As a husband, he monitors, absorbs, elicits, and limits instinctual drives and derivatives from the mother. He replenishes her affective well and allows her to attach, bond, and establish a symbiosis with, and then effect phase-specific disengagement from, the child. He serves as an external referent and alternative in the separation-individuation process. As a parent, he nurtures, disciplines, serves as a model for identification, and serves as a love object. His libidinal and aggressive availability, which is clearly variable in different men and a function of their previous experience in caretaking, determines how well or poorly he can function in all these regards, as well as whether or not he will be a good enough father. It appears from newer work, such as that of Abelin (1977) and Stoller (1968), that the father is also crucial in the formation of the child's sense of self and consolidation of core gender identity.

Finally, together with his wife, he provides his offspring with a protective shield that titrates the rate at which the child confronts reality. Albeit through the employment of a deficit model examining the material that emerges with the separation or disunion of things previously closely joined, I propose that the father serves yet another critical function. He is experienced by preoedipal boys and by oedipal-aged boys and girls as the modulator of aggressive drive and fantasy. The data presented here admit of many other interpretations. The departure of the father is by no means the only consequence of a divorce. It is, however, judging from the material that I have obtained, the etiological factor cited by the children themselves; therefore, it might well be worthy of consideration as an intrapsychic truth.

Conclusions

Children without fathers experience father hunger, an affective state of considerable tenacity and force. Father hunger appears to be a critical motivational variable in matters as diverse as caretaking, sexual orientation, moral development, and achievement level. The children studied in this sample all appear to evince father hunger. They feel that they lack something that they vitally need. Mothers and others can mediate the effects of actual father absence or psychological father absence. When the father is absent but revered (idealized or presented as an important and valued family member), as in times of war, or following death, the resulting state of father hunger seems less pronounced.

The ambivalence, hurt, and hatred characteristic of divorce seem to maximize for the child the felt absence of a masculine parent and to exacerbate father hunger. There is currently an epidemic of divorce and with it, sadly, an epidemic of father hunger. It is far from clear what the long-term ramifications of this state of affairs will be.

11

The Role of the Father in Gender Identity, Urethral Erotism, and Phallic Narcissism

Phyllis Tyson

The aim of this chapter is to consider the many ways in which father as well as mother influence and contribute to the gradual unfolding and establishment of gender identity in boys.

Components of Gender Identity

Gender identity is a very broad concept which, according to Stoller (1968), can include all those characteristics that comprise each individual's combination of masculinity or femininity. These characteristics may be determined not only by biological sex and anatomy, but by psychological factors such as object relations, identifications, intrapsychic conflicts, and bisexual conflicts—not to mention cultural and social influences. This broad definition might usefully be broken down into three parts: (1) core morphological or core gender identity, (2) gender role identity, and (3) sexual partner orientation. These factors, in interaction, produce the final broad sense of gender identity.

The establishment of gender identity begins with core morphological or core gender identity, which is the most primitive conscious and unconscious sense of belonging to one sex and not the other (Stoller, 1968, 1976). Recent research (Greenacre, 1950, 1958; Kohlberg, 1966; Stoller, 1968, 1976; Galenson and Roiphe, 1971, 1974, 1976; Money and Ehrhardt, 1972) suggests that core gender identity develops from a confluence of several factors, including innate biological and instinctual forces; sex assignment at birth; the nature and qualities of parental handling; earliest object relations; emerging ego functions; cognitive capacities; and the emerging body image. All of these combine to enable infants to establish a sense of their biological sex.

Gender Role

Gender role refers to one's characteristic overt behavior in relationship to other people vis-à-vis one's gender. Gender-role identity includes not only *role training*, or purposefully learned behavior manifested in stereotyped sex roles such as is discussed by psychologists and sociologists, but also subtle, complicated, conscious and unconscious exchanges of messages, reflecting interactions between the child and his parents. Parental attitudes toward the child's biological sex will influence the nature of these interactions, which in turn will affect the child's developing sense of gender and understanding of the appropriate role to play with others as a member of that sex. The establishment of gender-role identity also begins in the earliest months of life. Sandler and Sandler (1978) note that the infant develops, alongside the earliest representations of his or her objects and personal representations, "increasingly complex representations of the interactions, the relationships, the dialogues between himself and his objects" (p. 293). These representations of the dialogues become internalized and form an integral part of the representational world. Children will gradually begin to seek "self-like objects" (Kohlberg, 1966) as role models with whom to identify as their cognitive capacities mature, core gender identity becomes more firmly established, and they perceive that "biological givens" make them members of one sex and not the other. These identifications with self-like role models are added to the earliest representations of dialogues between self and object so that children build up an increasingly complicated self-representation, including a representation of their role in relationship to other people, especially their "habitual mode of relating" as a member of one particular sex. These representations become increasingly superimposed with cultural and social influences and expectations, and gender role finally comes to represent a combination of intrapsychic structure and culturally determined learned behavior.

Sexual Partner Orientation

Sexual partner orientation (Green, 1975) refers to a person's preference regarding the sex of a chosen love object, whether a person of one's own sex is preferred over a person of the opposite sex. Sexual partner orientation does not become a crucial issue until adolescence; however, precursors are evident before that time. Thus sexual partner orientation is established early in life when reciprocity develops between mother, father, and child; their relationship can be said to form the model on which all future love relationships are built.

The following discussion will focus on the epigenic unfolding of a broad sense of gender identity. Core gender identity, gender role, and sexual partner orientation will be distinguished in the hope that a clearer understanding may be derived of the crucial aspects of the father's role in the boy's establishment of gender identity.

Core Gender Identity

Core gender identity, the boy's sense of being a boy, is the first aspect of gender identity to develop and becomes the nucleus around which a sense of masculinity gradually forms. Apart from certain biological givens (neurophysiological organizing of the fetal brain), sex assignment at birth provides the first step in the establishment of core gender identity. Sex assignment has an unequivocal effect in convincing parents of their child's sex. Parental handling and the earliest verbal and nonverbal communications between mother and child, and father and child, will be influenced by the parents' conscious and unconscious attitudes toward a child of that sex. These earliest communications between mother and child as well as father and child form the anlagen around which gender-role identity also gradually takes shape.

Another very important ingredient in the establishment of core gender identity is the incorporation of physical and psychic dimensions of one's biological sex into the developing body ego. For the boy, this involves the discovery of his penis and its integration into his overall body image. Loewenstein (1950) describes a 10-month-old boy who discovered his penis through pleasurable contact. He repeated the contact and experimented with genital manipulation in the context of general body exploration; the tactile, kinesthetic, and visual instinctual stimulation helped him to confirm that his penis belonged to his body. Moments of uncertainty continued as the penis disappeared below his protruding abdomen; however, with growing cognitive maturity and a sense of object permanence (Piaget and Inhelder, 1969), it finally appeared that he had integrated his penis firmly and securely into his body image. Loewenstein describes the infant boy, during the process of discovery, as slowly touching his penis, then looking up at his mother, his face wreathed in smiles. Thus it appears that the reciprocal relationship between the mother and child is a primary ingredient in the pleasurable process of defining body boundaries and establishing genital awareness (Spitz, 1962; Kleeman, 1965; Francis and Marcus, 1975) with some evidence that a disturbance in the mother-child relationship may delay the establishment of genital awareness and general body image (Freud and Burlingham, 1947; Greenacre, 1953; Galenson and Roiphe, 1980).

Role Played by the Father

The father's role in this early discovery of penis, body delineation, and establishment of core gender identity is less clear, but perhaps inferences can be drawn from instances of pathological development. Greenacre (1953), after studying the early years of patients with fetishistic behavior, concludes that the first year to 18 months is a crucial time in determining a boy's ultimate gender identity. A disturbance in the mother-child relationship, repeated exposure to female genitals, or an overwhelming trauma may result in an insecure body image that predisposes the boy to severe castration reactions in later stages of development, disrupting the formation of gender identity.

Stoller (1979) comments on the disturbed mother-child aspect of problems in gender identity. He notes that in cases of very feminine transsexual boys the mother created and sustained a very intimate and unbreakable symbiosis with her son, while the father remained passive and distant. It appears, therefore, that the father plays a very important role during the first year, serving not only as a support for the mother, but as a shield to protect the child against mother's impulses to prolong the mother-infant symbiosis. Mahler (1966) also emphasized the nonsymbiotic nature of the father-child relationship, which enabled father to remain "uncontaminated." Thus one might consider that the father, by providing an additional and reciprocal yet nonsymbiotic relationship with the child, will implement the phase-appropriate separation of infant and mother. As the baby boy "hatches" with an increasing sense of separateness and individuality, he also begins to distinguish mother from father and to relate to each in slightly different ways, as a prelude to increasingly complicated dialogues with his parents.

Urethral Erotism Emerges

During the "practicing subphase," around 9 to 13 months, the toddler begins to experience greater control over and pride in every aspect of his body's function. He gains greater sphincter control, begins to experience greater pride and pleasure in urination, and shows increasing interest in father's urination. In general, the ambulatory boy develops a heightened awareness of all the properties of his penis; he becomes more aware of erections and begins purposeful genital manipulation.

The little boy's increasing fascination in his own urination and noticeable autoerotic pleasure have been frequently observed to arouse a degree of early castration anxiety (Fenichel, 1945; Roiphe, 1968). Fenichel notes that "the urethral erotic child necessarily becomes aware of the difference between the sexes with reference to urinating" (p. 68).

Father as a Sex-Role Model

Father has a second role in the prevention of pathology. If continued exposure to female genitals serves to confuse the boy and undermine his body image, father's penis can offer an alternative to female genitals, or he can actively mediate between mother and child to minimize this female exposure. The child then becomes more aware of his penis, labeling all parts of his genital apparatus and beginning to integrate them as a permanent part of his body. His cognitive apparatus becomes more mature so he can more easily and less anxiously compare the differences between the sexes and view father as a self-like object (Kohlberg, 1966). He now comes to seek father as an object with whom to identify.

Exposure to the female genitals may make the boy increasingly aware of anatomical distinctions, or he may experience the exposure as traumatic and fear that he may be in danger of losing his penis. His castration fear is set against the background of the earliest difficulties in the delineation of a body image, when the infant goes through moments of uncertainty as to whether or not the penis is an undissoluble part of his own body. On the other hand, viewing the adult male genital and urinary organ at this time may also intimidate the boy and undermine his pride. As Solnit (1979) notes, the difference in size may be as challenging as the sexual difference. However, it should be noted that preoedipal castration anxiety is generally related to fears of retaliation for anal and aggressive impulses directed toward the mother during the rapprochement phase. The mother, who is viewed as omnipotent and "phallic," is then feared, and rapprochement and toileting struggles may become organized around these early castration fears. However, the appearance of castration anxiety gives evidence that core gender identity has been established and that the little boy is aware that he is a male.

Assuming a Masculine Identity

We now turn to a consideration of gender role, which in some ways is a complicated process for the boy because of the need to change role models in order to assume a masculine identity.

Imitating Mother

The boy's first role model is his mother, and little boys are frequently observed imitating mother in her daily household tasks. Ross (1975) points out that during the anal-rapprochement phase there often appears a specific wish on the part of the boy to "have babies," and, later on, to bear and nurse babies as the mother does. Boys further reveal a fusion of anal-genital sensations associated with fantasies of having an anal baby. This transitory identification with mother and her gender role may be an attempt to establish a firm representation of mother, partially in order to cope with feelings of object loss engendered by the rapprochement crisis and partially in order to resolve feelings of ambivalence toward mother by becoming like her. Mother provides the first model of parental power. Her physical availability for the greater part of the child's waking days further makes her the most accessible object for role identification.

Identifying with Father

By the second year, however, father begins to have an increasingly important role apart from being the "uncontaminated caretaker" (Mahler, 1966). Abelin (1971, 1975) remarks that the father is important in encouraging the practicing toddler's exploratory and early phallic-like attitudes. During the rapprochement phase in particular, father may be crucial in countering the regressive pull back to symbiosis. But the father also plays an important role in helping the child begin to establish a male gender-role identification. With masculine core gender identity, the boy begins to seek self-like objects for identification; specifically, with heightened urethral erotism he turns increasingly to father and shows a fascination with father's urinary stream. Father, in being available as a figure for identification, can then take an active and concrete part in helping his son learn to urinate standing up and to take pride in the urinary stream that he too can produce. Father's participation, in fact, may help to "defuse" some of the toilet-training struggles that become entangled with rapprochement issues with mother, and may help the boy gain some measure of independence and autonomy. There is in fact some evidence to indicate that when father is absent or excessively passive, there may be a delay in the onset of urethral erotism (Galenson and Roiphe, 1980), a delay in upright urination, a delay in sex-role differentiation, and a retardation in the development of independence (Biller, 1976).

Upright urination in identification with the father might thus be considered as one of the boy's first steps in the assumption of a male gender role, as he begins to learn what it is like and what you have to do to be a male.

Clinical Example

If there is a marked disturbance in the mother-child relationship during this time, or a disruption in their contact because of separation, death, or divorce, the child may show a marked fixation at the stage of urethral erotism. He may then evince an emphasized erotic identification with father to such an extent that urethral erotic pleasures persist into later stages of life, perhaps coupled with a rejection of mother that may even extend to all women. Urinating may take on phallic or sadistic qualities, accompanied by fantasies of damaging or destroying; or it may serve to express a passive giving up or "letting flow" attitude, expressing the child's feeling of not being in control.

David was placed in full-day day care at 15 months. At 24 months his mother abandoned him and did not return for 10 months. After his parents' divorce, he began to live with mother 6 months and father 6 months until the age of 4 years and 11 months when he pleaded with the courts to be allowed to live with his father permanently and was allowed to do so. At the time of evaluation, at age 4 years and 8½ months, he declared that he hated women and felt that his father was the only reliable person in his life. There was little evidence that he had moved beyond urethral erotism. He wet his pants daily, sometimes many times a day, although he was dry at night. His daily wetting served as a reassurance that he had not been castrated, but it took on magical omnipotent phallic and eroticized qualities. Envy of his father's large phallus was evident as he pretended a baby bottle was father's phallus and he could go to outer space and "pee" on the entire world. The wetting had expressed elements of passive surrender to his domineering "phallic" mother. At times he felt he had no control over his wetting or over himself, especially in relating to his mother, and did not always realize he was wet.

With the resolution of the later phases of rapprochement and the establishment of relative self and object constancy, anal and urethral tensions tend to recede and to be replaced by increased genital tension. Genital masturbation becomes the primary autoerotic activity. Phallic exhibitionism emerges and the object's response to this becomes one of the boy's chief sources of narcissistic gratification. These developments mark the entry into the early phallic phase, termed the *phallic-narcissistic phase* by Edgcumbe and Burgner (1975; see also Greenspan, 1980).

Phallic-Narcissistic Phase

The phallic-narcissistic stage is distinguished from the phallic-oedipal phase in that although phallic-phase dominance has been reached, object relationships remain dyadic in the sense that, although both mother and father are important, triangular competitive situations are not yet apparent. Exhibitionism appears to be in the service of narcissistic gratification rather than the "seduction" of the oedipal object. During the phallic-narcissistic phase, an important task for the boy is to consolidate a narcissistically valued and firm male body image. The boy now frequently shows the counterpart of penis envy or penis preoccupation in the girl. He displays observable fascination with the anatomy of both sexes, and the boy's envy of the woman's ability to have a baby may reemerge (e.g., Kestenberg, 1956; Van Leeuwen, 1966; Ross, 1977). Although the boy may wish to bear and nurse babies as mother does, he does not wish to give up his own genitals. Indeed, because of the high value placed on the genitals at this time, castration anxiety may again appear.

Reemergence of Castration Anxiety

The earliest evidence of castration fear was seen at a time when the body image was still somewhat unstable, and when anal issues (the loss of feces) provided a model of lost objects. Rapprochement issues with mother were uppermost. Therefore the early castration fears specific to this era may be organized around rapprochement issues and fears of mother's retaliation for anal and aggressive impulses by abandonment. In contrast, at the phallic-narcissistic stage, castration anxiety arises not only from a fear of genital damage because of the high value placed on the penis and a fear of the envious woman; it also pertains to a fear of losing omnipotence (a remnant from the rapprochement phase and anal magical thinking) and to a general fear of narcissistic injury coupled with loss of self-esteem.

Need for Stronger Male Identification

Another crucial issue of this phase centers on the fuller assumption of a male gender role. Until this point, the boy's major role relationship has usually been with mother, who has been his primary object for identification. But if he is to move into the positive oedipal phase, the boy must identify with the father and embrace a male gender role. Identification with father began during the period of urethral erotism; now the boy must adopt other masculine behaviors and attitudes, as we see significant evidence of the boy's taking on father as an ego ideal. Freud said (1921): "A little boy will exhibit a special interest in his father; he would like to grow like him and be like him, and take his place everywhere. We may say simply that he takes his father as his ideal." Freud goes on to say that this behavior is typically masculine, and that "it fits in very well with the Oedipus complex, for which it helps to prepare the way" (p. 105; see also Ross, 1977).

Father's Actions a Source of Confusion. Often, however, a father spends little time at home engaging in his masculine activities, and a boy had little idea of the ingredients of a male gender role. He does not see his father "at work," where father may display many masculine attributes. Rather, a child typically witnesses the common stereotype of the masculine, hard-working father whose primary activity at home is passively watching football on television, or sleeping. The contrasts are very confusing to the boy's understanding of masculinity and the male role. Boys at this age often demonstrate role confusion by alternately playing with dolls and exhibiting phallically in imitation of the "superheroes" they see on television.

Biller (1976) points out that the quality of the father-son relationship, rather than the amount of time spent together, is what influences the boy's masculine development. A crucial factor in this development is the degree to which the boy's father exhibits masculine behavior in family interactions. Imitation of the father directly enhances the boy's masculine development only if the father displays masculine behavior in the presence of his son—not if the masculine behavior is reserved for peer and work relationships, and not if the father appears rather ineffectual in his interaction with his wife and children. On the other hand, masculine development is also facilitated when the father, as a competent yet nurturing masculine model, encourages and permits his son to be assertive and independent and to make his own decisions. A controlling and restrictive father who will not allow disagreement may prevent the boy from adopting an appropriate assertive male gender role. It appears that the optimal situation for promoting the boy's identification with the male gender role occurs when the father is warm, affectionate, and supportive, yet is assertive, active, and constantly involved in family functioning.

Parental Encouragement. The boy's optimal narcissistic investment in his masculinity and his assumption of a male role are further enhanced when both mother and father show visible pride in their young son's phallic prowess, phallic exhibitionism, and assumption of masculinity. Perhaps this stage is one of the most crucial for cementing a close father-son attachment. In fact, many fathers do not become actively involved with their children until this stage. The young boy's phallic exhibitionism in identification with father makes father proud; he sees himself reflected in his child and is moved to encourage masculine exhibitionism. The parents' pride is then internalized by the child, and the boy's self-confidence in his masculinity is enhanced; he consolidates a narcissistically valued and sexually differentiated body image and shows an increasing identification with father and father's gender role.

Parents' Relationship and Mother's Attitude Toward Men. The relationship between mother and father and the mother's attitude toward masculinity are important factors in the boy's assumption of a male gender role. Their relationship may be fraught with ambivalence. Mother may dominate and devaluate father and his masculinity. Father may be unreliable, passive, or absent altogether. In these instances, the boy may have difficulty in valuing and identifying with the male role. He may see little apparent narcissistic advantages in identifying with men, fearing that assuming a male role may mean being devalued, dominated, and belittled by mother; thus in doing so he risks losing his esteemed relationship with her, a relationship that may be based on a prolonged symbiotic tie. In this case, the boy may fail to make the shift adequately from identification with mother to identification with father. Feeling and believing that women are more venerated, the boy, for narcissistic considerations, may express a wish to be a girl.

Positive Oedipal Phase

If the boy has been successful in mastering the tasks of the phallic-narcissistic stage, he is then in a position to move toward the positive (phallic) oedipal phase. With assumption of more masculine attitudes and a male gender role, the little boy wishes for a different relationship with his mother. He wishes to assume a more masculine role in her eyes, rather than continue to be her baby in anaclitic dependency (Solnit, 1979).

As one boy said, "Mommy, me want to be your husband." When turned down, he thoughtfully replied, "Then I be your father."

Oedipal movement for the boy implies not a shift in object, but a transformation in fantasies about the object and a change of role in relation to the love object. The little boy now begins to wish for exclusive possession of mother, develops intense libidinal longings for her, and wishes to have father's large penis, to take father's place, to be mother's lover. As Freud (1921) noted, the boy's identification with his father becomes identical with the wish to replace his father in regard to his mother.

Because of the closer attachment to father, as well as father's increasing involvement with his son, these wishes toward mother are not without conflict. We now see the emergence of triadic object relationships in the classical sense, where affection for one parent arouses loyalty conflicts vis-à-vis the other.

Clinical Example

The boy then begins to differentiate the kind of relationships he wishes from different-sexed objects: Not only does he wish to be his mother's oedipal love object, but at the same time he wishes his father to be his friend—his "pal."

J., age 3½ years, during a short separation from mother at a time when positive oedipal fantasies flourished, was walking with his father but tripped and fell. Furious, he asked why daddy had pushed him. On the suggestion that he might be missing mommy, he broke down and sobbed. Later, however, he said to his father that perhaps it was good that mommy was away. "It gives us time to be together, Dad."

The extent to which the longing for father's love and attention exists alongside positive oedipal wishes is often underemphasized. Boys frequently are vocal about their wish to marry mommy, to have exclusive possession of her; or they behave seductively toward her. They also wish to be like father, to be with father; they long for father's attention. These longings to be like father, the idealizations of him, and the wishes for father's companionship should in themselves, however, not be confused with a bisexual wish. Freud (1921, p. 105) noted, "this behavior has nothing to do with a passive or feminine attitude towards his father; it is on the contrary typically masculine." But the closer attachment to father may serve to arouse bisexual wishes, which lead the boy to seek an exclusive relationship with father. Freud (1921, p. 106) noted: "The subsequent history of this identification with father may easily be lost sight of. It may happen that the Oedipus complex becomes inverted, and that the father is taken as the object of a feminine attitude, an object from which the directly sexual instinct looks for satisfaction; in that event, the identification with the father has become the precursor of an object-tie with the father."

Clinical Example

Although the boy may express so-called negative oedipal longings in which he pictures himself as feminine, this is usually of shorter duration than the positive oedipal phase. The reason for this is commonly understood to result from his castration anxiety; if he persisted in attempting to take mother's place and identifying with her gender role, it would entail the loss of his precious penis. Boys usually make it very clear: They want the penis *and* the baby. Furthermore, mother's place in father's eyes might jeopardize his oedipal position with her as well as his preoedipal, anaclitic attachment to her—an additional threat because of his continued need for "basic supplies."

T., age 4 years, with his most erotic look, exclaimed to his father after father had bathed him, "Daddy, I love you! I think I'll marry a man when I grow up." After some discussion, he realized that if he married a man, he could not marry a woman like mommy, would not be a daddy to a baby as his daddy was to him.

Therefore he changed his mind and returned to his former, slightly disguised positive oedipal resolution of marrying the little girl next door.

It is possible that cognitive maturation comes to the boy's aid in at least a partial resolution of the bisexual conflict. With an increased capacity to understand abstract notions, the little boy begins to gain a greater appreciation of father's role in procreation. With this he begins to understand how he can actually retain his penis and, by assuming a male gender role, have a baby. With pride he then begins to look forward to the day when he can, in identification with father, be a father himself and have a baby. Thus he adds an important ingredient to his concept of male gender role.

Blos (1979) points out that bisexual conflicts do not produce undue anxiety in young boys, and resolution is usually deferred until adolescence. However, a certain mixture of femininity might be added to the boy's sense of gender or broader "sexual" identity as a result of the bisexual wishes. It may be that this element of, or selected identification with, femininity is what helps the man in later life to be sensitive and nurturing his wife and children. This, then, indicates another very important function of the father in the boy's development.

Discussion

In this overview of the father's role in a boy's gender-identity formation, frequent reference has been made to identification with the father. The classic notion of the boy's identification with his father seems to be widely misunderstood. Its defensive function in protecting the boy against hostile impulses toward the father and against castration in the oedipal phase has been stressed. An identification with the father as the aggressor has been viewed as a vehicle for the resolution of oedipal conflicts. In more recent years, many authors have endeavored to point out that father is an important object even in the preoedipal years, and that identification with the father begins much earlier than the phallic-oedipal phase (Loewald, 1951; Greenacre, 1957; Mahler, 1966; Abelin, 1971; Edgcumbe and Burgner, 1975; Stoller, 1979).

Yet, if we return to Freud's 1921 thesis, we see that he depicted identification as "the earliest expression of an emotional tie with another person," and therefore not defense in and of itself. Furthermore, he saw identification as paving the way for the entry of the Oedipus complex. In addition, this earliest relationship was seen by Freud to be a very positive one. It was only much later, when "the little boy notices that his father stands in his way with his mother," that "his identification with his father then takes on a hostile colouring and becomes identical with the wish to replace the father." The oedipal boy's view of his father as a hostile figure, therefore, was understood by Freud as a projection of the boy's own hostility and not as an artifact of their real relationship. It seems, then, that we malign Freud and lose sight of the issues in statements such as, "In reviewing the literature at that time, I found that an early positive role of the father had been put forward only in recent years [beginning in 1951]" (Abelin, 1975).

Conclusions

This chapter has endeavored to illustrate some of the many ways in which the father plays a crucial role in the boy's establishment of core gender identity, in his assumption of a male gender role, and in his laying the foundation for sexual partner orientation. The boy's identification with his father is an important part of this process.

Identification with the father usually comes to the fore during the phase of urethral erotism. The first clear-cut assumption of the male gender role is betrayed in the boy's "upright urination." Further identification with father, idealization of father in the form of an ego ideal, and identification with the male gender role occur during the phallic-narcissistic phase; it is only by an identification with the masculine role that the boy can enter the oedipal phase and make the change from the baby role to the more masculine role of "lover" (in fantasy), choosing mother as love object. Identification with the father then continues throughout the oedipal phase, with certain vicissitudes caused by bisexual wishes. The father as an ego ideal becomes increasingly structuralized as a consequence of superego development. The resolution of the Oedipus complex is achieved by the boy's more fully identifying with the ego ideal, helping him gain greater autonomy and independence from parental figures.

By the time superego formation has taken place, the basic intrapsychic representations of gender identity and gender role have become structuralized. The final outcome of the boy's broad sense of gender identity, his assumption of a male gender role and his sexual partner orientation, will, of course, be determined by the processes and events of adolescence. The foundation, however, has been laid.

12

From Mother to Father:
The Boy's Search for a Generative
Identity and the Oedipal Era

John Munder Ross

It is Erikson's view that a sense of identity, indeed the sum of what we all are, is achieved by accretion, each structure resulting from what preceded it. The *paternal* identity of little boys—their would-be parenthood—follows this general principle as well, revealing a succession of identifications with the nurturing and generative functions of both mother and father. In this chapter, I shall sketch the unfolding of paternal identity in early childhood, a progression which climaxes during the oedipal era, presaging the psychological paternity of the adult man.

Infancy and Toddlerhood
As with any line of development, desires and convictions with respect to procreation may be seen to represent an individual's attempt to resolve conflicts between active and passive positions, progressive thrusts and regressive longings. A boy's (or girl's) interest in childbearing will express simultaneously wishes to be a baby and to have one, to be nurtured and to nurture. Throughout life, the wish to possess a child will at some level emanate from strivings to be a big, strong, succoring parent (mother or father), as well as from longings to be an infant, cared for and freed from responsibility.

The fluidity with which very young boys shift roles in relation to their dolls and teddy bears illustrates the duality. As one patient recalled, his brother's birth initially seemed to promise a chance to confer on him the

This is an abbreviated, revised version of "Toward fatherhood: The epigenesis of paternal identity during a boy's first decade," published in the *International Review of Psychoanalysis* 4:327–347, 1977. In this chapter, I have drawn on the contributions of earlier theoreticians detailed in Chapters 2 and 3, to which the reader should refer. Chapter 15 is a continuation of this chapter.

The work for this chapter was in part funded by the U.S. Department of Health and Human Services, Grant No. MH 05816, sponsored by the Department of Psychiatry, Downstate Medical Center, Brooklyn, New York.

status of "big brother." Yet it also reintroduced cribs and bottles into his home, the stuff with which he, as a near 3-year-old, might settle back into the passivity that he always tended to find more comfortable. Similarly, a father-to-be, proudly furnishing the nursery, found himself seized by an image of himself at his wife's breast, pondering just how her milk tasted, just how warm and wet it was.

Clinical Example: Henry

Henry, a 5-year-old, gives symbolic but poignant expression to this dichotomy. Full of boyish bravado, Henry was also, according to his parents, extremely concerned with babies. He loved them—his barber's, a family friend's, any baby at all. He was an only child, long awaited and much doted on by middle-aged parents, who joined with the child's teachers in wondering where, since his experience with babies was so relatively indirect, his fascination came from.

I interviewed Henry in an early research project I conducted (Ross, 1974, 1977), playing a game in which I pretended to be a genie who offered to fulfill any three of Henry's wishes. Eventually Henry would ask for a baby and two dolls; but first he recast the play:

Henry: No, No, No! I'm the genie and you're the Henry [the name the child had given to a boy bear in a picture, who was portrayed holding a baby, dubbed by the subject "Henry Two"]! You have to tell me the three things you want and I'll give it to you! [Pause] You tell me what you want! You're the baby!

JMR: Oh, I don't know, all the M&Ms [chocolate drops] in the world, or is that silly?

Henry: Silly . . . a baby?

JMR: Well, what about a baby?

Henry: OK, a baby. Abracadabra, into a baby! [He points and grins.]

JMR: I'm a baby? I meant having a baby.

Henry: I mean a baby. [He points again.] Wham!

JMR: Right . . . Tell me, what three things do you *think* Henry Two [the baby] would wish for?

Henry: He would wish for a doll.

JMR: And?

Henry: Abracadabra, another doll!

JMR: And what do I do with all these dolls?

Henry: Give it to the little baby.

JMR: And the baby plays with the dolls?

Henry: Yeah, they just move them around in their mouth. [He reaches for more candy, sucks on an M&M, and begins to crawl around pointedly, "playing baby" and grinning.]

Henry apparently wants both to be a baby himself and to have one. In having a baby, it seems he seeks power, not just an age-specific oedipal triumph but a more primary ascendance: the power to give, the privilege of parenthood. In short, Henry aspires to improve on his generational status in one way, one direction or the other.

Beginnings of Intentionality

The very young baby has little choice in the matter, not to mention little equipment or inclination to make choices of any kind. The experience of being cared for by the mother, however, establishes the foundation for later acts of self-help and gestures of self-parenting. Indeed, indicators of the infant's purposeful efforts to elicit maternal attentions actively occur as early as 2 or 3 months of age.

The smiling response described by René Spitz (1965) signals a first organizer of the infantile ego in relation to the mother and, quite possibly, the dawning sense on the infant's part that he or she can *act*, in Margaret Mahler's felicitous words, to "extract" maternal care and support. No longer does a baby merely react to sensations of hunger or satiation; no longer is his or her world known by "coenaesthetic sensing," as Spitz dubbed the neonate's gut responsiveness. Rather, the child begins to perceive the *gestalt* of mother's face in association with sensations of oral pleasure and bodily warmth. More importantly, an infant further reveals a rudimentary intentionality of sorts by returning the smile of a being who is, however, not yet clearly distinguished from the infant's own self.

I do not wish to ascribe too much in the way of intention to a behavior that is released by specific signs during a critical period and that is probably largely a function of instinctive patterning and maturational factors. Perhaps more telling are an infant's early "experiments" with transitional objects and phenomena, which begin after symbiosis proper, anywhere between 4 and 10 months, according to Donald Winnicott (1953); and which continue to serve a baby through differentiation and further separation-individuation from the mother.

Transitional Behavior

Not only do transitional activities—cuddling, cradling, cooing—testify to some primal "object relationship," as Winnicott put it, but, by betraying some of the major ingredients of their meaning and function, they also augur specific fantasies about having babies. Transitional behaviors define who the child is and where the child begins and ends. At the same time, they bespeak prototypal efforts on the part of children to *mother* themselves in the mother's absence, to comfort themselves with a soft rag or gentle cooing, to cuddle and cradle it, to incorporate or recreate the mother's breast in the fullest sense and to put it at their own disposal. Above all, these objects and activities serve to concretize personal relations in rudimentary or "proto-symbols," thus easing a baby's awareness of differentiation from the mother by perpetuating the *illusion* of continuing union with her. In a word, they enable the baby to create a "me" and, increasingly, to be his or her own baby.

No child at this stage is able to want a baby per se, of course. Inchoate wishes and imaginings are present only as ill-defined urges. It is evident, however, that the child has come to imitate motherly acts in the way that he or she understands them. In addition, although germinative impulses toward self-parenting share the fate of most preverbal and therefore diffuse and unbound experience—becoming inaccessible in their original form to later verbal recollection or even direct reconstruction—nonetheless their derivatives and continuing impact may be inferred from the less primitive, more articulate utterances and activities of older children.

Thus, for instance, many children in nursery school entertain the theory that babies are made from milk or some ingested substance or are born from breasts or carved out of the mother's body. Others, I have found, reveal more blatant desires to nurse babies, to put them down and give them bottles, to have "big pimples." Such beliefs and wishes need not be seen as expressions solely of naked hunger and spite, of "breast envy" alone. Rather, I believe, such evidence further indicates a young child's initial confusion and equation of nurturance with birth and productivity. It conveys, moreover, the vague sense that the child, or the child's ego, was somehow created from the love and gifts proffered by the mother— the *psychological* breast of the symbiotic era. When an older boy happens to see a baby fed and watches it grow, the notion that the two processes, nurturing and generating, are equivalent is confirmed.

An actual fantasy of bearing and suckling a baby requires the kind of symbolization in words, ideas, and images that is made possible by the birth of representational thought in the second half of the second year, and its growing ascendancy over coenaesthetic sensing, participatory representation, and sensorimotor intelligence. To construct a fantasy of bearing or rearing a baby, furthermore, a child must have developed a more certain awareness of body boundaries and of self and others; in this way, the child is led to represent both others and self as distinct objects, ultimately as full-fledged persons. His sense of gender has become more defined, as have his perception and definition of his own genitals, even though a child may continue to be more preoccupied with analerotic stimulation and sensations emanating from the "inner body," as Kestenberg has dubbed it (see Chap. 13). For a boy, the perception of himself as a boy will enable him increasingly to distinguish himself from his mother and to gain some understanding of their specific relationship as mother and child, and perhaps as female and male.

In addition, a boy must have appreciated the unique anatomy of his mother. Recognizing the existence of her breasts and genitals and aspects of their functions, although he may simultaneously endow her with a penis like his own, he may in turn adorn himself, in fantasy at least, with mother's recesses and perhaps also her protuberances. In some instances, the birth of a sibling may provide inklings of the nature of nursing and, more dimly, of childbirth. Defining bodies, his own and those of others, a boy can begin to intuit some of the connections between body parts—somatic sensations—and the production and sustenance of babies.

Because so much of his thinking remains dominated by primary process, the exact nature of the relationships cannot be understood; nor, for that matter, can desires and discoveries be distinguished as either fantasy or reality. It is only in the wake of the rapprochement subphase of separation-individuation, the dawning of preoperational representational thinking, and (from the psychosexual point of view) the maturation of sphincter control and anal preoccupations, that a child may first articulate definite childbearing and childrearing fantasies. Even then, these fantasies may be most evident in a 2-year-old's doll play, in a more active employment of transitional objects, or, perhaps, in pillows stuffed under shirts or mute cradling—not in elaborate verbalizations for which a little child is still conceptually and linguistically ill prepared.

Procreative desires at this stage will be related to anal urges in the broadest sense. Child though he may be, a little boy (or girl) would like to produce from within that part of the body that can never be known directly, something that is alive and valuable and not summarily disposable. In the words of Van der Leeuw, a child would identify with that "active, productive, purposeful mother."

Furthermore, possessing, bearing, or nursing a baby of one's own may symbolically allow the child to keep the mother near in the face of the painful but now nearly irrevocable realization that the two of them are not one and the same being. It is a realization which elsewhere provokes the sudden, often desperate clinging behavior typical of so many once adventurous 1½- and 2-year-olds. Further regressive undertones are discovered in the notions of reproduction through oral incorporation, in instances of the cloacal birth fantasies that seized Freud's attention, and in the ease with which a boy of this age switches roles in scenarios with his teddy bear or security blanket—now enacting provider and parent, now baby.

Clinical Example: Sam

Sam had never been a fearful boy, and his rapprochement crisis was not particularly troubled. Still, he did retreat more readily than before, running back and catching hold of his mother's or his father's welcome hands on outings to the playground or park. More noteworthy was Sam's interest in his stools: Undiapered, he waved bye-bye to them and, taken to the potty now and then at 2 years, he mumbled something to the effect of "Sam" and "baba." In fact babies began preoccupying Sam, and he would stare at younger children in the playground in rapt attention until he exclaimed in delight, "Baby!" He loved his doll, "William," and another doll made to resemble his father, both of whom began to attract him more than the "blankie" that previously had been his dearest love. By the age of 2½ years, he would hold these to his breast or stuff them down the front of his pants while singing softly. And he would refer to the dolls, each of his parents, himself, and his penis, interchanging the names: William, Sammy, Daddy, Mommy, Baby.

Hermaphrodites

Playing parent soon becomes complicated by a boy's developing perception of sexual differences. This discovery of his genitals and his boyishness is beset by feelings of helplessness, ambivalence, inabilities to understand as yet simple relations, and reluctance to give up former objects or to lose body parts. Sometimes, for example, when he saw his feces disappear down the drain, Sam would frown in fear and grasp his penis with one fist while clutching his mother's fingers in the other.

In his quest for omnipotence, his voraciousness whetted by an unrelinquished identification with a seemingly all-powerful mother, a boy hesitates to confine himself to a single gender. After the rapprochement and the anal phase, he may pass through a period similar to what Kestenberg (Chap. 13) has called "an inner genital phase." It is an era characterized by heightened perineal and inguinal sensations, problematic testicular changes, and, gradually, the uncontrollable states of penile tumescence to which he becomes ever more attuned.

Whether or not he is responding to heightened sensations and a *cathexis* or investment in the internal parts of his reproductive apparatus, remains to be determined. Rather, I would emphasize the little boy's *wishes* to be in possession of a mother's capacious recesses and resources, such as he imagines them. And here I differ somewhat from Kestenberg.

Cognizant now of anatomical differences, a boy between 2 and 3 years of age seeks at times to undo them through a variety of infantile fetishes—the sticks, marbles, and toy horses that line little boys' pockets. Heirs to transitional phenomena, these serve to express the illusion, and dawning delusion, of the phallic woman. A boy further seeks to endow himself with the gifts of both male and female and to fashion for himself an identity not simply, as Freud had it, of the polymorphous "little pervert," but somewhat more discriminately of a "little hermaphrodite." He

194

would have breasts like his mother's and use them as he sees her use them, to feed with or simply to "have." More intuitively, he would be full, possessed of her womb as he conceives of it, and bear babies just as she does.

Hermaphroditic motifs abound in mythology. There are, for example, carvings from the Creto-Minoan civilization in which vulva and penis are made to blend into each other as emblems of fertility. In certain simple societies in the South Pacific, the function of the man's penis in intercourse is misconstrued: His semen is believed to feed the fetus of the already pregnant woman. In the sophisticated Hindu culture, the god of the hearth, Ganesh, is a male figure with head and trunk of an elephant and a distinctly swollen abdomen. The impression is of a belly full of life, of self-contained providence and fertility.

Among the boys I studied at later stages of development, many tugged absently and dreamily at their tee shirts while speaking of women's "big pimples" and of nursing babies. One of these children, Chad (age 5), virtually deserted by his mother and cared for by his father alone, declared that he indeed was going to have a baby, which was growing in his belly and would emerge from what a classmate of his called "the special crease that people come out of." Even Henry, the boy described earlier who wanted to be the genie and not the baby, in an act of imagination and imitation may have been expressing his envy of "woman's painful prerogative." Perhaps this has been exaggerated by dim notions of a cesarean section. Moreover, in his reference to "two babies," he may be alluding to the male's testicles and to a wishful equation between these occupants of the scrotal sac and infants in utero.

Asked how a baby is born, Henry blew himself up and blurted out:

Henry: And then it grows and grows and grows and grows, and then it comes to be like that! Whush! [Looks behind him.] I can see what's in back there.
JMR: How do you think she [the mother bear in the pictures shown to these children] feels having that thing growing inside like that?
Henry: She's going to get fat. . . . [He puffs up his cheeks; laughs.]
JMR: But where does it come out of her, do you know? [Child points to his mouth.] Out of her mouth?
Henry: [Quickly] No! They have to open her tummy. . . . They make it open and then they put some more blood in, and then it's out. [He "operates" on himself by crisscrossing his belly with his hands.] . . . *He's* getting fatter, see? [In a later picture, Henry points to the father bear.] He's going to have the baby. . . . The door's open there. [He points to the door to the room, which is ajar.]
JMR: Do you want it closed? [Child nods.]
Henry: Yes, so nobody sees me. [He looks nervous, his attention appears to lapse, and then he whispers.] He's going to have a baby, too. . . .
JMR: [Quietly] So he's going to have a baby, and how does he feel about that?

Henry: He's going to put him right in there. [He points quickly to the father's belly, then to the baby carriage in the picture.]
JMR: He's going to put him right in there? So he can have a baby, huh?
Henry: [With great passion] Yeah, two babies!
JMR: What about the little boy, how does he feel?
Henry: He's going to get a baby too . . . and he-she too. [He indicates the girl bear in the picture.]
JMR: How are they going to get their babies, do you know?
Henry: I just told you. [In a hoarse whisper] They just open it up and they get a baby out and then they sew it back in again!
JMR: And how are they going to feel about having those babies? Are they going to like having them or not?
Henry: Yes. . . . [Absently] I got my new big wheel. . . . [He turns away.]

Clinical Example: Matt

Matt provides further evidence of how one boy, deprived of the normal family triad, struggled to relinquish his wish to be a mommy in favor of becoming a daddy. At 3 years of age, according to his mother's diary, Matt was living with his mother and 7-year-old sister; his parents had separated. Matt did not know what "a womans" was and, in fact, first equated her with the person who had one day stolen his mother's handbag. Woman was not synonymous with thief, his mother informed him. Rather, she was a person with no penis but breasts. He, a male with a penis, would grow up to become a man instead. "No," he countered, "a doctor." Once he had assimilated these distinctions of gender as categories, Matt believed that he had a choice in the matter. Initially, he decided that he would someday rather be a woman like his mother.

His mother noted in her diary, "Matt has got the sexes straight at last [when he] reeled off a list of all the humans he knows who have penises . . . including himself." With this discovery, however, the child was seized by a new anxiety. Naked from the waist down one blistering day, he grasped his penis and exclaimed, "It might come off!" That was what had happened to his sister, he declared, for all she had left was a hole. It was at this point that his mother explained to him "where babies come from and why girls are different."

More specifically, Matt's mother wrote:

When I was telling him about the place inside the mother where the baby grows, he said he wanted a place like that and a baby to grow inside him, too. So I explained the father's part in making a baby, and that you couldn't have a baby without a father. Sybil [her daughter] wandered into the room, and so I asked Matt if he could explain it to her. I wanted to see if he understood it. He hadn't. The daddy has semen in his tummy, he told her, and the mommy has an egg, and—"Mommy, what about chickens? They sit on their eggs." This morning Matt was getting dressed when he passed gas. "Oops," he said, "that must be the baby I have inside of me." I asked if he still thought he'd like to have a baby inside

196

him, and he said yes. Then he added that, as a matter of fact, he did have a baby inside him, "right now."

The birth fantasies of older boys like Chad, Henry, or even Matt appear to have been somewhat protracted by special life circumstances. In their original and probably "typical" form (i.e., in 2½- to 3-year-old boys) such desires or ideas serve several psychic masters. They can express the wish to have the mother's special power, yet presage a father's procreativity. They may represent an attempted mastery of the toilet training just then in process of completion: of the stools passed, the anxieties attached to their loss, and a restiveness at parental power over the moving of one's own bowels. In addition, in light of the connections in the boy's mind between his feces and his penis and the mother's strength and her imagined penis, the wish to have a baby defends, anticipates, and helps to master a boy's dread of another potential loss—castration. Thus it facilitates the difficult transition into the next libidinal stage in psychosexual development—the phallic phase.

Becoming a Boy

Between approximately 22 and 36 months, then, depending on both psychosexual and overall ego development, a little boy may reveal wishes to give birth to babies. At the very least, he will interest himself in rearing and even specifically nursing them. Just how sustained, acceptable, and conscious such fantasies of pregnancy, birth, and "ambisexuality" may be for any given child remains to be determined. In most instances, however, childbearing fantasies and, to a lesser degree, desires to succor babies, quickly become problematic for boys. (One may, however, see a resurgence of these feelings later in the oedipal period [around 4 years of age] perhaps as a consequence of "negative oedipal" or "homosexual" desires for the father.)

Whatever their residual and subliminal effects, maternal strivings are short-lived as conscious ambitions. In this respect, a "typical" boy differs from a "typical" girl, embarking on a diverging path of sexual and generative development.

Witness Matt's fear for his penis and Henry's secrecy. Even motherless Chad asserted that not only did he wish for a baby but also for "wings so I can fly . . . like a pilot." Stereotypically manly ambitions and constraints have begun to impinge on wishes now perceived to be "feminine."

Phallic Phase

The emergence of the phallic phase proper reflects a maturational thrust, progress in gender identity, and, I believe, a sense of resignation. Unable to compete with his mother's parental ascendancy over him, a boy must find an alternative route to parental authority.

Wanting babies no longer means having power, then, power that is within reach. A boy gradually learns not only that his mother lacks a penis, but also that he will never have a womb or breasts. In this regard he is destined to be "shortchanged" all of his life, to be physically barren or empty.

For some time he may (like Freud's Little Hans, or Matt) believe that he can determine his sexual destiny. But in time a boy will move from the hermaphroditic position and anticipate that to have babies is to be a woman and requires the sacrifice of his masculine attributes, specifically his penis, leaving him not with a womb but a wound. Rather than relinquish the valued penis, palpable and present as it is, he cedes the fantasied baby.

Subsequently, a boy may come to invest his tender yet ambitious maternalism in his genitals or inner spaces. He may at times imagine that they are his womb. He may even cherish them as if they were the child he cannot have (Henry's "two babies" may be his testicles). Some of these urges become diffused and are displaced onto infantile fetishes that have roots in transitional objects, but now also embody a boy's pride in his penis as well as his anxiety about preserving it. Other aspects of a boy's increasingly outmoded childbearing wishes are repressed by a rapidly developing defense repertoire. In any event, should a boy remain bent on being a mother, dissonant as this identification becomes with current psychosexual aims and cognitive capacities and with the fact that he *is* a boy, then the presence of such aspirations augurs a denial of sexual differences and of his own actual gender. Ultimately, such maladaptations may paradoxically come to inhibit the very procreativity for which a boy strives. That is, such inhibition may occur if his residual underlying maternal urges are not in some way largely satisfied.

To Be a Father: The Oedipal Era and Generative Identity

A boy's perception of his father, his attachment to him, and his identification with him are what make sex differences so evident in the first place. Having long ago singled out his father as a figure in his own right, indeed as a person of unique importance, a boy witnesses in him his own psychosexual fate and the impossibility of changing, choosing, or alternating his gender. If the masculinity promised by the father's presence entails certain losses, it does indeed offer undeniably sweet rewards. That same admixture of love and incorporative yearning a boy felt within his early symbiosis with the mother, in a lesser intensity, draws him away from her toward a father who becomes in his eyes less and less of a strange and peripheral figure. Identification with his father thus facilitates separation.

A son at this stage seeks more and more to drink in and enact for himself what he experiences as his father's manly strength; he too wants to be intrusive, erect, angular, mobile, and, of course, phallic.

First, I believe, during rapprochement and somewhat later during that particular phase described by some analysts as a period of "girlish dependency" on the father, a son would merely share adventures with him. "Homosexual" longings or, better, a more nonspecific object love for the father intermingle with strivings to be like him. Second, I conjecture that when the ambivalence of rapprochement has been superseded, then the aggressive urges initially directed toward the mother are displaced and projected onto the father, who is cast as a rival to be pushed aside in a boy's newfound quest for his mother's exclusive admiration. It is then that his identification becomes defined essentially in terms of competition and that the positive Oedipus complex is set in motion. In this respect, I would differ with Abelin's (1971, 1975, 1977) notions about early triangulation, emphasizing as he does the senior toddler's rivalry with father.

The major point is that a boy's father is present from the start in two guises, analogous to those of the mother. The "good father" is there to be loved, imitated, and introjected, and makes himself available as a model for the boy's developing gender identity. There also exists in the boy's experience a "bad father" who is absent, frustrating, punishing, tough, and eventually rivalrous, a stereotypical he-man.

Whatever illusions of strength and promise of greatness an identification with this aggressive, sadistic, or even "bad" image of the father may appear to offer, it remains an "identification with the aggressor," a primarily defensive maneuver designed to ward off a boy's fears for his nascent, still fragile masculinity and to counter his sense of inadequacy. Moreover, such an identification is fruitless: Even some measure of success in his effort to be strong in a bold but unproductive way will not enable a boy to feel fertile and creative, to fulfill his sensuality, and to assuage the hurts suffered as a consequence of his body's barrenness. Another sense of the father and of his own future is needed if a boy is to atone for these (potential) lacks within himself.

A father's physical and emotional availability to his son, to the family in general, and to the child's mother in particular, will influence his son's understanding of the parental relationship, the so-called primal scene, and the attitudes the child projects onto both participants. If the father seems remote, hostile, or authoritarian, his son may very well seize on sex as an altogether sadistic act more or less isolated from familial love, and may contrive for himself a variety of violent fantasies about it. As with the mother of infancy, parental absences incite rage, which is projected, coloring the child's image of the missing father. If, however, the father presents himself as a relatively caring, tender, and benign figure, able to absorb his son's hostilities without openly or implicitly threatening retaliation, then a boy will experience his as a nurturing presence. Such a relationship will, in turn, offset a child's more destructive conceptions of intercourse, which spring partly from the sadistic, intrusive components of his own phallic impulses. A boy may then intuit the more sensuous, pleasurable, indeed creative and generous aspect of the father in his sexual role. Having further acquired primitive logical capacities and thus more sexual knowledge, he may then identify with the father as a pro-creator possessed concretely and metaphorically of a "giving penis."

Clinical Example: Norton

Norton, a 4-year-old with a reportedly nurturing father and a rather sad and therefore less available mother, provides eloquent if still symbolic expression of a boy's search for masculinity and, indeed, for a penis, which are distinctly providential and nurturant. At the close of an interview session, during a free-play period, Norton wanted to stay in the room and play with the toys. He started pulling a tiny tractor onto which was attached a cart and said it "was pulling things to eat at home." He also held a toy cow that was going to "go into the rain and stand." He continued speaking about the "rain being nice" and the "rain stopping." Then he picked up a toy horse with a man on it and declared that the man wanted to "plant a seed" and would "dig a hole and drop the seed in." It was raining all over, he added, and seemed mournful for a moment.

JMR: What can the rain do?
Norton: [The boy was holding a toy cannon and matter-of-factly said] The cannon ball is broken.
JMR: The rain gives plants something to drink. . . . And what happens to them?
Norton: [With delight] They get bigger! [He was playing with the cannon and exclaimed] POW! [Still pulling things out of the toy box, he found a balloon and asked me to blow it up.] Can I take the balloon home?

Norton left, clutching the balloon to his breast, grinning, eyes sparkling. Later he was observed cradling the balloon, apparently, his teacher reported, "cooing to it."

A whole generative history seemed to be condensed in a few moments. Above all, it appears that Norton's wish to be succored, together with his desire actively to nurture, found expression in what he envisioned as the power of men to sow seeds and thereafter water them, to make things grow. Thus maternal and infantile aims, now outmoded, might be fulfilled by way of an age-appropriate masculine modality.

This identity remains precarious and uncertain: Norton's cannon ball remains at least momentarily broken. Yet Norton himself remains secure, his integrity assured by a continuing recourse to transitional supports, which now also preserve his boyishness.

And, once again, Matt is a case in point. His mother relates how her son came to accept his sexual fate:

I pointed out to him that he could be a daddy when he grew up and do all the same things to take care of a baby that a mommy does. The only thing he missed was carrying the baby inside him before it was born. He still looked a little forlorn, so I remarked that he'd never had a baby doll and would he like one? So he could play daddy and change its diapers and feed it? And he said eagerly that, yes, he wanted one, and seemed suddenly indignant that he'd never had one before. [Three days later she made the following entry.] Matt finally has the facts of life straight, and with a vengeance. Last night he paraded around with his socks stuffed down the front of his shorts, saying proudly: "Look how my penis has grown." He started asking me about his father's new wife. Does she have eggs inside her to make a baby? I told him she does have but reminded him that she can't have a baby by herself. There has to be a daddy too. "Yes," he explained patiently, "but she has my daddy! And he can put his seed in her, and it gets squashed together with her egg and makes a baby." He's beginning to feel good about his part—the man's part—in the whole reproductive process. This morning he spent 20 mintues with his new baby doll, walking around with it, rocking it and singing to it, and he finally tucked it into bed using his own precious security blanket. "Are you pretending to be a baby's daddy?" I asked him. "Oh, no, I'm the baby-sitter," he said. "And baby-sitter is good too." I've just started using a 15-year-old boy as a sitter and Matt is very taken with him.

Beneficent though a father may be, he cannot altogether quell the castration anxiety inevitable during the phallic and oedipal phases of psychosexual development. Nor will even the gentlest of fathers prevent his son from becoming for the time being an aggressive little male chauvinist, for such is the spirit of a boy's initial discovery of what it means to be a man. Thus even Norton, more ready with images of nurturance than many of his peers, is very much preoccupied with "cannon balls" that are broken. And Matt, too, is alternately proud of displaying his penis and anxious about losing it. Still unable to integrate bits of information into a complete understanding of stages in the reproductive process and unsteady in his burgeoning masculinity, a son with even a "better than average expectable" family, with a father who is a genuine libidinal provider, must struggle to organize sexual and nurturing images of himself that are still fragmentary and potentially contradictory.

This is a transitional period, then, a state of "dynamic disequilibrium," in Piagetian terms, a phase before his styles of defense have crystallized into a distinct character structure. During this transition, a boy will entertain a variety of wishes and identifications that will probably remain with him in more or less unconscious form throughout his life and that may possibly become pathogenic as far as his eventual genitality is concerned. Reaction formations, inherent sadism, and denials of maternalism or tenderness may predominate, leading to the phallic fixations so often associated with the stereotypical unfeeling, ungiving, often unproductive male.

On the other hand, a boy may retreat from assuming the man's role because it is unavailable to be internalized, because he fears retribution, or because he feels somehow that his mother does not accept him as a man. Homosexual longings and defenses may then serve to stifle the possibility of actual parenthood, and a boy may revert to the wish to make the baby in his own bowels.

Matt's case poses problems about the fate of maternal aspirations in a boy whose oedipal triangle is left incomplete. Certainly it leaves many unanswered questions: Did the mother's intervention catalyze latent pregnancy wishes that had perhaps contributed to Matt's castration fear and had found some fulfillment in Matt's pride in his penis, that is, *his* baby? Or was it, as Freud might have suggested, Matt's fear of losing his penis and longing for his father that forced him to retreat into a feminine identification in which having babies served as compensation for emasculation? One cannot say. Neither possibility excludes the other, in fact, and evidence for both is suggested. Actually Matt's childbearing fantasies are probably bolder and balder than many, and may result from the sporadic presence of his father, who had left his son at a crucial stage in the development of sexual identity, causing the mother to serve as a primary object of identification. She, in turn, by her well-meaning efforts to discourage male chauvinism and her evident rejection of Matt's father, may have appeared to devalue men and masculinity. Still, as his mother herself points out, father and son continued to spend weekends together, and other men, uncles and friends, were available to the boy. Nor did she actually frown on her boy's delight in his maleness.

Above all, Matt's mother provided her son with an understanding of a man's fatherly relation to his children. And it was, as she declared, "just what Matt needed." What the boy required was some awareness of the man's part in reproduction, of a man's sexual relationship with a woman, and of his active caretaking role whereby he might imagine himself to be a creative, nurturant "daddy" who shared in making and in tending babies. With this "sense of purpose," in Erikson's words, Matt might now overcome life's typical hardships as well as those peculiar to his unique circumstances, reconciling aspirations to generativity with the constraints and pleasures afforded by his being a boy.

The Mother's Role

Along with the "good father," then, a boy's mother must be present during the oedipal era as an essentially admiring and worthy, if not altogether available, object of her son's aspiring love. Her receptivity plays a vital role in determining the nature and quality of his libidinal object choices and of his sexual identity, and hence the possibility for future procreativity. Such a mother remains a constant figure who is both warm and appropriately detached: that is to say, maternal, womanly, sensual, and authoritative, all at once. She can be seen to be essentially the same person within her sexual relationship with the father as she is in her mothering. Neither she nor her son, then, become split in their sexuality, with pleasure divorced from caring or conception. She does not, however, become so accessible to her son (at least not directly) that she lets him take his father's place, thus depriving the son of ideals of what he would like himself to be and of the sort of woman whom he would choose to love.

Sexual Identity: The Resolution

Even a motherly mother and fatherly father cannot altogether spare their son from residual feminine or even homosexual wishes, or from his anxious, defensive, and often overcompensating protests against these threats to a newfound sense of masculinity. With luck, however, these and other potentially regressive, self-absorbing, and isolating responses will be transformed by the successful sublimations that accompany the oedipal resolution. Whatever their form, preoedipal urges toward productivity, along with selective maternal identifications, may now be subordinated to the paternal identification that climaxes the oedipal crisis and consolidates a boy's sexuality. It is this assumption of a would-be paternity, I am convinced, which promises to atone best for lacks inherent in being any one sex, and which thereby resolves inescapable conflicts in a boy's overall sexual as well as his more delimited gender identity (Chaps. 1, 15).

13

The Development of Paternal Attitudes

Judith S. Kestenberg,
Hershey Marcus,
K. Mark Sossin,
Richard Stevenson, Jr.

Therese Benedek (1959, 1960, 1970a,b; Parens, 1975), a pioneer in the study of parenthood, emphasized a man's role as provider and protector. From Benedek's perspective, fatherhood is rooted in the instinct for survival, and fatherliness derives from the reproductive-drive organization. Early experiences with the mother become integrated with memory traces of the boy's crucial early experiences with the father (Benedek, 1970a) and eventuate in a sense of and striving for "paternity."

Kestenberg (1965, 1975, 1980a, c) sees the biological roots of paternity unfolding in "tensions and impulses originating in cryptic, immature and maturing reproductive organs" (Kestenberg, 1974, 1981). These inner promptings provide the foundation for sex-specific parental roles, which are differentiated according to the diverging developmental pathways pursued by boys and girls. A boy establishes a primary identification with the mother and later with the father. Culturally determined and biologically rooted paternal attitudes include polarities based on dual identifications with mother and father. These attitudes, reflected in behavior, can be broken down as follows: (1) maternal or nurturant aspects that, based on a preoedipal mirroring of the mother, are often defended against; and (2) the provider-protector aspects that, based on imitation of the oedipal father, are often exaggerated. Although there is a good deal of overlap between maternal and paternal functions, we feel that there are consistent differences in the parenting styles of the two sexes that cross cultural lines.

This chapter, then, will define what is essential to a paternal identity, and then trace it through the boy's development. First, we outline the basic differences between men and women and examine how maternal

This chapter is based on observations from the "Father-Project" of the Center for Parents and Children, directed by Dr. Hershey Marcus. Its first director was Dr. John Munder Ross. Richard Stevenson, Mark Sossin, and Susan Tross participated from its start in 1975.

and paternal attitudes in men become incorporated in their masculine identity. The impressions reported are culled from observations of non-verbal as well as verbal behavior of children and adults of both sexes (Kestenberg, 1975a, b; Kestenberg and Marcus, 1979; Kestenberg and Sossin, 1979). Rather than introduce technical terms, however, we will present only clinical data that can be reconciled with the result of our movement research, but which readers can comprehend more readily.

Polarities Between Sexes

The more or less normal development of masculinity and femininity is based on bisexual patterns that are biologically anchored, but that decrease and increase with changing cultural trends. Thus in authoritarian cultures the purely "macho" male and the purely submissive female may achieve greater prominence than in the contemporary feminist culture, where men are encouraged to be tender and motherly and women are assuming greater responsibility for themselves and their children.

Exaggerated "monosexual" pure maleness (Kestenberg and Marcus, 1979) is characterized by aggression and activity; exaggerated femaleness, by indulgence and passivity. Being active or passive does not imply being assertive or immobile; rather, these are modes of interaction with the world in the service of personal aims and objectives. For example, activity as a modality of aggression is oriented to the overcoming of external obstacles, while passivity as a modality of indulgence implies accommodating to the forces of external reality. A "pure" male might demand that someone do something; a "pure" female would find a way to invite the other to want to do something. Both are directed behaviors toward goals, but the processes by which these goals are achieved are different.

Pure maleness is unsuitable for effective fathering, just as pure femaleness is unsuitable for good mothering. To become truly paternal or maternal, individuals of each sex must borrow certain characteristics from those of the other: That borrowing is the essence of their bisexuality. By assuming "pure" man's cautiousness and inhibition, the careless, "indulgent" woman becomes a caring mother who gives proper support to the child when she nourishes and carries him. The purely macho male is essentially unfatherly, since he is prone to injure himself and his child, whom he considers an extension of himself. The paternal man borrows an essentially female tendency to turn to the environment, which enables him to turn his aggression outward and to enclose mother and child into his sphere of safety. The bisexual feminine woman inhibits her drives in the service of maternality; the bisexual masculine man becomes the protector of his family against internal and external aggression. Both sexes are capable of aggression, but women frequently lose control when enraged and strike out randomly, whereas men are more apt to direct and control their aggression. Mothers are inclined to think of the child's needs, whereas fathers tend to see the child's behavior as related to themselves.

Further, we theorize that the adult man's paternal stance is determined by the interplay and successful integration of two tendencies. These involve (1) inner-genitality and an underlying identification with the nurturing mother, and (2) a phallic outer-genitality which is buttressed by the boy's identification with his seemingly self-sufficient father. We have observed that in phases wherein inner-genital needs are accentuated, and when there is identification with the mother as nurturer, there is a greater tendency to externalize inner-genital impulses into body care and affection. When phallic narcissism predominates and an excessive identification with the "pure" male is present, love tends to be considered demeaning and sentimental; rather, one's own and one's child's worth is measured by prowess.

Elsewhere, Kestenberg (1980b) has discussed the three faces of femininity—the maternal, the competitive (career-oriented), and the sensual—that together constitute integrated womanliness. Man becomes maternal in identification with his preoedipal mother; competitive with his preoedipal and oedipal father; and sensual in identification with his oedipal parents. His negative oedipal feelings allow him to identify, not only with his wife, but also with his daughter. The narcissistic pride of his achievement, born in pregenital phases and culminating in the phallic-narcissistic phase, extends to his children, especially his son, in whose achievements he basks. He sublimates his sensuality toward heterosexual and homosexual objects into fatherly affection and forbearance, while he converts his oedipal aggression into benign fatherly attitudes toward his children.

By sublimating some of his desires to reproduce himself and care for his offspring, man becomes creative in a number of ways, not only in artistic pursuits but also in the course of everyday work where he may assume a semi-parental attitude. When he does become a father, there arises a conflict between his desire for intimacy with the child and his sublimations in his work. His own creativity may suffer a setback, and he becomes more conscious of his role as provider and protector of the family. This is counterbalanced by his realization that he can neither become pregnant nor bear a child. Especially now, when man is no longer able to train his child in his own trade, men as well as women are continually beset by the conflict between the wish to rear the child and the wish to be engaged in productive work away from home. Currently we see the emergence of single-parent households, in which one parent assumes the role of two, as a solution to such conflicts. Together with Burlingham (1973), we believe that being brought up by only one parent robs the child of the richness of experience and also prevents the child from coping with the multidimensional relationships that constitute the backbone of community relations. Both parent and child suffer.

Development of Paternal Attitudes in Successive Phases
Pregenital Phases
From the start, the child senses the difference between the way he or she is held by the parents. Our research on movement patterns suggests that the male infant feels his father's motor rhythms as similar to his own. His attunement with his mother fosters orality, especially if she breast-feeds him. In terms of movement pattern, the oral rhythm is neither abrupt nor gradual, but the mother's movements add a gradual component, while the father's introduce more abruptness.

Needless to say, there are "abrupt" mothers and "gradual" fathers. We are generalizing here on the basis of what we have observed to be the more frequent preference in women and in men. On seeing fathers in the delivery room, one is impressed with their pride in their boys' sex and their greater "engrossment" (Chap. 5) when the child's movement patterns correspond more to their own. Despite the feeling of relatedness a father experiences when the infant moves as he does, he is more distant than the mother to the baby. Fathers frequently hold their newborns on their folded arms at waist height, whereas mothers will keep them close to their breasts or faces. Fathers are more inclined than mothers to hold babies with the baby's face facing forward or the baby's body stretched out on the thighs. Fathers also tend to toss their children up in the air, further increasing the distance between themselves and their children—a practice that serves as an exercise in separation between caretaker and baby.

Oral Phase. The neonate feels the father to be more active and aggressive, more abrupt, more daring, and more distant than the mother, thereby fostering independence and aggression. Over time, the father becomes less of an "accessory" to the mother (Kestenberg, 1971) and more of an entity in his own right, particularly as a play companion.

The father, perhaps along with siblings, progresses from being someone to turn to instead of the mother, to acting as a mediator of separation and a provider of a sublimating pathway for aggression through play. The infant develops an image of the mother by attuning to her rhythms and mirroring her facial expression in close proximity to her. In contrast, the development of the father image tends to evolve through distant observation and imitation. When a 7-month-old girl was asked where her mother was, she looked around as if amazed that she could not find her next to her. When asked where her father was, she reproduced a habitual head gesture of her father, which she had observed from her position across the table from him.

Our observations suggest that paternal behavior plays an important role in the child's progress toward regulation of aggressive drives and toward differentiation. Fathers promote aggression in the form of early infantile "hittings and meetings," which Winnicott (1964) linked to the establishment of a clear distinction between self and nonself. Fathers who attune with their baby boys will deliberately evoke clashes in a playful manner. If this does not occur, we may very well encounter a symbiotic attachment between father and baby.

Toward the end of the first year, many infants begin to show preference for either men or women. At this point, stranger anxiety is influenced by the mother's attitude toward the stranger (Chap. 8). Not only do infants begin to recognize sex differences in adults, but they also feel the undercurrents of affection or antagonism that exist among their mothers, fathers, siblings, and grandparents. A mother whose male infant seeks out men to play with may say, "He is a man's man," indicating that the boy is tough and masculine. The father's image is maintained in his absence through the mother's representation of him to her child. Some mothers will talk mournfully about a father's temporary absence, informing us that the baby misses his father very much. This attitude becomes a self-fulfilling prophecy, so that the child indeed feels sad in the father's absence. A mother may further delineate the father's functions, for instance when she indicates that daddy is needed to fix things. In such situations, a baby that has just begun to walk may clutch a screwdriver, linking it to his powerful father.

Some mothers have told us that they do not want to breast-feed their babies in order not to deprive the father of the pleasure of bottle-feeding. Such an attitude of mothers has multiple effects: on the father, who begins to see his fatherhood through the eyes of his wife (i.e., he should feed his baby and enjoy it); and on the child, who sees his father's function through the eyes of the mother. This indoctrinated father-child relationship must be distinguished from the direct, unadulterated experience between father and child. Similar complexities arise when a child observes the father's attitude toward a sibling.

Anal Phase. At the start of their second year, boys progressively identify with the father as possessor of valued qualities, such as strength and bigness. In the second year of life, a special relationship with the father leads to identification with certain of his external attributes, such as wearing a man's hat, the father's tie, or imitating a man's walk. Rough-housing with the father strengthens the toddler's feeling of having his father as a cohort, but he may experience some of the roughhousing as an attack on him and, in identification, as an invitation to attack children. In this, the anal-sadistic phase, attacks on babies who have become objects of great interest are not uncommon. Such assaults may be followed by transparent reaction-formations as the toddler instead "makes nice" to his victim. The incorporation of parental prohibitions is often accompanied by identifying with the disciplinarian and enjoining younger children from doing forbidden things. In this early behavior we anticipate the traits of the future strict father.

Urethral Phase. In the urethral phase which follows, the boy becomes achievement oriented, but this competitiveness is not yet phallic or oedipal. The boy may be tender with babies, but he may also push them down when they stand up or walk, to show that they belong on the floor below. In instances where the mother cannot cope with the boy's urinary interests, the father may figure as someone the mother relies on to train boys, in contradistinction to girls. This maternal expectation plays a big role in the boy's appraisal of the function of a father. However, his urinary interests and ambitions are not necessarily attached to the father as a model. He may be more interested in firemen and policemen than in the father's occupation. In many instances, he looks on the fireman as a rescuer and a policeman as a disciplinarian, whereas his father remains his big adult playmate. In this phase, as in the preceding phase, the father plays an important role in diluting aggressive impulses against the mother. The father offers himself as a benign recipient of aggression who is able to take it and can provide sublimatory outlets in aggressive fatherly activities, such as wrestling. The father's ability to survive the child's aggression emerges and continues to pervade the child's thinking, even at the height of his identification with the mother in the inner-genital phase that follows.

In pregenital phases, when a boy identifies primarily with the mother as a caretaker and with the father as accessory to mother, male figure, rebound object, and playmate, we see progressively increasing parenting behavior in identification with either parent, but especially the mother. However, the need to reproduce the baby that the child once was comes to a peak during the inner-genital phase, at a time when he is no longer a baby.

The Inner-Genital Phase

The 3 to 3½-year-old knows that daddies are men and mommies are "ladies." However, within the boy's conceptualization, it does not follow that boys grow up to be daddies and girls to be mommies. Many boys say they will be mommies when they grow up but will remain boys. Those who declare that they want to be daddies will frequently betray that they are merely bowing perfunctorily to convention. When asked whether they will go to work or stay at home to care for children, the future "daddies" declare they will stay at home with the children. Thus, they will be sort of mommy-daddies or "moddies" (Kestenberg, 1971).

In this phase, which follows the pregenital phases and precedes the phallic, children of both sexes mourn their lost babyhood. They may long to have babies in order to reproduce themselves and the mommies of their infancies. Also, they are afraid to shrink back into babies, and the progressive solution is to become mommy and have a baby. Thus the wish to have a baby arises at a time when the child is no longer a baby. The child must further provide this baby (Boehm, 1930; Jaffe, 1968) with a parent, most often the nurturing mother, with whom the child identifies. This identification is further encouraged by the dawning awareness that fathers cannot give birth to babies.

Children are not yet interested in how babies are made, but they want to know how and where they come out. They compare babies with other products and search for an orifice that would let babies out. They seem to identify their inner genital stirrings with live babies, an idea leading to a feeling that they are pregnant. All these ideas can occur earlier when toddlers are faced with a pregnancy, especially their mothers'. Boys do not readily accept the information that they cannot produce babies. A frequent imaginary location for emergence of a baby is the groin, where a boy feels the spermatic cords moving up and down, and the testicles, identified with babies, coming up and down. He imagines this in spite of the fact that the term *penis* is often reserved by the parents for the tripartite structure of the phallus and the testicles in the scrotum, as if to stress the external and deny the inner genital structures.

Nonetheless, the boy's awareness of inner movements lends credibility to his conviction that he has a baby inside. His care of his imaginary baby mirrors the movement he feels inside. Moreover, we conjecture that the later ability of the adult father to nurture a baby as a mother does is largely derived from feelings inside the body and from the kinesthetic memory of his own mother's ministering to him as a baby (Kestenberg, 1980b).

The boy who associates these inner feelings with delivering a baby inevitably becomes angry with his mother when he discovers that she has usurped all rights for reproduction for herself and the female sex. This period of dissatisfaction with his inability to produce babies is, however, much shorter than that of the girl. Encouraged by his parents and older siblings, he begins to aggrandize his penis at the expense of inner genitality, which he is then moved to deny. With this, inner genitality is depreciated, and the mother comes to be pitied rather than idealized as a bearer of children. As for himself, he no longer wants to become a mommy. Resting on the successful development through the inner-genital phase, and evolving from maternal identifications, a new phase is entered, earmarked by emerging phallic and subsequently paternal ambitions.

Phallic-Narcissistic Phase

In the phallic-narcissistic phase (Edgcumbe and Burgner, 1975), babies become equated with the phallus. The fantasy that mother lost her penis by producing a baby is more common now than before, and the renunciation of childbearing is reinforced by castration anxiety. Erections, which earlier had given rise to fears of loss of control over the phallus, are now welcomed. The boy becomes capable of producing them by masturbation, although he may also fear that his penis will become so big that it will fly away from him. Babies are seen as extensions of the penis, extensions often achieved in fantasy by an appropriation of the father's phallus. Thus the boy's imaginary baby becomes the bearer of his "grandfather's" phallic power.

The narcissistic attachment to the baby-phallus may betray itself in masturbatory activities involving a baby doll. The bouncing, jumping, leaping 4-year-old, we have found, may wish to jump on or jump with a baby. He may want to carry or embrace the baby with the baby's face in front of him, and keep the baby's rear end in front of his penis. Here the child tends to find a ready-made model in his father, who had acted similarly toward him and toward his younger sibling. The more narcissistic features of fatherhood, which emerge now, are the source of a man's transferring of his ego ideal to his son. The phallic boy acts as a father of his sibling, ruling over and, in fantasy, making himself the proud possessor of, the baby. He may try to take the baby from the mother, in a manner reminiscent of a father who wants to prove that the baby likes him better than the mother.

We thus tend to see an autonomous, but interdependent, transformation in self-image from a nurturing mother image to a playful, ideal father image. The playmate-father of the past and present combines to create a phallic-paternal need for aggrandizement through reproduction. This phallic reproduction is no longer modeled after women's pregnancies, but rather after the images of becoming bigger through a tremendous erection, and creating babies through a fantastical autonomy or cloning. As a result, paradoxically, getting a baby aggrandizes the future phallic father, while at the same time the baby's delivery threatens his body integrity by diminishing the size of his phallus.

Projection of wishes directed toward the father, whose penis he covets, plays a role in the boy's penis envy, which is stronger than that of the girl. When castration fear becomes very strong and a regression to the preceding maternal phase threatens, the solution may be to renounce the wish for parenthood, presaging a certain type of homosexuality.

Phallic-Oedipal Phase

In the second part of the phallic phase, the child reacts with aggression and rivalry to the father, who in his fantasy threatens to castrate him. He further becomes very interested in the procreative activities of the father and asks innumerable questions about how babies are made. He accepts the "seed theory" happily, because it reassures him that he would not lose any part of his phallus through procreation. His narcissistic competitiveness with his father now begins to give way to a rivalry for the mother's affection.

The competitive narcissistic phallic phase is followed by a sensuality in which phallic-genital excitement generates a desire to enter the mother and give her a baby. In the previous phase, father was needed as a continuous source of phallic wealth; in the positive oedipal subphase, by contrast, the father is wished away so that the child can be with mother alone. Fatherhood becomes incidental to having mother for a wife and replacing father. The murderous impulses toward the father become defensively transformed into a wish to shrink him into a baby. Thus the image of the baby is now modeled after a diminutive father. However, the baby of this phase is overdetermined. Giving the mother a "baby-father" as a token of generosity and a measure of love constitutes an identification with the father as mother's lover and provider. Giving the mother a son also compensates for her lack of a penis. The phallic boy not only wants to have a boy child as an extension of his father and himself, but he also cultivates the baby-son's phallic characteristics as a gift to the mother. The baby as a phallic gift is also a masturbation fantasy that prompts phallic-oedipal boys to seduce little boys and young sisters whom they teach to be boyish.

Not infrequently, the negative oedipal attitude precedes the positive or alternates with it. In the reversal from phallic superiority, a submissive attitude toward the father may be evidenced in which identification with the mother and a desire to replace *her* reigns supreme. The boy wants to marry his father and to conceive like his mother. This, too, is primarily based not on a wish to be a parent, but on a wish very similar to that of the girl, to be entered by the father's penis. The wished-for child then becomes a replacement for and a residue of the father's penis. The point of entry is usually the anus, sometimes the mouth. Through identification with the mother in the negative Oedipus complex, the boy becomes less adamant about possession of male children and becomes capable of identifying with girls, who, in his mind, are offshoots of his mother. Through reaction formation against the aggression toward the mother, a boy can also accept and wish for female children. The repression of the Oedipus complex engenders reaction formation of tender fatherliness and sublimations of narcissistic-paternal attitudes into pride in a child's achievement. Above all, the boy who enters latency identifies with his "fatherly father."

Latency

The latency boy is "all boy." When he overcomes the early latency regression to pregenitality, he projects all his pregenital wishes onto women and babies. This is facilitated by his transferring some of his feelings of dependency and admiration to his teacher. He also admires male heroes and older boys, and he is a good teacher to younger siblings.

The boy's expectations of himself are also largely tied to the father's expectations of him. Through heroic stories of war and death, attack by "bad guys," and escape from danger, usually shared with peers, the boy works through his forbidden oedipal wishes within the context of sibling or peer rivalry. The distance from the father in this respect contributes to his idealization in fantasy. The fantasy meets reality when the father is a scout leader who goes off camping with his boy-scout son and his buddies. Either way, the ego ideal of the latency boy shapes his images of his father and of himself as a future father.

Adolescence

In adolescence, regression to previous positions brings on a series of simultaneous contradictory identifications with mother, father, and siblings. One of the aspects of male personality, such as fatherliness, heterosexual or homosexual sensuality and interest in competitive work and games, can temporarily predominate over the others, but each exerts an influence over the other. A regression to pregenital, inner-genital, and phallic phases ushers in a diffusion of drives and identification in which inner genitality takes the upper hand and exerts an integrative influence on development. The father's acceptance of his own "insides" and his pride in his ability to procreate a good offspring, coming from a good inside, helps the growing boy to accept himself as a procreative person at the time when inner-genital sensations break through the defense barrier.

Pain in the testicles, ejaculatory stirrings, and constant comparison with the functions of other boys focus the child's attention on his genitals. In many cases, the first ejaculation results from masturbation; sometimes, however, it is associated with accidents, which are then equated with loss of control over feces and especially urine. All pregenital representations of a baby being born out of food, feces, and urine, which arose in early childhood, recur now with great force. The boy identifies with the "dirty old man" who sullies his mother. Linking his own "wasted" semen with children left around for the mother to clean up after is often directly connected with fantasies of creating children. Once there is psychic acceptance of the semen as the source of children that come from the boy's inside, we believe, there can arise a renewed identification with the mother and a repetition of the integration of various pregenital and genital stirrings, which was characteristic of the early genital phase that followed pregenitality.

A boy may reveal a homosexual attachment to a friend that has motherly qualities. A repetition of dyadic mirroring between mother and child forebodes a transition to a special relationship with the father, which is based on intimacy and parallelism as well as sameness. Being a pal of his father counters the boy's fear of becoming like his mother or a girl. Indeed, old fears of having female internal genitals are reawakened by the stirrings in the boy's own inner genitals and their behavioral manifestations. These are externalized partially to the surface of the boy and partially onto an alter ego: the pal, who takes the place of the baby of the early inner-genital phase. Through his pal relationship, the young adolescent rebuilds his body image and reintegrates his identity. Another source of reintegration through identification is the relationship to older, more mature boys or to older brothers who become idealized in lieu of the father, along with younger teachers or counselors.

The development of paternal attitudes within the framework of pre-puberty reintegration (Kestenberg, 1975, 1980a, c) draws on previous identification with the father and on relationships with parent-substitutes. The boy begins to look on his father as a man with varying interests and varying needs. The advent of fertility reinforces the old idea of changing places with the father as if it were the boy's turn to be generative because the father is becoming too old to be procreative. This, together with the soaring of sensuality to unknown heights, abets the revival of the Oedipus complex in midadolescence. The urgency to discharge tension in distance from the primary object is to some extent the motivating force in masturbation and masturbatory sex play. From the masturbation struggle, there evolve resolutions of conflict and sublimatory outlets, presaged in daydreams. Coming to grips with fatherhood is part of this struggle.

215

Because of current sexual mores, whereby adolescents more often engage in the consummation of sex, solitary masturbatory fantasies are engaged in less frequently, and sublimatory outlets become almost unnecessary. Worries about impregnating the girl and thus becoming responsible for the child and his mother are greatly diminished. The responsibility for the baby is shifted to the girl, who decides on the use of contraceptives, easily available abortions, or single motherhood. The boy is robbed of his chance to synthesize his father-identification with masculine drive and ego attitudes of a young man in transition to adulthood.

In later adolescence, there is an increase in aggression and consequently an increase in differentiation of sexual attitudes, career plans, and fatherhood. Parents are seen as real people, differentiated from what they seemed to be in childhood and early adolescence. The need to replace a lost parent image with a baby is not as great, and fatherhood is more easily postponed out of realistic considerations. There can be a fulfillment of paternal aspirations in creativity. Postponing fatherhood succeeds under optimal conditions of extending fatherly duties to the community and keeping it away from the family.

Young men tend to establish their own ideals of manhood and parenthood when they can maintain some measure of distance from their real fathers. When they develop a new relationship with a girl, they become paternal toward her. Reproductive wishes are then influenced not only by the man's need to reproduce his own babyhood and by his identification with his parents and siblings, but also by the consideration of his mate, who wishes to reproduce herself and her own parents or siblings.

Through these multiple identifications, paternal attitudes develop as integrated sets of functions that become, for the father, further differentiated and integrated in a successive adult parental developmental phase. With each new phase the child enters, a father and mother regress and have a new chance to deepen their parental commitments. A father who can integrate work and community responsibilities with love for his wife, with leisures and pleasures and pains of dyadic and triadic parenting, reaches a complexity of adulthood that single parenthood cannot attain.

Conclusions

This psychoanalytic investigation of the development of paternal attitudes draws from ongoing observational studies of infants, children, and adults conducted at our primary prevention center. Distinguishing essential and distinct paternal attitudes and behaviors from those that are maternal or nonparental, we have traced the developmental line of a boy's evolving paternal attitudes through psychosexual phases. The question of what is paternal has been broached, expanding on the work of Kestenberg and Marcus (1979), by elucidating the biological and cultural roots of those bisexual patterns that potentiate paternal and maternal attitudes (related to the polarities of masculinity-femininity and activity-passivity).

From the earliest phases, a boy experiences his two parents differently. The paternal father tends to introduce more active and aggressive interactive modalities than the maternal mother; hence he tends to foster differentiation and individuation. Precursors of paternal attitudes, developed in identification with the father, structure the child's inborn predispositions toward activity and motility. Examples have been tendered, illustrating how the nature of identification with the father varies in accordance with phase specificity and with variations in the psychological and communicational makeup of family systems.

Pregenital development lays a foundation upon which paternal attitudes develop through the interplay and successful integration of identification with the nurturing mother in the inner-genital phase and identification with the self-sufficient father in the phallic phase. In the urethral phase, it is especially important that the father meets the child's aggression by providing sublimatory aggressive outlets. The wish to reproduce, as it appears in the inner-genital phase, is in part derived from inner-body sensations; later, we think, it gives rise to the adult father's capacity to nurture. In the phallic-narcissistic subphase, the reproductive urge is transformed into a need for a phallic-paternal aggrandizement.

The phallic-oedipal phase brings a rivalry for mother's affection, replacing narcissistic competitiveness. A new prepaternal attitude develops in which the wished-for baby is an expression of affection and love from child to mother. In contradistinction, the negative oedipal attitude brings on a wish to receive a baby from the father.

Following latency's heightened idealization of the father-son relationship, adolescence brings regression to pregenital representations of babies. Prepubescent conflicts over wishes to grow up and still remain a child give way at puberty to heightened drives and sensuality, and only later to renewed separation and more integrated paternal aspirations. Procreative capacities are again linked to inner-genital promptings, and earlier pregenital baby representations recur in connection with experiences of ejaculation. Reintegration of body image and of identity are aided by the qualities of the "pal relationship" and idealization of older boys and men other than the father. Midadolescence often brings the development of a new father image, along with the revival of the Oedipus complex. It appears that a cultural-historical shift away from the need for sublimatory outlets has had the impact of heightening passive-narcissistic dependence, which interferes with the capacity to utilize sublimatory channels and to postpone fatherhood. Paternal attitudes may further develop as the young man enters adult relationships and chooses a new love object. Subsequent experience as a father increases the potential for a deepening of paternal attitudes.

A Note on the Father's Contribution to the Daughter's Ways of Loving and Working

Lora Heims Tessman

My heart ran so to thee
It would not wait for me,
And I discouraged grew
And drew away.
Emily Dickinson

This chapter focuses on a single contributing force (among many) in the development of a woman's ways of loving and working: the distinctive influence of her father. It raises the question of whether some deep, reverberating preparations for pleasure in loving and working potentially stem from the father-daughter relationship. Special attention will be paid to exploring the father's role in helping his daughter to transform her childish excitement into eventual initiative and vitality in work modes, and into tolerance for experiencing her passions profoundly in love. *Excitement* is used here to mean an inner state of aroused desire (rather than diffuse tension, agitation, or manic excitement). For example, in the excerpt above, Emily Dickinson (1945, p. 170) pictures excitement as an inner desire activating her "heart," but despairs about its acceptable integration into her character, or sense of "me" in actual loving ("and drew away"). The term *work* is used here to mean purposeful effort in which emotional, cognitive, or physical skills are directed toward the accomplishment of a goal that one has set for oneself, aside from the direct pleasures of gratifying relationships. The desire, in this case, is to use one's energies in some endeavor. It would be useful to discuss the fate of both "erotic excitement" and "endeavor excitement."

The qualities involved in a woman's particular way of loving and working may have increasing importance in the future. A number of social changes are converging to cause this development, including women's increased life expectancy, the growing inclusion of women in the labor force, the decreasing polarities in sex roles, and the decreasing birthrate. These factors are resulting in a longer span of adult years during which a woman's energies focus elsewhere than on the care of young children. Such shifts have been accompanied by a recent conception of the adult years as a period of continued emotional development, as opposed to the older view of adulthood as a period of unvarying maturity. For example, it has recently been recognized that women's erotic life continues to undergo changes throughout adulthood: There may be a resurgence of erotic intensity in midlife, the profundity of sexual response may deepen, and spontaneous sexual feelings (without immediate external arousal) may play a new role (Rubin, 1979). Hypotheses have been described both on physiological grounds (Sherfey, 1966; Rossi, 1980) and in terms of life-cycle role shift (Rubin, 1979). Such resurgence, however, may also mean that, in order for enriching adult development to proceed, previously settled conflicts and vulnerabilities may be reawakened in new forms and must be again resolved, or resolved at a deeper level.

The quality of emotional engagement between father and daughter frequently remains as a powerful undercurrent giving direction to that particular vision of happiness which becomes a guiding force in a woman's life and affects her perception of the value or futility of her own efforts in striving toward it. Emotional engagement is, of course, complex: It continually changes and occurs at many levels of consciousness, involving perception, fantasy, and overt interaction. The daughter responds to her perception of the father's attitudes and feelings about a complex of changing strivings within her. Some of the strivings are "gender linked" and some are not at all. She reacts to her perception of his general degree of interest in her versus his inaccessibility or withdrawal from her; his attitude, within their relationship, toward her attempt at various intimacies with him; her compliance or assertiveness with him; her developing capabilities, initiative, and autonomy with him; and his reactions to aspects of her development that extend beyond her direct relationship with him. In addition, for the daughter, the father's functioning in relation to her mother (or in some cases other love partners) and siblings, as well as in the wider world of "work" (making things, solving problems, approaching adventure and exploration, effecting change) becomes increasingly germane as well.

The Father-Daughter Dyad: Daughter's Side

The notion of gender differences—in this case, that fathers are different than mothers for daughters—has, in recent times, often been properly greeted with skepticism, and warrants a close examination of why fathers might have an especially salient role in the acceptance and transformation of excitement in their daughters. Cognizant of the necessary over-generalization and simplification, we can nevertheless consider what each member of the dyad (daughter and father) is apt to bring to the relationship. I believe that, for many little girls, the confluence of two kinds of excitement is directed toward the father, when he is available, beginning at a time when individuation from the mother is proceeding (more or less successfully) with some momentum. These two kinds of excitement can be termed *endeavor excitement*, which begins during the second year of life and is eventually associated with autonomy; and *erotic excitement*, beginning in the third and fourth year of life and gathering intensity throughout the oedipal period. These are the forerunners of later energies invested in work and love. Some degree of individuation is prerequisite to the girl's experiencing her excitement as inner in origin, though not necessarily in aim, and as having the potential for some mixture of expression and mastery. If, at the height of his daughter's desire for and interest in him, the father is able to enjoy her development as a growing person, this may help her to desexualize the relationship to some extent by motivating her to transform her excitement into some variety of collaborative pleasure with him, more or less mixed with aspects of identification with him in regard to the ego utilization of these very modes of transformation. However, if he responds to her interest with resounding rebuff or withdrawal, she may be left with a sense of futility about either her erotic longings, or the effort of transforming excitement in relation to a man, or both. Her ability to desexualize the relationship may be hampered if his need is to maintain the sexualization of the relationship.

Father's Role in Ego Ideal Formation

Both the modes of transformation and the libidinal connections frequently become assimilated to an ego ideal involving the father. Because the ego ideal remains more closely connected to desire than to prohibition (which characterizes the superego), and because desire becomes a central component of the little girl's wishes toward the father, she is particularly prone to involve him in her ego ideal, even when her major identification is with the mother. I have previously discussed the controversy regarding the role of such an ego ideal in contrast to the superego (Tessman, 1978), particularly in regard to its roots in the affectomotor period of development, its later continued closeness to libidinal excitement with associated images of others (object relatedness rather than identification), and the experiential sense of pleasure (rather than primarily of virtue as with the superego) when maintaining a sense of contact with it.

Nunberg (1932), Bibring (1964), Lampl-de-Groot (1967), and Blos (1974) all emphasize positive libidinal strivings as an impetus to ego-ideal formation, in contrast to the superego. Loomie and associates (1954) connect libidinal excitement, creative work, and the fantasy of the "benign attitude of the patron"; Snyder and Tessman (1965) note a common theme found among a number of creative adolescents and scientists: "the close relationship with an older man who encouraged and sustained the creative one at a crucial period." We spoke of "the search for this kind of relationship as part of the establishment of an identity through identification with an ego ideal" involving the father figure. Jacobson (1954) believes the girl conserves a lasting tendency to the reattachment of her ego ideal to an outside person; that is, her ego ideal becomes reenmeshed in the vicissitudes of her object relations in a way that the boy's does not.

Associated sex differences in ego ideal have been widely noted, though their origins are in dispute. For example, a woman's greater average concern with her relational nexus—that is, the great value she places on "caring" between people—is often central to her ego ideal and may conflict with what she perceives as dominant "male values," especially in the work place. The question of whether identification with an ego ideal involving the father is less conflicted for the woman who admires her father's qualities in relating to others as well as his work effectiveness, than for the woman who does not, will be raised later by way of clinical examples.

The quality of affective engagement in which the ego ideal originates seems later to become assimilated into the woman's ways of loving and working and into her particular vision of happiness. The daughter's valuing in itself the process of the transformation of libidinal excitement may make possible her eventual deidealization of the actual image of the father and of men without a concomitant loss in the potency of the motivating pleasure of their affective interchange per se.

Endless, less fortunate variations do, of course, exist. I will restrict myself to a few examples: If the father has sought early closeness with the daughter, and then suddenly engages in obvious erotic intimacy with someone outside the family (a common sequence when divorce occurs during the oedipal period), then a sense of rejection of her erotic feelings may become, for the daughter, an area of lifelong vulnerability, associated with various defensive reactions. In this case, the witnessing of the intimacy the daughter desires, the fact that she sees it but is not part of it, may "fix" it rigidly as a component of her wishes toward her father, which remain untransformed by the desexualizing influence of opportunities for further affectionate interaction. At another extreme, that of overt incest, the major trauma is usually not in the sexual act, but in the associated deficits and disruptions in the kind of sustaining relationship that both fosters overall development (Tessman and Kaufman, 1969) and aids in the transformation of excitement. In other situations, if a mother in a two-parent home actively interferes with the daughter's love for the father, either through her dominance and his passive acquiescence, or her devaluation of him, or other more subtle forms of inducing either fear or guilt about loving excitement per se, or as directed toward the father, the daughter may be deprived of the full force of her positive feelings (including erotic and endeavor excitement) for him; however, if the father does not reject her, the daughter often preserves these feelings in dormant form until they can flourish in a later love relationship.

I would now like to conjecture further about changes that affect the father-daughter relationship during her development, since these impinge on the fate of both erotic and endeavor excitement. In recent years, stultifying stereotypes of sex roles have loosened sufficiently to begin to allow both fathers and mothers to express to their children a greater range of responses both in feeling and behavior. Young couples now more frequently take for granted that fathers can be tender and nurturing, and that mothers can be the major role models for active competence in dealing with the outside world. Meanwhile, a growing body of research has addressed itself to the possible consequences of the differences in the socialization of sons and daughters (Hoffman, 1972; Maccoby and Jacklin, 1974). Also, interesting patterns of prevalent differences are postulated between mothers' and fathers' modes of interacting with their babies. For example, Brazelton's videotaped observations of parent-infant pairs suggest that whereas mothers, on the average, tend toward "modulated, enveloping, secure, and controlled" interactions, fathers are more "playful, exciting, and physical," displaying rapid shifts from peaks of involvement to valleys of minimal attention (Collins, 1979). Raising the possibility, then, that fathers may create an anlage to be sought out by their children beginning in infancy as exciting, how does this relate to the daughter's development in general, and to the transformation of excitement in particular?

From infancy through little girlhood, the child is prone to excitements varying in their pervasiveness, urgency, object of desire, or types of relief or fulfillment sought. Overly intense excitement can lead to a flooding of the ego, with a consequent sense of helpless dread and the need to invoke defenses against being overwhelmed. In contrast, when excitement is finally experienced as inner desire that can be identified and tolerated within a relationship, and also viewed as within the self, with the hope of at least partial (aim-inhibited) expression and mastery, the excitement may then contribute to ego strength and flexibility, perhaps analogous to the "tolerance for anxiety or depression" (Zetzel, 1949, 1965).

223

The baby learns from the earliest forms of diffuse excitement, indistinguishable at that time from body tensions, the degree to which a mutual adaptation with the mothering person can be expected to relieve or assuage the tension, or, alternately, to lead to prolonged or overwhelming distress. These earliest adaptations also form a nucleus of experience of the self in relation to a supportive or unsupportive environment (Winnicott, 1970). Of course, the child can derive such sensuous foundations of the self from interactions with both parents when both are available and involved. However, what the child most needs in infancy is the mothering person's (though it may be the father who is mothering) empathic alleviation of the tension of infantile needs. However, this need diminishes as the infant matures and begins to internalize the soothing qualities of the mother. The point is that when the foundations of the sensuous self have been soundly established with a mothering person, the quality of excitement directed primarily at the father may have different qualities. Or, as Kahne (1980) has noted, "a strong maternal introject protects her in dealing with the intensity of feelings about a man."

Development of Erotic Excitement

As the little girl progresses in her individuation from the mother, it seems to me that she develops a different kind of excitement, one that involves wishes much more complicated than being soothed or sated. By age 3 or 4 years, focal excitement toward the father appears to include both an active, loving exuberance and passive wishes to adapt to a new kind of mutuality with him. This inner excitement is not to be soothed, for it seeks not only acknowledgment and acceptance by the father as a feeling toward him, but in addition its utilization in a variety of loving collaborations. In her fantasy these collaborations may emphasize erotic, domestic, companionable, or "joint endeavor" adventures, and may be based on a beginning appreciative or hopeful perception of both similarities and differences between father and self. In fantasy the little girl makes her own contribution to the collaborative adventure. The degree to which this is focally experienced in terms of erotic aims may vary greatly among normal daughters. Specifically, the extent to which the momentum for these early loving fantasies about the father stems from her identification with the mother, or from her awareness of inner genital sensations clearly present in some little girls before adolescence (Barnett, 1966; Fraiberg, 1972), is often unclear. Active excitement toward the father is suggested by Edgcumbe and coworkers (1976): "Positive oedipal material showed some girls to be rather active in pursuing their fathers, and this seemed to apply not only to overt behavior, but also to the underlying fantasies and drive aims." For example, rather than the daughter's passively wishing to

224

receive a baby from father, the "material was often in terms of some form of 'making a baby together'." Both the nature of the erotic longings and the envisioned fulfillment in this period of development differ from those of an earlier period of active aims directed at the mother's body. Similarly, the quality of the wish for a baby tends to change as the girl develops. Little girls between the ages of 1 and 2 years may show their first intense interest in mothering infants or dolls (by holding, feeding, kissing them), replicating aspects of the mother-baby relationship. The father is not usually given a role in her interest in babies at this time. However, during the third and fourth years of life, the wish to create a baby specifically with the father is apt to have strongly erotic components, including the fantasy that the baby will bear his beloved imprint, or echo some aspect of his interaction with her (e.g., the fantasy that the baby will laugh in just the way he does). When such focal erotic excitement either is intolerable because of insufficient individuation, or prohibited by mother in the oedipal situation, or is rebuffed directly by the father, phobic or depressive symptoms may take its place. The meaning and resolution of such symptoms will depend on the level of ego integration and the flexibility that is at their source.

Much is known about the child's need to feel secure in receiving her parents' sustaining love as well as their guidance in progressive impulse control. It is this writer's opinion, however, that the little girl's desire to give love actively has been underestimated. The active desire does not mean an absence of passive aims, such as the wish to be lovingly penetrated. (For example, in dollhouse play the little girl may busily prepare a welcome feast while waiting for the doll father to "come barging in my door.") If the father can acknowledge her childish wish to bestow her love freely and seriously on him sufficiently to help her transform it into some kind of affectionate collaboration, he may have contributed to imbuing her later strivings with hope based on experience.

Development of Endeavor Excitement

Turning to the transformation of endeavor excitement, the role of the father in his daughter's developing capacity for pleasure in autonomous mastery and competence is complex. As women increasingly become role models for work outside as well as within the home, daughters increasingly synthesize their identifications in the world of work from characteristics of both parents. However, those aspects of her self-perception that stem from the affective bond with the father are particularly reactive to his role with the daughter. Unlike her erotic desires, the little girl's wishes to bring her developing skills to fruition with increasing autonomy are not primarily gender linked. If she views the father as requiring compliance or dependence as an essential aspect of her femininity, her autonomous competence may come into conflict with her erotic wish to offer herself to him. On the other hand, if the daughter perceives the father as valuing only her achievements and not her love, she may pursue achievements consonant with his values, yet never feel accepted by him. Work competence does not assuage a sense of oedipal failure.

The daughter's internalization of trust in her own capacities begins during the explorations of her toddlerhood, but is then still closely tied to the presence of the adult, perceived as powerfully protective and still only partly differentiated from the self. During this initial separation-individuation phase, the father's interest and care not only support the daughter's initial strivings toward autonomy and independence by forming a bedrock of secure identity away from the mother, but also represent for the daughter an important early experience of "differentness" (male instead of female) from the mother and the self. This helps her to differentiate her own identity from that of the mother and to expand her eventual choice of the adult traits and behaviors with which she can identify. Although the toddler daughter may require a certain amount of tender nurturing from the father in order to be able to utilize his encouragement of mastery or independence, she is also apt to look to him for both special caring and protective powers in the face of the unfamiliar or threatening.

Why little girls under 5 years of age frequently picture their fathers as more exciting, adventuresome (and at times frightening) links to the outside world than their mothers is not entirely clear. Of course, fathers have traditionally been considered as having a more active role than mothers in relation to the world outside home, with positions of power and importance that make them become representatives of initiative toward the outside world. Identification with these aspects of the father is not only socially rewarding for children of both sexes, but also ego strengthening in the sense that they lead to the effective use of one's inner resources rather than to retreat or manipulation through helplessness. However, this kind of explanation appears insufficient for those dual-career families in which mothers become role models for daughters in work, yet fathers do not seem to lose their special excitement as carriers of adventure. If recent shifts in sex-role expectations eventuate in women's greater self-acceptance of their excitement about developing independent capabilities, this may translate itself into greater average maternal support and enjoyment of such qualities in their daughters. If women change in this way, it will be interesting to see if this issue becomes less gender linked in the eyes of the daughter.

The father's involvement in the daughter's autonomous capabilities continues to be important in later childhood and adolescence. More salient than a distant pride in her achievement is his willingness to involve himself in the process. Such involvement provides a viable foundation for a continued good relationship during adolescence, when the more powerful force of sexuality and the struggle to affirm a more separate identity necessitate a greater distance between them in other areas. Women who emphasize their father's contribution to their enthusiasm in work usually stress the following aspects of their relationship: his treatment of her as an interesting person in her own right (this is often put in nonsexist terms such as "he didn't see me as just a girl"); his trust in her developing autonomous capacities during joint endeavors; his own capacity for excitement or enthusiasm about discovery in work or play; his invitation to her to participate in areas of mastery with him; and the emulated quality of his relationship to others, such as colleagues or friends, associated with work in the outside world. The particular area of interest developed by the daughter is, however, not necessarily shared by the father. Young women, for instance, are apt to draw on their experience of such an encouraging affective engagement involving initiative and mastery in work in order to seek out a mentor who might also appreciate these qualities, but in a quite different area of interest.

The transformation of endeavor excitement into later vitality in work optimally requires from the father something different than the transformation of erotic excitement into later passion in love. His view that her capabilities may not be gender linked is strengthening to her in the former, whereas an appreciation of her femininity is involved in the latter. Nevertheless, there are many connections between the two. For example, the wish to give herself erotically to the man can be expressed to some extent in an aim-inhibited and acceptable way if she is able to contribute positively to his or their mutual endeavors. Conversely, if he praises her skills, but keeps himself greatly distant, her achievements may feel barren to her, as though the essence of herself has been rejected. In later life, she, in turn, may need to disentangle these two types of satisfactions sufficiently in order to value appropriately her autonomous endeavors.

The Father-Daughter Dyad: Father's Side

Let us now turn to the response of the father. By the time a daughter is 3 or 4 years old, the father often becomes aware, with a greater or lesser degree of consciousness, that she is expressing loving excitement, accompanied by considerable affect and various wishful fantasies of emotional intimacy or joint endeavors with him. This puts the father in the position of having to respond to this excitement with whatever mixture of enjoyment and acceptance, rebuff and withdrawal, disparagement or overstimulation it kindles in him. His responses involve specifically the balance of his needs and feelings toward this daughter, and generally the whole gamut of his orientations toward desire and excitement, with their attendant emotionality; toward self-control and autonomy; toward emotional demands directed toward him; and so on. Thus the combination of his character structure and the specific meaning of his daughter to him will determine his response. For our purposes we disregard here such complications as the father's preference for another daughter, rivalry with the daughter for her mother's (his wife's) care, and negative feelings transferred from childhood relationships with his own siblings, in order to focus on interferences in the process itself of assimilating excitement in the relationship with the daughter.

Frequently aspects of issues that were laid to rest when the father left his own mother are reinvoked by his daughter's open, wholehearted interest in him. Sometimes, because the daughter is (in a more aim-inhibited way than his wife) also an oedipal object for the father without threatening maternal qualities, she may fall heir to the father's positive oedipal strivings, evoking a special reserve of tender pleasure in him. Then she is lucky. In other instances, problems associated with either his own identification or his early object relations prevent or distort the positive feelings. The identification issue—the father's general attitude toward the direct emotional engagement his daughter seeks with him—stems partly from the resolution of his own early identifications, as they relate to his sexual identity. As Miller (1973) has noted:

Psychoanalysts have said that a boy must first renounce early identification with mother, and then, later renounce sexual attraction to her. He must renounce not only the person, but the process in which she is engaged as well. A male baby is supposed to give up identification with certain ideas, e.g., passivity. He is encouraged to give up identification with those processes, e.g., the care of human life, which women are doing. . . . Underneath it all runs the interdiction of another even more basic process, which seems the most frightening prospect of all: close and direct emotional engagement with another human being who is different—and female. The boy is encouraged to turn to the world of men, where processes are structured to limit direct emotional involvement with anybody, male or female.

Such a favored resolution of a man's own identification conflicts may have the result that he will be more comfortable with his daughter's assertiveness and autonomy than with her loving emotionality. In such cases, he may, in fact, these days, be in favor of "women's liberation," except for their liberation to love him.

Regarding the object-relations issue: A father's reluctance about his daughter's excitement may be based on the particular kind of stimulation he has experienced in relation to his mother. Different sources of his reluctance will impinge differently on his daughter. For example, some inhibitions are based on the need to avoid being drawn into an oedipal excitement that is reminiscent of his experience with a seductive or over-stimulating mother and is associated with anxiety or guilt. In this case his need to affirm his autonomy or to control the emotional distance in re-gard to her may be great, but the daughter will have the benefit of feeling the bond as libidinous in some way. In this case, sometimes the defenses against intimacy do not become apparent until her adolescence, with its undisguised sexuality, makes its appearance. However, if, instead, the father's withdrawal from the daughter's wishes has been necessary in order to protect himself from experiencing vulnerability toward the image of a mother whom he has felt as pervasively unavailable, invasive, or de-structive to him, then his daughter is more apt to feel that he has a deep aversion to her excitement, a rejection that is more difficult for her to work through.

Mother-Daughter Dyad:
Relevance to Father-Daughter Relationship

Conversely, for the daughter, the degree to which her father's response is central to her total development will depend on the soundness of her relationship to her mother. For example, in the case of Wendy S. (to follow), the positive bond with father, superimposed on a reliable re-lationship with her mother and a lively love between her parents, was the bonus that led to her pleasurable vitality in working and relating. In con-trast, where sensuous interplay and mutuality have been lacking with the mother, perhaps because of the mother's own limitations in tolerating inner excitement, either the girl may react with deep-seated defenses against intimacy with the father (because the experience of intimacy has become dangerous in itself), or, in other father-daughter dyads, his re-sponse to her loving excitement may become more than usually crucial as the necessary force underlying her capacity for self-acceptance and ardor in adult life. He becomes essential to show her that happiness can exist. Again, it is the process of transforming excitement in itself (in such cases perceived as possible with fathers and not with mothers) which becomes internalized when the father-daughter relationship is effective in this way and contributes to her ego's strength and flexibility.

The daughter may utilize various enduring personality traits quite differently in accordance with the particular object relationship in which she is involved. To present one such pattern, the daughter may develop in childhood a kind of "vigilant empathy," which may function "in the service of defense" with the mother, and "in the service of pleasure" with the father. That is, if the girl perceives that the mother cannot welcome her and her childish wishes, she responds by denying, negating, or withholding such wishes from her, appearing quite self-sufficient while staying attuned to what she perceives or fantasizes the mother needs from her in order to stay as intact as possible. The need to "repair" the mother in this way (a common preoccupation for the children of depressed or otherwise disturbed mothers) is accompanied with more dread than pleasure, and the daughter's chance for a fulfilling life may be correlated with the degree to which she can separate herself, with the help of the father, from depending on this mother-daughter interaction. With the father, in contrast, the empathy functions to heighten her sense of freedom and pleasure in their emotional engagement with each other, and is accompanied by the feeling of happiness rather than dread. Although such a woman may be unusually vulnerable to rejection of her erotic passion, once she has more or less freed herself of earlier infantile longings, she is not apt to underestimate its role in her happiness. A brief example follows.

Clinical Example: Nicole G.
Nicole G.'s mother had suffered from a chronic, affectless depression with paranoid components, but her ideologically vigorous, exciting, playful father had maintained his interest in the child after a divorce when Nicole was 4 years old. Nicole learned early and habitually to eliminate all affect or excitement in interactions with her mother, with whom she became competent, self-sufficient, and carefully superficial in her communications. She reserved for visits with father her joyous excitement, intellectual curiosity, and pleasure in communication. As a vibrant, empathic adult with exceptional ability to understand and accept the consequences of her own and others' impulses, Nicole experienced a never-ending sense of delight and surprise at the mutually responsive interchange with her second husband. Within their strongly libidinous bond was also room for playful and aggressive components. In many ways her first bad marriage recapitulated her relationship with her mother, the second excellent marriage the relationship with her father. Lovemaking with her second husband was often accompanied by both the thought and affect of, "I feel so happy and in love with him." This tended to have

two components: his ability to receive her love, and her freedom to respond to his. One of her pleasures with him was to know him well enough to anticipate and fit herself in an erotic, playful fashion to his desires, in a way that would be as close as possible to what he wanted. For example, on his birthday she surprised him with a series of planned events that included a visit to an ethnic bar reminiscent of his childhood, with a ribald directness of interactions; a visit to a bookstore with an hour to choose an extra gift (this was a humorous, indulgent, aggressive-teasing gesture about his frustrating difficulty in making decisions within an hour, as well as support for his academic interests, which sometimes absorbed him without her); an intermission at home during which he could discover the semipornographic love poetry she had written and put under his pillow; and an evening at an elegant restaurant, appropriate for their identity as the young, successful professional adults that they were. In effect, her message was that she understood, accepted, and liked interacting (most of the time) with all the conflicting aspects of his nature. His enthusiastic response to her wish to give freely to him, as well as his initiative in showing he desired and cared about her, always touched her. One meaning of this had to do with her never-ending sense of pleasure at the contrast between his responsiveness and the unresponsiveness of her mother. That is, nothing she could have done or given of herself could ever make the mother happy or responsive to her. Another meaning lay in its evoking memories of her father, whose initiative and enthusiasm, in spite of certain insecurities she had about it, gave her the possibility of a happier kind of expectation.

For Nicole, the degree of abandon to sexual desire and excitement was a most sensitive barometer of perceived object relations. For example, her desire dropped instantly when she perceived in her husband transitory boredom or childish dependence, reminiscent of her mother, while it rose freely in response to his more usual initiative. The intricate association between echoes of the father (as well as consciously heightened essential differences) and her erotic responsiveness are too complex to include in this chapter. Although Nicole's depth of professional commitment and giftedness paralleled her investment in marriage, her work never had such power to move her.

The way in which adult love (e.g., marriage) can release the woman from remnant attachment to the father by finally sweeping away the love yearnings from the past will not be discussed in this chapter. What is significant here is that because of the deficits in the mother's relationship to Nicole, the involvement of the father was especially crucial for her rich adult development.

Clinical Example: Wendy S.

In contrast, Wendy S., a married mother, whom I discuss to exemplify a father's relation to ego ideal, began development with the benefit of a nurturing mother and a lively love between her parents.* As she put it, "I remember mother and father having fun together, her giggling and his chasing her around the house, around the dining room table. I remember only one real fight. My father was effective in communication, both his affection and anger were predictable." In addition, her own zestful relationship to the father included a sense of their special appreciation of one another revolving around the following: his support of her individuation and trust in her growing capacities; his acknowledgment and sensitive response to her libidinal wishes; their shared interests; and her love of the quality of his character per se. In adult life Mrs. S. showed an ego ideal connected with the quest for affects once shared with the father. This was in evidence not only in the refreshing quality of her emotionally direct interpersonal relations (where she too was "effective in communication"), but also in her career functioning, where her competence and leadership qualities were recognized in ways that led to unusually rapid promotions. Mother-daughter conflicts for Wendy S. did not gather momentum until adolescence, after father's death traumatized both mother and daughter.

During the initial interview Mrs. S. said: "People have always told me, 'you have something special to offer,' " but that her mother could never recognize this although her father did. She described father as having "a fine sense of humor and a lot of energy—and yet he was able to understand what people needed. Like on the first day of school, he packed a stick of gum in my pocketbook, and then I was able to be on my way. It was like he added a friendly touch to each event." One catches a glimpse of father's supporting her first major separation from home and mother. Holding onto the symbolic nurturance of the stick of gum, she could go confidently without holding onto an adult. Putting his "stick in her pocketbook" seems a charming version (in her fantasy or his action or both) of his adding "a friendly touch to each event" remembered by her.

In many ways she described her internalization of her father's trust in her autonomy. One day in therapy she talked of an argument with an indecisive colleague about an upcoming decision. She needed his agreement before action could be taken. She had the thought: "When I was on my own I could always make decisions because my father really trusted me." For example, after telling Wendy she could run the boat they were

---

*More detailed verbatim material from a period of therapy with Wendy S. has been previously published in *Children of Parting Parents* (Tessman, 1978).

renting one day and perceiving a wary friend's reluctance about getting in if the child was going to be in charge, her father insisted she be allowed to carry through rather than placate the friend. Another example: "My father and I loved kite flying; he would teach me tricks, but then let me do it myself. I once won a kite-flying contest when I was 7 or 8. It's not just that I wanted to do it on my own, but also that he let me. He had a certain trust and confidence that I've thought of as part of myself—that I don't seem to need that constant checking back about what people think . . . like at work, people have asked me how come I can keep coping under the stress of everybody else's opinion being divided." Having internalized the trust in her autonomy, she relates it to her freedom from the need for constant approval from others, a need from which many women suffer.

Mrs. S. also made clear that her father acknowledged and responded caringly to her disguised communications of libidinal excitement. She generally described him, unlike her mother, as having "a facility with all things at once, patience and a high tolerance for confusion." She was helped to tolerate her own erotic wishes by his responding to them as valid and nonthreatening, rather than by his needing to control or "organize" her at such moments. Anxiety about being disorganized by one's erotic sensations occurs not only because of their emotional power (which can lead in either regressive or progressive directions), but also because they are organized according to libidinal rather than secondary process logic. Mrs. S.'s father seemed comfortably cognizant of both: She recalls a variety of "elaborate games when I was very little, probably to get his attention away from others" when she was allowed to play in his office. She would experience the tension in either her own body (in bathroom games) or those of her dolls as a yearning for his attention. For example, she repeatedly locked herself in the bathroom "by mistake," waiting excitedly for him to come and take the hinges off and be the one to open her "door," knowing "he never left me long alone like that in there." She remembered the wish to be chased, like her mother, and to have him use his instruments on her. At times he interrupted his work to fix her dolls: When the dolls "lost their head" (associated for her with libidinal excitement replacing rational thinking), they seemed to have priority over work, as though he sensed that at such moments she needed his direct helpful intervention more than her "autonomy." However, in other interactions with him, she learned impulse control ("being quiet") as an aspect of reciprocity: "Then every night I would be on his lap while I listened to the news and practiced being quiet. But I knew he would read me a story after."

She states: "I think he would have liked the person I am. He is in his absence still an incredibly important part of my life. So much of who I am developed from him. It's funny, after my hour a few weeks ago I left feeling that I had developed a kind of aggressive survival instinct in regard to my brothers and sisters and coping with everything at home when mother needed me to do that after he died. Today, with the things we've said about my father, I feel different about myself, when I see how it came from him too, how it's a continuation of one of his strengths."

Mrs. S. makes clear that the self-esteem associated with aspects of her self-image changes in accordance with her awareness of the associated identification figures. She states she can value herself more (at that moment in therapy) when she feels identified with the father in a shared ego ideal. Such a shift in self-esteem is the crucial reason to explore, at different points in therapy, the shifting relationship between images of the self and parents. The unconscious aspects of such identifications may contain either valued or despised components of the self, but often they cannot be either evaluated realistically or given up until the identificatory links become clear.

In this brief summary the complexities of Mrs. S.'s ego ideal as related to father will not be traced further, except for the following consideration: Wendy S.'s most piquant conflict at work was between her own inclination for autonomy and leadership (evoking modes of identification with father), which, however, left her feeling "mentorless" (as she had been left fatherless after his death), and her desire for an enjoyable collaborative relationship in which she was sought out by others (evoking modes of the object relation with father). Nevertheless, she comfortably integrated in both modes the high value she placed on caring human relationships, which were mentioned previously as a common priority in the female ego ideal. She did not feel pressured, as many women do, to identify with a "male model" of efficiency or logic, necessitating the extrusion of personal compassionate responses in order to maintain efficiency or to gain the "respect" of men as an equal. It would be intriguing to inquire how frequently the seeds of such integration—for a woman— lie, as in Wendy S.'s case, in the character of the father who catalyzes her ego ideal. However, the meaning and consequence of prevalent sex differences in ego ideal in our culture is another topic.

Relationship to Father During Adult Development

During adult life many women do not repress their childhood love for their fathers as fully as do men for their mothers. This may be related to the following: The relationship to mother reactivates for both sons and daughters more archaic wishes and regressive ego modes than does the relationship to father. Hence for men, erotic wishes toward mother may remain closely linked to issues of dependency and control or, ultimately, to the psychic danger of a passive merger. For women, once individuation from the mother has proceeded, a maternal introject can be relied on and excitement can be tolerated, and the erotic longings for their father are more apt to remain linked to the progressive forces in their love of life.

Adult development confronts the daughter with several necessary changes in relation to her love of her father. First, she needs sufficient erotic detachment to make a free choice for passionate loving and then, later in life, for the deepening of her relationship to her partner in accordance with both the reality of the other and the limits of the self. Some deidealization of the person of the father is usually a necessary component, but those aspects of the ego ideal based on the process of affective interchange in the transformation of excitement can now be experienced by her either as sexual passion or as deep commitment to an endeavor in the world of work.

The Contribution of Analysis or Therapy

A final note about women lacking the sustained experience of a loving father: Sometimes a good psychoanalysis or therapy introduces the tolerance for the intensity of feelings of love or the encouragement for autonomy, which is inherent in a spirit of adventure and discovery toward inner psychic reality and which was either not provided in the father-daughter relationship or traumatically disrupted before the end of the oedipal period. In this context the woman may experience feelings of love for the analyst especially vividly, and her renunciation of them follows a different course than the more usual resolution of father transference. Frustrations of the unrequited feelings of love occur for her in the area both of being loved and of giving love. That is, the awareness that in this relationship she can do nothing to contribute to his pleasure or happiness may be felt as a particularly painful disappointment.

An additional complication is that as the incest taboo in the literal sense does not exist in the analytic situation when it is not primarily transferred from the childhood family configuration (e.g., when a father has been absent), the woman must renounce the erotic components of love for the therapist or analyst in a different way. That is, they are renounced because of the reality that they are not reciprocated (i.e., they are rejected), rather than on the basis of guilt in the oedipal situation or need to identify with the mother. Both the wishes and their rejection are apt to be less fully repressed than impulses associated with taboo. In addition, the adult rather than infantile nature of the erotic longings, when finally developed in their full intensity—associated with an advanced stage of autonomous identity and experienced in the context of a relationship that supports inner awareness—is a further difference from the usual father-daughter erotic undercurrents. In order to assimilate and constructively transform these feelings, the woman must either develop sustained tolerance for extreme inner love tension—a tolerance which is, in fact, strengthened by the analysis or therapy—or end the analysis at the appropriate time, with the ability to involve herself deeply and happily in living, but with such feelings still partially unresolved. In some cases, the analyst simply remains in her mind as a valued and loved figure, and in addition she internalizes many aspects of their interaction. A lively sense of gratitude may also remain tied to her awareness of what he has made possible for her in life. In other cases, the continued emotional development of adulthood—for example, the resurgence of powerful sexual feelings in late midlife, as described by Rubin (1979); or a renewed self-awareness following an at least partially gratifying and strengthening negotiation of major life issues, such as childrearing or career development; or the necessary libidinal disengagement from her children as they become adolescent—may intermittently reawaken directly erotic components of such feelings of love, and their painful renunciation becomes a repeated life task, even after earlier idealizations of the analyst have been resolved. Much as love for the father is normally never totally repressed by many women, for the women discussed above, some resonance of love for the therapist or analyst remains as a never laid-to-rest vibrato in their other love relationships.

Conclusions

The point of view presented here involves a shift of emphasis, rather than of content, in the usual portrayal of the oedipal period as essentially characterized by the little girl's romantic and sexual wishes for an exclusive relationship with the father, accompanied by intensified rivalry or hatred toward the mother. The difference in emphasis is focused on two aspects: (1) the nature of the excitement; and (2) the process of resolution of the oedipal desires.

Nature of the Excitement

It is postulated that the father is the focus of two kinds of excitement in the little girl, each having its own timing and pattern of development, though they are interrelated in important ways. One kind is the well-known erotic excitement, with its associated fantasies of love, which flourishes during the oedipal period. Clinically, stirrings of inner-genital sensations, as an impetus to erotic fantasies, are evident in some, but not all, little girls during the oedipal period, and the interpersonal factors associated with their distinct appearance are not yet clinically clear. Such inner-genital sensations may have different consequences (in sensation imagery, mood states, need for tension discharge) for the adolescent, the young adult, and the woman in late midlife. Empirically, the little girl does not "normally" disengage from her emotional or sensuous closeness to the mother during the oedipal years if their relationship has been sound and not overly restrictive or depriving up until this time. Erotic wishes toward the father more often coexist with, rather than replace, gratification with the mother at this time. Clinically, rivalrous envy of the mother more often gathers intensity in adolescence, pushed not only by now clear sexual forces, but also by the need for more definitive individuation from her.

In erotic excitement, the wish to give love may be as strong a component of the girl's fantasied fulfillment as the wish to be loved by the father. However, the quality of the wish to give erotic love will change throughout her life. For example, the mature woman, whose sexual experience and pregnancies have "increased her venous bed capacity" (Sherfey, 1966), while her emotional adult development in identity and object relations has proceeded, may experience (in prolonged pelvic vasocongestion) a physiologically mirrored depth and fullness of passionate longing in relation to a beloved, unknown to the little girl, adolescent, or young adult.

The second kind of excitement discussed is endeavor excitement, which begins during the period of individuation, prior to the oedipal period. The exuberance of the gleefully careening toddler, whose new motility has extended her accessible world, heralds the dawn of this new excitement. Unlike erotic excitement, it is not gender linked, but has to do with the anlage for autonomy, with growing freedom to experiment with one's skills. It is, however, linked to erotic wishes in many ways. Housed in a female body, its sensations, its imagery, and the impact of its assimilation will be different than for a boy. In addition, the degree to which it can be integrated into the father's view of the feminine may specifically affect the degree to which it will enhance or conflict with erotic desire. In adult life, endeavor excitement is more apt to be transformed into components of pleasurable identification with aspects of the father in ways of working; erotic excitement is more apt to be transformed into pleasurable object relations in ways of loving.

The daughter's sensitivity to the father's response to both kinds of excitement is probably heightened during the oedipal period and is associated with a new capacity both for rich fantasy and for identification with the feelings of others. Loss of relationship to the father during the oedipal period may "fix" the romantic fantasies of the wishes for interaction (Tessman, 1978) without the desexualizing influences of the later reality testing in the more usual father-daughter relationship.

Process of Resolution of Oedipal Desires

The experiencing and resolving of oedipal desires has a particular impact on the ego in addition to affecting object relations. The necessary shift in object relations involves the familiar renunciation by the little girl of the father as her beloved, and the acceptance of the mother both as her primary identification figure and as a continued source of gratifying supportive closeness. However, in addition, the resolution of oedipal desires optimally involves the internalization of an ego capacity for the transformation of excitement itself. The contribution of the father in this process revolves around his simultaneous role as object of her excitement and model in its transformation. If the daughter internalizes the ego capacity for transforming excitement in a way that is not only tolerable (e.g., developing capacity to delay impulse discharge), but also pleasurable through a vibrant and tender affective engagement with her father, then her knowledge of that potential happiness may remain as a guiding force in her later work and loves.

III

Developmental Perspectives: The Later Phases

In this section, the authors examine the relations between fathers and their children during later phases of the life cycle. The interchanges during these periods and the problems they pose will tend to be somewhat more familiar to many readers: the father's tutelage during middle childhood; the proverbial tempestuousness of the adolescent doing moral battle with his once idealized "old man"; the pure pleasure of a grandfather's delight in young children for whose care he does not have to assume a primary parent's absolute responsibility.

Less obvious is the adult's progression through the life cycle. Its course is less dramatic perhaps than the young child's rapid early growth. Nonetheless, grown men continue to grow and change, passing from youth to middle age and to senescence and death. Moreover, at each adult developmental juncture, a father will be influenced by his children. He will juxtapose their shifting and often urgent demands with the equally difficult and pressing tasks of his unfolding maturity; and he will comprehend them according to both the wisdom and the limits inherent in his particular place in the generational cycle.

In the first of these chapters, John Munder Ross pursues further his developmental line for paternal identity. His accent here is on the latency boy's rapprochement with the erstwhile rival of his Oedipus complex, and on the use he makes of "good enough fathering" to fashion his own sense of himself as a nurturing male and future father. In the process the boy is helped to learn more about the world in which he as an adult will have to make his way. In our culture, busy with work outside the home, too many men deprive themselves and their sons of this mutually enriching experience.

Ross's view tends to contrast somewhat with that of Charles Sarnoff, author of the next chapter. Sarnoff brings to this volume his theory of "the structure of latency," wherein middle childhood is characterized by externalization, symbolization, and the use of fantasy to express what have become the child's forbidden and, indeed, unconscious wishes and ideas.

In this scheme of things, the father is seen to figure as the purveyor of a boy's pragmatic, instrumental masculinity. Fathers are viewed as basically realists and providers, whereas mothers are believed to enfold their families with a woman's less purposeful, emotional receptivity. Where the distribution of such roles is not clearly defined, Sarnoff believes, boys and girls suffer cognitively, as well as in the crystallization of sexual identity.

Next, Aaron Esman, an analyst conversant with adolescence, turns to the scrutiny of fathers and teenaged sons. He outlines and illustrates the dialectics of a boy's early idealization of and subsequent rebellion against his father, a progression which tends to recapitulate the earliest years of a boy's development. Problems along the way, Esman demonstrates, can have a profound impact on the adolescent's sexual identity and on his choice of profession.

The following chapter is a revised and abridged version of Alan Gurwitt's groundbreaking paper on the analysis of a prospective father. In it, Gurwitt, one of the volume's editors, elaborates a specific sequence for the unfolding of paternity in young adulthood, one that resonates with the conflicting, often agonizing legacies of childhood.

Herzog, in a study of fathers whose children were born prematurely, pursues a similar theme. Taking Gurwitt's progression as a starting point and referring to Kestenberg and her collaborators' and to Ross's previous work on the early phases of caretaking in males, he demonstrates the importance of completing this second evolution of paternal identity. Precipitated into fatherhood before their time, many men may fail to embrace their proper place as providers and as figures ancillary to, rather than competitive with, a mother's role as essential caretaker for her infant. This perspective, then, challenges some current notions to the effect that men can tend young infants "as well as" women, or that there is "no difference between mothers and fathers" (see also Chap. 6).

In the next chapter, Colarusso and Nemiroff, psychoanalysts based in La Jolla, California, overview the interactions taking place between middle-aged fathers and, for the most part, their adolescent sons and daughters. The authors have long been students of the life span in a tradition established by others before them, most notably Erikson in 1950 and Linden and Courtney in 1953.

Stanley Cath, another of the volume's editors, then presents some of the vicissitudes of man's grandparenthood. He demonstrates how the revitalizing impact of the little child varies according to a particular individual's adaptation to old age.

It is fitting to conclude this section on the later developmental phases with Stanley Cath's and James Herzog's chapter on the dying and death of fathers. Suffering from their ambivalence toward fathers, growing children

240

(sons especially) will greet a father's death with great conflict. Their reactions to the loss will vary, Cath and Herzog demonstrate in their clinical material, depending on a host of factors. Some of these include the history of the particular child-father relationship, the other available persons in the surviving child's life, and the son's own generational status— whether he is himself a father or not.

15

Mentorship in Middle Childhood

John Munder Ross

Earlier I summarized a boy's progression toward a paternal identity from infancy through the climactic oedipal era. That line of development continues, however, extending through the entire life cycle. Of crucial importance in this evolution is the so-called latency period, a time when cognitive advances and the father's actual mentorship permit a boy to glimpse the facts of life.

The Riddle of the Sphinx

Just how and when does a boy come to comprehend what it means to father a child? As a boy's general ego development proceeds, his intellectual abilities, increasingly liberated from need and conflict, enable him, in Piaget's terms, to discover laws of causality for occurrences evident in the world. It is a child's emerging capacity for concrete operations that allows him to grasp some rudimentary facts about the reproductive process and to glimpse at least momentarily the chain of events that connects these elements.

The timetable is variable and debated among psychologists. But empirically I have found that boy between 6 and 7 years of age, who are now freed from many of the preemptive impulses and anxieties that still dominate their younger brothers, begin solving the "Riddle of the Sphinx." A middle-class, relatively savvy 6-year-old in our culture intuits that father and mother, male and female, conjoin in some way to produce offspring. He too, as a male, will one day participate in a sexual relationship with a woman whereby children are reproduced and tended, though, of course, the personal knowledge conveyed by ejaculation eludes his ken.

This, like Chapter 12, is based on a section of a paper, "Toward fatherhood: The epigenesis of paternal identity during a boy's first decade," which first appeared in the *International Review of Psychoanalysis* 4:327–347, 1977. Again references should be made to Chapters 1 and 2.

The work for this chapter was in part funded by the U.S. Department of Health and Human Services, Grant No. MH 05816, sponsored by the Department of Psychiatry, Downstate Medical Center.

The trouble is, such knowledge remains vulnerable to the kind of lapses and splits in awareness which, as Freud (1927) pointed out, may characterize even an adult man's perception of the facts of life, in particular of anatomical differences. The degree to which contemporary children merely parrot the knowledge fed to them by sophisticated, liberal elders, parents and teachers, without integrating it to pertain to themselves and those close to them, also remains uncertain. How much children want to know what they are told and how liable unwanted, burdensome facts are to distortion or repression, are still more elusive questions. Of course, even an understanding of "lovemaking" may serve other ends, more associated with the *machismo* and bravado typical of boys this age.

Clinical Example: Simon

Tough-talking 6-year-old Simon is the son of an aggressive businessman to whom he is very much attached. He is noted by teachers and parents for his "smart, hep" style, his braggadocio, and his unabashed striving for power. He is not, they say, among the more gentle and tender boys in his class. And yet:

JMR: [Showing a picture of a mother bear with her baby] How's she get that baby, do you think?

Simon: The doctor pulled her out of the uterus. How else, *dummy*? The vagina, it came out of! . . .

JMR: And how did it get in the vagina, do you know? How was it made?

Simon: They first . . . the father that has sperms . . . and the girl that has eggs . . . [Rapidly] I have a book all about being born, do you know that?

JMR: You do? So it tells . . .

Simon: [Interrupting] So when the sperm's alive and it turns into an egg, it moves over to the uterus when it's *black* [sic]! The baby moves over, rolls overboard! . . . You see there's a cord attached to your body button that will grow and live. . . . And then she is starting moving in the mother's body. . . . So, she felt it. Right?

JMR: Right.

Simon: And then she knew that a baby would come out soon. . . . [Thumps his abdomen]

JMR: Because she felt the baby move?

Simon: Yep. . . . And then!! You know what happened? [All is said with an air of great authority and drama.]

JMR: What happened then?

Simon: The doctor pulled the baby out of her vagina!

JMR: How do you think it feels to have the baby inside, do you think?

Simon: I don't know, but *she* does! Dummy! She's a girl!

JMR: Right. How does it feel to have a baby come out?

Simon: Well, she wouldn't even see it. 'Cause she would be asleep. . . . *Kook!* That's what you have to do, to be *asleep*, to pull a *baby* out from a *vagina!*

JMR: How does it feel to hold that baby then? How do you think she feels?

Simon: She feels happy. . . .

JMR: Why does she feel happy?

Simon: Ha, ha, ha!!! That's a *simple* question! [Very loudly] 'Cause she has a
new baby! Yeah! . . .

JMR: And that makes her feel happy, and what else?

Simon: What else? And what else?! Except *love*!

JMR: Love. . . . Okay, let me ask you: So who can have babies then?

Simon: Only girls can but [quickly, definitely] the father has to help, and the girl
has to be turned over sideways, and then, you see, the father sticks the penis
into the vagina, and the sperm starts coming out into the mother's vagina! . . .

JMR: How would he feel if he didn't have any role in making the baby?

Simon: Sad.

JMR: Sad? Why?

Simon: 'Cause . . . no baby would come out of her! . . .

JMR: Shall we see the next picture?

Simon: Hold on a second! I know how dogs were born too. The same way! They
need sperm seeds. . . .

JMR: Right. So that the man has . . .

Simon: And also chickens! And also things like that. [Later, he looks at a picture
showing a mother and father, an older brother and sister on an outing with a
new baby. When asked to describe the brother's and sister's states of mind, he
says they feel "fine." [Then Simon adds:] But, except they're mad too, 'cause
they get a better, 'cause they [points to the parents] own the baby and they
don't. [He points to children and frowns. Then he adds triumphantly:] 'Cause
if she gets a baby, then they [the children] will also own one and they
[parents] won't.

JMR: Huh? And the parents won't?

Simon: And I know what happens. When they're 18, they can't have any kids.
You're too old to have kids, dummy!

JMR: At 18 you're too old?

Simon: Yeah, when you're 80. . . . I think when they are grown-ups, these kids
will be their father.

JMR: Uh huh. . . .

Simon: And so their kids will be their father to the kids! . . . When he [the
brother] is a grown-up, the baby would be a kid. . . . And he would own
the kid. [Starts to turn pages again] . . . [Minutes later he looks at a picture of the
brother bear holding the baby, remarking:] He's fat . . . [Simon muses
for a moment] . . . He's going to grow up when he's a father . . . and take a
nap in the park!

In closing Simon endows the baby with "special spider powers,"
speaks of his wish to own a "baby leopard cub," and then describes the
feline pet already in his possession, a cat named by him "Black Power."

As Simon implies, being a "father" means to "grow up," although he
remains unclear as to whether, so to speak, the "poppa chicken" or his
"egg" comes first. Nor is he so certain, it seems, that such responsibility
will be altogether welcome—not without a moment's respite and regression.

No oedipal or postoedipal boy actually achieves the paternal identity
expressed in his "masculine" ideal (Freud, 1923a). A little boy is still, after
all, a child. As a child, he is excluded from the bedroom, from adulthood,
and from acts of creation for which his body is not yet prepared. Com-

pared with his parents, no matter how attentively they applaud his gestures at manhood, biologically a son *is* inadequate and infertile, and he must discover other modes of being or feeling strong and productive. Otherwise his only recourse would be that regressive, passive, and at the same time mysterious and powerful "nap in the park." When one is *asleep*, anything can happen!

Productivity and Learning in Middle Childhood

One such mode of productivity may be found in the creative play that typically occupies postoedipal boys and which, in most societies, ushers in their status as schoolboys, rather than preschoolers. Much of boyish play bespeaks phallic, intrusive contours and strivings, as Erikson has demonstrated. At the same time, however, certain of a boy's activities at this stage hearken back to his imitation of his mother's domestic, feminine activities. And still other creations, both plastic and dramatic, betray what appear to be transparent bisexual or ambisexual motives. In fact, they express exactly that union of identifications with both father and mother which Freud hypothesized in 1923 (see Chap. 1).

Play Styles

By 7 or 8 years of age at the latest, most boys have focused on gunplay, building of towers, and other activities associated with phallic, oedipal ambitions. But they also have begun to construct castles presided over by kings who sire royal families. They pirate and pilot rather womblike boats. Perhaps they manage hotels in which food and drink are served. And they play doctor. In many of these games, moreover, girls are invited to join and are active themselves as co-workers and playmates. And in many of their productions, intrusive, "inclusive," and inceptive forms and modalities are interwoven.

Sometimes, preoccupied with the world he has helped to create, a boy will "drift away," "give up the helm." When he does so, enacting the role of patient or simply riding in his buccaneer's galleon, he may be seen to reveal the kind of passivity that is a response to failure, temporary though it may be. He may be acknowledging, wordlessly, the sense of littleness and insignificance of which children of this age may be made all too aware.

Fantasies of Parthenogenesis

Confronted by the futility of his generative ambitions, a postoedipal boy, I conjecture, may be seen to embark on a regression in the service of the ego, as art historian and analyst Ernst Kris (1952) once put it in describing the creative process. In part, this is a defensive measure. But it is also age-appropriate and adaptive, both springing from and, in turn, fostering progress in other realms, specifically in a boy's ability to know and to act on an ever-widening environment. Thwarted in his wish to produce like his mother, a son further finds himself unable to possess her, or indeed to be productive in the manner of his father. Denied erotic entree as well as the privileges of parenthood, a little boy may then decide unconsciously to be his own inseminator, his own parents, and, more regressively, his own child. Thus a fantasy of parthenogenesis may be born, expressing a boy's inability to accept his generational status and, with it, his delayed generativity.

Less tolerable at this stage, nonetheless, a procreative fantasy such as this has become repressible. Ideally, wishes to produce babies and to be as nurturing as the idealized mother can now be sublimated in the form of a general productivity, in impulses to learn, act, and create *as if* independent of adult interference or advice. The goal is unattainable, "impossible," and, of course, no doubt springs in part from residual oedipal ambitions, from frustrated desires to be big and strong, triumphant. Yet a boy's labors mean much more.

Thrust Toward Industry

To describe the postoedipal period merely as a time of "latency," in the sense of dormancy, is misleading, especially in light of what Erikson has described as a boy's thrust toward industry (Shapiro and Perry, 1976; Chap. 16). The sensual appetites and aggressions of middle childhood and the fears these engender seem tamer and less transparent than those of earlier eras. But these never abate completely. More significantly, a boy's general interest in creativity remains with him, rendering the years of middle childhood a time of great excitement and accomplishment. During this time, the schoolboy is impelled to discover skills that will enable him increasingly to move freely within and occasionally act on his surroundings, to build a sense of "competence," which Robert White (1959) believes to be a prime mover and psychological mainstay throughout one's working life. Unable to "make people," as Erikson noted, to be "mama and papa," a boy becomes instead a student, a worker, a producer. At least this is one adaptive solution.

Middle childhood further encompasses a cognitive revolution during which a host of new realizations which may be forbidden or disheartening, uplifting or fascinating, must be integrated into the child's developing world view. New modes of thought are called on, according to Piaget; with new problems come different means of reasoning. The intense efforts of so many boys of this age to arrive at "right" answers and their chagrin at minor failures, indicate not only thinly veiled fears of oedipal catastrophe and preoedipal demands for "ideality" and perfection, but also a more autonomous, adaptive struggle to acquire knowledge and mastery. The arena of interest and conflict has shifted, but life tasks have not become any less pressing.

Specifically, the issues a boy now confronts are matters of life and death. On the unconscious level, his growing concern with knowing and manipulating the extrafamilial environment may originate, at least in part, in his striving to feel more creative and potent than he did within the family and its oedipal triangle. Outside this context, however, a boy also discovers his limits; that is, the finitude and relativity shared by him with all creatures. Of vital importance, as both Piaget and Freud suggested, is the child's crucial preoccupation with the origins and ends of life itself. However inchoate his emerging personal philosophy may be, an 8-year-old encounters the basic facts of life: Like everything else, he learns, he was conceived; he was born; he lives; he will die.

Detachment

In a boy's struggle to "solve" the "problem of life," issues of content resonate with modes of understanding. Challenged now is his egocentrism of feeling and of thought, a self-centeredness that becomes increasingly untenable and unserviceable in the real workaday world. By 8 or 9 years of age, a child requires an unprecedented objectivity, a decentering, if he is to become detached enough to class himself with other like beings and define his own limits in both time and space. Without such an appreciation of limits, as opposed to infantile or even later phallic omnipotence, effective action on his part would be impossible.

Indeed, far from being all powerful, a child's sense of self may even become momentarily lost in the dryness of style typical of latency boys. At times a businesslike, cool demeanor almost suggests affective isolation or even a false self. But this apparent emotional vacuum is adaptive, granting a young boy potentially painful, conflict-laden realizations about his human powers and inner limits without his either succumbing to despair or reawakening those self-seeking motives that continue partly to impel his curiosity.

A child of this age may err in the other direction from the self-reference of his earlier years, now removing himself from the problems with which he grapples, as if they had nothing directly to do with him. The primal scene, his parents' relationship, his own sexual feelings, and, for that matter, his wishes to be nurturant or generative: These no longer interest him. He is concerned instead with mates, that is, "the male" and "the female," chickens and anatomical tubes, as well as responsibility, work, and life's continuity. Finally, a boy's by now practiced use of concrete operations, which he has applied to physical problems, finally enables him to resolve more fully the "Riddle of the Sphinx." His capacity to form classes and relations allows him to begin to cope with life's complexity and to interrelate its various elements: anatomical differences, the origin of babies, the complementarity of man and woman, and the finality of death.

During adolescence these ideas will be personalized once more to include the boy himself, thereby regaining their emotional impact. In the meantime, the fact that his parents "did that" (to quote at least one 9-year-old boy), and by doing "that," made him, provides the greatest of shocks. The origins of at least a portion of these conceptual endeavors in a boy's own procreative strivings remain sublimated. Nor does he seem to recognize that, intellectually, he is discovering how one day he will in fact fulfill his biological destiny.

Nurturance and Mentorship: The Good Father

Throughout middle childhood, the possibility of tending babies remains important and redemptive. Although a boy cannot yet father a baby, nor feed it from breasts he will never have, he can care for a child or other creatures in a variety of ways. In fact, many boys in this age group enact and express an avid interest in caretaking, more readily than younger children still in the throes of the oedipal conflict, and more so than early adolescents beset by renewed dualities and rifts in gender identity and the need to compensate for their confusion. Many 8-, 9-, and 10-year-olds manifest this would-be nurturance by growing plants, succoring pets, and otherwise shepherding animals or children.

For some boys, however, the prospect of these activities arouses fears of femininity or emasculation, whereas for others such inclinations appear far more tolerable. Once again, the presence or absence of the father seems to be a major mediating factor, helping to determine both a son's readiness to tender love and his freedom to acquire the means to productivity in work. Throughout development, as I said earlier, "good" and "bad" fathers present discrepant models of masculinity. During middle childhood especially, a father's presence as a mentor comes to serve a specific, concrete function. A father may now help his son discover the skills with which to satisfy pregenital aims in a more acceptable fashion, to explore and experiment in the service of competence rather than to be driven, or inhibited, by some competitiveness. He may actually help his son become stronger and more adult; or he may not.

Indeed, this stage of the relationship between fathers and sons appears to parallel in some respects a boy's earlier rapprochement with his mother. Having been alienated from the father by his own rivalry and projections of his hostility, a son then returns to him for renewed guidance and instruction. It is closeness with the father and trust in him which ideally allow a boy to temper the aggressivity of both his curiosity and his assertiveness; nor will he fear that he will destroy for himself the father whom he loves and needs, or risk the loss, in an imagined retaliation, of his own boyishness. More secure in these ways because he experiences his father's care and because his father does indeed help him become masterly and manly, a boy may be further freed to fulfill creative wishes. In addition, he may expand and deepen his concept of manhood to encompass a variety of affects and activities which might otherwise become associated with the mother's exclusive province, with being womanly.

When a boy has as a model only a rivalrous "bad" father, it is often much harder for him, unless an alternative mentorship is found, to modulate his (phallic) aggressions in the service of discovery or industry. Nor can he integrate needs to produce or nurture with a sex-linked assertiveness. Heightened bravado, displays of aggression, and denials of tenderness, or a recession into an outworn feminine identification and homosexual orientation may be the consequences of this sort of failure.

In cultures other than our own, this mentorship is more often institutionalized. Boys are handed over to the tutelage of fathers or their collective male representatives after having been wrested from the virtually exclusive care of women. In our own society, patterns of paternal involvement with sons (and daughters) during the ontogenetic "age of reason" are more variable.

One boy, Willy, living alone with his separated mother and visiting his father perhaps once a month, passed through a particularly irksome phase during which he attacked, assaulted, and shouted down all comers while in fact accomplishing very little on his own. As his father made himself more accessible, Willy, by the age of 9, became calmer yet also less inhibited in his work. Jimmy, a 16-year-old boy whose father lived with the family but seemed to take little direct interest in it, found himself indifferent to school, work, sports, sex, or any active pursuit. His inertia compounded his sense of inferiority, and a vicious cycle set in of inactivity and sterility. Only drugs could capture his attention until, through treatment with a male therapist and an idealizing paternal transference, he found himself increasingly drawn to interests, schoolwork, and sex, which previously had been, in his words, "irrelevant."

Father's Effect on Creative Expression

Active fathering helps reconcile another division, again originating earlier in development. In part, a boy's generativity may be seen to follow two courses. One of these is object oriented, involving desires for the opposite sex and eventuating in genitality and fatherhood. The other more or less follows the "narcissistic" line, to borrow from Kohut (1971): At least in part, creative work stems from a sublimated love of self and the self's productions. Not that these two directions constitute diverging, distinct lines of development, however; rather, a *potential* tension exists between working and loving. This conflict is evident in the proverbial complaint of many adult men that involvement with family will erode their effectiveness as workers and material providers, or that being a father will rob them of their freedom to create. In our society there is a measure of truth to such prevarication; shop and house no longer blend into each other, and jobs do take men from the home. Still, this reality can serve as a resistance. Absorption in work may be tantamount to self-absorption; conversely, an exclusive interest in family may represent a retreat from a legitimate narcissistic pleasure in work achievement. Both are based in disappointments with respect to the preoedipal or "just-oedipal" mother: arrests, fixations, and regressions. But a father's comfort in being a father, his familiarity with the child, and his own self-fulfillment as a man may do much to heal old wounds and fill in the gaps, to repair the splits within his son's sexuality, and to offer future ways of adapting to the compartmentalizations inevitable in modern life. His presence may not synthesize a boy's procreative and creative identities as one—that is simply not realistic—but fathering may certainly make these seem more compatible.

It is not quite that simple, however. When one envisions the "ideal mother" during her toddler's rapprochement crisis, one sees her arms opening in welcome but then unfolding to let her child go again, leaving the child free to feel independent once more. The danger is twofold: For whatever reason, she may reject or rebuff her child; or she may seduce and reengulf him or her back into a symbiosis that precludes autonomy.

Fathering presents analogous problems during middle childhood, for not only may a father ignore or avoid his son; he may overcontrol him. His guidance, which is a form of nurturance, may become a force-feeding, an intrusion that disallows privacy and freedom of choice. Because of their own narcissistic needs, many men drive their sons, push them to succeed, steer them into activities toward which the boys are disinclined. The effects may not be so profound at this stage as they were earlier during rapprochement with the mother, or even during the oedipal era, because so much has intervened. With capacities such as object constancy secured, too much structuralization has already occurred to permit so great a transformation as the one whereby the good mother is internalized as one's own. But a boy's final assimilation of the good father and his triumph over the bad father are vital in divesting his images of, and identifications with, masculinity of excessive hostility, filial defense, or isolation. In so doing, he engenders a male identity, not merely phallic and intrusive, but caring, competent, fatherly in itself.

Toward Adolescence

As Bettelheim (1954), Blos (1962), and others have remarked, puberty is presaged by a resurgence of regressive and "ambisexual" yearnings, and by an increasing sense of uncertainty and resulting defensiveness. The tightening of defenses in preadolescence represents an overcompensation for a protest against the crumbling of a boy's brittle, posturing detachment, the pseudomaturity of so many late-latency children. Less consciously and less completely than before, children recapitulate many of the transformations in sexual and parental identity that are so visible and intense in 3- and 4-year-olds.

The differences, of course, are pronounced. For example, with the coming of puberty, boys anticipate realizable sexual impulses and social independence. In the interim, they suffer fragmentation and seek solace in allies, including fathers and their various incarnations outside the family. Peers also provide points of anchorage in the midst of those upheavals. At least these boys have behind them a decade of mothering and fathering, and of consequent identifications, from which to forge an identity that is their own and eventually to assume their status as a caretaker for the next generation.

16

The Father's Role in Latency

Charles A. Sarnoff

Latency: The Structure and the Age

The term *latency* refers to two distinct psychological entities. First, there is the state of latency. This is a behavioral state of calm, pliability, and cooperativeness, which makes education possible. It is maintained by a specific group of ego functions, the "structure of latency." This is the organization of ego functions, specific for the age period of latency, which provide discharge of drive through fantasy and symbol formation. It provides a pathway for an autoplastic response to frustration. It provides a conduit for the transmission of culture to the child. It presages realistic future planning as it appears in adolescence (Sarnoff, 1976). Through the structure of latency, distracting stirrings of drives are quieted.

The direct role of the father is limited in this essentially internal phenomenon. The maturational factors that make a state of latency possible by the age of 6 years have to do with ego and cognitive changes. Undoubtedly, the father makes indirect contributions to these factors during prelatency. The restless, angry, shouting father serves as a poor role model for the latency-bound youngster. Beatings, seductions, and excited behavior on the part of the father maul the state of latency. The drives are stirred beyond the capacity of the structure of latency to neutralize them. Conversely, the calm father who takes an interest in his child and his child's education strengthens the state of latency. The father who introduces hobbies and helps the child to collect pennies, baseball cards, pebbles, and the like, strengthens the ego structures on which the restraint and calm of latency depend. Encouraging the latency-age child to fantasize is relitively rare in fathers. The reading of bedtime stories and fairy tales is the most common of these activities. Few fathers reach the degree of involvement in stirring fantasy that characterized the father of Soren Kierkegaard, who responded to his child's request to go out by creating fantasy worlds in the house through which they both wandered.

The second psychological entity to which the term *latency* refers is an age period, usually from 6 to 12 years of age. (For a detailed study of and distinction between the structure of latency and the age of latency, see Sarnoff, 1976). During this period, the child acquires information about the world and his own relation to society as approved by the family. The age of latency is sandwiched between early childhood (1–5 years), when the child learns about what is expected from him in relation to his family, and adolescence (13–19 years), when the child learns about what is expected from him in relation to society as defined by his peers.

Importance of Parents' Roles
In the latency-age period, the tutelage of parents can define behavior and establish patterns of reaction that set the templates for adolescent drive-discharge patterns. For those adolescents in rebellion, these parental guidelines provide the armatures around which the person can reconstruct his identity in the years of maturity.

Implied here is the introduction of parental imagos after the age of 6 years. This implication is intensified when it is noted that patterns of speech, cognition, and memory organization mature during latency years under the tutelage of and in identification with the parents.

Although, as is well known, the basic structure of the personality is laid down by the age of 5 years, it does not follow that experiences subsequent to that time have no effect. Parents continue to mold the child until he or she reaches adolescence, and even beyond. Nevertheless, to set the latency-age period as a developmental stage against developmental stages already known would be like challenging the firmament with a handful of shiny pebbles. In this chapter, I shall delineate some of the areas in which the father influences the latency-age child.

One question must be constantly confronted in dealing with the role of parents in latency development. Can the role of the mother really be differentiated from the role of the father? The descriptions in this chapter are based on family units in which there is a strong differentiation of parental roles. The father can be recognized because he is male, physically stronger, feels less obligation to take primary responsibility for the child when the mother is present, is home less than the mother, and is, in his daily work, more directly confronted with the economic and financial stresses of supporting the family. As such, he is forced to interpret reality limitations for the family, and to be on the lookout for the intrinsic nature of things rather than take things on the face value of the words that represent them. This is the father role. However, there is no obligate connection between these tasks and the sexual biological assignment of the parent. Women have assumed this role as well as men, though typically it is assigned to the father. When the mother assumes the role, it is possible that sexual identity confusion will result in the children. In shaping the development of cognition, the father, by dint of the pressures of the pragmatic imperatives that confront him in the day-to-day process of earning a living, emphasizes the practical. He contributes heavily to the training of the child that involves the logical thought processes (i.e., magic, verbal conceptual memory, abstract conceptual memory) that are recognized by his particular society as the means for apprehending, interpreting, and recording truth. The classical mother lends greater weight to the transmission of tradition, while the father reinforces styles of cognition that mediate survival in new situations and in the marketplace. The distribution of these chores, so sharp in primitive societies, is blurred in ours. Either parent may contribute, but the weight of influence is the father's in any society in which the male must meet the world and wrest a living from it.

One must search in vain for a biological basis (correlate or determinant) that places males in the position of dominating the development of abstract conceptual modes of memory and thought. The opposite seems to be the case. "Females, on average, surpass males in several language skills, including articulation, comprehensibility, fluent production, use of verbal information in a learning task, and rapid production of symbolic codes or names" (Wittig and Petersen, 1979). Yet, these are the very skills that are developed by the father in teaching the child how to think about the world. Evolutionary reasons for woman's preeminence in word usage are offered by Mead (1958), who points out that delayed puberty, which evolved in mankind before language, shortened the childbearing period and thereby prolonged the woman's life. Man still hunted and died young. Woman was able to live long enough to develop and pass onto the progeny of the tribe patterns through which the evolution of new language skills could be guided (Sarnoff, 1976, pp. 355–357). Woman, consigned by childbearing and smaller physical stature to the hearth, became the guardian of the homely crafts and traditions, while man took up the bow and confronted the world beyond and its dangers. As society evolved in an organized marketplace, and the means of making a living shifted from wielding tools of strength to the manipulation of symbols and abstractions, the role of breadwinner did not shift to the better equipped female, but remained with the male, whose strength lay in physical power, size, and the more basic "superior performance on visuo-spatial tasks, mechanical and mathematical skills" (Wittig and Petersen, 1979, p. 50). Thus the female, who is better equipped to teach nimble feats of logic, is pushed aside. The male, whose strengths are elsewhere, is forced to hone his cognition; the classical mother is not. Therefore, the father typically (though not always) serves as the intermediary between the child and the real world "out there," in conveying to the child the styles of thought that the child will need to make his way.

The Father and Cognition in Latency
Memory Development

The cognitive progressions of latency-age children are many. Here we will focus on thought patterns associated with the child's apprehending, understanding, and coding for memory of the world as experienced. Awareness that the cognition of children differs from that of adults was reflected on by Vygotsky as quoted by Luria (1976). Vygotsky observed that although "the young child thinks by remembering, an adolescent remembers by thinking" (p. 11). Indeed, there are three levels of memory development that characterize the memory cognition of the latency-age child. At the earliest, the child remembers total experiences on a perceptual affectomotor level (*affectomotor memory organization*). With the development of the capacity for a state of latency, words and verbal symbols move into the primary position as the carriers of memory (*verbal conceptual memory organization*). As the child moves into late latency, about the age of 9 years, the ability to recall through coding, in the form of awarenesses of the essentials of what has been perceived, provides the child with an exceptionally accurate, undistorted, and highly efficient means of storing data for later use in interpreting new experiences (*abstract conceptual memory organization*). There is no requirement that this skill be developed. In many societies it is inhibited by the nature of the educational processes (Sarnoff, 1976). The father of the latency-age child is an important source of the pressure to develop this type of memory organization in our society. Industrial society is organized through this memory organization, just as religious societies are organized around the verbal conceptual memory organization. One should be alert not to confuse memories that are conveyed in words with the type of memory organization involved. All three forms of memory operation can be processed into words in order to achieve communication to another person. Only the second form codes awarenesses into words for retention in memory.

Effect on Therapy. This differentiation is vital for the therapist, who must at all times appreciate the memory modality that is being used by the child as well as the potential of the child to use more mature ones. At times it is necessary, as a therapeutic maneuver, to bring children to the most mature level in order to improve their ability to communicate, to function, and to use and retain the insights of child therapy (Sarnoff, 1979). There is a vicissitude set aside for the memories and motives of children that have been repressed before they have found their way to a form in which they can be understood and confronted. These motives grow and develop unbridled by reflection, wisdom, or logic, all of which relate to the abstract conceptual memory organization. The therapist can bring reflection, wisdom, and logic to bear on such motives only if they can be transformed into characters of rhetoric. Only then, when the concepts can be processed into words, can the logical capacities of the mind of the child in therapy be focused on them. More than words are involved. Words help to make what is knowable transmissible. Without the cognitive metamorphosis that makes motivation knowable and then transmissible, child therapy is limited to a set of simultaneous monologues. Therapy is then no more than a battle between a disciplined battalion in search of a woodland victory and a disinterested band of spirits cavorting in the forest canopy above their heads. There is no real contact.

When the therapist helps the child to find the concept and the words to express it, the role of the therapist and the role of the classic latency-age father become similar. To this extent, the therapy of a latency-age child transcends the ordinary goals of adult therapy. Even the ordinary pedagogical aspects of child therapy are transcended. In effect, such teaching is akin to parenting. Fulfilling cognitive potentials in a child expands the child's social and occupational horizons as would happen if the child had other parents.

Shakespeare placed words that convey this meaning well into a speech made by Prospero (or, according to some sources, Miranda) to Caliban (*The Tempest*, 1.2.350). Prospero, it will be remembered, has raised Caliban from a creature of beastlike sensibilities to the level of adult human awareness. In speaking of this feat, Prospero (or Miranda) says:

[I] took pains to make thee speak, taught thee each hour
One thing or other: When thou didst not, savage, know thine own meaning, but
    would gabble
Like a thing most brutish, I endowed thy purposes
With words that made them known.

The role of the parent goes beyond teaching the child words with which to name and remember. The parent can also help the child to find ways of understanding what he sees in terms of abstract reductions of the phenomena under study so that knowledge of the very essence of events can be coded into memory. From this grows a capacity to integrate and interpret new experiences in terms of their intrinsic nature. Past experience becomes the guide, and perceptions and interpretations based on verbal stereotyping are put aside. Because of his position in closer contact with the pragmatic world beyond the family unit, to the father falls the greater share of the burden of transmitting and encouraging these memory skills. We have already noted differences in the roles of father and mother in this area.

Now let us turn to some of the factors that cause latency-age boys and girls to respond differently to training in memory through abstract coding. Boys tend to be more successful in this pursuit than girls. Why do girls lag? As Harris has pointed out, "Given their earlier and superior linguistic abilities, it is conceivable that females, more than males, tend to code visual-spatial information linguistically—and, consequently, less efficiently in many instances" (1979, p. 52). Another factor is sex-role expectation. Boys are expected to perform better in math and spatial spheres, whereas girls are expected to excel in verbal skills. There is actually a pattern of results on aptitude tests that is called feminine patterning, "that is, a higher verbal than mathematics score" (Radin, 1976, p. 244). Although sociocultural factors have been blamed for this difference, Harris (1979) suggests that an "exclusively sociocultural analysis of male mathematical superiority cannot stand" (p. 52). Indeed, it is a repeated finding that in the absence of the father, boys take on the feminine pattern in aptitude test scores. The boy whose father is absent experiences a lack of the parental influence and model for the identification that could encourage the fulfillment of potential, which in girls appears to be on the average not as great (Harris, 1979).

Tolerance of ambiguity is more possible in the keeping of a home than it is in the world of business, where tolerance of ambiguity brings disaster. The classic father brings to the approach to new experiences a background of intolerance to ambiguity. The child who identifies with such a father has a strengthened approach to fresh and new problems. Absence of this demand for stringency in approach can lead to inexact interpretation of events and a willingness to let words and slogans influence the interpretations of events. The capacity for tolerating ambiguity, according to Radin (1976), "may well hinder the ability to solve complex problems; jumping to a solution before examining all aspects of a problem should surely reduce the child's problem-solving competence" (p. 247). The girl who identifies with her mother (in the classic sense of the term *mother*) would then bring less stringent demands to later tasks.

Clinical Examples
Now let us turn to some clinical situations by way of illustration.

Jimmy
Jimmy was 4 years old when his father lost his eyesight. Unable to deal with this sudden loss of function, the father, at the age of 35, withdrew from any attempt at gainful employment and took over the care of the house and the cooking, while his wife, who had been a lawyer, returned to work. The mother, who had been passive and dependent, looking to her husband to guide her steps even in matters as simple as voting, was thrust into the position of breadwinner. At first, she found herself taken advantage of in the business world, and even the object of a swindle that reduced the family's meager resources to the point of bankruptcy. The family home was lost and the children (there was one brother, age 8) placed briefly in a normal child-caring institution. Jimmy's mother learned quickly. She stopped taking people at face value and turned from using intuition to applying reasoned-out principles based on past experience to solve the problems of livelihood that confronted her. Her professional skills improved. Her husband, in the meantime, carried on the household chores, protected from the pressures of the outside world. In analysis, Jimmy gave clear indication that his identification was with his mother. Problems of sexual identity loomed strongly in his analytic work. His mother's role as the "classical latency father" transmitted to him the basis for a cognition that greeted the world with little room for ambiguity in the way he classified new information, and little in the way of vagueness in his later recall of the event.

Frank
Frank's father had deserted the family when Frank was 3 years old. Without a father in the house, the child had identified with the high tolerance for ambiguity that characterized his mother's approach to the evaluation of issues and situations. The mother returned with the child to live with her parents. Although she held a part-time, noncompetitive job, her main source of support was her father. At the time Frank was seen, his grandfather was living in Florida, as he had been for a number of years. His mother had recently remarried. For 8 years he had been a one-parent child. His own father was scarcely visible, contributing only minimally to his support. The boy was quite rejecting of his mother's new husband. In essence, his position of primacy in the household had been usurped. He was consciously resentful and took pains to disobey, provoke, and keep a distance from his "new father." When time came to go to camp, he expected to be sent by the "new father," who was expected to provide the money for something that was the "right of every boy" who lived in the affluent community into which they had moved. He did not feel that he needed to be polite or thankful. He held these views as a matter of course and without conflict. The fact that his real relationship with this man, with all the intrinsic characteristics that pointed toward a situation in which there were no ties and nothing owed by him or to him, could not support such a demand was beyond him. He proclaimed his right *de jure* and complained bitterly of mistreatment when his new father requested some sign of gratitude.

An example of the transmission of ambiguity tolerance from parent to child is revealed in the following interchange:

259

Q. (Therapist): What will you do for Thanksgiving?
A. Have dinner. People come to the house.
Q. Who is coming for Thanksgiving?
A. Company.
Q. Who?
A. I don't know.
Q. Doesn't your mother tell you?
A. When I asked, she said, "You'll see when they come."

According to Radin (1979, p. 249), "The literature on cognitive style tends to support the view that boys' approach to problem solving is influenced by their relationship with their fathers. . . . The link between fathers' behavior and girls' cognitive competence [is] negligible. Girls tend to establish a cognition in identification with their mothers." The father who responds to his daughter according to sex stereotypes (treating her in a fashion that elicits a traditionally feminine reaction) may retard her intellectual and academic development. If, however, the father sets up a relationship in which the girl can model her intellectual efforts and achievement motivation after the father's pattern, the father can heighten abstract memory skills in his daughter (Radin, 1979, p. 253). Too much paternal warmth may interfere with such development in a late-latency-aged girl, whose oedipal strivings must be counteracted by withdrawal from the father.

The Contribution of the Father to Self-Image

The image of the self and the self-esteem that is derived from it undergo a remarkable transformation with the onset of the latency-age period. Before 5 years of age, self-esteem was associated to an important degree, but not exclusively, with the attitude of the parent toward the child. This can sometimes be a precarious condition, for the depressed or uncaring parent may not attend to the child, which may leave the child feeling unworthy in spite of great competence. Parental love supports self-esteem; in turn, parental love is encouraged by behavior on the part of the child that demonstrates the child's ability to conform to the parent's demands in the behavioral sphere. After the age of 6 years, though this pattern persists and continues to contribute to the self-image, an important overlay is added. A portion of the child's self-esteem begins to be derived from the attitudes of society. At first this is made up of those areas that are preferred by the parents. Later, the influence and values of the teacher are felt. By the end of the latency years, peer pressure begins to define the skills and behaviors by which self-worth is judged. With the latency years, the larger world begins to define self-esteem, making the attitudes of the parent toward the child less important and, at times, least important.

Why this happens at this time is beyond the scope of this chapter. One thing, however, is certain: Parental expectations encourage this change, as does the child's desire to avoid passivity at the hands of the parents. When children begin to go to school, leaving home in the morning just as fathers ordinarily do, they leave the world of the mother and begin to explore the outside world. The behavior and the symbols that indicate success in this new world (if they are not too ambiguous) become elements to strive for. In addition, the ability to succeed in these pursuits becomes a measure of one's worth. Here is the key to the role of the father in the self-esteem and the self-image of the child. The child sees the symbols of success in society as tools to use in overcoming the sense of humiliation felt by small children thrust into a world populated and, in large measure, controlled by grown-ups. Children invoke parents' big cars, physical strength, large size, athletic ability, and stylish clothing in order to demonstrate their competence and shore up their self-esteem vis-à-vis their peers. At times these are private thoughts; sometimes they are so loudly espoused that one is reminded of the song duels of the Esquimaux.

An example of a "word duel" follows. Three children stood on opposite sidewalks. A girl and boy, both 8 years old, stood to the north. A 7-year-old boy stood alone on the south side of the street, the 8-year-old boy the target of his abuse. The girl cheered on the 8-year-old boy; her approval was obviously precious to him. "You don't know nothing," screamed the 7-year-old. "I do so," yelled his adversary. "What's more," said he, "my daddy is taller than your daddy." Immediately, the 7-year-old rejoined with, "Well, my daddy is a lot more richer than your daddy." Humbled, the 8-year-old looked down, blanched, mumbled, and then, recovering his composure, brightened as he threw the ultimate barb: "My daddy is fatter than your daddy."

I once worked with a youngster whose father beat him. I expected to hear him tell of his latest tragic confrontation with the father the day after a particularly severe altercation. Instead, the child busied himself with reinforcement of his shattered self-esteem through identification with his father who, that very day, had acquired a new car. A man of modest means, he had traded in his small car for a station wagon in order to facilitate the transport of his family. It meant something else to his 6-year-old son, who proclaimed to all who would hear, "My father has the biggest car."

Dostoyevsky, in *The Brothers Karamazov*, tells the story of a 9-year-old Ilusha, who has been exposed to a scene in which his father is humiliated and stripped of dignity. His father had been dragged from a tavern by the beard in the presence of the child and his classmates. The child rushed to his father's side and humiliated himself further by begging the assailant to release his father while kissing the hand of the attacker. The father later says, "At that moment in the square when he kissed his hand, at that moment my Ilusha had grasped all that justice means. That truth entered into him and crushed him forever, sir." The following days, the child was involved in teasing by the other boys. He engaged in rock throwing. He developed physical illness, depression, and intense fantasies of growing up to be a competent fighter, unlike his father, who would return to deal out vengeance on his father's attacker.

If the father cannot provide tools in the form of valued cultural elements identified with the father for use in bolstering self-esteem, lasting elements of lowered self-image are added to the child's character. The father's lacks must be truly severe, for most children use the ego mechanisms, "the structure of latency," to set aside their humiliations through the evocation of the fantasied image of the father as someone who could have the accoutrements of manliness and power if only he wished. Many times, while working in a residence for normal children, I was confronted with youngsters who pointed with pride to parents who had failed them completely. One child, a girl of 8 years, repeatedly returned from a visit to her parents with tales of the wonderful mush they had eaten, and complained bitterly of the steak we provided. An 11-year-old boy was taken from the "home" to an impressive mansion near Long Island Sound. The walls of the great room that formed the center of the mansion reached far above his small frame. He looked about as the guide spoke with self-impressed bravado about the cost and effort that the man who built the house had expended. She fell into shocked silence when he interrupted her to say, "My daddy could a' had a house like this, but he didn't want it."

In the normal child-care setting, we learned to delay visits to parents until the children were 14 years of age. It was then, we found, that the children's impressions of their parents' capacities were sufficiently realistic and sufficiently disengaged from the need to protect themselves from feelings of humiliation for the children's impressions to be useful in contributing to or responding to realistic future planning.

In early adolescence the child becomes big enough and physically mature enough to enter the adult world. Sexual expression with partners becomes a reality. In addition, intuitive responses to situations are replaced, as the result of cognitive gains, with realistic interpretations of events. At this time, the moment of disenchantment occurs. Fortunately, it is at a time when overvaluation of the father is not needed. At the moment of disenchantment with the need to overvalue the father set aside, overvaluation of the father is pushed aside by improved cognition and realistic symbolic elements in symbol usage, and the father is then seen in true perspective within the context of the world.

In brief, children need to overvalue the father in order to deal with their own feelings of humiliation. This is an effective manifestation of the "structure of latency." At times, events involving the father are so distinct and so strong that the defense fails and is followed by rage in reaction to the uncovering of the humiliation defended against. Children exposed to chronic humiliation of this sort (exposure to failure of family function or finances below the community norm) are often left with a permanent depression and a sense of low self-worth.

17

Fathers and Adolescent Sons

Aaron H. Esman

In *The Ghost Dance* (1970), his magisterial treatise on the origins of religion, the anthropologist Weston LaBarre writes (pp. 591–592):

The relation of fathers and sons is mysterious and terrifying. It has never been rational, nor will it ever be. It is not the only relationship that men must suffer. But father and son form the most critical and dangerous animal relationship on earth, and to suppose otherwise is to invite catastrophe. For it is by no means delivered to us that this species-paradigm will survive annihilation in blind self-slaughter through some displaced pathology of this relationship. No man ever grows beyond the reach of its influence. . . . How to accept and how to embody male *authority*, how to express and when to modulate aggressiveness against other men—how, in short, to be father and son, government and citizen—these still remain the towering problems of the oedipal animal.

In *Totem and Tabu*, Freud (1913) delineated a view of the primal relationship between the father and his adolescent sons, one in which the tyrannical authoritarian father is overthrown by the rebellion of sons eager to seize his power, and above all, to wrest from his possession the woman in the "primal horde." Freud here laid down the outlines of the model that has in large measure dominated the psychoanalytic picture of this relationship and, indeed, of adolescence itself; namely, that it represents essentially a recapitulation and reworking of the oedipal conflict. In more recent years many analysts and developmental psychologists (Erikson, 1950; Spiegel, 1958; Offer, 1969; Blos, 1978) have challenged this "recapitulationist" view, pointing out the failure to consider the multiple factors that make what Blos calls the "adolescent passage" a radically different experience from the oedipal situation.

In this chapter, I shall attempt to review some of the pertinent literature on father-son relationships in adolescence and formulate a picture of such relations within a developmental context. In particular, I shall venture to define some of the ways in which the father may facilitate and others in which he may impair optimal development, and to suggest some aspects of reciprocal influence of the adolescent son on the psychological development of his father.

Mozart and His Father

No more striking illustration of the complexities of such a relationship can be found than in the life of Wolfgang Amadeus Mozart, arguably the greatest creative genius in human history. Wolfgang had the good fortune to be born into a solid family happily thriving under the benignly authoritarian pedantic tutelage of Leopold Mozart, a moderately successful court musician and violin teacher. Quick to recognize his son's extraordinary talent, Leopold established himself as Wolfgang's only teacher, guiding his education not only in music but in basic academics and language as well. He was also, of course, quick to exploit the boy's genius for his own purposes, pecuniary as well as narcissistic, fulfilling some of his own frustrated aspirations by way of Wolfgang's extraordinary successes in the courts and capitals of Europe.

It was, indeed, through the impact of these triumphs and the steady nurturing of his talents by his parents that young Mozart developed an unquestioning sense of his own worth as a man and as an artist. Leopold, despite his paternalistic tendencies, seems generally to have refrained from stifling or subordinating his son's genius to his own. Wolfgang's self-confidence and his early idealization of his father are both expressed in his letter of February 28, 1778, in which he writes (E. Anderson, 1938):

I have full confidence in three friends, all of them powerful and invincible—God, your head and mine. Our heads, I admit, are very different, but each in its own way is good, serviceable and useful and I hope that in time mine will by degrees equal yours in those branches in which it is now inferior. . . . Remember that you have a son who has never, knowingly, forgotten his filial duty to you, who will endeavor to become more and more worthy of so good a father and who will remain increasingly your most obedient—Wolfgang.

This idealization was gradually modified during his late adolescence into an ego ideal capable of being not only attained but guiltlessly surpassed. The hostile rivalrous aspects of his oedipal conflicts with his father were lived out through his marriage to Constanze Von Weber, of which his father disapproved, and in a displaced rebellion against his employer, the bishop of Salzburg, against whose tyranny Mozart chafed in his young adulthood and from whom he finally broke away, leaving for Vienna and full independence in 1781 when he was 25 years old. His affectionate, deferential attitude toward his father persisted unchanged, at a respectful distance, until his father's death.

Until this point Mozart's relationship with his father would appear to have promoted his development. A powerful identification both on ego and ego-ideal levels, a confident sense of self, a fully developed craft, and a capacity for self-assertion and emancipation seem to have been the legacy of the Salzburg years. It was only in the Vienna period, following his apparent "emancipation" from his father, that the negative side of the picture became evident. He had, as Sitwell (1932, p. 138) says, "been far too long in leading strings. . . . He had no sense of the value of money . . . and he was not tactful enough. He would not seek out the right people or pay attention to them." He was, that is, quite incompetent in practical affairs and ultimately became dependent for his very survival on a succession of friendly father surrogates. In these respects, therefore, his father's influence had served to impair and restrict his development at his cost, and, given his sorrows and his untimely death, at ours.

Theories on Paternal Influence

As Malmquist (1978) has pointed out, most of the published studies of paternal influence have dealt with the development of sexual patterns; predictably, they tend to show that "boys from father-dominant homes display more sexual preferences according to the masculine sexual standard and are more identified with fathers than are boys from mother-dominant families" (p. 214). Further, there are suggestions from clinical studies that boys with absent fathers "appear to have difficulties in the realm of sexual identity." Illustrative is the study by Levi and colleagues (1972) of nine adolescent boys (and two girls) with problems of "underachievement," truancy, and the like. In all cases the fathers were seen as depressed and withdrawn, failing to defend their own values and expectations by engaging in "loving fights" with their children. Similarly, Teicher (1972, p. 407) described a group of *older* alienated college students (all adolescent males) who underachieved consistently: "All expressed a hopeless plea for relationship with a father who remained passive and distant, permitted self-depreciation and an impotent role. Always the father deferred to the mother."

Idealization of the Father

It is indeed with respect to the conflicting relationship with the mother that several authors have dealt with the father's role. In particular, Blos (1970) sees the adolescent boy's overidealization of the father in large measure as a defense against the dangerous attraction of the preoedipal mother. Anderson (1978), too, stresses the failure of the fathers of "borderline" adolescents to provide adequate support for their sons' individuation from the mothers; in this he transposes to adolescents the view of Forrest (1967) and Mahler (1975) of the father's crucial role in promoting separation-individuation during the preoedipal period.

There is wide agreement that the father plays a critical role as model and in particular as an idealized figure. Blos (1974) emphasizes the negative oedipal origins of this idealization and sees as one of the "tasks" of adolescence the gradual transmutation of this idealized image by means of reality assessment and internalization. R. Q. Bell (1968) found that those males whose fathers were important role models in adolescence functioned more effectively in young adulthood than those whose fathers were not. Blos sees as crucial here the adolescent's ability to cope with the "disillusionment" attendant on the correction of his early idealized image of the father. Meyer (1976) describes the rather extraordinary outcome of such a situation in the case of Houdini (née Erich Weiss), whose profound disillusionment in his ineffectual, inadequate father led him from age 12 years onward to seek to attach himself to idealized surrogates; he finally settled on the French magician, Houdin, with whom he identified to the extent of adopting both his name and his profession.

Reciprocity in Father-Son Interaction

In his comprehensive survey of the father-son relationship in adolescence, Siskind (1972) addresses himself extensively to the impact of the developmental changes in the boy on the father and vice versa. "Conflicts and crises in the father reactivated by those of the son have a tendency to make the father act unhelpfully or even destructively towards the son. Only by coping with his own conflicts and controlling his responses can the father counteract this tendency and help the son accomplish his adolescent tasks." Anthony (1969) develops a similar point, showing how many of the stereotypic and usually negative attitudes of parents toward adolescents are determined by the reactivation of their own poorly repressed conflicts by the developmental shifts occurring in their offspring.

Effects of Father Absence

In the sphere of psychopathology, attention has been directed retrospectively to the consequences of father absence, particularly with relation to delinquency. Recently, however, Lewis and colleagues (1978) have pursued a more detailed and focused approach. Their investigations of the fathers of delinquent adolescents have demonstrated a high incidence of violence and abusiveness, criminality, and psychiatric treatment for severe psychopathology in such men. Interestingly, they point out that these men tend to marry women who are themselves inadequate or ill (though rarely criminal); thus when they are themselves in prison or absent from the home, the son is left to cope with the disturbed mother.

Clinical Example: David P.

It is apparent from these citations of a growing literature that, as Siskind puts it in his conclusions, "The father is a powerful and integral force in the personality growth and dynamics of his adolescent son." A clinical illustration may serve to underscore his abiding impact on such seemingly diverse matters as career choice and sexual identity.

David P., a 22-year-old student, came for treatment in the throes of an intense obsessional crisis regarding his professional direction. Though matriculated in the first-year class of a prestigious law school, he was unable to decide whether he should remain there or transfer to another field of graduate study to which he had also been accepted. His father, a successful lawyer, had died several months earlier of a chronic debilitating illness, and David had chosen law school in part because of his father's expressed preference that he do so and despite his own leaning toward a different type of career. It soon emerged, however, that David's problems were more extensive. In particular, he proved to be preoccupied with the concern that he might be homosexual, a fear that rarely left him and that clouded his life with a persistent depressive cast. He was ridden with shame and guilt about all aspects of his sexual life, particularly his masturbation, which was frequently done without conscious fantasy and against intense struggles for control, and which he took as a further evidence of his homosexual bent. ("I am getting pleasure from myself, a male.") Further, he was profoundly concerned about his physical appearance, focusing on minute blemishes and imperfections as the basis for self-depreciation and shame.

David's father played a powerful role in his life. His mother had early shown signs of cyclical depression, which led David to attach himself to his father as a source of support and guidance. Mr. P. was a rigid, upright, and compulsive man who maintained the highest possible standards for his children and made clear his disappointment when they failed to live up to them. When 15-year-old David, beset by conflict over his masturbation, timorously asked his father whether he had ever masturbated, his father categorically denied having done so, thus intensifying David's shame and sense of personal failure. Intellectually, he knew that masturbation was a universal practice among adolescent boys; yet he could not deal emotionally with the disillusionment in his father that would be implicit in any doubt on his part about the veracity of his father's denial. He sought constant reassurance from me about his sexual concerns, but when it was pointed out to him that he already knew the answers to his questions, he felt let down and disappointed as he had when his father failed to offer him the reassurance he needed. At the same time, he was deeply mistrustful, constantly questioning time, financial, and physical arrangements of the analysis, intensely concerned lest he be exploited and taken advantage of.

In contrast to his perception of his mother as emotional and irrational, David viewed his father as a model of rationality and emotional control. He tended to regard emotionality as feminine, therefore, and to see any loss of affective control on his own part as further evidence of his defective manhood. It was therefore difficult for him to mourn his father's death; when, during one session, he burst into tears on recalling his father's funeral, it was with profound feelings of shame and self-reproach. He could not imagine his father doing anything of the kind.

In short, David had never overcome his preadolescent idealization of his father, nor had he by doing so succeeded in establishing an ego ideal capable even of approximate realization. His father's death intensified his feelings of guilt about deeply repressed hostile feelings toward him. His defensive efforts to ward off awareness both of these hostile feelings and of his passive longings for love and care led him to a submissive identification against which he fitfully but, ultimately, obsessively and in-effectually rebelled.

Subphase Variables in Adolescent Development
It is generally agreed that psychological development in adolescents is not uniform but that it can be best understood as proceeding through a succession of subphases in each of which particular developmental issues assume primacy. Following Blos (1962), it is customary to speak of three subphases (early, middle, late); for the purposes of this discussion, however, two divisions appear more useful.

Early Subphase: Separation from Mother
In early adolescence the father's primary role appears to be that of promoting, through enabling identification with sexual role patterns and through his availability as a love object, the process of separation from the primary dependent attachment to the mother. Through his support and encouragement and, particularly, through his empathic grasp of the boy's phase-specific needs (Paul, 1970), he encourages the boy's growing sense of self-growth and autonomy.

For the boy this process is not entirely without stresses. Although he derives reinforcement for his ego growth and the consolidation of his sexual identity from the relationship with his father, he is also confronted unconsciously by the threat of homosexual submission that this intimacy entails. Accordingly, gestures of autonomy and even rebelliousness are likely to appear as manifestations of the effort to disavow such wishes and, of course, of the process of "the second individuation" (Blos, 1967) that is intrinsic to the "adolescent passage," at least in Western cultures. Furthermore, the boy's disillusionment in the idealized omnipotent image of the father comes to prominence here in conjunction with the improved reality testing and heightened grasp of the world fostered by the growth of logical operational thought. This development, said by Piaget (1969) to occur in Western adolescents between the ages of 12 and 15 years, marks a major landmark in cognitive growth and is a major factor in promoting affective autonomy and adaptive competence. In allowing for a more realistic view of the parent, it encourages (barring interference by parental narcissism) the development of a more tolerant and flexible ego ideal. Experiments with alternative and sometimes deviant values (Esman, 1975) are characteristic of adolescent males (and, to a lesser degree, females) during this period. It is here that, as Levi and others (1972) point out, the father's integrity and consistency are essential in providing a sense of structure and stability from which the adolescent can deviate and to which he can, when needed, return. The father must steer the narrow line between acceptance and supine resignation, between empathic understanding and overidentification, between sensitive control and punitive restriction. It is not an easy task.

Late Subphase: Father as Mentor
When, in later adolescence, the struggle for autonomy and self-definition has been largely won, the adolescent then tends to see his father more consciously and pragmatically as a role model, teacher, and companion. The ambivalence of early adolescence will have been in considerable measure resolved, the idealization tamed, the disillusionment accepted. As the young man, more secure in his sexual identity, consolidates his heterosexual relationships, the need for rebellious negation of homosexual (or, in Blos's terms, "negative oedipal") longing subsides, permitting a more comfortable aim-inhibited attachment of equals to emerge.

The Father's Experience
It is a central theme of this volume that the father-child relationship is a reciprocal one in which each partner passes through critical transitions as the developmental process unfolds. Certainly this is true of the son's adolescence. Occurring as it does when the father is entering or passing through his middle years, it constitutes one of the significant issues with which he must deal, not only for his son's sake but for his own.

The experimentation and rebelliousness of his adolescent son will, as Siskind (1972) points out, challenge the father at the time when he may well be confronting and seeking to cope with critical conflicts in his own life (see Chap. 21). His son's apparent omnipotentiality (Pumpian-Mindlin, 1965) may seem to mock his own need to accept his limitations. His son's rebelliousness may arise just as he finds himself settling into the conformity required by corporate life and conventional social mores. The boy's sexual maturity and experimentation may present him with a challenge to what he, at least, may experience as the waning of his own pow-

271

ers. If he is uncertain or ambivalent about his own moral and ethical values, it will be even more difficult for him to permit his son to explore the range of possibilities without offering implicit sanction to antisocial or deviant behavior ("I was like that when I was his age") or resorting defensively to a rigid moralistic or punitive stance ("I couldn't get away with that stuff when I was his age"). If he is insecure about his occupational or educational achievements, he may drive his son to pursue unattainable goals, or set impossible standards and expectations in pursuit of which the boy may fall victim to depression or self-doubt (as in the case of David P.).

Empathic participation in his son's growth can help him to work through some of his own unresolved conflicts; he may, for instance, be enabled to attain a more flexible value system attuned to the realities of contemporary life. It may permit a reinforcement of his self-esteem through appropriate feelings of pride in his son's achievements. Above all, he may gain the gratification inherent in the tutelage and guidance of an evolving personality and the growing intimacy that can, where untrammelled by neurotic conflict, flower in such a context.

The Impact of Divorce

It is a commonplace of our time that fathers and their adolescent children must come to terms with the dissolution of the family by separation and divorce (Chaps. 29, 30). For both father and son (not to mention the other members of the family), the experience is likely to be a trying, even traumatic one, often necessitating major readjustments and sometimes leading to significant emotional disturbance.

The healthy older adolescent is not likely to be seriously affected by changes in a family from which he is already well along the road to emancipation. For the early adolescent boy, however, the impact of divorce is commonly severe. Still significantly dependent on his parents, he finds his security threatened by the disruption of family integrity. Often uncertain about aspects of sexual identity and of value formation, he is suddenly deprived of his primary role model. Further, the absence of the father may confront him with the anxieties attendant on an imagined oedipal triumph on the one hand, and a regressively tinged intensity of intimacy with his mother on the other. Both may be aggravated when the mother seeks unconsciously to use her son as a replacement for her lost husband.

In such circumstances, the early adolescent boy may experience a strong wish for paternal custody. With these longings may be mixed, consciously or unconsciously, less adaptive ones, such as longings for revenge against the mother, which require careful consideration. In many cases, however, it may well be desirable for the father to assume such custody, to help his son in achieving masculine identification and to reduce the sense of danger that may reside in exclusive or primary maternal custody.

This is not to say, of course, that such arrangements are without peril or complication. Angry at his father for what he experiences as a betrayal, the son may be exceptionally defiant or provocative. The father, anticipating a life of freedom and self-indulgence in his new single role, may find himself feeling encumbered by the responsibility of caring for a still needy and often demanding son, every ready to test his devotion and concern. If, as is so often the case, the divorce is emotionally incomplete and acrimonious, both parents may exploit the son as spy, informant, and agent provocateur, each against the other.

Nonetheless, when it is feasible, the custodial role for the father of the adolescent son is developmentally appropriate and often highly desirable. For the father, it can promote a sense of purpose and of continuing participation in a family life. For the son, it can have inestimable value as a buttress against what might otherwise be unmanageable oedipal conflicts and role diffusion. For both, it can offer the rewards of meeting and mastering a new system of relationships and interpersonal challenges.

18

Aspects of Prospective Fatherhood

Alan R. Gurwitt

Becoming a father is an important episode in the life cycle of a man and his family. The character of that episode draws on all that preceded and influences all that follows.

The very limited attention paid to prospective (or expectant) fatherhood (e.g., Jarvis, 1962; Blos, 1971; Colman and Colman, 1971; Arnstein, 1972) is thus remarkable, since it has long been recognized that the period of becoming a father is a time of important psychological transition (Boehm, 1930; Jacobson, 1950; Benedek, 1970a; Jessner et al., 1970). That there is significant stress in this transition is evidenced by the clinical literature on the pathological reactions to the achievement of fatherhood (Zilboorg, 1931; Freeman, 1951; Towne and Afterman, 1955; Lacoursiere, 1972a,b). Moreover, the phenomenon of the couvade that appears in various forms in different societies probably serves to regulate apparently powerful forces within men in response to birthing (Reik, 1919; Jones, 1961; Howells, 1971). Although some reports have focused on specific phenomena in male analysands (e.g., Eisler, 1921a,b; Evans, 1951; Rose, 1961; Jarvis, 1962; Jaffe, 1968), there has not been a case report on a male's reaction to psychological currents before and throughout pregnancy. It is the purpose of this chapter to describe such currents in a young man whose wife became pregnant and delivered a baby girl while he was in analysis.

The patient was 23 years old when he started analysis. He had been married for 6 months, and was in his third year of graduate studies in a scientific field at the time. His wife became pregnant during the last year of the 4-year analysis. Their daughter was born about 4 months before termination of the analysis.

His concerns at the start of treatment were difficulty in coping with daily demands, a sense of poor control over his emotional life, insecurity

This is an abbreviated version of an essay published in Ruth S. Eissler et al. (Eds.), *The Psychoanalytic Study of the Child*, Vol. 31. New York: International Universities Press, 1976.

in sexual relationships, problems in pursuing his graduate work, and problems in social relationships.

The patient had two sisters, one 2 years older, the other 2½ years younger. His father was a mechanic who never gained much satisfaction from his work. During the patient's first 2 to 3 years of life his father was rarely home because of the war-related nature of his work. He was home more often shortly after the birth of the patient's younger sister, and the patient became strongly bonded to his father. The strength of those ties was influenced, we learned, by his mother's pregnancy, the birth of his sister, and what probably was a period of depression experienced by his mother—factors which, conversely, cast a pall over his relationship with her. The closeness to his father was short-lived, influenced not only by the rise of oedipal conflicts within himself but by the father's increasing moodiness and alcoholic tendencies. Although he tried, the patient rarely gained his father's approval (at least after the age of 4 or 5 years), and often felt rebuffed by him. It was only later that we began to understand how the strongly sadomasochistic relationship between the patient's father and paternal grandfather, a martinet of a man, left the father rebellious but cowed, covered with a thin veneer of manliness. These cross-generational influences played a major role in the patient's attempts to achieve fatherhood with a different model of fatherliness.

The patient's mother grew up in a strict setting. Her own mother died when she was young. She was very attached to her stern father, but in college, where she excelled academically, she began to rebel. During that "gay and wild" phase of her life, she met and married the patient's "carefree father," a step that she later, resignedly, considered an appropriate punishment for her earlier wild ways. Her husband's later alcoholism, depression, and illness were part of the cross she had to bear, she once told the patient. Analytic work enabled us to see that the parents' marriage seemed to have changed after the birth of the patient's younger sister. As it soured, his mother devoted herself to being a "model" mother and housekeeper. A prominent theme during the early part of the analysis was his mother's strong prohibitions against most sensual pleasures. It was she, not his father, who overtly condemned his early masturbation. It was she who put the brakes on his early (and later) active voyeuristic researches into the great mysteries of life: anatomical sexual differences and reproduction as it pertained to humans. However, she actively encouraged and at times participated in his investigations into the nature of plants and animals. (Both parents were active gardeners.) Of equal importance in channeling the patient's endeavors and later career choice was his father's unvarying reply to his frequent questions about the nature of things: "That's the nature of the beast, son." This unsatisfactory answer spurred the patient on to a lifelong desire to find out just what was the nature of the beast.

The patient early became a devoted naturalist, roaming through nearby forests and exploring ponds. Fishing with his father and walks with his mother were key influences. He also furtively roamed through his home, where he had many opportunities to observe his parents and younger sister in the bathroom in varying stages of undress. These observations left him in awe and confusion, more frightened than pleased. Most of these experiences had been "forgotten," except for a relatively late one: his older sister exhibiting herself when he was 8 years old and the family was staying at a beachside cottage. He not only remained "disgusted" by her, but this and other earlier experiences raised more questions than they answered. Female anatomy, no matter how sophisticated his later education, remained an area of bewilderment and fear and also gave impetus to his choice of career. Equally important in his quest to comprehend the nature of beasts was how they arrived on this earth. We learned that he knew and did not know.

The patient's wife was a nurse whom he had met in undergraduate school. She was a warm and giving person, less threatening intellectually and sexually than the young woman with whom he had previously been involved. Although they experienced considerable conflict, external and internal, later in the marriage, their attachment to each other was basically solid and positive.

Early Phases of Analysis

The early phases of the analysis were concerned primarily with reconstructing the patient's developmental history outlined above. Much was learned about why he clung to infantile ways and why he felt small and flawed, but behaved with provocative arrogance. He realized how his research (then in biological areas) was inhibited by conflicts about seeing and understanding the prohibited; otherwise inexplicable difficulties arose whenever he attempted to use the most penetrating tool, the electron microscope. Related to this, increasing success in his career pursuits was associated in his mind with danger. He realized that his relationship with his wife was intertwined with remnants of the past and afflicted by ambivalence. He gained some insight into why he retreated from closeness to her and turned to men, only to flee from the threats of homosexual love and submission.

Issues around becoming a parent had come up from time to time. Indeed, one of the stated objectives at the beginning of the analysis had been the wish to be a good father. He often commented on how he and his wife would never become so all-involved as friends did with their children. He particularly berated his older sister's manner of parenting. Two years before the birth of his own daughter, however, he pushed away the thought of ever becoming a parent in spite of his wife's increasing insistence on becoming pregnant. He sourly anticipated being excluded during a pregnancy and the complications that would arise if they had a son. Following the chance observation of one of my daughters and myself going into a store, the negative tone seemed to alter. There was something remarkable about actually being able to help create a child, he commented.

During the summer before he began his third year of analysis, he spent much time with his nephew and was delighted at how well they got along and how well he understood him, in contrast with his "neurotic" and "self-centered" older sister. At first he did not see the connection between these activities and his announcement, early in September, that he and his wife were planning to have their first child the following autumn. That intention was played down as he reassessed his graduate work and career plans in a most positive way.

Perhaps the self-reassurances were necessary that autumn as he anticipated a new level and phase in the analysis in which he would "plumb the depths." Indeed, striking changes took place in the character of the sessions. Frequent dreams with deepening and more archaic associations led to earlier and earlier memories, fantasies, and theories of birth and body concepts. Body boundaries shifted, sexual and body secretions and parts were symbolically yet concretely equated. In retrospect, we were back to the time of his mother's summer pregnancy with his younger sister.

The Pregnancy

In descriptions of both psychological and physical events of pregnancy, a division into trimesters is commonly used. This division is clearly related to differential physical and psychological events in women. In approaching the primarily psychological phenomena in my male patient, I believe it is of value to rely on a similar division; in addition, I focus on the 2 months preceding the pregnancy, because in this preparatory period changes in the character of the analytic sessions took place.

In the 4 periods I describe (getting ready; conception, bridging, and the early months; midpregnancy; and coming-to-term[s]), two kinds of interrelated phenomena emerged: those clearly reactive to his wife's physical and psychological status and thereby influenced by the unfolding stages of her pregnancy; and those not so directly related to her immediate status but more broadly reflective of the very existence of the pregnancy and its implications for himself.

Getting Ready

Following a Christmas holiday break of one week, the patient returned after the New Year, declaring that a new phase of work was to begin. While ostensibly he meant finishing his thesis and embarking on new research, what unfolded were multiple aspects of concerns with impregnation and conception.

Shortly after his return he mentioned that his wife was now definitely planning to have a baby. Though the emphasis on his wife as the primary moving spirit partially reflected the overt nature of events, it was also indicative of his own ambivalence and defensive, innocent-bystander role against which he later protested.

In actuality he began to take an active role. The patient and his wife decided to move to a larger, more comfortable apartment. They chose a house situated near a pond. This quiet area, with the all-important water nearby and land for a garden, formed a setting that seemed to serve as a fertile environment for coming events. Although both the patient and his wife worked hard at remodeling the apartment, the patient in particular seemed to do so with a compulsive drivenness. It was the first time that he had taken so much interest in their living quarters. He was especially proud of his skill with tools, paying reluctant homage to his father whose mechanical and carpentry abilities were considerable. The move, the setting, and the settling activities had the quality of preparing a nest. Indeed, references to birds, nesting, and egg hatching, observations keenly made throughout his life, came up frequently during these hours.

A dream in which he had intercourse with the analyst's wife with his big, penetrating penis sent him running for psychological cover. Associations to this dream in later sessions further referred to his enfeebled and declining father, open criticism of whom (for being such a "lousy" father) would, he fantasied, lead to his father's suicide. Elements of a theme he repeated later were first seen in the transference: Namely, that to become an impregnator was not only the ultimate incestuous act but also a symbolic "doing in" of his father. The possible consequences of this dangerous action were reflected in concerns about accidentally injuring himself with the construction tools he used in his new home.

The sense of preparing for an ultimate act exhibiting his strength and ability was in the air, but it was fraught with danger from two sides: revenge from his father (or the analyst in the transference) and entrapment by his wife-mother (also the analyst in the transference).

Toward the middle of January, the patient's wife stopped taking birth control pills, but he did not mention this until the end of the month. It was introduced by several dreams. One dealt with two beautiful blonde women in revealing bikinis at whom he stared; the other starred his wife as a 10-year-old girl in a home movie. These two dreams, and others later during his wife's pregnancy, we gradually learned most prominently represented his mother, older sister, and wife as a mother-to-be; his sense of exclusion during the mother's pregnancy with his younger sister; fear of new exclusion during his wife's pregnancy; early voyeurism; and retaliation for his sexual activities.

His associations to the first dream introduced other key themes as well. They revealed that he and his wife had engaged in intense sexual activity during the preceding weeks. There was no doubt that she intended to become pregnant. Their sexual relationship seemed to serve less as a source of physical pleasure than as a means to pregnancy. While on the surface he was in agreement with the aim of their having a child, he bitterly resented both his wife's drivenness and his being used as a stud. Furthermore, although not for the first time, he began to think about the implications of a future pregnancy. He anticipated the future loss of exclusive control over his wife's body and attention. He expressed concern about the dangers of the pregnancy, labor, and delivery; and in his fantasies he saw himself as the perpetrator of a chain of events that was potentially mutilating.

The second dream, of the home movies, led to memories of "dirty" scenes in the past, including the episode of his older sister's exhibition. These memories stirred up oral, anal, and phallic fantasies that were tinged with sadistic overtones and contained primitive childhood concepts of reproduction. These archaic concepts, which coexisted with his sophisticated scientific knowledge, gradually were reworked.

He experienced renewed fears of the power women exerted by their sexual seductiveness. His wife's driven sexuality led to several biological analogies, such as black widow spiders in which the female kills and eats the male after fertilization. The male, however, could also do the mutilating, and he berated me for not making both him and his wife less dangerous and less vulnerable. As if in reaction to a sense of powerlessness, he began to retrace his own sexual curiosity as a child, recalling the warm and sensual summer evenings when his mother had allowed him to stay up late to investigate the wonders of fireflies. He remembered the combination of excitement and curiosity as he collected and squashed the fireflies to find out the source of their lights. He saw more clearly the merging of his curiosity, especially sexual, with the sadism of the scientific investigations as he attempted to understand and to master the mysteries of birth, life, and death, at least in these small creatures.

This theme could be seen repeatedly in his scientific research. Life, its beginnings, and the factors affecting it were key elements. Furthermore, the particular animals chosen for the research, types of amphibia, were linked in multiple ways to his childhood and both parents. The cloacal anatomy also seemed more compatible with his childhood concepts of anal reproduction, and its early embryological stages somehow were safer because of the sexual undifferentiation.

As a result of his current feelings of anticipated loss, he remembered and further worked through experiences of childhood deprivations. His mother was responsible for the loss of Pinky, the cherished soft, round, pink teddy bear that for years (probably up to the age of 5 years) had been his inseparable companion and comforter. He later recalled that he left Pinky at a neighbor's house and therefore might himself have played a role in its loss, but at this point he felt it had been his mother's insidious doing. When she told him Pinky ran away, he cried for hours. Indeed, in the sessions he seemed bereft. He later learned that she had asked the neighbor to throw Pinky into a burning trash heap. Bitterly, to emphasize the sense of maternal deprivation, he recalled being told that his mother breast-fed him for only 13 days. He was overcome by a sense of her cruelty, a feeling that spilled over and was related to the new depriver of his own needs. In this period he turned to the analyst (father?) in a dream:

I was in a strange country or place and in great danger. People are after me. A psychiatrist lived there. I went to his home, an elaborate home with office, beautiful internally. I felt pleased to be there, safe and happy because of the threats. Someone had tried to strangle me. The psychiatrist was not you. It was someone who seemed openly benevolent and was older. Then the scene shifts, yet is related. I discover, while in the Middle East, old artifacts of Babylonian civilization and am going to tell someone in a museum so that they could be put there. It's a detailed plot and I can't recall it all.

His associations again emphasized the dangers of new and impending events. The psychiatrist's office was a refuge and a womb. Babylonian civilization seemed a time and place of evil kings and weird events where one needed protection. He recalled other dreams about shores, lakes, being a fugitive. Most prominently he thought of the word *Babylon*, splitting it into *baby* and *lon* or *lone*. He felt like a baby not only in terms of the infantile aspects he recognized in himself, but in relation to the eventual termination. The latter was like a rebirth out of the womb of the analysis (and analyst), when he would be alone and scared.

The intermingling of themes related both to the coming pregnancy and to the nature of his relationship with me and the analysis (particularly its termination) came up repeatedly during the remainder of the analysis.

During this preparatory time, he was faced with his thesis deadline and thesis defense. He insisted on typing the thesis himself, although he knew that it was very time-consuming. As he wondered why he did so and in such a compulsive manner, we recognized his need to deliver that final product of his own creative endeavors by his own hands. At the time of the actual and successful thesis defense, although he had been lovingly and encouragingly sent off by his wife, he almost totally excluded her from the subsequent celebrations. He preferred to include only fellow, and mostly male, graduate students and faculty. But there was an important exception. He saw the thesis not only as his baby but as a creation of both his mother and himself. He briefly allowed himself to see his mother as an important source of his own creativity, though earlier in the analysis he had had to play down her significance.

Thus it gradually became clear that before embarking on the voyage of impregnation, he felt it was essential to complete his own creation, which derived from his own efforts and those of a symbolic union with his mother as well as identification with her as a creative being.

In summary, there was a period of a few months before impregnation-conception when intensification of external and internal activities seemed to be part of a process of getting ready. The marked ambivalence was apparent in the active preparation of a new home in a setting linked with growing things; yet the symbolic nature of the progenitor role raised problems. It was as if to impregnate was a surpassing and doing in of his father, a wished-for event, yet one that also precipitated fears of revenge and regression to a passive position and a denial of his own prominent role. It also raised fears of abandonment; of entrapment; of being overwhelmed by the power of women; of female seductiveness, past and present; as well as covert envy of the unique female creative capacity. His anger was great and was linked with potential destructiveness in his progenitor role. The completion of his own endeavors (research and thesis) before the pregnancy served as a declaration of his own creative abilities, which in a very special oedipal way were linked with his mother. Furthermore, as if he had turned passive into active, the increased tempo of scientific work was connected with a lifelong attempt to control and master the forces of reproduction, life, and death, forces so long out of his grasp. At this point, it was already clear that there would be a merging of currents related both to the coming pregnancy and the analysis, especially change and termination.

Impregnation-Conception, Bridging,
and the Early Months of Pregnancy
Shortly after the weekend during which impregnation probably took place (based on average length of normal pregnancies), the patient pre-

sented a copy of his completed and bound thesis to me. He looked on its completion as symbolic of the end of childhood and adolescence, the beginning of a new phase of life. He touched only briefly on the probability of his becoming a parent in the near future, and dwelt primarily on his career plans.

With the future and his independence very much in mind over the next several days, he began to think seriously about an appropriate time for termination. He wondered what work remained to be done in the analysis. He was particularly disturbed by a sense of being split, portions of himself being like his mother, others like his father. It seemed important to him to gain a better understanding of his past and present relationships with his parents. This aim led to a period of intense, though sporadic, working through of these relationships, a reworking that often occurred via the transference and was particularly colored by and perhaps intrinsically related to his wife's pregnancy. We saw that the split in himself pertained to each parent, who had had both good and bad attributes.

Early in this period he visited his mother at a time when his father "happened" to be away. They had long and pleasant conversations. Most important, they talked a great deal about parents and children and ways of childrearing. On his return, he began to soften his condemnation of both parents, but particularly of his mother.

Many more such visits and conversations followed. They were in marked contrast to previous times, when little visiting had occurred and the conversations had been limited and unsatisfactory. In the course of the next 9 months (and until termination), his view of his parents (and me) changed many times, but it remained important to revisit psychologically, now with a new purpose. Birth, children, mothers, fathers, were to have a new reality. In this context he reported the following dream:

I was anxious all week. It was weird, especially the sexual fantasies I experienced. A dream last night had the same tenor. In the dream I was in a town on Cape Cod, not far out, somewhere on the western part. I was going someplace close by, taking a shortcut. As I was walking across a bridge, I saw a girl not like anyone I knew before. She wore a bathing suit, possibly flesh-colored. Then I saw she had no suit top. She had incredibly beautiful breasts. Was she entirely naked? No, just her breasts were showing. I asked her how to get where I was going. I walked with her and was lost. Everything was confusing as if going away from my destination. Just a little bit off the track and yet so tremendously lost.

The locale reminded him of a place where he had done some research during his college years and where he met the girl who first stimulated his interest in intercourse. It also reminded him of the area where his family had spent the summers and where his sister had exposed herself. Bourne Bridge was exciting. It was a lift bridge. He wondered if he was anxious because he planned to visit his older sister the next day. It would be different from the recent visit to his mother. His father would be around. He then told of a recent party where he had experienced active sexual fantasies about both women and men, but had acted only on the former. All week long he had been preoccupied with "fantasy sex," with breasts, with masturbation. Did it have something to do with the visits to his mother? The associations then increasingly seemed "off the track." I said so, and brought him back to the dream. The sense of being lost was related to his confused sense of sexual identity and moving away, earlier in the week, from the closeness to his mother. I asked about Bourne. He thought of "to be born."

"Oh, by the way, my wife may be pregnant."

He said it in a monotone. He had tried to do a pregnancy test the day before by injecting urine into frogs. His wife's frog evidenced a vascularized cloaca; his did not. He then went on to elaborate thoughts about the girl known in college, reminders of his mother, then came back briefly to having been reading a book on obstetrics. It was unpleasant, frightening, especially pictures of female genitalia. It would only take a shortcut to be a girl. "Women scare the hell out of me. They, like my older sister, are so consuming."

Thus the pregnancy was announced by way of Bourne Bridge. Indeed, there was much to be bridged. Somehow he must bridge the male-female within, the real and the fantasized, the past and the present, starting life and the fear of injury and death, being a child-son-daughter and a parent-father-mother.

Over the next several weeks the pregnancy was most remarkable by its absence in the analysis, but by the fourth week there was no doubt that his wife was pregnant and that the pregnancy was having a major impact on them both. She had become very moody, nagging, demanding, preoccupied, unavailable—and just at a time, he complained, when he wanted to focus his sexual attention on her. After all, he had decided to give up masturbation to do so. Her breasts were sore; he could not play with them. As he had anticipated a couple of months earlier (indeed, 2 years earlier), she now was so much "more biological," and he at times felt enraged. The anticipated 3-month abstinence near and after term already loomed large.

He had a sense of familiarity, of similar things having happened before. His wife's ordering him about reminded him of his mother's behavior and his own volatile anger of his father's outbursts. His wife's expression of concern about his loyalty made him aware that for the first time there was severe strain on their marriage. This enabled him to recall his father's threats of leaving the family. More than anything, however, he felt apprehensive about his wife: She was so mysteriously different.

In spite of the turmoil, the realization of the fact of the pregnancy dawned slowly. As it did, he began to take small, conscious steps. He stopped smoking. Together, he and his wife spent much time that spring planting a garden. The analytic hours were filled with lectures on giving up being an indulgent, nasty little boy, on the joys of motherhood with condemnation of anyone who did not like children, on the responsibilities of fathers, and new sympathy for his father. He said the lectures were like those of a reformed drunk and wondered not only why he was suddenly such a straight-shooter, but also why he seemed so preoccupied with concerns about death, his own, his father's, and—well, he didn't know yet.

During the next several weeks he barely mentioned his wife, except to say that she seemed uncomfortable and more distant than ever. (The distancing was two-sided, but temporary.) The major focus was a recapitulation of his relationship with his father in the transference. Many elements of that complex relationship were reviewed, but with new understanding. The wish to be close to me, to be like me, to be a father as he fantasied me to be, further stirred up passive homosexual concerns. The agricultural mode evolved into his feeling like a plowed field, like Mother Earth. The more he wanted my strength and received "seeds of insight" from me, the more he was compelled to react with fight (attack and themes of violence and being violated) or flight (missed hours, or hours that seemed to go nowhere). For some time he fought off the inevitable conclusion of the negative oedipal relationship, the wish to have a (penis) baby by his father, by me.

Interwoven were multiple aspects of competition. Deep down he wanted to be superman, but was afraid of the repercussions. What kind of an analyst was I if I was not perfect (a superman) and able to make him so? Would analysis enable him only to be a human being, "though a better parent"? His (preoedipal) father, once admired by him as a little boy as being perfection personified, was far from such. Indeed, as a rival for his mother's attentions, the patient had won an easy victory; or was he victorious? Why was he so disturbed now by his father's weakness and his mother's babying of him, just at a time when he felt such a need for her, or his wife, or someone? Well, in any case, he had surpassed his father by his wit, and now, with his wife pregnant, he had shown that he and his penis could also beget a child. That was evident for the world to see as "she was beginning to show."

Gradually, he renewed his ability to see and tolerate feminine aspects in himself. Boundary strings, like those in his parents' garden that had stood for gender separation (trees and certain vegetables were male, flowers female), were falling away. The "all boy" image encouraged by his parents was a family denial of warm, nurturing aspects in men. His father seemed unable to tolerate these components, aspects both "feminine" (in the common but questioned use of the term) and passive-dependent in relation to other men. He began to wonder whether these were not only universal factors in men but also somehow important in his soon-to-be role as a father.

It was not surprising, then, when the theme of admiration for his mother and all mothers developed somewhat later. He once again became eloquent on the power and importance of mothers, not only in their ability to conceive and give birth but also to rear and mold children. The really important and powerful role in society was that of rearing children.

In June, toward the end of the first trimester, the patient's family visited on the occasion of his graduation. The "celebrations" were colored by the patient's anger and remorse about his father's too-eager anticipation of another grandchild and by his own fear of "contamination" of the child-to-be by his father. He also felt close to his mother.

A few days later he had a dream about a Cambodian child starving, while orgiastic partying adults ignored the child. The patient, however, tried to feed the child. His associations focused on his sense of starvation while both his mother and father cavorted. His parents' gluttonous ways required that children be protected from the evildoings of adults. Yet, whatever had been the case with his parents, it was he who was now gluttonous and wanted to cavort, because his wife was otherwise occupied and he lusted for other women to nourish him. His mother and his wife had not fully given of themselves to him and thus were prostitutes and deprivers. Nor did I do right by him, for I was about to leave on a brief vacation (to cavort), while he needed support and sustenance.

In summary, as the time of impregnation-conception approached, the tempo of preparation for career decisions, in part related to a future supportive role, picked up. He was aware, however, of inner splits on many levels, particularly in relation to his parents and their role as models of parenting. The need to bridge so much within himself also served to bring about the actual impregnation-conception. His feelings about the pregnancy were muted by a defensive pattern related to his progenitor role, but also by his attempt to cope with his sense of loss and anticipated change in relation to his wife. His wife's determination to become pregnant engendered anger. He felt used and deprived, especially as the normal physiological events of pregnancy took their course. She seemed different and mysterious, yet he felt it was like an old story, feelings that facilitated further reconstruction of the events around his sister's birth.

He reached out toward the analyst for support and, in the process, further worked through his relationship with his father, recognizing his positive admiration for the preoedipal father and the negative oedipal aspects that included the wish to be a girl, to be impregnated, and to procreate. Previous masculine-feminine differences were reappraised, the old boundaries no longer holding up. He struggled to be a good husband and father, viewing the analyst both as an idealized image of the good father and an example of the procreator gone awry. Signs of ominous, destructive forces began to appear, but for the time being remained unclear.

Midpregnancy
This period covers only about 6 weeks of the 3-month second trimester because it was interrupted by the summer vacation, after which the character of the analytic work changed.

Soon after he had again raised the question of a possible termination date, a visit by his wife to her obstetrician established a due date. As it happened, this date was a month too early, an error not discovered until very late in the pregnancy.

In late June, he chatted cheerfully about accomplishing so much in his research, as well as doing "father-like" things such as seeing that the car was repaired and saving money. He had gone fishing and found a tiny lost kitten along the road. His cheerful mood gone, he told of almost crying at its plight. He picked it up, took it home, bathed and fed it. He felt at one with that motherless and homeless creature. "Mothering" it had been important.

Around that time he reported the dream, "There is a big auditorium where people are making speeches. I want to go in and listen, but there is a guard at the door who won't let me enter because the auditorium is full. I knew I couldn't go against the rules, but I really wanted to go in."

His wife's uterus, we speculated, was the already filled auditorium. Not only was he left out in the cold, but he was prevented from looking inside. The guard at the door was me, the obstetrician, his father—and himself.

This was followed by a period of increasing lability, and rapidly shifting themes grew. One day, while looking back at the tempest of the previous weeks, he recalled two events. The day before had been his birthday; and 2 weeks ago not only was his wife showing more but the baby had begun to kick!

The pregnancy now was more real, but so was the fact that it involved a baby. As he had previously concealed the pregnancy state, he now avoided the existence of the fetus.

At this time much of the material in the sessions dealt with fat, ugly women: his wife and probably his mother seen from the vantage point of a 2½-year-old. Nevertheless, his repugnancy went to the point of his saying that not only did his wife seem ugly, but something about her appearance made him hate her.

Analysis of this disdain led to thoughts about the state of pregnancy and perhaps his mother's pregnancy as a kind of illness. He linked a recurrent childhood dream about crawling around in a sod-filled space, breathless and dying, with anal birth fantasies originating after his sister's birth at a time when he had been ill. Further associations to frogs clearing the cloaca and eating eggs added aspects of oral impregnation. Other dreams confirmed his envy of his mother's, sister's, and wife's ability to breast-feed.

Just before the vacation, another kind of interruption occurred that played on his worst fears and wishes. His father had what at first appeared to be a heart attack. Although, after a short while, no organic pathology was found and psychiatric consultation was recommended, the patient received the news with a mixed reaction. He condemned his weak, self-destructive father, who just wanted to get attention; he was like a baby. Yet the patient felt jealous, immobilized, and afraid.

In the last session before the vacation, he spoke of the tasks that he would have to deal with in the coming months. He already felt a sense of loss in relation to termination. He was to become a father in his own right, while at the same time having to struggle to deal with his father's need for help. He would have to make major career decisions as well.

To summarize this period, as his wife began to show and the baby began to kick during midpregnancy, the very reality of the pregnancy and an alive being could no longer be avoided. He felt excluded from his wife and from the creature within her, who now was increasingly seen as a rival. Reexperiencing the old sense of wonder and mystery, he revisited archaic, oral, and anal birth theories. The other source of his procreative and nurturing urge was now seen more clearly in his envy of women's procreative and nurturing capacities, the latter so marvelous when provided, so awful when withheld. His own nurturing wishes appeared most clearly in the incident with the stray cat. The further exploration of his bisexual origins and nature transiently heightened his castration anxiety, then mellowed even his concern about anatomical differences. He now felt sufficiently secure to bring about a rapprochement with his mother, identifying with her good parenting qualities.

Coming-to-Term(s): The Final Phase

The summer had been a bad time. There had been much to cope with, and he did not feel up to it. He blamed me for not enabling him to be "unflappable." Sadness and feelings of abandonment predominated. Termination and the last stages of pregnancy were interlocked, although the former experience was presently overriding.

His father was clearly depressed and, encouraged by the patient, had started therapy. His father's physical state was poor; he had partially lost vision in one eye. His mother rebuked the patient for not being more active in helping his father, as he now rebuked me. His wife and he felt apart and he was down on women. "I am not yet through being a son, let alone ready to become a father. Everything," he complained, "is awful."

Gradually, it became clear that this was not the case. Many significant steps had been taken; some openly revealed, others barely detectable, all played down. He and his father had begun to talk with one another. His father had, in one particularly emotional conversation, agreed that they had never been close as father and son, a fact that he regretted. During August there had also been an increase in the quiet observations of and interactions with married friends and their children. It was as if an active learning, practicing, preparing for parenthood was in process. And though he still had many complaints about his wife, their relationship was undergoing a transition; they felt closer to each other and intimately shared their experiences.

A week or two after he resumed analysis, his spirits picked up. That was embarrassing and sufficient reason to damn me, for it revealed the extent of his dependence on me. He was thus driven to throw his weight around, to engage in flirtations with young women, but his underlying self-doubts were clear in the sessions. In the vernacular of a current dream, could he "join the big boys of the hockey team of life" or was he "forever doomed to be subservient and have a short stick?"

For some time before a much-delayed trip to his family's home area to pick up hand-me-down items, he railed against his mother and other family members. Noting that he protested too much, he gradually became aware of his jealousy of his parents' new closeness and his reexperienced irritation about losing a favored position. These feelings were related not only to the events in his family, but to the baby coming and eventual termination. He could now understand how even before his own birth, but especially after it, when his mother put so much of herself into him, his father could have seen him as a threat.

At the time of the visit other conversations occurred with his father. He was delighted and yet uneasy about his father's new self-awareness. They talked about raising children. The patient was suspicious of his father's sudden enlightenment. He feared "contamination" from him. At one point during the conversation he said to his father that he loved him, only to have his father reply. "That's queer" (in the sense of homosexual).

The patient, as if instructing his father, explained that men, fathers and sons, can indeed love each other.

With the purchase of a cradle by his sisters, the occasion of a baby shower for his wife, and the increased kicking presence of the baby, he felt very left out from time to time: All those soft things and music boxes; it must be great to be an infant!

For a while toward the end of the second trimester (late September), his wife and he both felt more positive about everything. She seemed particularly tranquil and pleased, his work was going well, and they were looking forward to the baby. Quite striking was a gradual change in his perception of his wife. Far from being ugly, she now seemed very beautiful to him; she had a special kind of beauty that he thought was intrinsic to the pregnancy.

As the (incorrect) time for the expected birth came closer, the tempo of preparation picked up. His wife stopped working, they built more furniture in their apartment to set up a nursery, friends and in-laws visited, and they both felt more apprehensive. His wife again seemed different, as if the need to mother were biological. The patient felt his life was not his own. After all, since providing a sperm many months ago, he supposedly had had nothing to do with the course of events. His pleasure, goals, and work were being trampled on by women and "that baby," who now was viewed as a "pain in the ass." But he particularly resented his mother's instructions to him to be nice to his wife. What was he, some kind of monster? Did she know something he did not?

No longer able to ignore indications of destructive wishes, he began to see signs of his anger and jealousy in many areas. Thus he recognized that his homogenizing frog embryos in the laboratory was not just in the service of science. He half-jokingly spoke of competing with his wife, stating he could grow better embryos than his wife any day. His sense of sardonic bitterness led to some further reconstruction of probable reactions to the birth of his sister. Was not the gamut of his present feelings similar to his childhood destruction of his mother's flowers and his father's trees following her birth? Was the pattern of wanting to create and destroy born of that period? Bringing to life and putting to death seemed so intertwined.

In late October, he reported two dreams:

I forgot to tell you yesterday about an important dream I had Saturday night, before which I watched a horror movie about a brain that wouldn't die, a girl who had been killed in an accident, and body parts attached to other bodies. The dream was about my father, myself, and eyeballs. I had to collect two big eyes. My father went into the ocean to get the eyes for me, but in doing so risked losing one of his own eyes. My father did get the eyes and together we put them into a depression on a crab's back. Only then did I discover that my father not only had put himself in great jeopardy for me, but he may have had his right eye penetrated by a knitting needle. I was overwhelmed with love and said to my father, "You risked something very big for me," and then threw my arms around him, and we hugged one another and cried. It was a very emotional dream.

Last night I had another dream [recalled during the associations to the first dream]. Raquel Welch was madly in love with me. She had incredible tits, but all of a sudden she had two half-sized tits on one side, three altogether.

Although these dreams were worked on throughout the rest of the analysis, the initial associations disclosed the following: The ocean, water, represented a primordial source of origin and specifically intrauterine space; there was concern about puncturing the "bag of waters" either out of angry jealousy or wanton sexuality; people were at risk, not only the fetus and his wife but he himself and, in some way not yet clear, his father. He was apprehensive about losing his wife, but also about losing his position at the breast—he had been cheated by his mother, was about to be cheated again, and was gluttonous; women are untrustworthy and dangerous, so men must stick together; yes, he was envious of woman's reproductive capacity, but also filled with adoration, for his eyes "swallow [his wife] up as if to take her in and become part of her"; the whole business of a supposed lack of a role for fathers was "blurred," in part by envy.

Shortly thereafter, his father made a serious suicide attempt and was placed in a psychiatric hospital. These events set in motion a period of mourning for his father and concerns about dangerous thoughts and dreams causing harm to others.

In early November the patient began to take a new view of becoming a father. It was more than biological paternity, but the dilemma was, how much more? Gradually he was able to separate out his own sense of omnipotent influence, whether life-taking or life-giving, and to see that as his star and powers rose, his father's were declining. He had a sense of remorse and sadness, as well as new insights about future tasks of a parent. To be able to give, in spite of envy, to be able to shift and adapt one's needs and goals as one grew older and one's children came into their own were tasks of later parenthood. He cried for his father (it was perhaps too late for a reconciliation) and was able to go on to a better definition of his own goals. New ideals were being born, while old ones died.

The focus shifted back to his wife, the pregnancy, his work. One day he reported that he and his wife had gone to see a film on sexual practices in Denmark. In the movie was a scene of a delivery. He was overwhelmed with the skill and powers of the obstetrician. Could his father be reborn in the hands of a similarly skillful and powerful analyst? Was I so skilled that his analysis would result in a rebirth of a more perfect self? No, he later decided, I was merely human, and he would not become a superman. In any case, the latter event had supersadistic overtones, resembling a pact with the Devil of tyrannic aggression and submission, and would sustain the same pathology that had been passed on from his father's father and his father. Was that the cycle, the root of concerns about "contamination" from his father? In a telephone conversation his mother had predicted he would be a good father and not have his own father's hang-ups. Could it really be that the cycle would end with him?

Many of the sessions in November, toward the end of the pregnancy, were permeated by references to magic, mysticism, devils, and witchcraft. A dream that followed his seeing the film, "Rosemary's Baby," dwelt on pacts with the Devil. Not only were his father and grandfather in league with evil spirits, but malevolence was in the air and would inevitably affect the baby. For example, his father was trying to kill the patient's success; the patient and I were teamed up against his father; his mother was a witch; but most important, if my (magical) powers were greater, I would have protected him, his wife, the baby, and everyone else from his own malevolence.

During this period, it seemed that early childhood fantasies were at work, but not only destructive ones. The more important of these became evident in mid-November, close to the time of the initial and incorrect due date. One day he was mildly ill with chills, fever, abdominal cramps, and diarrhea. He remembered similar episodes when he was a child. He thought there was something suspicious about these physical symptoms and connected them with the imminence of the baby's birth. Later that month, after they learned that the real due date was a month later, he experienced constipation for several days, frequently said, "I don't give a shit," and had a dream with elements of producing a big shit. His intestines, we finally concluded, were producing birth phenomena. "Now that is the biggest trick of all, speaking of magic; intestinal and natal alchemy," he said.

In early December, 9 days before the birth of a daughter, he reported the following dream:

I was in some factory. It was a big, smelly one, which homogenized cats and dogs and dried them up for fertilizer. I was quite distressed, perhaps actually crying in the dream. There was a room for chopping up animals. A butcher came out, fat, with no hair, spattered with soup left over from homogenized cat. It was all over him, he was a mess. He handed me two kittens to hold before grinding them up. I went into another room, a classroom with youngsters of all ages and a male teacher who looked like a former history instructor. "Teacher," I said, "I'm sorry to interrupt, but I have a terrible problem." Then I told him about the butcher in the other room, starting to sob inconsolably as I spoke.

The dream was related to the baby coming and the birth process.

Both he and his wife were now impatient, wanting to get it over with; his wife had cried earlier in the week out of fatigue and apprehension. While waiting, he thought it best to finish some papers, and was surprised that he could be so productive in spite of feeling resentful of "this whole baby business." They had two cats, one of which had kittens. He ground up animals in the lab, and the butcher-monster in the dream was his father and himself. Would he be an intimidating father and, if not, what kind of father would he be? He would want to protect the baby from his father and himself. The history teacher might be me, helping in that protection. He twice sobbed in childhood as in the dream, once when his teddy bear was taken away, the other time after having been caught setting a fire; the latter was the most frightening incident in his life, while the former was the greatest loss and the most upsetting, as if it were his own baby.

The following week he concentrated on whether the baby and future children would impair his career, while at the same time coming to more definite conclusions about seeking a position where he would be in command of his own ship (family, living circumstances, research) and pursuing issues around termination.

A week later, after the birth, he indicated his new understanding of how children develop a sense of omnipotence. "Eight pounds of baby," he said, "are completely dominating 300 pounds of adults."

In summary, during the summer break that occurred toward the end of the middle trimester, the patient carried on more actively than ever his observations of other parents and his interaction with children. This continued on resumption of analysis in spite of some inner and outer turmoil, the latter related to the illness, depression, and suicide attempt of his father. His father's travails increased the patient's apprehensions about his own roles of progenitor and future father, as he again became concerned about his competitive strivings and successful deeds, especially his successful marriage and the fathering of a child. He mourned for his father and in the process began to clarify and separate out his own developmental tasks from the particular nature of his father's development (with a view of the vicissitudes of later stages of being a parent). Aspects of ending and beginning, of birth and death (Schafer, 1968), of creating and destroying were confronted anew, not only in terms of the pregnancy and the father's illness, but also via the transference, in relation to termination. He developed somatic, particularly gastrointestinal symptoms, which were couvade-like sympathy pains (Trethowan, 1965; Trethowan and Conlon, 1965). Termination was seen as a rebirth. All of these events, intrapsychic and external, with the enlarging fetus making its presence felt, seemed to invoke archaic mechanisms of splitting (Lichtenberg and Slap, 1973), introjection, and projection. In the latter part of the last trimester he had a sense of good and evil forces at work, endangering all, especially the baby. Against such powerful and seemingly magical forces, equally powerful counterforces were needed. The analyst was called on for all his wizardry, but was found to be only human, alas, a fact that would pertain to his own "rebirth" at the end of analysis. While these regressive phenomena transpired, progressive efforts were at work; for they, like the baby girl that was born, did not wait.

Discussion

Freud believed that the father was the most important person in a man's life, but Freud was thinking primarily of the father of the Oedipus complex. The recent rediscovery of the importance of the father in the development of young children also provided evidence that the father's import begins quite early (Abelin, 1975; Lamb, 1975). He exerts an influence, not only indirectly through support and protection of the mother, but also directly through his relationship and attachment to the infant. Furthermore, this relationship begins long before the conception and birth of the child. It is a process that is intrinsic to much if not all that occurred in previous growth and development, although it is likely that certain of these experiences and phases are more important than others. These prepare not only for fatherhood specifically but for parenthood in general, since overlapping of roles and functions, at least in contemporary American society, clearly occurs.

I propose that the period of impregnation and pregnancy constitutes an important developmental challenge for the prospective father, which, like other developmental crises, brings about internal upheaval and change. The outcome is of critical importance to the whole family (Ross, 1979).

These psychological events occur in the context of the special tasks of young adulthood. As was the case with the patient described, by that time important decisions about sexual identity, career, and marital partner have already been made. But when a man prepares himself to produce an offspring, it is likely that the equilibrium attained is challenged severely, although perhaps less noticeably than in the mother-to-be.

Ritvo (1971) describes how in early adolescence retreat from the object under the pressures of the upsurge of libidinal impulses leads to some degree of resurgent narcissism and ego disorganization. In late adolescence, there is a shift to new objects. The new object, the sexual partner, is an essential nutriment as well as an organizing influence. As a new task arose for my patient, that of becoming a father, the ensuing upheaval resembled that of early adolescence as well as other developmental crises;

as others in the past, it required a new reordering. It was clear that the previously organizing influence and progressive growth-promoting aspects of the new object, his wife, had suffered a reversal. We could see elements of a retreat to more narcissistic phenomena, some degree of disorganization, return of strong ambivalence, and resurgence of passive homosexual strivings. That shift was not new; indeed, it was all too familiar. However, the pregnancy and the child-to-be now seemed to serve as the new organizing foci.

Thus my patient's preparation for the pregnancy and the pregnancy itself initiated a major reworking of the past and current relationships with his mother, father, siblings, and wife, as well as a shift and resynthesis of his sense of self. All of these coalesced to color the psychological atmosphere into which his daughter was born.

The patient's mother came under new inspection. With the pregnancy of the patient's wife, the wonder of his mother's pregnancies and her creative and nurturing capacities was reexperienced both positively and negatively. He clearly envied yet secretly identified with these capacities. The links to her were stronger than ever, more satisfying, and yet more unsatisfying. The earliest preoedipal ties and disruptions, tidal waves of archaic affects, blurring of boundaries, primitive images of good and bad mother and self, and the primitive mechanism of splitting, projection, and introjection to cope with libidinal and aggressive forces—all these were aroused by the pregnancy. His mother's nature, her anatomy, her procreative abilities, her actions admired and feared, envied and repugnant, were comprehended anew. The cherished and dangerously seductive oedipal mother also reappeared in consciousness. The wish for this forbidden union, manifested at so many levels of productivity and with manifold repercussions, could no longer be easily disguised. Yet, in spite of all the upheaval, the patient began to sort out the desirable and undesirable aspects of, and experiences with, his mother, and thereby was enabled to form a new identification with her parenting role.

In relation to the patient's father, what came into view during this part of the analysis was not so much the father of the adolescent or latency years as the father of the oedipal and preoedipal years. The oedipal father, the rival on so many battlefields, now was engaged on more dangerous territories than ever. For this son to become a father like his father, yet not just like him; to become a procreator with a woman who now, more than ever before, was linked to his mother, was heavy work indeed. The real physical and psychological decline of his father made it all the more dangerous and difficult. It was no wonder that strategic retreats were necessary. The move to the preoedipal relationship, to the loving and beloved father, safely and at the same time dangerously strong, gained further momentum from the recurrent forces at work in relation to the preoedipal wife-mother.

Loewald (1951), Abelin (1975), and Lamb (1975), among others, in pointing to the early importance of the father in the child's development, indicate his modulating influence in the gradual separation-individuation process. Discussing the role of the father as a protector against aspects of maternal castration, Loewald (pp. 15–16) comments:

> Against this threat of maternal engulfment, the paternal position is not another threat or danger, but a support of powerful force. . . . The father figure, then . . . is not *primarily* hostile, representing the threat of castration with which the boy copes with passive submission and/or rebellion. Earlier, in my opinion more essential for the development of the ego (and reality), is his positive stature with whom an active, non-passive identification is made; an identification which lies before and beyond submission as well as rebellion.

With the resurgence of aspects of maternal envy, engulfment, and deprivation as a result of the pregnancy, my patient's admired preoedipal father stood as a protector, a refuge, someone who in fantasy actively sacrificed himself to rescue the patient from the primordial waters of the pregnancy. In addition, by taking over some of his father's specific and useful skills and attributes, forms of the ego ideal, the patient was able to begin gearing himself to become a supporter and protector of his own family, despite recognizing the flaws of his father of old and, especially, the old and sick state of his father of the present. His father was a model of fathering to whom he had to turn to sort out what was useful as well as to discard what would contaminate and impede. Further working through of the negative oedipal, homosexual coloration of his relationship with his father (and analyst) fostered reformulation of his ego ideals (Ritvo, 1971).

His older sister's mode of mothering and parenting was critically reviewed, as well as the import of earlier events in their relationship. Her old and new jealousy of him, as well as his sense of abandonment experienced around the birth of his younger sister, reemphasized the changes in exclusivity of attachment brought about by birth. His sisters' considerable involvement in his wife's pregnancy facilitated a reworking of his relationships with them. One outcome was a further moving away from the intense incestuous bonds to his younger sister, and a strengthening of his attachment to his wife.

The relationship between my patient and his wife underwent wide swings, which seemed to reflect reactions both to specific physiological and emotional changes in his wife as the stages of the pregnancy unfolded and to the more general fact and symbolism of the pregnancy. Before the actual impregnation and in response to predominant facets of each trimester, the mode of interaction shifted. Body changes in his wife, her normative emotional withdrawal and self-preoccupations, her sporadically increased dependency on him, her redefining of her own femininity, her varying enthusiasm for sexual relations, her concern about the intactness and health of her fetus and about her own health and body integrity—all of these were probably present, some actually reported by the patient, others only indirectly evidenced by his own concerns. In reviewing the careful descriptions by Bibring (1959), Jessner and colleagues (1970), and the Colmans (1971) of physical and emotional phenomena in women during pregnancy, I was struck by the fact that my patient experienced similar emotional (and in the last trimester, physical) reactions, seemingly arising entirely from within himself but clearly in part reactive to his wife. There was a remarkable sharing of psychological (and even some physical) events during the pregnancy. Through their new experiences and their reexperience of old issues, their relationship altered, faltered, and was strengthened as they underwent growth as individuals. This had to be. Whereas their marriage and heterosexual relationship had been initiated on a dyadic level of young adulthood, the joint creation of a child introduced a new level of relatedness.

Into this dyadic world peopled as it was by imagos in a state of transition, the child-to-be stepped gradually. At first it was more symbol than fact, yet at an early fetal age it already exerted powerful influences. As it got bigger and then finally made its kicking presence known, it gave warning to its parents-to-be to get ready. On the positive side, as a wondrous achievement, a marvelous experiment in the ways of nature, its existence was welcomed. Though often ignored as a new entity, it was what would make them a family, something they both desired. But in my patient these positive vibrations were buffeted by negative forces. For even before and certainly early in the pregnancy, the child-to-be stood more for the loss of hard-won position, a rival at the breast, a depriver of sustained support and attachment, an agent and accomplice of his father, an envious and envied sibling, an instigator of change ambivalently anticipated, evidence of dirty work, a potential mutilator or mutilatee, and thereby, all in all, an invitation for trouble. To add insult to injury, no matter how great an innovator and scientist he was, he could not do what his mother, his wife, his sisters could do. At times he seemed driven back to the infuriating role of a passive observer. This passive role was also welcomed, however, for he could take refuge and disclaim having had much to do with the baby.

It was remarkable that by the time of the birth and clearly in the months that followed, he came to terms with his child. Their relationship following the birth actually began on a most positive footing, the turmoil that had preceded being quietly and gradually covered by an amnesic blanket. The gender of the child was very important to the patient. A boy would have reactivated the range of conflicts that he had experienced with his father. He clearly wanted a girl and was much relieved when a daughter was born. Therese Benedek (1970a, p. 172) has commented on this phenomenon: "Not infrequently the desire for children of the opposite sex is motivated by an intuitive awareness of the wish to avoid reexperiencing with the child the conflicts that were incorporated through the developmental interactions with the parent of the same sex."

The analysis and the analyst via the transference probably influenced the nature of the experience of prospective fatherhood, as the latter influenced the former. I was at different times seen as each of the important persons of the past, with all their negative and positive characteristics. But I was also seen as an ally in the work of understanding, and as neutral in the war of conflicts, desires, and fears. The pregnancy and becoming a parent became an integral part of the analysis, a synergic interplay useful to both (Hurn, 1969).

Finally, I want to draw attention to an important phenomenon. In the second, but mostly in the third, trimester, my patient had the intense experience of powerful magical forces being at work. I believe that this type of experience is not limited to my patient. Bibring (1959), and subsequently Jessner and others (1970), have commented on the number of women who are haunted by the fear of producing a monster or a dead infant. Jessner and coworkers say, "These concerns . . . reflect the experience of the uncanny and of magic powers" (p. 222). In the third trimester, "most women experience the fetus now as an enemy, who is injuring the kidneys or the womb" (p. 223), and later, "experiences of anxiety in many forms and morbid preoccupations in women during the last weeks of pregnancy were observed in all pregnant subjects studied. . . . Delivery initiates in the mother fantasies of death and rebirth" (p. 224). My patient had similar fears, an expression of concern for his wife and of his own aggressive rage at his wife and child-to-be. The degree to which his fears were reactive to her fears is not clear. It seems to be particularly in relation to the commonly heightened apprehensions in the later stages of pregnancy that many societies exert the strongest ritual controls. The couvade phenomenon in its many forms would be an attempt to ward off the powerful internal and external forces to which all members of the society are subject.

One cannot extrapolate from one case and postulate the existence of universal phenomena. Moreover, the vicissitudes in the case reported here were colored by the particular complexities of this patient's life circumstances. The period of prospective fatherhood coincided with the terminal phase of the analysis and with the father's acute physical and mental deterioration—factors that exerted mutual influences on each other. Only further case reports can bring more understanding of the phenomena intrinsic to prospective fatherhood, at least from the vantage point of the analytic situation, unique though that may be.

Whatever the reasons for the past silence on fathers may have been, it appears that we are at last beginning to recognize the significance of the early role of the father. As a way to gain a better understanding of that role, we must turn our attention to the early developmental processes involved in becoming a father. Prospective fatherhood is a critical stage in that development.

19

Patterns of Expectant Fatherhood:
A Study of the Fathers of a Group of
Premature Infants

James M. Herzog

Men approach fatherhood by different routes. Each has constructed a kind of conceptual road map of what his life is to be. For some, family may figure predominantly; for others, life is organized differently, for example, primarily around career. A man experiences his wife's pregnancy largely in terms of his underlying views of his own life.

For men to whom caretaking is important, the development of this attitude is continuous, beginning with an early identification with their own mothers and undergoing character changes throughout childhood (Kestenberg, 1974; Ross, 1979). For other men it is more difficult to trace their particular line of development. Fathering fantasies and preoccupations of earlier years are either blurred or buried, negative, or perhaps never occur at all. In such cases fatherhood seems accidental and not experienced as being either an essential or a complementary aspect of life.

Overview of the Study

This work involves the study of a special variant of expectant and experienced fatherhood: The subjects were men whose wives gave birth to premature infants. In each case, however, the prematurity was not expected. These were all first fatherhoods, or at least first fatherhoods within the present marriage. The children were born between 25 and 39 weeks' gestation and the families were referred to the infant follow-up clinic that I administer. The technique used involved retrospective analytically-oriented interviewing of these new fathers.

The initial interview was often at a severely stressful time in the life of the family. The newborn's life often hung in the balance. Subsequent interviews occurred over the next 24 months during regularly scheduled return visits of the children and parents to our clinic. During this time, it was possible to form a unique kind of relationship with the parents. The great stress around the premature birth imparted a certain transferential element to the relationship with the interviewer. In many cases, this facilitated the revelation of deeply personal information, which might otherwise only be expected to be available in a well-established therapeutic alliance.

I set out to determine where each of the new fathers was in his particular expectant fatherhood, interrupted as it was anywhere from 26 to 39 weeks along its course, and I asked the new fathers to reconstruct what their earlier experiences during the pregnancy had been. Many of the new fathers considered this work important to them, both in dealing with the trauma of the moment and in consolidating the course on which they were embarking.

Studies have suggested that during pregnancy women experience a more or less orderly reworking of earlier issues involving intimacy, caretaking, and previous experience in the parent-child matrix. The character structure and style of the individual woman appears to play an important role in the intensity of this experience (Bibring et al., 1961). There also appears to be a rather close correlation between physiological changes and processes and psychological reworkings, regressions, and reintegrations (Kestenberg, 1976; Benedek, 1979).

Men's experiences of their wives' pregnancies have a somewhat different flavor (Gurwitt, 1976, Chap. 18). Men can choose how much they will be involved in the process, and thus to what degree they will respond psychologically to physiological changes in their wives. During this phase of the caretaking line of development in males, there appears to be more of a correlation between capacities for caretaking and intimacy in men than is necessarily the case in women. Men who have already tended to be intimate with their spouses are more likely to participate fully in the experience of anticipatory fatherhood than are those men not involved in such intimacy.

If one accepts the idea that a man need never know that a child has been conceived or can, even if he does have such knowledge, elect with greater or lesser success to ignore the fact—can one still then go on to say that there are inevitable patterns of expectant fatherhood that can be observed across men as well as in individual men (Marcel, 1962)? The results of the present study support a tentative yes. In the interviews with the 103 men in my sample, certain repetitive concerns, preoccupations, and general themes, which formed a relatively consistent pattern, emerge. These themes, feelings, and concerns were not equally felt by nor available to all the men. Rather, it soon became clear that the men could be divided into two distinct groups: those who were in touch with feelings and fantasies pertaining to the pregnancy, and those who were not.

An initial attempt to understand this dichotomy in terms of character type was not rewarding. It appeared, however, that a valuable discrimination was the nature of the marital relationship. Roughly speaking, men were cognizant of their own feelings about the impending arrival of their first child to the extent that they were empathic with and invested in their wives. It seemed, then, that fatherhood both qualitatively and quantitatively is related to the conjugal relationship.

A second feature, however, should also be noted: the individual, even idiosyncratic, meaning of each pregnancy for each father. One hundred and three separate stories of gestation and birth seemed to be intricately linked to as many separate life histories. Work with expectant mothers has also revealed tremendous diversity of meaning and processing of experience, but it was my sense that this was much more pronounced in the men than in the women. The fact that men can be at least once removed from the actual events of pregnancy, childbirth, and childrearing may imply that their psychological participation in these events and experiences bears a clear imprint of their previous experience, conflicts, and conflict resolutions. In women the life experience and meaning may be clearly detectable, but there is a stronger psychobiological cast.

The material that follows will focus primarily on the approximately 35 fathers who were deeply involved in an empathic intimacy with their wives. For purposes of convenience, I shall label this group as the "most attuned" group. I divided the remaining fathers into "less well-attuned" and "least well-attuned" subgroups. Mention will be made of some highly suggestive aspects of these latter two groups, but principally for purposes of comparison and contrast. I have also attempted to delete much of the more strictly individual or peculiar findings and will report the elements that the 35 fathers in the "most attuned" group seemed to have basically in common.

It must be emphasized that my conclusions are impressionistic and hypothetical inferences in need of corroboration by single cases studied in depth as well as the careful quantitative analysis of similar large samples.

The Getting Ready Period

There occurred a "getting ready period," to use Gurwitt's term (1976, Chap. 18). Among the 35 couples in the most attuned group, there seemed to be a distinct period in which both parties knew they would try to make a child soon. Husband and wife were sometimes on different timetables in terms of their lives in this regard, and this was worked out by the couple. Men reported that it felt different "having sex to make a baby" than "just having sex." "This is procreation," one father said. Several men reported that they and their wives discussed the difference between simply making a baby and being able to care for the baby. The distinctions between recreative, procreative, and "parentogenic" sex were explored and experienced. In my sample, this getting ready phase was recalled as a more "rational and controlled" phase of the total pregnancy than the phases that followed. Several men reported feeling they were embarking on something new and very foreign. One recalled the sensation that this was much different from "going off to college or graduate school, or even getting married." Some reported a sense of entelechy, that fatherhood was the reason for their being. About half of the men in the most attuned group were transiently concerned that they were sterile or would not have sufficient "stuff" to do it. Two men who were involved in a prolonged getting ready period related to reality constraints (e.g., financial and educational restraints) felt urgency "to get on with it before it was too late." Neither could recall what "too late" meant, but both, interestingly, noted the fact that their wives were over 30 years old. In the less well-attuned group, several men reported that it was their feeling that "a kid would be OK sometime," but that there had been no particular plan to have one now. Some of the men thought of suggesting abortion, but this option was not elected by their wives. Three of the pregnancies in the least well-attuned group occurred during serious marital rifts and were the ostensible reason for the marriage continuing rather than dissolving at that time.

Stage of Conception

The getting ready period was followed in the most attuned fathers-to-be by the stage in which conception occurred and was medically confirmed (Gurwitt's second phase). The affect characteristic of this phase was joy. "I jumped 3 feet in the air and shouted, 'Hurrah'," one quite staid gentleman reported. "We felt an inner glow," another said. Several of the men described an initial surge in their feelings of manliness. A physicist reported thinking as he was about to give a seminar, "I've got the cock that made her pregnant. My seed is sown." He felt very aroused at that moment and created quite a stir in his classroom when he wrote on the blackboard, "My physics is sexy," and then hastily recovered himself and went on the speak about quantum mechanics. Most of the men reported a substantial improvement in their sex lives with their wives in the ensuing weeks—and, with this, the wish to love and be loved seemed to expand. Several indicated that they became "quite hyper." "Making the kid was a high," one man reported. Only a very small number of men betrayed their ambivalence. One man said, "I kept thinking, it is true what my mother said that every time you open one door another is closed. The thought made me kind of edgy, like you know you can't go home again. You know I don't believe in abortion." In the less and least well-attuned groups, the news of the pregnancy elicited various responses. Seven women whose husbands were in the least well-attuned group elected not to tell their husbands that they were to become fathers. One man said, "She probably just hoped it would go away, the dumb broad, by the time she did tell me it was too late. I had no choice but to go along with her."

End of First Trimester

This initial mood began to change toward the end of the first trimester. The well-attuned husbands and fathers-to-be remarked on a perceptible change in their inner lives. Eight of the men remarked spontaneously, and the others concurred in response to directed inquiry, that they first became aware of this transition by way of an increasing incidence of new and different fantasies during lovemaking. Contact with the themes and issues of expectant fatherhood was, in fact, most often achieved in the sexual realm, which suggests the possibility at least of a connection between sexual expression and the caretaking in men.

Fantasies often intruded on lovemaking and were of several sorts. A number of men reported fleeting images of themselves as huge bottles of milk or as a cow's udder pumping necessary nutriments into their wives or into the fetuses. "I'm like that guy in the Philip Roth book," one man said. "I've become The Breast." The feeling of having to refertilize or nurture the pregnancy seemed to come to the fore (Bettelheim, 1954). "They need more and I've got it to give," one man recalled feeling. Another dreamed of the final scene from *Faust*, where Faust oversees the building of irrigation ditches. This same man, a psychiatrist, recalled the play's closing lines, "*Die ewige weibliche zieht uns hinan*" ("The eternal feminine draws us on").

For some of the men, this shift in their fantasy lives had an enriching or pleasing quality; others experienced it as distracting or irritating, with an obligatory or compulsive quality. Many of the fathers in the most attuned group revealed feelings on both sides. These fantasies, I conjecture, may reflect a reexperiencing of the earliest stage in a boy's caretaking line of development, his identification with the nursing mother, the furnisher of oral supplies. Of further interest was the fact that some men described themselves as nurturing both the mother and the fetus, almost as one. The differentiations between parent and child, between mother and father, seemed to have become blurred. In this fantasy of feeding

305

the fetus, the nurturing also appears to have become genitalized and heterosexual: Equations between penis and breast, and semen and milk seem to obtain.

In the other two groups, it was much more difficult to uncover these fantasies. In the least well-attuned group, an interesting variant occurred. Several men reported that they needed more sex than they were getting. "I'm hungry for it all the time," one man mentioned. Generally, these statements were couched in terms of the man's needs and deprivations rather than in terms of his spouse's.

The next characteristic to emerge among the most attuned men was an increasing preoccupation with their own insides. Several men reported a new quality to their ejaculatory experience, focusing on the sensations that just preceded climax. There was a new awareness of thrust and power. "It feels like a bull trying to get out; a volcano exploding; it hasn't been like this since I was 13 years old." One man recalled in vivid detail his first ejaculation as an early adolescent.

I was rubbing myself on my pillow. I was thinking of my girl—that we were in a swimming pool together, there was water all around—I was very close to her. Then I felt waves like the water was in me. The waves were coming stronger. I wanted to scream. I could feel it inside like it was travelling through my groin—pounding like the water harder, harder inside but wanting to get out, almost unbearable, then out, no longer in, but out. I can almost feel the march, the waves, from my testes all the way through me out my penis and into my wife. It reminds me of that movie "Fantastic Voyage"—but I'm not detached. I'm more there than ever. We should tell Masters and Johnson and those pleasure people about making love to your wife when she's pregnant.

There was also an increasing incidence of awareness of what was called aftersensation. "For the first time I felt an ache afterwards. There was a kind of rhythmic contraction sort of just inside my ass. I felt as though something inside me was letting me know I have insides too." Or, "There's something in me that has to do with this baby business. It's not just my prick and balls, but farther back. I mean really inside, not just out there." Or in more prosaic terms, one physician told me: "Look, if you are 30 and if you are screwing a lot more than usual, your prostate is going to let you know it's around. God, mine's reminding me that it is there constantly."

Midpregnancy

Several fathers reported more concern with gastrointestinal (GI) symptoms, in particular a feeling of fullness in the upper and lower GI tracts. I wondered if this trend, which seemed to be most evident around mid-pregnancy, had to do with the reworking of a successive stage in the caretaking line—a stage in which identification with the mother blends with the boy's "inner-genital" or maternal phase (Kestenberg, 1975b), when he becomes aware of early prostatic and seminal vesicle contractions. These are used to fuel his still powerful fantasies of being able to bear children (compare Little Hans [Freud, 1909a]). Residue of this phase of development often includes concerns about the order and connectedness of things such as body parts. One father reported: "I kept having these dreams of all these diagrams, a giant maze. Only I was both inside and outside." Another said, "How are all the parts of me connected. I've got to figure that one out. What I'm feeling, the baby, Ruth, my insides, and outsides."

This inner-genital stage appears to be followed by a hermaphroditic stage (Ross, 1977, Chap. 12). In childhood, the boy is likely to see himself as able to both fertilize and bear a child, as able to carry a baby like mother while sustaining his identification with the male role. Fathers in the most attuned group reported the wish that they could have it both ways. Several described new sexual techniques that allowed them to feel penetrated at the same time that they were penetrating: to give and get at the same time. One of the fathers related a dream in which an elephant reached around to his anus with his trunk and blew air into himself. He swelled up and ached. The father indicated that this is how he felt after he ejaculated now—both full and very empty. Men who reported that they felt empty when they were in touch with prostatic contractions, also spoke of fears that they would not have enough to give their wives or that they would not be good enough fathers. Many reported that they began to eat more, and several fathers gained significant amounts of weight during midpregnancy. In the less and least attuned groups, I did not find evidence of this reawakened inner-genital or hermaphroditic stage. There were some accounts of GI symptoms and several of the men indicated recurrent bouts of nausea. These were variously attributed to "the bug," its being contagious ("I caught it from my wife"), and a somatic metaphor ("I'm sick of the whole thing").

The Turn Toward Father and Fathering

At this stage of the pregnancy, roughly between 15 and 25 weeks, many of the men in the most attuned group reported an increased pressure to sort things out with their families of origin. A common preoccupation was that their own fatherhood would be blighted by difficulties in their relationships with their fathers. Over and over again, this motif was evident, often in terms of reestablishing connections: "How I hook up with my old man determines how the kid will hook up with me." There were analogies to plumbing, circuitry, and other kinds of connecting, and thus this sorting out phase, too, seemed to bear an earlier inner-genital imprint. There was another quality too. In order to envision oneself as a good father, many men strove to revive and reestablish contact with the good father of old. Often, this was the preoedipal father, but there was also present the mentor or masculine guide of the oedipal and latency years. Once more, I found that the male's caretaking line of development is fatefully affected by the presence of a good-enough male mentor-father, who helps the boy grieve the loss of his earlier identification and helps him to see what a man is and what a man does.

I have come to think of this turning to one's own father in a "straightening out" or even "refueling" manner during midpregnancy as a fateful landmark in anticipatory fatherhood. It is almost as if such an event signals a more masculine or less maternal quality associated with the second half of pregnancy. It is interesting to think in terms of Abelin's postulate (1977) that a boy is biologically programmed to turn away from his mother and toward the father at around 18 months of age to help dissolve his primary femininity and to embark on his anatomically determined masculine course. Something analogous may, I speculate, occur in midpregnancy when the turn to his father helps to launch the father-to-be on a more paternal course.

Men who did not go through this sorting out phase (primarily men in the less attuned and least attuned groups) seemed to become progressively less able to participate in their expectant fatherhood or what Max Deutscher (1971) called the alliance of pregnancy. Often these were men who had no father toward whom to turn. Much of their lives could be understood in terms of his absence. Those men who were father hungry, who had experienced a felt absence of their fathers or of those qualities associated with maleness in their growing-up years, seemed now to make a career of the pursuit of males and maleness. Paradoxically, such men were both most intolerant of their own feminine identifications and longings and most vulnerable to these in the second half of the pregnancy. Rather than being able to turn at this critical point with the help of an internalized male mentor to a paternal role that was nurturant, involved, and masculine, they tended at this time to fall into bisexual adventures, competitive strivings with their wives, or flagrant promiscuity. This finding was so striking—that the ability of a man to participate in expectant fatherhood is inversely related to his state of father hunger—that it emerges as the third general conclusion of this work.

Fantasies About the Coming Child

Sometime after quickening, a change in the fantasies and preoccupations of the father-to-be occurred. First, men began to think of the fetus as a child, separate from both themselves and their wives. For example, the sex of the child was now routinely conceptualized: In the most attuned group, approximately two-thirds of the men "expected boys"; in the other two groups, this figure approached 100 percent.

Blatantly aggressive fantasies also now made an appearance. One man reported a dream at 24 weeks' gestation. He was in Israel and saw a sign, "Ben Ramtitski." Where was this place? As he mused on his dream, his associations started with "Ram." He thought of Ramses, the prophylactic, and wondered why he had not used one. Then his thoughts turned to "ram tit," which called up sadistic feelings toward his wife. The "-ski" meant "son of ram tit," as did the "Ben" before. Assuredly this place was where he was going, but that it was in the promised land did not seem at all clear. He was aware of a wish to hurt the baby as well as to welcome it. After all, he had placed it safely in Israel, rather than in Eastern Europe, the land or origin implied by the -ski form of the name. The baby was now distinct and protected from his wrath by his wife's body. He had thought of wanting to hurt her body and then of wanting to venerate it. He remembered that he had felt a little afraid of making love to his wife then, lest he hurt her or the baby.

Many men reported variations of this theme from around 22 weeks onward. Their remembrances were especially vivid because of their closeness to the unexpectedly early arrival of the babies and because of the fact that in a not insignificant number of cases labor ensued in rather close proximity to the occurrence of these kinds of thoughts, feelings, fantasies, and dreams, as if they were responsible for the premature parturition.

As one possibility, this material might be seen to recapitulate the next developmental stage, when the oedipal little boy is forced to acknowledge the presence of three people and to bring together wishes to love and to hurt, to be nurtured and to be punished. In this vein, several men in the well-attuned group began to be bothered by stories and news having to do with child abuse. One pediatrician found it increasingly difficult to start intravenous infusions on his little patients. A number recalled having dreams in which they were administering well-deserved spankings to older children. One man reported that such a dream had been quite sexually exciting, although to the best of his knowledge he had never previously been aroused by such material. Variations on these beating fantasies involved the notion that the kid would beat out the father himself. "The little pisser," said one dad, "just wait till he's old enough to make me squirm." It should be added that the urethral and urinary imagery was quite pronounced in several fathers. One father reported the recurrent thought that he might now urinate into the vagina during intercourse, either drowning his baby or otherwise washing up the pregnancy. This father did recall having been a bed wetter until the age of 10 years. This material, which occurred after 26 weeks, is especially interesting to compare with Kestenberg's description (1976) of urethral reworkings in the third trimester in women. Once more, it was harder to devise impressions of the period after quickening in the men in the less and least well-attuned groups. It was my sense that there were hostile currents in these men, but that these were principally directed toward their wives. Two of the fathers mentioned their plans to get their digs in when the kids arrived, but this did not appear to be a phase-specific wish as it was in the most attuned group.

The End of Pregnancy
Some of the pregnancies ended at this point in time with the arrival of a very small, often sick, but usually viable baby weighing 750 to 1,000 grams at around 26 to 28 weeks of gestation. In those pregnancies that lasted longer, the third trimester seemed to bring with it a new kind of experience: the sensation on the part of many of the men that something "powerful, and magical and big" was going on, something beyond their ability to control. The intrusive fantasies seemed to decline, as did the frequency of lovemaking. There was a perceptible shift toward readying things in the real world for the child's arrival. Observations of children, concerns with patterns of childrearing, and preparations and activities related to the actual arrival of the child seemed to replace the preoccupation with inner processes of the previous months. "It's out of my hands," one father reported. "I've done what I could; now nature will take its course."

The theme of magic or mystery was echoed again and again. This varied in individuals from an emphasis on the sinister to an emphasis on the sublime. Also at this time, there reemerged a more defined notion of the differences in reproductive roles in men and women. The earlier sexual theories and reproductive fantasies seemed to be replaced by a general feeling of awe. Truth was more astonishing than individual fiction; the actual miracle of birth surpassed the childish fantasy. "Out of something that feels so good," one father said, "something that really has to be worked on. I have my part; she has hers. Together we make something new. The last 8 months have been hard work, but nothing, I'd wager, compared to the next 400."

In this later stage of pregnancy, men in the most attuned group seemed to be working on the differences between inner and outer, slowly coming to understand that which could be ordered and interpreted, while continuing to marvel at that which lay just beyond their grasp ("the eternal feminine draws us on"). I wondered if I were seeing a replaying of that stage in the boy's caretaking line of development when he sadly but surely gives up his maternal inner riches and invests his penis and the outside world with ever greater importance (Ross, 1977, Chap. 12). Thus, the expectant father gets back "in touch with his insides" and to some extent with those of his wife; yet he maintains his valuation of his penis, his exterior, and the outside world. Thus he grooms himself for his future role with his children as the representative of the outside world (i.e., the world beyond the mother-child symbiosis), but as provider who is also respectful of this symbiosis. He also serves as such as an external beacon to his wife, who may feel that she is being submerged in her own inner processes and concerns at the time of parturition.

The Premature Delivery

For all of the 35 men in the most attuned group, expectant fatherhood ended sooner than expected as a consequence of the premature births. All experienced varying degrees of anger, distress, fear, and grief. In this group, however, these affects were compatible with the ability to empathize with the comparable feelings in their spouse. These men instinctively felt that their wives needed more rather than less after the production of a premature infant. It was as if the process of expectant fatherhood, linked as it was to the shared intimacy with the wife, enabled the man to parent his wife at the very time when she most needed care. In this group, there seemed to be no gross disorders of attachment and parenting as have been noted elsewhere in the literature (Klaus and Kennell, 1976). The reciprocal fantasies and concerns of the new mothers have already been reported (Herzog, 1977).

Premature delivery triggered somewhat different behaviors in the men of the less well-attuned and least well-attuned groups. A variety of affects were reported, but two feelings predominated: intense anger, usually directed at the wife, but sometimes at the obstetrician and other health professionals; or the reaction that, borrowing from Greenberg and Morris (1974, Chap. 5) who defined *engrossment* as the father's rapt response to his full-term infant, I have called *superengrossment* with the newborn. This reaction occurred in fathers who had often been conspicuously disinterested in the pregnancy until this time. The baby looked "angelic," "full term," or "just beautiful" to these new fathers. In contrast, the fathers in the well-attuned group were often horrified at the fragility of their newborns, greatly concerned (and justifiably so) as to their lack of maturity and resilience. Among these so-called superengrossed fathers, what emerged was a competitive struggle with the wife for the baby's affection. Bitter denunciation of wives as "unfit mothers with bad insides" occurred with considerable frequency. The results of this state of affairs for the future of the family and for the initial mother-infant bonding were often disastrous (Herzog, 1977).

Was the orderliness of their reworking of old issues in caretaking disturbed by the lack of the prerequisite feature of a well-developed intimacy and empathy with their wives during the entire pregnancy experience? It was as if issues relevant to becoming a father surfaced in a less distinct and thus less workable fashion. In these cases, the strong affects aroused by the unexpected early arrival of the baby were turned against the spouse rather than being used as signals serving to strengthen the family unit. Missing in these men was the decisive turning from feminine to masculine conceptions of parenthood at the end of the second trimester and, with this, the experience of a mysterious external force: nature, or a miracle, or the sum is greater than the individual parts (the one becomes the two, the two becomes the three, the three becomes the one) that most of the well-attuned husbands had experienced around the seventh month. Interestingly, Jessner and others (1971) report a comparable feeling in pregnant women at this time of gestation. Instead of the feeling of awe, the women experienced themselves as responsible and culpable and, in a very real sense, they felt punished in being deprived of their babies. It seemed that less well-attuned men were compelled to act out what they were not able to remember or experience during pregnancy. In almost no cases did these fathers remember fantasies or feelings about feeding and refertilizing their wives or fetuses. Nor did they grapple with the wish to bear a child themselves, to hurt a child, or to hurt the woman who had had such great power during the preceding pregnancy. Instead, they manifested unintegrated aspects of all these urges in their superengrossment and competition with the "culpable–bad insides" mother.

Conclusions

As I review my impressions of 103 men whose wives delivered prematurely, it appears to me that certain characteristic stages of expectant fatherhood can be identified in at least one subgroup of these fathers-to-be. These stages do involve a getting ready period. This is followed by a time of fullness and ecstasy after an infant has been conceived. I then discerned a characteristic set of fantasies and feelings that clustered about the theme of nurturing woman and fetus along with an attendant worry about the adequacy of one's own supplies.

This gives way to a stage in which old issues from the inner-genital period of development and hermaphroditic fantasies come to the fore. And this in turn is followed by a time when the dialectic between the notion of a nurturing and a punishing penis ensues. It is here that the father-to-be is most aware of his own ambivalence toward the child and toward its mother. Concomitantly, a strengthening of the relationship with the man's own father serves to give prefatherhood a more masculine cast near the end of the second trimester. The mentor of old is revived. This stage is followed by an uncanny kind of feeling. That which has been willingly initiated has become larger than the sum of its parts, larger than the residue of past conflicts and resolutions (including perhaps the oedipal conflict), and large enough to quite literally become a life of its own. This feeling, which is often not exclusive to expectant fathers but rather is often shared with expectant mothers, strengthens the alliance of pregnancy and brings with it an appreciation of the division of labor in reproductive functioning and in subsequent parenting. It is almost as if this appreciation of the reality principle is ushered in by a recapitulation of earlier attempts at solving the "Mystery of the Sphinx," the dilemma of sexual differences and functionings (Freud, 1905b).

A striking feature of this work is the realization that this sequence seems to unfold with greatest clarity in those situations where the expectant father participated in an expanding mutual intimacy with his wife. Biological changes occurring in the wife are lent, as it were, to an expectant father. His attunement with her in turn allows the father to use these compelling occurrences to regress, to reassess, and to reintegrate erstwhile elements of his own caretaking line of development.

The second general impression gleaned from the work is that individual life experiences, both inner and outer, exert a powerful influence on each man's experience of prospective fatherhood.

A third general impression, a corollary of the first two, has to do with an apparently inverse relationship between the intensity of a man's father hunger and his ability to attune to his wife and to participate both intrapsychically and interpersonally in the progression toward parenthood. If you are always searching for a father, it may interfere with your ability to become one, although some men may make their own reparations and compensations for their defective childhoods by endeavoring to become superior parents themselves. In fact, a significant percentage of men in the less well-attuned group and an even higher percentage of men in the least well-attuned group came from families where the father was absent during part or all of the first 5 years of life.

313

Abelin's work on the critical role of the father in helping the young boy to dissolve his primary femininity and consolidate his masculine core-gender identity seems highly relevant. Without a father in one's personal past, it is more difficult to reconstruct a father in one's own pre-fatherhood, and this seems to have fateful implications for both intimacy and caretaking during adulthood.

The work of prospective fathers seems to center on the important questions of merging, borrowing, donating, feeding, relinquishing, hurting, feeling depleted, losing; recognizing what is self and what is other, how things are connected, and mechanisms of disconnection; tolerating bisexuality, yet retaining confidence in one's own core-gender identity; and becoming aware of the oedipal dilemma. These issues of ego boundaries, inside and outside, mourning and joyous anticipation, attachment and separation, are certainly the subjects of parenthood.

It is hoped that increased knowledge of expectant fatherhood and of the fathering process will allow therapeutic and didactic interventions that will assist men to function with greater freedom as lovers, husbands, and parents.

20

The Father in Midlife: Crisis and the Growth of Paternal Identity

Calvin A. Colarusso
Robert A. Nemiroff

Fatherhood is more than a biological event or a psychological state limited to one phase of life. As this volume demonstrates, it is a complex developmental task that extends throughout the life cycle.

The basic concept of this chapter is that midlife (ages 35–55 years) is a particularly formative time in the evolution of paternal identity because of the unique, phase-specific interaction between issues of midlife development in the father and adolescent development in his children. As a paradigm, the assumption is made that children of midlife fathers fall within this age range. It has long been apparent that middle-aged parents react strongly to their adolescent children. However, that the parental response is not only a reaction to the adolescent but also the result of equally (or more) salient developmental forces within the parent that are impinged on by the adolescent is not generally understood.

We believe that the relative absence of psychoanalytic theory of adult development has been responsible for the prevailing conception of the normal adult as essentially unchanging, a finished product in whom developmental processes are of little importance. Now a different understanding of adulthood has begun to emerge (Conference on Psychoanalytic Education and Research Commission IX [Coper 9] report on child analysis, 1974; Shane, 1977; Valliant, 1977; Gould, 1978; Levinson, 1978), one in which the adult as well as the child is understood to be subject to developmental forces.

In an earlier paper (Colarusso and Nemiroff, 1979), we conceptualized developmental processes in general as lifelong, having great significance for the adult as well as for the child. In a constant state of dynamic change, the normal adult is strongly influenced by both external and internal environments, reactive to previous life experiences from both infantile and adult past, and engaged in such new, uniquely adult developmental tasks as response to the aging process in the body and the heightened normative midlife focus on personal time limitation and death. These basic hypotheses underlie the picture of the midlife father we present here.

Studies on the Development of Fatherhood

Along with Gurwitt (1976, Chap. 18), we found the scarcity of psychoanalytic studies on fathers and fatherhood surprising (Chap. 1) in view of ample recognition that becoming a father is an important psychological transition. As sparse as the literature on becoming a father is, studies concerning the *continuous evolution* of fatherhood are rarer still.

Two significant psychoanalytic commentaries illustrating the developmental, evolving nature of parenthood are by E. James Anthony and Theresa Benedek (1970) and Gerald H. J. Pearson (1958). For Anthony and Benedek the biological root of fatherhood is in the instinctual drive for survival. Addressing herself specifically to the *developmental* role of fatherhood, Benedek (Anthony and Benedek, 1970, p. 167) wrote:

The functions which represent fatherhood, fatherliness, and providing are parallel to motherhood, motherliness, and nurturing. Fatherhood and motherhood are complementary processes which evolve within the culturally established family structure to safeguard the physical and emotional development of the child. The role of the father within his family and his relationship with his children appear to be further removed from instinctual roots than those of the mother. . . . Fatherhood, i.e., the human male's role in procreation, has instinctual roots beyond the drive organization of mating behavior to include his function as provider and to develop the ties of fatherliness that make his relationship with his children a mutual developmental experience.

For example, as documented over and over again by religious rite, custom, and socioeconomic organization, fathers search for immortality through their children, particularly through their sons. Paternal identification with a son is immediate and complex. The father "can project into him the aspirations of his ego ideal, anticipating unconsciously his future self realization in his own son" (Anthony and Benedek, 1970, p. 172). The experience of being a father also powerfully influences the evolution of the adult personality, as father engages dependent wishes stimulated by the inevitability of the adolescent's separation and further integrates childhood wishes to become like his own father.

Gerald Pearson (1958, p. 21) is one of the few analysts who has written specifically about dynamic conflicts and tensions within the middle-aged parent.

As middle age comes on, the adult feels that he is passing his prime. He observes that his adolescent child is growing rapidly into a vigorous young adult with all his success ahead of him. He contrasts his lessening opportunities for success and his now rather static capacities with the budding development of his child, and unconsciously he feels envy. In his unconscious his child now seems to be a replica of his own parent; *and he begins to act to keep the child in his place,* just as he wanted to put his parents in *his* place when he was a child. The adolescent therefore has to struggle against these unconscious motivated attitudes and actions of his parents and of other adults. [Emphasis added.]

In the real and unconscious battle for power that ensues, for the benefit of himself and his offspring, the parent must relinquish control of the adolescent's future. Poetically, Pearson describes an aspect of the conflict of generations as "two wounded narcissisms disliking each other" (p. 44). His advice to middle-aged parents is: "Probably it is better for the adolescent if the parents close their eyes and lick their narcissistic wounds in silence, as much as they possibly can" (p. 44).

The Impact of Children on the Resolution of Adult Developmental Tasks

It is clear that the experience of fatherhood during midlife is potentially a strong stimulus to continued adult development. The results depend on the individual father's reaction to the powerful sexuality, burgeoning body, and abundant future of his adolescent offspring, which stand in contrast to his own tempered sexuality, aging body, and heightened awareness of mortality.

Physical Aging

Acceptance of the aging body is a painful developmental task for every middle-aged man. The physical retrogression of midlife causes narcissistic injury (Cath, 1962) that produces, we hypothesize, a normative conflict between wishes to deny the aging process and an emotional acceptance of the loss of a youthful body. Because of his identification with them in the presence of adolescent offspring, particularly those who display themselves with phallic pride and narcissistic pleasure, the father's struggle is heightened by the painful contrast between their bodies and his own. The result may be regressive attempts to deny or compensate for the aging process, such as:

1. Magical repair of the body by methods such as plastic surgery or hair transplants

2. Search for a new body or parts of a new body through youthful heterosexual or homosexual contacts
3. Substitution for the body through excessive preoccupation with compensatory possessions such as bigger and better houses, boats, cars, and bank accounts

But the interaction can, by forcing an intrapsychic engagement of these issues, also serve to further the *resolution* of the normative conflict through a reshaping of body image leading to a heightened sense of appreciation of the pleasures that the adult body, properly cared for, can continue to provide.

Intimations of Immortality

Freud (1915) noted "our unmistakable tendency to put death to one side." There is nothing instinctual in us, he said, that responds to a belief in death. In the timelessness of the unconscious, we are convinced of our immortality. The first half of life is characterized by a tendency to deny the inevitability of death. In childhood and adolescence, that denial is bolstered by the immaturity of the psychic apparatus, by limited awareness and understanding of the concept of time (Colarusso, 1979), and by the progressive physical and psychological forces that characterize childhood development. There is little in the anabolic thrust of the early developmental process to indicate a personal end.

A major crack in the armor comes in late adolescence when intrapsychic loss is normally experienced through a loosening of ties to the parents. A sense of personal history develops with a recognition of past, present, and future (Seton, 1974). But the dawning realization is quickly defended against by the optimism and idealism of the young adult, attempts, as Jacques (1965) says, to deny "two fundamental features of human life—the inevitableness of eventual death, and the existence of hate and destructive impulses inside each person" (p. 505). Gradually the belief in the inherent goodness of man, a central characteristic of the idealism of youth, is replaced with increased awareness of the power of hate and destructive forces to contribute to human misery, tragedy, and death, by a "more contemplative pessimism" (p. 504).

By the fourth, fifth, and sixth decades of life, the defensive maneuvers alter, and the normal adult meets with his own finiteness as he recognizes and accepts the signs that confront him from every side: (1) Physical signs of aging, such as gray hair, wrinkles, slowing of reflexes, and moderation of sexual drive, appear and multiply; (2) it becomes clear that not all of life's ambitions and goals will be realized, and not enough time remains to achieve new ones of equal importance; and (3) the deaths of one's parents lead to a loosening of childhood introjects that had as a central component the internalization of a sense of continuance and security, provided in childhood by the good-enough parent. One is left alone with the recognition that he may die as his parent did. The death of a parent is a major change in an adult's life, bringing with it opportunity for internal reorganization, including increased separation-individuation, further oedipal resolution, and a new or altered relationship with the remaining parent. The maturing of one's own children into adulthood shatters the sense of perpetual youth because identification of the childhood self with young children is no longer possible.

In addition, as the middle-aged father observes his adolescent children beginning to contemplate and experience young adult aspirations such as work, college, courtship, marriage, and children, he repeatedly makes comparisons with his youthful experience, now 20 years or more in the past. The adolescent's focus on the present and future contrasts with the father's awareness of his lengthening past and draws him repeatedly to thoughts of his own limited life span.

The Effects on Fathers of the Reactivation of Childhood Development Themes and Conflicts: The Oedipus Complex

Just as the experience of being a father influences the course of major adult developmental tasks, so does it effect the reengagement of developmental issues and conflicts from childhood. Among the most prominent expressions of this intrapsychic process is the reactivation of the infantile oedipal complex, which we will now describe, and the separation-individuation process, which will be referred to later.

Pearson (1958, p. 177) has described the connection between adult developmental issues and the reactivation of oedipal conflicts:

By the time an individual is in his late thirties or early forties—usually when his children are becoming adolescents—he begins to realize that he will probably never fulfill some of his postponed ideals. He perceives that he has already started on the downgrade toward old age and death, and this realization invigorates his fantasy of the reversal of generations. . . . The parent's realization that he is past the peak of his powers with so many goals never achieved makes him feel frustrated. *The frustration re-energizes the fantasy of the reversal of generations, and with it the envies, jealousies, and hatreds of the oedipus period* [emphasis added].

The continuation of the oedipal complex into adulthood is not a new idea. Freud (1924) spoke of it in "The Dissolution of the Oedipus Complex," as have Pearson (1958), Benedek (1975), and others, but little has been described about oedipal phenomena as a central, continuing factor in normal adult development. One exception is the description by Leo Rangell (1953b, p. 13):

The oedipal complex has a continuous and dynamic line of development, from its earliest origin through various phases in the life of man, and the described phenomena are but stages in the continuing moving stream. By no means is it an event which plays a tumultuous but short-lived role limited to the phallic scene of the play of life, but it is rather a constantly reappearing character which comes across the stage in new and changing ways progressing with the ages of man.

There is much to describe regarding oedipal phenomena in the normal adult. Each parent reacts to the budding sexuality of adolescent children with at least occasional overrestriction or seductiveness. Aware of the muting of sexual prowess in midlife and unconsciously jealous of the adolescent's abundant future, the parent may retaliate against his offspring (Pearson, 1958). Reactivated oedipal sexuality, envy, and rage may be expressed directly through overrestrictiveness, neglect of the adolescent's interests, criticism of his views; or it may be expressed defensively through overprotectiveness, overconcern, and permissiveness. Competitiveness and envy of girlfriends or boyfriends, fiancés, and eventually wives and husbands of grown children provide ample evidence of the triangular relationships that exist among parents, children, and their spouses. Fathers' protectiveness of their daughters' virtue and encouragement of their sons' lack of it, and mother-in-laws' almost universal tendency to compete for their children provide all too obvious evidence of the nature of adult oedipal phenomena.

Father-Daughter Interactions

When the adolescent daughter begins to date, many oedipal feelings are stirred up in the middle-aged father by the introduction of a competitor, the boyfriend. Father's experience as a neglected outsider, observing a sexually charged relationship involving someone he loves, is similar to what he experienced as a child. Unlike the powerless child, the father may respond by attempting to dominate and control these dating relationships, or he may involve himself in them inappropriately through excessive interest or teasing:

An analytic patient complained bitterly that his adolescent daughter was keeping him in the dark about her relationships with boyfriends. He felt excluded and betrayed. His feelings grew in intensity and disturbed him since he recognized their inappropriateness and found it difficult to suppress powerful urges to repeatedly tease his daughter and her friends. Further associations led to negative oedipal material as the father described his anxious, angry response to his daughter's Halloween costume, which he described as "sexy and suggestive." Yet he wanted her to go to the party in question. Continued analytic work revealed his phallic pride for having produced such a sexually stimulating woman and also his attraction to the young males who would vie for her attention. He described his admiration and envy of their youthful bodies and sexual energy, which he hoped to capture magically for himself through his daughter.

Father and Son: Reworking the Negative Oedipal Constellation

As his teenage son becomes more insistent on independence and autonomy, a father must relinquish some of his active control over the son's life. A necessary shift in power balance between them occurs as the son tests, challenges, and eventually assumes mastery of his own life. This normative conflict stirs fears of failure within the positive oedipal constellation. It further reignites negative oedipal feelings within the father, who must deal again with feelings of hate, weakness, passivity, and helplessness in relation to another man who is important to him.

We believe that this largely unconscious process is an inevitable part of the normal father's reaction to his maturing son and is responsible for precipitating a necessary developmental shift in the midlife parenting process that adds a new dimension to the role of fatherhood.

Beset by feelings of impotence, loss, dissolution, and resignation, the father must gradually abandon his role as parent of a young child. Because many gratifications of that role were related to the direct expression and sublimation of feelings of aggression through domination and control, the transition can be a painful one. Overreaction may take the form of attempts to reestablish dominance or, through reversal, the opposite may occur whereby the father neglects the paternal limit-setting role, attempting to imitate the son rather than be his father.

It is our impression that the capacity for paternal generativity (Erikson, 1963) is determined in part by the resolution of this conflict. Through adult reworking of negative oedipal issues, generativity may be linked to masculinity as the passive, homoerotic caring trends within a father's character are expressed. His care, unintrusive support, and facilitation of the emerging sexuality, independence, and separateness of late-adolescent and young adult sons and daughters are crucial if he is to become an ally in his children's passage through these years. Since the adolescent son is dealing with his own oedipal feelings and the same active-passive dichotomy, this generative, supportive responsiveness in the father often stimulates similar feelings in the son. For example, one adolescent voiced his strong dislike for one of his father's friends who was competitive and challenging, but expressed affection for another whom he described as a "gentle giant."

For the father there is no final resolution of these issues, but a cyclic reengagement of them throughout adulthood. For instance, they peak again when the son chooses a partner, which may evoke feelings of jealousy and envy of, as one father put it "his luscious young chick." In the negative oedipal reworking, father may compete for his son by offering advice, money, and companionship, or, as in the case of one patient, by pleading (in a whining, helpless way) for his son's continued interest. Fantasies about the sexual life of the young couple may lead to conscious and unconscious identification with the son or possibly with his mate.

The nurturing, "feminine" side of the self can take on a new dimension, as it may have during the son's adolescence, and the result can be increased capacity for generativity now including the son's mate and eventually one's grandchildren as well. Continued self-object differentiation may occur throughout this process, leading to a more integrated, stronger sense of self, which now includes new aspects of fatherhood: the roles of generative father and father-in-law.

Many of the basic concepts presented above are illustrated by the following clinical examples.

Example 1

A 44-year-old father reported a wish to attend his teenage son's parties and dances. Through a series of fantasies about his son's sexual activities, it became clear that unconsciously he envied his young body and coveted his penis. As these wishes were interpreted in relation to his own aging process, he began to experience intense feelings of pain, anger, and jealousy. As these feelings became conscious the patient reacted by inappropriately attempting to restrict his son's dating and athletic activities. Only gradually was he able to assume a less intrusive, more supportive attitude. As he became more aware of the futility of his search for youthful powers and its negative effects on family relationships, he began to appraise and appreciate his own considerable middle-aged powers, his "stronger reality," as it is described by Helm Stierlin (1972).

Example 2

During his analysis, a 40-year-old business tycoon expressed a strong sense of worthlessness in relation to a powerful and very successful father. "My father was like a lion to me, an absolute king of the beasts." His own success, which surpassed his father's in many ways, had little effect on his sense of self-esteem. However, signs of healthy development in his latency-aged and adolescent sons impressed him. Could he really be so bad if he was man enough and father enough to produce them? As he analyzed his overidealization and fear of his own father, he was able to engage his sons in a more relaxed and easy manner. To his surprise and delight, they responded positively. "For the first time I really feel like a somebody. I'm a hell of a better father than I thought." As his children continued to develop they became living expressions of his self-worth. The recognition of the importance of his adult feelings toward his sons was the key to the successful analysis of his unresolved competitive "relationship" with his own father. This integration of adult experience and childhood conflict led to a more gratifying sense of fatherhood and was reflected externally in a marked increase in parental effectiveness.

322

The Adult Self and Fatherhood

In a recent paper (Nemiroff and Colarusso, 1980), we explored the nature of the adult self, concentrating on a description of its emergence and characteristics and the narcissistic issues that underlie its development. Agreeing with Saperstein and Gaines (1973) and Sutherland (1978) we saw considerable usefulness in conceptualizing a supraordinate self-system that mediates the interaction of the person as a whole with his environment and is recognized as the final determiner of action. It is our impression that the adult self evolves as the individual engages the major developmental tasks of adulthood. Narcissistic gratification and disappointment affect the evolution of the self as differences between idealizations and realities become clear.

The experience of fatherhood is a determining influence on the evolution of the adult self, because it is such a central experience, full of narcissistic gratification and disappointment. We are proposing here that the representation of the concept, father, within the adult self undergoes evolution as the experience of fatherhood changes. For example, there is a considerable difference between the experience and intrapsychic representations of (1) a 25-year-old father of a 3-year-old child with a young wife deeply involved in the care of her children, relating to a living father of 55, and (2) a 45-year-old father of late adolescents and young adults, relating to an aging or dead father and preoccupied with the aging process in himself and his wife. The experiences are so different and result in such altered intrapsychic representations that perhaps the only thing remaining the same is the name we give the experience: fatherhood.

The complex, evolving representation within the adult self is determined by many factors, among the most important of which are the following:

1. Experiences as a son: past and present experiences with one's own father and father substitutes (relatives, fathers of childhood friends)
2. Experiences as a father: past and present experiences with one's own children and the children of others
3. Related experiences: past and present experiences as a parent in concert with a spouse, as a sexual man, as a mentor and mentee

Paternal Response to Separation and Loss

To illustrate our premise of the evolving nature of fatherhood, we will use as an example the father's role in the separation-individuation process. We suggest that the father's involvement in the second individuation in adolescence (Blos, 1967) is quantitatively and qualitatively different from his involvement in the infantile separation-individuation process (Mahler et al., 1975), not only because the child is different but because father has changed as well (Chap. 17). The developmental processes taking place between parents and adolescent children require a more basic and involved participation on the part of the father.

The psychobiological events of pregnancy (Bibring, 1959) prepare a mother for the extremely intimate, symbiotic tie with the child. Primarily a participant-observer in the first individuation, the father serves as a buffer for both mother and child as they struggle against the powerful regressive pull toward symbiosis. During those oedipal and latency years, father plays a role of increasing importance as a protector, provider, and example for his young children. By the onset of adolescence, his position as a parent of equal importance to the mother is established in the minds of children, spouse, and self (Chaps. 2, 12).

The individuation of adolescent children, their movement from psychological and physical dependence to young adulthood, forces a reworking of the internal representation within the self of the father's role. He must transform the representation of himself as a protector, and caretaker of young children, and replace it with a different fathering identity as an interested facilitator, perhaps not as necessary or powerful.

This intrapsychic process is influenced by (1) paternal interaction with adolescent children around separation issues, (2) the father's reaction to separations and losses in his own life, and (3) his important involvement in the separation process occurring between mother and adolescent.

Separation Issues in Father-Adolescent Interaction
Some adolescents respond to the intrapsychic struggle over separation by an exaggerated, partly defensive, independent stance. For example, one high school senior insisted on handling all aspects of his application to college. He researched, filled out applications, and made a final decision entirely on his own, succeeding admirably in this task. His father's response to being so pointedly excluded was initially dismay and anger, and only later begrudging admiration. The appreciation of his son's adult competence and awareness that he would soon be leaving home precipitated a mourning reaction that gradually moved the father-son relationship toward greater equality and mutuality and redefined this man's understanding of himself as a parent.

Other adolescents struggle less against the separation process, and by so doing, facilitate a gradual, less abrupt, but still painful intrapsychic loss and redefinition of fatherhood. One adolescent, very much his father's son, in addition to being a straight-A student, was also a companion, sharing mutual interests in academics, sports, and cars. Their planning together for college led to a gradual, smoother intrapsychic evolution for this particular father, but also ignited intense feelings of grief over the loss of a son who was such a close friend.

Father's Reaction to Separation

The second major determinant of change in the representation of the concept of father within the self is the reworking of separations from his own parental past, particularly during adolescence. One father commented that he had moved across the country from his family, and he feared his daughter would do the same. In anticipation of his daughter's departure for college, another man remembered his own inability to express feelings about his leaving for college until a wrenching, tearful outburst of words and feelings at the airport. A third man, reacting to his son's aloofness, recalled homesickness when he himself had gone away from home for the first time at the age of 15 years. In each instance further analytic work revealed connections between these adolescent experiences and their antecedents from earlier phases of development, as well as their expression in the current reality with their adolescent children.

Another kind of dramatic midlife separation experience is that forced by death. The death of a parent, particularly his father for a man, leads to a loosening of childhood introjects, forcing a reworking of separation issues, a reengagement of positive and negative oedipal themes, often a new or altered caretaking relationship to a surviving, aging mother.

Father's Involvement in Mother-Adolescent Separation

The painful disengagement of adolescent children from their mother, and vice versa, also has a strong effect on paternal identity. Because his relationship to his children is not based on the psychobiological experience of pregnancy as much as on the powerful affective relationship of the first years of life (Spitz, 1965), a father usually can observe the maternal-child disengagement with some clarity and objectivity, even while he is engaged in a similar separation experience (Chaps. 6, 9, and 12).

Although his role as a buffer between mother and infant was important during the first separation-individuation process, during adolescence it becomes central, even critical at times, since both mother and child may turn to him for help.

While discussing his feelings about his adolescent daughter, one father said, "You know, it was easier when she was a baby. I just left it all to my wife and went to work. But I can't do that now. My wife won't let me walk away; she needs me to help her deal with Amy; she insists on my help. Amy won't let me off the hook either. She comes to me more often than her mother." With a mixture of pride and annoyance he said, "You know, I like it this way, but it sure as hell isn't easy."

Another reported his wife's anxiety when their son was late for breakfast while the family was on vacation. "He'll be here," he said. "Stop worrying; he's 16 years old."

A third father negotiated a more age-appropriate, realistic curfew for his 16-year-old daughter after mother and daughter had engaged in an intense verbal battle over the issue. Later he listened to his wife's sorrow and impotence as she verbalized feelings about her daughter's independence and sexuality.

Such interactions help the father to deal with his own sense of losing his children by allowing him to mediate actively similar feelings in his wife and children. They also lead to redefinition of the marital relationship, which becomes more exposed as a dyad when children are gradually removed from the internal conception of husband-father and wife-mother.

Intimations of Grandparenthood

The awe and amazement that a father feels as he sees his adolescent children become physically, sexually, and psychologically mature bring with them the first awareness of the potential of grandfatherhood and considerable ambivalence about so inevitable a portent of aging and of eventual death. Anticipation of the event is a major stimulus that acts in the healthy father as a psychic organizer (Spitz, 1965). Increased awareness of aging becomes connected with the concept of grandfatherhood through compensatory fantasies of living on through grandchildren, a kind of genetic immortality achieved through the narcissistically gratifying identification of one's characteristics in children and future grandchildren.

One father obtained great pleasure from his late-adolescent son's obvious imitation of his shaving habits; the little boy who asked to use his razor at age 3 years was now actually shaving just as he did. He was startled, somewhat pleased, and pained, by his growing awareness of a wish to have another little boy (his hoped-for grandson) copy his shaving habits.

As demonstrated by this example, the prospect of grandfatherhood brings with it the likelihood of recapturing the unambivalent admiration and love of young children, an attitude lost in the more realistic appraisal of older ones.

Another narcissistic gratification for the prospective grandfather is the reaffirmation of his sexuality through the fertility of his offspring. Their ability to produce children is a confirmation of his sexuality that takes on a special significance when physical retrogression and waning sexual prowess may be problematic.

Last, but by no means least, the prospect of "spoiling" the grandchildren—the fantasized expression of impulses without restraint—is, through identification, applied to the self as well. Here is an outlet for expression of loving, nurturing, and gratifying impulses toward the self (through the grandchild), which comes in the life cycle at a time of increased frustration and deprivation through the loss of children and the sense of physical retrogression and aging.

21

Vicissitudes of Grandfatherhood:
A Miracle of Revitalization?

Stanley H. Cath

In order to talk about fathers and grandfathers, it is necessary first of all to distinguish between the mythology of grandparenthood and its reality. The myth is of a benign, mellow, generous old man or woman hovering in the background, waiting to be called on whenever needed. Indeed, the stereotype is so prevalent that many grandparents feel obliged to adopt this role even though it is totally foreign to their nature. Actually, a grandfather can be in the prime of life, vigorous, active, productive, still an object for his son to reckon with.

Another discrepancy between myth and reality was revealed by a questionnaire (Robertson, 1976) addressed to grandchildren. Respondents said that they did not usually look to their grandparents for companionship, advice, as liaisons between themselves and their parents, as role models, or for financial support. The respondents nevertheless thought they would be missing a great deal if they did not have grandparents, but what they would be missing were emotional supporters, givers of gifts, and bearers of family history and tradition. The attitude of the grandchildren toward their grandparents applied equally whether the latter were physically fit and "with it" or old and feeble.

When the grandfather is portrayed in literature, drama, films, and the like, he usually emerges as peripheral to the mainstream of events and critical decisions. I question the accuracy of these conceptions of the grandfather. (Much of what applies to grandfathers applies equally to grandmothers, but the latter are not my subject here.) The grandfather may not be taking part in critical decisions, but his influence either is or has been crucial to the father who may be making decisions. When one has observed the conscious and unconscious dynamics operating in a three-generation family system, one finds it difficult to sustain the idea of grandfather as peripheral.

Is it possible that the myths surrounding grandparents can be attributed to the ambivalence felt toward them? That the ambivalence exists is obvious. Consider the ways in which old people are portrayed in mythology, literature, television, advertisements, and so forth. You will find as many ogres and fools as you will benevolent patriarchs.

Regardless of how vigorous and productive he might still be, becoming a grandfather represents a milestone in any man's life. He is reminded of his mortality, but is also assured of the continuity of his line. With advancing years, the basic anchorages a man has taken for granted—a healthy body, social and economic security, the meaningful activities to which his life has been devoted—may be threatened by the age-specific onset of either depletion or physical deterioration (Cath, 1962). The advent of a grandchild may reverse the downhill trend and revitalize the grandfather. He now feels assured of a future that is connected with his biological and psychological self.

It seems to me that the grandchild's ability to revitalize the grandfather, to compensate him for his failing powers, in part accounts for the grandfather's idealization of the grandchild. (The grandparent's willingness to rhapsodize over his grandchild is too familiar a phenomenon to require elaboration.) Certainly the father finds it difficult to understand this idealization, for it is in sharp contrast to the father's memories of his own childhood relation to his father, which he recalls as more fraught with parental disapproval.

Fathers envy the grandfathers' ready acceptance in the grandson of what was once not acceptable behavior in themselves. A grandfather picks up a grandson when he is hurt, comforts and soothes him when he is frightened. Instead of ridiculing the child, the grandfather empathizes with his anxieties and disappointments, his frustrations and failures.

One man watched with amazement this kind of relationship develop between his father and his own son. He had always been made to feel that he could never cry or show emotional distress. His militaristic father had taught him that a man stands up to anything and never shows weakness like women do. And so the son resolved that when he became a father his son would be allowed to cry if he were hurt. He was therefore astonished to find that his father no longer expected from his grandson the stoicism he had demanded 20 years earlier from his son.

With the advent of a grandchild, shifts occur in the family transgenerational dynamics. Grandfather (if he is beginning to decline) and grandchild are drawn together by certain similarities between them: They have fewer responsibilities than has the father, and their dependence on others is greater. Further, they are linked in their common resentment of the father whom they both have cause to envy. Indeed, another reason for grandfather to wax enthusiastic over his grandchild is that the latter is less threatening because of his innocence and ineptitude. A grandfather who has more time on his hands than he used to have will be grateful for the presence of a grandchild; the latter in turn will be grateful for the time and attention the grandfather has to give.

The grandfather's need to idealize the grandchild may also be accounted for by his need to compensate himself for guilt felt about his own inadequacies as a parent. He wants to believe that something better is possible than the conflict-torn relationship he experienced with his own father and with his own son.

A Selected Survey of the Literature

Abraham (1913) believed that grandparents had not played a decisive role in the lives of any of his patients. In his view, when a patient placed a special emphasis on a grandparent, he did so as a defense against a violent rejection of either father or mother. The patient, as a child, had the fantasy that the father would be disposed of and the grandfather would take his place. The child saw the grandfather's authority as even greater than that of the father. Abraham went on to speculate that displacement of authority from the father onto remote forebears might well be the basis for ancestral cults.

Jones (1913) stressed the child's fantasy that as he grows older his relative position may make him parent to his parents. From this the child draws many illusions of power and a strong identification with the grandparents. Jones also suggested that the custom of naming a child for the grandparent may reinforce this identification. He observed how infrequently analysts make inquiries about grandparents. In contrast to Abraham, in his clinical work, he realized how important grandparents really were, even if they had died before the grandchild was born. Jones' stance is consistent with the later direct observations of child analysts on the significance of the mother in the preoedipal phase and how she tends to repeat with her child experiences that she had with her parents.

Ferenczi (1913) agreed with Jones and Abraham that the grandchild will see the grandfather as an imposing old man who commands the all-powerful father, but Ferenczi thought the child's fantasy had another aspect: The grandfather was also a helpless, feeble old man, no match for the father, and therefore an object of disparagement. One of Ferenczi's patients had a patriarchal grandfather; the grandchild refused to submit to the father, treating him as an usurper who had robbed him (the grandchild-patient) of his rightful heritage. The patient had identified completely with the patriarchal grandfather. Ferenczi also noted that Freud's Little Hans had given his grandmother to his father in order that Hans might become his mother's husband.

Rappaport cited Flügel (1921) as pointing to several factors that reinforce the child's identification with the grandparent: (1) "the wish to become the parent of its own parent"; (2) "the wish to dispense with the parent and the projection onto the grandparent of the grandiose ideas formerly entertained with regard to the parent"; and (3) "the fact that the grandparents, as a rule, are less responsible for the child's upbringing and education and less stern and vigorous in the assertion of their authority." Flügel thought that the child's tendency to imitate the grandparent was "an important factor in molding the child's beliefs, attitudes, desires, and occupations" (Rappaport, 1958, p. 521).

Rappaport also observed how some aging men may try in vain to enforce their waning authority by increased rigidity and rage, or else they resign into states of apathy, depletion, depression, or disease, much as Shakespeare's King Lear did. He also noted that the bountiful, indulgent grandfather may be more like a mother figure, resembling mother in physical features, and more often than not surpassing her in generosity.

Case Material

Few grandfathers enter analysis. A quick survey of my own cases over 20 years reveals only two. I am, therefore, gratefully using cases from an unpublished paper by Samuel Lerner, "Grandfathers and Other Things," presented in Atlanta, Georgia, in 1979. Lerner reported on 4 cases that clearly illustrated the significance of the role of the grandfather in the child's development.

Clinical Example 1

The first case describes a middle-aged man in analysis because of "difficulty in his relationship." His overseductive, intermittently depressed mother had grieved continuously over the loss of her idealized father. The patient saw his grandfather as his mother's "boss." In the analysis, the grandfather became a key figure in the evolving transference. The analyst facilitated the patient's insight into the need for a grandfather in order to repair his feeling of inadequacy and incompetence vis-à-vis his powerful mother. An interpretation that both the analyst and the grandfather were being used in an attempt to shore up the patient's insecure masculinity led to a new phase of analysis and a better understanding of the nature of the patient's relationship with his mother.

Clinical Example 2

The second case was of a man who had won his oedipal battle, but had great problems, as many such men do, in relation to other men. He had regressed to a masochistic type of relationship with men, in the unconscious belief that he had the capacity to destroy them through his magical power. In his analysis, the character of the maternal grandfather emerged as mother's ideal. It was the death of this grandfather when the patient was 8 years old that consolidated the image of a magical, powerful figure with a tremendous hold over mother. Identification with this man had led to many exaggerated, almost mythological qualities in his own character structure. As the grandfather transference unfolded along these lines, certain narcissistic issues could be dealt with and much guilt relieved. It was the grandfather who had trampled over people, just as the patient had repeatedly done in his lifetime. His disappointment and grief at having a weak, incompetent father had been concealed in the tremendous admiration for his idealized grandfather.

Clinical Example 3

A third case was an anxious woman in psychotherapy, unable to communicate, especially with her son. The latter, by the age of 3 years, had identified himself with his maternal grandfather and had adopted this man's domineering, aggressive, and seductive qualities. The same charm and ability to manipulate people had led his mother to feel that her son was completely out of control. Further exploration showed that the mother had transferred the same kind of appeasement to her son that she had utilized with her father, and now felt similarly enslaved. This variation of the theme of the role of the grandfather and the bond between the generations led to a change within the family dynamics, especially between the patient and her son.

Clinical Example 4

The fourth case was a man who had difficulty in maintaining relationships with women and who complained bitterly about his passive father and became severely depressed. In contrast, the paternal grandfather had been an affable, entertaining, cheerful storyteller, who had spent much time with his grandson. A screen memory emerged of the patient stumbling into a room in which mother was giving grandfather an enema. Grandfather looked at the patient in seeming anger and confusion. In this patient's mind, the subsequent death of the grandfather was linked with a loud thump. He concluded that this is the way one dies: an enema followed by a fall out of bed. The screen memory seemed to have served to repress the truth of grandfather's later years. As the therapy proceeded, it became clear that the grandfather had gradually become demented. There had indeed been occasional violent episodes marked by "thumps." Lerner was able to help the patient realize it was more than he could stand to have his initial impression of his warm, affable grandfather changed so drastically.

Present Psychoanalytic Views

Lerner's cases show how far analytic thought has moved since Abraham's 1913 observation about the unimportance of grandparents in the patient's life (see also Finkelstein, 1975; Kornhaber, 1980). Today, researchers almost automatically take into account the parents' parents when trying to acquire a comprehensive understanding of an adult patient or infant or child (Mahler et al., 1975; Roiphe and Galenson, 1981).

Identification with the Grandfather

Rappaport (1958, p. 536) described the various sorts of identifications the child makes with grandparents:

If the influence of the grandparent is predominant because the parent still feels a need for guidance and protection, the grandchild has not only to cope with its own insecurity but also with the sensed deeper insecurity of the parent. Consequently, the position of the parents is reduced to that of siblings without authority. The grandchild, being the pampered favorite of the powerful grandparent, assumes there will always be a pampering grandparent, and finally by identification becomes this grandparent itself, prone to self-indulgence and lulled into a false sense of power.

Identifications with this form and with other kinds of grandparents appear in the transference, as Lerner's cases demonstrate so well. Inclusion of the role of grandparents in tracing the vicissitudes of the transference widens the scope of therapy and produces insight into behavior not otherwise understandable.

Grandfathers may particularly facilitate a boy's acceptance of the feminine side of himself. They may share their grandsons' play with objects traditionally regarded as feminine and seem to accept sucking of thumbs and bottles at rather advanced ages. Grandfathers also act as neutralizers of excessive parental demands for action, competitiveness, and other masculine ideals. They are less likely to engage a small child in competitive physical activities. Thus the grandfather permits the grandson a more yielding, softer relationship with a man and facilitates the expression of positive feelings toward other males in the preoedipal, oedipal, and latency child. Through gratification of these safe homosexual feelings, the grandfather facilitates the child's later trust of females, provided, of course, that the relationship of both grandfather and father with their partners were more positive than negative.

In both sexes, in the postreproductive period (the 50s, 60s, and 70s), a need for renewed relatedness to the same sex is very common, a need often triggered by the loss of a spouse. The ability to express this non-pathological homosexuality may be the unwitting gift of a grandfather to his grandson. If, on the other hand, a grandfather has never been able to accept his own passive side, and regards healthy, passive yearnings for a man's love and approval with disdain, the result can be an accentuation by both generations of the pseudoindependent male. Such an outcome may make grandfather's old age intolerable for all members of the family.

Effects on Relationship with Grandchild

As mentioned earlier, the age of a grandfather, the state of his health, and whether he is "disengaged" or retired may affect his attitude toward his grandchildren. One retired septuagenarian in cardiac decompensation, who had seemingly loved his grandchildren's visits in previous summers, began in May to dread their arrival in June. "When those hellions come, this peaceful retreat of mine will become a penal colony. They made too much noise at Easter. The baby was always crying. The older ones wanted too many things. I couldn't wait for them to leave. It becomes so peaceful. I felt better."

Another grandfather had many grandchildren, all of whom, like his children, he showered with gifts but emotionally ignored. When his life-style changed—that is, when some of the feedback he had obtained through organizational channels was no longer available to him because of "shifts in command"—much of his concern was turned to one adolescent grandson who was busy acting out a rebellion against his parents. Grandfather transferred his domineering and aggressive skills to the task of controlling this grandson's antisocial behavior. When grandfather found out that his own children no longer needed or desired either his money, his emotional support, or his intrusiveness, he allied himself with this grandson, recognizing they had the same targets for their hostility. For almost a year, while he attempted the seduction of this grandchild, he was plagued with many psychosomatic symptoms that his doctors attempted to medicate away. Because of his characteristics, he found himself deserted by peers and colleagues, rejected by his doctor and his children, and estranged from the other grandchildren. "Working only in the interest of others," he had always believed himself to be selfless. Now, with the determination that had marked his previous efforts, he encouraged his grandson to leave his family, to break away from home, and to move in with him. Having had some surgery on his eyes, he needed someone to drive, shop, and help cook. Focusing on the grandson with an intensity missing in the relationship with the other children and grandchildren, he gave him money, an automobile, and whatever else he wanted. This led to a tremendous amount of family discomfort and discord. In this "unholy alliance," in the words of the middle generation, the two traveled across the country for 6 months, living a rather extravagant life. During these 6 months, the grandfather's ailments cleared and the grandson behaved in a socially adept manner for the first time. The grandfather's sudden death in a motel brought an end to this unusual relationship, and triggered a major regression in the grandson.

The Reluctant Grandfather

The phenomenon of the reluctant grandfather has been observed in several men in their 50s and 60s. A formerly psychoanalyzed, remarried patient returned for psychoanalytic psychotherapy for several reasons, among them the news that his son and daughter-in-law were expecting a child. "I really don't want to be a grandfather. I just finished raising my own kids. They're just now independent. I rid myself of an impossible woman and found I'm enjoying it tremendously. I don't want to make commitments to any more children, especially if they're not mine. All my kids have shoved burdens onto me. Now I'm married for the second time and like some of my wife's children, and her grandchildren; that is, I enjoy seeing them . . . and seeing them go."

This case ended more happily than the one previously described, for when he became a grandfather in reality, the feeling of being exhausted, depleted, and imposed on (patterned after his relationship with the major figures in his life) was indeed negated by the real relationship with a responsive, smiling child. It turned out that he was able to enjoy his second wife's qualities, then her children, and his grandchild, and to be refueled by all of them. Although reluctant, he was a late-blooming grandfather.

I would like to close with two quotations. The first is from a letter written by a bright adolescent boy about the "most memorable day of his life." The second is a poem written by one of my more astute and sensitive patients.

The most memorable day turned out to be unforgettable because of a single event that caused these memories to find a memorable niche in the most important section of my cerebrum. . . . At my grandfather's funeral, the rabbi said we had the eternal memories of my grandfather to serve as consolation. This was true. If there ever has been such a thing as the gift of gab, he had it. When I'd give him the proper response . . . he'd always sing out "that's my boy." He could always entertain or tell me about our family history. It seemed to me that he alone was left to tell the stories. A whole world died with him, the world of people and events trapped within him, now to remain hidden forever. I like to think some of my grandfather rubbed off on me, he was the best person I've ever known. Maybe a little bit of him will help me achieve great levels before I die.

"Grandfather"

You lie in a suburb of Pittsburgh
nearly dead, an old opportunist

scraping breath from a bare air
like a boy exploiting a mixing bowl

in your wife's kitchen, where at Christmas
and other immutable times she kept

fudge as indigestible in you
as your prayers in me.

What fed you bored me; your daughter says
I made a circus while you prayed.

What we were too young or are too old
to remember or speak of she knows,

her middle word is all we have of it.
But I remember like a constant Sunday bell

Keep us, God, in the hall of Thy hand
*And under the shadow of Thy wing**

give your muted songs their end,
for now to think you up alive,

walking in a psalm beside
your Christ is no stranger

than your unremembered silence, which was usual,
and your medieval eyes.

David McDougall

*Emphasis added.

22

The Dying and Death of a Father

Stanley H. Cath
James M. Herzog

Throughout history men have insisted that at the end of the journey of life a door will open and a forgiving father-god will greet and enfold them. Cross-culturally, we also find an expectation of reconciliation with those who have gone before. It may be that this is because all through our lives we experience hellos and goodbyes associated with the formation of attachments, their ruptures (abandonments), and usually eventual reconciliations. It is assumed that achievement of a healthy ego within the first few years of life is reflected by a sense of continuity.

Some of these hellos and goodbyes are superficial, shallow, and make-believe; others are rich, meaningful, and at times very sad. As we age, final goodbyes become much more frequent and surprisingly more sobering and rich. This may be because *adieus* are tempered and blended by every past goodbye, as well as by the memory of all those to whom we have said goodbye before. For those who do assume we will meet again, the quality of separation may be more *au revoir*. We think this is a fundamental wish in the hearts of most people, reflecting and testing the depths of faith and the complexities of our ambivalent affiliations with those we love and those we lose. If, with each loss, we pause to ponder the meaning of the lost relationship, a serious change in our perspective may occur, along with a new level of anxious anticipation about those affiliations and attachments that still remain. The death of a father reflects the end of an era for some families and the beginning (at least partially if not totally) of an uncertain, unknown future for others.

As we grow older, our bodies may become more painful homes in which to live, and our daily activities more difficult to endure. All relationships and all age-specific tasks, including dying, contain not only the seeds of fulfillment, but all too often also the actualization of disappointments and a sense of things still undone:

To someone else my diagnosis would be senile depression. . . .
I see a cloud of disaster closing in on my world, even my

339

small one. . . . I have certainly taken a huge step out of the circle of life. . . . To live for one's health and preserve it like a national treasure is otherwise hard to bear. . . .

As for myself, I no longer want to live ardently enough, a crust of indifference is slowly creeping up around me, a fact I state without complaining. It is a natural development, a way of beginning to be inorganic, the detachment of old age I think it's called; it must be connected with a decisive crisis. . . .

The changes taking place are perhaps not too conspicuous, everything is as interesting as it was before, neither are the qualities very different but some kind of resonance is lacking. Unmusical as I am I imagine the difference to be something like using the pedal or not. . . .

There is a tendency to experience everything sub specie aeternitatis. . . . I still have important work to do but I must hurry. I must fight against the inexorable Chronos. I must do this before the resonance becomes even more muted.

Sigmund Freud

Painful existence—a slow death—enhances over time a sense of the incompleteness of human relatedness, imperfection in ourselves and our healing capacities, the inadequacy of communications, and poorly resolved ambivalences.

> When my father died I was high for 6 months. I had prayed he would die all along, then he would be at rest. I suppose I grieved in some fashion, but more for that which I never had. He had had a tumor, but it became cancerous. When we knew he was about to die, all of us came home. On Monday he lost the ability to speak. All he could do was say no. On Tuesday he suddenly began to go downhill. Watching him experiencing pain bothered me. I know that I felt guilty. I have always had to watch my tongue—I can get sarcastic and do damage. I rarely let loose or the rage will get into my voice. So I tried to write it all down. I like to write, rather than talk. Maybe because I can control it better. It was just so scary when I finally did come down from the high, I got depressed, and still do whenever I think of him.

Certain of our successes and most of our failures may plague our existence, as in the story just excerpted. In a more vulnerable cohort of people, however, losses through death may activate a regression associated with freezing of emotions and a refusal to emotionally reinvest. Sometimes all we see is a "refusal" to let dreams, fantasies, and emotions hold sway and become paramount again. In some fashion, this blunting of affect may be a preparation for the end, reechoing Freud's words: "If we want to endure life, prepare for death." On some level, men do know that they owe to life a death. Weisman (1972b), in his work with dying patients, described the phenomenon of half-knowledge. That is, a person may know he is going to die, but can only tolerate the thought in consciousness for a short time; then, for another period of time, this same individual may act as if death were not a reality. Thus on one level we may know that death is real, while on another it is always dreaded and denied.

The Meanings of a Father's Death

From an early age, the dying of a father is something anxiously expected, often fantasied, and possibly vicariously experienced. It is rarely prepared for, however, or even experienced at the time as a reality. When it happens, it may release a grieving, not only for the real person, but also for what neither ever existed nor will be possible in the future. In some circumstances, such a death brings the realization that one has truly lost the opportunity to obtain what a father might have given, had the relationship been different or had he lived longer. In the words of one patient, "I said to my father, 'I'll miss you.' He was dying. He just looked at me and couldn't say anything. It was one of the saddest moments of my life. I couldn't tell if he was too sick to answer or, like it's always been, just that he couldn't show any emotion towards me."

Thus in the late years of a father, a middle-aged son may have the last chance to "undo" ambivalences, earn his father's respect, return what he wished to return so as to make reparations for that which he took, or to express feelings of simple compassion or gratitude (Cath, 1972). In a futile midlife attempt to reach his father, Franz Kafka wrote "A Letter to Father." In it he expressed both his hope and despair of learning a secret withheld, namely, why his father had acted toward him the way he had. In this letter he decried his father's shortcomings, especially the discipline of public humiliations and father's failure to understand why Franz could not value Judaism. Equally important, however, Franz confessed a secret of his love reflected in his work. "My writing was all about you: all I did there, after all, was to bemoan what I could not bemoan upon your breast" (Kouretas, 1967).

In his magisterial treatise on the origins of religion, *The Ghost Dance*, the anthropologist Weston LaBarre (1970) says:

The relationship of fathers and sons is mysterious and terrifying. It has never been rational, nor will it ever be. It is not the only relationship that men must suffer. But father and son form the most critical and dangerous animal relationship on earth, and to suppose otherwise is to invite catastrophe. For it is by no means delivered to us that this species-paradigm will survive annihilation in blind, self-slaughter through some displaced pathology of this relationship. No man ever grows beyond the reach of its influence. How to accept and how to embody male authority, how to express and when to moderate aggressiveness against other men—how, in short, to be father and son, governor and citizen—these still remain the towering problems of the oedipal animal.

This rather typical oedipal view of the father-son relationship might, happily, seem anachronistic in light of the material presented in this chapter and elsewhere throughout this volume. The *potential reciprocal ego enhancement* of sons by fathers and fathers by sons from birth even unto death is one of the major themes of this treatise. During the dying and death of a father, a son may feel a special urgency to "set things right." This should be appreciated as a significant maturing opportunity in the care of the dying father for all of his family. In these circumstances, a frequently encountered wish is that fathers would verbalize not only their vision of their world, but their concept of what their son had meant to them, conveying directly or indirectly, "I love you. I appreciate what you have done for me. It was worth having you."

Unfortunately, a deficiency of such communication shapes the grieving period of many men.

As long as I can remember, my father told me that one day he would write me a very special letter. But he never mentioned what the letter would be about. I used to speculate about it, about what great secrets the letter would reveal, what great surprises, what intimacy we would share. I knew what I hoped the letter would contain. I wanted him to tell me where he had hidden his affection, but then he died, and the letter never arrived, and I never found that place where he had hidden his love.

Duane Michals, "A Letter from My Father"

More often than not, the effects of such a silent father's death are more internal and are hidden away in ritualistic negotiation of the felt demands of the outer world, for example, a funeral. These outer shoals seem much less difficult to navigate than the inner shoals of psychological turmoil and some of the almost universally felt deficiencies in hidden father/self-love which we hope to illuminate in this chapter.

Thus the approaching death of an aging person may elicit a deep longing for that person to stay, but (depending on circumstances) an equally deep longing for him or her to go. When life appears over for a particular person one loves and hates, especially if this ambivalent phase is extended over time, intrapsychic inventories are taken as to what may be or will be left to sustain the self; what reservoir of introjects, conscious and unconscious memories—either creative or destructive—remain as an inheritance. Some grieving men having assessed both sides of this dilemma during the dying of their father, and, after the death have been stimulated to even greater heights of creativity or achievements. They seemed released from an internal bondage and subservience. Others felt unable to continue alone, and still others set out on a self-destructive path. To the outsider it seemed as if they were bent on joining their father. Some may be swept up with intense feelings of emptiness, regret, and depression for not having known their fathers, and "decide" that a fatherless existence is no longer tolerable. They immediately set out to search for a replacement. This is especially likely when they cannot assume the father role itself, thereby grieving through the loss by becoming that which was lost. Some reproach themselves for not having probed deeply enough to obtain what was necessary to know themselves and their roots with conviction. Some family secrets indeed are interred with father's bones, but their irritating residue may form a nidus of uncertain shame: Relationships sometimes outlive people. Others, more fortunate, inherit an enhanced sense of self and pride in having endured their father's death in life.

LaBarre's rather pessimistic viewpoint, reinforced by Freud's earlier writings on the oedipal period, must be taken into account. We would stress, however, the reciprocal enhancement of self, core-gender identity, and consolidation of reasonable masculinity that men are capable of experiencing as sons who pass through the death of their father. Accordingly, we assert that the meaning of the dying and death of a father depends on the balance and residue of affectionate and hostile affects between father and son, as related to the modulation of aggression in the earliest triangulations within their family. This "most terrifying, critical, and potentially dangerous of human relationships" may also have the potential for one of the most creative and reciprocally valuable of human interactions. In that achievement, interpersonal, verbal, and nonverbal communication does not take place in isolation; however, we cannot ignore the contributions that mothers, sisters, and brothers, as well as other family members including grandparents, may make both in critical times and in the foundation of mental representations of father-son bonds.

A tragic example of family residues and the complex difference between an interpersonal, public response and a private isolating intrapsychic reality evolving in the circumstances of a father's death is suggested by a letter from Abraham Lincoln to a friend, "Fanny."

Dear Fanny:
It is with deep grief that I learn of the death of your kind and brave father. Especially that it is affecting your young heart beyond what is common in such cases. In this sad world of ours, sorrow comes to all and, to the young it comes with

bittered agony because it takes them unawares. The older have learned to ever expect it. I am anxious to afford some alleviation of your present distress. Perfect relief is not possible except with time. You cannot now realize that you will ever feel better. Is this not so? And yet, it is a mistake. You are sure to be happy again. To know this, which is certainly true, will make you less miserable now. I have had experience enough to know what I say, and you need only to believe it to feel better at once. *The memory of your dear father, instead of an agony, will yet be a sad sweet feeling in your heart, of a pure and holier sort than you have known before.** Please send my kind regards to your afflicted mother.

Your sincere friend,
Abe Lincoln

This letter presents us with a paradox. Did Lincoln's father ever become a sad, sweet memory in his mind? Did he ever come to terms with the death of his mother, his father's remarriage, and the issue of illegitimacy? We can really never know. What is known is that when Lincoln's father felt himself close to death, correspondence reveals how Lincoln consistently ignored his father's increasingly urgent written pleas to see him. Even when his traveling duties brought him nearby, he refused to come to his father's side. This has led to speculation by students of American history that much of Lincoln's idealization of other great contemporary and past leaders represented a polarization of and a split in father images. That is, he had a desperate need to idealize some father figures, though he simultaneously degraded, punished, or retaliated against others. One wonders whether this conflicted relationship may have contributed to his serious, sometimes suicidal, depressions. Much evidence seems to point in the direction that, in contrast to a sad, sweet feeling of a pure and holier sort than known before, which he indeed may have wished for, Lincoln retained a deep sense of shame about his own paternal heritage.

The Responses to a Father's Death

Not all sons react to the reality of the decline, the dying and death, of a father in a stereotypical way. The range and circumstances of meanings involved lead to a variety of significant conscious and unconscious characterological changes. Our experiences have led us to organize this delicate balance around six criteria:

1. The age and circumstances of the survivor son in terms of his life progression, having to do with the management of impulses and defenses, maturation and libidinal investments, cohesiveness and continuity of the self

*Emphasis added.

2. The degree of the father's psychological aliveness before, during, and after his death, a characteristic that is often related to the depths of the attachment, affiliation, or distancing that had taken place during life, and may well determine the quality and intensity of mourning during the last years of the father's life
3. The intactness and availability of internalized parental images, "male caretakers," in the son's psychic structure, whatever their source
4. The stabilizing intimacies remaining in the surviving son's milieu, including psychoanalysts and therapists
5. The question of subjective and objective accountability of the father's contributions to the residual interpersonal assets and liabilities in the mind's eye of the son; may be most evident in ongoing attachments within and without his family
6. The issue of whether or not the surviving son has achieved fatherhood as yet, and, if so, what he conceives his death would mean to his own son; may determine how he colors, modulates, and deals with the residual angers, hurts, and gratitudes in ongoing father-son relationships

Many grieve the loss of the idealized preoedipal father long before the father's biological death. As in Lincoln's case, more perfect intrapsychic replacements may be found. All too often, however, disillusionment, denied initially, is inevitable. Some sons are reluctant to retrace the intrapsychic paths of reciprocally relating to men no longer imagined to be grandiose and pure; these men may never again trust a male friend. This degradation of the image of the real father into an incompetent, inadequate, unethical, or evil mental representation may contribute to specific vulnerabilities in the father-son constellation in midlife and beyond. Shakespeare, according to some historians, had a father who rose to a minor political office, but, probably afflicted by alcoholism, ended his life in disgrace. It was after this that the bard is said to have changed the direction of his life. We can only conjecture about the meaning of some of the figures in his literature as reflecting some of these concerns.

Those unfortunate enough to watch their parents lose cognitive and social skills, or to become demented before death, may experience a prolonged period of anxious guilt, marked by unwelcome wishes for death to come as soon as possible (Cath, 1976). The feeling of having no parents, even though they are alive, present, and sometimes influential, may create in offspring a sense of depersonalized and justified aggression. Some feel lost in time and space, wish for time to pass as quickly as possible, and experience deep feelings of guilt. Others turn to religion or to younger women, who traditionally revitalize the self and may neutralize feelings of emptiness or anger. However, the missing or special qualities of a father often determine the character of the father hunger and the replacement search. Preoedipal, oedipal, and postoedipal children will attribute entirely different meanings to circumstances surrounding a father's demise; for example, some adolescents, sexualizing their search, still look for certain paternal qualities in their love objects. It is not surprising that an extremely troubled relationship with such a father's successor, especially if of the opposite sex, may soon develop.

Death may come in many forms: quiet and natural over a period of time; abrupt through accident or disease; a tormenting death in which personhood has been long lost and doctors seem helpless; or the finality of rejection brought about by suicide. Some clinical vignettes are offered.

Clinical Examples

A Father's Psychological Death; A Son's Rebirth

David, a 29-year-old psychologist, entered analysis because of difficulties in his relationship with women. He is the third son of survivors of the Nazi holocaust. The initial transference featured repeated references to the fact that David felt nothing for the analyst because the analyst could not reciprocate. This led to a notion that the often-quiet analyst was often "dead wrong" in his approach, and then to the notion that he was actually dead. David's perception of the analyst as "dead wrong" and then actually dead made some sense in the following context. David's father had been profoundly depressed, unavailable, most of the time totally silent. He had lost a family during the war and, in a sense, had "died" himself.

The second phase of the analysis evolved both within and outside of the transference. It featured repeated efforts to get a rise out of a man, to bring him back to life by provoking a response. The sexual mode proved most amenable to this acting out, and David entered into several active homosexual relationships. They were all short-lived and proved to be quite unsatisfactory.

In the fourth year of the analysis, David's father, advanced in years and seriously ill for a long time, died. The son's response was to feel liberated, in that his father had been released from his suffering and so had he and the rest of the family. He was not sad. In fact, the sadness that had characterized his earlier father hunger seemed to give way to a more varied affective state, and he now felt that he could get on with his life. He became very interested in a number of women, including his mother. He felt that his father's premature psychological death prevented his comfortably relating to women, especially mother. Now, with father's actual demise, he could use the alliance with the analyst to this end. As he became alive, he began to revel in things feminine. A wish to become a father emerged, and for the first time, David spoke of wanting to marry and someday have children.

Father: "A Bee-Heading"

Lawrence, 36 years old, was referred to psychotherapy by his wife's therapist. After 10 years of marriage, including 3 years of twice-weekly psychotherapy, his wife had arrived at the point where she wanted to have a child. Lawrence felt this would be an impossibility. Other chief complaints, presented on a list compiled by his wife—herself a psychiatrist—included lack of interest in sex and indecision about a career. Lawrence, pursuing his second doctoral degree, was considering yet another professional change. Interestingly, this intelligent, obsessional man soon advanced the idea that perhaps psychoanalysis was the treatment of choice. He complained of lack of affect, citing particularly his total lack of feeling when his father had died 17 years earlier. At this time, embarking on his first doctoral program, he felt he had drive and energy enough to take anything; a mere loss could not bring him down. A number of dreams featured, in more or less distinct form, the theme of infanticide. He appeared to be involved in an oedipal drama in which anal-sadistic outcomes predominated. In one dream, he reported the existence of a midget assassin who was on the prowl. A headline in the newspaper read: "Who is Killing the Great Professors of Europe?" Further newspaper text read: "A Bee Heading in This Direction. Alert! Alert!". As Lawrence associated to this dream, *bee heading* became *beheading*, and the thought of killing the great professors enchanted and then consternated him. He then had the association to the name Lawrence Geist. As we analyzed the dream further, we learned that Geist, the German word for spirit, meant his "Lawrence" spirit. He feared the murder of this spirit by a midget assassin, a son, who would even behead one of the great professors of Europe. At this moment he was overcome with grief and wept for the first time that he could remember. "My father, my father. How can I become a father if I have killed my father?"

Father: The Only Source of Warmth

At some point during this narrative, the patient, Elmer, began to sob. His voice reached a pitch never heard before in the consulting room.

My father was the source of the most positive or truly the only warm feelings I have ever known. It was he who picked me up and comforted me when I was hurt as far back as I can remember. His eyes gleamed when I came home from school, and it was into his arms I always ran to be hugged. For some mysterious reason, my mother never meant the same, never came to my graduations or any of the games I played in. By contrast, my father was always there. It's funny, she still tends to ignore me, turn away when I come in the house. Even her body movements like that infuriate me. When I walk in the door she goes on with what she is doing and doesn't say anything. I keep thinking maybe it was because I was illegitimate. Maybe I'm supposed to feel I forced them to marry. Rather, I have the feeling she tricked him into marrying her by getting pregnant, and I didn't have anything to do with it. But, you know that my father is in the hospital with cancer. I really know he is going to die and what will happen to the source of little warmth and pride I've had in the past and may still have? He is the only one who shared it with me, shared my pleasures, even though he couldn't share my griefs. He never could stand it when I was sad. We never really could talk, but I always enjoyed just being with him. It always seems as if my mother was saying to my father, "You go off with him . . . take him off my hands." He didn't seem to mind as long as I behaved myself. I'll never do that to my child or let my wife do what my mother did.

"A Thirty-Year Wake"

Harold dreamed that the door was halfway open. He was in a bed and wanted to get up and close the door, but felt paralyzed. His associations led to mother, who was now old and threatened by strokes, having had several transient ischemic attacks. Mother had always plagued him about neglecting and not appreciating her. He thought of his mother in a coffin, unable to move, waking up as he did in the dream, and feeling paralyzed. He wondered if he would still feel responsible for all of his mother's miseries, even after her death. When father died 30 years ago, he had left the patient in the position of having to care for mother, with no parent to love. The only one he had cared about was his father, who was a highly narcissistic and selfish man. Yet Harold gave him what love he could. The door was halfway open, but he had not closed that door or gotten out of that room. He had not been able to break the guilty bondage he felt with mother. Even when his father was alive, Harold could not keep from feeling this way. He thought to himself many times that father's death had started a 30-year wake, 30 years of mother's dominance, still churning up his life. He had wished over and over again that mother would die. In his words, "the wake continues."

Father the Entertainer and Son the Coach

I [Charles] always knew my father was a fraud; he loved audiences so much. I tried to keep away from him and often I was glad when he was not around. I never knew if it was my anger at him or his at me, but one thing was sure—he tore into me with meaningless sarcasm that would bite deep. Like, that expression I hate so much: *Darf mir gehen zu college?* (Do you have to go to college?). I don't know if you're Jewish or not, Doctor, but what he really meant was, how can you be so stupid and go to college and come out with things like that? I wanted to vomit. I wanted to quit school and never go back. Words never did me any good. I knew he

348

never listened. He talked continuously and saw me as somebody who interfered with his ability to entertain others. I just hated company because I knew the show would go on. When he died, I was so relieved. The only trouble is, my wife says I have become more like him as I age. Here I am, 35 years old, never interested in my own kids, always coaching someone else's kids down the block in the little league. But, even there I put them down, just like he did with me. Christ, does that mean he's not dead? That he is living in me? God damn it, there has to be something I can do about it. I feel like I'm a fraud; I can't be friends with anyone easily. The best friend I have, my only friend, is just like my father. I know I didn't trust him. He puts up such a front with people, he's so smooth, always talking, a know-it-all. But, Doctor, more important, is there any substance in me that is not my father?

The Father Who Lived "Long Enough"

I [Jason] am so glad my father lived long enough for me to come around to feel like an adult. I had a real hard time as a teenager, acting up. He always reacted like a tyrant, autocratic. I defied him, but everyone else respected him and even loved him. Everyone except me. I needed somehow to spoil his life. To spit on him. I never knew why I did that, but right now I feel such a mixture of sadness, nostalgia, and guilt, as if I want to go back and undo it. Do it all over again, do it better. At last I did the right thing. I made something of myself. It wasn't what he wanted, wasn't business, but the last few years before his death, he was so proud of me he couldn't stop talking about it. I guess, somehow, I gave him something he wanted. I am glad, at least, of that.

Suicide of a Father

Maurice, a middle-aged, very self-assured internist, had been in analysis for 4 years for sexual problems when his father committed suicide. He seemed determined to deal with it "maturely," and grieved little. As his analysis continued, he began to try to readjust his life and to put the pieces together, entering a new relationship with a woman who had many of the qualities of his father. The transference evolved in such a way that idealization of the analyst became more pronounced than it had been before. The analysis took a turn in which, in contrast to the past 4 years, it seemed he was constantly trying to please the analyst and do the right thing. An interpretation that this was the case and we might explore whether or not he had some concern about the analyst, led to associations about how tired and haggard the analyst had looked and whether or not suicide was on his mind. For the first time, the patient began to grieve openly for his father and to express some love for the very early years in which father had seemed strong. The loss of the analyst as a real possibility by termination had raised in his mind the notion that maybe someone worth grieving for could be lost. In the past, he had been so angry with his father and his weaknesses that he could not even begin to express his feelings of tenderness. He wondered how people could be so ex-

349

hausted as to be depleted of all inner loving feelings for their own kin, to take their lives and ignore the consequences of guilt that suicide brings. He was able to reveal some of his own suicidal preoccupations, which had antedated his father's death.

The Alcoholic "Immortal" Father

I [James] had no choice. My mother was helpless, had always been incapacitated. My father, sick unto death in the hospital, claiming he was immortal. As I had done so many times before, I took over without thinking. I arranged for the private duty nurses, consulted with the doctors and called my Aunt Sue to have her come over to stay with mother. Then I went to the hospital for what I was sure would be the last visit, at least if the doctors were correct. Imagine how I felt when I found him sitting up in bed, grinning from ear to ear, eating like food was going out of style. I was so furious. I coughed my way out of the room and began to cry. "Not again! How could we go through these alcoholic binges, the detox centers, the brushes with death, all over again? How I wish he had just died."

Discussion

In almost all men everywhere, there seems to be a prolonged universal adaptive process related to fathers' decline, dying, and death. Balancing the nurturing, loving aspects of the father-son relationship are punishing, retributional features. The latter reflect disappointment and frustration of realistic and egoistic aims, often attributed by one generation to the other. This balance marks a progressive developmental process which, in some instances, can be said to have begun during the neonatal phase, for example, the prediction that Laius need fear his unborn son, Oedipus.

Although parents may expect children to be perfect when they are born, to develop along a predetermined path not always appropriate to that particular individual in his time, and somehow to bring some enhancement to the aging, parental self, they simultaneously fear the opposite. The child, in turn, asks that his parents meet increasing demands for care as well as legitimate needs for idealized objects in order to build a cohesive, continuous self, especially to gradually feel known and valued by a significant, powerful father. In this elaborate mutual, reciprocal progression of changing needs, fathers and sons construct various mental representations of each other—some accurate, some inaccurate—and they pass through different phases at different times in their lives in which these needs and images may or may not be constant. At times, either one may focus more on what has been lost than what has been gained, what can be restituted or what needs to be renounced.

A father's destiny in his late years often generates in a son a feeling of what his life is destined to be, of what is to be gained by living long or through those phases the father has just traversed. The usual pattern is for the balance to shift from fathers in power, "the command generation," to younger men through a gradual transition in which a reversal of roles, prestige, and command is likely to take place. Shakespeare presented a compelling drama in which an aging, weakening King Lear turned to his daughters and sons-in-law in order to pass on to one or more of them his accumulated wealth and kingdom. First, however, he tested his family: "How much do you love me?" Two daughters responded, in essence, "unequivocally." His third daughter, Cordelia, answered in a way that seems dynamically true, even though it did not please him. She responded, "according to our bond, your majesty." In essence, the dying and the death of a father interrupts certain reality aspects of this bond, even as other aspects of the bond continues. Toward the end of the father's life, the father-son relationship may be detoxified or intensified by the presence or absence of a third generation, that is, grandchildren. Under these circumstances, a softer side of the homosexual bond between men may emerge (Chap. 21). That is, a father can split off and accept his need for a male figure to complete and enhance his bisexual self from his son onto a grandchild. In many cases, the father can never turn to the son in this same tender way. One father realized this was happening. "Seeing my father with my own children affects my view of him tremendously. They have a relationship beyond the conflict that we knew. It must have been my fault. I can now imagine that were I to die first they will not miss me as much as long as my son is around. But, if he should die first, they will miss him in a way that they will never miss me. I don't know what to make of it." The dying father who has become a grandfather and knows a more positive, affective interchange with another male may have an entirely different feeling about his death than one who has never known a positive relationship with his own father, with his son, or with any other male member of his family. I even suspect it may color his conception of the world beyond and his representation of God (Chap. 23).

Conclusions

From one point of view, the father dies as he has lived: a real figure, an important actor in the internal and external world of his children. From another point of view, the father lives on intrapsychically, reflecting the vicissitudes of father-child relationships within the context of longitudinal generations of fathers. These variations are reflected in the reaction of the child whose male parent dies, as well as the adult man's reaction to his father's death. When fathers have been absent for long periods, the likely resultant father hunger, despair, confusion about masculine identity, and

351

role will affect offspring significantly. Any father's actual death interdigitates with the intrapsychic circumstances, wherever his child is in his long line of efforts to make restitution to his father and father-gods, in understanding his own mortality, and in coming to terms with the earliest abandonment, hostilities, or strains he remembers in his own father-child relationship. Often, as in the case of David, above, there is relief that reality, internal and external, may be now more concordant.

Although the capacity to be a father might be thought of as genetic, the destiny of fatherhood and the quality of fathering depend on how the tender shoots of masculinity have been cultivated in the family matrix of a mother, father, and siblings. Actual fathering is thus usually nourished in the context of the spouseship and of children. Furthermore, because of sex differences in life expectancy, more fathers than mothers will die in a similar context. Thus a father's death has a unique contextual meaning as well as an actual one within every family, reflecting the realities of the developmental phase and stage of relationships between caretakers and father. Often paternal death occurs after a reversal of roles played by members of an original dyad or triad and an assumption, partial or complete, of protective responsibilities by a child or children.

This chapter has explored the ramifications of paternal loss through the stages of dying, death, and merely surviving. We have stressed the distinction between psychological and actual death as important explanatory concepts, which may illuminate mourning patterns that differ in temporal sequence. That is, the death of personhood may long antedate biological death. In addition, reactions to the father's death tell us something quite important not only about the father's life, but about his unique role and function for his survivors at all ages. No matter when death occurs, there is revived between father and son a prototypical reciprocal conflict, a tension between being and becoming, between declining and dying.

We can distinguish many themes, but four areas of disruption appear to occur regularly with the death of a father. First, throughout life, each individual uses other individuals to help in the management of impulses, affects, reality testing, and the maintenance of homeostasis. The good use of the father object by a son approximates what Kohut calls the good selfobject. When this is lost, the issue becomes one of finding others to help in the continued effort to modulate, titrate, and manage the currents of inner masculine life as well as the threats of annihilation that living long enough will inevitably bring. Psychoanalysis and the fields traditionally related to it, by extolling the independence and autonomy of the individual, have perhaps underestimated the criticalness of the intimate dyadic and triadic relationships for maintenance of self structures over the life span. We must recognize the ongoing use of others by the self in spouseships and among peers. Our own understanding of such phenomena tends to emphasize an individual's ability to define one's own well-being or completeness in terms that include the well-being and completeness of offspring and spouse. We would emphasize, then, not so much the masochistic aspect of parenthood as the particular ability to empathize with, extend the self in time and space, and experience the intimate connection between self and others, implicit in the making and caring for new generations.

IV

Cultural and
Historical Variations

Our choice of chapters on the social, historical, cultural, and literary variations on the theme of fatherhood has perforce been highly selective and indeed rather arbitrary. To encompass a fuller range of topics, much less a comprehensive treatment of fathers and fathering at different times and in different places, is clearly beyond the scope of the volume. Rather, our intent has been to provide a context for and some counterpoints to the preceding essays, whose points of reference are, inevitably, historically and culturally bound.

Psychoanalyst Ana-Maria Rizzuto's chapter on the godhead representation and the father's role in its formation derives from long-term research (readers should refer to her book for further details). She sees such a structure as an essential, inevitable accompaniment of personality development.

Critic Paul Schwaber also reveals an epigenetic view of the religious impulse in his exegesis of the patriarchal tradition as chronicled in the Old Testament. His piece and Rizzuto's to some extent complement the views of other analysts who have studied the irrational and pathogenic aspects of institutional religions with their authoritarian, hierarchical organizations. This perspective on patriarchy within the family is represented in Nathaniel Ross's contribution (Chap. 33) on dominance and submission.

Sylvia Brody, an analyst who has studied extensively the progressive interplay between infants and mothers, offers a welcome serendipity of poignant vignettes and excerpts from the nineteenth-century English novel. She has long emphasized the psychosexual roots of the self-sacrifice inherent in mothering, and now gives testimony to a man's struggle with and abiding tendency to retreat from analogous promptings in himself, compromising his paternity in the process.

Sudhir Kakar is both a psychosocial historian and an analyst and has been both a student and a teacher in Germany, the United States, and his native India. A disciplinary and sociocultural breadth thus converges on his deceptively simple essay on fathers in India. Chosen as a case in point of cultural differences, this chapter is nonetheless consistent with the rest of the volume. Like other authors, Kakar emphasizes the father's early incarnations as an ally and developmental facilitator, in addition to his preordained role as a rival and overlord.

Like Kakar, American historian John Demos has been a student and collaborator of psychohistorian Erik Erikson. Here he surveys the history of fatherhood in America. He underscores the but gradual removal of men from the home and, with this, the initial role of fathers as primary parents responsible for their children's moral and emotional development.

23

The Father and the Child's Representation of God: A Developmental Approach

Ana-Maria Rizzuto

Psychoanalytic literature has neglected not only the role of the father "in the flesh" (Freud, 1913, p. 147) but also the "exalted father" (Freud, 1910, p. 123; 1913, p. 147; 1914, p. 243; 1923c, p. 85) whom children transform into a God.

As though two neglects were not enough, psychoanalysts since Freud's time have paid no attention to what children do with their parental representations when they transform them creatively into a God. The psychic services provided by a God who the child believes exists and who is, in turn, even more knowledgeable and powerful than the parents themselves, have been ignored and bypassed. Declaring ourselves to be progressive nonbelievers in illusions, we have blinded our eyes to each child's developmental need to create publicly or privately his or her own God; surely there is a developmental reason for children to be so persistent. The most poignant case is that of a girl of 7 years, born to parents of a large family of committed atheists and militant communists. The girl was so afflicted by the insistence of her parents that there was no God that she would lock her bedroom door, lie face down on the floor, and say, "Please, let there be a God."

Fathers do not come without mothers. Fathers and mothers do not come without a child. These simple facts of life make any ordinary parental group a triad (of united and symbiotic relatedness) and a trinity (of distinct individuals). Each of the members of the family group has, obviously, a reality of his or her own as an existing individual proceeding through a life cycle of epigenesis and transformations. Each of them, also, experiences the others as well as him- or herself in a private psychic reality, in which the representation of him- or herself and the other two members of the group renders a particular version of each of them as the result of weaving into a representational form the wishes and fears, the memories and anticipations, the fantasies and the interpretations about what they are like as spouse, parent, or child. The complex intertwining of those two realities creates for the family and each individual member a particular universe of shared facts and subjective interpretations of them, linking father, mother, and child forever to each other. The child starts this experience not only at the beginning of historical life but without any other previous experience to use for comparison. His or her biological endowment and immersion in the triadic and trinitarian relationships become the very substance of the child's psyche, and elicit through the accumulated modes of relatedness, memories, fantasies, wishes, and fears his or her lifelong basic modality of relating to others and to him- or herself.

As though this process is not complex enough, the child's developing capacity to represent and symbolize allows him or her to create imaginary beings made out of both self-representations and representations of the parents. For the child, these imaginary beings have a powerful reality of their own. There are monsters, whose scary qualities may come either from the projected badness of the child or the displaced fears of the parents; there are strange, wonderful, or worrisome creatures such as gnomes, elves, boogey men and women, fairy godmothers, and devils (the very bad child); and there are the Devil (the very bad father) and the witch (the very bad mother). Also, there is God, one more creature in the long parade of concocted characters. They all appear sequentially from 18 months of age onward and continue well into latency, to disappear quietly early in prepuberty if the development has been normal.

One of them, however, does not go away: God remains with most children for factual and subjective reasons. The culture at large accepts the actual existence of God. No small witness of this cultural acceptance are the many religious buildings and temples of diversified religions that dot the landscape of every town in America. What impresses children the most, however, is not the landscape, but their parents' belief (or explicit nonbelief) in this superior being. Children notice parents' references to (and many times reverence for) this God whom they consider bigger than themselves. Having no sensory experience of God, children are forced to create the representational characteristics of their God out of the most extraordinary beings they know: their parents. Subjectively, God may remain even in the context of a militantly atheist family because the young believer needs the psychic services God provides privately to the child.

The process of creating a God representation out of self and parental representations follows an orderly and demonstrable sequence like any other line of development. The process may also include other adults closely related to the small child. The parents, however, whether physically present or present only in the desires and the imagination of the child (as in the case of a parent deceased before the child was born), are the main source for the psychic attributes bestowed on the Godhead. I have shown (Rizzuto, 1979) that, properly investigated, a detailed and careful reconstruction can trace God's representational characteristics to experiences in reality, wish, or fantasy with primary objects.

Representations does not refer to a mental content, an idea, or a feeling. The term is meant to include the totality of experiential levels gathered in the course of growing up under a given name, whether it be father, mother, self, or God. Representations of people always include visceral, proprioceptive, sensorimotor, perceptual, eidetic, and conceptual components. These components are present in the God representation created by the child and attributed to God as well-fitting character traits. Examples are the subjective experiences of feeling "watched" by God's piercing eyes, supported by feeling "in His hands," or "afraid of" His anger.

The child first creates his or her God representation by linking some of the parents' representational characteristics to some nonvisible being called God. The earliest representation used by the child originates in the mother. Later, a compound representation of the parents may be created and used to form a God representation. Finally, the paternal representation may lend some of its traits to the Godhead. Other important family members may also join in. In normal circumstances, however, contrary to what Freud described, the father alone is never used to form the God representation. Once the child has created his or her particular version of what God is like, the "character traits" attributed to Him will remain as the baseline of the child's feelings about God.* Psychic life, however, is not static, and the changes brought about by the epigenetic transformation of functions and structures at all levels (physical, intellectual, emotional), environmental influences, and historical events must have an impact on the individual's need to update, modify, transform, or repress his or her available God representation. In the last chapter of my book I have described in detail the usual transformations that take place during the entire course of life (Rizzuto, 1979).

Research

This chapter aims to present and discuss the conditions necessary for a child to be able to use his or her father to form and transform the God

*"Him" is used here only because it is customary. God, in the representation of the child, may as well be female.

representation. The clinical material reviewed to investigate the topic is the same I used for the book: 20 individuals (men and women) whose entire lives were studied in the most exhaustive manner in order to provide a comprehensive and detailed description of their earliest, as well as later, object relations and object representations. The God representation was investigated as carefully as the early objects so as to compare and to trace God's characteristics to their human sources.

The sample included 10 men and 10 women from 18 to 60 years of age. They encompassed all diagnostic categories, from schizophrenia to phobic reactions, reactive depressions, and intense adolescent turmoil. Before discussing the theoretical implications of the findings I shall describe and classify the individuals according to the facts of their life situations in relation to their fathers and mothers.

Table 9 presents the findings about the 20 individuals whose life histories were studied. The information included is limited to those essential facts that permit establishment of a correlation between the father in the family and in the child's subjective experience, as well as his contribution to the individual's God representation and belief.

Interpretation of the Data
Six individuals (30%) have a representation of God made up almost exclusively from their idealized maternal representations. One other individual also used the parental couple and her father.

God Representation Derived from Mother
Clinical Example 1
Donna Marconi (case no. 13) formed her God representation exclusively from her idealized, wished-for mother. In talking about an ideal mother, she rejects her own and replaces her with a real person, a nun and teacher who was of great help to her. In actual life, her father had died when she was 5 months old. Her mother worked and was always involved with different men, leaving her daughter alone through the night even during her childhood illnesses. The patient felt very distant from her mother and felt that she needed her very much. When she was 5½ years old her mother acquired a permanent male friend, who moved in with them. The little girl liked him very much and was quite willing to take him as a father. However, after numerous fights with the mother, one day he left without announcement or farewell, never to be seen again. Her older brother tried to help her, but he did not qualify to be exalted into a Godhead.

Table 9. Formation of the God Representation

Case No.	Age (Years)	Diagnosis	Belief in God	Actual Mother	Ideal Mother	Actual Father	Ideal Father	Actual Parents	Ideal Parents	Self	Other Source
Females											
3	20	Neurotic depression (suicidal gesture) in a passive-aggressive personality; adolescent turmoil	?	+	My mother. Any changes in her? I wish she understood the way I felt [refers only to adolescent behavior]	Distant. Controlled, proud of controlling his feelings. Hardworking. The dominant figure in the family. Away from home a lot. (+)	My father. But I wish he understood how I felt. A father I was not afraid of. I wanted his affection.	++++	–	++	–
6	41	Schizophrenic reaction; undifferentiated	Yes	+	My mother. I wish she could have taken me shopping with her when I was younger.	Religious school principal. A strict and busy man. Totally devoted to the school. Hard person to get to know. A shy man. (+)	My father. I wish he talked to me more. It must have been hard on him to talk to me as a daughter.	++++	–	–	–
7	34	Borderline character disorder; committed suicide	Yes	+	My mother. She is wise, loving, and hardworking.	Businessman. Drank heavily. Volatile. Good provider. Very sociable. "A house devil and a street angel." Very jolly and charming; also very angry and frightening. (++++)	A man who is peaceful, loving, and enjoys his children. A wise man who would listen to and help you.	++	–	Assigned to father since birth	–

Table 9. (*Continued*)

Case No.	Age (Years)	Diagnosis	Belief in God	Actual Mother	Ideal Mother	Actual Father	Ideal Father	Actual Parents	Ideal Parents	Self	Other Source
9	49	Neurotic reactive depression	Yes	++	Not my mother. A very efficient mother. A mother who shows love through talk. A mother with whom I can talk about my problems.	Worked hard. He was the provider who gave his wages to mother. Big, fat, robust, and quiet. (The patient attached herself to him.) (++)	A big, jolly man. A strong, warm, loving man. (Not the actual father.)	+++	−	−	−
10	18	Adjustment reaction of adolescence	No/Yes +		Not my mother. One who is less of a martyr and does not complain all the time. One who does not baby her children.	Good provider. Improved his condition. He built up my self-confidence. I felt myself his intellectual peer. He has a great sense of humor. (++++)	My own. No changes whatsoever. He always understood me and had time for his children.	++	−	Assigned to father very early (+++)	−
11	46	Alcohol addiction; passive-aggressive personality	Yes	−	Not my mother. A mother who conveys to me completely that she loves me. One I could respect and who would accept my love in return. One who gives me guidelines and values. One who does not try to live her life through me. (+++)	Incapable of separating from his parents. Insecure. Unable to provide for the family. Poor working record. Sexualized the relation with the daughter in adolescence.	I want him to be in love with my mother. I want him to love me as a person, to take me on his lap. A strong person, who would listen and understand. A very special man.	−	+	−	−

362

12	27	Borderline character disorder	Yes	–	Not my mother. Another who wanted me, took care of me, liked me, and was happy. (+++)	Alcoholic. No generational separation. Competed with the children for the mother. Frightening, impatient. Dependent, insecure. The boss in the house. Punished the children. (+)	An older father, who was 30 when I was born. A man who works all the time, likes my mother and me, and wanted me to be a girl. Calm, quiet, spanked me when I needed it, but usually tried to find out why I did things wrong.	++	–	–	–	Grandmother (++)
13	25	Passive-aggressive personality with reactive depression	Yes	–	Not my mother. But Sister Mary Michael. She is warm, understanding. She listens. She cared for and understood me. (++++)	Died when the patient was 5 months old. At 4 years, patient became aware that she did not have a father.	A daddy who loves you, punishes you, cares about you, talks to you, gets mad at you, makes you feel you want to be good.	–	–	–	–	Jesus (+) Older brother
14	60	Involutional depression	Yes	–	My own mother. I could not have gotten a better one. I do not make any changes in her. (++++)	Died of tuberculosis when patient was 16. He was a teacher and contractor. He was the provider. Mother and father always knew what to do. He was the member of my family I disliked the most.	Not my own father. A man like Hubert Humphrey or Franklin D. Roosevelt. A man of great understanding. Well educated, religious.	+	–	–	–	—

Table 9. (Continued)

Case No.	Age (Years)	Diagnosis	Belief in God	Actual Mother	Ideal Mother	Actual Father	Ideal Father	Actual Parents	Ideal Parents	Self	Other Source
16	58	Anxiety neurosis; phobia	Yes	+	My mother, but a little less strict.	Extremely hardworking. Quiet, gentle, warm. He was kind. He was an angel. He was a lovely man. (++++)	My father. I would not change my father in any way.	+	–	–	–
Males 1	38	Obsessive-compulsive personality with manic behavior	Yes	+++	Not my mother. A mother who loved my father and from whom I can sense what it was to see a woman loving *another* man.	Manic-depressive illness, manic type. Religious delusions. Very violent. Constant quarreling and physical violence with wife. Inefficient. Always in debt. Unpredictable. (++)	A man who taught me how to compete, how to go out into the world and stand on my own two feet, who supported me, who would go sailing and camping with me. Someone I was not frightened of because of his anger. (++)	–	–	–	Jesus (+) Brother
2	39	Obsessive-compulsive personality with reactive depression	?	++++	Not my mother. One who realized she had a younger son, who was interested in me as an individual, not as a number. One who makes you feel that you belong.	Outgoing, affable. Very competent. Loved and respected in the community. Close to his wife and children. Very involved and perceptive. He knew people and his children.	The one I have.	–	–	++	–

364

4	27	Passive-dependent personality with somatic reaction: testicular pain	Yes	—	My mother. Few changes. (++++)	Worked regularly. Provided well. Quarreled with wife. The child was afraid that the father could hurt mother and himself. Aloof and distant. The child could not talk with him.	A father who takes interest in you, listens to you, takes you places, gives you the feeling you are the son.	—	—	—	—	—
5	26	Schizoid personality; psychophysiological disorder	Yes	Committed suicide when child was 5 years old	My mother. No changes. I love the memory of my mother and me, and it is unfair she had to go. (++++)	Alcoholic when patient was 5 years old. Remarried. No communication between father and son. Constant quarrels over stepmother. Provided well and "was there when needed." (+)	My Uncle Ray. He is a heck of a nice guy. For awhile he took care of me and my sister.	—	—	—	—	—
8	46	Obsessive-compulsive personality with reactive depression	No*	+++	My mother with some changes, such as less preoccupation with personal complaints. Not so concerned about us. She was a great mother in the main.	Hardworking. Provider, boss, disciplinarian. The person who had everybody's respect. Strong and self-reliant.	My father. I was always proud of my father. I always liked and loved him. I still do. I have deep affection for him.	—	—	—	—	—

Table 9. (Continued)

Case No.	Age (Years)	Diagnosis	Belief in God	Actual Mother	Ideal Mother	Actual Father	Ideal Father	Actual Parents	Ideal Parents	Self	Other Source
15	27	Passive-aggressive personality with traumatic neuroses	Yes	–	My mother without any changes. There is no one like her. I have the ideal mother.	Mildly violent. Good-hearted. Constantly quarreling with spouse. Inefficient. Crippled by accident when patient was 7 years old.	I like the same father. I want to change his hitting us, his hollering. I wish he worked and that his accident had not happened. He was a good-hearted man.	++++	–	Wished to be God's special son	–
17	57	Obsessive-compulsive personality with reactive depression	Yes	++++	My mother without any changes.	Hard and efficient worker. Left money, house, and children in his wife's hands, but set all the rules. Physically absent most of the time. An angry man with a quick temper, who could get furious. "A good man at heart." (+++)	My father, the one I had. Changes? To be closer to me, setting me on his lap, teaching me something. I would change his temper.	–	–	–	–
18	47	Obsessive personality with reactive depression	Yes	–	My mother. I don't think she could be any better to me.	Rugged, hard-working. Tried hard to make the family happy. Good, kind. Always did the right thing. Patient admired him. Did not show his emotions. Physically very big.	My father was the best father. He was a wonderful person, and I don't want anybody else.	++++	–	–	–

366

19	29	Schizoid personality with reactive depression	?	+	My mother with some changes. A mother who is not so protective and fearful for my welfare and who treats me more as an adult.	Worked very hard. Provided very well. Devoted to work and family. Very domineering, demanding, controlling, given to outbursts of rage. The absolute boss. Very ambitious for his son. (++++)	–	–	I get another father. A father who likes children, is not too preoccupied with success, is more open about discussing things with his children, and can admit he is at fault.	–	Father tyrannized the family	–
20	19	Borderline character disorder with acute depression	Yes	–	My mother. I wish only that she did not work. (++++)	Worked very hard. Provided acceptably with great effort. Devoted to work and family. Passive, calm, emotionally hungry, low self-esteem. Physically absent most of the time.	–	+	I want my own father. I wish I could talk to him more. I wish he were younger so we could participate together in sports.	–	–	–

*"Do you want to be united to God? From what I hear from believers, union is the ideal, a Nirvana sort of thing; and if it is a good thing, I want it."
+ = God representation; – = absence in God representation. See text for the patients' names.

The father was never mentioned in the household. In spite of it, the child became aware of her absent father when she was 4 years old. She does not seem to have been able to use fantasies about her father to form her God representation. Perhaps her fear of her mother's numerous lovers interfered. She did long for a father who would love her, punish her, care about her, talk with her, get mad at her, and who would make her want to be good. That ideal, wished-for father made no contribution to her God representation. Her need for the presence of a caring mother took precedence. The urgency of the need at the time of the study is illustrated by the following statement: "The love of God towards me is important because I need his guidance *now*. . . . The feeling I get from my relationship with God is one of Hope because I need that *now*."

This woman as a small child was exposed to many adults who had compassion for her predicament and helped her in whatever way they could. The patient always felt that adults were willing to help and she always accepted their help. Nonetheless, she wanted a mother (not her own mother) and a father (she knew close to nothing about her own) who could treat her like a child. In her later life she has not sought fatherly figures, but only substitute mothers, who listened to her, understood her, and cared for her.

Her God representation was created from her experiences with her mother. Two quotations suffice to illustrate: (1) "I believe in a personal God because I feel His presence is with me" (the prevalent, wished-for, good mother she used to form her God representation), and (2) "I have felt that I hated God because He forsook me at times" (the characteristics of the actual mother that constitute the hateful side of God).

From this patient, one may conclude that when the experience of early mothering has been so massively traumatic, the individual's life preoccupation becomes one of finding a mothering object. In the total absence of a fathering figure that could be used for mothering, the patient's only choice when the time came to flesh out the representation of God was to use the images and experiences available from her rejecting and abandoning mother and her wishful fantasies for a caring mother. The urgency of the need seems to have left no room to create an imaginary father or a fatherly God. Her God fulfills only the maternal function.

Clinical Example 2

The next patient, Richard Renard (case no. 5), is of the same age as Donna Marconi. His representation of God is made up almost exclusively of his greatly idealized *real* mother, and it also includes some minor traits of his actual father. This young man describes best the core of his psychic life when he says: "I love me* and the memory of my mother, and it's unfair she had to go." In real life his mother had a severe mental illness, neglected the children, and finally committed suicide when the patient was 5 years old. He managed, nonetheless, to keep alive a real memory of sitting on his mother's lap while she was tending gently to him. He forgot his childhood suffering and idealized her to the point of saying that "she was perfect." He always felt that his father "was always there when I needed him most. He saved my life from choking to death." He could not forgive his father for remarrying, however, and has carried on a relentless 19-year war with his stepmother. In selecting an ideal father, he rejected his own and selected his maternal uncle, who took care of him and his sister the entire year immediately after his mother's death. This man had already included several paternal traits in his God representation. His God, at the level of images and wishes, is made up almost exclusively from his memories of his relation with and idealization of his mother. God and his mother, at the more intellectually elaborated level, are by no means identical, but rather different. God had power over the mother: "What I resent the most about God is that He took my mother when we were children"; further, "The most important thing I expect from God is to see my mother."

That his mother died when he was in the developmental phase in which a grandiose self prevails in the context of an idealized object is best illustrated in his naive description: "Emotionally, I would like to have the power that God has because I would like to fly, lift heavy objects, etc." Because he attributes power and the ability to perform feats of strength to God, there is probably more in his concept of God than the representation of a maternal object, however perfect it may be. The power he wants has to do with self-mastery and mastery of the world, and that seems to be precisely what God has. I suggest that in the mind of the child those attributes are related to paternal representations. Besides, he had described how, at a very early age (before the death of his mother), his father's efficient intervention saved his life.

In Richard's case it seems that the earliest of God's representations still available for closeness ("Prayer is important to me because it gets you closer to God") originates in his own idealized representation of his mother; together with it, but not integrated with it, is the other side of the powerful God, capable of great deeds and, more than anything else, of taking his mother and giving her back to him. In the long run, the true appeal rests in the mother, as illustrated in his revealing answer to the

---

*"Me" is the patient's written misuse of the pronoun. The misuse is age-appropriate for a young child.

question of whether or not he wanted to be united with God in heaven: "Oh, sure! I guess I want to live. I guess there is a life after death. I want to be happy and in eternity, and, as I said, I want to be with my mother." I repeated the question, and he said, "I don't know. . . . When you say God . . . I can't quite picture it. What kind of a person is God? He is a man. I want to be with my mother."

This young man's representation of God indicates that, in spite of his massive early trauma with his mother (before her death), he had not remained exclusively attached to her. The caring presence of his father permitted him to admire his father's deeds and to assess him objectively. ("He cares for me and J. and would do anything for us.") He was able to use that paternal representation to form another aspect of his God representation. It is interesting to note that at no point did he talk about his mother and father as a couple. In the same manner, his God has most of the traits from his idealized mother and some from his father. The two components of the representation are obviously opposed to each other and not integrated. I wonder if he believed unconsciously that his father had "sent" his mother to heaven, where she is waiting for her children, to replace her with the stepmother. I have no evidence for this possibility.

Psychologically, Richard's God representation indicates that it had been formed at the time when he could include some limited aspects of his interactions with a "powerful" father, beyond the solitary need for mothering.

Clinical Example 3

Stephanie Russell (case no. 11) is a 46-year-old woman who has been an alcoholic for several years, especially after the birth 11 years ago of her last child, a girl. The child was conceived immediately after the paternal grandmother's death and was experienced as a grandchild and not her own child. This woman had been given to her grandmother when she was 2 years old, never to return to her own parents. The parents lived on the second floor of the same house as the grandparents, but the child was considered part of the grandparents' family and not of her own. She never forgot the intensity of the rejection she experienced, including the day of her mother's death, which was a couple of years before her admission to the psychiatric unit. She had a profound bitterness that her mother had died without saying that she loved her, and an equal disappointment over the fact that her mother had not heard that *she* loved her mother.

Her God representation is formed mostly from the counterpart of her experiences with her abandoning early mother. God is most of the time the idealized good mother she never had; what she does not like about her God are those aspects of her mother that the realities of life did not permit her to idealize. The best illustration of this point are the following quotations. The psychiatrist said about her, "A major theme in her life has been the search for her mother's love." The patient said, "I never lived with my mother." (It is important to notice that she did not say "with my family," or "with my father.") Then she stated, "What I resent the most about God is the searching for Him, because I get frustrated and discouraged when I cannot find my way to Him." God has all the earmarks of the ideal mother of a small child:

1. "*His presence* is the most rewarding feeling I ever had—more love than one can bear" (emphasis added).
2. "God provides for my needs because *He knows what they are*. That is His nature" (emphasis added).
3. [He had] "a complete understanding of how I felt."
4. [He had the] "ability to fulfill my needs. . . . The way in which He fulfilled my needs (I knew it was motivated by love) made me feel alive."
5. "I have experienced the reality of His knowing me personally."
6. "The feeling I get from my relationship with God is one of love, peace, assurance, stimulation, creativeness, confidence, guidance."

When asked to describe an ideal mother, this woman did not want her own mother, but one who "conveys to me fully and completely that she loves me; one I could respect and who would accept my love in return. Who gives me guidelines and values." Her God representation does not include any traits of her father as an individual. It only included the wish for a parental couple, an idealized parental couple with a child as a part of the Godhead. When asked to draw a picture of God, she drew a circle with a very small child in the center, holding hands with adult stick figures, one on each side (of the child). She described the drawing: "Trinity . . . God is omnipotent but [notice the "but"] at the same time, we are meant to be His children . . . to live as brothers."

She has an idealized version of her experience with the parental couple that portrays a happy threesome: "[I have] a very vague feeling that during the first year after father and mother were married [and they had] just the baby [herself] . . . there must have been happiness and I was loved. . . . I needed to feel close to them."

The role of the father in this situation is to provide triangulation, another adult for the mother so that the two, together, can love the child.

In fact, when asked to describe the ideal father, she talked about the father of a very small child: "I want him to be very much in love with my mother; he also loves me as a person. They will enjoy watching me grow. I would like to hear that they have a life of their own; that I wasn't their whole life." (The parents married because the mother was pregnant with her.)

From this evidence I conclude that her God representation was formed during the time when her experiences, fantasies, and wishes were in the period called by Abelin (1975) early triangulation. The loss of the mother (and father) at the time when the prevalent need was still for mothering contributed to the creation of a God representation with marked maternal traits, which also includes the idealized triangulation of loving parents and child.

Clinical Example 4

Mabel Brook (case no. 14) represents a similar case. The difference is that the triangulation used is the *actual idealized memory* of the *actual parents* in the real environment where they lived. Her major trauma occurred at age 4 years. She was the oldest child of a black family from the South. There, apparently, they were doing well, with both parents being teachers. She remembered with fondness going to school to her mother's class, holding hands on the way over. They decided to go to a city in the North, where they found crowded living conditions, very different from their rural background. The parents worked all day long, and she barely saw them. Her entire life seemed to have remained attached to the earliest years, feeling that in those days life was happy and she had her parents. She never forgave her father for leaving their hometown.

Her God representation is made almost exclusively of her experiences with and representation of her mother. There is a component of God that is derived from her experiences with the parental couple and "their ruling with a strong hand."

Clinical Example 5

For reasons of space, I will not describe Domenic Pappas (case no. 20), whose God is very similar to Stephanie Russell's. Joseph Gordon (case no. 4) offers a most interesting variation. God is directly derived from his idealized version of a mother he loved and feared. His father, in turn, has provided all the characteristics of the Devil he hates and fears. The patient's hospitalization occurred as the result of his experiencing intense testicular pain of psychic origin. The pain had started after his father was

372

declared cured of a prostatic carcinoma, which had appeared a year earlier just after the patient had cursed his father in a fight and called him a bastard. On learning that the father was ill, the patient started to pray frantically for his cure. As soon as he learned that his father was free of danger—a cure he attributed to God—he developed his symptom.

The father was a distant, aloof laborer, who drank considerably and quarreled frequently with his wife. The mother was a housewife and was very close to the patient. Both parents complained to the child about each other. The child always preferred his mother, but feared her too. He was always fearful that his father would harm his mother, or that he would himself be injured if he tried to intervene.

That he had a tremendous involvement with his mother is best illustrated by the fact that soon after his marriage he had an affair with his mother-in-law.

When asked to describe the ideal parent he would have wanted, he said about his mother, "I couldn't have any better mother. She was . . . terrific!" He rejected his father and asked for a father that "is interested in you, takes you places, and gives you the feeling that you are the son."

That he was struggling with intense oedipal wishes is best illustrated in the solution he thinks would eliminate his problems: "For me to fully please God I would have to change my whole way of life. . . . If I could change myself I would like to be like my pastor because he is a clean-living man." He feels that God loves him and that God is "all good and deserves my love." Instead, he is "committing sin" and feeling that "I hurt Him." Hurting God is the specialty of the Devil: "I think that he wants us to sin because he enjoys hurting God."

His conflict with his father is naively illustrated in his unconscious confession when he completed the following sentence: "The member of my family whom I dislike the most was . . . I never disliked my father."

Contrary to what Freud (1923c, pp. 85–86) said, this patient's God and Devil representations are not the result of the splitting off of the good and bad representations of the father and "exalting" them, respectively, into God and Devil. God has His representational sources in a very loved and idealized (but feared) early oedipal mother, with whom no oedipal resolution has been worked out. The Devil, on the other hand, has all the attributes of a "bastard," like father, who "tries to deceive people" and "enjoys hurting God."

One can easily see that a God formed at the highest hot point of an oedipal crisis that is still going on cannot make any room for the parental representation of a couple. The hated and dangerous rival becomes a sadistic phallic Devil. In this conflict the parents as a couple are not used to form a God representation.

Clinical Example 6
Douglas O'Duffy (case no. 2), 39 years old, presents yet another variation. He formed his God representation directly and undisguisedly from his direct real experiences and representations of *his actual mother*. He loved her, but he resented bitterly her inability to celebrate him personally and to acknowledge him as a special individual. He had a most loving father, whom he adored and who loved him in turn. The parents were a stable and loving couple until they died in their 70s. The family was close and the patient was among the youngest of eight siblings. He has been unable to use his paternal representation to contribute to his God representation. He is so stubbornly determined to deny existence to a God who, like his mother, would not acknowledge him first that he has no psychological space to do anything else. His case shows that a major psychic trauma of lack of personal recognition at an early age so colored his character structure that he could not use his otherwise caring parents, particularly his adored father, to integrate into a representation of God (Chap. 7; Rizzuto, 1979).

Clinical Example 7
Bernadine Fisher (case no. 12) has also formed the prevailing and most desirable traits of her God representation from her idealized version of her mother, who in real life had very little mothering to offer. Her God is capable of loving but has a low opinion of her. She also used the parental couple and some traits of her father, whose punishing went into the punishing aspects of God and whose ability to "never let any of us be happy" went into the Devil, who "wants us to be bad because then we can't be happy." She was the first child, conceived before the marriage of two confused and dependent adolescents, whose entire marriage was founded on clinging mutual dependency and a total inability to live as adults or to have a generational distance from their children. Both parents competed with the children for mothering and constantly displaced their own fear, anger, and frustration onto them. There was in that confusing household a moment of rest for the patient; that was when her paternal grandmother was around. The grandmother made the child feel special and had a protective and affectionate relationship with her. That grandmother seems to have lent her characteristics to another representation of God, totally unintegrated with the prevailing one. That God and the grandmother are liked by the patient because they are "always there." With that God she can communicate only when she is alone, and then she feels close to Him. The other God is "my enemy because He doesn't think much of me." One may see in this case that the extremely frustrating relationship

of a small child with a mother who is always angry and unable to mother her child because she is so concerned with herself and her husband, creates a situation of a child alone, facing an inimical situation with her parents. The child then may use that experience to create one of her God representations, while the exchanges with the grandmother would be used to create the representation of another more available, but less needed, private God.

Clinical Example 8

Samuel Wolf (case no. 8) is a nonbeliever who remembers having believed between the ages of 4 and 10 years. The traits he ascribed to God are all traceable to his maternal representation, although, in the picture of God, he drew a vaguely differentiated face if it were not for an added beard. He called it "a patriarchal figure."

He is an extremely ambivalent man with a long love-hate relationship with his wife. He listed "sex" as his most unsatisfied need from the age of 15 until the present time. He said that the sex he had "was not enough to satisfy me." He had always been his mother's favorite. He described her as "a good mother in the main" and as "a pain in the ass." He complains that as a child "she did not grab me or kiss me or anything." He respected his father and was proud of him; and he thought that if he could change himself, he would like to be like his father, who "was strong and self-reliant." He kept both of his parents as the ideal parents. This brief description suggests that this man belongs to that group of patients who never renounce their oedipal wishes, keep a sexualized representation of the oedipal mother, and submit in fearful obedience to the parental couple, while they remain entitled to their revengeful anger for not having obtained satisfaction of their sexual desires. Their self-esteem is low, and they constantly feel inferior to their fathers. Such sexualized representation, as Freud pointed out (1918a, pp. 115–117), cannot be used for a lasting transformation into a God representation. The sexual object has to be debased and rejected, with the accusation that it is not good enough to satisfy the individual's desires. In his case, the mother who did not "grab" him, the wife who is not "enough" for him, and the maternally sexualized God representation must be rejected. In his case we are talking about a libidinal fixation that must have reappeared in puberty when he ceased to believe. It is my suspicion, though I have no evidence for it, that the child believer was able to utilize the patriarchal components of his respected father to lend belief to his maternal-paternal God representation. If this is the case, like the God of the Wolf Man, the more paternal God could not sustain itself in front of reawakened sexual wishes. A representational regression must have occurred to that maternal, sexualized God representation. That regression required repression and made belief impossible.

God Representation Derived from Parents

There are five individuals whose God representation derives mostly or exclusively from the parents as a couple. The five persons—two men and three women—are very different from each other in almost every respect. What they seem to have in common is the way they perceive their parents as a couple. Each of them deals with the couple in a different manner, but none of them deals only with one parent individually. Mary Kehoe (case no. 3), an adolescent female, keeps both her parents as the ideal parents, with some modifications. Victoria Russo (case no. 9) rejects both of her parents, while she is always busy searching for the occasion to say: "I am the big me." Ula Boden (case no. 6) keeps her parents, with some modifications. She was never able to get close to them, but never ceased trying. In the main, she has remained a fearful child, terrified of trespassing her boundaries. Paul Lally (case no. 18) greatly admires his father and feels that both parents were "the best ones" one can get. He is a devout and dutiful person, totally dedicated to his work and family. Finally, Frank Luppo (case no. 15) feels that "there is nothing like" his mother. She is the ideal mother. He makes only some changes in his father, but he feels that "he was a good-hearted man." All of the five are firm believers, with the exception of Mary Kehoe, who believes when somebody loves her, but either does not believe or doubts when there is nobody there. Victoria Russo has a peculiar way of believing. She believes intensely when she is in need. Then she completely forgets about God until her next need arrives. Ula Boden suffered from schizophrenia and numerous religious delusions. Her father and mother had been totally committed to a fundamentalist religion, coloring every aspect of their family life. Fear prevailed over every other emotion in their upbringing.

In summary, regardless of the level of pathology, the child's realization that the parental couple is there as the adults who rule the world creates a new psychic situation. When the child—whether through fear, need, admiration, or submissive retreat—accepts the fact that she or he is the child, and they the united adults, then the representation of God may be transformed to accommodate the new change. Later situations may provide the occasion for regression to earlier maternal representations of the Godhead; but while the situation of acceptance of the role of a child prevails, the God representation has maternal and paternal traits.

Clinical Example

Gerald King's (case no. 1) is the only case that offers a very different picture. His God has maternal and paternal traits, including the traits of an idealized, wished-for father. His father was a violent manic depressive who physically hurt his wife although he never touched his son. The mother was alternatively sadistic and abandoning. The child became a loner, in constant contradiction with himself, at times identifying with the sadistic father, at times fearing him; always loving and hating his mother. In the midst of it all, he desperately wished for a man who would truly father him: protect him from his infuriating mother and guide him in the task of becoming a man. He was also always searching for religious experiences and religious leaders who would be guiding fathers for him. He could neither idealize his mother nor see that the parents were a couple. In his terrified escape from his fascination with his mother and his obvious terror of his father, he understood that only a real father could protect him. His God has all the painful and frightening contradictions of his parents. That his God has a heavy representational component from the wished-for father is best illustrated in the following quotation: "What I like the most about God is His forgiveness, because unlike my own father, I can come to God in prayer saying: 'Father, forgive me'; and I feel better—forgiven or not!"

It is not that the earlier components of his God representation do not derive from his mother first, and then from his father; it is that this man knows he needs protection from his mother and father alike. A reelaboration of his God into an idealized father permits him to believe and to pray, as well as to protect himself from his dangerous parents.

God Representation Derived from Father

Finally, there are four persons whose God representation was formed predominantly from the paternal representation. No individual had used, contrary to what Freud suggested, only the representation of the father. Marion Keefe (case no. 7) and Eva Kaplan (case no. 10) were children assigned from birth to their father, and it was clear to everybody involved that the child (in both cases the second offspring in the family) belonged to the father and that the mother had assigned herself to the firstborn child. Daniel Miller had a totally ineffectual mother who required the assistance of a nurse to care for him during the first month of his life. The mother had the role of an older sibling, totally submitting to her husband in obvious fear of his violent and domineering temperament. Fiorella Domenico (case no. 16) was the fourth of eight children of a very stable, traditional Italian family, who considered the father "the head of the family" and considered him "the most important person." He was described as "closest to my mother because he was married to her." The same was said of the mother in relation to the father. The "children were considered as children and we did what we were told." The father was described as "kind and warm" and a "wonderful person," who was the boss "because we looked up to him." The patient loved her father very much and found him "great" and wonderful. She also loved her mother, but not without a mild ambivalence. Most of the traits of her God came from her father, including his whiskers, which she confessed she forgot to draw in her picture of God. She had as good and as loving a relation with her God as she had with her father. She was devout but capable of enjoying life with her husband and children. The only restriction she had was that she could not get angry with her God, and when the possibility of losing her husband to death confronted her she avoided her God by producing a church phobia.

Clinical Example 1

Eva Kaplan (case no. 10), an 18-year-old girl in transition to college, was assigned to her father from birth. She was expected to become the doctor he had been unable to be. The father's attachment to the girl was such that when confronted with some adolescent misbehavior on her part, he told her that he had "ceased to exist." Her intense adolescent turmoil seemed to be her attempt at separating from her father to form an identity of her own. In this period of intense crisis with her father (she had decided not to become a doctor) and her mother, she was actively searching for a God that would make sense to her. She was Jewish, but was interested in Buddha, while consulting with a rabbi. The most important components of her God representation can be traced to her paternal representation and her self-representation. The parental couple and the maternal representation make a lesser contribution.

Clinical Example 2

Daniel Miller derives his God representation exclusively from his father, if one is to disregard a cryptic remark that may link Him to his mother. The couple makes no contribution to his God. Psychologically the parents did not form a couple, because the mother related to the father as a frightened child who could neither oppose him nor protect the children. The father's presence occupied the entire psychological space of the household. He also had decided to take his son's life into his hands and make him into the doctor he had not been able to be; the desire was so intense that he would do his son's homework for him. He was critical, mocking, and inclined to humiliate the boy. He would go into frightening rages, screaming and throwing things around; his wife and children were cowed by his behavior. The patient admired, feared, and despised his father in equal proportions. Although Daniel Miller has a very vivid representation of God, he is a nonbeliever for whom God is the object of some rumination without his really asking whether or not there is a God. When he was a child, the God of the Old Testament felt "revengeful" and frightening to him, and he did not want anything to do with Him.

Conclusions

The answer to the question of the role of the father in the child's formation of a God representation is not a simple one. The complexities arise from the fact that there are infinite manners of being a father, a spouse, and a man. Children, too, provide new additions to this complexity by the way in which they experience their parents in the context of a web of family interactions and under the unpredictable vicissitudes of life's events. War, illness, poverty, job promotions, death in the family, and other ordinary and extraordinary occurrences bear on the manner in which children experience their fathers. The mother constantly provides the children with her own version of what kind of person the father is as a spouse, a father, and an individual in the world. The child organizes this many-faceted experience of the father around issues of paramount importance for the subjective integration of his own psychic life. When the psychological moment arrives to create or transform an already existing God representation, the child may attribute some of the paternal characteristics to God.

Developmentally the first God representation is made from the real or wished-for good mother of a small child. That God is a kind and loving presence who is always there.

On reaching the stage of early triangulation, the child seems to require a stable enough couple to integrate the feelings of belonging to a triadic trinity into a God representation related to a protective Godhead. When major trauma interferes very early, as happened to Richard Renard, the child who is already very aware of the presence of a caring and "powerful" father cannot integrate the experiences, and carries with him or her, parallel God representations: one made of the maternal traits and the other of paternal traits. When the child's self-awareness increases and the child has his or her love affair with the world, desires for power and grandiose feats emerge with special intensity. The father seems to provide a model for boys and girls alike to imitate in their desire for power and self-aggrandizement. The power attributed to the father soon gains entry into the God representation, as well as into the greatly idealized self-representation. Soon after, the first oedipal move begins. The God representation that had already included aspects of both parents may become sexualized, together with the relationship with the parents. When this is the case, the child may repress the representational components of God that bring forth the conflict, and then narrow the God representation at the preconscious level to those parental traits that are ego syntonic. The child's acceptance of the fact that he or she cannot win in the oedipal situation leads to self-acknowledgment that he or she is a child, that the parents are first related to each other, and that the children are to be under the care of the couple. In this case, the God representation draws its characteristics from the parental couple.

If the oedipal conflict is resolved and the parental representation is desexualized and "exalted," as Freud said, into a Godhead, the person, as shown with Fiorella Domenico, may have a most pleasant and satisfying relationship with her God. In her case, God was predominantly formed from her paternal representation. I do not know if it is possible that a boy who has found a similar resolution would use his maternal representation preferentially to "exalt" it into a Godhead. I am inclined to believe that the boy would use either a much-reviewed representation of his mother under the scrutiny characteristic of the latency period, or a more balanced, parental couple type of representation of God to which the father may provide some easily recognizable traits. If the oedipal conflict with the parental couple cannot be resolved, the God representation includes the traits of one or both parents, but none from the parents as a couple. The sexualized father representation may contribute elements to the representation of the Devil, as Freud suggested (1923c).

Three cases were described in which the paternal representation seemed to prevail in the formation of the God representation. In these the father was from the very beginning of life the person who literally had taken possession of the child. These individuals show that when the father is an overwhelming figure in the child's life, the God representation is predominantly made from the paternal representation. I wonder if Freud was not misguided to generalize about God being an "exalted father" by his acquaintance with cases like Dr. Schreber, whose father was very much like the father of the patients just presented.

The last variation in the sample is Gerald King, whose God representation obtains a good number of its traits from a wished-for father, some from his frightening actual father and mother, but none from the parental couple. It seems that when a child is confronted with a very dangerous mother (seductive and abandoning) and a violent, manic-depressive father, the hope left to the child is that a strong and kind man will come to protect him from both parents.

In adolescence, some individuals, just before entering the adult world, attempt to see their parents with new eyes, trying to understand the many vicissitudes of their lives together. The process brings about intense doubts about self-value and the meaning of life. The parental representations now fused into a God representation are tested under the disguised name of God while there is a search for God in the philosophical or religious sense. Together with it, the young individual resorts to peers and romantic love to provide him- or herself with new sources of love. Then, as with Mary Kehoe, belief in God depends on the presence of a romantic lover.

At the end of adolescence the God representation has acquired its basic traits that are to last for life, though many new additions and transformations are still possible. At this point the God representation is complex and made of innumerable exchanges between the individual and both parents. If the necessary conditions are given through regression, remembering, reenacting, or simply through shifting some of his or her own feelings, the individual may find in his or her God representation very private emotional experiences of the past. Fears and consolations from earlier days reappear in the context of religious experiences that keep him or her in touch, for better or for worse, with the child he or she has been, as well as with his or her parents. That religious reexperiencing may also contribute continuity to the emotional and intellectual structuring of one's present and future. Lack of religious belief is only another manner of dealing with the parents and the God representation formed in childhood.

24

The Patriarchal Tradition:
Creation and Fathering in *Genesis*

Paul Schwaber

Wondering about his older sons who grazed the flock far away, Jacob called to Joseph. "Here I am," the lad replied—exactly as Abraham had when summoned to sacrifice Joseph's grandfather Isaac; as Jacob himself had when directed by God to return to Canaan, where his feared brother Esau lived. Joseph's generational echo signals danger and readiness because his task had its terrors. His brothers, not without reason, despised him. All commentators agree that Jacob had spoiled the long-awaited son of his favored wife Rachel by loving him above the others, singling him out, for example, to receive a coat of many colors. The text is unarguable: at seventeen, Joseph—the only biblical figure the rabbis would call a *Tzaddik*, a righteous man (Leibowitz, 1972, p. 430; Wiesel, 1976, pp. 141–142)—was full of himself. He tattled on his brothers. He insisted that they listen to his vainglorious dreams. Their sheaves, he reported, bowed to his in the field; the sun, moon, and eleven stars bowed down to him. Even Jacob rebuked him for that one. Nevertheless, when sent to seek his brothers he set out at once, persisting when he lost his way. Injudiciously and tauntingly, he wore the coat of many colors. Young Joseph was galling, assertive—a difficult brother.

We need not detail his ensuing adventures to recall him thrown into a pit, seized by Midianites, brought by wandering Ishmaelites to Egypt and sold to Potiphar, a kind man and an officer of Pharaoh. The Lord being with Joseph, Potiphar's household prospered under his direction. But when Potiphar's wife desired him, he landed in prison, where yet another well-disposed man, this time the chief jailer, benefited by allowing him to run things. It was there that Joseph's talent for dream interpretation became apparent. Soon called on to interpret Pharaoh's ominous dreams, he did so convincingly and was appointed to oversee planning in all of Egypt for the famine the dreams foretold. We learn little of Joseph's anguish during his trials. Instead the text stresses that he recognized God to be guiding his ācumen and decorum. Eventually the brothers who betrayed him arrived seeking food, and he severely tested them before revealing who he was. This magnificent episode, to which we shall return, illuminates important transformations in his character. "I am your brother Joseph," he says to them startlingly, "he whom you sold into Egypt." Quickly he reassures them: "Now, do not be distressed or reproach yourselves because you sold me hither; it was to save life that God sent me ahead of you." And having comforted them he explains further: "It is now two years that there has been famine in the land, and there are still five years to come in which there shall be no yield from tilling. God has sent me ahead of you to insure your survival on earth, and to save your lives in an extraordinary deliverance. So it was not you who sent me here, but God; and He has made me a father to Pharaoh, lord of all his household, and ruler over the whole land of Egypt" (45 : 4–8). Joseph bestrides this moment: frightening, assuring, and clarifying, all while fulfilling his early aspirations. From a spoiled son and hated brother given to arabesques of grandiosity, however, he actually has become God's preserver of life, "a father" to Pharaoh, and, impressively, a feared and powerful man capable of forgiveness. His development, coming as the climax of *Genesis*, amplifies recurrent motifs in the lives of his forebears, the Patriarchs Abraham, Isaac, and Jacob—indeed, no motif more than the process of development itself.*

The Bible famously starts at the beginning. God creates the world, declares it good, rests on the seventh day, and, growing enraged with its human occupants, all but destroys it: "All flesh that stirred on earth perished—birds, cattle, beasts, and all the things that swarmed upon the earth, and all mankind. All in whose nostrils was the merest breath of life, all that was on dry land, died. All existence on earth was blotted out— man, cattle, creeping things, and birds of the sky; they were blotted out from the earth. Only Noah was left, and those with him in the ark" (7 : 21–23). When the waters abate, God grants dominion to Noah and his sons and with them makes a moral covenant: "Every creature that lives shall be yours to eat; as with green grasses, I give you all these. You

---

*Dealing with the text as a mimetic whole, as I do here, hardly gainsays and can build upon the momentous contributions of historical, archeological, anthropological, formal, and sociological scholarship to biblical studies during the past 200 years (Rosenberg, 1975; Alter, 1975, 1976, 1978). Such scholarship, which was given major impetus by Julius Wellhausen's classic formulation of the documentary hypothesis (1883), has been ably surveyed by Hahn (1954). Wellhausen's fundamental notion has been disputed by Cassuto (1941) and, on different grounds, by Kaufmann (1937–1956).

All quotations are from the Jewish Publication Society's translation, *The Torah: The Five Books of Moses* (Philadelphia, 1962), supplemented by *The Soncino Chumash: The Five Books of Moses with Haphtaroth*, ed. A. Cohen (Hindhead, Surrey: Soncino Press, 1947).

must not, however, eat flesh with its life-blood in it. But for your own life-blood I will require a reckoning; I will require it of every beast; of man, too, will I require a reckoning for human life, of every man for that of his fellow man!" (9 : 3–5). Correlatively, God promises never again to destroy the earth or its creatures by flood, and as a sign He shows Noah a rainbow. Forgiveness and self-restraint seem qualities that God, no less than man, had to learn.

The Flood story follows that of the primal parents banished from Eden and immediately precedes the Lord's confounding of Babel. Together these establish, early in *Genesis*, a pattern of creation, destruction, compensatory dependability and uneasy trust, a basic rhythm of human experience and expectation. Thus when the Patriarchs of Israel emerge, they stand in one aspect as survivors, a remnant. Their lives, moreover, prove dogged as well as glorious. The Patriarchs struggle repeatedly with dangers that include famine, scarcities of precious water, adversary neighbors, rivalrous kin, temptations, and a demanding—at times angry—God. Importantly distinct from their contemporaries and different one from the other, Abraham, Isaac and Jacob share the crucial task of survival as a responsibility, a grounding ethic. Each of them amasses goods, wealth, and, to the extent possible, allies, as if testifying insistently, by deed, to an exigent need for security and well-being.

For their burden and destiny were special. "Go forth from your native land and from your father's house to the land that I will show you," God said to Abram:

I will make of you a great nation,
And I will bless you;
I will make your name great,
And you shall be a blessing.
I will bless those who bless you;
And curse him that curses you;
And all the families of the earth
Shall bless themselves by you [12 : 1–3].

The *Avot* (fathers) hear variations of this promise often. They may not always feel sure, but they are to produce the Jewish people in history. Their survival bears on the sacredness of all human life, their specific progeny and purpose, and moral and spiritual efficacy for others. To them survival means more than personal safety, although, of course, never less than that.

Through generations they evolve an informing and quite flexible style of behavior that supports not classical heroism—deeds of war, courage and attendant fame, and death—but the knowledge and cunning necessary to preserve life. It is as though once Adam and Eve ate of the tree of the knowledge of good and evil, bringing death, woe and history into the world, the basic human value became just that difficult knowledge in its relation to deeds; or so the unfolding stories of *Genesis* suggest. To be sure, Abraham must have fought hard when, moving by night with his men, he rescued Lot from kidnappers. But this action is exceptional and gets less narrative prominence than his refusal of reward from the local king, his hospitality to guests, his trials of faith, his bargaining with God for the wicked city of Sodom or with the Hittites for the Cave of Machpelah, which he buys for a burial site. The Patriarchal style is diplomatic. Abraham, Isaac, and Jacob cultivate subtle arts of peace. They size up persons and situations. They work out agreements. When Abraham's shepherds dispute with Avimelech's over a well, he negotiates. Again over wells, his son moves away and later agrees to a treaty, with the same king. Lot and Abraham separate rather than quarrel over grazing rights. Jacob pledges with Laban to respect a boundary between them; and after Jacob's return, he and Esau finally and sensibly decide to live apart.

This family tendency to avoid clashes, to find areas of compromise, proves tenacious during Jacob's extended and trying dealings with his uncle and eventual father-in-law, Laban. We know how strong Jacob is. He falls in love with Rachel the moment he sees her and moves the massive stone covering a well for her, one that all the local shepherds could budge only together. Nonetheless, he works seven years for Laban in order to marry her. In many ways shrewd and observant, he can't be in all, because he notices only too late that he has been given Leah, the firstborn, instead. At last, instructed by God to leave for Canaan, he flees with his wives, his children, and all his goods while Laban is far from home, to get away at all.

Such behavioral biases in fathers and in sons who become fathers aggregate as a continuum of traits: cunning, alert awareness, practicality, planning, ingenuity, balance, intelligence, and a capacity for aspiration. Taken together they amount to a small and ambitious group's resources, its idiom of operation. Yet like all diplomacy, the Patriarchal kind encompasses complexities and can be distressing. Auerbach (1946, pp. 3–23) has shown that the spare frame and telling details of *Genesis* invest the Patriarchs with mystery and grandeur without idealizing or sentimentalizing them. They can act shabbily. Twice Abraham passes off his wife as his sister, fearing first that Pharaoh and later that Avimelech will kill him to seize Sarah. Lest this maneuver seem unique to Abraham, we see Isaac act identically because of Rebekah's beauty. Avimelech, in fact, remonstrates that Abraham's lie brought suffering to others because God intervened, to which Abraham offers only that Sarah is his half-sister, daughter of his father by a different mother. However derivative of ancient marital codes (Sarna, 1966, pp. 102–103), this is embarrassing. But the issue reaches deeper than shame. It stuns. At dreadful moments the Patriarchs chose to stay alive, by wits alone if necessary, to endure.

Except when they had no choice. From God's unfathomable wish for certainty, He demands a culminating act of faith from Abraham, who time and again had proved loyal both to God and to the promise of descendants. He had left his father's home as asked, dealt fairly and wisely with others, fought when he had to, lied when he needed to. Devoted to his wife and to Lot, he loved his son Ishmael by Sarah's handmaid Hagar and then, urged by Sarah to send them away and advised by God to heed the request, sadly did so. More equably than Sarah, he trusted God's assurance of a son after her childbearing years. Surely he had earned the increment in his name from Abram to Abraham, signifying that he had merged his fate with God's word. Then in his old age, having watched the boy grow, he was told to sacrifice him—that is, to kill him and to burn him as an offering: "God put Abraham to the test. He said to him, 'Abraham,' and he answered, 'Here I am.' And He said, 'Take your son, your favored one, Isaac, whom you love, and go to the land of Moriah, and offer him there as a burnt offering on one of the heights which I will point out to you'" (22 : 1–2). God appreciated how hard this would be for Abraham: his son, his favored one, Isaac, whom he loved. And silently the Patriarch obeyed, the man who had pleaded with God for Sodom by citing God's own standard of justice. Yet for his dearest son, his only link to his promised posterity and the still-living sign of the purpose to which he had committed his life, the old man Abraham would not plead. Profound minds have groped to understand. Is he silent because outraged? Does he hate, give up, privately renounce? Can Abraham still trust? Does he here test God? Does God betray? Do Abraham and God commune beyond the ethical? (Kierkegaard, 1843; Sarna, 1966, pp. 154–165; Leibowitz, 1972, pp. 188–205; Wiesel, 1976, pp. 69–97). The passage supports all these premises.

Undeniably, Abraham proceeds with determination. Early the next morning he saddles the ass, splits the wood and takes two of his servants and his son Isaac. Later he carries the knife and the firestone, builds the altar, lays out the wood, binds Isaac and picks up the knife to slay him. "Here I am," he had said. The aged father is the moral agent for this responsibility. On the third day at the appointed place, Abraham leaves the servants behind with the animals and goes on with Isaac: "Then Isaac said to his father Abraham, 'Father!' And he answered, 'Yes, my son.' And he said, 'Here are the firestone and the wood; but where is the sheep for the burnt offering?' And Abraham said, 'God will see to the sheep for His burnt offering, my son.' And the two of them walked on together" (22 : 7–8). Isaac understands and says nothing—for chapters. Although an angel intervenes at the moment of sacrifice and once again promises Abraham descendants as numerous as the stars of heaven and the sands of the seashore, Abraham walks down the mountain alone. Isaac is not mentioned: "Abraham then returned to his servants, and they departed together for Beersheba" (22 : 19). The *Akedah*, or Binding of Isaac, often is thought to represent an advance of civilization—the renunciation of human sacrifice (Leibowitz, 1972, pp. 201–205; cf. Sarna, 1966, pp. 157–163). We may add that it gives expression to paternal murderousness as well as to its inhibition. Yet a strong midrashic tradition holds that Isaac in fact died, that the angel spoke too late, and that later the story was patched over (Spiegel, 1950). This extreme tradition has emotional truth, for certainly Isaac did not return with Abraham. Perhaps he would not, terrified, furious, and scarred internally, a victim of both his father's faith and God's test.

Thereafter Isaac barely fulfills his Patriarchal role. His silences and his deeds suggest conflict, unwillingness, unhappiness, that he lives burdened by his destiny as son to that father and chosen of that God. Uniquely among the Patriarchs, he does not find his own wife. Abraham sends the servant Eliezer back to Haran for that purpose. A Canaanite woman would not do. Moreover, Abraham makes Eliezer swear not to take Isaac out of the promised land, should the woman not wish to return with him. Later God forbids Isaac to leave Canaan, though famine is in the land. The implication seems strongly to be that Isaac would leave all too quickly, given the chance. He disappears from view after Moriah and reappears to greet his bride Rebekah, having settled in Beer-lahai-roi, a place earlier associated with his repudiated half-brother Ishmael (16 : 14). We can surmise that he grieves when Sarah dies, for "Isaac loved [Rebekah], and thus found comfort after his mother's death" (24 : 67). When Abraham dies, we learn only that he and Ishmael bury their father at Machpelah. Subsequently Isaac breaks silence with God to pray for Rebekah, who is barren. As husband and father, he provides handsomely, accumulating wealth, negotiating and compromising in the family style. Of his twin sons, however, he prefers Esau and has to be fooled into blessing Jacob. So Isaac continues the covenant. But he suffers it.

His trickster son Jacob earns the name Israel, and Jacob's morally problematic sons, who betray Joseph, sire the twelve tribes. Again, *Genesis* does not sentimentalize, though many readers of it do. No Pa-

388

triarch so troubles the conscience as the man who deceitfully displaces his brother from the line of *Avot*. The developed intelligence and capacity for love Jacob shows later in life are less apparent in his youth, when he seems devoted to his mother alone, who in turn favors him. He began pushing for priority in her womb, and God told Rebekah in her pain:

Two nations are in your womb,
Two separate peoples shall issue from your body;
One people shall be mightier than the other,
And the older shall serve the younger [25 : 23].

Surprisingly, perhaps, Jacob grows into a mild tent-dwelling man whose apparent passivity contrasts sharply with the rugged hunting of Esau, whom Isaac prefers. Still, Jacob early outwits Esau easily, trading bread and lentil stew to his famished brother for the latter's birthright. Then, instigated by Rebekah and disguised as Esau, he garners Esau's rightful blessing from their blind old father. Later Isaac pointedly tells his older son: "Your brother came with guile and took away your blessing" (27 : 35).

True, Jacob acts at his mother's urging and, inferentially, according to God's providence. Esau may not have been the man needed. But the brother's deed remains. What meaning can Jacob's duplicitous elevation have? The rabbis, troubled, have pondered the text for answers. They have interpreted Jacob's long duress with Laban and his being duped into marrying the firstborn, Leah, as ironically fitting retribution for his treachery (Leibowitz, 1972, pp. 317–324). Moreover, as Elie Wiesel has observed, Jacob continues to be dominated by strong women (1976, pp. 110–112). Rachel and Leah merely pass him between them for their competitive purposes. They send him to bed with their handmaids to tally up sons on their respective accounts. Even the aged Jacob's doting love for Joseph seems yoked to Rachel's memory, for she had by then died giving birth to Benjamin.

Neither his grandfather Abraham nor his father Isaac proves so morally mercurial as Jacob. Yet Jacob alone, his exile completed and his family large, wrestles with the mysterious Man on the border of Canaan, is hobbled by him, and demanding blessing as the price for letting go, is called Israel, or striver with God (32 : 29). God subsequently confirms the name (35 : 9–12). As Adam assigned names to the creatures, so Jacob would provide his to the people of Israel. Wiesel (1976, pp. 130–135) remarks two poles to this Patriarch's mature character: that of Jacob and that of Israel. The highest attainment of the man, the family, and the people—the spiritual ego ideal—is Israel. But even after being renamed he continues, from inner consistency and realistic appraisal of circumstances, striving with himself, to plan, to plot, to observe. As Jacob he divides his camp in two and sends staggered presents to Esau, who approaches with 400 men. As Jacob he foregoes Esau's offer of escort and eventually lives apart from him. Old Jacob prefers Joseph and latterly the youngest, Benjamin, to his other sons. But as Israel he lives his final years in Egypt. And it is Israel, the congeries of slaves who will share a religious destiny, that Moses will lead from captivity to Sinai. Survival for Jacob, through a tortuous life, included attaining to the spiritual heritage and passing it on—discernible and named—to all the descendants of the Patriarchs. His development issued on the dialectics of the people Israel's spiritual identity.

Abraham, Isaac, and Jacob differ markedly. As sons they break from their fathers, and as fathers they produce sons who break from them. Such fathers nurture and necessitate sons who separate, who emerge through the arcs of their own lives as unique selves. Each of the Patriarchs bore the covenant differently, and at least one, we have seen, may have hated it. Jacob, corroboratively, swears by "the Fear" of Isaac (31 : 53). But as affected as they were by their experience, which always included the requirements of a divine father and a not very hospitable or easily nourishing world, they decisively shaped their experience as well. They were chosen, admirable, could be frightening and even embarrassing. They were loyal, had doubts, could be treacherous, could be frightened. Unusual as they were, they always seem human, in part because they developed a family style for transmitting a larger family's aspirations.

We tend to keep our guard up when reading the Bible and may not appreciate the remarkable imaginative achievement of *Genesis*, how cogently it presents experience in a world without precedent. It deals with the beginning, the world created by God who, somehow askew, thought He gave dominion to a race of creatures that was good but consistently turned out not to be. God too, then, has to learn His way, for all behavior is new. How, through *Genesis*, God and humans interact has enormous significance for gauging value, for estimating the worth of modes of behavior. God moves from principal actor to a far more reserved one. Talking easily with Abraham and less often with Isaac and Jacob, He is only referred to, though frequently, by Joseph. This distancing provides both tension and opportunity for the development of the Patriarchs. It gives them room to emerge, through willed effort, into a viable group with spiritual and earthly purpose. Divine and human fathering serves as the shaping principle of *Genesis*, the way meaning and pattern are imposed on possibility. The Patriarchs father children, a style of continuity and spiritual ideas—and thereby themselves. They assume responsibility, can say "Here I am," as the first man and woman could not. Questioned about their forbidden deed, Adam blamed Eve and she blamed the serpent. Cain, too, having murdered Abel, answered God evasively: "Am I my brother's keeper?" By contrast, each of the Patriarchs takes on density and outline through the times of his life, until the first book of the Bible ends with Joseph successfully grappling to preserve life on a massive scale during Egypt's prolonged famine, regarding himself, appropriately, as "a father" to Pharaoh. Problematic and consequential though fathering proves, in its range of meanings it provides the locus for development, for caring, and for self-definition.

The clearly related matter of human sexuality, although receiving much recognition, gets far less firmly patterned treatment, in part because one of its depicted qualities is that it resists patterning. From the first, sexuality is *there*: active, crucial to life, wayward, and bewildering. It informs the events in the Garden involving primal parents, the serpent, the fruit of the tree, eating, the wish for mysterious and restricted knowledge. When Adam and Eve eat the fruit of knowledge of good and evil, they cover their nakedness, feeling shame. Even the two versions of creation, Chapters 1 and 2 of *Genesis*, imply not only amalgamated sources but ambivalence. In one, the first man and woman appear jointly as the culmination of God's labors; in the other, God makes Adam, then draws woman from his rib while he sleeps unawares. Her mysterious origin prefaces their desire to taste the knowledge of good and evil. Thereafter the ranges of sexual mystery stretch widely. Why are some women barren and others not? What does it mean that God helps, permits, or delays pregnancy? The *Genesis* narrative encompasses impressive vagaries. Noah, who saves mankind, uncovers his nakedness while drunk and is spied on by one of his sons, whom he later curses. After fleeing Sodom with him, Lot's daughters get him drunk to have children with him. Earlier Lot tried to protect the messengers by offering his daughters to the crowd at the door: "The men of Sodom, young and old—all the people to the last man—gathered outside the house. And they shouted to Lot and said to him, 'Where are the men who came to you tonight? Bring them out to us, that we may know them" (19 : 4–5). In Hebrew as in English, the verb "to know" links cognitive to physical qualities. Knowledge stems from the body. And *Genesis* recognizes varieties of sexual desire— voyeurism, incest, and homosexuality in the instances cited. It includes onanism—providing the name for it, like that of sodomy, to the world. In the Dinah episode it presents rape and retaliatory massacre for rape. Joseph's brothers perpetrate the latter. When their father protests, they

391

fiercely reply: "Should our sister be treated like a whore?" (34 : 31). Sexuality in *Genesis* has power. Never totally tamed or constrained, it pulsates intrusively. When Rachel dies giving birth to Benjamin, and Jacob, who has attained the name Israel, buries her, we read immediately: "While Israel stayed in that land, Reuben went and lay with Bilhah, his father's concubine, and Israel found out" (35 : 22). Now Reuben was Leah's firstborn, and Bilhah, in addition to being Jacob's concubine, was Rachel's handmaid and the mother of several of Reuben's brothers. The possibly avenging and triumphant motives in Bilhah and Reuben remain implicit, as do Jacob's feelings when he finds out, for that cryptic account is all we learn of the matter. Anywhere, at any time, sexuality can erupt.

Repeatedly we see God and men trying to structure sexual energy for sustaining and enhancing purposes. They symbolize crucial commitments between them bodily. The covenant with Abraham, for example, includes circumcision for all males of his descent; and it is just that which Jacob's sons exploit to avenge the rape of Dinah. When Eliezer departs at Abraham's behest to find a wife for Isaac, he swears a solemn oath by touching Abraham's thigh. Joseph promises on Jacob's thigh to bury him in Canaan. Similarly, Jacob is hobbled at the hip as he strives with God, crippled by way of his very attainment to the identity of Israel. Allowing for slight displacements, these interactions seem to testify to perceived awesomeness of the male genitals as a source of life and focus of vulnerability. Circumcision and the image of Israel's injury suggest a defense against retribution—recall the serpent's punishment and Adam and Eve banished from Eden, the Tower of Babel, the Flood, and Moriah—a psychology of partial sacrifice for enablement. Concomitantly, the attitudes toward women, though rich, seem neither comfortable nor definitive. After Sarai becomes Sarah, the delineation of suitable wives for the Patriarchs gets emphasized. Avimelech attests insistently when he returns Sarah to Abraham that he never touched her. Rebekah's virginity is mentioned prominently, along with her hospitality and her being of the family. Although for differing reasons, it is clear that Canaanite wives will not do for Isaac or Jacob; indeed, when poor Esau hears the stated reason for Jacob being sent to Haran, he touchingly takes additional wives from beyond Canaan, still trying to please his father. But suitability remains an unresolved issue. Joseph takes an Egyptian wife. Abraham and Jacob have children with handmaids and concubines, and Judah unintentionally does so with his daughter-in-law. Jacob's adored Rachel, the mother of Joseph, uses the excuse of menstrual difficulties to hide her theft of her father's household gods. *Genesis*, in brief, proves as preoccupied with sexuality as it is with survival, development, and knowledgeable responsibility. But warily, less confidently, because sexuality is markedly anarchic and recidivist.

While bearing squarely on choices that both enlarge and demarcate the group, sexual desire and wish, broadly understood and in a psycho-analytic perspective, can be seen to vitalize the inner motives and feelings of persons presented. From the time Abel and Cain make offerings to God, children vie impressively for recognition and love. Jacob and Esau compete, as do Joseph and his brothers, with abiding consequences. Rachel and Leah struggle jealously together in their marriage to Jacob. Jealousy, indeed, is taken very seriously in *Genesis*: Cain's provokes the first murder; Sarah's determines the fate of Hagar, Ishmael, Isaac, and all their descendants, to say nothing of affecting Abraham's happiness.

Similarly, the intensity of loving attachments and their aftermaths work through lives and generations. No less than his preference for Esau, Isaac's depressed reserve after Moriah correlates fascinatingly with Rebekah's importance for Jacob, as it does with the latter's eventual marriage to two strong-willed sisters. Rachel's death seems resonantly to inform Jacob's special devotion to her long-delayed firstborn, young Joseph—and even, thereby, Joseph's self-regard, which is unique in *Genesis*. Ironically but believably, Jacob ends up favoring one son, as his father did, as Abraham did with greater sadness. And although this is perhaps speculative, Joseph's ultimate vocation—sustaining, nourishing, and literally feeding masses of hungry people—may derive from his mother's death when he was very young. May we speculate further? Could Abraham's having to renounce Ishmael ("Oh that Ishmael might live by Your favor!" he had cried when God promised him a son with Sarah) provide yet another current for his willingness to sacrifice Isaac: the father, with the knife, scarring his son for life?

What can be certain is that in the presence of Isaac's reserve, Rebekah emerges decisively; and that Jacob's passivity with women enables Leah and Rachel to thrive, agitate, compete, play tricks, and work out agreements. These contrasts articulate the larger pattern of *Genesis* in which God recedes as men move into prominence, fathers willy-nilly give way to sons who become fathers, and suggest that characterizing aspects of masculine and feminine roles, even as depicted in this book of the Patriarchs, prove available, regardless of gender, for internalization and self-definition.

Genesis presents persistent problematics of sexuality while showing its ranging force in human interactions, feelings, motives, and growth. As such it is crucially part of the Patriarchal style for getting by and adapting. The focus is on fathers, who arduously solve their negotiations with the natural landscape, other peoples, themselves as political beings, and their God more thoroughly than they can master sexual variousness. The Patriarchs' women and wives remain secondary, although important, challenging. Usually that bias gets historical explanation: our notions of equality would be aberrant. The imaginative reality of *Genesis* enriches the view. The Patriarchs coped with their difficult and unprecedented world. They apparently depended on men and women having different aims and expectations. But the narrative of their lives and generations seriously addresses human sexuality and in impressive ways explores it. For sexuality too was new.

Overt sexual behavior posed no besetting problem for Joseph, despite Potiphar's wife. She tried hard to entice him but, spurned, accused him falsely. Later Pharaoh gave him Asenath, daughter of a priest of On, and Joseph married and had sons without stress put on the matter. Such ties, whether legitimate or illegitimate, seem not to have engrossed him. The narrative structure suggests as much by suddenly juxtaposing the memorable Judah and Tamar episode, which early interrupts the account of Joseph's life. Replete with fearsome genital desires and demands of commitment, that episode continues a preoccupation in *Genesis* but contrasts sharply with Joseph's dominant concerns, as if calling attention to the difference in emphasis.

For reasons already suggested, Joseph from the first takes himself as a major object of regard. Narcissism infuses his character as depression does Isaac's. His brothers and father could not have known how well he would learn from experience; or that, protected in turn by fatherly benefactors (Potiphar, the chief jailer, and Pharaoh) he would increasingly merge his singular self-awareness and pleasurable, guiltless ambition with alertness, intuitive intelligence, shrewdness, and a remarkable capacity for planning—which is to say, that he would redeploy the Patriarchal style of operation creatively in Egypt. That is one way he became "a father" to Pharaoh.

Doubtless he paraded his dreams foolishly before his brothers, and he paid for it. He was more decorous with Potiphar, whom he served admirably. But his nascent diplomatic skills faltered when Potiphar's bold wife pressed him, and his strategy during their decisive encounter backfired. Invoking loyalty to his master and fear of God, he was sent to prison. Perhaps even then he lacked sufficient self-control, discernment, and tact. We read that "Joseph was well built and handsome" (39 : 6), and the rabbis gloss that he dressed to highlight his good looks (Cohen, 1947, p. 242; Leibowitz, 1972, pp. 413–415). Thereafter, however—in jail, at

Pharaoh's court, and second in command in all of Egypt—he aided his benefactors adeptly and advanced himself without provoking envy, anger, or retaliation. He was a consummate minister of state for Pharaoh, planning for the lean years he foresaw by storing food, then exchanging it over time for the money, cattle, and land of Egypt, except for that of the priests. Thus Joseph sustained everyone, skirted potential trouble, and aggrandized his master: another way he "fathered" him. The people of Egypt testified to his extraordinary political achievement, saying: "You have saved our lives! We are grateful to my lord, and we shall be serfs to Pharaoh" (47 : 25). Joseph proved comfortable with power. He used it well and displayed it shrewdly. He not only liked center stage, he learned to keep himself there. Just as if he'd said openly: "Here I am."

The qualities we come to associate with him shape the drama and meaning of his reconciliation with his brothers in Egypt. Obviously he has a score to settle with them, and though he does not forgive easily, he aims to test them, to see whether they have grown through experience, as he has. Earlier God tested Abraham. Now a perceptive, powerful man, who likes being in charge, tests his brothers, who do not know who he is. At first he jails them as spies; after three days he speaks to them through an interpreter, maintaining distance and implying that he does not comprehend their language: "Do this and you shall live, for I am a God-fearing man. If you are honest men, let one of your brothers be held in your place of detention, while the rest of you go and take home rations for your starving households; but you must bring me your youngest brother, that your words may be verified and that you may not die." Terribly distressed, the brothers lament: "Alas, we are being punished on account of our brother, because we looked on at his anguish, yet paid no heed as he pleaded with us." Reuben adds accusingly: "Did I not tell you, 'Do no wrong to the boy?' But you paid no heed. Now comes the reckoning for his blood" (42 : 18–22).

Joseph turns away weeping, moved that their betrayal burdens them still. Yet he tests them further, having more in heart and mind than proof of bad conscience. To heighten their wonder and fear, he has Simeon bound before their eyes and their money put back in their sacks with the provisions for the journey home. By demanding the youngest, he involves Jacob, for the father will have to permit Benjamin to return as commanded. When they do return, Joseph sustains the uncertainty to the moment Benjamin stands accused of stealing his silver goblet. Judah rushes forward, pleading, offering himself instead—as years before no one did for Joseph:

Your servant my father said to us, "As you know, my wife bore me two sons. But one is gone from me, and I said: Alas, he was torn by a beast! And I have not seen him since. If you take this one from me, too, and he meets with disaster, you will send my white head down to Sheol in grief." Now, if I come to your servant my father and the boy is not with us—since his own life is so bound up with his— when he sees that the boy is not with us, he will die, and your servant will send the white head of your servant our father down to Sheol in grief. Now your servant has pledged himself for the boy to my father, saying, "If I do not bring him back to you, I shall stand guilty before my father forever." Therefore, please let your servant remain as a slave to my lord instead of the boy, and let the boy go back with his brothers. For how can I go back to my father unless the boy is with me? Let me not be witness to the woe that would overtake my father! [44 : 27–34]

So Joseph orchestrates a cruel test, a suspenseful and dramatic one in which his role is central, and they pass. They do not repeat their crime, having become better men. But he has made them suffer for betraying him. By reviving Jacob's grief as well, he punished the father who endangered him, perversely assured himself, furthermore, that the father could be forced to endanger the second of Rachel's sons—that he would not, in other words, prove to love Benjamin more. Then and only then does he reveal himself, and forgive. His telling first words are: "I am Joseph. Is my father still well?"

Joseph's story, like that of Israel in Egypt, continues. The moral climax of *Genesis*, however, the culmination of the themes we have been tracing, comes in this drama of reconciliation. The family style of survival, the struggle to develop, the singularity of persons, the fate of self-regard in Joseph, the need to *know*—others, circumstances, one's own continuities—in order to act responsibly and wisely, focus here. Learning about his brothers as they do about themselves, Joseph shows that he knows himself. He respects his own anger, his desire for revenge, his very temperament. By not forgetting the past or himself, he can forgive— exactly because he now knows that his brothers and father, no less than he, remember. Hence he fuses conscious knowing to ethical action, epitomizing what it means to study good and evil. One must understand all the words: *Here I am* (cf. Wiesel, 1976, pp. 139–169).

Even at the close, *Genesis* does not sentimentalize. Joseph secures the land of Goshen for the family of Israel, skillfully staging that benefaction from Pharaoh. When old Jacob dies, though, the brothers feel frightened again: "What if Joseph still bears a grudge against us and pays us back for all the wrong that we did him!" They send a message to him. It is a lie, but a diplomatic one: "Before his death your father left this instruction: So shall you say to Joseph, 'Forgive, I urge you, the offense and guilt of your brothers who treated you so harshly.' Therefore, please forgive the offense of the servants of the God of your father" (50:15–17). Joseph weeps. Eloquently he reassures them. But clearly he has not surrendered an iota of his power. Neither he nor they, all the children of Israel, forget their past or what is signifies of human capacities. Again we see remembered knowledge informing their responsible action. It is a small instance of many in *Genesis* that allow us to appreciate Freud's modest and accurate remark that imaginative writers understood the unconscious long before he found another way to talk about it.

25

Fathers in Nineteenth-Century Novels: Some Portrayals of Unconscious Conflict in Paternal Attitudes and Behaviors

Sylvia Brody

Because in these times more and more young families are coming apart, fathers are often choosing to take more daily care of their children. Many feel a normal uneasiness about their new functions, which historically and culturally have been relegated to females. Some may still be able to carry out their tasks with enough satisfaction to balance the difficulties that naturally occur. Others are apt, however, to be hampered from experiencing satisfaction by vague anxiety, from which they may have been protected in the past by traditional patterns of child care. Clinical experience shows that the anxiety about involvement with the daily demands of children derives in part from hidden conflicts about accepting what may appear to be a feminine identification. Such anxiety may interfere seriously with a father's competence and pleasure with his children, and may arouse a variety of defense maneuvers. For this reason I wish to draw attention to the ways certain unconscious conflicts that have a source in unconscious beating fantasies may be observed in the behavior and attitudes of fathers (Brody, 1956, 1970; Brody and Axelrad, 1978).

To put it very simply: A man may perceive yielding to the young child's wishes to be looked at, caressed, talked to, listened to, as if these were indulgences that might touch off latent homosexual or feminine fantasies that consciously are repellent. This is why I think that, generally speaking, a father who feels his masculinity to be vulnerable must set up firmer, and sometimes more rigid defense measures than a mother against a child's natural demands. Indeed, he may go so far as to regard

The study reported by this author was supported by the National Institute of Mental Health (MH 1429) and the William T. Grant Foundation. Parts of this chapter were presented at a meeting of the Denver Psychoanalytic Society in October 1978, and at a Congress of the Gesamthochschule, Kassel, West Germany, in November 1979.

the child as an exploiter, and himself as a victim. Alternatively, some fathers unconsciously give way to pseudofeminine identification, and submit too easily to the child's demands, or even become seductive.

To illustrate these conflicts I have chosen several novels of the nineteenth century, a period in which the novel first became a prominent literary medium and reflected changing values that were affecting most social institutions: family, church, labor, and leisure. A high premium began to be placed on school attendance and on education both for material progress and for the cultivation of taste and refinement, as avenues toward rational pursuits. The Utilitarian principle of the importance of good conduct as that which advances the greatest happiness for the greatest number was much esteemed. These ideals are directly relevant to paternal behavior because in the Victorian family it was usually the father more than the mother who spoke for and was expected to enforce standards of conduct and morality, at least during postoedipal phases of development.

Thus I have decided to describe several fathers in novels by Jane Austen, Charles Dickens, Anthony Trollope, George Meredith, and Samuel Butler, in which the maintaining of those standards, especially in the family, were essential themes. This selection has been made with the further consideration that the novels' appearance preceded the influence of psychoanalysis, so the behaviors of fathers they portray may be compared with present-day fathers, about whom I shall later report briefly. And where defense measures against unconscious conflicts may be recognized in the fathers, their fictional portraits may be seen to reflect the kind of artistic insight that conveys psychological truth.

Austen's Fathers

The character of Mr. Bennet in *Pride and Prejudice* (1813) is a benign father of five daughters. The first two are to his liking: Jane is sensitive, tolerant, and steady; Elizabeth, his favorite, is enjoyed by him for her good sense and spirit. It was only fair to expect his third child to be a son, but when instead three more daughters come along, Mr. Bennet does as much as he decently can to retire from the presence of all except the two elder girls. His wife was once young and attractive, but early in their marriage he found her to be empty-headed. He humors her with mild condescension. As the three younger girls become as silly as their mother, Bennet regards their mindlessness with detached amusement and leaves them to her foolish influence. His only demand of them is not to disturb him in his study.

Elizabeth . . . had never been blind to the impropriety of her father's behavior as a husband . . . she endeavoured to forget what she could not overlook and to banish from her thoughts that continual breach of conjugal obligation and decorum which, in exposing his wife to the contempt of her own children, was so highly reprehensible . . . she had . . . felt . . . strongly the disadvantages which must attend the children of so unsuitable a marriage [pp. 252–253].

It is when the giddiest of the three girls elopes and precipitates a possible scandal that Bennet is suddenly appalled by the indifference he has shown to their way of life. He feels guilt for having carelessly allowed them to find a primrose path. He takes steps at once to see to it that the next wayward daughter conducts herself properly, and the story ends well.

This father has recognized that he erred seriously in failing to elicit his children's affection and trust and, in this, to protect them from becoming as flighty and as empty as their mother. As a result, they have been driven to seek frantically for idle pleasure among opportunistic associates. Avoidance and denial are the mild defenses with which Bennet protects himself from involvement with the girls whose love he felt could give him no pleasure. These defenses shortchanged his paternity.

In *Mansfield Park* (1814), Austen portrayed Sir Thomas as a typically formal upper-class father of his day. He is depicted as a man of sturdy ethical purpose, seriously involved in international business matters, with little relation to his family. He arranges for his sons to prepare for vocations, and expects his daughters to make proper marriages; meanwhile, he leaves the girls to their own amusements, and in the care of a selfish aunt whose flatteries he tries to complement by his severity. The result is not the even balance he has hoped for, but a damaging insincerity in the daughters. It transpires that they have only pretended proper behavior in his presence. Too late he realizes that he never taught them the necessity for self-denial and humility, or the need to govern inclinations by a sense of duty, or according to the religious instruction they had received. He had been too concerned with their elegance and social accomplishments. His absence of conflict, until the final remorseful insight into his errors, may be understood as a successful repression of any wish to enlist the affection of his daughters, or to take note of their needs for emotional support or intellectual guidance. Father and daughters have experienced no mutual affection, make few demands on each other, and the girls' personalities are left impoverished.

Dickens' Fathers

Dickens' *Dombey and Son* (1848) presents, in greater depth, a father's internal crisis.

The wealthy, arrogant "marble monument," Mr. Dombey, is in a state of exaltation, for he has a son. Great plans are in his mind about the boy's future and the firm of Dombey and Son. That his wife is dying, that 6-year-old Florence sobs as she clings to her unmoving mamma, these do not trouble him. It is only too bad that the baby, Paul, will not have his own mother to nurse him. A uniquely loving woman is hired for the purpose, with the proviso that she and Paul not become attached to one another. It does vex Dombey to see the nurse's pity for the forlorn little girl, of whose existence he prefers not to be reminded. One day he learns that the nurse has also dared to visit her own devoted children. He dismisses her at once, ignoring Florence's pathetic cries for her. From that day, the robust Paul begins to decline and wants only to be with Florence. She seeks always for a sign of affection from her father, perceives his uneasiness with her, and dreads offending him; she dares not look at him, and trembles in his presence. Dombey is told that Paul, near age 5, still is not thriving. So preposterous an idea angers him; he refuses to believe it, but agrees to Paul's going away to a school at the seashore. He does not mind the exceedingly disagreeable, hypocritical schoolmistress and her very harsh regimen; he rather feels sure that the pressure of discipline and hard work will make Paul stronger. The child tries with all his energies to do what is expected of him, becomes sadder and weaker, and finally dies.

Dombey's world is now bleak and cold. He never speaks of his terrible wound, goes to his business, rigid and self-important as ever. At home he closes himself up in his room alone in gloom. The sight of the dying Paul holding on to Florence as once she had held on to her mamma, keeps returning to his memory irksomely. From both scenes he feels strangely disconnected, and as if reproached. Florence, lonely and desolate after her second bereavement, yearns to talk to him, at least to be near him in his despair. Night after night she secretly goes toward his room, crouches outside it on the cold stone floor, and presses her lips against the closed door (pp. 229–259):

In her one absorbing wish to be allowed to show him some affection, to be a consolation to him, to win him over to the endurance of some tenderness from her . . . she would have knelt down at his feet, if she had dared, in humble supplication . . . . She had been unwelcome from the first; she was an aggravation and a bitterness now . . . . He rejected the angel, and took up with the tormenting spirit crouching in his bosom. Her patience, goodness, youth, devotion, love, were as so many atoms in the ashes upon which he set his heel.

It galls him to look at her beauty and see her alive, with Paul dead.

Florence thinks something is lacking in her, that she cannot express her love for him and gain his. She watches other children with their fathers, aching to find out how they succeed where she cannot, then decides she must study how to please him, and so engrosses herself in books, music, and prayer. She is agonized when she overhears herself spoken about by someone kindly explaining to an orphan that "not an orphan in the wide world can be so described as the child who is an outcast from a living parent's love." She remains resolute, however, in her determination to bring her father to know of her love for him. Meanwhile she will give him no cause to be troubled by her, or thought ill by anyone.

Dombey marries Edith, a proud woman who soon despises him but who loves Florence dearly. Florence entreats her new mamma to teach her how to become deserving of her father's love, and again her hopes are dashed by Edith's saying it is an impossible task for her; Florence takes this to mean she is unlovable. Edith, moreover, is forbidden by Dombey to continue in her preferment of Florence. The marriage deteriorates; there is an angry quarrel that ends in Edith's running away with a manager of Dombey's firm, whom he had trusted in everything. At the news Dombey, in rage at this dishonor, tears out of the house.

Florence is bursting with grief for him, and hearing him come back, is impelled by her compassion to rush to him: "Oh, dear, dear Papa!" In his frenzy he strikes her, and as she falls, tells her what Edith is and bids her follow Edith, since they have always been in league. So Florence sees at last that she has no father, and at 17 flees from home. Old friends protect her. Later she finds love and marriage to the young man whom her father disliked because he had befriended Florence. Dombey never looks for her.

His affairs worsen. He takes no warning about the dire state of his business (brought on by the manager), and then his world is smashed: He is bankrupt, gossiped about, ignored, humiliated, and friendless. Day after day he sits in the big empty house, shattered, lost in solitary confinement.

He begins to remember the past, and experiences a kind of catharsis. A great change comes over him as he realizes what it is to be rejected and deserted. Through all the bad times, Florence alone was always gentle and faithful to him. "She had never changed to him—nor had he ever changed to her—and she was lost." He keeps wandering about the abandoned mansion, agitated, weeping, not knowing which room was hers, fearing that if he should see her pass on the street he might still be too proud to speak to her.

And suddenly Florence is on her knees before him, tearfully begging his forgiveness. On the birth of her baby, whom she named Paul, she knew how much she loved him; so she also knew she should never have left her father. She admits her guilt and pleads with him not to cast her off. Dombey is crushed by shame, misery, and yet, oddly, some rapture. He can only groan in his suffering until at last he looks upward and cries, "Oh, my God, forgive me for I need it very much!" They clasp each other silently for a long, long time. In later years, he loves to watch the new Paul "free and stirring." The story of their bond is well known. But Florence knows the measure of his affection for her little Florence, another frank "revenant": "He hoards her in his heart. He cannot bear to see a cloud upon her face . . . . He fancies that she feels a slight, when there is none . . . . He steals away to look at her, in her sleep . . . . He is fondest of her and most loving to her, when there is no creature by" (p. 798).

Florence is artless, earnest, courageous, and openhearted; all are stirred to love her, except her father. She epitomizes pure love, he the ambitious, exploitative merchant made morally insensible by pretentiousness. His defensive isolation supports a brittle pride, which at times is in danger of being sundered by vague guilt or anxiety. Still he tries to act as if there were no place in him for a wish to be needed, much less loved. He asks the reverse: Others must obey his commands and admire his supremacy. ("The idea of opposition to Me is monstrous and absurd.") He seems to believe that he has chosen to restrict his emotions and actions, yet there are moments when he perceives that he is too inhibited to feel spontaneous emotion. It is as if he is oppressed by a chronic struggle against a return of an unsuccessfully repressed longing for intimacy. At the end he wins it, by virtue of Florence's steadfast trust in his availability. *She* has suffered his aggression and rejection, and *she* persists in her readiness to receive his love.

In *Hard Times* (1854), Dickens expressed revolt against the human suffering brought on by the industrial order and by a false pragmatism it often nourished. The story deals with the evil effects of an education intended solely to advance economic success, unadulterated by any trace of emotion, fantasy, or imagination. Thus, for Mr. Gradgrind, who runs an elementary school, education demands absolute exclusion of affective experience. Play is useless, even dangerous, because it distorts reality, and he sees the children in his school as "little pitchers . . . to be filled with facts." He places highest importance on learning plain facts about the material world, and feels dignified by his opportunity to prepare children to live in a world of economic growth.

His own children must study calculation, metallurgy, botany, mineralogy, and other subjects at home, where learning consists of memorizing series of names and definitions. Gradgrind allows them no choice of activities and asks nothing from them but to learn what he tells them to. Love is displaced by order, obedience, and hard work. Gradgrind represents an extreme of grinding severity based on a sincere trust in the value of education based entirely on rigid attention to hard facts. He is proud of being known as "eminently practical." When his daughter, aged 9 years, begins to say to her brother, "Tom, I wonder . . . ," Gradgrind, overhearing, steps forth and says, "Louisa, never wonder!" "Herein lay the spring of the mechanical art and mystery of educating the reason without stooping to the cultivation of the sentiments and affections. Never wonder. By means of addition, subtraction, multiplication, and division, settle everything somehow, and never wonder. Bring to me, says M'Choakumchild [teacher], yonder baby just able to walk, and I will engage that it shall never wonder" (pp. 37–38).

The obedient Louisa, benumbed by her education and having no alternative, submits to marry a rising factory owner, Bounderby. He is a coarse braggart whom she loathes, but accepts, because he will further the career of her brother Tom, whom she loves. But Tom, who has always chafed more than she against their father's rigidity, commits a felony. A poor long-suffering laborer, a heroic figure of the novel, is accused of the crime and as a result accidentally succumbs to a miserable death. Tom blames his father for his criminal behavior. Gradgrind should not be shocked, his son tells him cynically: "So many people are employed in situations of trust; so many people, out of so many, will be dishonest. I have heard you talk, a hundred times, of its being a law. How can I help laws? You have comforted others with such things. Comfort yourself!" (p. 216).

A former student of Gradgrind tries to arrest Tom for what he admits to be his own selfish reason. The father pleads for his son's freedom and hears a bitter response: "I am sure you know that the whole social system is a question of self-interest. What you must always appeal to, is a person's self-interest . . . . I was brought up in that catechism when I was very young, Sir, as you are aware" (p. 218).

Cissy, a girl traveling with an itinerant circus, one whose way of life is in utter contrast to everything Gradgrind finds worthy, at last illuminates his feelings and thinking and reawakens his basic kindness, but too late to save his children from broken lives. Isolation is Gradgrind's most conspicuous defense against his own and his children's instinctual drives, except for aggressive drives to achieve economic progress. His adamant obstruction of his children's freedom for any joyful experience has a quality of a caricatured reaction formation against any activity that might lead to sloth. The isolation is undone on two occasions: when he befriends Cissy, whom at first he treated harshly; and when, at the end of the story, he emerges from his defensive position and has access to feelings of humility and sorrow.

Trollope's Fathers

Trollope's *The Warden* (1855) concerns a quite different father. Mr. Harding lives modestly with his younger daughter Eleanor. He is loved for his kindness, dignity, and the wisdom with which he carries out his duties as church warden.

The discovery of a minor legality in an old document vaguely suggests that his post may have been given to him improperly, and an inquiry is spearheaded by one John Bold. Eleanor, seeing her father shaken by bad news, begs him to tell her his trouble, but he does not (p. 77):

> Mr. Harding was not the man to judge harshly of any one, much less of the daughter whom he now loved better than any living creature; but still he did judge her wrongly at this moment. He knew that she loved John Bold; he fully sympathized in her affection; day after day he thought more of the matter, and, with the tender care of a loving father, tried to arrange in his own mind how matters might be so managed that his daughter's heart should not be made the sacrifice to the dispute which was likely to exist between him and Bold. Now, when she spoke to him for the first time on this subject, it was natural that he should think more of her than of himself, and that she should imagine that her own cares, and not his, were troubling her.

He tells her that he can in no way disapprove of her love and apologizes for Bold, even praises him for his energy and good intentions. But actually Eleanor's fear is for her father, not for herself. At a later point she again begs her father to share his torment with her, and again he asks, why should she be unhappy before it is necessary? Why should her young days be clouded? So she entreats him to give up the struggle, as her only wish is that he should be at ease; he should not think of her but proceed in this affair only if his honor is in question. She is ready to give up Bold if he proves to be an enemy of her father. Bold is no enemy, says Harding; maybe his charge is justified.

He gently rebukes Eleanor for thinking of casting Bold away. Much affected by her love for himself, however, Harding finally acquiesces to her wish to know the cause of his sadness, but insists he must undergo privation if necessary, for her sake, to save the honor of both. Without his knowledge she takes steps to clear his name and succeeds. Nevertheless, Harding has been unable to avoid an idea that there may be some bit of truth in Bold's charge, although Harding could have known nothing of it, and so in spite of remonstrances on all sides, the warden's conscience brings him to give up his post. His children must never have any cause to feel shame for their father.

In his surrender of the wardenship he is sad. His motive may seem masochistic, yet he also finds legitimate relief in doing something for his daughter, and he continues with a good and satisfying life. Harding is exemplary in his unalloyed wish to receive the love and respect of his daughter, and in his acknowledgment of her claim to help him carry his emotional burden. The single defense here may be a reaction formation against a need to protect himself from an undeserved attack on his integrity, so that without Eleanor's intercession he might have sacrificed his excellent name.

In *Framley Parsonage* (1860) and *The Last Chronicles of Barset* (1867), Trollope presents a father whose moral exactitude is extreme. Mr. Crawley is a desperately poor curate of a small parish and an uncommon classical scholar who keeps to his studies rigidly and obsessionally. Often, however, he feels prostrated by the austerity in which he lives and by his inability to do more for his wife and children. "This father, though he loved his offspring with an affection as intense as that which human nature can supply, was not gifted with a knack of making children fond of him . . . . Such men are not always the best fathers or the safest guardians . . . . Bur Mr. Crawley was a stern man, thinking ever of the souls and minds of his bairns—as a father should do" (Vol. 2, p. 169). His children, put off by his sternness, sometimes avoid him, "adding fresh wounds to his torn heart, but by no means quenching any of the great love with which he regarded them."

When Mrs. Crawley becomes ill with a contagious disease, Crawley insists on caring for her and the children alone in virtual starvation, rather than accept help of gifts from his kind, well-to-do neighbors. Standing in his doorway, holding his youngest child in his arms, he sees the neighbors approach and is immediately ready to fend them off for fear they bring food, money, or advice. They ask only to remove the children temporarily from the sick mother. Crawley absolutely refuses; he cannot sacrifice what little pride he has left. "It is very sweet to give . . . . But the taking of what is given is very bitter. Gift bread chokes a man's throat and poisons his blood, and sits like lead upon the heart. You have never tried it" (Vol. 2, pp. 179–180).

When a sum of money is mislaid by another man, Crawley is found to have used it and is accused of theft. He knows he is innocent but cannot account for the money's having come into his pocket, and months of suffering ensue. A wealthy major of excellent character loves Crawley's daughter, Grace, and asks consent to visit her. Crawley, knowing no way to prove his innocence, abjectly explains that in view of the circumstances he is unworthy to have authority over his daughter, nor can he encourage a gentleman to take her hand. After the major goes, Crawley sits motionlessly, his face turned to the wall, in misery for his "poor darling" who has been soiled by his impurity and therefore must be robbed of the fine man who loves her. He feels his children's claim that he should act honorably, and is so hounded by his conscience that he declares himself responsible for the theft before he comes to trial. All the signs suggest it and most people have come to believe it; so he must have stolen the money. He is ready to go to prison. In the end his honor is vindicated and his integrity rewarded.

Crawley, one of Trollope's finest characterizations, is exceedingly masochistic, as the name implies. The rigidity of his reaction formation endangers his family. He is no model of a father's healthy capacity to resolve his instinctual conflicts. Yet his story does dramatize a father's refusal to compromise his children's entitlement to an upright father.

Meredith's Fathers

Meredith's *The Ordeal of Richard Feverel* (1859) again deals with the pitfalls of a father's moral control. The Principles of a Science of Humanism are here transformed into a naive tyranny.

Sir Austin Feverel's wife has run away with their best friend, leaving her infant son, Richard. The father loves the boy dearly. To shield him from the follies of women and other moral dangers, he sees to it that the boy's education is carried out entirely in the seclusion of the family estate, monitored by Sir Austin's Principles of Scientific Humanism, in order "to germinate in Richard the love of every form of nobleness." All moves fairly well until Richard, at the age of 14, takes part in a serious escapade. His father soon hears of it, believes the act was "unprovoked and wanton," but will let Richard have a fair trial by not confronting him directly: "The Baronet's possession of his son's secret flattered him. It allowed him to act, and in a measure to feel, like Providence, enabled him to observe and provide for the movements of creatures in the dark . . . and young Richard saw no change in his father to make him think he was suspected" (p. 57).

Still completely optimistic about his Experiment, Sir Austin says to the father of Richard's accomplice, pointedly, "I find . . . there are fathers who are content to be simply obeyed. Now I require not only that my son should obey; I would have him guiltless of the impulse to gainsay my wishes, feeling me in him stronger than his undeveloped nature, up to a certain period, where my responsibility ends and his commences" (p.

130). Lofty motives have led the father to deny his son's right to feel and think autonomously.

A few years later Sir Austin goes on a secret errand to find just the right young woman for Richard. In his absence Richard by chance meets and falls passionately in love with a neighbor, Lucy. Learning this, Sir Austin is self-accusatory: It is all because he has not been enough of a Preceptor and Friend to his son. His pride tells him to be tolerant, and so he appeals to Richard to look out for the snares that beset him, reminding him of his own deep love for Richard, for which Richard should be grateful, and should thus accommodate to his father's wish to renounce Lucy. Richard does not agree, and the mutual trust of father and son is weakened. Shortly thereafter, each again misinterprets the other's intentions and their estrangement grows, for Richard has identified himself with his father in being too proud to surrender. Sir Austin feels that his system of values is failing fast—but no (pp. 314–315),

Just because he suffered and decreed that he would suffer silently, and be the only sufferer, it seemed to him that he was great-minded in his calamity. He had stood against the world. The world had beaten him. What then? He must shut his heart and mask his face . . . . He might well say, as he once did, that there are hours when the clearest soul becomes a cunning fox.

He pretends to be unforgiving, which causes him great pain, but he feels a Spartan comfort in it. Actually he is in a profound struggle, for he bears his son no malice, feels magnanimous in not withholding funds from him, and yet cannot relent to see him. He rather tests Richard's capacity to wait obediently many months after Richard has been ready to reunite and make amends.

"The Baronet was conscious of a certain false gratification in his son's apparent obedience to his wishes and complete submission, a gratification he chose to accept as his due, without dissecting or accounting for it. The intelligence reiterating that Richard waited and still waited, Richard's letters, and, more, his dumb abiding and practical penitence" vindicate the father's course of action. Finally the father's love almost brings him to yield. Inwardly he takes credit for his softness, but wants no one to suppose him soft. "And the last tug of vanity drew him aslant" (p. 368). To the end he has no doubt that the cause of Richard's rebellion was his giving the boy too much liberty during his childhood. The System is still correct. Sir Austin's later efforts to rekindle it with Richard's wife and son lead to tragedy.

Sir Austin is complex. He has believed that his deepest wish is to be loved by his son and to do everything in his power to ensure the son's future happiness. He gives up his personal pleasures and rears the boy in a way that should prove his virtuous intentions, earn the son's love and gratitude, and show the world by means of the System he has created, a uniquely superior human being. But he nourishes the boy's allegiance too seductively, and when the allegiance falters, he becomes moralistically punitive. Further moral cruelty sustains the punishment, always guided by a rationale that credits the father for a steadfast loyalty to his high-mindedness. He comes to grief because actually he has *demanded* his son's love and has expected his son to respond fully to his (the father's) needs. He forces himself to act on impulses that I have referred to as moral sadism (Brody, 1970): that is, achieving satisfaction by inflicting mental pain, for a moral purpose. He longs to be loved and needed but is inhibited from accepting either pleasure in a form that does not meet the claims of his overly strict superego. His unconscious wish for self-aggrandizement, and the sadomasochistic gratification he reaps, are clear.

Butler's Fathers

Butler's *The Way of All Flesh* (1903), written near the end of the century, tells of two generations of fathers, each of whom has implacable demands to be free of paternal obligations. Old Pontifex was a benevolent villager of exemplary character. He agrees to have his young son, George, go out into the mercantile world of London. George becomes a wealthy man of affairs, proud, stern, self-righteous, penurious, and aloof from his children. He is willing to pay for their upbringing and education, as they thus become dependent on his wishes in all things. When they do anything he dislikes he considers them disobedient, and several times a week thrashes them. Theobald, the eldest son, is threatened with disinheritance if he does not obey his father; so very reluctantly he submits to being ordained, and very reluctantly he allows himself to be pulled into a marriage.

Like his father, Theobald, who is the central father in the story, never liked children: He might tolerate them better if they were born grown-up or could be chosen for sex and age at a shop.

As a father, Theobald is far more severe than George ever was, more colorless and affectless, save in his rush to feel righteously indignant at any sign that *his* children may show wishes of their own. If he has children, they must at least be properly trained from infancy, so that all indications of self-will should be scotched. His eldest son, Ernest, is his main victim (p. 128):

Before Ernest could well crawl he was taught to kneel; before he could well speak he was taught to lisp the Lord's Prayer, and the general confession . . . . If his attention flagged or his memory failed him here was an ill weed which would grow apace, unless it were plucked out immediately, and the only way to pluck it out was to whip him, or to shut him up in a cupboard, or dock him of some of the small pleasures of childhood. Before he was three years old, he could read and, after a fashion, write. Before he was four he was learning Latin, and could do rule of three sums.

As a child Ernest was allowed one treat: On Sundays he could choose his own hymn. Theobald feels much put upon for having to carry the financial burden of Ernest's care and education, and repeatedly charges the boy—who is disappointingly small, shy, and sensitive—with not expressing to his father the gratitude Theobald deserves for his singular indulgences. He coldly resents Ernest's seeming not to consider how fortunate he is to have the advantage of so worthy and concerned a father. The mother supports her husband's severity, and enjoins their children to show their father "obedience, affection, attentiveness to [his] wishes, self-denial and diligence . . . . This was how it came to pass that their children were white and puny; they suffered from *homesickness*. They were starving, through being over-crammed with the wrong things" (p. 158).

During Ernest's adolescence an episode occurs that brings him to act with spontaneous kindness to a servant whom his father has treated cruelly; afterward he trembles in anticipation of his father's rage, although he has had to promise his mother never to fear his father. Theobald confronts the boy cruelly, somewhat as a spider traps a fly. "It never occurred to Ernest to ask his father why did he not hit a man his own size, or to stop him midway in the story with a remonstrance against being kicked when he was down" (p. 258). Ernest can only stammer out that the father's accusation is true and he is strictly punished. His parents "had chapter and verse for everything they had either done or left undone." His childhood was one of (p. 393):

long and savage cruelty—cruelty none the less real for having been due to ignorance and stupidity rather than to deliberate malice; of the atmosphere of lying and self-laudatory hallucination in which he had been brought up; of the readiness the boy had shown to love anything that would be good enough to let him, and how affection for his parents . . . had only died in him because it had been killed anew, again and again and again, each time that it had tried to spring.

As a lonely, self-effacing young man, Ernest drifts about for a way of life after he, like his father, is reluctantly ordained. A series of accidental events leads him to temporary social disgrace. Theobald at once disowns him, and learning that Ernest has also been duped and may now also be penniless, the father is pleased. He has always wished Ernest to make requests of him so that he can have the opportunity to refuse them and castigate his son's unregenerate qualities. Eventually Ernest unexpectedly inherits a fortune. His father, furiously jealous, expects Ernest to share his wealth at once and freely with his family, not one of whom has ever treated him kindly. Ernest gives up his parents, lives alone, reading and writing on most serious topics, and knowing he can never enjoy an intimate human relationship.

Theobald is an ideal example of a father's conscious repudiation of any wish to be loved or needed. Perversely, he commands Ernest to love him and to receive his harsh strictures submissively. Here we see an identification with the aggressor: Theobald's own cold, autocratic father; a hostile projection of his own incapacity to feel kindness or generosity; and a severe and anxious repression of libidinal aims with regard to his children. (An opposite example of a father's yearning for his children's love, and repression of aggressive aims toward them, paid for by masochistic surrender, appears in Balzac's *Pere Goriot*.)

We do not expect to find paternal responsiveness to the instinctual drives of a child in so pure a culture, and yet *The Way of All Flesh* is not a fairy tale, but a thinly disguised autobiography up to the period of Butler's ordination. It was completed in 1885, but because his sister was still alive, the book was not published until 1903, a year after Butler's death.

Ernest Pontifex's mother is an insidiously castrating female, a woman who undermines men. All the other mothers in the novels I have mentioned are ineffectual, dying, or missing, so that the fathers act alone.

Discussion

In each father we can see degrees of passivity that lead, or almost lead, to disaster. Bennet and Mansfield are least affected; Harding and Crawley would have been dishonored unfairly were it not for the good offices of loving daughters and friends; Dombey, Gradgrind, and Feverel suffer profoundly for having failed to appreciate their children's longing to be loved and needed for their own sakes. And Theobald Pontifex remains obdurate, providing an exquisite picture of the negativism, blocking of affect, and fear of emotional surrender that Anna Freud (1952) has described.

The examples I have presented from literature of a century ago have many congruities with research findings (see the following section, Empirical Support). Here, in view of the unconscious conflicts and defenses that I have emphasized, and that appear to me to have major effects on fathers' behavior and attitudes, often to their regret or sorrow, I am prompted to make a few general remarks about the mutual relations between fathers and children.

Consciously, a father may dearly wish for the ability to allow his children freedom to express love for him and to rely on him for active help in acquiring ego and character strengths. His goal is to lead the child gradually to establish lasting values. To help build those strengths and values in the child's early years, a father needs to have his own inner freedom to nourish the child's affection and trust, and to recognize the child's legitimate (and often unspoken) demands. To these he must, ideally at least, respond without fear of being made excessively passive, and without resenting the practical and emotional efforts that he may thereby initiate or to which he may accommodate. Then the normal conflicts between father and child in the preoedipal and oedipal phases are less likely to threaten either one's masculine or feminine aims.

As the child grows into latency, he or she can more spontaneously look to his or her father more for gaining skills and knowledge. At the same time, the child can gain an appreciation of the father's wishes, needs, and values. By means of the child's responsiveness to the father's emotional and intellectual availability, the father can now have increasing opportunities to influence the child toward the foundation of a firm but benign conscience. If, during this period, infantile wishes or ego regressions of the child mount instead of receding, however, the father-child relationship may be weakened considerably. A father is liable to feel acute disappointment in the child and in himself, with perplexity as to which of the two has failed the other. The situation can be very painful to both. He may rationalize that things will change as the child matures. Nevertheless, he may be aware of unquiet feelings or anger toward the child, and feel impulses to reject him or her. Above all, he may feel shame that the child is reflecting the father's, or the grandfather's, inadequacies.

During the child's prepuberty the father can have one more chance to win favor with the child and facilitate his or her further development. More than ever before, the child has become able to be realistically critical of the father's personality, and the father's vulnerability may again be sparked. I have observed, in treating patients from latency to adolescence, that fathers who can bear their own as well as the child's shortcomings without condemning either, and who can allow the child to realize his or her potential without envy, do come through this trying period with a refreshed respect and concern for each other.

The arrival of adolescence produces a major shift in the father's attitudes, one related to the revival of his own oedipal conflict. It touches again on the issue of supremacy, and on the unconscious dilemma, the

413

wishes and fears about being loved and needed (imposed on). The shift is brought about by a reversal of aim and object of the wishes. The father, who in the child's past can have felt a wish to be loved and needed, now wishes that the adolescent should seek to gain *his* love, and should show a need for *him*. The father, who once may have enjoyed accommodating to the child's demands, now feels it is time for the adolescent to accommodate to *his* demands. When these desires are not realized, or when a father's normal narcissistic aims for the child's successes are frustrated, his inner conflict may rise sharply. He may accuse himself of failure, and be faced with the possibility that he has not been so good a father as his own father was. Or, what is more painful, in spite of a longstanding vow to act differently from his own father, he may find himself harboring attitudes exactly like those he deplored in his father, but to which he may have unwittingly surrendered. Then he is apt to feel deserving of rejection and to give way to sad moods. Or he may relinquish his hopes for his children and detach himself from them emotionally. It is as if he feels that damage has been done to his already compromised ego ideal. Although our mores about sexual roles are undergoing change, hostility toward sons for failure to fulfill the father's expectations is still observable far more often than toward daughters. One other outcome of a father's aspirations may also bring mixed pleasures for him: that is, when a son, again more than a daughter, surpasses the achievements of a father whose self-esteem has been precarious.

The problem of present-day fathers who have more responsibility for a child's daily care consists of much more than a lack of experience in sharing maternal obligations. Problems arise, as I have tried to show, when a father is assailed by conflicts about giving and receiving love and setting limits, mainly in the preoedipal phases; about respecting the child's needs as well as being obeyed, mainly in the oedipal phase; about being admired and emulated, mainly during the latency period; and about being rivaled in spheres of realistic activity, mainly during adolescence. In these ways, the father's own preoedipal and oedipal character conflicts stream together as the child grows older, and help to shape the adolescent's capacity for his own eventual fatherhood.

We may say that to be a good father means to provide enjoyments while keeping the child from fixation to infantile pleasures; to help the child bear appropriate frustrations, in consideration of his or her age and maturity; to be a masculine figure, firmly, without having to prove strengths by harsh measures or by maintaining distance from the child; to see that it is natural and desirable for mothers and fathers to enjoy mutually supportive but different contributions to childrearing; and to let the son or daughter know that to be loved, the one need not be hypermasculine nor the other hyperfeminine.

Empirical Support

The foregoing propositions are supported by data drawn from interviews with fathers of children of ages 2 to 7 years, in a longitudinal investigation (Brody and Axelrad, 1978). It demonstrates the high frequency with which fathers may defensively avoid awareness of their children's needs.

Of 127 fathers who were invited to speak about their children annually, 104 agreed to do so at least once; of these, only 62 did so with firm interest. A father's involvement in his child and in childrearing were assessed according to his knowledge of the child's daily life, the quality of his relationship to the child, his ability to perceive the child as an individual, his understanding of the significance of experiences in early childhood, and his ability to provide control in a way that could permit minimal identification with the father as aggressor.

By their own accounts, a majority of the fathers had limited knowledge about their children. They reported little or no enjoyment of the child's company, and poor acquaintance with the child's interests, frustration tolerance, fears, or negative character traits; little or no sympathetic awareness of his or her emotional states or of the impact of emotionally significant events; and little or no interest in offering appropriate sexual information or in lessening the child's anxiety. Only a minority clearly encouraged the child's self-esteem, expression of appropriate affects, positive feelings toward the fathers or other persons, or toward learning in the larger sense; or showed distinctly positive and objective feelings about the child. Only a minority appeared to nourish a superego structure in the child that was firm, stable, and benign; in more cases it was strict, or weak, patchy, and perhaps defective. Fewer than half of the fathers believed methods of childrearing were important, and only a few more than half were found to be thoughtfully involved in their interviews.

The strengths they had as fathers, mentioned most often yet in less than one-third of the sample, were understanding; having moral, educational, or religious ideals; love; and discipline. Only a few mentioned honesty, fairness, consistency, and being good providers. Only one said he had thought out rational ideas of childrearing. Eleven did not know what their paternal strengths might be, or said they had none. The weaknesses mentioned in almost half of the sample were not being or wanting to be with the child enough, or being too busy or too lazy to do things with him. Others said they were too lenient, too strict or demanding, short-tempered, impatient, lazy about discipline, lacking in confidence, or having other neurotic reactions. Eight did not know what their weaknesses might be or said they had none.*

As may be seen, most of the strengths they cited represent superego commands, indicating that they had conventional ideas about what fathers should be like. Most of the weaknesses they cited implied that in actual dealings with their children many fathers felt unequipped, awkward, impatient, or distant. By and large, it appeared that a majority could not show appropriate feelings to their children, and could not recognize or accede to the children's normal claims for concern beyond those that might be related to habit training and academic progress. At the same time, many fathers showed or expressed embarrassment, guilt, sadness, or fear of losing the child's love as a consequence of their parental insufficiencies.

*Numbers for each item named are available from the author on request.

26

Fathers and Sons: An Indian Experience

Sudhir Kakar

To speak of fatherhood in India, as distinct from fatherhood elsewhere, involves the implicit assumption (and admission) that fatherhood can be a cultural construction as much as a biological one. In other words, a man's fatherhood is not only influenced by his life stage and his uniquely individual life history: It is also shaped by the cultural matrix—family type, cultural norms, values, and ideals of parental behavior—in which fatherhood is embedded. Before I proceed to elaborate on the cultural construction of fatherhood in India and its impact on the developmental fate of sons, let me first note that I am fully aware of the problems in making any generalizations on fatherhood in a society as complex and heterogeneous as India, which has such a welter of distinct regional, linguistic, caste, class, and regional subidentities. Yet there are a number of accounts of childhood in different castes and classes from all over India—anthropological studies of growing up in villages in many parts of the country, sociological studies of childrearing practices in a few towns and cities, clinical case material, regrettably limited to certain classes in the large cities—which lead to the conclusion that certain tentative generalizations on fathers and sons in traditional India, in the sense of describing a dominant mode in a variable range, are indeed possible. Parenthetically, I must also add that in the following observations, "Indian" primarily refers to Hindu India, although, in fact, other religious groups in India have been profoundly influenced by the dominant Hindu culture.

Ideals of Fatherhood

If there is one predominant father-son theme in the texts that are commonly regarded as the repositories of Hindu cultural values (e.g., the *Mahabharata* and the *Ramayana*), it is the importance attached to, and the intense longing expression for, the birth of a son (Kakar, 1979). A number of myths and didactic passages repeatedly emphasize that begetting a son is one of a man's highest duties and the only way he can discharge the debt he owes to his ancestors. Even the very name for the son, *putra*, means "one who delivers from the hell called *put.*" Consider the story of Jarat Kuru.

The renowned ascetic Jarat Kuru, full of merit and great spiritual power derived from his sustained asceticism, was wandering around the world when one day he came across a deep pit. In this pit, the spirits of his ancestors, the *pitris*, were hanging head down, their feet tied to a tree trunk by a single skein of rope that was gradually being nibbled away by a large rat. It was evident that the *pitris* would fall down into the deep darkness of the pit. Moved by their pitiable condition, Jarat Kuru inquired whether he could somehow save them from this fate, expressing his readiness to do so even if he had to give up all the rewards to which his great asceticism entitled him. "Venerable *brahmacarin*," the *pitris* answered, "thou desirest to relieve us! . . . O child, whether it is asceticism, or sacrifice, or whatever else there be of very holy acts, everything is inferior. These cannot count equal to a son. O child, having seen all, speak unto that Jarat Kuru of ascetic wealth . . . tell him all that would induce him to take a wife and beget children" (*Mahabharata*, pp. 107–108).

Sons in the *Mahabharata* are not only seen as instrumental in the fulfillment of a sacred *duty* which, however agreeable and meritorious, still carries the connotation of religious necessity and social imposition. They are also portrayed as a source of emotional and sensual gratification. Listen to Shakuntla asking Dushyanta to acknowledge his son whom he has forgotten because of a curse (pp. 177–178):

What happiness is greater than what the father feels when the son is running toward him, even though his body be covered with dust, and clasps his limbs? Even ants support their own eggs without destroying them, then why shouldst not thou, virtuous as thou art, support thy own child? The touch of soft sandal paste, of women, of [cool] water is not so agreeable as the touch of one's own infant son locked in one's embrace. As a Brahmana is the foremost of all bipeds, a cow, the foremost of all quadrupeds, a *guru* the foremost of all superiors, so is the son the foremost of all objects, agreeable to the touch. Let, therefore, this handsome child touch thee in embrace. There is nothing in the world more agreeable to the touch than the embrace of one's son.

Classical Sanskrit literature, too, contains many lyrical accounts of a father's love for his son. Thus, to take two well-known examples, Bhavabhuti describes Rama's love for Lava and Kusha, while Banabhatta rhapsodizes over Prabhakarvardhana's love for his son, Harsha. The greatest of all Sanskrit poets, Kalidasa, too is lyrical about the father's feelings for his child; for instance, in his descriptions of Dushyanta's feelings for his son Sarvadamana and of Dilip's love for Raghu in *Raghuvamsha*, Dilip responds joyfully to Raghu's birth (3. 45–46): "He went in immediately [on hearing the news] and as the lotus becomes motionless when the breeze stops, he gazed at his son's face with the same still eyes. Just as a tide comes into the ocean when it sees the moon, similarly the King [Dilip] was so happy on seeing his son that he could not contain the happiness in his heart."

These accounts from ancient texts (but also from many modern folktales) are evidence of a strong projective identification of fathers with their sons. It is an identification that is explicitly recognized by many passages in the *Mahabharata* that maintain that the father himself is born as the son, and with the placing of his own seed in the womb he has placed his own self.

However, as I attempt to show below, the cultural emphasis on a father's intimate emotional involvement with his son may well be the expression of the Hindu son's intense, unfulfilled wish for his father's presence at a critical stage of his childhood. In itself a universal wish, the need for the father becomes a pressing and lifelong theme in India because of certain features of Indian infancy that need to be elaborated in some detail.

The Second Birth

One of the most striking features of male childhood in many parts of India is what I have elsewhere called the "second birth" (Kakar, 1978). The second birth refers to the sudden widening of the world of Indian childhood from the intimate cocoon of maternal protection to the unfamiliar masculine network woven by the demands and tensions, the comings and goings, of the men of the family. The abrupt separation from his mother generally occurs around the fifth year of a boy's life. Even more than the suddenness of the transition, the *contrast* between an earlier, more or less unchecked benevolent indulgence and the now inflexible standards of absolute obedience and conformity to familial and social standards is the most striking feature of the second birth. As an anthropological account of a Hyderabad village describes it, "The liberty that he was allowed during his early childhood is increasingly curtailed. Now the accent is on good behaviour and regular habits. The child is more frequently spanked for being troublesome" (Dube, 1967, p. 149). And a northern Indian proverb, which has its counterparts in the oral traditions of other regions, pithily conveys what the boy has now to face: "Treat a son like a king for the first five years, like a slave for the next ten and like a friend thereafter."

Whereas until this time the male child is enveloped in, and often overpowered by, his mother's protective nurturing and love—a love abundantly lavished (and ideally unconditional)—whatever approval or appreciation he can now hope to receive from the men in the family who now take responsibility for his care and instruction is much more qualified. Relationships become more businesslike, and affection is a token in each transaction. It is conditional on the boy's behavior, something he has to earn by learning the formalities of correct relationships with each member of the family and by conforming to the norms of family and caste behavior. Without any preparation for the transition, the boy is literally banished from the gently teasing, admiring society of women into a relatively stern and unfeeling male world full of rules and responsibilities in which he cannot be quite so cocky. Little wonder that this transition of the second birth is associated with intense bewilderment and uprootedness.

This critical shift takes place, of course, within a psychosocial dimension; it is one of the emotional frontiers in the inner world of experience. Insofar as the daily logistics of eating, playing, sleeping, and taking care of himself are concerned, the 4- or 5-year-old Indian boy retains for a while longer the leeway to be with sisters and to seek out his mother. Although he must spend even more time in the exclusive company of boys and men, going back to his mother less frequently, and basically for reassurance, he begins to learn to dilute his need for emotional support and succoring and to turn for these needs now to one of the grandparents perhaps, or possibly to an uncle or aunt. This process of intimacy diffusion, the replacement of the exclusive nurturing attachment to the mother with a variety of less intense relationships with any number of others in the extended family circle, is yet another characteristic of the second birth.

The second birth, then, is the stage for the Indian boy's oedipal drama. We must, however, note that the emissary of the culture demanding that the Indian boy relinquish his intimate status with his mother is not just the father but the whole assembly of elder males in the family. The boy's fury at being separated from his mother is not directed toward his father alone; it is diffused against all the male authority figures who are collectively responsible for taking his mother away. Thus it makes sense, symbolically, that in Indian mythology, Ravana, the abductor of the "good mother," Sita, has not 1 but 10 heads.

Because it is diluted and diverted to include other elder males, oedipal aggression against the father, in its "classical" intensity, is on the whole not common in India. For instance, in an analysis of 166 folktales from seven Indian provinces, it was found that the father-son conflict in India was of a low intensity as compared with similar figures from 42 other societies (Kakar, 1974). The intensity of the conflict varies, of course, from region to region and among different social groups. In communities that emphasize manliness in its *machismo* elaboration and keep their women in the seclusion of *purdah* (e.g., the Rajputs), and who thus exact from their sons a dramatic and total renunciation of the feminine world of mothers and sisters and aunts, the oedipal dimension of the boy's rage against the father and other males tends to be more pronounced than in communities where the second birth is a more relaxed and gradual process.

The son's anger against the father in the Indian context has thus less to do with the vicissitudes of the oedipal complex than with the father's ambiguous role within the family. For the narcissistic injury inherent in the abrupt dissolution of the mother-son bond can be tempered through the reinforcement provided by the boy's identification with his father. A father, as Erikson (1958), Fromm (1971), and others have emphasized, is not only the counterpart of little Oedipus, but the guardian and sponsor of the boy's separation from his mother at a time when his courage for such an autonomous existence is both new and tenuous. Indeed, "The affirmation of the (father's) guiding voice is a prime element in a man's sense of identity." Given the intensity, duration, and ambivalence of the mother-son connection in an Indian setting that I have discussed elsewhere (Kakar, 1974), the need for the father's presence and for his guiding voice becomes even more pressing, the necessity of this father-son alliance outweighing the hostility of the positive Oedipus complex. In fact, the deeply buried need for such an alliance against the overwhelming, omnipresent, and sexually threatening mother of early childhood often emerges during the analysis of male patients. It may be helpful to illustrate through a case vignette.

D. was a 26-year-old engineer who had come to analysis because of a general loss of interest in work, inability to relate to people, and suicidal thoughts. He was the eldest son of parents who had spent the first 3 years of his life with his mother at the home of his maternal grandfather. In the fourth year of his life, D., along with his mother, went to live with his father in a distant village where his father was a policeman. D.'s first memories of his father were of a harsh and authoritarian man who had broken the blissful intimacy between mother and son, but who was, fortunately, rarely at home. As the analysis progressed, however, D.'s memories and feelings about his early years began to change. He discovered that under the overt hostility against the father, there were considerable feelings of affection and admiration. Concomitantly, the mother's image began changing from a loving woman absorbed in her son's welfare to a devouring, overpowering mother who clung to her son and belittled his efforts at individuation. D.'s resentment against his father, he discovered, had less to do with his earlier "oedipal rage" and more with the fact that the father was so often away and did not permit his son emotional access. Once, when after his marriage D.'s feelings of helplessness in face of overpowering femininity had been again stirred, D. had the following significant dream: "I am in our village home when a gang of decoits led by a girl attack our house. The female leader of the band is chasing me through the rooms of the house. I pass my father in the hall. He is lying on the bed with a gun but it is not effective and he cannot help me though he wants to. I am very afraid as the girl bandit runs after me, laughing and mocking me for not being able to defend myself."

Another, a borderline patient, who was struggling desperately against his incestuous impulses toward his mother, dreamed: "I am lying on my bed when I see my mother approaching. She is almost naked and has a laughing, gloating expression on her face. I am very scared. Then I see you (the analyst) sitting in a corner of the room with an enormous penis next to your chair that rises from the floor and goes up to the ceiling. I hold the penis and feel safe." Besides other themes, this dream also echoes a Hindu mythological motif, depicted in temple sculptures, in which a boy holds fast to his father's penis to escape the god of death.

The guiding voice of the father can become effective and the alliance succeed only if the father allows his son emotional access to him—that is, if he allows himself to be idealized at the same time that he encourages and supports the boy's own efforts to grow up. Identification is a process, however; it requires that over the years the father be constantly available to his son, a criterion fundamentally at odds with the rationale and structure of the Indian extended family. For the strength and cohesion of the extended family depend on a certain emotional diffusion; it is essential that nuclear cells do not build up within the family, or at the very least, that these cells do not involve intense emotional loyalties that potentially exclude other family members and their interests.

Thus the principles of Indian family life demand that a father be restrained in the presence of his own son and divide his interest and support equally among his own and his brother's sons. The culturally prescribed pattern of restraint between fathers and sons is widespread in India, sufficiently so to constitute a societal norm. In autobiographical accounts fathers, whether strict or indulgent, cold or affectionate, are invariably distant. In the analysis of many male patients, the father often appears as a shadowy figure, his paternal presence a childhood blur.

Behind the requisite facade of aloofness and impartiality, an Indian father may be struggling to express his love for his son. Fatherly love is no less strong in India than in other societies. Yet the fact remains that the son, suddenly bereft of the "good" mother and needing a firm masculine model with whom to identify as a means of freedom from the "bad" mother, is exposed to bewildering, contradictory messages of simultaneous love and restraint, emanating from his father. He does not have that necessary conviction that his father is a dependable constant to learn from, be loved by, and emulate. The son often lacks the affirmation of that one guiding masculine voice, as it becomes diffused among many. The unconscious anger of sons against good but "intangible" fathers, their individual paternity muffled in the impartiality required by the extended family, is one of the major themes in the father-son relationship in India.

27

The Changing Faces of Fatherhood: A New Exploration in American Family History

John Demos

Fatherhood has a very long history, but virtually no historians. Its only invariant aspect is the biological one; all else is fluid and changing. No two individuals father in precisely the same way; similarly, no two cultures, or historical epochs, support identical styles of fathering. Of course, there is always overlap—shared elements of purpose, of practice, and of emotional style—especially in adjacent settings. Moreover, where the settings are historically adjacent, we may reasonably expect continuities as well as contrasts. Still, the point remains that fatherhood, no less than other parts of human experience, bends to the passage of time.

But if this serves to define history, it does not automatically give rise to scholarship. Historians choose from a huge field of topical possibility, and they have not as yet chosen fatherhood. Public events and collective experience have traditionally claimed their interest—history as "past politics." Indeed, for earlier generations of historians fatherhood would scarcely have been legitimate—and perhaps not even conceivable—as a center of serious investigation. Even with the recent flowering of a so-called new social history, fatherhood remains out of view. There are no focused treatments of the subject in print—no monographs, articles, or compilations of data, let alone synthetic overviews. The historical study of fatherhood is waiting to be born.

Fortunately, the wait will not last much longer if current trends and portents hold firm. The new social history carries within it the seeds of gestation, and the larger scholarly environment looks more and more favorable. Interest in personal, even private, experience has been clearly legitimized. Recent work in family history, women's history, and child-

I would like to acknowledge my profound debt to E. Anthony Rotundo, currently a member of the doctoral program in American Civilization at Brandeis University, and also to Rachel Cramer, a recent alumna of Brandeis. Their research underlies much of what I have attempted in this chapter.

hood history has raised implicit questions about fatherhood, and has thrown up promising material for answering such questions. Points of intersection with each of these lively subspecialties are obvious; they are also advantageous. Problems and lacunae will be more an inducement than a hindrance to study. In fact, younger scholars are already busy around the edges of the field, and the results of their work will be available within a few short years.

The present essay is, then, a prediction of birth—although not the event itself. It anticipates progress, raises questions, flags problems, and tries finally to fashion an outline for the history of fatherhood in America. Hence it qualifies as what one scholar has called "hypothetical history"— that is, an informed guess, in advance of the requisite base in monographic research. This is the way things *probably* were—no more, and perhaps less.

A vast gulf of change separates early American fathers from their counterparts today. The differences embrace underlying goals and values; prescribed methods and styles of practice; the shape and quality of personal interaction; and the larger configuration of domestic life. Consider the following entry in the diary of a New England clergyman near the end of the seventeenth century (C. Mather, 1969, pp. 239–240):

I took my little daughter Katy into my study and there I told my child that I am to die shortly, and she must, when I am dead, remember everything that I said unto her. I set before her the sinful and woeful condition of her nature, and I charged her to pray in secret places every day without ceasing that God for the sake of Jesus Christ would give her a new heart . . . I gave her to understand that when I am taken from her she must look to meet with more humbling afflictions than she does now [when] she has a careful and a tender father to provide for her.

This vignette of "tender fatherhood" startles us: to invoke for a young child the spectre of parental death seems thoughtless and manipulative, if not patently cruel. In fact, the parent in question was young and in good health; his actual death lay decades in the future. But viewed in context, his admonitions seem less peculiar and unsettling, and may even make a certain sense. Death was an active presence in the lives of early Americans, old and young; and a father who did not prepare his child for such possibilities might well be considered negligent. Note, too, that discussion of death was directly linked to moral and religious instruction; the end in view was the child's improvement in "grace," and even her ultimate "salvation." Whether tender or not, this father seems concerned, involved, active for the welfare of his children. And other evidence of his family experience points strongly in the same direction.

In fact, the picture sketched here fits nicely with a large corpus of prescriptive statements from the period. When ministers and others in positions of leadership wrote about fatherhood, they emphasized a broad range of tasks and responsibilities. Father must be centrally concerned in the moral and religious education of the young. He must impart the rudiments of reading and writing—to the extent, at least, of his own literacy (*father as pedagogue*). He would also have the primary responsibility for guiding sons in the choice of an occupational "calling" (*father as guidance counselor*). And he would play a key role, for both sons and daughters, in courtship and marriage making: approving (or disapproving) a proposed match, and allotting "portions" of family property to secure a couple's future (*father as benefactor*). By contrast, mother's part in all this was rarely, and barely, mentioned. Some authorities felt obliged to caution that she should not be "exempted"—in implicit but clear recognition of her lesser role (Bloch, 1978).

There is the further point that most such prescription was addressed to men (or to parents generally, but with the operative pronoun "he"). And if we ask why this was so, we must turn to larger questions of gender. Beliefs about maleness and femaleness are also historically variable, as we ourselves can testify from recent social experience. Our forebears of two and three centuries ago maintained some characteristic attitudes toward gender considerably at variance with our own. Men, they believed, must "overrule" women, in domestic affairs no less than other spheres of activity. For men had received from their Maker a generally superior endowment of "reason." Both sexes were liable to be misled by the "passions" and the "affections," but women were more liable because their rational powers were so weak. The biblical account of creation, and of Eve's temptation in the Garden, made this point clearly enough, and there were numerous personal examples from everyday life. A well-known passage in the journal of John Winthrop (first governor of Massachusetts) describes an unfortunate lady thought to have gone insane "by giving herself largely to reading and writing." To woman's intellectual inferiority was added her special *moral* vulnerability. It was no accident that most witches turned out to be females (Morgan, 1966; Demos, 1970b, 1971).

This complex of belief and practice carried important implications for parenting. Children came into the world inherently "stained" with sin; moreover, their "passions" were immediately powerful, their "intellectuals" miserably underdeveloped. The steady hand of fathers was necessary to restrain the former, while encouraging and molding the latter (*father as*

427

moral overseer). Unfortunately, the influence of mothers frequently ran the opposite way. "Indulgence," "excessive fondness," a tendency to spoil or "cocker" the children: such were the common *maternal* failings (Bloch, 1969). Carried to and fro by their inordinate affections, and lacking the "compass" of sound reason, women could hardly provide the vigilant supervision that all children needed. Too, men were better positioned (than women) to understand the young; as one authority put it, "Father ordinarily has the most share in procuring, and most sense in perceiving, the wisdom of his children" (*father as psychologist*) (Bloch, 1969). Finally, fathers provided the best examples of good character and right behavior (*father as model*). In all these ways and more would men predominate as parents.

To be sure, the pattern was modified by particular circumstances—for example, the age and gender of the children. We can safely assume that infants were largely in the day-to-day care of mothers. For breast milk was their chief source of nourishment, and this alone must have dictated a substantial maternal presence. Moreover, daughters remained (in general) closer to mothers than did sons. Their common gender, and a shared round of household tasks, forged emotional bonds of lasting strength. Still, these are *only* modifications, not refutations, of the basic rule. Once infants were past the age of breast-feeding, their fathers came strongly into view; and girl children, no less than boys, required moral supervision from a man. It was chiefly for this reason that the common law affirmed overall rights of child custody to the father in cases of marital separation.

The closeness of fathers and sons can be studied, and tested, in several ways. Patterns of correspondence are notably revealing. Teenage boys serving apprenticeships, as well as young men officially on their own, would maintain contact with their families of origin chiefly through letters to fathers. Often they would ask to be "remembered" also to their mothers—but in terms that seem (by our lights) formal, or downright perfunctory. Of letters written directly to mothers there were very few. One man whose father had just died wrote home to a brother and included the following message to their mother: "I sincerely condole with . . . [her] on the loss of her husband; please tender my duty to her." Here in a single sentence, and especially in the reference to "her husband," is palpable expression of the distance thought appropriate to the relation of mothers and sons (Gay, 1809).

It appears, too, that fathers—not mothers—were particularly identified with the prospects of sons. The latter, when young or newly born, were commonly described by their fathers as "my hope" or "my consolation." Sons were seen as continuing a man's accomplishments, in-

428

deed his very character, into the future. Thus would a successful son reflect credit on his father—the credit of a "good name" or "good repute." However, these same effects might well reverse directions, with "the sins of the fathers" being found in the sons as well. Drunkards and gluttons, fornicators and thieves, would naturally reproduce themselves (*father as progenitor*) (Rotundo, 1981).

With so much at stake on both sides, it is not surprising that father-son relationships rested heavily on notions of "duty." Paternal oversight of education (in all aspects) was invariably portrayed in this light; sons, for their part, owed "respect" and "honor" in return. (A more tangible filial "duty" was assistance to fathers in their old age.) Yet this need not exclude "affection" of a deep and lasting kind. Affection *and* duty, affection energizing duty, duty controlling affection: such were the common formulas. Again, personal correspondence, when carefully read, displays the one no less than the other.

We would like, finally, to envision actual fathers and children caught up in the routine experience of everyday. Unfortunately, the records afford only sudden glimpses here and there; but these nonetheless are revealing. A father and his 10-year-old son carting grain to the mill; a father counseling his adult daughter on her impending marriage; a father and his son "discoursing" on witchcraft; a son and daughter joining their father in an argument with neighbors: from such small nuggets a cumulative picture emerges. It is a picture at once consistent with the prescriptive materials cited previously and with our larger understandings of early American life. It is a picture, above all, of active, encompassing fatherhood, woven into the whole fabric of domestic and productive life. Indeed the critical point is that domestic and productive life overlapped so substantially—and were, in some respects, identical. The vast majority of seventeenth- and eighteenth-century fathers were, of course, farmers; of the remainder, all but a handful were local artisans and tradesmen. In either case, productive endeavor was centered in or around the family hearth, and it seemed natural, even necessary, that children should be directly involved. From an early age boys and girls began to assist their father in the work of farm or shop. Fathers were thus a visible presence, year after year, day after day (*father as companion*). The same pattern obtained for leisure-time experience as well. Families attended church, went visiting, and passed the long hours of stormy winter days or summer evenings, largely as a unit. Fathering was thus an extension, if not a part, of much routine activity.

Additional aspects of "actual" fatherhood were rooted in demographic and ecological circumstance. In the first place, all adult men expected to become fathers, and only biological infertility might disappoint those expectations. (Perhaps 10 percent of colonial American marriages proved "barren.") Moreover, most would be fathers many times over. An average couple produced about eight children surviving past infancy— though with some variation between one region or time period and the next.) This, in turn, meant that fathering might continue up to, or into, old age. (Often a man was past 60 when his youngest child married and left home; of course, a considerable number did not live long enough to see that day.) Most fathers would have to suffer the loss of one or more of their children to some form of mortal illness (Demos, 1970a, 1978).

These statistical realities can be demonstrated with precision, but their meaning in emotional terms is far from clear. Some scholars contend that parents must have hedged, or limited, their investment in children whose prospects of survival were so uncertain (Shorter, 1975; Stone, 1977). Yet fragmentary evidence suggests otherwise. An occasional diarist or correspondent can be glimpsed in postures of extreme parental concern: for example, a prominent New England merchant who sat up and "watched" overnight whenever one of his children became seriously ill (*father as caregiver*) (Sewall, 1973). The depositional records of local courts afford scattered impressions of the same phenomenon: for example, a village craftsman who remembered that "when his child was sick, and like to die, he ran barefoot and barelegged, and with tears" through the night to find assistance (Drake, 1967). Such materials raise, but do not resolve, important questions about the *interior* dimension of colonial fatherhood. Controversy will no doubt continue, and will hopefully spur additional research. In the meanwhile we should be wary of inference from demography alone, that our forebears were uncaring toward their young.

The foregoing sketch of early American fatherhood is highly compressed and simplified. It presents, at best, a set of mainstream trends or norms, without allowing for variance across space and time. That such variance was real and in some respects substantial cannot be doubted. "Puritan" fathers of seventeenth-century New England were not indistinguishable from their counterparts in the southern colonies or along the Appalachian frontier; nor were they exactly reproduced in their "Yankee" descendants of the following century. Even within the same region and the same time period there might be important differences: One recent study posits coexisting but contrasting styles of "evangelical," "moderate," and "genteel" childrearing in colonial America (Greven, 1979).

Yet no summary could possibly comprehend all such distinctions, and for present purposes the mainstream elements are the important ones. Almost everywhere fatherhood displayed the same active, integrated orientation. And in this, there was little apparent change through the several generations of our "colonial period."

When the story is carried forward into the national period, however, change appears as a central motif. It did not come all at once—indeed, its pace can be easily exaggerated—but its cumulative force seems, in retrospect, unmistakable. Indeed, the sense of change, with all its possibilities and perils, was widely manifest in the period itself.

The early decades of the nineteenth century brought a new burst of writing on domestic life. "Advice books" on courtship, on marriage, on homemaking, and above all on childrearing, fairly gushed from printing presses all across the land. Of course, advice of this type can never be directly equated with behavior, but it does—and did then—express prevalent attitudes and concerns. The concern of nineteenth-century writers about childrearing was partly a matter of nationalism: received (i.e., English) models were considered, in principle, unsuited to "republican" families. But something more was involved as well. The urgent tone of the new advice betrayed deep anxieties about the evolving shape and future prospects of the family. Change was actively embraced, and covertly feared, at one and the same time. And even as Americans envisioned new family forms, they wished to shore up the ways and values of the past (Sunley, 1955; Wishy, 1968).

Significantly, this divided message was directed with special force toward mothers. *The Mother at Home, The Mother's Book, The Young Mother's Companion*: thus the titles of leading examples of the genre. Many of them contained a passage, or a chapter, on fathering; and there were companion volumes, at least a few, aimed primarily at fathers. However, the overall emphasis was clear, and was markedly different from the pattern of earlier times. Mother was now the primary parent. On her fell the chief responsibilities, more urgent and important than ever, for proper "rearing" of the young.

These changes were underscored—indeed were prompted in part—by new ideas about gender. Virtually all human relationships were now reshaped by a massive system of (what modern sociologists would call) sex-role stereotyping. Women and men were thought to occupy different "spheres" appropriate to their entirely different *characters*. The female sphere was, of course, the home—and nothing more. Feminine character was calm, unselfish, in all ways "pure." It was woman's purity that, from a moral standpoint, elevated her far above man. It was also her purity that especially qualified her for motherhood (Welter, 1966; Cott, 1977; Degler, 1980).

Ideas about human development were changing too, with convergent results for childrearing. Ministers, physicians, and advice writers increasingly stressed the formative influence of early—*very* early—experience. The Reverend Horace Bushnell, whose enormously popular treatise on *Christian Nurture* was published in 1843, expressed the reigning wisdom on this point: "Let every Christian father and mother understand, when the child is three years old, that they have done more than half of what they will ever do for his character" (Bushnell, p. 48). In fact, if not in so many words, such statements declared the transcendent importance of *mothers*. For mothers were now, more than ever, the leading caregivers to infants. The roots of maternal influence were seen as extending even in utero; thus numerous authorities believed that a mother's experiences during pregnancy might shape the destiny of her unborn child. Did she wish, for example, to bear a future architect? Then she might spend her leisure hours gazing at fine buildings or pictures of buildings. Such, at least, was the strategy followed in one particularly famous instance—by the mother of Frank Lloyd Wright (Wright, 1932).

As mother's importance waxed, father's inexorably waned. Many of the leading advice writers addressed this trend directly, disapproved it, and wished at the very least to retard its progress. But their words have the ring of special pleading, which only underscores the change. "I cannot believe," declared one clergyman-author, "that God has established the relation of father without giving the father something to do" (Alcott, 1841, pp. 88–89). Another urged simply that fathers "be careful not to under-rate [their] own duties or influence" (Dwight, 1835, p. 29). (Recall the quite similar words of caution—but about *mother's* role and influence—that had issued from comparable sources in the colonial period.)

And how were father's remaining "duties" described? First, and possibly foremost, he was still expected to set an official standard of morality for his family as a whole. He would conduct the family prayers (where that custom survived); he would lead in "edifying discourse" around the dinner table or fireside (Cramer, 1980). He was also the final arbiter of family discipline. Of course, in many routine matters mother's authority was sufficient, but when the stakes were high father must step in. These themes were frequently elaborated in domestic fiction: for example, a mother who threatens her recalcitrant child with the prospect of father's punishment ("when he returns home"). On other, happier occasions father would offer himself for play. He and his children might then enjoy "innocent games" or "romps" on the parlor floor (Cramer, 1980). Or he might simply observe and applaud; thus one father in an actual case commented, "Three such rosy-cheeked children are not to be found as ours . . . . I wish you could have seen them this evening dance, while their mother played on the piano" (Lusk, 1840).

Although fatherhood on these terms was hardly insubstantial, it diverged in obvious and important ways from the earlier pattern. For one thing, it became part-time (*father as discussion leader, father as playmate*); for another, it opened some distance from the everyday workings of the household (*father as disciplinarian, father as audience*). The links between parents were reshaped accordingly. Thus a leading advice book urged that fathers question their children every evening along lines such as the following: "Have you obeyed your mother in all things today? . . . Can you remember any case . . . in which you have tried to help your mother without her asking you to do so?" (Abbott, 1848, p. 149). And a popular work of domestic fiction described a woman's discussion with her husband about the "rearing" of their temperamental young son: "'Persevere, Anna, persevere,' were usually her husband's encouraging words. 'You are doing well. If anyone can mold right the disposition of the wayward child, it is you. I only wish that I had your patience and forebearance'" (Arthur, 1846, p. 44). What actual women might make of such "encouragement" is difficult to say. But here lies another strand in the newly emergent pattern: *father as moral support*.

If distance and part-time involvement had come to characterize fatherhood (at least in some cases), it was preeminently for one reason. Beginning in the first decades of the nineteenth century, and increasingly thereafter, men were drawn out of their families toward income-producing work. The growth of large-scale commerce, of industry, and (later) of service enterprise—indeed, all the dynamic tendencies of economic modernization—yielded this overall effect: home and the workplace would no longer be the same. On the contrary, they became very different places, each with its own designs and purposes, its distinctive values and modes of activity. Around home was drawn an implicit but keenly felt boundary. On the far side lay "the world," including shops, factories, offices of all kinds. Passage across this boundary seemed difficult or dangerous, and must therefore be limited to necessary "occasions." Most of the latter involved men in their pursuit of "gainful occupation."

The wrenching apart of work and home-life is one of the great themes in social history. And for fathers, in particular, the consequences can hardly be overestimated. Certain key elements of premodern fatherhood dwindled and disappeared (e.g., *father as teacher, father as moral overseer, father as companion*), while others were profoundly transformed (*father as counselor, father as model*). Meanwhile new postures and responsibilities emerged from a general reordering of domestic life. Some of these are noted in the immediately preceding pages; but one remains as yet unmentioned—and is perhaps the most important of all. The "man of the family" going off to work and returning with the money needed to support an entire household, the "breadwinner," the resourceful fellow who "brings home the bacon": behind these now-tiresome clichés stands the figure of *father as provider*. Of course, fathers had always been involved in the provision of goods and services to their families; but before the nineteenth century such activity was embedded in a larger matrix of domestic sharing. With modernization, it became "differentiated" as the chief, if not the exclusive, province of adult men. Now, for the first time, the central activity of fatherhood was sited outside one's immediate household. Now, being fully a father meant being separated from one's children for a considerable part of each working day.

That there was paradox, even painful contradiction, in this evolving pattern of experience seems plain in retrospect. But several generations were needed to work out its effects. At first, the "provider" role appeared to have enhancing implications for fatherhood. Providing could be seen and felt, on both sides, as an enlargement of paternal nurturance. The father who "brought home" the bacon, no less than the mother who cooked it and put it on the table, was supplying the vital needs of his children. What he actually *did* in his shop or office was little known to other members of his family; yet its product (income) was known, and was critical to their personal well-being. His ultimate "success" would depend on his strength of mind and will, his endurance, his moral fortitude—and perhaps on other qualities that women and children could but dimly imagine. As a result his work seemed mysterious and wonderful, and his ability to negotiate the treacherous routes through "the world" might be positively heroic.

In short, father's intrinsic connection to all that lay outside home gave him a special status within it. Whenever he returned to the "sacred hearth," he commanded attention, affection, respect, deference, devoted care. The sacrifices he had made, the risks he had run, the experience he had accumulated, the recognition he had achieved: all this made his opinions especially worthy to be heard (and accepted), his orders to be followed. A poem from midcentury will serve to exemplify such larger-than-life fatherhood:

Father is Coming

The clock is on the stroke of six,
    The father's work is done.
Sweep up the hearth and tend the fire,
    And put the kettle on:

The wild night-wind is blowing cold,
    'Tis dreary crossing o'er the world.

He's crossing o'er the world apace,
    He's stronger than the storm;
He does not feel the cold, not he,
    His heart, it is so warm:
For father's heart is stout and true
As ever human bosom knew . . . .

Nay, do not close the shutters, child;
    For along the lane
The little window looks, and he
    Can see it shining plain.
I've heard him say he loves to mark
The cheerful firelight through the dark.

Hark! hark! I hear his footsteps now;
    He's through the garden gate.
Run, little Bess, and ope the door,
    And do not let him wait.
Shout, baby, shout! and clap thy hands,
For father on the threshold stands.

Howitt, p. i.

Alas, such deeply idealized images are often problematic in relation to practice, and this one was especially so. It imposed, first of all, a standard of performance that only a portion of fathers could expect to meet. Success as provider did not come easily in nineteenth-century America. Popular formulas stressed "self-making," as noted previously; but, in fact, opportunity was limited, if not foreclosed, by objective circumstances of race, class, ethnicity, place, and blind luck. And failure exacted a heavy price in self-, and social, esteem. To make matters worse, that price was shared with the families involved. A man who could not find his way in the world was likely to seem a failed *father*—in his own eyes, and in the eyes of those who mattered most to him.

How such disappointment was managed in individual cases is hard to imagine, and harder to study; but the rapid growth of the tramp population—a veritable "army," in the period phrase—suggests one (presumably extreme) line of response. Meanwhile, domestic fiction was full of failed fathers, their shortcomings as providers admixed with intemperance, improvidence, and plain malice. A common plot line, for example, featured a hard-pressed father forcing his children to marry not for love but for money, as a way of relieving his own debts. The cost of these maneuvers was measured in broken hearts and otherwise blighted young lives, and death itself sometimes appeared as the ultimate result. One could well say of this literature that its most vivid portraits of fatherhood were destructive ones (*father as murderer*) (Cramer, 1980).

435

Even for the best of providers there would be problems and pitfalls in fathering. Achievement in the world and constructive involvement at home: these made *separate* goals, often in conflict with one another. A key point of conflict was time: How much time could, or should, a busy father spend with his family? And, assuming that the quantity of such family time would be limited, what of its quality, its use in specific activities? Again and again prescriptive writings picked up the tension. Here is one fictive father, so driven by a "rapid increase in trade, and the necessity of devoting every possible moment to my customers" that he can no longer manage to conduct family prayers. (Subsequent events bring him back to his senses and his duty: "Better to lose a few shillings," he concludes, "than to become the deliberate murderer of my family, and the instrument of ruin to my soul") (*Parents Magazine*, 1842a, p. 198). There is another, who cannot leave his business worries in the office and thus spoils the evening hour supposedly reserved for his children. (Dinner finds him "full of a restless impatience, . . . hurrying through . . . in silence, . . . with an occasional suggestion to others to make the dispatch of which he sets so striking an example") (*Parents Magazine*, 1842b, p. 174). At least occasionally, personal documents display the same conflict against the backdrop of actual experience. Thus a correspondent observed of Boston business families that "the points of contact between husbands and wives . . . were so few that a husband might 'become the father of a large family and even die without finding out his mistake'" (McGovern, 1975, p. 85). And the wife of one such man complained (in a letter to relatives) that "his own business, and then that *dumb* committee, take every moment . . . . Every eve'g he is out either at caucus or drinking wine with the Gov. at some gentry folks. So you see the evils consequent upon being a distinguished man" (Russell, 1845).

Of course, some fathers would manage to work through, or around, these demands on their time and energy. The advice literature furnished many hopeful models of "household management," designed to forge openings to fatherly interaction for even the busiest of men. Yet beyond the reach of any such contrivance lay deeper, more disabling problems. For sustained contact with the world touched men's innermost experience, indeed their very *character*. Many of the qualities most readily associated with success in work—ambition, cleverness, aggressive pursuit of the main chance—had no place in domestic life. At best, a man would have to perform an elaborate switch of role and behavior on crossing the threshold of his home. (It is notable that thresholds became a recurrent preoccupation in all sorts of writing from this period.) At worst, he would have to choose between effectiveness in one "sphere" or the other. And, given the convergent effects of practical need (i.e., for income) and cultural stereotype (i.e., about gender), most men instinctively preferred to concentrate on work and public affairs.

There was, moreover, an explicitly pejorative meaning to the contrast between home and the world. Home would exemplify the "purity" of women and the "innocence" of children. The world seemed deeply suspect from a moral standpoint—disordered, unstable, full of "traps" and "temptations" to vice in many forms. Personal integrity was largely discounted there. The struggle for success presented many inducements to abandon "true principle"; and one compromise led easily to the next. The men who lived and worked in this environment were necessarily imperiled, and maleness itself seemed to carry a certain odor of contamination. This, too, greatly complicated father's role and whatever substantive contributions he might hope to make at home.

In order to strengthen his contributions and lessen the complications, father must fight down some of his deepest masculine tendencies. In doing so, he might well be guided by the example, if not the overt tutelage, of women. Thus men seemed characteristically "impatient of results," which was fine for business, but inappropriate to childrearing. Women, by contrast, were exemplars of patience, owing both to their "natural endowments" and to their cultural role and training. Similarly, men were given to sharp and severe methods of command, whereas women were better at the "gentle arts" of persuasion. Again, of course, it was women's way that best suited the home environment.

The prescriptive and fictional literature overflowed with illustrative cases. A typical story describes a troubled relationship of father and son. The father seeks an attitude of cheerful obedience to his generally reasonable commands. The son obeys, but not cheerfully. The father grows increasingly irritated, and the situation worsens—until a woman visitor, a certain "Aunt Mary," offers some helpful advice. Father's commands are usually given in "a cold, indifferent, or authoritative manner," but a "softer" approach, expressing "the sunshine of affection," might work to better effect. The father listens, and changes his tone; and his son's attitude improves remarkably (Arthur, 1854, p. 249). Other stories have less happy endings. In one the father imposes on his timid and sickly son a harsh regime of physical toughening—mostly outdoors, in wintertime, and late at night. Eventually the child dies, as much from "terror of his natural protector" as from overexposure and overexertion (Sigourney, 1834). In a second story the father comes home "wearied and vexed" after "a hard day's labor," and finds his son covered with dirt and grime. Reacting too fast, he "taxes . . . and scolds [the boy] severely, only to learn a little later that the dirt has come from the performance of a particularly good deed. In the meantime the boy contracts pneumonia and dies before the father can make amends (Graves, 1845). Such lugubrious tales expressed for nineteenth-century readers a profound and pervasive anxiety about fathering. Bad fathering was a matter not just of indifference or irrelevance, but of potentially deadly peril.

But this, we should remind ourselves, was the dark side of a highly variegated picture. Anxiety about fathering, fantasies of bad fathers: such things stand at some distance from the actual experience of individual families from one day to the next. Again we need behavioral evidence to set alongside the prescriptive and fictional materials; and again, such evidence is less available than we might wish. Still, current scholarship is beginning to sift and sort through quite voluminous quantities of personal documents from the period; and some early results can be summarized in a tentative way.

It is apparent, first of all, that many fathers throughout the nineteenth century continued to have affectionate relationships with their children. Indeed their affection may now have been more openly expressed than in premodern times (when "moderation" of feeling was a touchstone of human relationship, and especially of childrearing). There is also much evidence of fatherly interest and involvement in the lives of children—insofar as other commitments allowed. Fathers continued to articulate for their sons and daughters an official code of conduct. They seemed to accept an implicit division of responsibility for the moral training of their young: the outside aspects fell chiefly to them (e.g., formulating specific precepts, punishing major infractions), while mothers took care of the inner-life dimension (e.g., nurturing "conscience" and the growth of "steady habits"). Fathers also played an added role, with sons, in providing advice about "occupations" and public affairs (which, after all, were defined as exclusively male preoccupations) (Rotundo, 1981).

Yet, when considered *in toto*, the behavioral evidence appears to confirm the trend toward limited fatherhood. Certainly it shows a shift in the relative weight of fathers' and mothers' parental contributions. Consider the following points of contrast with the pattern of premodern times:

1. *Then* fathers were the chief correspondents of their (adolescent and adult) children; *now* (i.e., during and after the mid-nineteenth century) mothers played that part at least as often (Rotundo, 1981).
2. *Then* fathers played the central role in guiding, or fully controlling, the marital choices of their children. *Now* autonomy was the reigning principle in most aspects of courtship; and, to the extent that either parent was involved at all, it was usually the mother (and usually vis-à-vis her daughters) (Rothman, 1980).

3. *Then* mothers seem to have been little concerned with any aspect of their sons' lives after childhood; *now* letters and diaries show them emotionally entangled with sons who were well into adulthood (Rotundo, 1981).

4. *Then* it was common to give the largest share of blame or credit for adult outcomes to fathers; *now* the same judgments were made about mothers. "All that I am I owe to my angel mother": thus a favorite period cliché, echoed in one form or another by countless diarists and correspondents reflecting on their own childhoods (Demos, 1974; Bloch, 1978). Moreover, maternal influence was clearly associated with the special closeness of mothers and children. After all, wrote one man near the end of the century, "most people are on more confidential terms with their mother than with their father" (Ricketts, 1896).

The law of child custody presents one final way of tracing the same shift in parental roles and influence (Zinaldin, 1979). Part prescription, part behavior, this evidence seems particularly vivid and compelling. In the premodern era, as noted above, custody belonged exclusively to fathers, reflecting their acknowledged status as the primary parent. However, this pattern was progressively altered by the courts of nineteenth-century America. At first, the changes were ad hoc and limited to cases of manifestly "unfit" (i.e., "immoral" or "profligate") character. But in time the issue was more fully joined, and broadened. A Pennsylvania decision of 1810 rejected a father's claim to custody, for the reason (among others) that children of "tender age" need the "kind of assistance which can be afforded by none so well as a mother." A case in Maine two decades later elicited judicial opinions that: (1) daughters should be treated as "requiring peculiarly the superintendence of a mother," (2) sons "may probably be as well governed by her as by the father," and (3) "parental feelings of the mother toward her children are naturally as strong, and generally stronger, than those of the father." By 1847 a New York court could declare simply that "all other things being equal, the mother is the most proper parent to be entrusted with the custody of a child." To be sure, the older principles died hard—some courts asserted as late as 1834 that "in general, the father is by law clearly entitled to the custody of the child"—but the trend was more and more in the opposite direction. By the end of the century the law, no less than common opinion, affirmed maternal preeminence in childrearing (Zinaldin, 1979).

To speak of common opinion for any part of the nineteenth century is admittedly to oversimplify a complex and ever-changing situation. In fact, the United States of this era embraced a growing variety of groups and traditions, with a corresponding variance in family life. For those who lived in farm households, still a very large number, there was some carryover of earlier patterns. The image of the "family farm," validated in social and political terms by Jeffersonian ideology, lost little of its appeal; and where reality conformed to image, fatherhood might well retain an active, integrated orientation.

Immigrants made another important source of cultural and familial variance. Generalization about such a diverse mass is perilous; assuredly, all of the major ethnic groupings maintained their own styles and forms of domestic life. Still, it does seem clear that most nineteenth-century immigrants were of "peasant" background, and as such reflected a broadly premodern tradition. Integrated fatherhood was their way, too—or at least their expectation. However, the process of immigration was itself profoundly unsettling for family relations. Fatherhood, in particular, was tested and challenged by all the transitional steps from the "old country" to the new. Typically, fathers were responsible for decisions to migrate, in the first place. Then, too, it was their responsibility to justify such decisions by converting American "opportunity" into tangible "success." Yet they were hampered again and again by their unfamiliarity with the language, the customs, the whole cultural ecology of the host country. Moreover, as fully formed adults they were necessarily limited in their adaptive capacities; younger people found it easier to learn and to change. More than their own children, immigrant fathers (and mothers) would remain "strangers in the land." They might even become a kind of embarrassment—the visible reminder of an outlived and outmoded past (*father as anachronism*). And this was an especially potent source of pain and tension, within families and across generations (Handlin, 1973).

Black families must also be mentioned here, if only to clear the record of inherited misunderstanding and prejudice. According to some accounts, black families were severely damaged, if not destroyed outright, first by slavery and later by the combined effects of rural poverty, mass migration, and the disordered environment of inner-city ghettos. The brunt is thought to have fallen with special force on black men, that is, fathers, who responded by simply opting out of domestic life: thus the myth of black "father absence." Black women were supposedly stronger, more authoritative, more responsive and responsible to family: hence the complementary myth of "black matriarchy" (Frazier, 1966; Moynihan, 1967). But myths these were, and are. Recent historical scholarship shows a different picture altogether: a people that even in the midst of slavery incorporated many domestic values of the dominant culture (while retaining at least some "Africanisms"); a household system in which the presence, and leadership, of fathers was very much the norm. To be sure, some portion of black men cracked, or compromised, under the strain. But the vast majority were no less fully *fathers* than their white counterparts. Indeed, some may well have been more so. In their case, fatherhood carried special responsibilities for protecting the young (*father as shield*). Black children must first be guarded from, and then be armored for, the bitter shafts of racism (Gutman, 1976).

So it was that immigrant experience and black experience conditioned fatherhood in special ways. Yet, when seen in the longest perspective, these effects made for quantitative—not qualitative—difference from mainstream norms. Many families of certifiably "native stock" paid the price, in intergenerational conflict, for rapid social change. Each new cohort of children rendered its own fathers to some extent anachronistic. (Hence the implicitly pejorative term of reference for fathers: "my old man.") Similarly, most nineteenth-century fathers felt called on to protect their young from an uncaring world. True, the dangers were less immediate for white children than for black ones, but a fatherly shield would be needed all the same.

It should be clear, in any final view of the nineteenth century, that changing styles of fatherhood belonged most especially to a "modern" vanguard. The members of this group were largely white, Anglo-Saxon, and Protestant. They lived in cities. They worked in the new commercial and industrial "occupations." They belonged to what would later be called the "middle class." To them were directed the advice books and novels, from them came the diaries and letters, which have bulked so large in the present discussion. Relatively few at the outset, their numbers swelled prodigiously as the century passed, and they played in any case a style-setting role. Other groups observed, envied, resisted, adapted—and ultimately followed.

Many of the themes and tendencies just described were joined in a single cultural figure that has considerable resonance even today: the famous (or infamous) "Victorian patriarch." Here one feels the aura of authority surrounding nineteenth-century fatherhood, as well as the distance—even the danger—attaching thereto. The "patriarch" image also captures a certain isolation: father's elevated position exposed him to scrutiny by many others, not least by his own kith and kin. When, in premodern times, his responsibilities to family had been more immediately nurturant, he had been harder to see whole. Subsequently, however, he came out in the open—"available at last," as one study puts it, "for conscious examination" (Weinstein and Platt, 1969).

The process of examination, spanning the interval from the Victorian era to our own, has yielded much doubt and worry, and a steadily growing fund of direct criticism. The "patriarch" has been scaled down, and certain of his leading qualities have been modified. Still, in large measure he survives. Or at least the figure survives, and with it many consequences for actual experience. There is space in what follows only to outline this most recent part of the story.

In the first place, the end of the nineteenth century and the start of the twentieth produced a substantial elaboration of Victorian beliefs about gender. Maleness was defined more and more in terms of ambition and achievement, of what contemporaries called "push and go" or even "animal energy." As before, energy seemed invaluable in "the world" but irrelevant to family life, and the qualifier "animal" (sometimes rendered "animalistic") carried a menacing undertone (Rotundo, 1981). Men must somehow be "tamed," or else be excluded from home and hearth. In his natural state the "male animal" could only disrupt the "family circle" (*father as intruder*).

The force of these images was augmented by change in the social environment. Work experience and domestic experience became ever more distinct, for greater and greater numbers of men. Large-scale, highly differentiated, "impersonal" organization was the pattern of choice in many forms of productive enterprise. Moreover, the late nineteenth century brought the first great boom in suburban living, as street railways (later buses and private automobiles) opened new vistas to "commuting" (Warner, 1963). Suburbs would soon become the epitome, in spatial terms, of the work-home dichotomy. "The suburban husband and father," noted one writer as early as 1900, "is almost entirely a Sunday institution" (*Harper's Bazaar*, 1900, p. 200). Since such fathers spent so little time at home, they could not acquire savvy and skills in "domestic employments." They burbled and bumbled, and occasionally made fools of themselves. They were cajoled, humored, and implicitly patronized by long-suffering wives and clever children. Dagwood Bumsted (of the "Blondie" comic strip), Ozzie Nelson (of the popular radio show "Ozzie and Harriet"), and the faintly ridiculous hero of Clarence Day's Broadway play *Life with Father* made well-known variants on the general type (*father as incompetent*).

The snickering attitude that infused this imagery betrayed as well a deeper tension in father-child relations. With family size greatly shrunken (as compared to premodern times), with family boundaries ever more tightly drawn, with family values expressed more and more in psychological terms, domestic relations assumed a particularly intensive form. It was no accident, for example, that Freudian theory, with its cornerstone concept of the "Oedipus complex," found its most receptive hearing in the United States (Demos, 1978b). To be sure, intensive families were increasingly common throughout the Western World by the early twentieth century; but American experience created special, and amplifying, effects. One of these was "anachronistic" fatherhood, as noted above: fathers who seemed "old-fashioned" alongside their more open and adaptable children. In fact, such differences acquired a normative significance from progressive views of historical development. The hope of America, so widely and fervently proclaimed, was its future—which was to say its "younger generation." Other aspects of cultural ideology also played in here—most especially the "cult of success" and the manifold encouragements to social mobility (Wyllie, 1954; Cawelti, 1965). Success was measured in terms of distance from the starting point to the finish in any given life, and the starting point was the position of father. Here lay an inducement to competition between the generations, powerful and pervasive—however covert—and uniquely American (*father as rival*).

Does this seem too harsh, this portrait of intrusive, incompetent, and competitive fatherhood? In fact, there were other elements that must also be weighed in the balance. Most important perhaps was the continued salience of "breadwinning" in men's personal and domestic experience. The image of *father as provider* was, if anything, stronger in the opening decades of the new century than ever before. Moreover, it conferred on many individual fathers a special status, expressed in attitudes of respect, of deference, of grateful love on the part of other family members.

In addition to exploiting these traditional advantages, twentieth-century fathers have also accepted—have created, in part—one new role of a "softer" sort. In the hours left over after their work and public duties—on evenings, weekends, and vacations—they have sought to engage their children in a variety of comradely activities. Much of this is by way of recreation (attendance at movies or sports events, camping, fishing); some involves projects of household maintenance or improvement (gardening, redecorating, repair work). One hears echoes of the old "companionate" theme in father-child relations, but with a difference. The modern pattern is more contrived and self-conscious, and altogether more confined. For example, it is confined chiefly, or only, to sons; the relation of fathers and daughters, by contrast, has no clear focus and little enough substantive content. Nonetheless, shared recreation can be—often is—deeply meaningful on both sides. The aim is to discount for a time differences of age, of experience, of status—to find some neutral ground on which father and son can meet more or less as equals (*father as chum*). Perhaps this underlies the spread of a relatively new term of address for fathers, the now almost ubiquitous "dad" or "daddy." There is a note of affectionate familiarity here. But there may also be some implicit tendency to patronize: "dad" slides easily into "poor dad."

This brief sketch of developments in our own century has scarcely touched "events" as such. Did the Depression, then, have no effect on fathers *qua* fathers? And the two world wars? And the political turmoil of still recent memory (with its specifically "generational" confrontations)? A short answer would have to be that such events did most certainly affect many individual men in their personal experience as fathers, but did not alter fatherhood as a category of social experience. The Depression attacked, and sometimes shattered, fathers in their central role as providers; but the role itself survived until the return of better times, and flourished thereafter. The wars separated millions of fathers from their families for months or years at a stretch, but the ensuing peacetimes brought a renewal (even a reinforcement) of traditional domestic arrangements. The reform and countercultural movements of the 1960s challenged authority of many sorts—including, and especially, the paternal sort—but with little long-term effect.

Still, this is not to say that fatherhood is wholly uninfluenced by larger currents of change. And two changes, recently begun and still in progress, deserve special notice here. Both bear strongly on the experience of individual fathers; either, or both, may alter the category as well. The first is the entry of women—most strikingly, of married women with small children—into the working world outside the home. The second is the growing incidence of divorce and thus of single parenthood (even, in a small portion of cases, of single *father*hood). As a result of these trends the vast gulf between the experiences of men and women, anchored in more than a century of our history, has finally begun to close. Also, and paradoxically, divorce has led in some cases to an enlarged experience of fatherhood (even where the children involved live primarily with their mother). Indeed, maleness itself (including fatherhood) is increasingly subject to reconsideration of a very elemental sort. The old verities about hard, striving, emotionally invulnerable men seem dubious in fact and distressing in result. And it is precisely these forces that have limited the range and depth of fathering in the past.

Can history help us to visualize the fathers of the future? Could it even yield "lessons" of some value in coping with that future? No lessons in the literal sense but, for those who would welcome further change, a measure of hope—and a caution.

The hope is founded on the plain fact that received models of fatherhood are not writ in the stars or in our genes. Our ancestors knew a very different pattern from our own, and our descendants may well have another that is no less different. Fatherhood, history reminds us, is a cultural invention.

The caution is that all such inventions are deeply rooted in contemporaneous structures of society and culture, of belief and custom, and even of "depth psychology." Thus change in the role, broadly conceived, can only be slow, incremental, painful. Change in individuals may come more quickly, and go deeper—but still within some limits.

As always, history allows us to be hopeful and compels us to be humble, at one and the same time.

V

Clinical Problems and Applications

The editors have determined to close this volume with some clinical excursions, touching on the father's role in psychopathology, on the psychic consequences of bad or deficient fathering, on specific aberrations in fathering, on problems posed by single parenthood, and so forth. Once again, we have not attempted a complete coverage of the field. Nor, given the exploratory nature of the research and theory described in previous chapters, can clinicians prescribe with confidence or certitude presumptive modes of prevention and intervention in contending with these various problems. Nonetheless, cognizance of the depth and complexity of father-child relations and their familial context, and of the importance of fathers, does carry with it practical and, indeed, therapeutic implications. Thus it is fitting, we believe, to conclude by highlighting some of these practicalities.

The first chapter, by Judith Wallerstein and Joan Kelly, condenses their pioneering extensive studies of divorce, which are more fully reported in their recent book, Surviving the Break-up: How Children and Parents Cope with Divorce. *The chapter is quite comprehensive in its own right. Here we would only underscore one point: the discontinuity of father-children relations before and after the break. Clinicians should thus be alerted to the danger of possible deterioration in the father-child relationship, and those charged legally with determining custodianship should entertain the possibility at least of an amelioration in parenting once the father (or mother, for that matter) has been extricated from the tensions and hostilities of a discordant marriage.*

Stanley Cath, an editor of this volume, then turns to a case in point of a child's struggle to come to terms with his father's absence as a consequence of divorce. Many of the strains merely outlined in the previous chapter are brought into living relief. The case has the further advantage of demonstrating the importance and viability of working with our patients as parents, of working preventatively and therapeutically with their chil-

dren, not actually in treatment, much as Freud did with his famed case of "Little Hans."

Brandt Steele, the analyst noted for his comprehensive studies of child abuse, then focuses on the abusive father's inner world. Each abused child, he demonstrates, tends to find a predetermined place in a parent's representational system, one that prompts or seems to satisfy his punitive, sadistic distortion of fathering.

In the next chapter, Irving Kaufman, who in the past has been noted for work with delinquents and their families, looks at another alternative typically deemed an abuse: incest. With their wives (mothers) complicit openly or covertly in the sexual encounter, fathers and their daughters may turn to each other for the only solace and succor possible in a schizoid and unnurturing family climate. Thus a clinically tempered empathy is required in working with all participants in the incestuous act.

Charles Socarides discusses the role of fathers in his chapter on homosexuality. It is a topic that he has studied in depth, hitherto underlining the homosexual's incomplete individuation from his mother and his later search for a compensatory external masculinization through the sexual act with another man. Obviously, a father's abdication or absence, or both, is only one possible etiological factor in sexual disorders of this kind, but a significant one indeed.

Nathaniel Ross, an analyst who has in the past cast a Freudian eye on religion, turns in his chapter to the clinical legacies of "patriarchal" domination and filial submission. One striking feature of the cases reported by him is the sense of inner weakness and effeminacy which the men in question seek to obscure by way of their posturing braggadocio and more pernicious cruelties. The father's sadistic actions and "pseudohypermasculinity" move sons to recoil from embracing their manhood wholeheartedly, yet invite the boys to assume a brittle identification with man merely as aggressor.

Robert Stolorow and Frank Lachmann, who have written extensively on developmental arrests, present a case history of a little girl who lost her father early to a most terrible fate: death in a concentration camp. Their focus on the father has precluded an equal emphasis on the patient's mother. Although the vicissitudes of the holocaust have been beyond their scope, their accent on father-daughter relations and their exploration of the interplay between persons and part objects, or body parts, in a young child's experience are important contributions.

Sheera Samaraweera and Claire Cath, actively concerned with early training and especially prevention, present a case from their Tufts Family Support program. Their work is in quite a different mode from that of the *traditional clinical or analytic consultation. Immersing themselves in the daily life of their "client" during pregnancy and early parenthood, they demonstrate the critical nature of these periods for adult development and thus for the subsequent growth of the child.*

Finally, Julian Ferholt and editor Alan Gurwitt, child psychiatrists, both of whom have directed child psychiatric services, turn to a knotty problem plaguing child work: the exclusion of fathers from treatment. It is fitting that the book should conclude with some attention to the causes and consequences of this most insidious problem. We shall let the chapter speak for itself.

28

The Father-Child Relationship: Changes after Divorce

Judith S. Wallerstein
Joan B. Kelly

One legacy of divorce is discontinuity in the parent-child relationship. The many changes of the separation and divorce, and their extended aftermath, are reflected in unexpected and far-reaching changes in the child's relationship with both parents, and not only illuminate the evolution of the postdivorce family, but also throw light on the parent-child relationship as it occurs within the intact family. In the same way that the clinical setting enables us to learn about normal and psychopathological behaviors by magnifying both psychological stress points and responses, similarly family disruption, by showing us where the lines of cleavage develop within these relationships, enables us to examine their nature more closely and to learn from these cleavage planes about family relationships under normal or less stressful conditions where the component parts, being more firmly in place, conceal the nature of their inner workings.

The parent-child relationships after the marital rupture are not continuous with those that were forged previously. The greatest change occurs in what is, in fact, the altogether new relationship between the visiting parent and the visited child, which has no counterpart in the intact family structure. The nature of this postdivorce visiting relationship is often not predictable from that which existed before. Because discontinuity is most dramatically highlighted in the vicissitudes of this visiting relationship, we have selected it for our focus: its previous history, its evolution into visiting status, and its various forms as crystallized 5 years down the road.

Our research has been supported since 1971 by the Zellerbach Family Fund, San Francisco. The project staff consisted of Judith S. Wallerstein, Ph.D., principal investigator; Joan B. Kelly, Ph.D., co–principal investigator; Angela Homme, Ph.D.; Doris Juvinall Schwartz, M.S.W.; Susannah Roy, M.S.W.; and Janet West, M.S.W. A full report of the project appears in the book *Surviving the Break-up: How Children and Parents Cope with Divorce* by Judith S. Wallerstein and Joan B. Kelly (New York: Basic Books, 1980).

Nature of the Predivorce Parent-Child Relationship

In order to examine divorce-related change, it is important to look back briefly at the relationships that obtained during the failed marriage, and to hold these in mind as a baseline for the ensuing changes. Our findings in this regard are at some variance with the commonly held conception.

A complex balance of psychological forces governs the relationships between parents and children within failing marriages. We soon learned that the parent-child relationship did not mirror the unhappy marital ties, and that the stresses of the marriage did not necessarily spill over into the relations with the children. It is evident from our findings that parenting can swing free, relatively unencumbered by marital unhappiness; or, put technically, parenting can be maintained as a relatively conflict-free sphere of behavior within a very deprived and unhappy marriage. We were interested, in this connection, to discover that men who readily resorted to violence in response to their wives did not necessarily beat or even spank their children. We have found that parenting can be used, appropriately or inappropriately, to offset the marital unhappiness through cultivating a special close relationship with one or more children. On the other hand, we have also found that the parenting capacity can be captured and destroyed by the anger and unhappiness of the adult in the marriage.

In a significant number of conflict-ridden households, the parents were loving and supportive of the children's physical and emotional development.* The quality of father-child relationships ranged from good enough to exceptionally good for at least a fifth of the children. Similarly, the mother-child relationship was good enough, or exceptionally good, for a third of the group. One-quarter of the children had two committed parents. Furthermore, whereas a tiny fraction (only 5 percent) of the married couples were able to communicate well with each other, at least a quarter of the fathers and a third of the mothers were able to communicate very well indeed with their children.

Adults who disagreed strongly with each other about a great many issues were often able to cooperate in the care of their children. Child-rearing issues were not a source of disagreement for over a third of the parents, and half of all the children had experienced relatively consistent handling by both parents. We were sometimes surprised to find as a repeated occurrence that two parents who related poorly to each other were able to share in the parenting and caring function, and to maintain the other partner at his or her best as a parent. For a number of the couples in

---

*The data are taken from a sample of 131 children, aged 3 to 18 years at the time of the marital separation, who came from 60 divorcing families and were followed over 5 years in the Children of Divorce Project, Northern California, 1971–1977.

our study the highest point of adulthood that they had been able to achieve revolved around their parenting functions.

At the other end of the spectrum, over 40 percent of the children had had exceedingly poor relations with their fathers, marked by gross psychopathology or neglect. Some of these men corroded the child's self-esteem; others were physically or sexually abusive. At least a quarter of the mother-child relations were also very poor, marked by serious neglect and threatened abuse. Where physical violence occurred between the parents, children were often witness to the fighting. Physical abuse between the parents, mainly beating of the wife by the husband, was an ongoing part of life for a quarter of the children in this study. Several children lived in terror in the families of habitual violence, worried whether one or both parents would be hurt by the other, or when the police would next be called on to separate the angry parents. Children were also often privy to the sexual acting out of one or both parents in families where this occurred, and provided the audience for the accusations and counteraccusations of promiscuity.

Children brought up in families where the marriages were failing thus had experienced a diversity of relationships, ranging from those emotionally restrained to those rocked by bitter fighting and violence. Some families were isolated and lonely places; others were nurturant and appeared harmonious, and a good quarter of the children did not even know their parents were unhappy in their marriage. Children from these different kinds of families thus came to the divorce with different views of what was at stake as well as varying ideas about what they stood to lose.

Nature of the Postdivorce Father-Child Relationship

Although different custodial arrangements are emerging throughout the country, the dominant shape of the postdivorce family in the 1970s has been that of the custodial mother with whom the children reside, and the father who has visitation rights. We shall be describing, therefore, the visiting father. We should stress, however, that the characteristics we describe are not primarily, in our view, sex linked. Our experience points to their being tied only in part to the sex of the visiting parent, and just as much, or perhaps more, to the visiting role.

We begin with Wendy. A year after her parents separated, 5-year-old Wendy recognized the interviewer, greeted her warmly, and spent most of the hour playing a lively and exciting fantasy game she called, "Wait till your daddy comes home." The story was about a household full of people (dolls in the dollhouse), all of whom kiss, jump for joy, and dance around with gay abandon when the daddy doll comes home. Wendy volunteered that she sees her father a lot "because he loves us so much." She said that he would return to live with them when he (the father) was all grown up. Noting a little ivory Buddha as she left, the child rubbed its belly, making a secret wish which she then immediately confided to the interviewer: that her father would return home.

The child's fantasy was not nourished by the father's behavior toward her. Wendy's father visited infrequently, and his interest in his children was secondary to his own concerns. Wendy's mother, a highly competent businesswoman, worked full-time, as she had throughout the marriage. The children were cared for by a devoted housekeeper who was referred to, on occasion, as "mommy." Nevertheless, the child's undiminished, and perhaps intensified, hope for the return of the departed father emerges clearly in this vivid fantasy play. Powered by her passionate oedipal strivings, which had continued in full force and, in fact, had become more intense since her father's departure, Wendy's statement that "He will return when he is grown up" mirrors her hope that she will live with him when *she* is grown up.

Seen again at age 7 years by the same interviewer, Wendy had grown into a tall and graceful child. Asked for her three wishes, she responded gravely, "I would like to see you a whole lot more; I would like to see my daddy a whole lot more; I would like my mom and daddy to get married again." The child's yearning for her father appears to have persisted, encapsulated by the ego achievement and growth of early latency, but essentially undimmed by time and undiscouraged by the father's erratic and still infrequent visits.

To Wendy and the other children we followed, visiting and the continued contact with the absent father were crucial issues, both at the time of the separation and during the years that ensued. The parent-child relationship and its significance to the child outlives the marriage and continues during and after the divorce. By his or her presence or absence, the visiting parent remains central to the psychic functioning of the children, and separation at a critical time in the child's development may indeed intensify the child's psychological tie and commitment to the relationship.

Effects of Father's Absence and Departure

A potent force links the child's self-esteem with continued contact with the father in the postdivorce family. At the 18-month follow-up mark, and again at 4 to 5 years afterward, we found a significant connection between low self-esteem and depression in the child, and continued disappointment with the father's infrequent or erratic visiting. Conversely, we found, especially emerging at the 4- to 5-year mark, a significant tie between high self-esteem and good ego functioning in the child and a good father-child relationship at that time.

To most children the father's visits soon represent the depth of his love and commitment. Especially in the period immediately following the separation, the frequency of the visiting itself becomes a significant measure, and the children keep careful count.

The father's departure from the household is an extraordinary event. For the many children who feared abandonment by their father following the separation (about half of our sample), the continuity and the frequency of the visiting provided the desperately needed assurance of his continued interest. For others, especially the younger ones, the departed father appeared to have a somewhat disembodied quality and, like the father of the Chagall painting, he appeared to be hovering somewhere in space over the roof of the house, without fiddle and without joy. One 7-year-old boy, who had been told that his father had moved to Oakland, looked worried for days and finally confessed his profound confusion, asking whether Oakland was in Mexico, and where, indeed, was Mexico. Therefore, for many children, the visit from the father and the visit to the father to locate where he is in space—and that indeed he *is*, and has a bed, and a refrigerator—are immensely important in allaying the intense anxieties of the postseparation period.

Differences Between Pre- and Postdivorce Relationships

Despite the urgency of the children's request for visiting and the intensity of their yearning, we have found a striking and unexpected discontinuity between the predivorce father-child relationship and what continues into the postdivorce period. The new visiting relationship, although presumably rooted psychologically in the former relationship between father and child, often fails to reflect the continuity that psychological theory, developed from study of the intact family, has led us to expect. Thus men who had been close to their children during the marriage and had spent time with them failed to visit or arrived infrequently and irregularly. Conversely, other previously distant fathers, who had hardly acknowledged their children during the marriage or were frequently irritated by their presence, began to visit with a regularity that surprised both their children and us.

The visiting relationship has no counterpart within the intact family. Its parameters, its limitations, and its potentialities are new and remain to be explored.

The Phenomenon of Funneling. Following the marital separation, an abrupt break in the continuity of their daily contact, the father and child must without rehearsal or guiding script adapt their feelings and mutual needs within the narrow confines of a visit. Their success or failure to construct a relationship under the severe constraints imposed by the visits will determine the course of their future together. We conceptualize this process as a *funneling*, which requires complex and sometimes exquisite maneuvers from the several participants. The difficulties inherent in this compressive or funneling process have been insufficiently appreciated. If anything, the courts and the embattled partners and their respective attorneys have directed their energies toward imposing restrictions and conditions that further encumber a relationship which, under even the best of circumstances, requires care and encouragement.

From the outset the relationship consists of the practical problem of where to go and what to do, the bewildering sense of no place to go and no idea of what to do. This is sometimes compounded by the combined presence of children of different ages and colliding interests, by the absence of the mother who had often served as interpreter of the children's needs. Many fathers found these practical problems, at first, insurmountable. What to do with young children needing nurturing care? Or with older children who appeared to need continual stimulation and entertainment in order to stem their restlessness? Some confused men changed their entire routine for the children's visits; others changed nothing; and others, equally perplexed, expected the children to take full responsibility for the agenda. "I feel like a camp director," said one exhausted father.

Adaptation to the Visiting Father's Role. The broad parameters of the new role were also unclear. To what extent is the visiting father a guest, a favorite uncle, or a parent? More explicitly, to what extent does the visiting parent continue to take responsibility for setting behavior and moral standards? To what extent does he register approval or disapproval, or enforce discipline or even homework, and how can he do so without the built-in safeguards and bedtime rituals of intact family life, which mute disappointment and soften anger and provide safe channels for alleviating the inevitable conflicts and frustrations of the relationship? Hurt feelings are more likely to continue, and misunderstandings are more likely to remain unclarified. Men who were accustomed to commanding their children experienced a new sense of impotence and frustration. All of these complexities combine to keep the father's sense of who he now is unsettled and unsettling.

Changed Sense of Time. The sense of time as a component of the parent-child relationship has also changed. For parents and children who share the repeated tasks of daily living together, time is part of the unobtrusive background of family life and provides a steady muted rhythm that, by its very unobtrusiveness, conveys the comforting notion that the present will endure. For the visiting parent and child, time is a jarring presence. The constraints of time and space may impose a severe burden or, in some instances, a welcome limit on the interactions of the relationship. Both parent and child must now find time for their meeting and must part on time. Both meeting and parting have acquired new meanings, and also accompanying anxieties that may long endure.

Other Stress Factors. Many other factors also threaten the fragile relationship and generate stress. At this time children take on special significance as economic or psychological burdens whose presence is resented; as important sources of self-esteem whose reassurance is sought and whose absence is feared; as friends, needed helpmates, and even counselors during lonely, stressful decision-making times; as prizes to be fought over; as the only reliable allies in the marital battles. The complex dependence of adults on children for their own self-esteem is especially apparent as fathers become vulnerable to their children in new ways that sometimes radically change the balance of the relationship. A quarter of the men were afraid of rejection by their children. They were worried about the children's disapproval and anger because of the divorce. In addition, over a third of parents were in active competition with each other for the affection and loyalty of their children.

Men were uneasy about what to do with their lovers at visiting time. How would their children and the developing relationship with the woman be affected by her presence? They did not know how to arrange for privacy in close quarters, and they often failed abysmally to understand or to be aware of the consequences of their own behavior or to anticipate the children's response:

Mr. Z. had a large waterbed in his apartment, which he and his 7-year-old daughter shared during her weekend visits. Occasionally, when he invited a woman friend to join them, he peremptorily sent the child to an adjoining room for the night, replacing her with his friend. He was annoyed and mystified by the child's tearful protestations.

Visiting parents also found that the visit itself became an arena that readily evoked in both parents the ghosts of the failed marriage and the fantasies of what might have been. Raw feelings of both marital partners are exacerbated by these visits even without contact between former spouses, or when the contact is fleeting. The visit is an intense, multi-determined event, which is continually available for replaying of anger, jealousy, love, mutual rejection, and longing between the divorcing adults. Although the majority of parents tried to honor the children's visiting time, a fifth of the women saw no use in the father's visits and actively tried to sabotage each meeting. This fighting between parents reached pathological, even bizarre, intensity. One gently bred matron smeared dog feces on her husband's face when he arrived to see his children. A third of the children were consistently exposed to intense anger at visiting time. The tension generated by the parents burdened the visits and caused stress to everyone involved.

Psychological Complications. Parallel to the external complications of setting up the visiting patterns, subtle inner psychological forces had a profound influence on the nature and frequency of the visiting relationship, and contributed to its fragility. Both the father's own psychological conflicts and, more important, the father's feelings about the divorce were at stake. The father's role in the divorce decision, his eagerness for or vigorous opposition to ending the marriage, were crucial influences in determining the future of the visiting relationship. Contrary to what many children believe, the pattern of visiting immediately following the separation is not an accurate reflection of the father's love. Indeed, what makes the visits difficult are the father's many psychological dilemmas, not necessarily directly related to his feelings about his children.

Men depressed following the divorce found it painful to visit their children and often did so irregularly or not at all. Their children rarely understood this and experienced the inconstancy as the father's lack of interest in seeing them. The depression that frequently occurs following divorce is a serious hazard to establishing a continuing relationship. Fathers who had been rejected by their wives often expected the same from their children. Men preoccupied with their own shame, grief, lowered self-esteem, even their own expendability, found that visits with their children deepened their depressions by bringing back painful memories of the marriage and its disruption. Some depressed men lacked the energy to mobilize themselves for the stresses and demands of the visit. Visits occasionally brought a flare-up of somatic or other depressive symptoms, such as increased drinking, which lasted for days after the child returned home.

Men who felt consciously or unconsciously guilty at having ended the marriage had great trouble initiating and maintaining visits with their children. This group included fathers who had been devoted to their children and where, in fact, the preexisting father-child relation had had a special importance because the deprivations within the marital relationship had brought father and children together. The father's guilt was often profound at having left an especially strong parent-child relationship. Others felt guilt at leaving their children with a psychologically disturbed or otherwise incompetent mother, or to pursue a different lifestyle or lover.

Guilt had a twofold effect, leading either to a decline in visiting or to a flurry of visiting immediately following the marital separation, but not sustained. A decline in visits, owing to the father's guilt, further reinforced the guilt and led the father deeper into his impasse. It was not uncommon for fathers to project their guilt onto the children, to magnify moderate misbehaviors of the children, and to find in these the justification for discontinuing their visits. One such father referred with irritation to the bourgeois values of his 5-year-old child, a child he had cared for tenderly during the marriage.

Characteristics of the Successful Visiting Relationship

All these factors were counterbalanced by the passionate, persistent yearning of the children, especially those under the age of 9 years; by the commitment of many fathers to their children; and by the interests of about half of the women in maintaining the visits. Thus the visiting relationship that successfully outlived the marriage reflected, not so much the character of the predivorce relationship, but the father's motivation, the child's motivation, and the psychological capacity of fathers and children to adapt flexibly to the new conditions. It was usually those men who could bend to the complex logistics of the visiting; who could deal with the women's anger and the children's capriciousness, without withdrawing; who could involve the children in their planning; who could walk a middle ground between totally rearranging their schedule and not changing their schedule at all; and who felt less stressed and freer to parent, who continued to visit regularly and frequently.

Other factors led fathers to visit frequently: concern for children who had been left in the care and custody of depressed or psychologically troubled women; fathers who were lonely, psychologically intact, and not depressed; fathers who were economically secure and educated; fathers with young children; fathers whose children were not angry at them; and fathers and families where the relationship between the parents had calmed down and was no longer marked by intense animosity. All tended to visit more, although the mother's attitude toward the visiting was a factor of fading significance over time. Finally, it is reasonable to assume that the interventions of our project played a significant role in encouraging the father to visit more frequently and in facilitating the development of better relations with the children.

Nature of Relationships 4 to 5 Years Postdivorce

The patterns that emerged 4 to 5 years after the separation are not concordant with the widespread community expectation that contacts between fathers and children tend to drop away steeply. Although the external dimensions of the visiting, the frequency and length of time spent together, do not capture the entirety of the parent-child relationship, such measures nevertheless do provide a baseline for assessing continuity and change over the years.

Frequency of Visits

Most of the men continued at 4 to 5 years postdivorce to visit their children. At that time, three-quarters of the fathers continued to reside within an hour's drive of their children. Less than 10 percent lived more than an hour away by air travel.

A quarter of the children were visited once a week or more. Forty percent were visited once a month or more, usually once or twice a month. An additional 10 percent saw their children on vacations and holidays because of geographical distance. About a fifth of the children were visited erratically and infrequently, an average of once every few months or less. Ten percent of the children had no visits at all. Over the 4 years there was a general decrease but no precipitous decline. For a small group there was an increase over time. Most of the children were happy to visit with their fathers. A small subgroup rejected the overtures and refused the visits. Overall, a quarter of the children were continually disappointed by the father's disinterest, which they related to his insufficient visiting.

Visiting Patterns

We turn now to a brief consideration of some of the visiting parent-child patterns that emerged at the 4- to 5-year postseparation mark. By this time it was apparent to us that the relationship had settled into a number of patterns, that new factors had helped to shape these, and that there were new consequences for parents and children. The visiting pattern itself is no longer of overriding importance, in part because the children are older and the fear of abandonment is no longer central. What emerges rather at this time are two sets of considerations. The first concerns those children who *are* visited, with whatever frequency or pattern. The issue here is the extent to which the ongoing father-child relationship continues to contribute to the child's unfolding development. In effect, to what extent and in what ways is the visiting father still a parent and what kind of a parent is he? Alternatively, are there visiting relationships that are destructive rather than helpful in impact, or perhaps of little influence? The second consideration concerns children where visiting has enormously diminished or even stopped: What is the impact of the father's absence?

At the 4- to 5-year mark we found several broad categories. Within the framework of a visiting relationship, many were good, but the majority were impoverished or had failed to keep pace developmentally, or both. Among the one-quarter who were visited insufficiently or not at all, the majority yearned to see their father; but there was a smaller group who actively rebuffed the father's wish to visit. An additional group were children whose visiting father was psychiatrically ill, a fact that posed a particular kind of problem.

Helpful Visiting Fathers

Despite all the perils of the visiting parent-child relationship which we have presented, at the 4- to 5-year mark some 30 percent of the total sample of the children had fathers who played a significant parenting role in their lives. Lacking the full authority of the parent in situ, these men had by dint of sustained effort and capacity succeeded in earning or maintaining a respected place in their children's lives. Because they lacked both daily contact and direct authority to intervene, their role was limited compared with that of a custodial parent. Moreover, the role had its price within the father's second marriage. However, these men maintained a presence that could be used as needed, as a separate resource, which lent greater security to their children. These children, in turn, had made good developmental progress and been spared the acute sense of rejection that other children suffered.

The demands of this role were not light. Most of the men who survived its tests over time not only were seriously committed to their children, but had the emotional maturity and the psychological intactness to perform well within a relatively ambiguous role and in the absence of a coherent family structure. On the other hand, they were not necessarily psychologically astute or people of unusual sensitivity. Although the group included blue-collar workers as well as professional men, and many worked long hours during the week, none held two jobs and all had some leisure to commit to seeing their children. Perhaps most important in terms of the significance, especially to the older child and adolescent, these men were able to build a relationship that, by its very nature, supported the child's continued growth toward maturity and independence. By not binding the child to a previous dependency, by establishing a relatively new base for the relationship outside the confines of the family home, founded on a mutuality of shared interests and affection, these visiting fathers came to be identified in their children's minds with growing up. A good number of these children in fact modeled their career choices after their fathers. With the younger children, the father at his best provided a second home and a relationship that was often less stressful than that with the custodial parent.

461

Shirley, an 11-year-old pragmatist whose parents were divorced when she was 7, reflected 4 years later about her parents' divorce. "I didn't want my parents to get a divorce, but they weren't happy so they probably needed it. But I get to see my dad so I don't miss him. It's not better, but it's not any worse." Shirley spent every other weekend at her father's home and called him or saw him informally in between. Actually, she and her father were much closer following the divorce than they had been during the marriage, and she did not feel deprived.

These fathers were a mixed group with regard to history of their relations with their children during the preexisting marriage. Some had been close to their children in the predivorce family and had then successfully negotiated the treacherous currents of the visiting relationships. Others had hardly known their children, had spent most of their time away from the household during the years of the unhappy marriage, and had only begun to be close to the child after the separation. Still others were galvanized into a new awareness of their children by their own anguish at the time of the marital separation, especially their sense of an impending loss of a relationship they had theretofore taken for granted. A small number found the very limits imposed by the visiting more congenial than the constant exposure during the marriage.

In addition, some fathers were able to make a special effort to remain active in their children's lives in conscious recognition of the distress and disorganization of the custodial mother. Where the custodial mother was not too distraught, the visiting could be helpful and in supplementary ways strengthen the children or provide the mother with needed relief. Given a more severely disturbed or disorganized mother, the constraints of the visiting severely inhibited the help the father, however devoted, could provide. A good father-child relationship within the framework of visiting is not sufficient to sustain the child's development if the relationship with the custodial parent is poor. Even at its best, the role of the visiting parent remains psychologically secondary and supplemental.

Poor Visiting Relationships

In almost half of the total sample, the relationships of the children with their fathers, all of whom were visiting, but with exceedingly varied patterns, had become emotionally less nutrient, offering little or no help to the children in addressing the complex developmental tasks of childhood and adolescence. Approximately half of these poor relationships had been poor during the marriage and merely continued their previous course. An equal number had ranged from outstanding to good enough during the marriage, but had deteriorated markedly in quality during the subsequent years, despite the continuity of contact.

Ironically, the visiting itself appeared to increase the possibility of fixation of the relationship to the mode and level that had been attained at the time of the marital rupture. Our findings suggest that somewhat less than half of these relationships had kept pace developmentally with the child's growth. In a good number of these high-contact but relatively impoverished father-child relationships, child and parent continued to perceive each other as each had appeared at the time of the separation, and to respond accordingly. One father still held his 8-year-old daughter in his lap at the dinner table; she had been 3½ years old when the marriage ended. We suggest that parent-child relations that evolve within the matrix of the growing family are conducive to more flexible growth than a visiting structure, which can easily acquire a fixed and stereotyped quality. The visiting parent is often less perceptive, less interested in change or aware of change, or may need to make time stand still because of his own unresolved conflicts. The intensive time and space constraints of the visiting relation and the absence of the modifying presence of the other parent may create a climate that fosters a regressive relationship between parent and child, one that runs counter to the child's developmental needs.

Mr. C. began to visit his daughter immediately after the marital separation. He was motivated in part by his genuine concern regarding the mother's disorganization, and he saw his role as that of a stabilizing influence on the child. During the 4 years following the separation, Mr. C. visited every weekend without fail. Seen at 13 years of age (4 years after the divorce), Kim, giggling, said, "My daddy, he's so sweet; he's a cutie, I adore him, I could eat him up. I do everything for him. He's just perfect in everything he says and does." This child looks forward with high excitement to the weekly visits and dinner at a restaurant as the highlight of her week, which was otherwise without much interest for her in school or with her peers. She was immature in her general deportment and becoming increasingly obese.

Some father-child relationships that we deemed poor during the postdivorce years were very similar in form and quality to the relations that had obtained during the marriage. These fathers could not be reliably counted on; on the other hand, they could not be discounted in the event of a pressing need or an emergency. They did not reject their children but remained somewhere in the background as inconstant figures. Although they played an insignificant parenting role, we found them nevertheless an important presence to their children, who continued to be attached to them. They gave little and little was expected of them; when they did give, they met with real gratitude, and the children often held them in real affection over the years. Moreover, their continued presence, reassuring even if inconstant, served to ward off for these children a sense of complete loss and of consequent depression.

Six years after the divorce we interviewed Edward, age 14 years, who, despite the fact that his father had hardly been home throughout the marriage, told us, "The divorce made me go bananas. I would still wish it never happened, but I suppose not having all that yelling is better." Asked whether he sees his father much, the boy said, "No, not very much—once a month." He then brightened, adding, "Dad came up yesterday and took me out for a prime rib dinner." At that time Edward had serious school problems and had just been arrested for shoplifting, but it had not occurred to him that any of these problems would be of concern to his father.

Many of the youngsters who had poor relations with visiting fathers did quite well over the years within the framework of a nurturant, competent mother and, sometimes, stepfather. The children as a group did not suffer the sense of having been rejected by their father. They were, however, almost entirely dependent on the sometimes strained capacities of the custodial parent, as well as the availability of other supports, and their own resourcefulness in utilizing these. There were a number of other patterns of poor father-child relationships, including those related to the remarriage of the father, but we must turn now to what happened when the father was absent.

Disinterested or Rejecting Fathers. The psychological development of children who are visited infrequently or not at all because of the father's disinterest or active rejection during the years after the divorce seems to be severely burdened. The great majority of these unwanted children, who amounted to a quarter of the total group, experienced intense and continuing disappointment, and their self-esteem was seriously diminished. The younger children were most vulnerable, and many became depressed, showing different symptomatic behaviors including obesity, poor learning, and pervasively sad affect. At the 18-month postdivorce mark, this response was seen primarily among little boys; at 4 to 5 years postdivorce, we found it among boys *and* girls between the ages of 7 and 12 years. For the adolescents, the same connection between continuing disappointment and low self-esteem was present, but weaker. There seemed no question that the absence or disruption of contact with the father will exercise a chilling effect on children's self-esteem. The most stressed were those children whose relations with the father during the preexisting marriage had been loving; the blow seemed an impossible one for the child to absorb. Young boys seemed to be the most vulnerable to this effect.

Children struggled hard to explain and to understand the father's disinterest. They missed good fathers, they missed not such good fathers, and they missed very poor fathers. They continued to yearn for many years. Some youngsters employed poignant and vivid fantasies to fill the emptiness they experienced in their lives. Others were bitterly angry, referring to their fathers caustically. "He has time for everything but me. I'm sure not waiting for him anymore." The anger spilled into their relations with peers and teachers and, at adolescence, brought some into conflict with the law and into sexual acting out.

Bobby, aged 8 years at the 4-year mark, had been seeing his father, who lived a few blocks away, irregularly and sometimes only for a few minutes at a time over the years. The clinician reported, "I asked Bobby if he was seeing his father. He looked blank and became suddenly vague and difficult to understand. A police car went by just then with the siren screaming. (Bobby's father is a policeman.) The child lapsed into a preoccupied silence. I waited a few moments and suggested gently that the police car had reminded him of his father. Bobby started to cry and continued to sob without stopping for a full 35 minutes."

Exceptions to this intense continued longing for the father sometimes occurred with those youngsters who felt rejected in the postdivorce family by a father who had rejected them, demeaned them, or abused them during the intact marriage. These youngsters sometimes had an easier road and then seemed able, by their own efforts and with the help of a competent mother and sometimes a good stepfather, to strike out for themselves, especially at adolescence, with some verve and independence, and to turn their back on their father and counterreject him. Where this occurred, the divorce was clearly beneficial in its physical separation of the psychologically disordered father from daily contact with his children. A central issue in the ability of such children to separate themselves from a traumatic or a nonexistent visiting relationship was in the capacity to disidentify with the father and to achieve a sense of individuated psychic integrity and therefore of restored self-esteem.

Rejecting Children

The final category, to be very briefly mentioned, included a small group of children in our sample who from their side rejected their father although he wished to visit them frequently. These children shared the bitter anger of their mothers, and we were impressed with the staying power of this anger over many years.

Larry and his sister were both devastating as they mimicked their father's efforts to woo his children and elicit their interest in his visiting. Then, in sober reflection, Larry, now age 14 years, said, "My father has to understand that when he shoots arrows at my mother they first have to go through our bodies before they reach her. Tell him," they said, "there's no hope at all."

Active rejection of parents by children was rarely seen as clearly in the intact family, which brings us full cycle to our conclusion.

Conclusions

We have, in this all-too-brief review, attempted to capture some of the salient points of the changing relationship with the noncustodial parent at three different junctures: in its diversity in the predivorce family; in the discontinuity associated with the complex funneling process and associated psychological fragility of the visiting relationship; and in the changed and changing diversity of relationships at the 4- to 5-year mark.

Psychological theory and clinical wisdom have conceptualized the parent-child relationship within the intact marriage as broadly continuous, subject to fluctuation by virtue of the vicissitudes of the child's development and the echoes and residues of childhood conflict evoked anew in the parent by the child's developmental progression. This theory and wisdom have dealt as well with the absent parent, primarily within the framework of the effects of loss and mourning on the child's psychological development. Our findings suggest the need for new models to conceptualize the phenomena in divorced families marked by altered continuities, unexpected discontinuities, and new kinds of relationships: those of visiting parent and visited child or part-time parent and part-time child. We are back to fundamental questions of continuity and discontinuity of human relationships and their internal representations.

29

Divorce and the Child: "The Father Question Hour"

Stanley H. Cath

The little boy Jeff whose quest for a father during the first 5 years of life is reported here was never seen in therapy, although I met him on one occasion in my waiting room and was most favorably impressed with him.

After a divorce had become a foregone conclusion, the mother became my patient while in her final trimester of pregnancy, and continued for the first 5 years of the boy's life. This, then, is an example of "intervention psychoanalytic psychotherapy" of a vulnerable child carried on through the parent.

For a child, one of life's greatest tragedies is the loss of a parent. Such loss brings conscious and unconscious pain that is often felt throughout a lifetime. To desensitize the loss and master the void pose one of the greatest challenges to the child's further ego development.

The story of Jeff illustrates vividly and concretely some of the problems facing both mother and child as the latter perceives and then conceptualizes his or her loss. We will see how it is not just external traumata that determine the outcome of loss in terms of eventual ego strength or weakness, but, more often, how events are handled by the victims; how resolution is usually achieved not through one single explanation or one set of attitudes, but rather through the day-to-day adjustment in family interaction. A continual conscious and unconscious interpretation of how the loss has been experienced may finally bring some understanding of the puzzling question, "Why did it happen to me (or to us)?," an open question in that it contains the potential of a frightening undermining of self-esteem. Indeed, such day-to-day handling of the problems created by loss may provide eventually for a resolution of that haunting question, "What happened to my father?," which can be answered, at best, only qualifiedly and then only with some degree of acceptance by those whose ego strength has grown despite their pain and vulnerability. The loss of a parent usually brings a temporary or permanent regression with varying degrees of ego impairment; in some cases, it may prove to be an impetus toward achievement and creative effort, for in the resolution of his or her grief, the child may forge new strengths while trying to repair the wounds. In the process the child needs to maintain faith in the growing capacity of his or her own ego, as well as in the stability of his or her residual surrounding world.

This story might never have assumed its particular interest had not two preconditions existed: an intelligent mother, alert to her young son's needs and courageous enough to acknowledge them; and an intelligent child natively endowed so that he was able to respond to the mother.

The Dawning Awareness of Something Missing

Although the separation of his parents was not culminated until he was a year old, Jeff rarely saw his father after his first 6 months. The only visible sign he gave of remembering that someone else had lived in his home came when he was about 9 months old; toward evening, if he heard the outer door of the apartment house open, he would turn toward the door as if expecting someone to enter. This sign, which his mother took to mean that he was "missing someone," was apparent for only a few weeks. There were two or three more visits from his father, but they ceased shortly before his second birthday. Nevertheless, before this time, much conversation about his father flowed all around Jeff.

Awareness of the Meaning of Divorce: A Double Loss

Grief, as a human asset, permits us eventually to reach a relative emotional detachment from the painful feeling of loss and of memories of the past, in order that we may live more in the present and direct our energies to new sources of love, approval, and affection. It is generally assumed, not always correctly, that a year is needed to detach oneself from old objects and begin new relationships.

However, the process of mourning, whatever its time span, brings with it special problems for the divorced parent living with a child. More often than not, the mother (or the father) is not capable of giving much love to others. Absorbed by the loss, sometimes attributing that loss to personal failure, the remaining parent has little energy to love or to empathize with the child, especially if the child resembles the lost object in any way. The child then feels a double loss. Sensing the withdrawal of the parent into depression or into self-centered bitterness, the child may feel a confirmation of his or her own badness and lack of value or worth.

For the child, as for the primitive human, death or depression related to loss does not come about by chance, or by "natural means." In his unconscious, fears of being abandoned are activated by threats of withdrawal in everyday life. If such loss is threatened, if fantasies are realized, then the cause must be guilt-laden needs, wishes, or both, or some wrongdoing. The haunting and ponderous questions, "Why did this happen to me? Why did my father or my mother go away? What could I have done to prevent it? Did I lack something in giving or in demanding too much?," are universal manifestations of attempts to put things in some form of perspective that will leave one whole.

Early Awareness of Mother and Father Differences
Although it is impossible to know how soon a child forms mental representations of the differences between mother and father, it has been reported that infants as young as a few weeks of age seem to respond differently, quantitatively and qualitatively, to the footsteps or the voices of their parents (Chap. 6). Fairly convincing arguments can be presented for "preverbal conceptual mental representations" of both mother and father well within the first few months, if not weeks, of life. Before 12 weeks of age, a child usually does not seem to be presented with overwhelming problems should a loving mother be substituted, but it is unquestionable that after this age, mother becomes increasingly indispensable and focused on. Even though father may be increasingly significant, as evidenced by specific responses to him, the presence of mother becomes increasingly more essential and her interaction more difficult to interrupt or to replace. Whether as an infant Jeff "realized" the early loss of his father as a specific presence or memory can never be known.

A Later Awareness of Fatherlessness and the Beginning
of the Search for a Father
In all likelihood, a toddler may not consciously remember a parent who has been away. Mother's willingness to let herself be questioned repeatedly about Jeff's lost father, her unflinching honesty and candor in the face of his persistent need for a male figure, mark moments of significant choices. In addition to signifying her own refusal to turn entirely inward or away from the loss, they allowed her small son to develop greater freedom in verbalizing his needs. But she also invited him to participate in establishing greater freedom in mutual grieving for a man, thus creating a freedom for both in their relationship. A rejection of Jeff's questions might well have resulted in distorting his development.

In fact, Jeff's mother's deliberate search for new relationships was yet another important option for both mother and child. There were, of course, awkward moments. At about 2 years of age, Jeff seemed to become especially aware of men and became markedly attached to his only uncle and to Peter, a neighbor. Both men had a child about Jeff's age. His mother noticed that when he was with these children they seemed openly more possessive of their fathers and talked constantly about their "daddies." Jeff's failure to participate in this kind of conversation indicated to his mother bewilderment, which she interpreted as his awareness of loss, or at least of "not having something." She shared his pain when, in his presence, her friends took care not to use the word "daddy" when speaking with their children. If the word sometimes slipped out, she was conscious of the long silences or side glances. She sensed self-conscious embarrassment often felt in the presence of a fatherless child. The lump in the throat, she said, was for both of them, a lump that decreased in size as time wore on, but never entirely disappeared. Her ever-present willingness to recognize Jeff's unhappiness is evidence of her own refusal to give in to self-pity, and it was clearly an important factor in the ongoing lively interaction between her and her son.

It was apparent to her long before Jeff could verbalize the concept of "fatherlessness" that he realized other children had something he lacked. As soon as he was able to talk clearly, some time after 2 years of age, she learned that his sense of difference had indeed been translated into feelings of deprivation and loss.

Bedtime and the Father Question Hour

Jeff did what most children do when afraid to talk of their feelings: He introduced the subject that was closest to his heart by using safer substitutes or displaced objects. One night while preparing for bed, he heard Peter's daughter, the upstairs neighbor, crying. "Is Jane crying for her daddy?" he asked. "It sounds that way," his mother replied. "Is Jane's daddy home?" was the next question, betraying that his real concern was with daddy being home. The many questions about Jane's daddy following questions to which they already knew the answers, revealed to his mother that this was his way of wanting more or different kinds of answers for himself. She finally asked, "Is there something you would like to ask me?"

Thus began what we came to call the "father question hour." It was a time for questions and answers, of open and honest dialogue between mother and child which usually, but not always, took place at bedtime when play and activity were not so available to distract or to stem or neutralize anxiety. Jeff's mother, as if sensing their importance, began to keep a record of these sessions.

Jeff's response was an immediate yes, followed by, "Where is my daddy? Why doesn't he stay here the way the other daddies do?"

Mother: Because we are divorced, and he lives somewhere else.

Jeff: What is "divorced" mean?

Mother: Sometimes when two people get married, they find out that they didn't love each other and would be happier living apart or being married to someone else. The divorce was between your father and myself, and you had nothing to do with it. Your father wants you to be very happy, just as I do.

Jeff: Does he live far away from here?

Mother: Not very far away, but he lives away from here.

Jeff: Where?

Mother: In an apartment.

Jeff: Will he come to see us?

Mother: No, we both thought that since we would be happier living apart, it would be better to start again. That is why I date, so we can find a man we will love, and who will love us. You can kind of pick your own daddy, won't that be fun?

Jeff: Did Karen [his cousin] and Janie [Peter's child] pick out their daddies?

Mother: No, but your other friend, Louise, can pick out her daddy because her parents are divorced too.

Coping with Realized Loss of Father

She thought that his struggle to grasp the concept of divorce would be aided by his knowing of another child in a similar situation. Again and again he sought to understand "separation," "not living with us," and in his bedtime questioning indicated a regressive clinging and a need for mastering his mother and his situation. Although one might question the wisdom of promising him that he "might pick his own daddy," she felt it was a promise that truly made him different in a "superior" way from his small friends and that it seemed to bring him important support. The fact that the promise later "came true" tended to augment Jeff's sense of omnipotence. At least it gave him an answer for his friends: "I am looking for a daddy and I can pick my own."

Children of Jeff's age can be most concrete. Everyone must live somewhere, and since trains are for going away and daddy was away, Jeff understandably concluded, "My father lives on the train tracks." That he was trying to place his father in space as he tried to comprehend the concept of "living or not living with mother" is seen in his question: "How come I'm living with just you?"

Mother: Because your father and I are divorced.

Jeff: Why didn't I live with him?

Mother: Aren't you happy living with me?

"Then," wrote his mother, "pulling my emotions together for the time being, I added to that overly sensitive, guilt-ridden question of mine, 'Also, Jeff, your father works all day and mothers usually take care of the children.' Jeff said, 'I want to live with you, all of us together, I mean.'"

Jeff's immediate sensitivity to the hurt he had given his mother did not go unnoticed. "I would venture to say," she commented,

This conversation was not exactly my finest hour! Inside I was screaming (to myself). Here I was, left alone with the child, to explain why he can't see his father; left to make the excuses. I knew I wouldn't hurt Jeff that badly to tell him that his father just couldn't care. And yet, I couldn't be a martyr, and take all the blame my son would most understandably place on me. I had to learn that nothing I could say would be the right thing, because Jeff was not in a right or normal situation. But I could say the wrong thing! Somehow, I had to find a middle ground where I could be honest with Jeff, without deliberately hurting him or his opinion of himself. I would try to have us live together with as little resentment as possible.

Children of Jeff's age can abandon painful reality as easily as they can sometimes be most concretely aware of it. In his attempt to cope with the fact of fatherlessness, Jeff revealed his need to secure a family for himself. He and his friend Louise began to call each other brother and sister. He called other men "daddy." At this age, ego boundaries can be diffuse and separate identities easily interwoven. His maternal grandfather had recently died. In the small boy's mind, his mother's father and his own father were one and the same, and the death of one explained the absence of the other:

Jeff: Who is that man in the picture?
Mother: Your Grandpa, Jeff, and my father.
Jeff: Where is he now? Why did he go away?
Mother: He died because he was very sick and he's with God now. You have his name because you were named after him.
Jeff: He is my father, too, because my father is dead.
Mother: No, this is your grandfather; your father did not die.
Jeff: No, my father is dead, too.

A Child's Narcissistic Demands on a Divorced Mother

Jeff's anger made him very emphatic, but his mother insisted on the truth. "I gave the same answer as the previous one, just a little more definite sounding." Around the same 2- to 3-year-old stage, he openly resented his mother's leaving at any time. His distress (lightened for a moment by his unconscious pun and his mother's laughter) was evident in a dialogue that was almost typical of this period:

Jeff: Are you going out tonight?
Mother: Yes, I am going out on a date.
Jeff: I want to be your date and go out too!
Mother: You're my son, but we still go places together.
Jeff: Do I shine?

His mother wrote,

> This was too much, and I laughed as I tried to explain the difference between *son* and *sun*. I had to reassure him many times that I would not just "go away." I knew I felt guilty about hurting him by insisting that I also needed a life of my own. But I forced myself to go, knowing that the outcome would be tragic if I didn't.
>
> I learned he would manage to be rather rude to my dates, if he was in a certain mood. I had tried to make it a big treat for him to meet my new friends, but it obviously wasn't. For example, coming home from a date with a man Jeff had met several times and had seemed to particularly like, I would find my son still awake. As I said goodnight to my date at the front door, we heard him happily singing out from the other room, "damn, damn, damn" over and over again! I hadn't heard anything like this from Jeff before and I didn't make too much of it right then. I couldn't help laughing, but the man was appalled. That was the last time I ever saw him.

This comic scene was truly more complex. Children may act out mourning by devious means, by searching for substitutes through exhibitionistic sexuality, by psychological or psychosomatic regression, or by persistent and provocative or bad behavior. Jeff's provocative behavior was, of course, a sign of other things as well: his sensitivity to the fear of loss of his remaining parent; his demands (more than ordinarily excessive because of his singular situation) for the sole possession of his mother; and also his resentment at the threat of another man replacing his lost father (for occasionally a child may deify and idealize a lost parent to the extent that it becomes impossible for anyone to compare with or to replace the lost ideal). Certainly Jeff made it very difficult for his mother's dates and for her. In spite of his mother's reprimands, he did not hide his jealousy or his desire to wipe out all competition. "I always want to live with you; and I don't want you to get married." His mother's candid and clear reply, "I'm not marrying anyone yet, but no matter who it is or when, you will always be with me, and you will have a daddy besides," brought forth the firm assertion: "I don't want one."

This conversation took place while the date waited in the living room, the mother torn between two people demanding her attention. When the date left, she sat down and cried, "very hard. I didn't know who to hate first." But she did know that, in spite of his loud assertion, Jeff indeed wanted a daddy and she wisely determined not to yield to her son's possessiveness.

Separation-Individuation Issues

A son left at an early age with his mother will begin, inevitably, to rebel against maternal domination. His need to reject his mother as the ideal model for male behavior has been reinforced by the discovery of the differences between the sexes. Around 3 to 4 years of age, Jeff gave renewed evidence of the significance of his hunger for a father and began to reveal the degree of his vulnerability. This was, indeed, a critical time. Mother's despair, depression, and the equally frantic "search," combined with feelings of failure, consumed tremendous amounts of her psychic energy, leaving her child depleted of his mother's interest.

Role Reversal

This neglect was intermittent, however: It alternated with an opposite (and apparently contradictory, certainly confusing) reaction—an excessive dependence on the child by the parent. In such a situation, a child may find himself unconsciously called on to "give to" his parent what he senses correctly is felt by her to be missing, lost, or gone. This reversal of roles made him into a little mother, or "a motherly father," in order to alleviate the despair he sensed in his mother, and to allay his ongoing intense fears of further abandonment by the sole parent remaining. Some children attempt to meet parental needs by offering to sleep in the place of the missing one. Many times, a child inadvertently reopens wounds by gestures, mannerisms, or other resemblances to the now-hated partner. Sometimes a parent's hostility to the departed partner is so great as to lead to false reconstructions of the events leading to the divorce or to the constant devaluation of the departed partner. A man or woman may try continually to prove he or she was the "better parent." For deep psychological reasons, a woman may set up or feel called on in repetitive situations to play the role of the father, thereby bitterly reiterating both her and her offspring's independence of him.

Mother's very real "shattered faith in men," no matter how unconsciously reinforced by her past, may create for a son a bewildering awareness of her unconscious hostility to him as another male figure. In some circumstances, this constellation of unverbalized affects may contribute to the abandonment of an identification with a male figure, who would "do such a thing as impregnate a woman and then desert her." Mother may often remind her child that, in contrast to his father, she has "stuck by him." This may add to the burden of guilt he may feel for having his fantasies actualized in having "won the oedipal struggle." Too often boys raised in such atmospheres become "mother's sons" with problems centering on masculinity, potency, and a limited capacity to relate to and fully love women. The image of the mother as seductress or vampire seems almost proportional to the child's fear of his own sexuality and the degree of overstimulation he may have experienced. The latter can be neutralized or modified by a father or father substitute whose presence bears witness to having survived his own oedipal struggles (Chaps. 7, 32).

Yet if a child has only fantasies to supply a partial answer as to the why of father's disappearance, he may supply quite a frightening answer indeed. We have seen how Jeff's mother openly explained his father's nonpresence by defining over and over again the word "divorce." That Jeff continued to grapple with the concept for a long time is clear from the following evening conversation which took place when he was 3½ years old.

Jeff: Why doesn't my father live here the way other fathers do?

Mother: We're not married any more, Jeff, and I think your father is planning to marry someone else now. Someday I will marry again, too, and then that man will be your daddy.

Jeff (demanding):   You call him up and tell him I said he is married and he should move in here now!

Mother: I'm sorry, but I can't do that. Your father is marrying again because he wants to. This is his choice, as it will be my choice when I marry again, as it was his choice as well as mine to get a divorce. I know this is hard for you to understand now, but this was your father's choice, too.

Jeff: Well, then, marry someone now! (Then he began to list his choices starting with his uncle and then including every one of his mother's friends' husbands.)

Mother: Those men are already married. But we'll find someone who is not married, someone who is unattached.

Jeff's mother concluded later, "My own guilt about his fatherless situation made me continue to convey the feeling that he could choose the man as much as I. Thinking about it now, I believe I overdid it. This was another example of my trying to make it up to him."

Jeff, by almost inevitable logic, had arrived at the conclusion that mother's "meanness" had been the cause of his father's going away; an appropriate punishment, therefore, was in his power. "I'll run away, too!!" A preoedipal child who has only begun to learn to curb his impulses, to accept restrictions, to differentiate cruelty and kindness, feels the conscience he possesses is the same as that possessed by others, child or adult. Like himself, then, mother can be simultaneously destructive or loving. Concepts of destruction and murder do not seem to upset a small child to the degree parents often anticipate, because the child's superego has not yet reached full development, which may also account for children's tolerance for violence and sadism in stories or on television.

The Challenge of Ambiguity on a Child of Divorce

A new phase in Jeff's search was triggered when he noticed on staying overnight with Peter and Sue (the upstairs neighbors) that they shared the

475

same bed. Surprised and puzzled, he sought out his mother for questioning. "I explained that married people share the same bed, or bedroom," she says. To Jeff, this was obviously a tantalizing idea. Now, when he awakened during the night, he sometimes walked into his mother's room, saying, "I want to sleep with you because I feel sick," or "Let me sleep in your room because I'm lonely." She writes,

I always felt sorry for him when he said he was lonely, but I knew I had to be firm about this. I would tell him he had a lovely room of his own, and there was no reason to sleep in mommy's room. After awhile, I just insisted strongly, "March back into your room immediately." Once when he had a high fever, and I had been up almost all night, out of sheer exaustion, I let him sleep in the other bed in my room. I realize now that, had I been married, I never would have done this: However, had I been married, there would have been someone else to share the responsibility.

With awareness of parental emotions and needs, a child intermittently desires to please and caress, provoke and destroy. He may feel limitless in power, but his omnipotence brings terrifying problems that generally precede and highlight the oedipal stage. If the child learns he can control either his parents or his anxieties by one or another means, he is prone to overdevelop that part of his personality. Jeff's mother insisted that if possible he be prohibited from adopting the role of "the man in the family," a decision that, if not "lifesaving," was certainly "psyche-saving."

Jeff's unconscious need for a male in the family became more and more dominant by the time he was 4 years old and began to show signs of winning out over his desire to have his mother all to himself. He began to ask men to sleep over at his house. The arrangements he proposed were varied, but each one ensured him his exclusive possession of his mother. Invariably the men were married and thus clearly unavailable. The invitation was made doubly safe by his proposal that they could sleep with him in his room, or, better still, his mommy could move in with him and the man of the evening could sleep in his mommy's room, alone. The time was both an amusing and a trying one for his mother. Among some of the motivations for this "new phase" were the fluctuations in his identification, possibly wondering what it was like to be a woman and to sleep with a man, and what it was like to have a baby, a conjecture that seems validated by another conversation recorded by his mother. For Jeff was indeed making important connections now between men, women, bed, babies, and the role of fathers. He began by confronting the important question of his own birth. "I want a baby," he said to his mother one day.

Mother: Perhaps after I'm married.
Jeff: Was I a baby once?
Mother: Yes, you know you were. Everyone is, in the beginning.
Jeff: Were you married when I was born?
Mother: Yes.
Jeff: Who were you married to?
Mother: Your father.
Jeff: What does a man do about the baby in your stomach? Did that man do that to you?

"I believe I must have looked as stunned as I felt," wrote his mother. "First to hear him put all of this together; then because I was reminded that he was not my son alone! It was sometimes easy to forget he ever had a father. It was also the first time in close to a year that he mentioned his father directly."

Adjustment to Stepfather

Then Jeff made up his mind he had found the man he wanted for a father, and, as his mother remarked, the man was "surprisingly available!" Jeff had "selected" for this important role Murray, a man who was clearly attracted to his mother, in no small degree because of her remarkable relationship with her small son. It was as if he could relive through Jeff the kind of relationship he might have wished for himself. He was truly kind to the boy and from the first was a positive influence. Jeff made clear in every way he could contrive that he wished Murray was his father, his impatience with his mother's cautious deliberation finally leading him to exclaim in exasperation: "Why can't we get married now?"

But when Jeff learned that his mother and Murray were really going to fulfill his own impatient wish for marriage, he was silent. In his ambivalence he refused to go to the wedding. Once more his mother revealed her awareness of the importance of the moment. Knowing that reality, however painful, is always easier to bear than fantasy, she insisted that he be there. Although upset by his apparent change of attitude and, for a while, hesitant about her course of action, she reported, "I approached my son again and told him I was buying him a new suit for the wedding. 'I'm not going!' 'Yes, you are going because we will all be upset if you're not there. You won't have to do anything but stand there and watch. Afterwards, your grandmother is taking us out for a lovely dinner party."

At the wedding, Jeff tried to stand between his mother and Murray as if he were the one getting married, or perhaps as if making one final attempt to eliminate the rival male by separating the bridal couple. In truth, the marriage was a new contract for him as well. For after the ceremony he asked, "Are we married already?"

For a time after the return of the newlyweds, Jeff revealed his need by devoting his "question hour" once more to sleeping arrangements. He became, in effect, a night watchman, listening for signs of activity between his parents, and in the morning could often be found sitting at their bedroom door. However, compared to many similarly reestablished families, the complex process of transition to a new family group took a relatively short time. The movement from overt concern with the question, "What will that man do to mommy?" to acceptance of the newcomer as "daddy," was for Jeff a progression from negation through puzzled anxiety to neighborhood announcements of the new family structure, including descriptions of the new sleeping arrangements. Opening the window that faced the parking lot to say hello to some friends, Jeff yelled out with obvious joy and pride, "My mommy is married now, and I have a new daddy, and my mommy has one bed now instead of two, and my mommy and my new daddy sleep in one bed together!" His mother, though recording her "bright red" embarrassment at the sudden publicity, rejoiced in her small son's acceptance and evident happiness.

Much as a sleeper deprived of dreams for several nights dreams in great quantities as if to satisfy a basic biological need, a child deprived of a male pattern on which to model himself or in need of one to aid separation-individuation from mother, craves such an object. Jeff, at an age when his hunger for a male figure was becoming most critically acute, began to devour his new father, as if to make up for the lost and lonely years. With remarkable patience, the newlyweds handled his need, as he sought to adjust, to readjust, and to redistribute emotional love and attention within the family. He demanded the sole attention of his new idealized father with the same intensity he had once demanded his mother's. As time went on, Jeff grew less demanding, less insistently possessive. Murray's continued presence, his being with him "in the flesh," made him a "real daddy" in Jeff's mind. The following conversation illustrates:

Jeff: Did Karen pick her daddy, too?
Mother: No.
Jeff (persisting): Is Don her first daddy?
Mother: Yes, he is.
Jeff: Does that mean he is her "real daddy"?
Mother: Yes. If he is her daddy, then he's a real daddy. Your daddy is your daddy now, so he is a real daddy, too.
Jeff: Does that mean he's not my first daddy, though?
Mother: No, he's not your first daddy, but that doesn't mean that he's not a real daddy to you.

According to his mother, Jeff seemed satisfied.

A particular form of guilt characterizes children such as Jeff. This was rather poignantly revealed when Jeff, hearing of the birth of a new cousin and consciously aware of the link between babies and hurting, as well as between babies and punishment by spanking, once more asked about his father, "Was there a man here when I was born?" Told that there was, he asked, "Did he go to work?" An affirmative reply brought the next question: "Who was he?" His mother wrote, "I just looked at Murray. What should I say to Jeff in front of Murray?" "His name," Murray took up the question, "was Raymond Pierce." Jeff, knowing that Pierce was his own last name, turned to his mother once more:

Jeff: Did that man spank me when I cried?
Mother: No, why would anyone spank you as a baby, if you cried?
Jeff: Did he spank me?
Mother: Of course not. You were my wonderful, adorable baby, and there was no need to spank you. You were my baby and I loved you very much, as I do now.

Jeff was once more betraying guilty anxiety about his own father's disappearance and linking the birth of his cousin to his fatherlessness, to spanking and punishment, then all together, to intercourse, babies, and what "was done to mother," for, although Jeff was proud of his new father and still bragged about him, he still sometimes resented him and wished he had his mother to himself. It is probably because of his wish to eliminate competition and his awareness that it is possible to suffer punishment (spanking) from a man, that the ancient disappearance of his first father is recharged by aggressive guilt normally found in the oedipal situation.

The full integration of Jeff's stepchildedness with the mysteries of birth, of maleness and femaleness, with concepts of activity and passivity, with curiosity about and respect for ancestral tradition, will not take place until adolescent years, during which time his quest for his real father may be expected to reemerge. One can only hope the solidly meaningful relationship with his stepfather will carry him through this difficult period with a minimum of strain, for it is still possible that this particular child may feel a burden of guilty hostility that may challenge his "belongingness" and "maleness" with unusual severity.

30

Abusive Fathers

Brandt F. Steele

The Child Abuse Syndrome

Maltreatment of infants and children is one of the most maladaptive forms of behavior that parents can express toward their offspring and one that is most distasteful and difficult for both laypersons and professionals to comprehend and to handle. Despite studies in recent years that have increased our knowledge and understanding, abuse remains a problem much outside the general stream of social concern. Many people still find it hard to realize that a significant number of fathers and mothers physically injure or neglect the children under their care, or abuse them sexually or emotionally, thereby seriously distorting their subsequent physical and psychological development.

Statistics

According to our best estimates, approximately one million children are physically abused and neglected each year in the United States, and probably a nearly equivalent number are sexually mistreated. Some 2,000 to 3,000 children die each year of repeated injury or prolonged neglect. Other countries have similar patterns of abuse, although often a lower incidence of reported cases. There is abundant evidence that maltreatment has existed since earliest human history in various forms in most cultures of which we have knowledge, and it cannot be attributed in any way to "modern" stresses and social change, although possibly modified by them.* It is reassuring to realize that the human race has survived and increased as well as it obviously has for thousands of years despite the damage done to an enormous number of the infants who formed the successive generations of our species. One can only admire the adaptive

---

*Editors' note: See de Mause, *History of Childhood*. The specific ideas of Lloyd de Mause about the history of infanticide and abuse are controversial, but family historians do generally agree with the appalling history of the treatment of children, as will be evident in other chapters of de Mause's anthology.

abilities and capacities of growing children to survive all kinds of trauma, albeit with far less than ideal results.

The maltreatment of offspring by "fathers" is displayed not only by biological fathers but also by stepfathers, adoptive fathers, and others such as temporary or long-term paramours and covivants who are assuming the social role of the "man of the family" and are involved as surrogate fathers in the child-care situation. Other male figures, such as older brothers, baby-sitters, teachers, male relatives, camp counselors, and others may also be involved in abuse, but this chapter will concentrate on fathers.

A Species-Specific Disorder

Maltreatment is essentially a human phenomenon. Males of some lower species of animals may attack or destroy their offspring, but this usually occurs only in those species in which the male is not ordinarily involved in the care of progeny. In species characterized by a "family" group, the males do not damage the offspring for whom they provide significant caretaking functions. An interesting exception to this general rule that bears some resemblance to human patterns is that of the Langur monkeys in India observed by Hrdy. She describes the actions of young male monkeys who overthrow an existing dominant male and take over the deposed predecessor's role as head of the tribe and possessor of the harem. Such young males then proceed to kill existing male babies and those born in the following few weeks, seeming to allow survival only for those males who might be the product of their own sexual activities subsequent to obtaining top position. Such actions also make females more quickly available for copulatory activity rather than prolonged inactivity resulting from infant nursing.

This is reminiscent of the historically common human pattern of a newly conquering monarch eliminating all vestiges, especially male children, of a previous dynasty. It also seems similar to the not infrequently observed behavior of a father being particularly punitive toward a child of his wife's previous husband. The wife's attachment to this child is seen as interfering with her attachment and loyalty to the new husband. Infanticide as a result of repeated abuse by fathers is no different in its essentials from that caused by mothers.

Intrafamilial violence perpetrated by both men and women is extremely common, and there is no good evidence that abusive, aggressive behavior toward children has any significant gender-linked biological basis. There is no demonstrable correlation between abusive behavior and androgen levels, or the presence of XXY chromosome patterns, or the existence of recognizable central nervous system lesions.

Types of Abuse

Under the general title of "abuse" we subsume several forms of maltreatment. There is *physical abuse*, which includes nonaccidental injuries ranging from minor bruises through lacerations, burns, fractures, and damage to the central nervous system and other internal organs. There is also *neglect*, resulting from a failure to provide adequate food, shelter, clothing, medical care, psychological stimulation, or general protection in situations that cannot be accounted for by inescapable external environmental factors. One of the common serious types of neglect is that of "failure to thrive" in infants as a result of maternal deprivation. *Sexual abuse* ranges from simple excessive fondling to all varieties of masturbation, oral, anal, and genital activities, genital intercourse, and rape. It can be either heterosexual or homosexual. By far the commonest form of sexual abuse is that of incest (Chap. 31). *Emotional abuse* is subtler and much harder to define. In simple form it is the excessive, repetitive, verbal and attitudinal denigration, belittlement, disparagement, and humiliation of a child by the caretaker. It is also the inevitable accompaniment of all other forms of abuse. Fractures and other physical injuries, unless they are unusually severe and deforming, or damage the central nervous system, do not necessarily lead to long-lasting harm. The emotional trauma, however, of being attacked, injured, and uncared for by those caretakers to whom one must look for care and protection, is profound and persistent in its effects. The damage from sexual abuse is much less that of physical damage or anything directly related to the sexual impact, than it is the general distortion of psychological development and maturation resulting from the exploitation of an immature child for caretaker satisfaction.

Emotional and nutritional neglect are much more common during the first 3 years of life and become especially evident and damaging during the normally rapid growth period of the first few months.

Physical abuse, too, is most common in the first 3 or 4 years, and head injuries during the first year are particularly serious in their long-term effects. It often continues through later childhood and into adolescence in the form of severe physical punishment, more commonly with boys. Sexual abuse seems to be quite rare before the age of 2 years, but thereafter it increases in frequency on into puberty and adolescence, and is much more common in girls than in boys. In essence, maltreatment of children includes all acts of either commission or omission that interfere with the child's optimal physical, emotional, cognitive, and social development.

Sex-Determined Variation in Abuse Patterns

Fathers and mothers are quite similar in the general aspect of their abusive behaviors, but there are also significant differences. Mothers are more commonly involved in the neglect of infants, especially nutritional neglect leading to failure to thrive. The father is, as a rule, much less involved in the feeding role, but a lack of his emotional support and understanding can be profoundly destructive to the mother's nourishing ability. There is also a relationship between a state of depression in the mother and her deficits in caretaking ability. This is especially true of postpartum depression, which usually does not occur in the same way with fathers. Fathers are much more frequently involved in sexual abuse of children of all ages than are mothers; father-daughter, stepfather-daughter incest is by far the most commonly seen form of sexual abuse. Often fathers will repress sexual feelings relating to their own children, and then through mechanisms of displacement act out such sexual impulses toward other children who are either more distant relatives, acquaintances, or strangers. Sexually abusive acts may be in the form of exhibitionism, pedophilia, fondling, genital intercourse, orogenital contacts or various perversions, and rape; they may be either heterosexual or homosexual. In matters of physical abuse, fathers do not show any significant consistent difference from mothers, except for a general tendency of men to be more aggressive and to display violence more than women. It is also true that many physically abusive fathers show less than average aggression and assertiveness in their general lives; they are often quite meek, mild, and noncompetitive, and express violent behavior only at rare intervals toward one or another of their children. It is very specifically directed aggression rather than indiscriminate discharge. In cases of physical abuse there is roughly equal distribution between mothers and fathers of responsibility for the actual abusive acts. Some fathers confine their maltreatment to physical abuse, others only to sexual contacts. Some physically abuse daughters early in life and later sexually abuse them with or without accompanying physical abuse. It is not uncommon for some men to abuse spouse as well as children.

Psychological Characteristics of Abusive Fathers

Men who manifest aberrant behavior in the form of child abuse are far from a homogeneous group, and many of the common stereotypes of child abusers derived from sensational stories in the media are highly inaccurate. It is helpful to consider the problem as a disordered pattern of childrearing—that is, an abnormal parent-child interaction that exists rather independently with or without many other varieties of normal or abnormal behavior.

Sociocultural Background

Abusive fathers come from all social and economic classes and all walks of life. They may be wealthy, living in luxury in a large suburban home, or barely existing in abject poverty in a center-city slum. They may be professionals with graduate degrees or illiterate unemployed laborers; devoutly religious or atheistic; white, black, or red; absolute teetotalers or heavily involved with drugs or alcohol; living in a stable marriage or in a series of short liaisons; highly successful or recurrently failing in their jobs; in urban or rural settings, with superior IQs or mental deficiency; or they may be at any point on the wide spectra between these listed extremes.

Mental Disorders

There is a small percentage of abusers who suffer from schizophrenic or depressive illness of psychotic degree, or from any of the various types of neurosis or severe borderline states. It is our impression that these disorders occur among abusers in about the same frequency as in the general population. A great many have significant problems in the sphere of narcissism, sometimes severe enough to be categorized as a narcissistic character disorder. Chronic, mild, anaclitic depression is very common but much less overt than in women abusers. There is also a group of fathers who might best be included in the vague class of "sociopaths." They have frequent brushes with the law, a tendency to impulsive-aggressive behavior, excessive selfishness, and extreme disregard for the rights and welfare of others. Their job records are spotty, and they may often be involved with substance abuse. Overall, fathers who abuse children are not greatly different from a cross-section sample of the general population of men, and it would be misleading to try to categorize them as a specific sociocultural subgroup or as suffering from any single commonly diagnosed psychiatric disorder.

Common Traits

Although no specific psychiatric diagnostic classification is usefully applied to child abusers, it is possible to describe a constellation of psychological traits that are commonly seen in both men and women who mistreat children. They have a poorly developed sense of identity and a very low self-esteem, which may sometimes be overcompensated for by exaggerated self-assurance and braggadocio. Longstanding feelings of emptiness and being uncared for are evidenced by excessive neediness, dependency, and an atmosphere of immaturity. They have little basic trust or confidence that the world can be safe or good to them; they tend to be lonely, have few friends, and express a pseudoparanoid attitude toward authorities, especially those to whom they must turn for help. They have difficulty in finding pleasure for themselves or in allowing their offspring to have pleasure. They expect too much compliant, satisfying behavior from their infants, much too soon in the baby's life; further, they have a strong belief in the value of physical punishment as an agent to improve behavior. There is a corresponding lack of empathy and a resulting inability to respond sensitively and correctly to the infant's state, needs, and age-appropriate abilities.

The source of this derailed parent-child interaction lies in the parents' own earliest childhood experiences. We have rarely seen an abusive caretaker who does not give a history of abuse or neglect, or both, during the earliest years of his life. The deprivation was essentially a lack of empathic care, an emotional deprivation, although it can also be nutritional deprivation or lack of other material necessities. It is out of the great pool of neglected and abused children that the next generation of maltreating caretakers develops, although not all children subjected to maltreatment become abusive parents. Either because maltreatment was less severe, or, more important, because of significant contacts with other more caring persons during childhood, they become able to be adequate caretakers. There are also some children who seem to have constitutionally "stronger egos" and more adaptive techniques for survival without damage. The transmission of maltreatment patterns from generation to generation indicates that such behavior is acquired or learned rather than genetically determined and instinctive. Such learning begins in the earliest months of life and continues through infancy and childhood, and the unconscious memories of what it was like as an infant and how one was cared for become the most powerful determinants of later parenting behavior. Most basic is the identification with the parent of the earliest months of life, and this is enhanced or modified by more cognitive social learning in later years after the child has acquired language.

Clinical Example

An example showing many of the aforementioned factors is that of a Marine sergeant who had fractured the skull of his 18-month-old baby boy, during punishment for a mistake in toilet training. He said, "He knows better; he did it deliberately. I'll show him who's boss; who does he think he is, anyway?" And "You have to teach kids to respect authority, otherwise they'll grow up spoiled rotten." If it were not so sad, it would be almost amusing to see a 200-pound, over 6-foot man acting as if he were dangerously threatened by a little toddler. He had felt that his own mother was a cold, aloof person who never went through more than the mechanics of taking care of him and never really cared about how he felt or what happened to him. His father, on the other hand, had been a strong, aggressive person who demanded perfect behavior from all of his children, and was very free with physical punishment by straps and boards. In simple terms, the sergeant is now an unempathic, demanding, punitive parent, reliving some of the experiences of his earliest life. He is submissive, obedient, angry, and fearful toward higher authorities, and punitively unfeeling and demanding toward underlings in his charge. His blustering, aggressive exterior hides many inner feelings of low self-esteem, loneliness, and yearning for love. This man treats his own baby boy the way he was treated as a child.

The transmission of child-caring patterns from generation to generation is not in itself abnormal. Both good and poor patterns are transmitted in the same way. In the child-abuse syndrome we see the poor parenting practices experienced in early childhood being repeated with the caretakers' own offspring.

Misperceptions of the Child

Misperceptions of the child are ubiquitous in abuse cases, and are based on several different dynamics. The child is often viewed as the reincarnation of the father's own bad childhood self, endowed with all the nefarious traits for which he was punished in early years. This is not a projection, but rather a sort of reverse identification (i.e., "He is like me"). The father, then, in identification with his own punitive parent, can punish the child with full superego approval. Fathers often tell us, "I was never abused. I deserved every beating I got," and punish their children for the same infractions with the same techniques that were used on them. The child may also be perceived, through displacement and transference, as a new edition of a much-hated sibling, and thereby become the victim of angry, revengeful feelings that were never expressed against the original object but had been smoldering in a repressed state. The sex of a sibling may also determine the father's propensity to focus his abuse on either a boy or a girl child.

Role Reversal

Abusive fathers commonly look at their offspring as sources of comfort and satisfaction of narcissistic needs, much as their own parents. This is the well-known phenomenon of "role reversal," in which the parent behaves as if he were a needy child, expecting his own offspring to be the caregiving, nurturing adult. So long as the child behaves well, the father feels satisfied and his self-esteem is enhanced. But sooner or later the child is bound to fail in this impossible task, and is then punished for disobedience and for deliberately producing what is felt by the father as a narcissistic injury. The transference to the child of quasi-parental qualities carries with it the hazard of the child being seen as the bad parent, who not only failed to care adequately, but also actively demanded and criticized. Thus an unsatisfied, crying infant can be responded to as if he were the angry parent of the father's early years. Rage that could never be expressed to the real parent may be released on the infant. In order to accomplish this, it seems that there is a rapid shift in identifications. The father identifies with his own punitive parent and the baby is justly punished as the equivalent of the bad childhood self.

Most parents see in their babies—consciously or unconsciously— qualities that are like those of themselves, of grandparents, or other relatives. If these are good, admired qualities, then all is well. If the qualities seen are the bad ones of a disliked person, however, they are an ominous stimulus of trouble for a father with the potential for abuse. The baby is thought of as "bad" from the very beginning and will constantly be at greater risk of abuse for failure to meet expectations. The perception of the child as somehow unsatisfactory or unsatisfying is a common thread in all instances of abuse, sometimes related to reality factors but more often to the discrepancies between the actual baby and the father's fantasies and wishes for a child who would satisfy his own needs. Babies can be seen as "failures" because they are of a different sex than hoped for, or because they are too active, too passive, born at an inconvenient time, premature, a rival for the mother's attention, or anything else that strikes an unpleasant chord in the father's mind.

The variable and rapidly shifting identifications just described are manifestations of the father's own insecure, poorly integrated sense of identity. Because of exposure to varying degrees of emotional deprivation and abuse in early years, he has not been able successfully to accomplish the developmental tasks of separation-individuation and mature ego formation. There is neither an adequately coherent sense of self nor a firm continuing identity. His good and bad images of himself, his parents, and his child are fluid and rapidly interchangeable. His responses to environmental stimuli, although seemingly "impulsive," are really unconsciously determined by the psychic patterns developed in early years. He is still, to a great degree, a child whose attempts to be an adult parent are seriously hampered and distorted by the relics of early childhood conflict.

Circumstances for Abuse ·

Although always having the potential to do so, fathers attack a child only under specific circumstances that stimulate feelings of deprivation, low self-esteem, helplessness, and narcissistic rage. Precipitating events include such things as severe criticism by wife or boss, breakdown of home appliances or automobile, loss of job, frustration of plans by weather or people, financial crises, loss of an important person by death, or extra demand for performance. Under such circumstances, the father, with no one to turn to for help and comfort, looks to his child for behaviors that will make him feel better. If the child fails to show proper respect, obedience, and appreciative response, he or she is seen as unsatisfactory and abuse is likely to occur. Exceptions to the foregoing are the more "sociopathic" fathers who more persistently and constantly abuse a child without apparent relationship to any stress or crisis. Although they may punish more severely for messiness, toilet errors, or other forms of disobedience, they also "torture" a child by hitting or pinching each time they pass, touching with a lighted cigarette, teasing, ridicule, and verbal denigration of extreme degree. Often they will abuse severely when under the influence of alcohol, and sometimes through repeated severe abuse —especially with injury to the head—cause death of the child.

Men with backgrounds that provide the potential for abuse usually marry or develop liaisons with women of similar background and abuse potential. We rarely see abuse by one spouse that is not either consciously or unconsciously condoned and tolerated, if not actually abetted by the other spouse. We have known fathers who, while complaining of a wife's abusive acts, are unconsciously doing everything to stimulate her attacks, and who begin to be abusive themselves if the wife stops her maltreatment.

The abusive father's attack against his child is not related simply to the strength of his aggressive drive as much as it is a reflection of his lack of empathy for the child's immaturity, dependency, and helplessness. All parents have a potential for aggressive discharge and abuse if placed under sufficient stress and provocation, but most do not do so. Empathy for the child and libidinal attachment to him or her are the forces that inhibit the release of such aggressive impulses, and these are the very qualities characteristically deficient in the abusive parent. Insufficient empathy, evidenced by the subtle, repetitive pattern of giving priority to parental needs over those of the infant, is the usual sequel of poor attachment to the baby, which is apparent during the first actual contact between father and child at the time of birth or later. Warning signs of poor attachment are negative attitudes or rigid, specific, high expectations expressed prenatally while the infant is still in utero. Failure to meet such expectations means the infant is "unsatisfactory" and may not be attached to and sufficiently libidinized.

Most of the literature on attachment behavior deals only with the attachment of mother and child, but fathers also go through the attachment process with either positive or negative results. Men do not have the same preparation for attachment or the same experience of feeling a child inside as a part of themselves as mothers do. Their attachment may be more similar to that of adoptive and step-parents of both sexes, a process that has not to our knowledge been adequately investigated. A father's poor attachment and poor empathy seem directly related to his own early life when he experienced poor attachment and inadequately empathic care from his parents. The abuse syndrome can easily be described as a "disorder of attachment," and the perinatal period is a pivotal time when the potential for maltreatment patterns is transmitted to a new generation. The recent trend of fathers being more actively involved in the mother's pregnancy and delivery apparently enhances their attachment and empathic responses to their babies, and preliminary observations indicate there is a corresponding decrease in the abuse potential (Chaps. 18, 19, 35).

This chapter has described the major themes of behavior and psychodynamics commonly seen in fathers who physically abuse the children in their care. In addition to shared general characteristics, each abusive father is an individual. There are as many different kinds of fathers as there are different experiences during the life cycle, and such variations must be considered in all diagnostic and therapeutic efforts. It is most important to realize that one is not only dealing with a father who has injured his offspring, but also trying to understand a grown-up abused, neglected child who is seriously hampered in his parenting ability because of deficits in his early life.

31

Father-Daughter Incest

Irving Kaufman

Sociological, Legal, and Medical Considerations

Masters (1963), in his book on *Patterns of Incest*, pointed out that "there is a great diversity of opinion, among students of the subject, about incest: about why it occurs and why it is prohibited; about the effects of incest behavior and the effects of the incest prohibition; and about whether the law should concern itself specifically with incest at all" (p. 3). In the same book there are many illustrations of incest occurring as a regular part of the lives of various people. Incest is a subject of religion, literature, and psychology. These same questions persist today.

Freud (1905) discussed incest as an integral component of the Oedipus complex and attributed major psychological issues to the conflict between the incest wishes and the prohibitions. Freud (1913), in *Totem and Taboo*, further illustrated the psychological power of the incest taboo where marriage was forbidden between members of the same totem whether or not they were biologically related.

Whether the physical sexual act of incest has ill effects or not is still questioned by various authorities. However, the psychological implications have great impact and lead most societies to legally prohibit incest. Nonetheless, it still exists, even where it is prohibited.

In a presentation of the epidemiology of childhood sexual abuse, N. H. Greenberg (1979) states that "the number of children abused sexually in the United States each year is estimated to be between 50,000 and 100,000 in one study, and 360,000 in a more recent report. In about 38% of the cases he stated the offender was either a parent or a relative of the child" (pp. 16, 18–19). Most investigators believe the incidence to be much higher, with many cases never discovered or reported. Although incest occurs in all socioeconomic strata, persons of lower class are more likely to be reported by health personnel. Lukianowicz (1972) stated that incest is an international problem with features in the family patterns, mean age of onset (usually around 11), and length of time incest continues similar in most countries. In contrast to rape, which mostly occurs outside the home and is a single or rarely repeated phenomenon, incest almost always occurs within the home and goes on for varying lengths of time, averaging at least 6 months and often years. In contrast to rape, in my observations, incest usually does not involve overt coercion, force, or aggression. The coercion, however, may be more covert because of the authority position of the parents. Father may be seen by the daughter in this authority position, and this is regularly reinforced by the authority of the mother who may unconsciously condone or even encourage the incest.

Incestuous families are at all socioeconomic levels. However, despite the pathology of the parents, they tend to stay together until the incest is acknowledged and some outside agency interrupts the incest. In a paradoxical way, one could almost assume that the incest enables the various family members to cope with their interpersonal pathology, and that the daughter is the bond holding them together. When there is a threat of interruption of this pathological process the tendency is to try to reestablish it whenever possible, such as at the time of father's release from jail. Incest then is syntonic to the family and serves special pathological purposes. The overt actions of these families cover a wide range of disruptive behavior. Some of the families are chaotic; others appear quite "respectable." In a very large number alcoholism, especially on the part of the father, is part of the pathology. Sometimes, but not always, incest occurs while the father is under the influence. Some of the combinations and permutations of the family patterns will become more evident as we review the behavior of the individual family members.

According to Lloyd (1979), a criminal justice specialist, the legal definition of incest is narrow and specific. He states that the law "focuses on four issues: the age of the victim, whether sexual penetration has occurred, whether sexual contact occurred, and the circumstances surrounding the episode" (p. 88). The police investigation focuses on these questions. It has been my observation that this investigatory process can in its own way be extremely traumatic, especially to the girl being interrogated, particularly if she is old enough to realize that her testimony might lead to lengthy incarceration of her father, the hostility of her mother, and the disruption of the family unit. According to David Lloyd, the law defines penalties according to the kind of sexual interaction; so the police need to know "whether the defendant's penis entered the labia of the victim ('carnal knowledge,' or statutory rape), whether the defendant's penis entered the anus or mouth of the victim, or whether the defendant (in the case of a male) took the victim's penis into his or her mouth or penetrated the daughter's labia or anus with his tongue (sodomy or 'the crime against nature')" (p. 89).

The girl is subjected to many other questions surrounding the circumstances of the alleged incest, for example, attempts to arouse or force the victim by touching various parts of her body. It cannot be emphasized too much that the need to determine the legal issues because of the seriousness of the charges, the severity of the penalties, and the impact of this detailed probing of the girl's experience are very traumatic. In some instances, unlike the incest itself, this highly personal interrogation, with the implication that the girl is either lying or a "whore," feels more like a rape than the incest.

All states have enacted laws that prohibit sexual interaction with children. The penalties can be severe. David Lloyd states that forcible penetration of a child (whether vaginally or rectally) would be "sexual assault in the first degree" and carry a potential of life imprisonment. If the child is of the age of consent (usually 16 years), the penalty could be only 8 years of imprisonment.

All health care persons are required by law to report suspected child abuse, and David Lloyd goes on to state that the physician is liable to fine or imprisonment, or both, if he fails to report such an incident. In addition to criminal liability, the physician who fails to diagnose and report child abuse may be civilly liable to the child for malpractice. David Lloyd reassures physicians that there is no ethical problem for them in reporting suspected sexual abuse. (This issue is covered in Section 9 of the *Principles of Medical Ethics* of the American Medical Association.)

A related issue, increasingly observed in incest cases, is venereal infection, adding a medical problem. Sgroi (1979), in her study of pediatric gonorrhea beyond infancy, found that in children under the age of 13 years with gonorrhea, sexual abuse was the presumed cause. This is consistent with a 1979 United States Public Health recommendation that "with gonococcal infection in children beyond the newborn period the possibility of sexual abuse must be considered" (U.S. Public Health Service, Treatment of Recommendation for Gonorrhea, 1979).

Family Dynamics and Patterns of Incest

The daughter normally needs an appropriate amount and kind of libidinal loving interaction with her father for healthy personality development. When the relationship is too little, too much, or distorted, then the normally expected developmental sequence can be adversely affected.

Father-daughter incest is one example of an excessive and distorted interaction between father and daughter, which must be understood as related to the mother as well. The presence of incestuous fantasies in both fathers and daughters is frequent; however, the actual acting out of these fantasies occurs only under special circumstances. In the majority

493

of cases I have seen, the common pattern of families of incest is one of collusion among all the participants, and a major tendency toward introversion. The incest is one component of a family structured so that the members primarily use each other to express major emotional needs.

Some investigators, such as Nakashima and Zakus (1979), state that incest was part of a general pattern of child abuse. Father either threatened or actually forced the daughter by violent verbal or behavioral threats to submit to his sexual advances. However, they also agree with my observations that incest is frequently a search for nurturing and mothering for both father and daughter, as well as an expression of anger at mother for deserting them. The role of family members leading to incest will be discussed in greater detail.

It has been my impression that in child abuse, whether it be aggressive or sexual, the intense affectual interaction tends to bind the family members to each other.

For many reasons, the intense emotional impact of libidinal or aggressive interaction between father and daughter leaves intense imprints on their egos. The paradoxical tendency is to repeat the experience. There is a general assumption in the community that the child battered or sexually involved by the parents would wish to interrupt this process. In my experience, we found just the opposite. This may be why incest and physical abuse continue for so long a time.

For example, an abused child placed in a foster home often tends to run away and return to the abusing parents. By the same token, interruption of the pathology of physical or sexual abuse without treatment of the participants tends to lead to family disruption or a strong effort to re-establish the pathology. This is a pattern seen in the dynamics of other types of psychopathology. The pathology in the family is serving special needs, disturbed as they may be. Merely arresting the external manifestation of the pathology tends to lead to widespread reverberations in the personalities of all the participants. The complication this poses for management and therapy will be discussed in that section.

Incestuous Fathers

An understanding of the fathers who commit incest with their daughters is based on a psychophilosophical evaluation of the meaning of the sexual encounter. The following are examples of the wide range of perspectives.

The "Power Play" Theory

Some investigators present these fathers as chauvinists and the incestuous act as part of the process of male domination and devaluation of the weak and helpless in the sexual arena. A female child would be most vulnerable. This is parallel to the sociological studies of prejudice, destruction, and subjugation of one segment of society by another. For example, Dollard describes in *Caste and Class in a Southern Town* (1957) the need of the whites to dominate and subjugate the blacks in terms of the gains to the whites. The first gain was economic, where the blacks were relegated to the poorest paying, most menial jobs. The second was the sexual power this gave whites over blacks. The third was prestige and social position. All black women had to submit to the sexual advances of white men, and if they resisted they were in danger of serious physical harm. In summary, this point of view is based on the concept that people have a need for power. Physical and sexual abuse of women, especially female children, which occurs in incest, is an example of this power drive.

If one takes this power view, attempts to change, control, or modify the behavior would be based either on legal controls or some attempt to modify the sociocultural attitude of the males who engage in this practice.

The Regression Theory

Mohr, Turner, and Jerry (1964) studied males who commit pedophilia, including sexual relations between father and daughter. Among the many interesting and valuable observations the authors presented, I would like to emphasize the following.

Males who commit pedophilia fall into three major age groups: the very young, the middle-aged, and the elderly. Middle-aged men far outnumbered the elderly or the very young. One could speculate that pedophilia could be a form of regression. Freud had pointed out that women during menopause can regress from the adult heterosexual level to an anal level. The same regression could occur in men.

The nature of the sexual act of the male with the female child (particularly in reference to the prepubertal girl) takes on the form and characteristics of the sexual fantasies and practices of the child at that given age. Exhibiting, touching, and looking are the major forms of sexual behavior, such as what a girl of 11 years old often displays. Although intracrural, oral, anal, and genital contacts have been reported for very young girls, the majority of the cases in this study were pregenital in nature, corresponding to the developmental level of the child. This finding could reflect a fixation, or more likely a regression, on the part of the male to a more infantile way of functioning. The treatment, then, would have to deal with this infantile pattern and what it means in the psychic economy of fathers who behave in this fashion toward their daughters.

As would be expected, as the daughters become adolescent and pubescent, genital contact becomes more frequent and the relationship takes on a different character with different meanings.

The Psychodynamics of Incest

Considering incest in the framework of the psychodynamic meaning of the act, incest falls into three subcategories:

1. The largest number of participants appear to be depressed, with both father and daughter reacting to the loss of mothering and turning to each other sexually to deal with the void and loss. Obviously this phenomenon is very complex, and it is discussed in detail in this section.
2. A smaller group of fathers and daughters are schizophrenic, and the sexual union is part of a symbiotic process. This too is discussed and described with a case example.
3. The third group are the fathers who are operating in a sadomasochistic way where the sexual act is part of a perversion. This is psychologically parallel to the view that incest is a chauvinistic act. The difference here is that the motivating factor is viewed as a fusion of libidinal and aggressive drives where the sexual release requires this particular set of aggressive circumstances rather than as a power drive.

The Systems Theory

Incest is viewed in terms of a systems theory where the sexual act is part of a total family process and may even be necessary to maintain the family equilibrium. This latter point is illustrated by the major family disruption that occurs when the incest is terminated. This "systems" orientation to incest is discussed in some detail in this section.

The "Amoral Fiend" Theory

A very popular point of view, which in my opinion is the least useful, is that incest is committed by individuals lacking in the development of a moral sense, as postulated by Kohlberg. These men are viewed as amoral fiends who should be punished for their misdeeds, and the major approach is legal. This point of view neglects the fact that incest is much more complicated, occurring in the home over a long period of time with a total family interaction and a psychodynamic meaning.

Incest as a "Harmless Aberration"

Some authorities feel that incestuous impulses are so universal that they are not pathological and that there is no evidence that it causes any harm. This point of view is difficult to comprehend, although there is evidence of cases of incest where the pathological effects have not been as severe as one would have anticipated. However, in a culture where incest is illegal, immoral, and contrary to the values of the culture, it is difficult to believe that it does not arise out of the types of pathology in the father that have been discussed, and that it does not have repercussions on the daughter.

Categories of Incestuous Fathers

Fathers who commit incest are not all alike. In my studies I generally found that they appeared to fall into three separate categories. Nakashima and Zakus (1979), in a study of incestuous families, also describe three groups of men who commit incest. Their classification is related to the age of the child when incest occurred. (These observations were derived from Gebhard's book, *Sex Offenders*.)

The first type was a father who committed incest with a daughter under 12 years of age. These men were "rather ineffectual nonaggressive dependent men who drank heavily, worked sporadically, and were preoccupied with sexual matters" (p. 33). They were classified as "dependent" and used sex to meet their emotional needs.

A second group of men committed incest with daughters between the ages of 12 and 16 years. In this group, preoccupation with sex did not appear to be the overriding issue. Many were alcoholic, others of a subculture that tolerated incest, and in some instances circumstances were defended as "situational." Thus these fathers were so diverse that it was difficult to tease out common characteristics.

The third group were fathers who committed incest with daughters over 16 years old. They were described (p. 33) as "conservative, moralistic, restrained, religious, devout, uneducated, with disorganized lives." Many came from cultural backgrounds "wherein sexual morality was publicly emphasized but privately breached with relative impunity."

In my experience, however, three types of fathers emerged. One was a very nurturant, overtly dependent man who was concerned about his family, which tended to be introverted. The second type of father was often aggressive and controlling (domineering), who once again acted in ways that he defined as in the best interests of his family. His deep infantilism and dependency were often covered by his dogmatic lecturing and overt aggression. In either type the family was often closely tied to each other, with minimal contact with the extrafamilial environment. The third type of father does use overt aggression.

Regardless of the personality of the fathers, they acted as though they were entitled to sex with their daughters. This seemed related to the fact that they felt abandoned by their wives and had turned to the daughters for need fulfillment. Although their pathology took a genital path, the basic personality issues were preoedipal, and the more overt needs seemed to be for basic nurturance. These fathers rationalized and condoned, and some made remarkable excuses for their sexual relationships with their daughters. These included teaching their "daughters about sex in the right way," and "giving them love and affection." These infantile men used their daughters for their own infantile needs, and seemed incapable of sufficient differentiation of their needs from their daughters' needs.

Clinical Example 1. An example of the first type (a more passive, overtly nurturant father) was a man who complained to his daughter that her mother constantly left him to visit her own mother. Mother relied on this daughter, reversed roles, and placed her in the parent role, forcing her to do much of the caring for younger siblings, cooking, and housecleaning. Both father and daughter, missing mothering, turned to each other for an affective response that rapidly became sexualized. Father said he was concerned about the rest of his children, and helped his daughter as she cared for them. At first he spent many hours talking with her, and eventually they began to have intercourse.

In most of the cases I studied, mother was a passive, dependent person who either needed her own mother or turned to her daughter for mothering. Yet other mothers are more aggressive, hostile, and openly rejecting of their husbands. These men may cling desperately to the rest of the family, seeking their love and affection, and finally find a loving relationship with one of the daughters.

Clinical Example 2. The second type of father may be illustrated by a quite disturbed man who terrorized his family with his aggression. Owning a gun collection, at times he would shoot over the heads of various family members. The mother was passive, sickly, unavailable, and had long since retreated from the scene. Much of the responsibility fell on the older daughters, and soon father had sexual relations with two of them. He did not use overt aggression to force the relationship, but they became emotionally attached and dependent on him. In an interview with one of the daughters after she had become impregnated by her father, now in jail, she could barely talk. A very bright high school senior, obviously in a grief reaction, she could only say, between her sobs, "I want my daddy."

In general, the common pattern of families of incest, then, appears to be one of collusion with a major tendency toward introversion. For example, one of the above controlling types of fathers would not allow the daughter with whom he had incest to have an independent life, and even accompanied her when she went on an errand.

Clinical Example 3. There is a third type of father who actually forces his daughter to commit incest. This often is a domineering, aggressive type of man who devalued his wife and took the stance that he was superior and lord and master of his household. Many of these men were alcoholic, and became even more domineering and grandiose under the influence. In one such case a father came home drunk. Mother told her 11-year-old daughter to put father to bed because she was his favorite and he would listen to her. Obediently she led him into his bedroom and he dragged her into bed. When father masturbated her she felt overwhelming anxiety. This anxiety is typical of the reaction we observed in girls sexually overstimulated before they were able to have an orgasm. When daughter informed her mother, she was told father would never do anything like that, but the scene was repeated many times. The daughter's attitude toward father was that she feared and idolized him. She later felt she was a femme fatale, that no man could resist. In therapy this was traced to her feelings of having won over her mother in the oedipal triangle.

The Pedophiliac Component of Incest

Sachar and associates (1979), working at the New York Psychiatric Institute, conducted a study of child molesters. The issue was raised concerning the personality structure of a man who chooses a child as his sexual object. There was a comparison between men who choose any child (pedophiliacs) and those who choose only adult women. A series of tests was employed to try to determine what was sexually stimulating to these men and to men who did not choose a child. They found no difference in sexual excitement response between the pedophiliacs and those men who commit incest in contrast to those who choose adult women. This group postulated that men who were pedophiliacs or who had committed incest, or both, despite having had sexual relations with adult women, had a conflict about trusting women and saw the child as pure and innocent. This group felt that the treatment had to include working with these issues and helping the man through conditioning techniques in order to resolve these conflicts and, ultimately, to be able to direct his sexuality toward adult women rather than children.

Pedophiliac tendencies thus play a very important part in the incestuous relationship between father and daughter, and the associated personality structure has to be understood in this context for treatment to be effective.

Mothers of Incestuous Families

Many of the people who have reported on their studies of families where incest occurs are struck by the part the mother plays in the process. In an earlier study Kaufman, Peck, and Tagiuri (1954) found that the mothers of the girls were extremely dependent, still struggling with feelings of desertion by their own mothers. Despite their depressed and often dull appearance, on further contact we were surprised to find that they appeared brighter than average. As rejected daughters themselves, mothers used their daughters as substitute mothers, demanding care, nurturance, and self-sacrifice, and displacing their hostility from their own mothers onto these same daughters.

Nakashima and Zakus (1979) described the mothers of incestuous families as having feelings of worthlessness and as being depressed. Browning and Boatman (1977) described the mothers as being depressed and withdrawn from the wife-mother role. In many ways these mothers are threatened by the sexual wishes of their husbands (probably because they feel too much like children themselves or were sexually abused), and pursue their own infantile needs into adulthood.

In some instances mothers were openly hostile and cold toward their husbands, much as with the second group of men we described. The hostility seemed to be reactive to their own needs for mothering, with an attendant inability to meet the needs of their husbands and children. The needs of others seemed to arouse feelings of invasion and stimulated hostile reactions in these mothers.

Because of her own problems, the mother plays a part in the onset and perpetuation of incest by not functioning in the more mature wife-mother role. This may help explain why she denies, avoids, and resists attempts of anyone to call attention to the fact of the incest. When incest did occur, and one daughter told her mother about it, mother responded with "Your father would never do that," and became overtly angry at the daughter for being "a troublemaker."

Another mother, noticing her husband was not in bed with her, went directly to her daughter's bedroom. She looked in and saw father on top of daughter. Closing the door quietly, she went back to sleep. Examples of mother's knowledge of incest and the need to deny it are repeatedly observed in many studies.

Daughters of Incest

For some reason, then, incest occurs when mother, father, and child are in unconscious collusion. The daughter, facing her own oedipal drives, should normally be helped, taught, and conditioned to control and sublimate such wishes. Instead, she is picked by both parents to act out their conflicts. This double condoning of instinctual forces leads daughter into incest, with the result that she complies, often for years, sometimes without a proper sense of its being a forbidden act.

Consequences of Incestuous Experiences

There are several general and specific consequences for maturation and subsequent object relationships inherent in this situation for the daughters. The close incest experience ties the daughter to the father, a tie that lasts, sometimes literally but often emotionally, for most of the daughter's life. Yet in some studies of adults it has been discovered that incestuous experiences appeared to have had no serious effects on the personality of the young women. This finding was confirmed by Yorukoglu and Kemph (1966), who described two such cases.

Schultz (1980) questioned whether "we have underestimated children's capacity to adjust to early sexual experience and are overeager in our psychological and legal need to get at all the details" (p. 12). He further states, "In some cases, intervention causes 'iatrogenic trauma' more severe than what the child has experienced in the sexual encounter" (p. 12).

Karasic (1979) describes various forms of child abuse and "has found from clinical experience that the child's ego may remain intact because of an ability to mobilize protective resources."

Money (1980) says, "A childhood sexual experience, such as being the partner of a relative or of an older person, need not necessarily affect the child adversely."

Character Disorders. Lukianowicz (1972), in a County Antrim, Ireland study of women who had had incestuous experiences, found that none of them had become psychotic or were seriously neurotic. Rather, many had character disorders. This might be consistent with an unresolved, depressive reaction going back to the loss of parenting by mother and father.

In the cases I have seen, confirming the Irish study, the most frequent personality problem in girls with incestuous backgrounds has been character disorders associated with a great deal of acting out. It is my impression that the major contributing component of this type of pathology results from the extent of disturbance within the family, where incest is only one of the pathological features. It is true, however, that in many instances the sexual experience itself seems to have caused later pathology. To illustrate this, we found that some of the girls as adults became homosexual, which seemed to reflect their need to find the missing mothering. Others had difficulty in their marital relations. One of my patients, who had had incestuous experiences with her father, later became very promiscuous and was proud of her ability to give and receive sexual gratification. She married several times, but each marriage ended in divorce. She became frigid and extremely hostile at the sexual advances of her husband, but she was able to have enjoyable extramarital affairs. In therapy it became evident to both of us that each husband was supposed to have been the nonsexual father she did not have. Wanting a nonsexual caring relationship with her husbands, she acted out her disappointment at not having had adequate fathering from her own father. It took considerable therapy to get to these underlying issues and finally to reach a resolution.

We have repeatedly found that girls involved in incest often function relatively well while the incest is occurring. Not all but many do well in school and handle peer relationships quite well. However, it is at the point where incest is discovered, and particularly during the process of legal intervention, that a major disruption may follow. With the threat of loss of father, the family fears falling apart. In addition, many of the mothers become especially hostile to their daughters for causing such severe family problems; in short, they continue to be nonsupportive or nonempathic or reactive to the daughters' needs. In some of my cases this is the time the girl becomes depressed, and in her regression has a great deal of difficulty managing her life. Needless to say, this is the time she needs the most help and support.

Affect Hunger. As some of the girls get older, they still possess and express a great deal of affect hunger. This may be manifest in either promiscuity, homosexuality, or both. It is my impression that the sexualization of relationships to either men or women has several sources. In the first place, sexual acting out with the father was condoned and, in that sense, self- and family-syntonic. However, the longing for missing mothering created by the abandonment of a mother in need of mothering herself often plays a part in the woman's turning to homosexuality and attempting to find a female who can care for and please her. One young woman, as a teenager, had incestuous relations with her father and uncle. When it was finally reported to the authorities, the family broke up. She became extremely upset, and was placed in a group setting. There she developed an intense attachment to a member of the female staff, and later described to me the homosexual relationship that developed. Possessed by an inordinate yearning to be in bed with this woman, she had a compulsion to hold onto her breasts, which she associated to the need for maternal nurturance. Gradually, she developed other homosexual relationships. However, when she worked through the underlying depression related to her mother's actual desertion by being out of the home, and emotional desertion by not helping her avoid sex with father, she gave up homosexuality and began to date men. She then went through a period of heterosexual promiscuity while dealing with depressive feelings that she did not have an adequate father who cared about her as a daughter. She eventually resolved enough of these feelings to get married, and had several children of her own.

Schizophrenia. Contrary to other reports on later consequences of incest, I have found several cases of psychosis, mostly schizophrenia. There were also some women who developed depression. In one such case of depression the woman had made a serious suicide attempt. Incest with her father occurred in her latency years. Having resolved her acting out to the point where she could marry, she had a child. When the child was old enough to go to school she felt deserted and depressed at home. Finding a job with an older man, a well-known scientist, she developed a very strong attachment to him that she tried to develop into an affair. He rejected her, and gradually she became depressed and quit her job. Her suicide attempt followed. She had embodied in this man all of the idealized qualities she had built up in her mind for her father, who had recently died. It would seem she was trying to deal with her feelings of loss of both father and daughter by reenacting the sexual relationship with this older man. The conflicts of her attachment to her husband played a significant part: She tried to split the relationship between the idealized father and the frightening incestuous father-husband.

In the cases of schizophrenia I have studied, incest appeared to have occurred in the context of an extremely disturbed family pattern. In the symbiotic fusion, the sexual relationship is one part of the family pathology. The sexual union between father and daughter takes on the quality of a concrete acting out of the symbiotic tie to each other. It makes them feel that they become "one." Such a symbolic acting out negates the natural separation-individuation that normally reaches its peak at 18 months of age. The parents are acting out for each other and the sexual union of father and daughter meets the same needs for the mother, who is also in unconscious collusion with the incest. Since the normal separation-individuation phase requires a solid ego and a nonpathological management of the aggressive and libidinal drives leading to their integration as the child progresses, the sexual acting out covers over the aggressive components. Under stress, the aggression breaks through, and these schizophrenic family members are particularly prone to violent acting out in the form of suicide or homicide. In the clinical example that follows, suicide was the major issue in the family.

A 14-year-old girl was admitted to a psychiatric hospital for firesetting. This acting out occurred after the incestuous relationship with her father had been exposed and he had been sent to jail. Feeling that she was a criminal, she wanted literally to set herself on fire and to destroy herself. In this fashion she expressed her rage at the loss of father, and her feeling that she could not live without him. She developed hallucinations that her father was speaking to her, along with delusions that he would soon be with her. Her present fantasy was to grow up, have his child, and in this way reconstitute a family, but in an idealized, perfect manner. Her mother had been withdrawn, nonresponsive (in all probability a schizophrenic woman), nonreactive to either the needs of her husband or her daughter. The husband had omnipotent fantasies that he could manage everything. Usually he came home from work, made dinner, and told his wife she could go to bed, an invitation she readily accepted. He and daughter turned to each other with the idea he would teach her about sex in a way she could never learn from anyone else. This would help her to become the ideal woman. The daughter developed an intense symbiotic tie to father, and readily agreed to sexual relations. Therapy and the transference ultimately had to focus on the absent mothering and deal with her symbiotic tie to her father.

Other Family Patterns of Incest or Near-Incest

Tessman and Kaufman (1969) studied and compared some cases where incest did not actually occur, but some of the preconditions that often lead to incest were present. We discussed three such groups and I am adding a fourth.

When one sister was chosen for incest and another not, the unchosen one showed an extreme reaction to being in this position of being overstimulated but unfulfilled by her awareness of the sexual relations occurring between father and sister. These nonchosen girls often become anxious, hostile, or extremely upset. Such a setting particularly provokes high levels of anxiety, and becomes a potential precursor for the later development of somatic and phobic symptoms.

In other girls, if the mother pressures the daughter toward incest because of mother's unconscious needs, and father resists these pressures, another pattern emerges. The father may handle this pressure either by becoming hostile and rejecting toward his daughters, or by denying a loving response to their femininity. Fathers often express this denial by trying to make buddies out of their daughters, whom they may ask to help change a tire or go fishing. This type of girl, when faced with feminine desires or needs, often becomes sullen and withdrawn. She frequently has difficulty in articulating thoughts and feelings. She is more comfortable in motor activity and nonverbal behavior, often showing considerable interest in sports.

In another group, if mother creates the conditions where incest may occur but the father does not have physical contact with his daughter, there may be an intensification of incest fantasies. Mother may encourage incest by abandoning father and daughter, turning daughter into a mother surrogate, and pushing father and daughter into increasing closeness. If the father has no pedophiliac wishes, and an ego strong enough to control his own unconscious incestuous feelings toward his daughter, he will not participate in a physical relationship. However, he may feel emotionally drawn to his daughter. This closeness was expressed in one case by lengthy and deep conversations into the late hours on the daughter's bed. The consequence of this kind of interaction is frequently a more classic psychoneurosis, in which oedipal wishes are stimulated but not actually acted out. These fathers may remain obsessively attached to their daughters and become jealous and critical when the daughters start dating. The daughter in turn may have difficulty finding men who are good enough and have the deep empathy and understanding she experienced with her father. Such women, if they do marry, may be frigid because the sexual relationship has incestuous implications. They also are prone to the classic psychoneuroses, particularly phobias.

In cases where the father has a strong pedophiliac urge and sees his daughter as a sexual object, the actual physical incest may not be consummated because mother has a more mature ego and has resolved her own incest-oedipal conflicts. Incest is abhorrent to her, she is acutely aware of father's intentions, and she actively takes steps to prevent the actual incest. This leads to another pattern of family pathology which is exemplified by the following case.

Father came home drunk and moved toward his adolescent daughter, about to make sexual advances. The daughter stood paralyzed. Mother quickly moved in and put father to bed, telling her daughter to set the table. Characteristic of this type of girl, she passively obeyed and was preoccupied with being "good."

In this type of family where father has difficulty controlling his pedophiliac and incestuous drives, he is viewed as the "monster" in the family by both mother and daughter, and an intense hostile passive-dependent tie develops between mother and daughter. Father, who feels frustrated, excluded, and devalued, frequently turns to alcohol and may have the equivalent of temper tantrums. When these girls grow up they often remain excessively attached to their mothers. They frequently become phobic, displace the fear of father onto the outside world, and have extreme difficulty in leaving home. The attachment to mother remains as their major libidinal involvement. A few have homosexual relations, but any threat to the attachment to mother is frightening. Despite their fears, they often do surprisingly well in structured school and work settings. Most of them do not marry and retain a fear of heterosexual relations.

Conclusions

The libidinal and aggressive drives within all persons play a major part in the interpersonal factors of human relations. These include the incestuous elements and the aggressive punishments for these forbidden wishes, as expressed in the oedipal struggle. In the normal parent-child relationship these forces, when under the control of the ego, contribute to the daughter's development. This process ultimately leads the daughter to identify with her mother as a woman and later to seek for herself a man like her father. It is not the presence of the drives but inadequate or distorted ego development that leads to pathology instead of maturity. Incestuous urges exist in all fathers and daughters. Their successful management results in the resolution of the Oedipus complex. This allows the child to develop the necessary boundaries for her continued separation-individuation growth and development. Excessive rejection or inappropriate expression of these urges can create developmental problems. Sublimation of the normal father's positive sexual feelings toward his daughter can be gratifying to both of them in furthering their sense of self-esteem. The father can feel love and pride toward his daughter, and the daughter can feel she is valued as a woman. The fathers who need to and do act out these incestuous drives with their daughters are struggling with an ego deficit symptomatically manifest in an infantile pedophiliac way.

It appears that when incest actually breaks through it is in the context of a special kind of family pathology where in some way mother, father, and daughter are all caught up in a pathological interaction that includes incest. The pathological interaction that I most frequently observed is a disturbed family in which mother and father are seeking mothering from their daughter because they had not received it from their own parents.

The physical, emotional, legal, and social consequences of incest are extremely varied. Some are immediate, others long range, varying from minimal to severe. Family disruption may be among the most devastating consequences. The degree or severity of the consequences of incest depends on the personality matrix of the family and the girl who has been the object of the incest.

Therapy

Treatment must be inclusive in order to help with the physical, legal, psychological, and social issues, which are extremely complex. In order to be maximally effective, the professionals who treat cases of incest need to be aware of their countertransference feelings. Incest stirs up intense hostile countertransference feelings, especially toward the father, as well as shock and anxiety in relation to the act. Because the helping professions get caught up in their own feelings, they can overlook the overall emotional needs of the family members. There often is a lack of appreciation of the depth of the attachment of the daughter to her father, and father to the daughter. This sometimes has serious consequences. For example, one girl whose father had been arrested was informed he was a criminal and deserved to go to jail. In a group foster home at the time, she jumped out of the window in an abortive suicide attempt. After she broke her leg, she stated she missed her father and felt she was as guilty as he.

Management of these cases requires careful consideration of the personal and familial issues confronting each of the family members. Ideally, a program would include individual and/or family therapy for all. Treatment must deal with the underlying needs, sometimes an unresolved depression, of the family members based on their reaction to past family losses, or a schizophrenic reaction with wishes for symbiotic fusion. Unless the underlying issues have been handled and ongoing treatment arranged, there is considerable likelihood that incest will continue, either with the same or another daughter.

One significant point related to family dynamics and maturation remains to be clarified. In my experience, awareness and detection of the ongoing incest most frequently occurs when the girl involved begins to move toward increasing autonomy and differentiation from the family. This move threatens the precarious family balance, father's equilibrium, and his narcissistic balance. In one case, an adolescent girl started to date boys her own age. Father became furious and ordered her not to date boys. Daughter responded by saying, "If you try to stop me I will tell mother." After "not noticing" for 6 years, mother at this point asked what daughter was talking about. When she was told, a breakup of the family seemed imminent. Then mother sought counseling, which, among other things, led to incarceration of father and an overt depression in daughter. Treatment was needed to deal with all these issues. Part of the ultimate goal of therapy is to further the separation-individuation and autonomy of the daughter, as well as to deal with the unresolved pathology in the parents. This treatment includes helping mother and father with their passive-dependent needs for mothering, and helping both parents with their own unresolved incestuous wishes. In addition, the father needs special help with his pedophiliac impulses.

32

Abdicating Fathers, Homosexual Sons: Psychoanalytic Observations on the Contribution of the Father to the Development of Male Homosexuality

Charles W. Socarides

A disturbed father-son relationship has long been alluded to as contributing to adult male homosexuality. Freud, at several intervals, commented on the importance of the father in the psychogenesis of homosexuality. As early as 1905 he predicted with remarkable prescience the family constellation so commonly noted in subsequent decades (Bieber et al., 1962; Socarides, 1968) in the psychoanalysis of homosexual patients: a domineering, psychologically crushing mother and an absent, weak, hostile, or rejecting father. In *Leonardo da Vinci* (1910, p. 99) Freud observed, "In all our male homosexual cases the subjects had had a very intense erotic attachment to a female person, as a rule their mother, during the first period of childhood, which is afterwards forgotten; this attachment was evoked or encouraged by too much tenderness on the part of the mother herself and further reinforced by the small part played by the father during their childhood." He stated that the mothers of homosexual men were frequently masculine women "who were able to push the father out of his proper place" (p. 99). He was "strongly impressed by cases in which the father was absent from the beginning or left the scene at an early date, so that the boy found himself left entirely under feminine influence. Indeed, it almost seems as though the presence of a strong father would ensure that the son made the correct decision in his choice of object, namely someone of the opposite sex." Again, in a 1915 footnote to the *Three Essays* (1905b), he reflected that the presence of both parents played an important part in normal development and that "the absence of a strong father in childhood not infrequently favours the occurrence of inversion" (p. 146). Freud concluded that homosexual men show a lack of regard for the father or a fear of him. Their motivation in turning toward other men was in all likelihood a result of their need to diminish castration anxiety secondary to oedipal conflict. They sought reassurance by the presence of the penis in the sexual partner, avoided the mutilated female, and denied all rivalry with the father (Freud, 1921).

In subsequent decades, numerous analysts, though corroborating Freud's impressions, increasingly noted the homosexual's inability to make an identification with the father. This inability was apparent not only in his lifelong poor relationship with the father, but also in his pervasive conscious and unconscious feelings of femininity or deficient sense of masculinity, or both, reported during psychoanalytic treatment. A fuller comprehension of the significance of many of these clinical observations was contingent on advances in our theoretical knowledge of psychic events that antedated the oedipal phase (Mahler and Furer, 1968; Abelin, 1971, 1975; Galenson et al., 1975; Mahler et al., 1975).

From 1967 to 1977 I had the opportunity to study a large number of adult homosexual men. During this period I treated psychoanalytically 63 male homosexuals (term of analysis averaged 3 to 5 years) and saw 350 homosexuals in consultation (average one to three sessions). Two-thirds of all these men were suffering from a preoedipal type of homosexuality, which I call the *well-structured perversion*; whereas one-third suffered from the oedipal type (Socarides, 1980). A small number (10) were *schizohomosexuals*, that is, schizophrenics with coexistent homosexuality. More than 214 homosexuals were suffering from the preoedipal type of homosexuality, and it is with this group that this chapter is concerned.

I have found that in oedipal homosexuality, in marked contrast to the preoedipal form, a structural conflict exists, that is, a conflict between the major structures of the ego, superego, and id—between the subject's aggressive, sexual, and other wishes—and his ambitions and ideals. The nuclear conflict in oedipal homosexuality leads to a renunciation of oedipal love for the mother and the assumption of a negative oedipal position. The faulty sexual identity in these cases is secondary to a retreat from an active phallic position. However, these patients are not the relatively pronounced cases in which perverse development is clear and definite (i.e., the well-structured perversions). Nor are occasional perverse acts the only avenue the oedipal homosexual has for the attainment of sexual gratification; for them, perverse acts are not obligatory for the alleviation of intense anxieties, as in the preoedipal homosexual perversion.

In this chapter, I describe what is specifically *homosexogenic* in the families of male prehomosexual children as reconstructed from their analyses, and depict the resulting nuclear conflict of these patients. The developmental issues confronting the preoedipal child are dealt with extensively elsewhere in this volume (Chaps. 11, 12, 15). Though my intention is to focus on the impact of paternal forces on maturation, it is readily apparent that I must take into account the larger context in which they occur, especially the mother-child interaction; thus frequent references to the interlocking effect of both maternal and paternal attitudes will be made.

Homosexogenic Families

My psychoanalytic studies reveal that each of the families of the 214 preoedipal homosexual patients I observed was markedly deficient in carrying out many of the functions necessary for the development of an integrated heterosexual child. Despite the varied environments of each family, specific distorting influences could be isolated, influences that led to emotional and cognitive difficulties characteristic of preoedipal homosexuality. I invariably found in my homosexual patients an interlocking family pathology dating back to the patient's early years of life, and affecting the child's separation-individuation process, profoundly interfering with his capacity to resolve his primary feminine identification, and producing severe ego deficiencies. The specific homosexogenic factor in the great majority of these families was the dominant mother in the area of childrearing and influence.

Indeed, the father's resignation of power, authority, and rightfully held influence may well be termed an "abdication." Paternal abdication, when it occurred in the context of a psychologically crushing mother, had especially severe consequences, for it made the task of separation from the mother extremely difficult, and left the child structurally deficient and developmentally arrested.

Two specific consequences emerge from this family matrix:

1. The boundary between self and object, the self and mother, is blurred or incomplete, with a resultant persistence of primary feminine identification with her and a disturbance in gender-defined self-identity.
2. This developmental deficiency produces an *object-relations* type of conflict, one in which the patient experiences anxiety and guilt associated with the failure of development in the phase of self-object differentiation. The nuclear conflict of preoedipal homosexuals consists of a desire for and dread of merging with the mother in order to reinstate the primitive mother-child unity, with its associated separation anxiety.

The father's libidinal and aggressive availability is a major requirement for the development of gender identity in his children, but for almost all prehomosexual children the father is unavailable as a love object for the child. Nor is he available to the mother as a source of emotional support. If physically present, he rarely limits or prohibits, but is often exquisitely passive (Prall, 1978).

Although most homosexual men portray their fathers as weak, passive, or unable to stand up against the mother, it should not be assumed that all abdicating fathers give the appearance of submission and defeat. Some adopt an affective stance of arrogance, hostility, and superiority, compensatory defensive reactions to what they unconsciously and/or consciously perceive as the insurmountable challenge of fatherhood (Chap. 15). As one patient noted, "My father never can say, 'I do not want this' against my mother's wishes. So he rationalizes not doing it, but I've seen through that. I am angry at what he doesn't allow himself to be. He is weak in front of my mother. Weak means he's afraid of her. The façade he may present is that he is the master of his house, but mother is the boss."

Some homosexuals complain that their fathers actively disliked or disapproved of them, resented them, or thought of them as "sissies." If the father attempted to introduce masculine activities into their lives, he did so in an abrasive manner, with little empathy and often with open derision. In order to avoid, lessen, or eliminate disagreements and confrontations often bordering on violence with their wives, many fathers willingly relinquished the entire supervision of their sons to the mother. In effect, the fathers sacrificed their sons in order to escape their wives.

In some instances, the elder of two male children raised in such an atmosphere does not become homosexual if during the middle to late preoedipal phase another male child is born. The control over the older male child is then loosened, and his male identification with an inhibited but partially available father is reinforced, while the newborn becomes the recipient of the mother's endless domination and manipulation and ultimately becomes homosexual (Paul, described later, is a case in point). In all homosexogenic family settings there appears to be a disturbed, unsatisfactory heterosexual relationship between the parents.

Many mothers of homosexuals suffer from a sense of low self-esteem and from castration anxiety and penis envy. These attitudes and fears profoundly influence their approach to their young male children. They may regard their sons' bodies as penis substitutes or symbols of their own masculinity, "attaching to [them] either positive or emotional valence" (Mahler, 1975a, p. 245). They commonly treat their sons' bodies as if they were part of themselves, or put obstacles in the way of the child's individuation and self-expression, especially during the quasi-negativistic phase beginning at the age of 2 years. Behaving comtemptuously toward the phallic masculinity of their sons, they interfere with the formation of self-identity as well as that of sexual identity by crippling phallic self-assertion and self-esteem (Chap. 7). The abdicating fathers do not interfere with the crushing attitudes of these mothers.

Unless the father shows his readiness to be identified with, and the mother respects the father's masculinity and permits him to act as a role model, the little boy is unable to disidentify (Greenson, 1968) with the mother and establish an identification with the father. This shift requires the mutual cooperation of mother, father, and child; and, in Abelin's words (1971), may well be "impossible for either [the mother or child] to master without their having the father to turn to" (p. 248). These findings confirm Greenacre's earlier (1960) impression that the life history of perverse patients is one in which the father has indeed suffered a severe and chronic, often unremitting devaluation by the mother, especially during the earliest years of the child's life.

In the rapprochement subphase of separation-individuation, the child uses the mother to fulfill regressive fantasies, but she simultaneously arouses intense feelings of resentment and frustration. In contrast, the father, although taken for granted, may represent "a stable island of external reality, carrying over his role from the lost practicing paradise" (Abelin, 1971, p. 243). This is because there is less discrepancy between the child's image of the father and the real father at this age. During this period, toddlers, when they are disappointed by their mothers, begin to evoke their fathers in their play through drawings, calling them on the telephone, playing games with them, and other methods of spontaneous father play.

Such play is almost completely lacking in the histories of prehomosexual boys, as reconstructed during their adult psychoanalyses or elicited from histories obtained from their families. Furthermore, it is strikingly apparent that prehomosexual children have great difficulty in attaching themselves to "father substitutes," compared with normal children, who easily substitute older brothers, grandfathers, and older males for the father.

Dramatic reenactments of rapprochement crises secondary to attempts at intrapsychic separation from the mother are a frequent occurrence during psychoanalytic treatment of homosexual men. The patients feel threatened, as they regress, with maternal engulfment. Regressive experiences of this type are also a reflection of the father's earlier failure to function as one of a wide range of nonmaternal objects helping the child to establish and hold onto reality. They are ameliorated and ultimately mastered through the new object relationship created in the transference with the analyst-father. For it is the father's love that helps diminish the child's fear of loss of the mother's love and the loss of the object, a fear that can become so intense that the child's developmental spurt is completely blocked or frustrated and his reality functioning disturbed. If the child does not have the father to turn to, he experiences a severe deflation of his developing sense of self-esteem, caused by overwhelming feelings of weakness and the painful realization of his own helplessness. A self that has been rendered helpless and fragile by such developmental interferences is likely to develop extreme narcissistic vulnerability. A spurious sense of self-cohesion and self-esteem is then maintained by the construction of a pathological grandiose self (Kohut, 1971). Narcissistic personality disorders are commonly found in association with preoedipal homosexuality.

To recapitulate, a normal boy must find his own identity as a prerequisite to the onset of both true object relations and partial identifications with his parents. To the male homosexual, the mother has, in infancy, been on the one hand dangerous and frightening, forcing separation and threatening the infant with loss of love; on the other hand, the mother's conscious and unconscious tendencies are felt as working against separation. Anxiety and frustration press for withdrawal of libido from the mother and increased aggression. The resulting introjected "bad" mother image leads to a split in the ego in order to maintain the image of the "good" mother. In his narcissistic object choice, the homosexual not only loves his partner as he himself wished to be loved by the mother, but also reacts to him with the sadistic aggression he once experienced toward the hostile mother for forcing separation, and often forces separation repeatedly from his many "lovers."

The unconscious hostility reinforces denial of any of the mother's loving and giving aspects. The homosexual seeks to rediscover in his object choice—in the most distorted ways—his narcissistic relationship with the different images of the mother (and later of the father) as they were first experienced.

Homosexuality can, therefore, be seen as an attempt to separate from the mother by running away from all women. The homosexual is trying to undo whatever separation he has achieved and remain close to his mother in a substitutive way by utilizing the male. Of central significance is that the male sexual partner represents the father, to whom the son is looking for salvation from engulfment. He is seeking a reduplication of himself as an object through the sexual partner.

Case Material

Clinical Example 1

Roger, a 25-year-old homosexual, described the severe devaluation of his father by his mother, the father's ultimate abandonment of him, and its consequences. He was an only child, conceived during the father's military leave during World War II. Because the father was in combat overseas, Roger did not see him during the first year of his life. During that time he lived with his mother, who was intermittently employed in an administrative capacity in an industrial plant. When his father returned, there were frequent arguments leading to severe violence between the parents. His most significant memory was of witnessing, at age 4 or 5 years, a physical fight between his parents. By this time his father, after many arguments with his mother, no longer lived with them and on this occasion was visiting them.

After this incident the parents eventually divorced, and the patient saw his father again on only two occasions. The first was at the age of 8 years, when he and his mother accidentally encountered his father on the street: "Mother abruptly turned me around and we ran for the subway."

At the age of 11 years,

Father called her and told her he wanted to see me, and then she tells me, of course, he never really wanted to see me. She always tells me that, that he never cared for me. That my father was an alcoholic, a sick man . . . I feel so sorry for him. She said that she married him only out of sympathy. He said that he really wanted to see me, and she said she just wanted to protect me and that he was a bad influence; he was a drunkard, and so she got rid of him.

Roger yearned and wept for his absent father. One of his earliest dreams or memories, he could not tell which, was of being with his father in the bathroom. The father was urinating and the boy was looking at his father's penis. The father had a pleasant smile on his face. This represented the boy's desire to be loved by the father, and to be endowed with masculinity through identification with the father and his penis, which he accomplished later in the homosexual act. During analysis, Roger became aware that he was angry with the father and that in his homosexual relations was trying to find and love him. His homosexual partner represented a fusion of maternal and paternal images. In sucking a man's penis (father's penis), he was not only possessing the good and giving maternal breast through substitution, but also relieving aggression by forcibly seizing the penis and becoming whole again through identification with a male partner.

Roger was unable to give up the security of closeness and identification with the mother because of the absence of an accessible father. The father failed to offer a motive for identification, namely, pleasure and joy in masculinity, resoluteness, and commitment to the welfare of his son. Strikingly absent was the most profound motive for the child to identify with the father: the love and respect the mother shows for him (A. Freud, 1965).

Clinical Example 2

Throughout childhood, Paul was dominated by a mother who was in complete charge of the family and responsible for all decisions. Her husband was passive and yielding, obviously afraid of his moody, irascible, and uncontrollable wife. The mother dominated the social and academic life of the patient and his brother, but concentrated mainly on Paul, the slightly younger of the two by 2½ years. Until his entrance into analysis, every decision had first to be discussed with his mother and approved by her; no secrets were allowed.

Paul's childhood was marked by endless parental bickering, violent arguments, and, during his early years, physical assault. On at least two occasions the mother provoked her husband into a physical attack with a kitchen knife. She also threatened the patient with abandonment and divorcing his father if he did not comply with all of her requirements and desires. Paul could not handle his mother's aggression and soon began to identify with her, taunting his father at times, making fun of him, and siding with his mother on nearly all occasions. Paul learned that silence was his best recourse in protecting himself from his mother's vicious outbursts.

His mother constantly stimulated his aggression in early and late childhood by teasing, ridiculing, slapping, and clawing him. Whenever he tried to defend himself, she beat him to the ground, sitting or lying on top of him, scratching his arms and face, and hitting him in the stomach. Fighting back in self-defense only produced more physical damage.

He had difficulty eating during infancy and recalled that at 3 and 4 years of age he was often force-fed when he did not "clean up" his plate. On two or three occasions he vomited his food and was forced to "eat the vomit." Subsequently he vomited often on becoming even slightly upset.

Until he was 16 years old, Paul's mother often slept in the same bed with him. He would fold his arms around her from the back and feel as if he were merging with her and her body's warmth. She frequently disrobed in front of him; at other times, half-dressed, she would walk around with her breasts exposed; in his late childhood and early adolescence, she constantly asked his opinion of the shape and size of her breasts and of her general physical attractiveness. She occasionally made fun of his penis, stating that he would never be able to function as a man with a woman in his later years. She criticized all his friends, especially girls, in an attempt to isolate him.

During Paul's adolescence, his mother constantly jeered at him for failing to rival his brother academically. The brother successfully eluded the mother by staying in his room. The father sided with Paul's brother, and they both teased Paul for his attachment to his mother. Paul's brother and father spent a good deal of time together, often playing ball and attending athletic events together. (The brother married in his early 20s, moved with his wife to a different city, and showed no signs of homosexuality.)

Paul achieved success in graduate school. He was somewhat feared by his colleagues for his angry, aggressive verbal attacks on those he felt were inferior to him or who tried in any way to take advantage of him. He took great delight in verbal onslaughts similar to his mother's, and in revealing to people in authority their "falseness and weakness." His pleasure in this was a result of his identification with the aggressor (his mother), as well as his wish to heap abuse on his father for the latter's weakness and his failure to protect him as a child.

Paul entered psychoanalytic treatment at the age of 27 to seek relief from the futility he felt was ahead of him were his homosexuality to continue. He complained that such a course did not lead anywhere and that his only friends were homosexuals. He was extremely unhappy and suffered intensely from his inability to desist from his homosexual practices. In a somewhat defiant way, he announced to his parents, shortly before entering treatment, that he was a homosexual, and requested their help. His father was alarmed, saying that he could not understand how his son could "live in a sewer." The mother apparently accepted his pronouncements, but felt that his homosexuality was "only a passing stage" and that he did not need treatment.

Paul was unable to disidentify from his mother during the preoedipal and oedipal years because he did not have a father to "go to." This produced both severe difficulties in separation and an excess of aggression. The father was unable to serve as a buffer against the mother's aggression toward the child and the child's aggression toward her. Paul dealt with this aggression by libidinization via the homosexual object, which represented both the maternal penis and the paternal body. By running to men and escaping engulfment by the all-powerful mother, he sought refuge and salvation.

As Paul was helped to face the mother's ruthless, irresponsible, negative, and destructive behavior, he was able to lift himself out of his unconscious masochistic sexual submission to her. Feeling threatened by his mother, he felt threatened by all women. As a result of his treatment, he gradually developed affectionate feelings for women.

During the course of treatment, Paul's father told him that when Paul was 2 years old the father thought of divorcing the mother, but didn't because of "us children. . . . The fact that he could think of leaving us makes me feel lonely now." Loneliness frequently led to massive anxiety, which was then neutralized through libidinalization in the homosexual act.

Paul continued to relive occasions in his past when his father "sided" with the mother. This represented a complete capitulation to the hateful, destructive mother in order to "save himself. . . . My father tells me that I should be a 'good son to her.' He wants me to go all out and give myself to my mother in order to protect *him*. Recently he took away from me the promise that he was going to give me money for the treatment." It was his belief that his mother was the only potent force in his life and his father an essential incompetent. "In my homosexuality I think I'm giving in to her. I do not take another woman, I take a man. . . . I remember how she used to treat me, but it seems at least she loved me." His despair at feeling unloved by his father, previously unconscious, was extreme.

As the analysis progressed, Paul felt increasingly liberated from both his destructive aggression toward his father and his hatred of his mother. "It's not a nice feeling to hate someone, but what was there is still there. She was a very sick woman and still is, and this is what she did to me. I called my father after I felt these things last night, and I told him I was all right. When I spoke to him, however, he still seemed frightened. He suggested that I not come home as often as I did in the past because it upset my mother!"

The full range of Paul's destructive aggression and murderous feelings toward men made their appearance in the middle phases of the analysis. "I often have fantasies about hitting a man, hurting him. I thought about this guy that I had sex with the other night, screwing him in his office, and sometimes it even changes from sex to pure aggression, just like jabbing him. And after I talk of these feelings I feel somewhat kindlier toward men."

His aggression toward men served multiple functions: It protected the breast of the mother by displacing aggression onto a substitute, the male with a penis; it punished the father for denying him his masculinity, for failing to protect him against the crushing mother; at the same time, having intercourse with men forced love and affection from father substitutes. His homosexual activities constituted a severe sadistic assault on men (his father) and were highly overdetermined. Anxiety, which always preceded homosexual arousal, was libidinized and neutralized through homosexual activities. Desire for homosexual relations occurred whenever he felt frustrated by life's disappointments and fearful of abandonment by his mother. The act quieted fears of loss of the mother and gratified sexual wishes toward both parents. He felt assured of their love in a substitutive way and warded off fears of castration by acquiring a potent and strong penis from the male partner.

Paul felt that his father threatened him with his mother in order to "get off the hook himself." For this reason he harbored profound feelings of bitterness and hatred toward his father. Protected by the confidence and trust in the analyst, he mustered enough strength through identification to consummate his first heterosexual experience, which he perceived as a triumph. He realized in therapy that his mother's dismissal of his homosexuality when she was first told about it was tantamount to sanctioning it. If he were interested only in men, he would never leave her for another woman.

In the ensuing months, Paul began to enjoy heterosexual relations more fully. He reported that the "bond between my mother and myself, that crappy bond was being broken. But it's like losing something when I tell you about my interest in women and when I begin to think of having sexual intercourse."

In the later phases of the analysis, Paul recalled a crucial memory, deeply repressed, of the beginnings of conscious homosexual desire. The incident occurred at the age of 7 or 8 years: "The children used to take a nap in the afternoon in an afterschool group where *Mother left* me, and there was something about a bigger boy. I wished to have him as a *substitute for my* father and for a friend, and he would do something in bed with me. The other boy was 12 years old and he lay on top of me and I liked that. Before that I was a sexless kind of kid" (emphasis added).

Paul could gradually remember that in the earliest years of his life, "my father loved me a lot and he loved me most, and that's why my mother took it out on him." This reappraisal of the father-son relationship, his recognition that his father had attempted, even if only for a short while, to fight the mother's undue attention and domination, provided considerable relief from his hostile feelings toward his father and led to a gradual turning toward the father once again. He realized that his father did love him during an early period of his life, that his father was not completely helpless and weak, but eventually had to "sell out" to the overwhelming, hateful mother. Yielding to the mother became a means of survival for both father and son.

Of crucial significance was Paul's identification with the aggression of the mother. This further acted to isolate him from his father: "I began to make my father feel like shit. He was a skunk and a shit, and I would hurt him and embarrass him and it would give me satisfaction and my mother satisfaction, too. If I couldn't fight my mother, it seemed to me I could join with her. I would fight and hurt my father, and this would please her. I feel terrible and ashamed when I realize what I did."

Paul realized that sex with men arose from aggression, whereas with women aggression did not create desire. He began to comprehend that sexual intercourse with men was really a repetition of the incident in childhood that he had transformed into a childhood fantasy. It was not the erotic experience per se that he sought in his homosexuality, but its reassuring and reaffirming function. He recalled that, harassed, threatened, and subdued by his mother and unprotected by his father, he would lie on his bed face down, violently move his body, and say, "Fuck you, father." He added, "I had similar things happen to me with my mother, and when I was younger and angry with her I'd lie on the bed face down, and I'd get a general feeling and I'd have to say, 'fuck you, too, shit-ass mother.' These angry feelings always translated into sex, and finally I'd masturbate and take up some of the hate and then I could relax [erotization of aggression]." The substitution of men for the mother produced a quieting of hatred and was an essential factor in helping him retain his mental equilibrium.

A major insight was achieved in his discovery that, when angry with his mother, he developed homosexual desire: "It is obviously that I do not have a father to stand between me and my mother, and the only way I can get one is through homosexuality, and the only way I can enjoy her is through homosexuality. The homosexuality has to do with my need for my father: Wanting my father and hating my father and wanting my mother and hating my mother."

He noted that "the worst thing my mother could say to me and the worst thing she could do which made me homosexual is when she told me, 'You are just like your father.' She would tear him down and then by saying this with a terrible smile on her face she makes me feel just awful." The homosexual act helped to restore Paul's self-esteem, but it only functioned as a temporary alleviating measure.

Long-repressed incestuous desires of the oedipal period and feelings of destructive aggression toward the mother began to emerge into consciousness and to be assimilated:

I know I wanted to have sexual intercourse with her for years. It brings tears to my eyes when I say this and I'm crying now. I'm loving her all over but I wish my mother had my father and my father her, and I could just let it go at that, the two of them . . . . I didn't feel I did anything wrong as a child, but I see now that in loving her I'm killing her and destroying her. The killing of her and below that is the intercourse with her. But I feel there is a good reason to kill her, that is, to kill our relationship, to get her out of my life, and let my father have her. There is an expression, "Go in health and peace." If it could happen that way, my mother could have my father and my father her.

In the later phases of the analysis, Paul began to perceive his father's good qualities, to enjoy them and to love him.

I guess I really put him down in a way, as I didn't think I could get anything from him, any support from him against my mother. I really didn't think he had a lot to offer in certain respects, but my mother put these ideas in my head, that he was weak. She can no longer do this, but she doesn't stop trying . . . . If I had to choose now between parents, who would be alive—and this may sound cruel—I'd rather it would be my father than the other way around because he really knew how to enjoy a lot of things. She knocked a lot out of him. For example, he loved music and art, loved going to the park and watch people play ball. She didn't like any of these things and always criticized him and said he only took me to free things, making him a cheapskate. In actuality, he tried to get for me those things he could offer. He tried to get me to enjoy them, even if he could not afford to take me to 'paying things.' He took me to concerts that didn't cost money, and museums.

In a follow-up interview years after the end of his psychoanalytic treatment, Paul attributed much of the success of his treatment, the removal of his homosexuality, his ability to enjoy heterosexual intercourse and love a woman, to the fact that he "reacted very strongly" to the analyst. He had to trust somebody and the analyst was the only person he could trust. He also felt a sense of accomplishment throughout the treatment, just being able to stop and think about himself in a more realistic way. He was profoundly affected by the tremendous encouragement he received from the analyst (father). Throughout the treatment, except for short periods, Paul was confident that the analyst was on his side completely, "that no matter what happened, [he] was always there." In effect, a new object relationship had been achieved.

Conclusions

I have described one factor in the complex and multifactorial genesis of adult male homosexuality: the father's unwillingness or inability to function appropriately during crucial phases of his son's early development. The preoedipal homosexual has failed to achieve separation from his mother. He has been unable to disidentify from the mother and identify with the father. Although the mother plays a vital part in the separation-individuation process, the father's role is also decisive.

33

Domination-Submission Patterns in the Patriarchal Family Structure

Nathaniel Ross

Ethologists have accustomed us to the concept of the pecking order (Lorenz, 1966) in animals, administered in the vast majority of cases by the males of various species. This order is reflected in the behavior of primates (McLean, 1973; Sagan, 1977), as well as that of mammals that rank lower on the evolutionary scale. Primates adapted to the open fields, such as baboons and macaques, show distinct domination-submission types of behavior (Starr, 1971), not only in the drastically different sizes of males and females, but in the pecking order of the males themselves. Among wolves, adaptation in the interest of survival is demonstrated in the totally submissive response of the weaker, smaller, or younger wolf, who lies on his back in a completely vulnerable posture when play between him and a dominant wolf reaches the point of the possibility of a dangerous attack by the latter. On the assumption of the vulnerable position by the submissive male, the dominant male stops threatening the submissive one. Needless to say, the females are regularly dominated by the males. Among birds, the pecking order is a matter of common knowledge. Again, the males are usually the dominant ones, although as in kites and crows, the female mates of dominant males may lord it over lower male members of the pecking order.

Interestingly enough, ethologists have discovered that there are centers in the brainstem, the lowest segment of the triune brain, that monitor the executive functioning of these hierarchical orders (Sagan, 1977). McLean (1973) terms this most primitive part of the brain the *reptilian brain*. When such centers are extirpated in dominant animals, their aggressive behavior disappears.

Until modern times at least, the same types of domination-submission phenomena have been the rule in human society, no matter to what degree our cerebral equipment has enabled us to transcend the limits of animal behavior. Except in rare and isolated cases, such as that of the Trobriand Islanders, fathers are the dominant forces in families, and men the ruling forces in society. Such dominance, although under attack during the twentieth century, especially within recent years, remains the order of the day. This is especially true not only in countries dominated by theocratic regimes, such as Islamic countries, but in those with ancient absolutist traditions, like the Soviet Union (in spite of its Marxist pretensions), similarly in modern China, in Latin America, and even in some Western countries. In the latter, a battle against the patriarchal domination-submission forces in our culture is being waged in the interests of the chief subjects of domination: women and children.

Before proceeding to clinical illustrations of domination-submission patterns, I should like to call attention to a recent ethological discovery that illustrates the thesis of this chapter, and another historical fact that strikingly illustrates the resemblances between a royal personage and male squirrel monkeys (McLean, 1973).

In *Freedom at Midnight* (1975, p. 169), L. Collins and D. Lapierre write*:

Centerpiece of the great collection of the Sikh Maharaja of Patiala was a pearl necklace insured by Lloyd's of London for one million dollars. Its most intriguing item, however, was a diamond breastplate, its luminous surface composed of 1,001 brilliantly matched blue-white diamonds. Until the turn of the century (the 17th) it had been the custom of the Maharaja of Patiala to appear once a year before his subjects naked except for his diamond breastplate, his organ in full and glorious erection. His performance was adjudged a kind of temporal manifestation of the Shivaling, the phallic representation of Lord Shiva's organ. As the Maharaja walked about, his subjects gleefully applauded, their cheers acknowledging both the dimensions of the princely organ and the fact that it was supposed to be radiating magic powers to drive evil powers from the land.

During the same century it was inconceivable for a Japanese man to acknowledge love for a woman, but entirely proper for her to cut off a finger or two from one of her hands to demonstrate her adoration for him. When a male squirrel monkey feels in any way threatened, he shakes the bars of his cage, lifts one leg, and exposes an erect penis. On the walls of the caves of Altamira (Hays, 1962), there are drawings of ithyphallic warriors. These are soldiers going into battle, their spears thrust forward, their penises in full erection. I have often observed little boys, under 4 years of age, frequently clutching their penises as they do battle with swords or spears or guns. This observation deserves further study.

*I am indebted to Dr. Richard Atkins for having called this historical item to my attention.

Case Material

In order to illustrate a number of the far-reaching effects on individuals of this powerful form of dominance, which has so deeply affected human life, I shall present clinical cases illustrating its origins, subsequent effects on the life cycle, vicissitudes in forms of psychopathology, the ironies and paradoxes attendant on its exercise, and a few of its social and cultural implications.

Clinical Example 1

The first case is that of a man who came to treatment in his 30s because of neurotic symptoms consisting of acrophobia and travel phobias; sexual dysfunction consisting of tendencies to premature ejaculation and fears of uncontrolled ejaculation in certain interpersonal situations; a lack of self-esteem in spite of conspicuous material success; and tendencies to become anxious and depressed whenever he succeeded in any venture. Although he was a very tall, powerful young man who had been voted the most handsome student in a prestigious preparatory school, he had felt very often that no woman would ever desire him. He was constantly plagued by the desire to look down on his wife—who had been graduated from an Ivy League college with conspicuously rigorous scholastic standards of admission, considered by his friends extremely attractive—as limited in intelligence and cultivation, and not especially good-looking.

This man's father was a financially successful businessman, arrogant, hot-tempered, and very egotistical. Extremely limited in his formal educational background, he was contemptuously anti-intellectual. He never praised his children for any of their educational achievements, although he seemed to place great value on the social prestige arising from admission to preparatory schools and colleges with very high scholastic standings. When the patient came home to report truly significant academic achievements, he was greeted with either indifference (by both father and mother) or sneering remarks about the probable superiority of his classmates. This father would tolerate no differences of opinion. When, after a few years of analysis, the patient one day confronted him with the latter's intransigent dogmatism, his answer was, "If I'm wrong, I'm dead." The father was invariably critical of his own relatives and acquaintances. As a result, he had no friends. He was intensely competitive, to the point of ultimate financial self-destructiveness. On one occasion, when the patient, who worked for him after his graduation from college, differed with the father about certain business decisions, the latter proceeded in his own way despite the most obvious prospects of failure. He wound up losing a large sum of money. As a child the patient remembered coming home from school frequently to describe facts he had learned, only to be greeted with scorn and derision by his father. If the patient cried, he was laughed at by the father and called a coward and a crybaby. Throughout his childhood he was terrified at the thought of physical injury. The mother, who never failed to boast to her son about his father's "brilliance," was extremely seductive and indeed took him into bed with her when the father went off on business trips. This went on until he was 12 years old. During adolescence she would often sit before him in her nightgown while she cut his fingernails. On several occasions later on, while having his nails manicured, he had ejaculations (without erections) in his trousers. At the same time as these seductions went on, his mother would enjoin him against making love to girls until he was married. She would constantly interrupt him with a frown on her face when he had telephone conversations with girls. The patient remembered his childhood illnesses as the happiest times in his life.

With regard to love, the father would openly express his contempt for any man who presumably loved his wife, stating that any man who claimed to do so was probably covering up the fact that he was having an affair. The patient never saw any manifestation of affection between his parents.

In addition to being terrified of rebelling against his father in any way, the patient was continually trying to appease him. The analysis was characterized by working through difficult negative therapeutic reactions in which masochistic temptations to fail were prominent. He experienced great difficulty in giving up identifications with the sadistic father that had, in part, acted as defenses against severe castration anxiety. He began to recognize that the wish to surrender, to fail, to succumb to the father's domination, represented desperate attempts to obtain love from a man totally incapable of giving it to anybody. In this particular case, two of the truly surprising effects of this move toward liberation were (1) his success as a result of sheer professional superiority in getting a large corporation to finance the buying out of his father (he thus succeeded to the ownership of the business), and (2) his deepening interest in intellectual and artistic pursuits in which he had already shown real giftedness during his school years but which he had not dared to express in any overt way because of the scorn and contempt to which he had been subjected when displaying such interests. As for daring to feel like an adult inwardly and to love his wife, this took much additional analysis.

This patient had been thoroughly demoralized by the arrogant, sadistic, and totally domineering behavior of a father who, it could easily be deduced from many of the incidents and attitudes described by the patient, was at bottom a weak, frightened, inadequate man, totally incapable of facing his own problems. The overwhelming narcissism, with a complete incapacity for loving anybody, was extremely destructive to others and to himself, and indeed, he ended up in his old age totally subservient to his sadomasochistic wife.

Another basic point to be made here is that paternal domination of this degree, which seriously damaged the patient's attempts at separation-individuation, and a failure to achieve the capacity to enjoy life, attendant on the inevitable vicissitudes during the rapprochement phase, succeeded in storing up a reservoir of violence and hostility within the patient that again and again was directed inward, resulting in repeated states of depression. Evidences of such hostility, together with great fear of it, also took the form of intense competitiveness with his classmates, friends, and business associates. This had made it impossible to establish any satisfactory levels of friendship. The slightest evidence of success in anybody he encountered immediately engendered feelings of envy, denigrative attitudes, and involuntary expressions of such resentment, not always successfully concealed. In other words, identifications with the aggressor were the order of the day. The social implications with the accumulated hostility will be discussed after the presentation of other clinical material.

Clinical Example 2

A man of 50, married for many years to a woman who had frequently admitted having lovers, came to analysis after several years of unsuccessful therapy, designated as analysis. He was one of the younger of five children in a family dominated by a father who had, according to the patient, never brooked opposition by anybody, male or female, and had never hesitated to express contempt and ridicule toward his wife and children and friends. The patient's mother was totally at his beck and call, extremely passive and very proud of her meticulous, compulsive keeping of domestic financial records. She openly showed preference to the patient, always sat him beside her at the dinner table, and made admiring comments about his physical attractiveness.

Despite the father's conspicuous financial and social successes, he suffered a "breakdown" during the patient's adolescence when an important assignment given to him by his state government proved too much for him. He seemed depressed for many months but was never hospitalized or treated by a psychiatrist. He then stopped formally working and retired, becoming increasingly wealthy through financial investments. Later, this type of early retirement was to become one of the patient's principal ambitions, but he was never able to achieve it.

This man stated at the first interview that he had been unhappy as far back as he could remember. As a schoolboy he would sneak around the main paths to the schoolhouse because if he met his schoolmates he would often be teased and attacked. He was very unpopular, a "loner." It was difficult to ascertain the reason for this, until it gradually emerged that he had a very sharp tongue and very quickly became defensive in any social situation, with both men and women. His father, too, although he achieved great social prominence and was selected for many prestigious (nonpaying) positions, had the reputation of being biting and sarcastic.

When he grew up, despite outstanding academic and professional success, the patient felt inhibited and anxious in social situations. He longed to give up his job and retire to a farm like his father. His feeling among his peers, at successive levels in his career, was always that of being a child. In this respect, his failure to achieve a sense of adult identity was exactly like that of the patient described as the first case. His relation to his wife was that of the underdog. She herself had a sharp tongue and was known for her formidability in social situations. The first patient's wife was quite opposite to this, but the patient frequently felt toward her, as he did toward all women, that they were "big" and overwhelming, especially their breasts. Both these men suffered from serious sexual difficulties, never having had confidence in their potency.

Conclusions

The openly experienced hostility of both these men to their fathers was bitterly expressed during their analyses. Frequently the second man, while using tools or driving a car with his father nearby, would have an almost irresistible impulse to strike him or run over him.

The first man was intensely competitive, not only with his father but with other men. Every game felt like a contest to the death in which any loss might be followed by a period of actual sexual impotence. The father himself was constantly betting and gambling, whereas the son expressed his competitiveness in games in which his conspicuous athletic skill was often damaged by feelings of fear, inhibitions, "tightening up," and subsequently losing.

The second patient had no more faith in his ability to win a woman than did the first. Yet both were their mother's favorites. They had both been extremely submissive and unconsciously hostile to women. A common feature reflecting the powerful urge to submit and to surrender themselves, not only to men but to women, was reflected in different ways in each of these patients. In the first, if his wife was at all active in sex play, he would lose his erection. In the second, on several occasions when in a passionate embrace, he would suddenly be overcome by panic, by a fear that he would lose consciousness and be "swallowed up." At this point he would lose his erection. Without entering into the complexities of the analytic situation, it can be stated at this point that these two sons of extremely cruel and domineering fathers had retreated from the oedipal conflict through intense fears of castration, had returned to their mothers for succor, and had in turn been powerfully tempted to submit to these mothers by being swallowed up in symbiotic fusion. Among the many results of this situation were a sense of isolation from other men; an intense underlying hatred and competitiveness with them, in which they felt doomed to failure; a persistent feeling of lack of a sense of identity as adults; marriage to women by whom they felt continually dominated; and failure to enjoy life. With regard to the last-named phenomenon, there was abundant evidence of very unhappy experiences during the rapprochement subphase, in which the mother's joy in the child's ability to achieve separation is reflected in the latter's elation and exultation in its age-appropriate achievements. Both mothers, deprived constantly of opportunities to be admired and genuinely loved by their husbands, evidently turned to their sons for substitute gratifications they could not obtain from their husbands.

At bottom, in both of these cases, there was clear evidence of an intense longing for acceptance and love from the father. In the first case, this was evidenced by a persistent tendency to overidealize surrogate fathers, which came out strikingly in the tranference neurosis. For a long time, the first patient could not conquer his insistence that the analyst was totally without flaws, that he was a man of impeccable scholarship, who invariably made the "right" decisions in every life problem. He could not imagine that his analyst ever engaged in sexual activity, that he ever had any professional or marital difficulties, nor that he had ever been ill. He was quite obviously displaying the well-known defense of splitting between the good and bad object, in order to cling desperately to the former. The intensity of this attitude was much greater than average. As it turned out, it became inescapable that his father was actually extremely dishonest, hypocritical, ungiving, unloving (including his feelings or rather lack of feelings for his grandchildren); and that he became increasingly depressed and unsuccessful as his son began to attain prominence in his chosen field. The situation had been continually compounded by the patient's mother, who never failed to praise the father to the skies for his alleged "brilliance," even to the extent of inventing obvious prevarications that the father was a "great scholar." In any event, it was necessary to evoke underlying negativisms and hostilities in the transference before the patient slowly began to take pride in his own achievements, in his work as well as his handling of family situations, before it began to be possible to consider termination.

The second patient's underlying desperate need for a good father was also reflected in his idealization of the analyst in the transference. During the first year, his attempts to flood me with referrals of his colleagues and relatives had to be repeatedly dealt with. But further than that, numerous dreams revealed homosexual longings for the father (he had had a number of homosexual experiences in adolescence, which he had been terrified to relate to me); and every once in a while, especially on birthdays and holidays, he would burst into tears, longing for words of warmth and approval from the father. Finally it became clear to him that he had continually demeaned himself, not only to the father, but both inwardly and outwardly to other men, and that his insistent feeling that he had remained a child in spite of dramatic evidences to the contrary, all represented attempts to achieve the impossible—namely, to extract love from a man who appeared quite incapable of giving it to anybody. Not until then did the patient begin to feel that he was "growing up." This conviction was manifested in a great surge of relief when he went home on the occasion of one of his mother's birthdays. At the dinner table, on this presumably festive occasion, the patient listened to his father ridiculing not only his children but his wife and suddenly "got fed up." Turning sharply to his father, he exploded, "For Christ's sake, Dad, can't you ever stop being so nasty?" There was shocked silence and to everyone's great surprise, the father said meekly, "Gee, I was only joking." Obviously, a great deal of analytic work had been achieved before this denouement took place. From then on, the patient began to experience more and more elation in his telephone conversations with his father (they lived in different cities) when the expected acerbity on the latter's part continued to diminish in frequency and intensity as the patient became more and more able to converse with his father on equal footing.

The patient divorced his unfaithful wife and began to establish increasingly intimate and satisfying relationships with his children. He ultimately married a woman who was far more suited to him in temperament, stability, and commonality of interests.

Space does not permit the detailed description of two other cases (among many others of a similar cast) that illustrate various facets of what I have designated as the "domination-submission pattern," but I shall briefly mention them for the sake of illustrating several common features.

Clinical Example 3

In one, a man who had suffered from lifelong anxiety, insomnia, rage, contemptuous attitudes, and verbal attacks on others, ultimately had a heart attack despite prolonged previous analyses that apparently had not resulted in effective approaches to his preoedipal experiences as revealed through transference phenomena. He finally discovered that his crucial underlying wish was not only to discover that the expression of his death wishes toward the analyst would not only not bring retaliation, but would make the latter understand fully his desperate need to be held and cradled in parental arms. In other words, no matter what he did or felt, he would be unconditionally accepted. Like the two fathers who were described in the first two cases, his father had been unrelentingly absolute in his insistence on always being right. The mother had died when the patient was 5 years old. Afterwards, he had had several operations for chest wall infections over a period of years. These were unconsciously felt as punishments for his having "killed" the mother, who was later described to him as a rigid, compulsive, distant woman, often unable to care for her children because of illness. The father was constantly making verbal attacks on his children, competitors, customers, relatives, and friends. The patient's identification with this aggressor was reflected throughout his life in the same kind of behavior, but as we can see, despite this he felt like a helpless infant, always crying out for love. Not infrequently he would have a sudden feeling in the analytic situation of affection for the analyst, to be succeeded by a panicky fear that he was "becoming a homosexual."

Clinical Example 4

Another patient, again a man of achievement, had seriously compromised his career by hostility, sarcasm, intolerance to subordinates, hypercritical attitudes toward friends who might have helped him, and a generally aloof and superior demeanor. He was married and able to have intercourse successfully, but had periodically had passive homosexual experiences (per anum) since adolescence, accompanied by strong orgasms. This man too had an extremely domineering father, who had divorced the mother when the patient was in his 20s. The father was not a very well-educated or highly intelligent person, unlike his bright children, but would not tolerate any contradiction by them on matters in which they were obviously much better informed.

This patient revealed in analysis the deepest longing for love by a father figure. Indeed, he had been "in love" with a man in his field whom he greatly admired and had finally timidly confessed this to him, hoping to have his homosexual longings reciprocated. The other man said he was not homosexual and that such a relationship was impossible. During analysis, at times of crisis in his marriage, and in extramarital affairs, he would suddenly be overwhelmed by powerful fantasies of being a baby, held in a strong man's arms with loving care. This patient was, like two of the others described, a tall, strong, outstandingly impressive-looking man of decidedly handsome appearance.

531

Discussion

What do these patients have in common that reflects certain results of the domination-submission pattern so ubiquitous in the patriarchal families that prevail in most parts of the world today?

1. All of the individuals described suffered from serious disturbances in their sense of identity as adults. Even when they presented themselves to the world as effective, successful men of recognized achievement, they were uncomfortably aware of feeling less than men among their peers and in relation to women. In all four cases, they were either acutely conscious of an intense desire to be a helpless, cared-for child, or this fantasy emerged during their analyses.

2. Serious deficiency in sexual potency was present in three of the cases. In the fourth there was seldom if ever a feeling of tenderness in lovemaking. In one of the cases, the first cited, potency had been maintained only when he felt sadistic and contemptuous toward his wife.

3. In all cases, loving was felt as a weakness, not a strength.

4. Strong homosexual tendencies existed in all four. In one of them it was overt, although he was also heterosexual in his relation to women and had actually experienced feelings of love toward his wife during courtship and for a few years after marriage.

5. Intense competitiveness toward other men was a feature of all four, resulting in all cases in severe restrictions in their capacities for friendship.

6. The constant feeling of being tested as to their masculinity haunted and harried the lives of all these men, often making daily living a torture. The theme of incessant threats of castration pervaded their lives. They all found it very difficult to lose in various challenges, at work, in physical activities, in courting women, and in their sexual experiences. The sensation of being watched and judged was common to all of them.

7. Masochistic tendencies took the form of temptations to surrender to more powerful or what were imagined to be more powerful individuals, and in two cases to women.

8. Except for the first patient described, who had maintained his marriage at a fairly stable level, the three other men were married either to more dominating, castrating women, or inappropriate partners of decidedly socially depressed levels. In the first case, as stated above, the patient could feel fairly comfortable only by imagining his wife to be intellectually and culturally inferior, which she was not.

9. A strongly ambivalent attitude toward the analyst, with a drastic split-

ting between overidealization and underlying denigrative tendencies, characterized each analysis.

10. A deep-seated need to be loved by the unloving fathers characterized each case, despite persistent evidence that the fathers were conspicuously incapable of loving either their wives or their children. The ultimate impossibility of satisfying this need and the discovery that the stated or explicit demand on the part of the father to be loved, admired, or respected in the face of his resentment and intolerance for any attempt at autonomy by the son—in themselves evidence of his inability to love—finally convinced these patients that they had been living under the aegis of the most self-destructive illusion all of their lives.

11. Identification with the rejecting, domineering, hostile, aggressive father dominated all four men. They were completely unconscious of this force within themselves and it was necessary to reveal this defense to them in the most tactful and gradual way before they were able to accept its validity and begin to emancipate themselves from its influence.

12. Three of the four patients had sons toward whom they were unconsciously repeating the behavior of their fathers toward them, as might have been expected. In one case, although the son was grown when the father came to analysis, the insight came in time for the patient to establish a real reversal of the relationship, whereas in another, the child was young enough for the analysis to prevent real damage from taking place.

Conclusions

It must be obvious that the problem of domination-submission presents innumerable complexities that should be and, indeed, in numerous instances have been explored. There is, for example, the benignly despotic father who is capable of some transcendence of his narcissism in relation to his offspring and who is not as cruel and intolerant as the fathers described in this article. One would have to study cases of this type to determine the ramifications of the psychic development. There is the knotty question of variations in native endowment and their effects in counteracting the destructive effects of domination-submission at various phases of development. The factor of object loss of either parent must affect ultimate personality structure, depending on the phase of development when it takes place. What are the effects of domination on the female child's development? Here there does exist a body of clinical material in my experience, but space does not allow its elaboration. Then there are the results of domination by the mother to be considered. Here, too, ample material is available, but I have confined myself to discussing the role of the father because of the specific subject of paternity that is the theme of this book. Of course, it is also true that in most of the contemporary world the great majority of children have been brought up in families dominated by males. Living in the Western world, we have become less aware of this fact, but it remains true that Oriental, Islamic, Latin, and Orthodox religions and African cultures are dominated by male chauvinism. The social, political, and cultural implications of this fact are staggering, but such discussion must be reserved for future studies.

34

Early Loss of the Father: A Clinical Case

Robert D. Stolorow
Frank M. Lachmann

The psychoanalytic literature on child development and object loss has focused on the effects of the presence or absence of the mother during the early preoedipal period, emphasizing in particular her contribution to the structuralization of self and object representations. The psychoanalytic treatment of a young woman whose father had died when she was 4 years old illuminates the crucial developmental importance of the father for a girl of this age, and illustrates as well the specific consequences of losing him just before entering the oedipal phase.

When Anna began her 4-year analysis, she was 31 years old. She had been married for 12 years and worked as a real estate broker. She complained of both diffuse anxiety and states of acute panic, the content of which centered around fantasies that her husband would leave her for another woman.

Anna was born in Europe and lived in her early years through the horrors of the Second World War and the Nazi occupation. When she was 4 years old her father was taken to a concentration camp, where he eventually died. During an analytic session, while exploring the ways in which she kept alive aspects of her relationship with her father in her current experiences with men, Anna made a startling discovery that proved to be pivotal in her treatment. She suddenly realized that she had never accepted the reality of her father's death. Indeed, she exclaimed, even now, she had a feeling of absolute conviction that her father was still alive. Much of the remainder of her analysis was concerned with uncovering the genetic roots and characterological consequences of this firmly embedded conviction.

The case presented here is a considerably revised and expanded version of material first published in *The Psychoanalytic Quarterly* (44:596–611, 1975). It also appears in a book by the authors, *Psychoanalysis of Developmental Arrests: Theory and Treatment* (New York: International Universities Press, 1980).

At the age of 4 years Anna had not yet developed the cognitive capacities that would have enabled her to comprehend the meaning of the terrible events that were taking place around her, especially the sudden and inexplicable disappearance of her father. The surviving adults in Anna's environment, particularly her mother, failed to provide her with sufficient assistance in the task of assimilating the grim realities of the war and her father's incarceration and death. The mother falsified the reality of the war, telling Anna that the exploding bombs were just doors slamming. She also pretended to Anna that her father had not been taken to a concentration camp, and tacitly perpetuated the myth that he was alive by never directly discussing his death with Anna and never openly mourning his loss. These experiences left Anna with a feeling of confusion about what was real and what was unreal, a feeling that was reanimated in her analysis with the discovery of her unconscious conviction that her father was still alive. It was left to Anna's own fantasy life to fill the vacuum left by maternal omissions and falsifications in order to make some sense of these incomprehensible and tragic events and to regain some feeling of comprehension and mastery: "I had to find some reason. It all seemed so crazy. I couldn't accept that such things could happen and there was nothing you could do. I was trying to understand what was happening. None of the adults would tell me. No one sat down with me and told me my father was in a concentration camp or dead. So I made up my own explanations."

The specific content of the fantasies that Anna elaborated to "explain" her father's disappearance and continued absence developed as the complex consequence of several factors, including her level of cognitive development, the particular circumstances surrounding her father's disappearance, the nature of her relationship with her father, and her psychosexual organization at the time of her loss of him.

With regard to cognitive development, there is evidence that a child at age 4 has not yet attained the abstract concept of death as a final and irreversible cessation of life. To the extent that a death is acknowledged at all, it is typically conceived of as a potentially reversible departure to a distant geographic location. A common element in all the conscious fantasies with which Anna explained her father's absence was the notion that he was living somewhere in a distant land and might someday return to her. Throughout her childhood and on into adulthood, at first consciously and later unconsciously, she "waited and waited" for him to come back to her and feared that she might "miscalculate" or "do something wrong" that would make her miss her "last chance" to see him.

Consistent with this level of cognitive and moral development, Anna, in her fantasy explanations, blamed herself for her father's depar-

536

ture and continued absence. The particular circumstances surrounding his departure contributed to the content of her fantasies. Anna recalled that she had found a notice and had brought it to her father. She did not understand what it was and took it very lightly. She even felt excited about the opportunity to deliver something to her father. When she gave the notice to him, she danced around him in a very happy and excited mood. She came to believe that the notice had instructed him to report to the Nazi authorities. After he was gone, she developed a fantasy that he hated her for being happy when she delivered the notice because her happiness meant she did not care about him. "He stayed away because I was such a rotten little kid to have acted happy, and he was glad to be away from me. If only I had given him a proper farewell. I missed my last chance to make him want to come back."

As an older child she continued to blame herself for the tortures she perceived he must have experienced in the concentration camp and, later, for his death. She imagined that if she had not delivered the notice or if she had been miserable, upset, and hysterical when she delivered it, her father would have been magically spared. In the transference, whenever she was faced with a separation from the analyst, Anna revived these elements of her fantasy. On such occasions she worked herself up into a state of acute panic and frenzied worrying as a kind of "ritual sacrifice" in order to "prevent disaster"—to ensure that the temporary separation would not turn into a permanent one as it had with her father.

The guilt-ridden, self-blaming elements in Anna's fantasy explanations must, of course, be placed within the context of her relationship with her father at the time of his departure. Anna recalled that she loved her father dearly, but that her boundless love for him had been only partially requited. He was often away on long business trips and was sometimes preoccupied, irritable, distant, and rejecting of her affectionate overtures and demands for attention. Anna sometimes felt hurt and left out because her father and mother were very devoted to each other and often went out together. On occasion she had a guilty wish to be "relieved" of the strain of the thrilling but sometimes painful "game" of trying to win expressions of love from her father. Clearly, to the extent that her great love for him had been disappointed and rebuffed, she had harbored angry wishes to be rid of him. When he was taken away, her feeling of guilt contributed to the content of her self-blaming fantasies.

The final elements for Anna's fantasy explanations of her father's disappearance—perhaps the most fateful ones for her characterological development—were provided by the vicissitudes of her psychosexual development. Because her father had been taken away when she was 4 years old, Anna's explanations of his absence included features of both the castration-anxiety period and the oedipal stage. She developed fantasies that her father stayed away because she was defective, repulsive, and totally valueless, or because he had met another woman and had chosen to live with her; if Anna could just win him away from the woman who had stolen him, he would return.

Material that unfolded in the course of her analysis suggested that castration imagery played the more prominent role in her interpretation of her father's absence. The loss of her father intensified and magnified the feelings of mortification and self-devaluation characteristic of the castration-anxiety phase, in that it occurred at a time when Anna had turned to her father as an idealized "selfobject" (Kohut, 1971, 1977) whose phallic grandeur she could share and thus regain a feeling of wholeness and self-worth. The lost father was not primarily the sexual father-as-lover of the fully blossomed oedipal phase. Rather, he was the strong, powerful, glorious, presexual father-as-protector of the phallic phase, from whom she sought shelter against a threatening world, along with reparation of her narcissistic wounds. The importance of castration feelings in Anna's reaction to the loss of her father was evidenced both by her pattern in adult life of forming attachments to powerful, protective phallic father figures, and by the important role that a distinct illusory penis played in her development. From her early childhood, Anna had maintained a fully conscious conviction that a small penis protruded from between her vaginal lips, a conviction that held serious consequences for her developing self-image and sense of sexual identity.

Although the exact time at which the illusory penis was crystallized could not be established, it can be fairly safely assumed that its rudiments appeared as a direct response to her father's disappearance. The illusory penis is subject to two complementary explanations. According to the first, Anna imagined that her father stayed away because her defective and "castrated" genital made her disgusting and valueless to him: She was "only a girl," she had no penis. She then developed the fantasy of possessing a penis in an attempt to repair her imagined "defect" and as an expression of her wish to make her father value her and return to her now that she was "whole." However, the penis fantasy only exacerbated her feelings of defectiveness. Later in life Anna made further efforts to repair her "defect" by forming ties to aggrandized, phallic father figures, union with whom would undo her imagined castration (Reich, 1953).

According to the second explanation, the penis fantasy was an attempt to restore her father by enshrining a part of him in her own body image. She developed the illusory penis to make restitution for the loss of the whole object by incorporating a highly valued part object, her father's penis. Indeed, the tenacity with which she later clung to her illusory penis was paralleled only by the tenacity with which she maintained her conviction that her father was still alive.

The various explanatory and restitutive fantasies discussed so far cannot technically be described as defensive denial fantasies. Primarily, they represent attempts on the part of a 4-year-old child to adapt to a state of cognitive and structural insufficiency; that is, to fill in with phase-specific fantasy elaborations the vacuum left by an immature psyche inadequately supported by the surviving adults in her environment.

At some point after the war, during her latency period when cognitive and emotional maturation and expanded sources of information had enabled Anna to begin to comprehend the realities of her father's incarceration and death, she indeed began to construct an elaborate defense system, which, until its dissolution by analysis, functioned to keep her father alive. Her efforts at this later time can properly be described as a denial that prevented the mourning process of which she was now becoming developmentally capable. The denial was promoted by the multiple components of her complex, ambivalent attachment to him. She wished to keep him alive because she wanted to spare him a horrible death and also to keep alive the hope that he would return and she would again enjoy his love. She wished to keep him alive because she felt terribly guilty and magically blamed herself for his death. And she wished to keep him alive because she needed once again to feel sheltered by his protection and united with his phallic grandeur.

In order to deny his death, she now had to cling to both the castration imagery and fantasies of oedipal defeat. And to maintain this denial system, she had to select and cling to negative memories of her father's devaluing, rejecting, and excluding her, while repressing all positive memories of his loving, caring for, and valuing her—lest they contradict and jeopardize her denial fantasies. The repressed, split-off imago of the good, loving father was displaced to the memory of a kindly uncle to whom Anna attributed gifts from her father and other expressions of his love. In her adult life, Anna further buttressed her denial system by clinging to real or imagined experiences in which a father surrogate devalued or rejected her or left her for another woman. This in turn supported her conviction that her father was rejecting her or chose another woman, but was still alive. Furthermore, she warded off experiences of feeling loved, valued, or chosen by a man so that her denial fantasies and her devotion and loyalty to her father would not be jeopardized. Clearly, when Anna's denial fantasies coalesced into a static defensive system that had to be maintained at all costs, it had extremely deleterious consequences for her self-esteem as a woman, as well as for her characterological patterns of relating to men.

It was between the age of 10 and early adolescence that circumstances necessitated the final solidification of Anna's denial fantasies into a static and unassailable system. When Anna was 10, her mother remarried, and Anna's denial fantasies dovetailed with a host of oedipal-competitive and sexual conflicts, greatly intensified and complicated by her hope that her stepfather would substitute for her lost father. At this point Anna, in reality a bright and pretty child, began to feel ugly, stupid, defective, and "freaky," and became obsessively preoccupied with her illusory penis—symptoms that remained with her until they were removed by the analysis.

These castration themes served multiple functions for Anna during this crucial period in her development. The oedipal triad quickly evolved into a highly dangerous situation in which her stepfather openly expressed a preference for Anna over mother, and met her blossoming sexual fantasies and provocativeness with overt seductiveness. Her mother, an insecure, subservient, masochistic woman, was an inadequate oedipal rival who promoted rather than discouraged the developing sexual bond between Anna and her stepfather. Quite consciously and deliberately, Anna used her feeling of being defective and possessing an illusory penis to prevent a dangerous oedipal victory and to avert the possibility of overt sexual activity with her stepfather, reassuring herself that he would not want her once he discovered her "deformity."

Additionally, feeling ugly, stupid, and undesirable to her stepfather warded off Anna's wish—and averted the possibility—that her stepfather would become a father substitute and thus intrude into and jeopardize her deep bond of devotion and loyalty to her real father. Anna felt ugly, hated herself, and developed talionic dreams of being buried alive, partly because she felt tempted to commit her mother's crime of burying her real father by accepting her stepfather as a replacement.

Her mother's remarriage represented to Anna the first tacit acknowledgment of her father's death by the adults in her environment. This threatened abruptly to obliterate her denial fantasies. Anna was thus forced to redouble her efforts at denial and restitution and to fortify all the mental operations by which she was keeping her father alive: feeling defective, freaky, and worthless; brooding over her illusory penis; imagining that boys would reject her and prefer other girls. Moreover, she had to mobilize feelings of being totally unloved and abused by her stepfather, because to recognize and accept his affection and caring would mean accepting that her father, too, had loved and valued her, and was, therefore, absent because he was dead. By fending off her stepfather with castration imagery, Anna not only protected herself and her mother from the dangers of oedipal competition, she also ensured that she would not

540

"miscalculate" by accepting her father's death and accepting her stepfather. She ensured as well that she, unlike her mother, would be ready
and waiting for her father when he returned.

The final solidification of her denial system occurred during Anna's
early adolescence, as her pubertal development exacerbated the threat of
overt sexual activity with her stepfather. In response to her stepfather's
sexual intrusiveness and seductiveness, Anna would think to herself, "My
real father would never do such things," and she wistfully yearned for her
real father's return. She elaborated fantasies in which he would return,
her mother would choose to stay with her stepfather, and Anna would
remain with her real father and enjoy his care and protection. Anna, like
Freud's Dora (1905b), called on the imago of the idealized protective
father to rescue her from an incestuous threat. This necessitated the final
cementing of her denial fantasies, through which she kept her father
alive, into a static defensive system with all its unfortunate consequences
for her self-image, self-esteem, and patterns of relating to men.

Much of this history was recapitulated in the transference. During
the period when the analytic work consisted of active confrontations with
the denial fantasies and encouragement for Anna to accept the reality of
her father's death, she became immersed in rage-filled transference
struggles in which she cast the analyst in the image of the sexually intrusive stepfather who threatened to destroy her loyalty and devotion to her
real father.

The therapeutic alliance withstood the impact of these transference
storms, and Anna was eventually able to work through the transference
and to give up her denial system. The most immediate consequence was
that she experienced a belated mourning process as she permitted herself
to imagine the tortures and horrible death her father must have suffered
at the hands of the Nazis. (At this point she also began to fear that the
analyst would die.) Coincident with this unfolding mourning process was
Anna's dramatic recovery of positive memories of a loving father; along
with these memories, she also retrieved repressed memories of loving devotion from various other men. Anna now clearly recognized that she
had elaborated a complex denial system in which she viewed herself as
defective and sacrificed her memories of her father's and other men's love
in order to spare her father the terrible, agonizing death she now realized
he must have experienced. Just as the sacrifices she endured to keep him
alive were a measure of her great love for her father, so now was her pain
in belatedly imagining how he died.

As Anna accepted and mourned the death of her father, she also
began to give up the feelings of being defective and undesirable. The
working through of her denial system and her father's death had made

possible the uncovering and reintegration of the repressed, split-off imago of a loving father. This in turn resulted in marked and lasting improvements in her self-image and self-esteem and in increasingly strong feelings of being valued and desired by men in her current life.

Conclusions

The case of a young woman whose neurotic personality structure evolved from the trauma of the death of her father when she was 4 years old has illuminated the crucial developmental importance of the father as an idealized selfobject for a girl of this age, and has illustrated as well the specific consequences of losing him. The loss of her father during her transition from the period of castration anxiety to the oedipal phase eventuated in specific disturbances in her self-image, her sexual identity, her self-esteem, and the pattern of her relations with men. However, as evidenced by her capacity to maintain a therapeutic alliance during difficult transference struggles, the loss had not obliterated the stable and differentiated self and object representations, which reflected the developmental achievements of the relatively benign years before her father's death. Hence, for Anna, the loss of her father affected the content and affective coloration of self and object representations, but did not interfere with their structuralization.

At age 4, Anna had been developmentally incapable of comprehending the death of her father, and the fantasies with which she attempted to explain his absence became the heir of the lost father and underwent the psychosexual transformations to which the imago of the actual father would have been subjected had he been alive. Hence her explanatory fantasies were shaped by her psychosexual organization at the time of the loss. Later she wove these fantasies into an elaborate denial system, which constituted the nucleus of her neurotic personality structure. The discovery and dissolution of this defensive system were pivotal to her analysis, making possible a belated mourning process and lasting improvements in her self-image and self-esteem.

35

Fostering the Consolidation of Paternal Identity: The Tufts Family Support Program

Shera Samaraweera
Claire Cath

The basic aim of the Family Support Service is to attempt primary and secondary prevention of psychosocial problems in infancy and early childhood and to facilitate the continued growth and maturation of the parents. We operate on the hypothesis that prepared couples can do a better job as parents and can better enjoy their child and their parental role. This preparation is not merely a cognitive process, but involves emotional shifts as well. Our program tries to bridge the gap between clinician and researcher as well as that between the research and the baby and family in need by utilizing a multifaceted, multidisciplinary team approach. One arm of the team works out of the child-guidance clinic, where a child psychiatrist (or clinical psychologist) and pediatrician work with the family's counselor (or social worker) to offer an initial evaluation of the whole family, followed by periodic monthly assessments, including Bayley Testing of the infant. Ongoing interventions are based on the findings of these assessments and are usually implemented by the family's counselor, who forms the outreach arm of the team. The family also forms ongoing and important relationships with a child psychiatrist or psychologist, and a pediatrician, who offers well-baby care and pediatric consultation to the family. The family counselor is supervised by the team leader, who is usually the child psychiatrist or clinical psychologist on the team. The family counselor makes weekly home visits with the primary aim of establishing a warm, supportive working relationship with the family in the context of which "education" and early interventions can be achieved. This multipronged approach to the family's needs and problems ensures better physical and emotional care for the new baby.

We serve a range of families, from normal couples to those who already have some psychopathology and for whom both educative and psychotherapeutic measures are needed.

We believe that parenting (skills) cannot be taught or improved by cognitive input alone, but can occur only when accompanied by some changes in unconscious fixations and identifications (Chap. 36). Hence prospective parents are encouraged to examine and discuss their relationships with each other and with their own parents, as well as their aspirations, fantasies, fears, and more realistic expectations in connection with the birth of their baby, so that problem areas and past conflicts still extant may be identified early and worked on. We help them to assess what the pregnancy means to each of them and to form a mutually supportive "alliance of pregnancy," so that they can turn to each other for nurturance and emotional support. The counselors also help parents deal with *new* conflicts that might be activated by the pregnancy or the child's birth. More active support is offered during the childbirth process (with the worker attending the birth where indicated) and early postpartum period, when many unexpected crises can occur.

Weekly home visits continue after the baby's birth, but the focus now includes issues around the infant and parent-infant interaction. The infant's unique characteristics are demonstrated to the parents in order to help them form an early and enduring attachment to the baby. Interventions are geared around the early diagnosis of problems in the infant, in the parent, or in the parent-infant interactions.

We have gradually begun to appreciate what types of interventions may be helpful and meaningful to individuals in accepting their parental roles and achieving a sound parental identity.

In the Family Support Program we have had the opportunity to work with and observe expectant couples in first as well as subsequent pregnancies. In most cases, we strive for a longitudinal viewpoint, following the family's formation from early pregnancy to the child's second birthday. We believe we have been able to observe and isolate some of the factors that favor and promote the man's positive conception of himself as both husband and father, and of the new threesome as "his family," rather than as a competitive triangular relationship.

The first pregnancy presents the initial challenge and opportunity for the man to begin achieving a paternal identity. The birth of his baby, and his interactions with his spouse and his child will ideally consolidate this process. Subsequent pregnancies may be even more complicated, however, if they revive the significance of ordinal position relationships with siblings, which are then replayed in the new family setting.

We have begun to develop interventions that may help individuals in accepting their parental roles. In this chapter we will present a case in depth, describing these strategies and the progression from individual lifestyles to couple formation to early family development. We will delineate those aspects of the prospective father's participation in the pregnancy and birth that enhanced or impeded the creation of an "alliance of pregnancy" (Deutscher, 1970). We will show how this in turn led to effective attachments between parents and infants and between spouses themselves over a period of 5 years. We will then offer a general discussion of how intrapsychic phenomena in each member of a couple influenced their ability to relate to each other and to their child, and to accept their parental roles. This approach evolves from and depends on psychoanalytic theory, as well as on the new research of many workers in the field of pregnancy, birth, and early infancy. In the Family Support Program our focus is ideally on primary prevention and early intervention to prevent problems between spouses, and between parents and children. Over recent years the role of the father has been increasingly appreciated.

Clinical Example

Although ideally we work with couples from midpregnancy to the child's second birthday, we accepted this both late- and short-term case because the couple was so eager for help and had many strengths on which we could build even in the relatively short time available.* The period in which we could work was a crucial time. It meant fostering a bond between the parents and between them and their child. With this couple we felt we would be making a worthwhile contribution to their lives, although we would not be working with them as we usually do. We felt we could assist them in the working through of already strongly ambivalent feelings toward each other and the pregnancy. Although the program focuses on the couple, the infant, and the maturation of the family as a whole, in this chapter we will focus more on the father. We will begin with excerpts from a letter from the father sent shortly after their departure from our program.

Dear Claire,
   It's been nearly three months since we met. . . . We often think of you. Many times I intended to write. . . .
   People say that the 21st and 22nd years of a person's life are apprehensive ones. For me they are confusing as well. Sleepless nights filled with doubts of my future and our future. . . . Urges to be accepted and to accept in this adult world. . . . A sense of aimlessness. Occasionally I am delighted in realizing that I am growing up. Yet growing up seems so painful. . . .
   Suddenly I began to realize what I went through in that fiercely competitive environment of Boston. This morning was the first time in 5 years that I had a

*This couple was seen by Claire Cath and supervised by Shera Samaraweera. We have used first names in keeping with the important informal aspects of the program.

sense of "belonging." But there still is a problem. I am too young, too confident of my own abilities to believe. . . .

Our life has its happier moments too. Milly and I often go picnicking. We both like to explore nature. The baby has 4 teeth now. He can stand, sit, crawl, get into many things and give us lots of misery. But all unhappiness is instantly resolved when he stares at us with his big brown eyes, cuddles us tight and says "adada, amama."

How is life in Boston?

As a reminder, we are both eagerly waiting for your words.

Affectionately yours,
Wing-Gong B.

In this chapter, 2½ months of work will be much condensed. In retrospect, we realize that the interventions resulting in the progress in the couple sound too easy, but in all probability this represents both an artifact of condensation and the limits of reporting verbally complex family interventions.

In May, Milly and Wing-Gong, a mixed racial unmarried couple, aged 20 and 21, were referred from a local university by a staff psychiatrist. Claire's first visit found them in his dorm in a state of panic and chaos. She learned that Wing-Gong was the eldest of three brothers, had come from Okinawa as a child with his parents and paternal grandmother, and had lived with them until college.

However, this was no time for history taking. He couldn't stop talking about his fear of what marriage would be like and his unreadiness to be a father, especially as he would be starting a university fellowship in the fall. He asked Claire in several ways, "What will it be like to try to study with a crying baby around?" It happened he was turned away by his family when he asked them for help about the issues involved in marriage and having a baby. His father coldly replied, "What is there to tell? You know it all already," and his mother had never been a person to whom he was able to turn for information or help. In his fiancée's presence he admitted he felt trapped and unready for marriage.

Milly had come as a child with her family from a middle European country. She looked very pregnant and very frightened. She and Wing-Gong were trying to finish their exams, planning to graduate on June 2, marry on June 21, have the baby about July 14, and move to the West Coast in the middle of August. In addition, it was soon clear that they had remained socially quite isolated although they had been at the same university for several years.

To Claire's question, "How were you disciplined as a child?" Milly casually replied, "Oh, they beat me." Her description of herself was of a very good girl who always did what her family wanted, including being an excellent student. Indeed, she had just completed a difficult major in 3

546

years. We quickly realized that Milly and Wing-Gong were struggling in an emotional tug-of-war between each other and two sets of angry and controlling parents.

Related to this was the decision not to attend their own graduation. They said sadly, "No one is coming, anyway, because they all have to come to the wedding." Wing-Gong was further conflicted about the marriage because he felt he would be less likely to be invited into his father's business with a non-Oriental wife. Although he was studying for an entirely different career, he rather saw himself someday living a wealthy man's life like that of his father.

As a family, they would need more money than his fellowship allowed. He could not see a mother working: "She should be home with the child." With their financial situation that would be impossible. This marriage did not fit his image of what a marriage should be or what his parents' marriage was like. Because they had never shown emotion in front of him, he had no clue of how his parents fought or demonstrated affection. He had received much approval by learning to write his own name at 5 years of age. The most outstanding thing he remembered his parents having said about him was that he exhibited a terrible temper, which he alleged was handled by admonishing him to use more control.

Deprived of parental love, the couple made an immediate transference to Claire as a wise, noncritical mother who found them likeable and who possessed a good sense of humor. They worked well and quickly with her, separating from their families of origin, building an alliance around plans for the infant's birth, and preparing for the wedding. In the Family Support Program we usually help couples by applying some of the recent research of Klaus and Kennell (1976) on maternal attachment, and that of Greenberg and Morris on paternal engrossment (Chap. 5), which stress the value of fathers' involvement in planning for birth and being present at delivery. Because of the nature of Milly's and Wing-Gong's relationship and his not being ready yet, it seemed particularly important to help the father become invested in planning for the delivery. So Claire spent a great deal of time talking with him about the pregnancy, prenatal care, and the childbirth process, and how a man can help himself achieve certain goals once he learns about the process and decides how much he wishes to participate.

Milly, on her part, was anxious to breast-feed her baby but was discouraged, especially by her mother, who warned her that breast milk can poison babies. Milly was furious. Claire permitted her to ventilate her anger freely and then told her that Milly's own milk would be the best for the baby. She added that she had seen many women either confused or jealous of a nursing mother and giving bad advice. They talked about the importance of the feeding experience and its meaning to the infant in terms of the tactile and visual experience as well as nourishment. Claire talked of how a baby learns to love by the way in which parents hold him, stroke, cuddle, speak to, and look at him.

Having attended one prepared childbirth class at the hospital where the birth would take place, they pronounced the classes "dumb" and refused to go back. But it was possible to influence them as to the importance of preparation for the birth, especially emphasizing the value of the father's role, and how knowing what was going to happen would help them both feel less frightened and more in control. Wing-Gong avidly read *Husband-Coached Childbirth*, and Milly read a book on breast-feeding that Claire brought. Claire talked again about the importance of the feeding and the early bonding as a social event for the *whole* family. She indicated that it was an experience in which all the senses were involved, i.e., through the feeling of the parent's skin against the baby's, through eye-to-eye contact, through the parents' voices, and mother's smell. Claire suggested that a father should not miss the chance to enjoy the holding, cuddling, talking to, smiling at, and the joy of the baby's response, even though he is not the one offering the food. They wanted to know more about handling the baby. Wing-Gong especially was unaware of what an infant is like at different stages of development. He was concerned about sharp things in the room on which the baby might get hurt. He had no knowledge of when a baby can sit, stand, walk, and he wanted to hear more.

Arriving one day to find them angrily attacking each other over details of the wedding plans, Claire told them she could easily see how everything must seem too much. She knew several people who had organized weddings and clearly remembered how anxious they were that everything should turn out well. She stressed that none of these people were preparing their own wedding, nor were they graduating, having a baby, or anticipating a major move all at the same time. No wonder they were overwhelmed. Anyone would be. Claire helped bring the problems into focus by encouraging them to vent their feelings, and offered suggestions for the wedding plans, which were examined together as options, leaving the final decision to them. It seemed important to help them hold up their heads under the venomous attacks of their families. They were able to lean on Claire for information, practical support, clarification, and interpretation of feelings. At times when she arrived, they seemed close to falling apart, but always pulled together during the interview. It seemed clear that a handsome wedding, a feeling of competence around delivery, the father's active participation in the birth process, and success for Milly in breast-feeding were all crucial in helping them build confidence in themselves and in their ability to parent.

Once things were talked over, both handled most of the details with dispatch. As Wing-Gong seemed able to become decisive and take a leadership role, the issues were clarified and placed in some orderly sequence.

Later, at the wedding, Milly's mother's anger was clear on her face as she walked down the aisle, her eyes ablaze. Otherwise, everything went beautifully. It was a sunny day, and there was a lovely buffet luncheon in an open courtyard of the university chapel. Milly's family left the very next day, but Wing-Gong's family stayed 10 more days and then left an elderly grandmother with the newlyweds.

About a week before Milly's due date, another crisis developed. This involved their future exclusion from university housing following the birth of the baby. They worked this out themselves, but not without turning to Claire to vent their anger and fear, and to discuss plans about what to do. They moved into a new apartment just in time for the delivery.

Claire received a call on a Sunday morning from a very excited and pleased Wing-Gong. He had been through the entire delivery with Milly, and they had a son. Wing-Gong had been there for the entire 30-hour labor, which had begun Friday about 4:00 P.M. On Saturday afternoon he had taken Milly to the hospital, where she was sedated at 6:00 P.M. when she was only 3 cm dilated and in considerable pain. The medication had the effect of stopping the labor for 3 to 4 hours. At the time it seemed to Milly and Wing-Gong that the staff had been in a state of confusion before they finally decided against a cesarean section; a spinal anesthetic was then administered and an episiotomy performed. The baby was finally born with the help of forceps. After all this, Milly was too weak to hold the baby but Wing-Gong was allowed to carry him to the recovery room, where he "played with him and got to know him." Since Wing-Gong had learned of its importance, he was able to make the most of this opportunity and tried to interact with his child through every sensory modality. Then he took the baby to Milly for her to "play with" for a while. But Milly had felt "spaced out" after the delivery. The baby had been somewhat sedated and not interested in the breast although they had pushed the nipple into his mouth. Claire's reassurance that when a baby is sedated he is unlikely to be interested in feeding took the onus of blame off her shoulders.

Milly also told Claire that although she had "panicked several times" during the delivery, "Wing-Gong kept me going by doing the breathing with me and sustained me in many ways and I couldn't have made it without him." This indeed was eloquent evidence of an "alliance of pregnancy."

On Claire's next visit at their apartment she was sorry she had not made a second hospital visit. The postdelivery period can be an especially vulnerable time for the parents and infant, as other emergencies often arise. They may need help when frustrated by certain institutional procedures. In this instance, they had been sent home while the infant remained hospitalized because of an elevated bilirubin level. The infant had to be kept under lamps with his eyes bandaged. On a practical level, however, they had handled the emergency well, having rented a car and delivered breast milk to the infant. This was particularly striking in that on the occasion of Wing-Gong's parents' visit when Claire had suggested renting a car to take them around, his response had been, "What! Me drive a car in this city?" But finally they had the baby home, and Milly was struggling to build up a milk supply that had lagged because of the separation from the baby and the lack of stimulation of nursing. Still she was reluctant to supplement. A complicated crossfire of seemingly conflicting advice was heard from the La Leche League representative, the pediatrician, and the paternal grandmother. Claire, to defuse the stalemate, said to Milly, "I guess it makes you feel a failure to think of supplementing." She nodded, the angry, defiant look disappeared, and tears began to roll down her cheeks. Then Wing-Gong gave Claire a useful clue: "She's so tired because she takes the baby into bed at the 1 or 2 A.M. feeding, falls asleep and keeps waking up through the night. . . . Neither she nor I get a full night's sleep and she's exhausted all the time." Claire pointed out what a long way she had come, how well she had done with all obstacles so far. They were able to reason out together why her milk supply was lagging and to conclude how a supplementary bottle for the middle of the night feeding would enable her to get a night's sleep and waken in the morning with full breasts.

This was not the only issue, however. Wing-Gong also wanted his turn to talk. He was angry both at Milly and his son and appeared quite jealous. He needed time from Milly for himself too, especially because he didn't like his sleep or hers to be so disturbed. Recognizing his need for time too, Claire said, "I know how you must feel. So many fathers, especially when deprived of sleep, get angry at babies and even jealous. One father in our program told us he was so angry at the baby when woken up at night that he wanted to throw it against the wall. Of course he only thought about it but didn't act on it!" "Exactly!" Wing-Gong exclaimed excitedly, "That's exactly what I said. Last night I said to Milly, 'Milly, throw that baby against the wall.'" They talked more about how hard it was to have to share Milly with the baby. It is sometimes as hard for a baby's father to share his wife with their baby as it is for an older brother to share his mother with a new baby. This led him to talking about his younger brothers and how he felt when they were born. During this conversation about his childhood, Wing-Gong brought up previously latent concerns about the mischief little boys get into. He told of an incident where he threw a flaming paper kite into a window in his parents' home. They began to appreciate together how parenthood revives all the fantasies as well as the real worst and best sides of selves, both as fears and expectations. How much we imagine things going wrong needlessly, especially when we are upset, tired, or impatient. Claire also pointed out that it was probably harder for Milly and Wing-Gong than for lots of other couples because they had not even had time to adjust to being married before they had to start adjusting to being parents. There would be many tasks and adjustments as new parents for them to work on, including finding suitable outlets for their own needs. Claire pointed out that it is important to find new ways to give to each other and to themselves in order to be refueled enough to be able to give all that a baby needs. They talked about the things each of them liked to do for fun and how they could get to do these things while they were still in the city and later when they moved.

The issues around supplementary bottles and their solution seemed to turn the tide, and a refreshed Milly was soon able to be both mother and wife and soon discontinued the bottles. In the last few visits, in addition to talking about their feelings about leaving, travel plans came up for discussion. They had planned to take the night coach to save money. This meant they would arrive at 3:00 A.M., West Coast time, with no one to meet them after having been up all night. Claire pointed out potential pitfalls of this plan, hoping to persuade them to go in the daytime. But when they said goodbye to her, they were still planning to leave Monday at midnight. On Monday afternoon Claire called sadly to say another goodbye and to wish them luck. Milly sounded surprised when Claire mentioned the midnight coach and said, "Oh, we're not going until tomorrow morning. We decided to go in the daytime after all." For Claire, the delay, reflecting a more mature judgment, was a lovely going-away present.

Discussion

Having exhausted the options of family and the university's counseling resources, this couple, especially the father, was absolutely overwhelmed by the news of the pregnancy. With no one to turn to, the expectant father felt he was going crazy. His feelings of isolation and inadequacy were reduced partially by Claire's effort to make every next challenge seem possible. She helped them proceed step by step through what initially had seemed insurmountable chaos to establish some sense of priorities, so that whatever strengths were present could emerge from within themselves. By themselves they seemed to lack the capacity to order priorities. This state of ambiguity, indecision, and chaos, as well as the nascent alliance of pregnancy and marriage, was eventually confirmed in the father's letter quoted in the beginning of the case: "The 21st and 22nd year of a person's life are apprehensive ones. For me confusing as well . . . sleepless nights filled with doubts of my future and our future."

In anticipating parenthood, spouses and prospective spouses face a crisis that often involves images of changing roles and real self-sacrifices in lifestyles that can be frightening. Fantasies of what the new role will be and the balance between demands or joys may be far from reality. In some couples, models for loving parenting may be entirely missing. Hence they do not know what to expect and have difficulty visualizing themselves in the parental role. Thinking through some of these issues ahead of time, especially with the reality-based caring insight and knowledge of a mature worker, can considerably ease the transition to parenthood. We have found that mental visualization or activation of fantasy of what to expect under the best of circumstances, as well as how problems can be ameliorated or corrected under less than ideal conditions, is important. Correction of uncontrolled fantasies and fears about the unknown, therefore, is one of the most valuable tools in this process.

We knew that the lifestyles of each partner in this couple were very different before they came to college, even though at this point in college they shared some similar interests. Both had been born in foreign lands and their first language was of another country. Their culture, childrearing practices, and family lifestyles were quite disparate. Still, though there were many conflicts, they shared the strong desire not to give up the baby or their relationship. Milly's style of dealing with her anxiety around significant changes was to hold in feelings and repress anxiety until she exploded. Wing-Gong's style of handling anxiety was to become distraught and panicky and to lie sleepless. He blamed his disorganization on not knowing what to expect. For people like Wing-Gong, for whom marriage and parenting are ambiguous states clouded by secrecy ("because my parents never showed emotion to each other or to us"), the worker needed to be more open, and through reassurance be more licensing of emotional expression. Claire sensed and capitalized on the increasing bond between the couple. While discussing the issue of intimacy, Milly noted that she tended to have only one friend at a time, and it became Wing-Gong, even though her mother had told Milly, "Men are out for all they could get." We helped Wing-Gong to become warm and giving by utilizing his obsessive-compulsive defenses to master his anxiety. By learning more about pregnancy and the childbirth process, he could feel in control and not "crazy." He was then able to become more warm and nurturing to Milly.

This improved his self-confidence and enhanced his self-image. He also began to feel that the role of husband and father was not totally terrifying after all. However, at first he was concerned about his career and wanted to put his energy into establishing it. Fearing that a baby would consume them, neither father nor mother had their mind on the real needs of a child at this point. The unexpected pregnancy was a poor fit in their lives indeed. Their families were unempathic, distancing, and threatening. It was the worker's task to determine whether something about these dreaded expectations could be altered; and whether each of them, especially the father, could be helped to accept the pregnancy and view the unborn child in a more positive light. During pregnancy, even in the best of circumstances, each member of the couple undergoes a great turmoil and psychic reorganization. We have found that the father-to-be, like the mother-to-be, faces many new tasks and unique feelings never experienced before (Chaps. 18, 19). If these feelings are appropriately handled, with the arrival of the child a sense of mastery and delight strengthens the familial bond. In Wing-Gong's words, "All unhappiness is instantly resolved when he stares at us with those big, brown eyes."

In our program, we create an atmosphere in which the father's ambivalent feelings toward the unborn baby, his spouse, her pregnancy, and her closeness to the baby can be expressed, tolerated, and worked through. We have found that it is completely within normal limits for some fathers to experience at some level one or more of the following range of emotions: fears of being abandoned by the spouse for the baby, jealousy of the unborn child, rivalry about the mother's ability to produce a baby, concern about having a defective baby, notions of having damaged the wife, fear of the wife's continuing and indefinite dependency, concern about financial burdens, role conflicts, and so on. When we have a clue as to which of these feelings exist, such concerns can be explored and worked through in order to release the positive feelings that may coexist; for example, many fathers may then feel a sense of pride and accomplishment and a sense of taking their place in the line of the generations.

With these interventions, the young prospective father in this case was able to overcome his wish-fear to drop out of school and his fantasy of leaving Milly. As we helped them focus on getting ready for the birth, dreaded fantasies were replaced by visualizing an interaction with a newborn that would not only be gratifying to them as well as to the baby, but in some way would also help them live up to mental representations of how they felt parents should receive and raise a child. These mental representations, both conscious and unconscious, are part of the heritage of every human being. However, each person's fantasy is based on a constellation of ideas and memories of how he or she was welcomed into the world, as well as how he or she would have liked to have been received and accepted. This constellation forms part of the ego ideal of each expectant parent and, if tapped, contributes to a gradually increasing positive alliance in planning for the delivery. By activating these images of what good parents they desire to be, an increasingly vivid mental representation of the baby as a product of their love rather than an intruder into their lives comes alive. Then the child seems less demanding of a sacrifice of self-interests and goals.

Planning for the parents' visit for the wedding helped this couple to establish a beginning working alliance needed to counteract the negative parental imagery that was so much a part of this case. This alliance freed them of guilt and joined them to focus on what had to be done to get ready for the delivery and the early postpartum period with the help of the worker. They began to make physical and emotional space for the baby. Father's active participation in the prenatal care and the childbirth preparation enhanced his perception of himself as a loving and welcoming father. Although at first squeamish about being at the delivery, he was able to reverse his position when assured that he did not have to witness the blood, and that his purpose in being there would be to comfort and coach his wife while standing at the head of the bed. He would also be helping himself to be in control of the situation by being actively involved in acting as a coach.

In this particular case, because of the complications of sedation and the prolonged and difficult delivery, mother was in no position immediately after the birth to initiate and make contact with her child. It was the father who first welcomed the baby into the world and had the incredible high described as one of life's most memorable experiences. His excitement about fondling, making eye contact, and getting to know his infant no doubt contributed to the couple's ability later to rally in bringing milk to the baby, not allowing themselves to be separated from the child in spite of the elevated bilirubin. It appears, then, that fathers can play a role of inestimable value, not only in bonding themselves to a child, but in facilitating the bonding with a mother that might otherwise not have happened. In this case we speculate that had the father been absent from the birth, it is highly likely a postpartum depression could have ensued in the mother. His enthusiastic presence reassured both parents of the vitality and ongoingness of their new family, as well as of his dependability.

Conclusions

The work in this case suggests a paradigm in that, had not intervention been offered and accepted, the latent ability of a father and a mother to parent might have been aborted. The paradigm illustrates how an overwhelmed father still in active contest with his own father, to whom he could not turn, was able to become a loving one. It may be that it was possible for such a man to turn to his lover for compensation and comfort, up to the time of impregnation and the demand for marriage. But once the impregnation happened, the nature of the relationship changed and the lover was now seen as more hostile, demanding, and intrusive. At this point many men reject the situation and drop out in some form or other, as indeed was threatened here. Others may begin a new level of relatedness as a lover, husband, and father. In this case, there is reason to believe that with our intervention the latter path was made possible.

We have kept in contact with this couple by letter and occasional visits over the past 5 years. We can document that the spouses are relating more closely to each other and forming a stronger parental coalition. With a second child, they show clear evidence of a closely knit family in which both parents have managed to work out a balance between their professional lives and parental roles.

36

Involving Fathers in Treatment

Julian B. Ferholt
Alan Gurwitt

The recent interest in fathers on the part of clinicians and social scientists must contend with what in effect has been traditional neglect. It is probable that the factors responsible for this neglect still exist, for it is our impression that the renewed interest in the father has not yet resulted in adequate change in clinical practice. In this chapter we shall first examine some aspects of the importance of the father in the etiology of children's psychological problems, then factors that lead to his partial or full exclusion from intervention, and, finally, steps that could lead to greater involvement of fathers in treatment.

Father's Effect on Child's Psychic Development

The father is a crucial member of the family, one who has profound effect on the child's personality development. His impact begins before the child is born and extends throughout the child's life. Common sense, bolstered by new scientific evidence, tells us that we were wrong to dismiss the father as only a provider, a protector, and a support to the mother, or as having little direct impact until the oedipal years.

The aspect of the young child's nurturing environment that has most impact on personality development is the emotional atmosphere, or the feeling tone, surrounding a broad range of "good enough" child care. Of course childrearing practices have bearing on the development of a child's personality. However, the emotional tone of the interactions between parent and child, a reflection of the inner life of both, almost always determines the meaning of any childrearing practice.

The emotional atmosphere of the child's care is in large part made up of subtle nuances of nonverbal behavior, which communicate the feelings of the parent directed toward the specific child. The behaviors that communicate feelings in a love relationship are usually idiosyncratic to each parent-child dyad based on their accumulated experience together. Many of these behaviors are not under the parents' conscious control.

Inadvertently each parent communicates to the child the powerful thoughts and feelings, conscious and unconscious, that constitute the meaning that child has for the parent.

These parental ideas and feelings make up a mental portrait of the child, and these mental portraits are primary factors in determining the parents' impact on personality development of their child and their role in the etiology of mental illness.

A conviction about the importance of the inner life of all family members leads to the conclusion that, regardless of how little time the father actually spends with the child doing child care or interacting in other ways, he is inevitably a crucially important person in the child's environment. From the moment the mother knows she is pregnant, she psychologically experiences the fetus growing inside her body both as part self and part father. The real interaction with the father, as well as the feelings and thoughts that are attached to him in the psychic life of the mother, are thus significant determinants of the meaning that child has for the mother.

In addition to the father's particular significance to the mother, the inner lives of all family members are connected by a body of family beliefs and myths; that is, a family culture, by which we mean a system of shared symbols that allows individuals in the family to organize, give meaning to, and communicate about certain aspects of their experiences of themselves and of the world around them (including each other). A large component of any particular family's culture is the shared features of a "mental portrait" each member has of each other, including the specific child who is in treatment.

The father is a participant, however active or passive, in the family social system. He has an influence on its culture and in particular on the shared aspects of the mental portrait of a child. Of course, to the degree that the mental portrait of a child is shared completely and uniformly by all of the family, it is an extremely potent force in determining the emotional tone surrounding the child's interactions with family members. We can best influence the emotional tone of the child's nurturing environment by having an impact on the mental portrait of both parents. Therapeutic intervention, although not the only way, is an important way to do this (Chap. 35).

Child's Effect on Father's Psychic Development

Most fathers themselves are significantly affected when there are family tensions and problems for their children, though they and their families may not acknowledge it. In addition to the suffering of emotional pain, their own growth and development as adults are threatened by these difficulties.

Children have a tremendous impact on the psychic life of their parents. They may dominate a large segment of the adults' physical, social, and emotional environments. Indeed, most parents actually depend to some extent on their children for love and support. In addition, the health and development of children represent goals and accomplishments for parents, and the problems children manifest threaten the parents' self-esteem.

Most importantly, children are psychologically a part of their parents. The child stimulates further evolution of the parents' psychosexual development and the separation-individuation process, leading not only to the reexperiencing and reworking of earlier phases but also to the advance of adult phases (Chaps. 1, 2, 12, 15, 17, 20).

Although there are areas of similarity, it is probable that the nature of the impact of children on fathers is also different from that on mothers. One supposed difference between fathers and mothers is that work and career priorities, at least in the past, were considered to be of greater importance to men than was parenthood, whereas for women the opposite was the case. There is evidence not only that changes are occurring for men and women as to their priorities, but also that much of the lifelong interaction already common between fathers and children has, in any case, been unrecognized. For example, we now know that, for a man, becoming and being a father constitutes a series of profound psychological experiences (Chaps. 10, 18). The strong but muffled reactions of men to pregnancy, labor, and delivery, as well as the intense sharing of sensual symbiosis with the newborn infant and developing baby, are among those many areas where the father's intrapsychic responses and development have been insufficiently acknowledged—in part because they are rooted in early feminine identification that undergoes normative repression (Chaps. 1, 2, 11, 13). It is such muffling in fathers and society, along with stereotypes (see below, Rationales for Excluding Fathers from Treatment), that probably contribute to the fact that our society has neither fully recognized nor given full license to the expression of key paternal experiences and influences. Fathers deserve our attention in treatment for their own sake as well as for the sake of their families.

Father's Importance in Evaluation and Treatment

We now turn our attention to the particular importance of the father in each phase of therapeutic contact.

In the evaluation phase, fathers are indispensable sources of information. Interviewing the fathers and direct observation of fathers with their wives and their children give us data that are critical in our assessment of the father's personality and his relationship with his children and wife. This information both supplements and contrasts with data about the father from other sources; indirect data about the father is necessary but never sufficient. Fathers offer information about the family system that, if unnoticed at the onset of treatment, may never become clear again. They often remember aspects of the past history of the child and other family members that the mother has not observed or has repressed. They highlight aspects of the mother-child relationship by their own reports of the mother and child together. Fathers also confront us with the similarities and differences between the mother-child and father-child relationship with the same child, which can be extremely useful in understanding the dynamics within the family and the child's self and object relations.

Once treatment begins, the father's involvement is important. The treatment of the father results in changes in the father-child relationship and in the family system that can be extremely helpful to the child. In addition, the father's relationship with the professional person often helps to sustain an alliance with other family members. Failure to establish an alliance with the father may doom or skew the treatment. The more disturbed the family, the more critical it is to involve the father, if feasible, directly from the onset. It may be absolutely essential to involve the father when one parent (or both) is a seriously disturbed person, or when there is a defect in parenting such as a persistently negative mental portrait of a child with the associated predominance of rejecting and hostile feelings toward the child. (Unfortunately, this problem is not at all rare in our society, and is by no means limited to cases of physical assault, sexual assault, and gross neglect.)

An alliance with a very disturbed mother and her children will frequently break down just at the point where change is possible and the family system is threatened. In cases where the father is a seriously disturbed person, the problems in the father's relationship to the child may never become clear in the treatment if he is not involved directly. On the other hand, when the father's problem is finally recognized by the therapist, the mother and children may be unable to relinquish the denial that is protecting them from facing the potential uncoupling of the family unit and the possible psychological decompensation of the father (with the potential to hurt himself and others), unless the father is also directly involved in treatment. If it is not made clear from the beginning that the father's role is crucial, at a later time the mother may not be able or willing to bring the father to treatment and the father will be less likely to form an alliance because of the therapist's preceding relationship with the mother and child.

As we mentioned above, some parents with an early developmental deficit—with borderline, narcissistic, or psychotic personality organization—develop a symbiotic, psychologically fused, or almost exclusively narcissistic object relationship with a particular child. This is reflected in the parents' inability to separate the child's needs and other aspects of the child's inner experience from his or her own. The pain of the parent's own deprivation, the intense unmodified aggression, the primitive need for nurturance, his or her depression and guilt are stimulated by parenthood with a specific child. This may be more so at a particular time in the parent's or child's life. In order to prevent fragmentation of a tenuous and rigid defensive structure in the face of the psychological demands of parenthood, the parent may develop a pathological relationship with the child. This parent depends on sustaining a pathogenic mental portrait of the child to buttress his or her psychological stability.

These vulnerable adults typically form a very tenuous alliance in treatment because of their unstable object relationships and their limited ego capacity. Therapeutic work on the parent-child relationship with a parent like this can be very limited; sometimes it is completely impossible unless the spouse has his or her own alliance with the therapist to sustain the treatment. The spouse can then force the issue for the resisting parent in order to protect the child. When the spouse is not involved, he or she will frequently support the resistance in order to protect the parent in treatment, or "defend" the pathological integrity of the family, or both.

Though we believe it is very important to establish a working alliance with both parents early in the treatment of a child, the timing and intensity of contact with any one parent should vary according to particular needs of that family. It may be some time, for example, before a mother or a child can allow the father to become actively involved; even with the family's encouragement, the father may be unable to become involved. This should be the exception rather than the rule.

Thus it is clear that including the father in mental health intervention can be essential to the establishment and effectiveness of both evaluation and treatment. For similar reasons, it is important to include the father in other medical and educational services to children and families. For instance, when a very vulnerable parent develops a defect in parenting, it often begins before the child's birth or in the neonatal period, and then crystallizes in the first year into a rather fixed mental portrait. The father is a very important element in this process. We think it crucial, therefore, that obstetricians and pediatricians involve fathers in their medical and psychological evaluations and interventions long before the family's problems become severe enough to bring the child and family to a mental health professional (Chap. 35).

Cases of Father Exclusion

During recent years many professionals have come to agree that they should involve fathers in treatment, but in actual fact fathers are very often not effectively involved. Extensive pediatric liaison experiences— including consultation, teaching, and direct services in a large pediatric training setting—have provided the authors with a good deal of firsthand data about the failure to include fathers in the pediatric hospital and office practice (fathers are absent from 97 percent of pediatrician office visits [Duff, 1980]). Supervision of child psychiatrists in training, consultation to a variety of child mental health services, our own private-practice experiences, and informal communication with child psychiatrists in other geographic areas also confirm the absence of fathers from so much of child psychiatric work. The involvement of one of the authors (Ferholt) in clinical child development and in infant psychiatry (studying problems in newborn babies and associated postpartum reactions in their parents) has uncovered the same deficit. Essential to understanding the relative absence of fathers in these settings are the many ways in which the milieu of the clinic, the beliefs of clinicians themselves, and concepts of fathering roles within fathers and their families act to exclude fathers from meaningful participation, even when they are physically present. Besides the more obvious factors at work, exclusion may occur even when the clinic leadership and staff are explicitly committed to actively involving fathers in treatment, suggesting unconscious forces at play.

Too often when fathers do come in, the atmosphere of the service setting, as well as the behavior of the professionals directly involved in treatment, communicate an insensitivity to the vulnerabilities and needs of the fathers.

The following examples illustrate the varied character of father exclusion in different settings.

Mr. Jones was present at the delivery of his first son, Jonathan. He had been included in some prehospital classes and had met the obstetrician for the first time during the labor. However, in the hospital he was abruptly excluded from the labor room by the nurse, who was in a hurry to perform her routine admission procedure. The nurse finished with the mother and then left the room and forgot to tell the father that he could go back. He waited a long time, wondering whether he was allowed to go in or not, but nobody ever spoke with him or greeted him or told him what his role was in the hospital. When later he was allowed into the delivery room, as previously arranged, nobody told him where to stand. It *seemed* clear from the layout of the room and the talk of the professionals that he was not only unimportant to the procedure, but that he was in the way and an interference to their work.

Another example of a father's feeling intimidated was given by an experienced pediatrician in private practice:

He told how, after following a child for 1½ years, he learned that there was a serious family problem and that the child was vomiting because of it. As he took the history from the mother he learned that the problem had begun 6 months before and that she had failed to tell him about it during previous well-child visits. When he asked to meet the child's father, the mother was reluctant at first. During the interview that finally was arranged, the father explained that he had been in the car during that 6-month well-child visit and had not been able to bring himself to come into the pediatric office to meet with the pediatrician because he "knew" that the office was for mothers and babies. In thinking about this father's comment, the pediatrician recognized that his office and his instructions to his patients did not make it clear that fathers were welcome.

Another pediatrician who worked in an outpatient clinic serving poor people told us that fathers frequently did not come to the clinic. When they did, they usually would remain in the waiting room; if they did come into the crowded examining room, they would often sit in a corner looking at the floor and not participating in the interview. Since the clinicians saw this behavior as "cultural," few made any attempt to involve the fathers in what was happening.

In the last example, although there are important cultural variations in the role and function of the father, these do not rule out his involvement. The nature of the intervention and the proper point of entry do need to be adapted so as to be appropriate and effective in that particular culture. We believe that too often cultural differences and language barriers are used as rationalizations for inaction, one result of which is exclusion of fathers.

When young children are in the hospital, it is often desirable for their parents to live in the hospital with them. In our experience, when a father takes a shift living in with his sick child, it is not unusual to see him watching television either in the hospital room or in the parents' lounge, and therefore not involving himself actively with his child. In pursuing this matter, we found that fathers frequently find themselves being ignored by the nurses instead of being helped to know what they could do to assist their children. Although it is true that the physical layout and psychological environment may not really welcome the physical presence of parents with their child, it is particularly the father who is the less accepted parent. This is unfortunate because such stressful experiences especially call for close, supportive total family involvement.

In all of the examples given, the professionals involved simply did not create an atmosphere where fathers were welcomed and respected. Important opportunities to facilitate vital family participation on the part of fathers were missed.

When fathers are being subtly excluded from mental health interventions, therapists may describe fathers as passive, insensitive, or merely "compliant" in the psychotherapy. Often fathers are viewed by clinicians as uninvested in their own internal growth, while mothers seem more ready to move ahead in treatment. Hence it is not at all unusual for fathers to be allowed to drift away from a treatment, and for the therapist to find more satisfaction in treating the mother alone. His predictable resistances to psychological treatment, even when obvious (like missing appointments), are not challenged as vigorously as they would be for the mother. Certain aspects of the family's view of the father may be left unquestioned. These might include the family's seeing him as being uninvolved in family matters, as insensitive, or as impulsive. In consequence, the role of other family members in encouraging these behaviors (if, indeed, they are present) may not be recognized.

Reasons for Excluding Fathers from Treatment

How is it possible that clinicians, even when they profess otherwise, do not effectively engage fathers? We believe there are multiple reasons, which we have classified as follows.

Administrative Constraints. Administrative and procedural practices, informal and formal, that are operant in clinical settings contribute to the exclusion. These include such obvious practices as: lack of scheduling service time when working fathers could more readily be seen; intake procedures that reflect a bias toward mothers (for example, self-report forms that do not specifically ask for fathers' opinions); the absence of male staff members even when it is obvious that for certain ethnic groups or certain families it is vital to have male therapists. Even seemingly minor arrangements, such as waiting rooms without magazines appropriate for men, carry the message of a lack of welcome.

Shared Stereotypes. Stereotypes about masculinity, parental roles, and gender functions that are common in American society at large and shared among many clinicians, families, and fathers themselves also contribute to the exclusion. These include such assumptions as: Fathers and young children have limited impact on one another; fathers who are truly masculine would have little interest and participation in childbirth and early child care, and should maintain a certain aloofness; the primary childrearing parent is the mother, with the father's role limited to protective and supportive functions only.

Theoretical Barriers. Few clinicians have been trained to translate into practice a theoretical formulation that acknowledges the multi-determined etiology of any psychological disorder. A great deal of clinical practice is guided by very simplistic notions, which depend on ideas such as linear causality, the mind-body dichotomy, and the nature-nurture dichotomy. When a child's problems are seen primarily as physical in origin, then biochemical, structural, or genetic formulations seem sufficient; thus involving the father in treatment does not appear critical. When behaviorist learning theories are relied on too exclusively to plan interventions, then treatment that focuses on behavioral change for the child may involve only the adult who interacts most with the child. In this paradigm, fathers again may be seen as unimportant. Even intervention focused on the inner life of the child may discount the importance of fathers by viewing personality development as an epigenetically consistent unfolding of innate maternally-triggered maturational events. Variation and deviation may then be understood primarily as the result of endowment or an intrapsychic developmental structure little influenced by specific child-care practices or the nuances of parental feelings toward a child.

Countertransference. Intrapsychic phenomena within the therapist, old or new, unconscious or near-conscious, color and may skew the therapist's work with families, particularly as regards fathers. (It is our belief that there is too much controversy about attempts to define more stringently the term *countertransference* to restrict its use here.) Most simply, clinicians have their own powerful personal experiences that affect if and how they treat fathers. Those experiences, past and present—whether in the form of unconscious neurotic conflicts or overt discomfort—are an inevitable part of our having been sons and daughters, or our being husbands, wives, fathers, and mothers.

Both male and female therapists share reactions such as memories of the painful yearning for more attention and appreciation from our fathers; or the sense of loss, self-depreciation, abandonment, and anger sometimes associated with deprivation of active father participation in childhood. Lingering distress at having been (or having fantasied so) less favored by our fathers is not easily put aside when dealing with similar patterns in families we treat.

For female therapists, especially common themes include strong reactions, when treating a wife and mother, to themes of abandonment by, or lack of support from, a husband; identification with the anger and envy felt by a female patient for a husband's or father's power, independence, and stature; or discomfort with and avoidance of father patients because of forbidden oedipal wishes to be intimate with those fathers as well as to gain superiority over the mother patient.

For male therapists, commonly occurring reactions include negative oedipal conflicts when treating fathers, with the stirring up of old prospects of intimacy with strong and dominating or stern and punishing fathers; and oedipal rivalries that skew work with fathers and mothers in well-known triangular fashions.

Transference. All of the reactions described for the clinician may occur within the father patients or their wives as transference phenomena that prevent or skew the involvement with male or female therapists.

Thus operating at any one time are unconscious forces within the therapist(s) and family members that may undermine the effectiveness of treatment of fathers. The experience and training of the therapist may not be sufficient insurance against such distortions.

The following example illustrates many of these factors:

Mrs. M., a social worker in a mental health clinic for young children and their families, was working with Mr. and Mrs. S. in a treatment focused on their parenting of their 7-year-old son, Henry. He was being seen by a child therapist in the same clinic because he suffered from severe anxiety and behaved in an extremely demanding and disobedient manner. As Mrs. M. got to know the couple, both mother and father agreed that Mr. S. was important to his son, but that his relationship with Henry was both erratic and often unpleasant. Mr. S. was absent from the family a great deal; furthermore, he often changed scheduled time with his son without sufficient warning. When father and son were together, Mr. S. hurtfully teased Henry, took him to scary places or movies, and, when disciplining him, would do so explosively. Clarification and advice from Mrs. M. in therapy did not result in change of the behavior. However, in sessions he was reluctant to discuss openly his own reactions and feelings. He and his wife agreed that his preference for privacy and his tendency to distrust others were characteristic "masculine" patterns in his family, but these patterns were not therapeutically questioned by Mrs. M., in part because they troubled her. Subsequently the father's participation in therapy waned, leading to a decision by the therapist to treat the mother more intensively and to include Mr. S. only in sessions that dealt specifically with Henry's progress and management.

After several months Mr. S. complained to the director of the clinic (a man) that his wife was not getting better (though she was), and that Henry was only slightly better (which was true). Mr. S. wanted the case management to be reviewed. The director agreed to do so, although he cited both Mrs. M's competence and the clinic's pattern of monitoring clinical work. Mr. S. emphasized his sense of being criticized as being passive, inadequate, or negligent, or as someone without feelings. He very much felt he had been "kicked out" of therapy, whereupon he angrily asked the director if he (the director) was a father and whether he thought fathers were really important to their children. He quickly followed with an admission of major faults as a parent and husband, as well as problems in his business. Mr. S. told of his fatigue, fear, and sadness about his unhappy relationship with his son Henry, his wife, and his own parents and siblings.

Mr. S. soon started in individual therapy with his own therapist (in the same clinic). The whole family situation, including the child's symptoms, improved rapidly, and the child's internalized problems became more accessible in his psychotherapy.

Mrs. M., an experienced therapist, discovered with surprise her failure to explore the father's resistance to treatment, as well as her exaggerated sympathy for Mrs. S.'s "aloneness" with her difficult child. She began to see her dislike for Mr. S. as a reflection of her disappointment with and anger at men in her own life, especially their withdrawal from and lack of support of her.

All this occurred in spite of Mrs. M.'s sincere conscious commitment to including both parents in treatment, and her competence as a therapist.

Early Father-Child Developmental Phenomena. Three additional factors also interfere with the work of therapists. They could be classified as transference and countertransference phenomena, but their occurrences are so common in patients *and* clinicians that they deserve special emphasis. First, the early developmental steps in young boys involve identification with the mother and her maternal functions, especially her reproductive capacities, which is later renounced as part of the growing boy's male identity. The second phenomenon is the tendency to see the father as a remote or "twilight" figure. The third phenomenon is the common but rarely conscious fear and awe on the part of men of pregnancy and the birth process (Chap. 18).

Biological Factors. It may well be that men as parents react differently to children as compared with women as a result of neurobiological differences. These might include such factors as: cognitive strategy differences; greater capacity for spatial orientation in men; differential hemispheric functioning; motoric differences; and the possibility of greater inherent aggressiveness (Chap. 6; Cath, 1980).

Of course, some of these are speculative (at least in our view) and they are modified by experiences. These factors could interefere with the outcome of the treatment of a father.

The conclusions we reach, however, about all of the above phenomena affecting the character of clinical involvement of fathers, is that a cacophony of factors can stand—and have stood—in the way. The most effective inclusion of fathers will depend on active appraisal and awareness of those factors.

Methods to Encourage Inclusion

Although there are many practical administrative problems that present obstacles in clinical settings, the more difficult task is to address attitudes of the staff that reflect unrecognized stereotypes and conflicts. In order to do so, we believe there must be not only a personal commitment by the staff and its leadership, but also discussions about practical administrative issues that reflect a concern about fathers; consultation, individual supervision, staff conferences, and in-service education; and awareness of how the culture and framework of the clinic may themselves reflect sex-role stereotypes that may aggravate problems. Regarding the latter, the distribution of authority and responsibility in the clinic, and interaction between personnel that might, for example, demean or exploit men or women colleagues, could well cause resentment that affects the way families are treated.

Conclusions

To summarize, the commitment to involving fathers in treatment is not just a nicety, but a fundamental necessity. The lack of such commitment or capacity to implement it reflects incorrect beliefs and attitudes about the role of the father in the child's development as well as the powerful intrapsychic forces at work in clinician and patient alike. There is no simple remedy. As clinicians and administrators, we need to be aware of the beliefs, attitudes, and forces that coalesce about and within us to press for the exclusion of fathers. This awareness requires our sustained attention. Our efforts to overcome these forces require a strong commitment.

Afterword

E. James Anthony

Fatherhood and Fathering: An Overview

During the Yayoi period in Japan (200 B.C.–300 A.D.), when the inhabitants began to engage in rice-based agriculture and to acquire holdings of land, a dramatic shift took place in the structure and function of the family. The previous Jomon or neolithic period was a maternal system in which the role of the father was scarcely recognized, and he lived separately away from the "main house" where the woman stayed. The word for "parent" indicated only the mother. By the advent of the Yayoi period, the adult males had gained in economic and working power, had assumed a dominant role, and had established a paternal system. The word for "parent" now included the father with a suffix to imply that he labored in the field. By looking at the original forms of Kanji, the hieroglyphic characters derived from China over 3,000 years ago and adopted by the Japanese, the character representing "father" was formed by a combination of the symbols for "right hand" and "stone axe." Therefore, the etymological meaning of the character for "father" is "having a stone axe in hand and working":

Right hand
Stone axe
Father

The character for "mother" was created at around the same time and formed from a combination of symbols for "woman" and "breasts." Thus, the etymological meaning of the character for "mother" is "a woman nursing a baby":

Woman   Mother

I am indebted to Dr. Kosuke (1978) for this interesting piece of information illustrating the first of a series of transitions that have taken place in various cultures and that have followed similar sequential patterns: The man is first recognized as a father; then gains admission into the family circle; takes over the leadership of the household in relation to other families; plays an increasingly intramural as opposed to extramural role; and, finally, in this age, has invaded the nursery and has become a caretaker along with the mother of both infants and children (cf. Chap. 27). The dynamic impact of such transitions on the developing offspring must be considerable and switch the emphasis from preoedipal to oedipal upbringing. In a wide variety of ways, this book deals with the different effects of too little and too much father in the family and with all the different proportions in between.

Thus there is no single definition of fathering that fits every society and every culture both present and past. Cross-cultural studies have shown how relative the label is both qualitatively and quantitatively, making any attempt at generalization impossible. The mother role, in contrast, is far more consistent and less culture bound.

As father participation in family life has increased, so has the function complexity of fathering, although this correlation may result from our increasing knowledge of parenting and child development. Our concept of the father has proliferated along with our theories. We can observe him, for example, participating empathically in the pregnancy of his wife, manifesting at times a host of psychophysiological *couvade* symptoms, accompanying her to her childbirth classes and learning the elements of infant care; we can watch him as he tries unsuccessfully to establish a symbiosis with the neonate similar to that of the mother and feeling that his lack of breast does not allow his "holding" to convey to the infant or to the observer the confidence and competence of the mother; we can infer from his emotional comfort that he is far more happy to substitute at times for his wife and relieve her periodically from the incessant demands of the newborn; we can observe him making things easier for her so that she can preoccupy herself with her primary task; we can assess the degree of altruism that he exercises in sacrificing some of his rights to the infant but not without some rivalrous strivings within him-

self. In terms of theory, his functions can be delineated a little more succinctly. Psychocognitively (Piaget), he tends to talk more "operationally"
to the child, to eschew fantasy and to enhance reality. From early on, he
teaches the "logic of relationships" as exposed through secondary processes. Psychosexually, he plays a major role during the preoedipal phase
in determining gender identity, and, during the oedipal phase, his role is
central in the child's conflict. During latency his external, reality-ori-
ented, and "instrumental" importance becomes apparent to the child and
crucial in the child's further development as a productive and cooperative
member of an ever-growing community. But it is during adolescence that
the total concept of the father as a synthesis of authority, power, prohibition, and manliness becomes both a challenge and an impetus to the
individual's further emotional maturation.

From a study of the views presented in this book, it is clear that the
concept of fatherliness and fathering has undergone as many vicissitudes
as that of motherliness and mothering, and the misperceptions on the
part of the developing child as well as the clinical investigator, together
with the fantasies woven around them, have been determined by the age
of the child and the scientific epoch during which the research has been
carried out. Parents are largely projections of their children and every
culture has created its own brand of parental mythologies. Clinicians and
ethnologists have found that fantasies and folklore have a lot in common.
Children dream their dreams, by day and by night, of being loved and
favored, protected and enriched, abandoned and left alone, beaten and
exposed, and later, when grown-up, they codify the various types of
"family romance" into the compelling enchantments of fairy tales,
thereby perpetuating parental myths from generation to generation.
There is no such thing as "real" parents: They are always amalgamations
of fact, fantasy, and folklore.

The evolution of fantasy into theory takes a similar pathway as the
genesis of fantasy into folklore, but in both cases the adult makes an attempt to operationalize unfulfilled childhood yearnings. The image of the
father as internally incorporated or externally projected is therefore in a
process of constant modification and it is not easy to separate the
psychological dimensions of internal, external, and transitional father
figures as they impinge on experience. Psychotic, neurotic, psychopathic,
abusive, incestuous, authoritarian, and neglectful or uninterested parents
add their complications and confusions to the already murky conceptualizations of parenthood. The child's developmental task, crucial to his
own psychological survival as a future parent, is to reconcile the good
introjections and projections with the bad introjections and projections, as
well as the good realities of nurturance and protection with the bad

realities of beating and battering. The question to the child, sometimes posed by the clinician, of "What do you feel about your father?" opens up an endless vista of father images with each perspective invested with its own ambivalences. If one structuralizes these images and fixes them to a moment in time, one then hears the voice of conscience and behind that the voice of God.

These profound metamorphoses are illustrated in the case of Freud's long internal struggle with his father and the various ways in which he came to terms with it eventually. As a toddler, he had fleeting memories of walking in the woods with his father and already being able to run away too fast to be caught, which were a comment on his father's grandfatherly age. He was really too old for his young wife who was the same age as his daughter. During latency, there is a mixture of memories and feelings: His father was "the wisest, most powerful and wealthiest" man around and yet he remained passive and humble in the face of anti-Semitic abuse. At the age of seven, Freud deliberately urinated in the parental bedroom and was reprimanded by his father who exclaimed angrily, "That boy will never amount to anything." This narcissistic trauma was worked through in a succession of dreams all contradicting the prophecy of doom and failure. From adolescence onward, his conscious attitude remained consistently affectionate, admiring, and respectful, and it therefore came as a great shock to him a year after his father's death, when he himself was in his forties, to discover from the analysis of his Oedipus complex that his unconscious mind had taken a very different view of his father (Jones, 1957).

His father had to die before he could discover the internal etiology of his neurosis, and what he referred to as his "little hysteria," his wish to kill his father, suddenly came to the surface following the death and relieved the repression. The father as the internal aggressor replaced the father as the external seducer in his formulation of theory. As he remarked, "The old man's death affected me deeply . . . he meant a great deal in my life . . . I feel now as if I had been torn up by the roots." On the fifteenth of October, 1897, he made his shattering discovery. "I have found love of the mother and jealousy of the father in my own case too, and now believe it to be a general phenomenon of early childhood . . . the gripping power of *Oedipus Rex*, in spite of all the rational objections to the inexorable fate that the story presupposes, becomes intelligible . . . every member of the audience was once a budding Oedipus in phantasy, and this dream-fulfillment played out in reality causes everyone to recoil in horror, with the full measure of repression which separates his infantile from his present state . . . the idea has passed through my head that the same thing may lie at the root of *Hamlet*" (Freud, 1897). ("Conscience doth make cowards of us all.") His father had died exactly one year prior to this momentous piece of insight.

In some ways, it was probably easier for Freud to discover his Oedipus complex than it would have been for someone else bent on the same introspective course. Jakob Freud was, as Freud's stepbrother pointed out, more of a grandfather than a father and Freud's family romance took the form of believing that the father of the hateful sibling who displaced him was his stepbrother, who therefore probably carried the bulk of the oedipal rage while Jakob was afforded some degree of "diplomatic immunity." In this three-generational system, the question of fathers could be confusing to the small child.

Jakob reappears in the psychomythology as "God the Father." The child "looks back on the memory-image of the overrated father of his childhood, exalts it into a Deity, and brings it into the present and into reality. The emotional strength of this memory-image and the lasting nature of his need for protection are the two supports of his belief in God" (Freud, 1933).

In *Totem and Taboo* (1913), Freud depicted a titanic struggle between the younger males in the primitive horde and "the old man" who inevitably gets killed and then eaten by his sons. Their actions made it difficult for the brothers to live together without renunciation and thus led to remorse, repression, and inhibition, all of which contributed to a conscience transmitted to future generations. Freud did not find it difficult to accept this anthropological theory since the impulses of murder, cannibalism, and incest postulated in primitive man were also to be found in the young child. After all, it was 200 years since the writer Diderot surmised that if a little boy were left to himself and possessed the violence of a man, he would strangle his father and sleep with his mother! The earliest religions were therefore rooted in a totemism. With the development of Mosaic religion, the father came into his own again as the Almighty Creator, but then Christianity appeared, replacing the father religion with a son religion. "The old God, the Father, took second place; Christ, the son, stood in his place, just as in those dark times every son had longed to do . . . from now on, Jewish religion was, so to speak, a fossil" (Freud, 1913). The killing of the father is a fantasy in the mind of the oedipal child; the death wish becomes more preconscious and nearer to reality when the child is undergoing the adolescent process. As Winnicott (1971) puts it, "Growing up means taking the parent's place. It *really* does. In the unconscious fantasy, growing up is inherently an aggressive act." He takes as an example the game "I'm the King of the castle" that starts in play during early latency but is transformed into a life situation at puberty. Becoming an adult implies "the death of someone" and further personal development can take place only over the dead body. Freud could not accomplish the major breakthrough in psychoanalysis before the death of his father. Thus, according to Winnicott, murder is the theme implicit to adolescence and a prerequisite to the process of maturation. "This makes it difficult enough for parents and guardians. Be sure it makes it difficult also for the individual adolescents themselves who come with shyness to the murder and the triumph that belong to maturation at this crucial stage. The unconscious theme may become manifest as the experience of a suicidal impulse or as actual suicide."

Winnicott's preoccupation with mothers makes him seem somewhat uninterested in fathers, but in thinking of the importance of good-enough mothering, his frame of reference is entirely preoedipal. Fathers are there but not in a crucial sense. They can be done without. He goes on to say "the term paternal must necessarily come a little later than maternal. Gradually the father as male becomes a significant factor. And then follows the family, the basis of which is the union of fathers and mothers in a sharing of responsibility for this that they have done together, that which we call a new human being—a baby" (1971). Many infant psychologists and psychiatrists are currently challenging this assumption. They would insist that the father, mother, and baby, given the opportunity, the proximity, and the license, form a preoedipal triangle that has a different structure and function than the later oedipal one. The father is seen not only as a substitute, a support, and a standby at times of crisis but as an integral part of the emotional bond between the infant and mother. Abelin (1975) has referred to this as "early triangulation," indicating that the infant and toddler have to apprehend and internalize the relationship between their two most cathected objects, mother and father. Mahler and Gosliner (1966) also envisaged an earlier positive role for the father: Since he was not "contaminated" by the symbiosis of the mother and baby, he could assist the infantile ego to disentangle itself from the regressive pull of the symbiosis. As a Victorian father, this type of paternal role was not conceivable to Freud, and it was certainly not within the conceptualization of Winnicott. Neither of them could have thought of the father as someone who had specific object libido and specific "emotional refuelling" to offer the small child or that the toddler of the preoedipal era had a deep need to get and keep his parents together.

To establish an enduring sense of completeness, the child from the beginning needs both parents. Talcott-Parsons (1954) formulated the mechanism of an internalization of sex and age roles in the development of the human personality. On both sides of the gender axis, the child assimilates the maleness of the father and the brother and the femaleness of the mother and the sister; on both sides of the horizontal axis, the age differences between the parents and children are internalized. There is a need for a "generation gap" so that the child can have its parents "in front of it." In this psychoanalytically-derived paradigm, the father is once again important from the beginning, although most theories of development would subscribe to a gradually increasing importance in the role of the father. In some cultures, the father, together with the men in the tribe, ritualistically rescue the male offspring from the mother and the household of women. Before the boy can enter the man's world, he must give up his ties to the mother symbolically. In many primitive societies, there are "making of man" ceremonies in which the boy who has previously lived in the company of his mother and women is snatched from them in a dramatic repudiation and is born again as a man out of the men's ceremonial "baby pouch." Again, in southern New Guinea, among the Karaki, no boy can attain full adult stature without a culturally prescribed childhood sequence of passive and active homosexuality, restricted to fellatio, after which he is permitted to become completely heterosexual. Since the Karaki believe that pregnancy can result from the swallowing of semen, a ritual is performed at puberty in which the pregnancy is burnt out of the boy by pouring lye down his throat (Herdt, 1981). The central theme in many of these rituals involves the father's role in actively bringing about the transformation of the growing boy from womanliness to manliness. (What is of extraordinary importance for the theory of homosexuality based on the formulation of "too much of mother and too little of father" is the fact that the long practice of childhood and adolescent homosexuality apparently does not, to any significant degree, affect the adult heterosexual adjustment.)

Although there are physical practices emphasizing the boy's entry into the man's world, there is also a strong psychological component indicating the importance of the father in shaping the adult personality of his son. The following is an example of the advice given to his son at puberty by a West African father (Laye, 1955, p. 21):

There is a certain form of behavior to observe, and certain ways of acting out in order that the guiding spirit of our race may approach you also . . . if you desire the guiding spirit of our race to visit you one day, if you desire to inherit it in your turn, you will have to conduct yourself in the selfsame manner; *from now on, it will be necessary for you to be more and more in my company.**

Here we see in practice the father's role in transmitting the values of traditional belief. One can admire the consistency, constancy, and continuity involved in the process, contrasting them with the doubts

---

*Emphasis added.

regarding moral standards, religious beliefs, and traditional behavior characteristic of fathers from advanced technological societies. In such discontinuous cultures where the process of transmission fails, the children are particularly prone to a diffusion of their identities at adolescence (Erikson, 1957) and may become for prolonged periods what Mitscherlich (1969) has termed "passengers," that is, individuals who passively adopt the frames of reference of any group in which they find themselves and that carries them along for a while. Under such conditions, the sense of self is in real jeopardy.

Although this book is about fatherhood and fathering, one cannot at any time avoid helpful or invidious comparisons with mother care since the spirit of parental competition is very much in the air at present as parental roles become less defined and delimited. The increasing number of single-parent families has made it incumbent on fathers and mothers to attempt to become androgynous in interactions with their children. Thus, they will "mother" them at bedtime and "father" them in the playground, but the change of parental hats is not made without a certain amount of internal psychological discomfort. Many will openly confess that it is hard for them to play both roles and that not only are they confused themselves but a source of confusion to their children. Being a motherly father or a fatherly mother does not involve a long history of developmental preparation and generally represents little more than an ad hoc adjustment to a novel circumstance. It would seem that parenthood has different degrees of depth for the two sexes. Stephens (1912) states the conventional view clearly and succinctly: "Men are not fathers by instinct but by chance, but women are mothers beyond thought, beyond instinct which is the father of thought. Motherliness, pity, self-sacrifice—these are the charges of her primal cell."

The counterview, as stated earlier by Abelin and others, is not in favor of an exclusive maternal mystique that originates almost at the tissue level. In France, Badinter (1980) has generated a major controversy in her thesis questioning the existence of a maternal instinct since history, according to her, has amply demonstrated that mothers can often relinquish their babies to wet nurses and others with comparative indifference. If the instinct is questioned with regard to the mother, there would certainly seem to be no case for the father's possession of it. Whether instinct has been replaced by learned behavior, highly susceptible to cultural influences and equally available to both sexes, remains to be conclusively demonstrated. Even with regard to learning, there are those who claim that the mother is in a better position since pregnancy and the concomitant "hormonal avalanche" appear to sensitize her to the needs of the infant. In addition, other sex differences (still to be

576

confirmed as differentiators) help to amplify this sensitivity further. Women, for example, are considered to be more empathic, more intuitive, and more in touch with the primary processes than men, and therefore in better contact with the primitive organisms in their care. It has also been claimed that the mother-child relationship fosters an unrealistic preoccupation with fantasy. At the right moment, said to be at the beginning of latency, the fathers bring law and order, organization, and reality into the family circle, sometimes at the expense of feelings. The so-called authoritarian complex, caused by a dictatorial father, may produce children with strong compulsive and organizational tendencies on the one hand or children inclined to daydreaming, dawdling, and aimless distraction on the other. A negligent father, in contrast, may also generate ineffectual children who have not experienced enough tension in the relationship with the father to enable them to discipline themselves and develop a reliable conscience structure. What the good-enough father bequeaths to his child is a ground plan for the orderly development of a functioning moral system and a realistic practical life.

Whereas psychodynamic theorists in the United States have emphasized a preoedipal paternal renaissance, the European Mitscherlich (1969) has emphasized the gradual "disappearance" of the father from society in terms of his paternal educational function. He has not been lost through divorce or death but has simply faded away into the outskirts of family life. Gorer (1948), examining the American scene from the European vantage point, has discerned an underlying contempt for the father against the general background of "Momism." American society, according to him, rejected the father as a model and as a source of authority. In turn, he expected his sons to reject him. There is no doubt that the father-son relationship had a very special position in paternalistic societies that more or less assumed a tilted relationship between the two—ruler and ruled, master and slave, God and man, and omnipotent one and impotent one. The father may be an authoritarian personality or become addicted to the dominant-submissive mode of relating, but in many cases the reasonable father will grade his demand for absolute obedience in accordance with the child's stage of development. If the father has performed his job well during the early stages of life, control from without gradually gives place to control from within. The command-and-obey system is needed but not natural even in the toddler. The process of domestication or adherence to family rules and regulations is gradually internalized through imitation and identification until it becomes part of the personality. When Martin Luther remarked that he would "rather have a dead son than a disobedient one" he was overlooking his own harrowing experiences during childhood, and later found it necessary to restate his opinion. "Children should not be too severely flogged; for my father once flogged me so severely that I fled and became averse to him until he accustomed me to him again." Still later he added, "My parents treated me so harshly that I grew quite dispirited. My mother once flogged me until the blood flowed all because of a nut, and the hard and severe life they made me lead caused me later to enter a monastery and become a monk." It also led him to challenge the whole authority of the Roman Catholic church and attempt to replace it with a more fallible system. His notion of better dead than disobedient indicates how tenaciously an unconscious identification with an aggressive father can persist in the mind of the individual.

The wish on the part of the child to kill the father is paralleled by the generally unconscious wish in the father to destroy the son. The destructiveness may take psychological forms and injure the spirit irreparably. To a child, the father's severity means retribution for his or her own aggressive wishes directed against him. These wishes are inevitable even with the most loving upbringing, but when the father's aggression far exceeds his manifest love, the child's own death wishes may become uncontrollable and completely undermine his or her internal sense of security. Throughout life, the child will be unable to shake off the memories of a terror-filled childhood and will remain intimidated, lacking in self-confidence and mistrustful not only of others but of him- or herself.

The writer Kafka was a striking case in point. When he was small, he was a fluent speaker but as he came increasingly under the dominance of his father, he was eventually unable to either think or speak in his father's presence. Here we have a case of too much of father and too little of mother. Kafka regarded his mother as the catspaw of her husband, unable in any way to alter his implacable management of the children. He saw life as a direct battle between him and his father with himself as the casualty. The conflict was grossly unequal but he was aware of his own strong wishes to hurt his father. The difference lay in the father's lack of insight. "What was always incomprehensible to me was your total lack of feeling for the suffering and shame you could inflict on me with your words or judgements. It was as though you had no notion of your power. I, too, I am sure, often hurt you with what I said but then I always knew and it pained me but I could not control myself, could not keep the words back, although I was sorry even when I was saying them." But his father was never sorry. He was aware of his son's pitiful psychological state but did not hold himself responsible for it, and this is what hurt his son most. "I am the result of your upbringing . . . you unconsciously refuse to acknowledge it."

No physical abuse was involved but, for a hypersensitive individual, the verbalized threats were by themselves devastating. "How terrible for me it was, for instance, when you would say, 'I'll tear you apart like a fish,' and although I knew that nothing worse was to follow (as a little child I may not have known that), it fitted exactly my notion of your power and I saw you as being capable of doing it . . . one could only remain alive as a child through your mercy."

The syndrome of too much father was agonizingly documented by Kafka and contained a series of indictments:

1. He had constantly to examine the "terrible trial" pending between himself and his father in all its detail, from all sides, on all occasions, and from far and near. It was a trial in which the father was judge and jury and Kafka was the bewildered plaintiff.
2. Because of his father, he had lost all his self-confidence, and in its place was a boundless sense of guilt.
3. His father had instilled in him a distrust of people and of himself and a perpetual anxiety about every little affair of life.
4. He could not escape from his father even as an author. "My writing was all about you; all I did there was to bemoan what I could not bemoan upon your breast. My writing was a 'long-drawn-out leave-taking from you' and yet 'I could never escape from you.'" Kafka likened himself to a prisoner who wanted to escape but simultaneously wanted to rebuild the prison as a home for himself. "If he escapes he cannot rebuild; and if he rebuilds, he cannot escape."
5. Sexuality in any form was barred because it lay, like so many other vital things in life, in his father's domain. "Sometimes I imagine the map of the world spread out and you stretched diagonally across it. And I feel as if I could consider living in only those regions that either are not covered by you or are not within your reach."

But without this kind of father, would Kafka have been anything but another neurotic nonentity? One is reminded here of Proust's remark that the neurotic sufferings of creative writers allowed the rest of the world to enjoy the creations vicariously and without pain.

Another highly creative individual, the philosopher John Stuart Mill, offered a different aspect of the too much of father and too little of mother syndrome. His father took complete control over his life and stressed only the cognitive, the rational, and the analytic aspects of it. He began the study of Greek when he was three and had covered most of the world's literature by the age of twelve. Yet, so important did his ideas eventually become that Freud took the time and effort to translate his work into German. In Mill's own autobiography, three things stand out: the lack of any mention of his mother; the absence of any reference to feelings; and a prudishness so extreme "that one would never learn from his writing that humanity was divided between men and women" (Freud, 1880).

Mill's identification with his overwhelming father was almost complete, but at the age of twenty, the austerely intellectual lifestyle created by the two of them together broke down, and he became depressed. He asked himself the critical question, if all the objects that he and his father pursued in life were realized, would this be an occasion for great joy and happiness, and his honest answer was no. "At this my heart sank within me: the whole foundation on which my life was constructed fell down . . . I seemed to have nothing left to live for" (Mill, 1874). He realized that the habit of analysis inculcated by his father had a tendency to wear away feelings. "My education, which was wholly his work, had been conducted without any regard to the possibility of its ending in this result: and I saw no use in giving him the pain of thinking that his plans had failed, when the failure was probably irremediable, and, at all events, beyond the powers of *his* remedies" (Mill, 1874).

Before he could recover from defeat and depression, he had, in fantasy, to kill his father. He did this in an extraordinary way. He accidently came upon a book in which he found a passage relating to the death of the father and its impact on the family. The major impact was on a boy who was now to become his own man and head of the family, no longer under the domination of the father. When Mill read this, he wept; his depression immediately grew lighter and he began to feel that not all was dead within him. As Freud had discovered the oedipal system following the death of his father, Mill discovered his whole philosophical system following this fantasied death of his father. This second system represented not only a liberation from his father but also a discovery of his mother. He did not want to relinquish the analytic mode stemming from his father but he now wished very strongly to leaven it with feelings deriving from his mother. A combined analytic-affective system then became the basis of his philosophy, or what he called "the internal culture of the individual" (Mill, 1874). He ceased to attach an almost exclusive importance to the training of the human being for speculation and for action. "The cultivation of feelings became one of the cardinal points in my philosophical creed" (Mill, 1874). Soon he was able to find a comfortable and caring mother figure with whom he lived for the rest of his life.

If the father-son relationship is fraught with fear, frustration, and fight, the father's relationship with the daughter is not without its rough passages during development, although catastrophic upheavals are much less common. Ekstein (1980) has described his own fathering with respect to his daughter. He begins with the idea that not only do children need parents but that parents need children in order to round off and deepen their personalities. The children need to exist in the minds of the parents before parenthood begins and after childrearing concludes. The same is true of children. In order to function ultimately as parents themselves, they have to construct and reconstruct parental models that derive primarily from their own parents and then from the long line of surrogates who imbue them with different kinds of parental attitudes and behavior. Grandparenthood brings the parental cycle to a close, although some are fortunate to achieve great-grandparenthood—by this time, however, parental feelings are becoming markedly attenuated.

In the beginning, according to Ekstein (1980), the father-daughter relationship exists merely in the mind of the father as he daydreams about the future. When his daughter becomes an actual entity, with her mother in the background, an emotional cycle is set into being. His feelings for her will determine to a large extent her feelings about her own femininity and cause her to feel attractive and wanted. Deutsch (1945) in fact goes so far as to suggest that the girl's sexual awakening is to a significant extent a function of the father's seductive attention to her. Within the bounds set by incest laws, he must make her both psychologically and physically conscious of his masculine interest in her as a female. Without this seductiveness, the daughter may remain inhibited. There is some truth, especially with regard to the father, in the old adage that "the son is a son 'till he gets a wife but a daughter is a daughter all her life." According to Freud (1933), the girl never resolves her Oedipus complex in quite the same dramatic fashion as the boy, and it lingers on into adolescence when oedipal wishes may become powerful once again and generate the risk of incest. A surprisingly large number of babies born out of wedlock to teenagers have been fathered by the girl's parent. Toward the later end of the life cycle, the daughter may become, as in Freud's case, a mothering figure in the life of the aging man. Four years before he died, Freud wrote to his friend Lou Andreas-Salome, "Naturally I am more and more dependent on Anna's care of me, just as Mephistopheles once remarked: 'At the end we depend on the creatures we made.' *At all events it was very wise to have made her*" (Jones, 1953).* At this point, the daughter's anxiety mounts as death approaches since now she feels she will not only lose her father's love (her oedipal anxiety) but lose him altogether.

The son's attachment is, in general, not so dependable. The compe-

*Emphasis added.

tition with the father is always there, never fully resolved. The father remains a measure of all things for the son, whose strongest wish is to succeed the father as "king of the castle." When the son turns to a different occupation, the relationship is easier and mutual respect may grow between the two, which helps to strengthen the libidinal tie and with it the family equilibrium. The father needs to detach himself from the aspirations he has for his son and to realize that the work model he has to offer may be obsolete for the new generation. If he insists on maintaining his position of omnipotence, it may act as a millstone around the son's neck. Piaget's son, the infant who became famous as Laurent in the studies, entered his father's field and failed miserably to the father's great disappointment. Martin Freud, Freud's oldest son, avoided this predicament (M. Freud, 1958, p.9):

To have a genius for a father is not a common experience. . . . I am a member of a small minority, the object of some curiosity, but not necessarily looked upon with much favor by society. Society is not, it would seem, prepared to cheer loudly when any one of us tries to climb to fame and glory. Personally, I make no complaint. I have never had any ambition to rise to eminence, although, I must admit, I have been quite happy and content to bask in reflected glory. Nevertheless, I believe that if the son of a great and famous father wants to get anywhere in this world, he must follow the advice given to Alice by the Red Queen—he will have to go twice as fast if he does not want to stop where he is. The son of a genius remains the son of a genius, and his chances of winning human approval of anything he may do hardly exist if he attempts to make any claim to a fame detached from that of his father.

In my experience, it is much easier for daughters than sons to bask in reflected glory and not become intimidated by an impossible rivalry. Sartre (1964) declares in his autobiography that he was very fortunate to have lost his father before his birth; otherwise, like other sons, he would have had to imitate Aeneas by carrying his father on his back throughout life.

Many fathers and many sons have said to themselves later on: if only we could go back to the beginning, how much better we would be with each other, how much more we would appreciate each other and how much more we would have benefitted from the relationship. In Ionesco's *Victims of Duty* (1958), there is a scene in which a son goes back into his memory and meets his father again. The son says, "Father, we never understood each other. You were hard. Perhaps you did not mean badly. Perhaps it was not your fault. It was not you, your violence and selfishness that I hated; it was your weakness with which I had no sympathy. You used to strike me but I was tougher than you. My contempt hit you much harder; it killed you. We might have been good friends. I was wrong to despise you. I am worth no more than you. Look at me. I am very like you. If you were willing to look at me, you would see how like you I am. I have all your faults." The father, in turn, speaks to his son, "My child, I was a travelling salesman. My job sent my roving all over the world. From October to March I was in the Northern Hemisphere and from April until September in the Southern. So there was nothing but winter in my life." Here we have a monologue between father and son who cannot see or understand each other and between whom there is only an exhaustion of hatred and a grudging forgiveness.

I cannot do better than end this overview of the complex and convoluted fathering function by quoting Samuel Butler (1903), part of whose work was translated by Freud. This passage represents one of the most gentle analyses of fatherhood on record and touches on the ambivalences that haunt the father and son relationship throughout life. The father is speaking:

"I shall be just as unkind to my children," he said, "as my grandfather was to my father, or my father to me. If they did not succeed in making their children love them, neither shall I. I say to myself that I should like to do so, but so did they. I can make sure that they shall not know how much they would have hated me if they had not much to do with me, but this is all I can do. If I must ruin their prospects, let me do so at a reasonable time before they are old enough to feel it." He mused a little, and added with a laugh: "A man first quarrels with his father about three-quarters of a year before he is born. It is then he insists on setting up a separate establishment; when this has been once agreed to, the more complete the separation forever after the better for both." Then he said more seriously: "I want to put the children where they will be well and happy and where they will not be betrayed into the misery of false expectations."

The Father Transference in Everyday Life

After reading the extreme reactions of Kafka to his father, one is surprised to learn from contemporary sources that the father in question was a very typical Victorian parent, perhaps no worse and no better than many other fathers of the time. Neighbors regarded him as a kindly if somewhat pompous man with many of the characteristics of his class and creed. Yet in Kafka's "Letter" he is portrayed so monstrously that one immediately suspects the operation of some distorting mechanism. This could have been Kafka's constitutional hypersensitivity, but it is so reminiscent of what a patient projects onto the analyst that one can imagine some mode of transference process was at work. Some grossly disturbing image derived from early childhood was being transferred to the adult father-son relationship. Even Kafka seemed to be aware that something in him was creating the monster.

As if to confirm this, we have detailed data on another famous father and son struggle as depicted by Gosse (1907). The correspondence, in this case, was reverse: The father sent a long letter to the son complaining bitterly of his behavior. He wrote:

When your sainted Mother died, she not only tenderly committed you to God, but left you also as a solemn charge to me, to bring you up in the nurture and admonition of the Lord. That responsibility I have sought constantly to keep performing: I can truly aver that it has been ever before me—in my choice of a housekeeper, in my choice of a school, in my ordering of your holidays, in my choice of a second wife, in my choice of an occupation for you, in my choice of a residence for you; and in multitudes of lesser things—I have sought to act for you, not in the light of this present world, but with a view to eternity. For awhile, all appeared to go on fairly well . . . but of late, and especially during the past year, there has become manifest a rapid progress towards evil . . . when you came to us in the summer, the heavy blow fell full upon me; and I discovered how very far you had departed from God. It was not that you had yielded to the strong tide of youthful blood, and had fallen a victim to fleshly lusts . . . it was not this; it was worse. It was that horrid, insidious infidelity.

When one recalls Butler, one realizes that here again is a typical Victorian father. The son's image of him many years later was as vivid as if he was still experiencing it as an adolescent. He complained of his father's incessant cross-examinations and of the fact that all his personal relations with his father were poisoned by this insistency. "I was never at my ease in his company; I never knew when I might not be subjected to a series of searching questions which I should not be allowed to evade." His feelings were ambivalent, like Kafka's. He yearned for the tender side of his father. "What a charming companion, what a delightful parent, what a courteous and engaging friend my father would have been, and would preeminently have been to me, if it had not been for the stringent piety which ruined it all." He revolted against "the police-inspection" to which his views were incessantly subjected. Replies were often violent and hysterical. He often had no clear recollection of what he had said. "I desire not to recall the whimpering sentences in which I begged to be let alone, in which I demanded the right to think for myself, in which I repudiated the idea that my father was responsible to God for my secret reports and my most intimate convictions."

Having gone through a huge crisis, not dissimilar to those of Butler, Kafka, and Mill, Gosse reached the conclusion that there were only two alternatives to be considered. Either he must cease to think for himself; or his individualism must be instantly confirmed, and the necessity of independence must be emphasized. There could be no question of a truce; it was all or nothing. And so, as respectfully as he could, "without parade or remonstrance, he took a human being's privilege to fashion his inner life for himself."

All these young men appeared to be fighting for their autonomy, but behind it, as if to sustain them, there seemed to be a transference exaggeration, almost amounting to irrationality at times, making it clear that it was not only the external father with whom they were struggling: It was the deeply imbedded father of early childhood.

Some sons (and the syndrome seems not to include daughters) are apparently fated to carry their fathers not on their backs like Aeneas but inside them all their lives, continuing the struggle, the endless mutually recriminatory dialogue, that can never be resolved even by death.

References

Abbott, J. S. C. Paternal neglect. *Parent's Magazine*, March, 1848, p. 149.

Abbott, L. Paternal touch of the newborn: Its role in paternal attachment. Boston University School of Nursing Thesis, 1975.

Abelin, E. The role of the father in the separation-individuation process. In J. B. McDevitt and C. F. Settlage (Eds.), *Separation-Individuation: Essays in Honor of Margaret S. Mahler*. New York: International Universities Press, 1971.

Abelin, E. Some further observations and comments on the earliest role of the father. *Int. J. Psychoanal.* 56:293–302, 1975.

Abelin, E. The role of the father in core gender identity and in psychosexual differentiation. Read to the American Psychoanalytic Association, Quebec, 1977.

Abraham, K. Some remarks on the role of the grandparents in the psychology of neurosis. *Clinical Essays* 44–47, 1913.

Abraham, K. Manifestations of the female castration complex (1920). In K. Abraham, *Selected Papers*. New York: Basic Books, 1953.

Abraham, K. Infantile sexual theory not hitherto noted (1925). *Selected Papers*. 1953.

Ainsworth, M. Object relations, dependency, and attachment: A theoretical review of the infant-mother relationship. *Child Dev.* 40:969–1025, 1969.

Ainsworth, M. The development of infant-mother attachment. In B. Caldwell and Ricciuti (Eds.), *Review of Child Development Research*, Vol. 3. Chicago: University of Chicago Press, 1973.

Ainsworth, M., Bell, S. M., and Stayton, D. Infant-Mother Attachment and Social Development: Socialization as a Product of Reciprocal Responsiveness to Signals. In M. Richards (Ed.), *The Integration of the Child into a Social World*. Cambridge: Cambridge University Press, 1974.

Alcott, W. A. Woman but a helper, designed for fathers. *Parent's Magazine*, Dec., 1841, pp. 88–89.

Als, H., Tronick, E., and Brazelton, T. B. Analysis of Face-to-Face Interaction in Infant-Adult Dyads. In M. Lamb, S. Suomi, and G. Stephenson (Eds.), *The Study of Social Interaction*. Madison: University of Wisconsin Press, 1979.

Alter, R. A literary approach to the Bible. *Commentary*, Dec., 1975, pp. 70–77.

Alter, R. Biblical narrative. *Commentary*, May, 1976, pp. 61–67.

Alter, R. Character in the Bible. *Commentary*, Oct., 1978, pp. 58–65.

Alvederdes, F. *Social Life in the Animal World*. New York: Harcourt Brace, 1927.

Anderson, B. J., and Standley, K. A methodology for observation of the childbirth environment. Presented to the American Psychological Association, Washington, D.C., 1976.

Anderson, E. (Ed.). *The Letters of Mozart and His Family*, Vol. 2. London: Macmillan, 1938.

Anderson, R. Thoughts on fathering: Its relation to the borderline conditions in adolescence and to transference phenomena. *Adolesc. Psychiatry* 6:377–395, 1978.

Andry, E. J. Faulty paternal- and maternal-child relationships, affection, and delinquence. *Br. J. Delinq.* 97:329–340, 1960.

Anthony, E. J. The Relations of Adults to Adolescence. In E. J. Anthony, *Adolescence: Psychosocial Perspectives*. New York: Basic Books, 1969.

Anthony, E. J., and Benedek, T. *Parenthood*. Boston: Little, Brown, 1970.

Anthony, E. J., and Koupernik, C. *The Child in his Family: Children at Psychiatric Risk*, Vol. 3. New York: Wiley, 1974.

Anzieu, D. *L'auto-analyse de Freud*. Vols. 1 and 2. Paris: Presses Universitaires de France, 1975.

Appleton, T., Clifton, R., and Goldberg, S. The Development of Behavioral Competence in Infancy. In F. Horwitz (Ed.), *Review of Child Development Research*, Vol. 4. Chicago: University of Chicago Press, 1975.

Arnstein, H. S. The crisis of becoming a father. *Sex. Behav.* 2:42–47, 1972.

Arthur, T. S. *The Mother*. Boston: 1846.

Arthur, T. S. Aunt Mary's suggestion. In T. S. Arthur, *Home Lights and Shadows*. New York: 1854.

Auerbach, E. *Mimesis: The Representation of Reality in Western Literature* (1946). Transl. by W. R. Trask. Princeton: Princeton University Press, 1953.

Austen, J. *Pride and Prejudice* (1813). New York: Heritage Press, 1940.

Austen, J. *Mansfield Park* (1814). London: Folio Society, 1959.

Bach, G. R. Father fantasies and father-typing in father-separated children. *Child Devel.* 17:63–80, 1946.

Badinter, E. *Love Plus: The History of Maternal Love*. Paris: 1980.

Bak, R. Further fantasies and father-typing in father-separated children. *Child Dev.* 17:63–80, 1960.

Bak, R. The Phallic Woman: The Ubiquitous Fantasy in Perversions. In Ruth S. Eissler et al. (Eds.), *The Psychoanalytic Study of the Child*, Vol. 23. New York: International Universities Press, 1968.

Ban, P., and Lewis, M. Mothers and fathers, girls and boys: Attachment behavior in the one-year-old. *Merill-Palmer Q.* 20:195–204, 1976.

Barnett, C., et al. Neonatal separation: The maternal side of interactional deprivation. *Pediatrics* 45(2):197–205, 1970.

Barnett, M. C. Vaginal awareness in the infancy and childhood of girls. *J. Am. Psychoanal. Assoc.* 129–140, 1966.

Barry, W. Marriage research and conflict: An integrative review. *Psychol. Bull.* 73:41–55, 1970.

Baumrind, D. Current patterns of parental authority. *Dev. Psychol.* [Monograph] 4:1–103, 1971.

Bee, H. L., Van Egeren, L. F., Streissguth, A. P., Nyman, B. A., and Leckie, M. D. Social class differences in maternal teaching strategies and speech patterns. *Dev. Psychol.* 1:726–734, 1969.

Bell, A. Additional aspects of passivity and feminine identification in the male. *Int. J. Psychoanal.* 49:640–647, 1968a.

Bell, A. The role of modelling of fathers in adolescence and young adulthood. *J. Counselling Psychol.* 30:30–35, 1968b.

Bell, R. Q. A reinterpretation of the direction of effects in studies of socialization. *Psychol. Rev.* 75:81–95, 1968.

Bell, R. Q. Stimulus control of parent or caretaker behavior by offspring. *Dev. Psychol.* 4:73–88, 1971.

Bell, R. Q. Parent, child and reciprocal influences. *Am. Psychol.* 34:821–826, 1979.

Bell, S. The development of the concept of object as related to infant-mother attachment. *Child Dev.* 41:219–311, 1970.

Benedek, T. Parenthood as a developmental phase. *J. Am. Psychoanal. Assoc.* 7:389–417, 1959.

Benedek, T. The organization of the reproductive drive. *Int. J. Psychoanal.* 41:1–15, 1960.

Benedek, T. Fatherhood and Providing. In E. J. Anthony and T. Benedek (Eds.), *Parenthood: Its Psychology and Psychopathology.* Boston: Little, Brown, 1970a.

Benedek, T. Parenthood During the Life Cycle. *Parenthood: Its Psychology and Psychopathology.* 1970b.

Benedek, T. Depression During the Life Cycle. In J. Anthony and T. Benedek (Eds.), *Depression and Human Existence.* Boston: Little, Brown. 1975.

Bernays, A. My brother Sigmund Freud. *Am. Mercury* 51:335–342, 1940.

Bettelheim, B. *Symbolic Wounds.* Glencoe, Ill.: Free Press, 1954.

Bibring, G. Some Considerations of the Psychological Process in Pregnancy. In Ruth S. Eissler et al. (Eds.), *The Psychoanalytic Study of the Child,* Vol. 14. New York: International Universities Press, 1959.

Bibring, G. Some considerations regarding the ego ideal in the psychoanalytic process. *J. Am. Psychoanal. Assoc.* 12:517–521, 1964.

Bibring, G., Dwyer, T. F., Huntington, D. S., and Valenstein, A. F. A Study of the Psychological Processes in Pregnancy and the Earliest Mother-Child Relationship: I. Some Propositions and Comments. In Ruth S. Eissler et al. (Eds.), *The Psychoanalytic Study of the Child,* Vol. 16. New York: International Universities Press, 1961.

Bieber, et al. *Homosexuality.* New York: Basic Books, 1962.

Bigner, J. J. Fathering: Research and practice implications. *Fam. Coordinator* 19:357–362, 1970.

Biller, H. B. Father absence and the personality development of the male child. *Dev. Psychol.* 2:181–201, 1970.

Biller, H. B. Paternal Deprivation, Cognitive Functioning and the Feminized Classroom. In A. Davids (Ed.), *Child Personality and Psychopathology.* New York: Wiley, 1974.

Biller, H. B. The Father and Personality Development: Parental Deprivation and Sex-Role Development. In M. E. Lamb (Ed.), *The Role of the Father in Child Development.* New York: Wiley, 1976.

Biller, H. B., and Borstelmann, L. J. Masculine development: An integrative review. *Merill-Palmer Q.* 13:253–294, 1967.

Biller, H. B., and Meredith, D. *Father Power.* New York: McKay, 1974.

Bird, B. A study of the bisexual meaning of the foreskin. *J. Am. Psychoanal. Assoc.* 6:287–304, 1958.

Bloch, R. H. American feminine ideals in transition: The rise of the moral mother, 1785–1815. *Feminist Studies* 4:101–126, 1978.

Blos, P. Preoedipal Factors in the Etiology of Female Delinquency. In Ruth S. Eissler et al. (Eds.), *The Psychoanalytic Study of the Child,* Vol. 12. New York: International Universities Press, 1957.

Blos, P. The Second Individuation Process of Adolescence. *The Psychoanalytic Study of the Child,* Vol. 22. 1967.

Blos, P. *The Young Adolescent.* New York: Free Press/Macmillan, 1970.

Blos, P. The Genealogy of the Ego Ideal. In Ruth S. Eissler et al. (Eds.), *The Psychoanalytic Study of the Child,* Vol. 29. New York: International Universities Press, 1974.

Blos, P. *The Adolescent Passage.* New York: International Universities Press, 1978.

Boehm, F. Homosexuality and the Oedipus complex. *Int. J. Psychoanal.* 12: 66–79, 1926.

Boehm, F. The femininity complex in men. *Int. J. Psychoanal.* 11:444–469, 1930.

Bowlby, J. *Attachment and Loss*, Vol. 1. New York: Basic Books, 1970.

Bradley, N. The doll. *Int. J. Psychoanal.* 42:550–556, 1961.

Bradley, R. Fathers' presence in delivery rooms. *Psychosomatics* 3(6):474–479, 1962.

Bradley, R. *Husband-Coached Childbirth.* New York: Harper, 1965.

Brazelton, T. What makes a good father. *Redbook,* June, 1970.

Brazelton, T. *Neonatal Behavioral Assessment Scale.* Spastics International Medical Publications, Monograph, no. 50. Philadelphia: Lippincott, 1973.

Brazelton, T., and Als, H. Four Early Stages in the Development of Mother-Infant Interactions. In Ruth S. Eissler et al. (Eds.), *The Psychoanalytic Study of the Child,* Vol. 34. New York: International Universities Press, 1979.

Brazelton, T., Koslowski, B., and Main, M. The Origins of Reciprocity: The Early Mother-Infant Interaction. In M. Lewis and L. A. Rosenblum (Eds.), *The Effect of the Infant on its Caregiver.* New York: Wiley, 1974.

Brazelton, T., Tronick, E., Adamson, L., Als, H., and Wise, S. Early Mother-Infant Reciprocity. In R. Hinde (Ed.), *Parent-Infant Interaction* (Ciba Foundation Symposium, no. 33). Amsterdam: Elsevier, 1975.

Brazelton, T., Yogman, M., Als, H., and Tronick, E. The Infant as a Focus for Family Reciprococity. In M. Lewis and L. Rosenblum (Eds.), *Social Network of the Developing Child.* New York: Plenum, 1978.

Brenner, C. A Case of Childhood Hallucinosis. In Ruth S. Eissler et al. (Eds.), *The Psychoanalytic Study of the Child,* Vol. 6. New York: International Universities Press, 1951.

Breuer, J., and Freud, S. Studies on Hysteria (1895). In *The Standard Edition of the Complete Psychological Works of Sigmund Freud,* Vol. 2, Transl. and ed. by J. Strachey with others. London: Hogarth and Institute of Psycho-Analysis, 1955.

Brody, S. A Mother is Being Beaten: An Instinctual Derivative and Infant Care. In E. J. Anthony and T. Benedek (Eds.), *Parenthood: Its Psychology and Psychopathology.* Boston: Little, Brown, 1970.

Brody, S., and Axelrad, S. *Mothers, Fathers and Children: Explorations in the Formation of Character in the First Years.* New York: International Universities Press, 1978.

Bronfenbrenner, U. The changing American child: A speculative analysis. *J. Soc. Issues* 17:6, 1961.

Bronfenbrenner, U. Developmental research, public policy, and the ecology of childhood. *Child Dev.* 45:1–5, 1974.

Bronfenbrenner, U. Who Cares for America's Children. In V. Vaughan and T. B. Brazelton (Eds.), *The Family: Can It be Saved?* Chicago: Yearbook, 1976.

Bronfenbrenner, U. Contest of child rearing problems and prospects. *Am. Psychol.* 34:844–850, 1979.

Brooks-Gunn, J., and Lewis, M. Person perception and verbal labeling: The development of social labels. Presented to the Society for Research in Child Development, Denver, April, 1975.

Browning, D., and Boatman, B. Incest: Children at risk. *Am. J. Psychiatry* 134:69–72, 1977.

Bruner, J. Organization of early skilled action. *Child Dev.* 44:1–11, 1973.

Bruner, J., Jolly, A., and Sylva, K. (Eds.). *Play.* New York: Basic Books, 1976.

Bruning, J. L., and Kintz, B. L. *Computational Handbook of Statistics.* Glenview, Ill.: Scott, Foresman, 1968.

Brunswick, R. M. The preoedipal phase of the libidinal development. *Psychoanal. Q.* 9:293–319, 1940.

Bryan, C. Bisexuality. *Int. J. Psychoanal.* 11:150–166, 1930.

Burlingham, D. The Preoedipal Infant-Father Relationship. In Ruth S. Eissler et al. (Eds.), *The Psychoanalytic Study of the Child*, Vol. 28. New York: International Universities Press, 1973.

Bushnell, H. *Christian Nurture*. New York: 1843.

Butler, S. *The Way of All Flesh* (1903). New York: Heritage Press, 1936.

Caplan, G. Patterns of paternal response to the crisis of premature birth. *Psychiatry* 23:365–374, 1960.

Caplan, G. *Prevention of Mental Disorders in Children*. New York: Basic Books, 1961.

Cassell, T., and Sander, L. Neonatal recognition processes and attachment: The masking experiment. Presented to the Society for Research in Child Development, Denver, 1975.

Cassuto, U. *The Documentary Hypothesis and the Composition of the Pentateuch*. Transl. by I. Abrahams. Jerusalem: Magnes Press, The Hebrew University, 1941.

Cath, S. H. Grief, Loss and Emotional Disorders in the Aging Process in Geriatric Psychiatry. In M. A. Berezin and S. H. Cath (Eds.), *Geriatric Psychiatry*. New York: International Universities Press, 1962.

Cath, S. H. Personal communication with Alan Gurwitt, 1980.

Cath, S. H. The institutionalization of a parent—A nadir of life. *J. Ger. Psychiatry* 5(1):25–46, 1972.

Cath, S. H. A testing of faith in self and object constancy. *J. Ger. Psychiatry* 9(1):19–40, 1976.

Cawelti, J. J. *Apostles of the Self-Made Man*. Chicago: University of Chicago Press, 1965.

Charlesworth, W. R. The role of surprise in cognitive development. In E. Elkind and J. H. Flavell (Eds.), *Studies in Cognitive Development: Essays in Honor of Jean Piaget*. London: Oxford University Press, 1969.

Clark, R. W. *Freud: The Man and the Cause*. New York: Random House, 1980.

Clarke-Stewart, K. A. The father's impact on mother and child. Presented to the Society for Research in Child Development, New Orleans, March, 1977.

Clarke-Stewart, K. A. The Father's Contribution to Children's Cognitive and Social Development in Early Childhood. In F. A. Pedersen (Ed.), *The Father-Infant Relationship: Observational Studies in a Family Setting*. New York: Holt, Rinehart & Winston, 1980.

Clower, V. The development of the child's sense of his bisexual identity (panel discussion). *J. Am. Psychoanal. Assoc.* 18:165–176, 1970.

Cohen, A. (Ed.). *The Soncino Chumash: The Five Books of Moses with Haphtaroth*. Hindhead, Surrey: Soncino Press, 1947.

Cohen, L. J., and Campos, J. J. Father, mother, and stranger as elicitors of attachment behaviors in infancy. *Dev. Psychol.* 10:146–154, 1974.

Colarusso, C. The development of time sense—From birth to object constancy. *Int. J. Psychoanal.* 60:243–251, 1979.

Colarusso, C., and Nemiroff, R. Some observations and hypotheses about the psychoanalytic theory of adult development. *Int. J. Psychoanal.* 60:59–71, 1979.

Collins, G. A new look at life with father. *New York Times Magazine*, June 17, 1979.

Collins, L., and Lapierre, D. *Freedom at Midnight*. New York: Simon & Schuster, 1975. P. 169.

Colman, A. D., and Colman, L. L. *Pregnancy*. New York: Herder & Herder, 1971.

References

Conference on Psychoanalytic Education and Research. Commission IX. Child Analysis. *Am. Psychoanal. Assoc.* 1–20, Mimeo. 1974.

Conn, J. Children's awareness of the origins of babies. *J. Child Psychiatry* 140–176, 1947.

Cott, N. F. *The Bonds of Womanhood: Woman's Sphere in New England, 1780–1835.* New Haven, Ct.: Yale University Press, 1977.

Cramer, R. D. Images of the American father. Brandeis University Honor Thesis, 1980.

Crawley, S., et al. Developmental changes in the structure of mother-infant play. *Dev. Psychol.* 14:30–36, 1978.

Degler, C. N. *At Odds: Women and the Family in America from the Revolution to the Present.* New York: Oxford University Press, 1980.

Demos, J. *A Little Commonwealth: Family Life in Plymouth Colony.* New York: Oxford University Press, 1970.

Demos, J. Underlying themes in the witchcraft of seventeenth-century New England. *Am. Hist. Rev.* 75:1311–1327, 1970.

Demos, J. The American family in past times. *Am. Scholar* 43:422–426, 1974.

Demos, J. Old Age in Early New England. In J. Demos and S. Boocock (Eds.), *Turning Point: Historical and Sociological Essays on the Family.* Chicago: University of Chicago Press, 1978.

Demos, J. Oedipus in America: Historical perspectives on the reception of psychoanalysis in the United States. *Annu. Psychoanal.* 6:23–39, 1978.

Deutsch, H. Genesis of agoraphobia. *Int. J. Psychoanal.* 10:51–69, 1929.

Deutsch, H. *The Psychology of Women.* New York: Grune & Stratton, 1946.

Deutsch, H. The Significance of Masochism in the Mental Life of Women (1930). In R. Fliess (Ed.), *The Psychoanalytic Reader.* London: Hogarth, 1950.

Deutscher, M. Brief family therapy in the course of first pregnancy: A clinical note. *Contemp. Psychoanal.* 7(1):21–35, 1970.

Deutscher, M. First Pregnancy and Family Formation. In D. Milman and G. Goldman (Eds.), *Psychoanalytic Contributions to Community Psychology.* Springfield, Ill.: Thomas, 1971.

Devore, I. Mother-Infant Reactions in Free Ranging Baboons. In H. Rheingold (Ed.), *Maternal Behavior of Mammals.* New York: Wiley, 1963.

Dickens, C. *Dombey and Son* (1848). New York: Heritage Press, 1957.

Dickens, C. *Hard Times* (1854). New York: Norton, 1966.

Dickinson, E. *Bolts of Melody.* Edited by Todd and Bingham. New York: Harper, 1945.

Dixon, S., et al. Early infant social interaction with parents and strangers. *J. Am. Acad. Child Psychiatry* 21:124, 1981.

Dollard, J. *Caste and Class in a Southern Town* (3rd Ed.). New York: Doubleday, 1957.

Drake, S. G. *Annals of Witchcraft in New England.* New York: Benjamin Blom. 1967.

Dube, S. C. *Indian Village.* New York: Harper & Row, 1967.

Duff, R. Personal communication with Julian B. Ferholt, 1980.

Dwight, T., Jr. *The Father's Book.* Springfield, Mass.: 1835.

Earls, F. The Fathers (Not the Mothers): Their Importance and Influence with Infants and Young Children. In S. Chess and A. Thomas (Eds.), *Annual Progress in Child Psychiatry and Child Development.* New York: Brunner-Mazel, 1977.

Earls, F., and Yogman, M. W. The Father-Infant Relationship. In J. Howells

(Ed.), *Modern Perspectives in the Psychiatry of Infancy*. New York: Brunner-Mazel, 1979.

Edgcumbe, R., and Burgner, M. The Phallic Narcissistic Phase: A Differentiation Between Preoedipal and Oedipal Aspects of Phallic Development. In Ruth S. Eissler et al. (Eds.), *The Psychoanalytic Study of the Child*, Vol. 30. New Haven, Conn.: Yale University Press, 1975.

Edgcumbe, R., Lundberg, S., Markowitz, R., and Salo, F. Some Comments on the Concept of the Negative Oedipal Phase in Girls. In Ruth S. Eissler et al. (Eds.), *The Psychoanalytic Study of the Child*, Vol. 31. New York: International Universities Press, 1976.

Eisler, M. J. Womb and birthsaving phantasies in dreams. *Int. J. Psychoanal.* 2:65–67, 1921a.

Eisler, M. J. A man's unconscious phantasy of pregnancy in the guise of traumatic hysteria. *Int. J. Psychoanal.* 2:255–286, 1921b.

Ekstein, R. Daughters and Lovers: Reflections of the Life Cycle of the Daughter-Father Relationship. In E. Kirkpatrick (Ed.), *Women's Sexual Development*. New York: Plenum, 1980.

Emde, R. N., Gaensbauer, T. J., and Harmon, R. J. Emotional expression in infancy: A biobehavioral study. *Psychol. Issues* (Monograph 37): 1976.

Erikson, E. H. The problem of ego identity. *J. Am. Psychoanal. Assoc.* 4:56–121, 1950a.

Erikson, E. H. *Young Man Luther*. New York: Norton, 1958.

Erikson, E. H. *Childhood and Society* (1950b). New York: Norton, 1963.

Erikson, E. H. Identity and the life cycle: Selected papers. *Psychol. Issues* (Monograph 1): 1959.

Erikson, E. H. Eight Ages of Man. In E. H. Erikson, *Childhood and Society* (2nd ed.). New York: Norton, 1963.

Erikson, E. H. *Insight and Responsibility*. New York: Norton, 1964.

Erikson, E. H. Womanhood and the Inner Space. In E. H. Erikson, *Identity: Youth and Crisis*. New York: Norton, 1968a.

Erikson, E. H. *Identity: Youth and Crisis*. New York: Norton, 1968b.

Erikson, E. H. *Ghandi's Truth*. New York: Norton, 1969.

Eron, L., Banta, T., Valder, L., and Laulicht, J. Comparison of data obtained from mothers and fathers on child rearing practices and their relation to child aggression. *Child Dev.* 32:457–472, 1961.

Esman, A. Changing Values: Their Implications for Adolescent Development and Psychoanalytic Ideas. In S. Feinstein and P. Giovacchini (Eds.), *Adolescent Psychiatry*, Vol. 5. New York: Aronson, 1975.

Evans, W. N. Simulated pregnancy in a male. *Psychoanal. Q.* 20:165–178, 1951.

Fanaroff, A., et al. Follow-up of low birthweight infants: Predictive value of maternal visiting patterns. *Pediatrics* 56:544–550, 1970.

Fenichel, O. *The Psychoanalytic Theory of Neurosis*. New York: Norton, 1945.

Fenichel, O. Specific forms of the Oedipus Complex. In *The Collected Papers of Otto Fenichel*, Vol. 1. New York: Norton, 1954.

Ferenczi, S. The Grandfather Complex. In *Further Contributions to the Theory and Technique of Psycho-Analysis*. New York: Brunner-Mazel, 1913.

Ferenczi, S. *Thalasse: A Theory of Genitality* (1924; 1938). New York: Norton, 1968.

Ferholt, J. B. The Parental Negative Mental Portrait. In preparation, 1982.

Filene, P. G. *Him/Her Self: Sex Roles in Modern America*. New York: Harcourt Brace Jovanovich, 1975.

Finkelstein, L. Awe and premature ejaculation: A case study. *Psychoanal. Q.* 44:232–252, 1975.

Flügel, J. *The Psychoanalytic Study of the Family* (1921). London: Hogarth, 1948.

Fock, N. South American birth customs in theory and practice. In C. Ford (Ed.), *Cross-Cultural Approaches: Readings in Comparative Research*. New Haven, Conn.: Human Relations Area Files Press, 1967.

Fodor, N. Fire and begetting. *Am. J. Psychother.* 2:240–249, 1948.

Ford, C. *Field Guide to Study of Human Reproduction*. Behavior Science Field Guide, Vol. 2. New Haven, Conn.: Human Relations Area Files Press, 1964.

Ford, C. A *Comparative Study of Human Reproduction*, Vol. 32. New Haven, Conn.: Yale Publication Anthropology, 1964.

Forrest, T. The paternal roots of male character development. *Psychoanal. Rev.* 54:277–295, 1967.

Fraiberg, S. Libidinal Object Constancy and Mental Representation. In Ruth S. Eissler et al. (Eds.), *The Psychoanalytic Study of the Child*, Vol. 24. New York: International Universities Press, 1969.

Fraiberg, S. Some Characteristics of Genital Arousal and Discharge in Latency Girls. In Ruth S. Eissler et al. (Eds.), *The Psychoanalytic Study of the Child*, Vol. 27. New York: International Universities Press, 1972.

Fraiberg, S., et al. Ghosts in the nursery: A psychoanalytic approach to the problem of impaired infant-mother relationships. *J. Am. Acad. Child Psychiatry* 14:387–424, 1975.

Francis, J., and Marcus, I. Masturbation: A Developmental View. In J. Francis and I. Marcus (Eds.), *Masturbation from Infancy to Senescence*. New York: International Universities Press, 1975.

Frazier, E. F. *The Negro Family in the United States* (2nd ed.). Chicago: University of Chicago Press, 1966.

Freeman, T. Pregnancy as a precipitant of mental illness in men. *Br. J. Med. Psychol.* 24:49–54, 1951.

Freud, A. Studies in Passivity. In *The Writings of Anna Freud*, Vol. 4. New York: International Universities Press, 1952.

Freud, A. Normality and Pathology in Childhood. *The Writings of Anna Freud*, Vol. 6. 1965.

Freud, A., and Burlingham, D. Infants Without Families: Reports on the Hampstead Nurseries. *The Writings of Anna Freud*. 1947.

Freud, M. *Sigmund Freud: Man and Father*. New York: Vanguard Press, 1958.

Freud, S. (1880) Translation of "Enfranchisement of Women." In J. S. Mill, *Gesammelta Werke*. Leipzig, 1851.

Freud, S. (1887–1902) *The Origins of Psycho-Analysis*. New York: Basic Books, 1954.

Freud, S. (1892–1899) Extracts from the Fliess papers. In *The Standard Edition of the Complete Psychological Works of Sigmund Freud*, transl. and ed. by J. Strachey with others. London: Hogarth and Institute of Psycho-Analysis, 1966.

Freud, S. (1896) Further remarks on the neuropsychosis of defense. *Standard Edition*. 1962.

Freud, S. (1899) *Standard Edition*. 1962.

Freud, S. (1900) The interpretation of dreams. *Standard Edition*. 1953.

Freud, S. (1901) The psychopathology of everyday life. *Standard Edition*. 1960.

Freud, S. (1905a) Fragment of an analysis of a case of hysteria. *Standard Edition*. 1953.

Freud, S. (1905b) Three essays on the theory of sexuality. *Standard Edition*. 1953.

Freud, S. (1908) On the sexual theories of children. *Standard Edition*. 1959.

Freud, S. (1909a) Analysis of a phobia in a five-year-old boy. *Standard Edition*. 1955.

Freud, S. (1909b) Notes upon a case of obsessional neurosis. *Standard Edition*. 1955.

Freud, S. (1910) Leonardo da Vinci and a memory of his childhood. *Standard Edition*. 1957.

Freud, S. (1911) Psycho-analytic notes on an autobiographical account of a case of paranoia. *Standard Edition*. 1958.

Freud, S. (1913) Totem and taboo. *Standard Edition*. 1955.

Freud, S. (1914) Some reflections on schoolboy psychology. *Standard Edition*. 1955.

Freud, S. (1914) On narcissism: An introduction. *Standard Edition* 1957.

Freud, S. (1915) 'Our attitude toward death' in thoughts for the times on war and death. *Standard Edition*. 1955.

Freud, S. (1916) On transformations of instinct as exemplified in anal eroticism. *Standard Edition*. 1955.

Freud, S. (1918a) From the history of an infantile neurosis. *Standard Edition*. 1955.

Freud, S. (1918b) Contributions to the psychology of love: III. The taboo of virginity. *Standard Edition*. 1955.

Freud, S. (1920) Beyond the pleasure principle. *Standard Edition*. 1955.

Freud, S. (1921) Group psychology and the analysis of the ego. *Standard Edition*. 1955.

Freud, S. (1923a) The ego and the id. *Standard Edition*. 1961.

Freud, S. (1923b) The infantile genital organization. *Standard Edition*. 1961.

Freud, S. (1923c) A seventeenth-century demonological neurosis. *Standard Edition*. 1961.

Freud, S. (1924a) The dissolution of the Oedipus complex. *Standard Edition*. 1961.

Freud, S. (1924b) The economic problems of masochism. *Standard Edition*. 1961.

Freud, S. (1925) Some psychical consequences of the anatomical distinction between the sexes. *Standard Edition*. 1961.

Freud, S. (1926) Inhibitions, symptoms, and anxiety. *Standard Edition*. 1959.

Freud, S. (1927) Fetishism. *Standard Edition*. 1961.

Freud, S. (1930) Civilization and its discontents. *Standard Edition*. 1961.

Freud, S. (1931) Female sexuality. *Standard Edition*. 1961.

Freud, S. (1933) New introductory lectures on psychoanalysis. *Standard Edition*. 1964.

Freud, S. (1938) An outline of psycho-analysis. *Standard Edition*. 1964.

Freud, S. (1939) Moses and monotheism. *Standard Edition*. 1964.

Freud, S. (1940) Splitting of the ego in the process of defense. *Standard Edition*. 1964.

Frodi, A., Lamb, M., Leavitt, L., Donovan, W., Naff, C., and Sherry, D. Fathers' and mothers' responses to the faces and cries of normal and premature infants. *Dev. Psych.* 14:490–498, 1978.

Fromm, E. Sex and character. *Psychiatry* 6:21–31, 1943.

Fromm, E. *The Crisis of Psychoanalysis*. London: Jonathan Cape, 1971.

Furman, E. *A Child's Parent Dies: Studies in Childhood Bereavement*. New Haven, Conn.: Yale University Press, 1974.

Galenson, E., Miller, R., and Roiphe, H. The choice of symbols. *J. Am. Acad. Child Psychiatry* 5(1):83–96, 1976.

Galenson, E., and Roiphe, H. The Impact of Early Sexual Discovery on Mood,

Defense Organization, and Symbolization. In Ruth S. Eissler et al. (Eds.), *The Psychoanalytic Study of the Child*, Vol. 26. New York: International Universities Press, 1971.

Galenson, E., and Roiphe, H. The Emergence of Genital Awareness During the Second Year of Life. In R. C. Friedman, R. M. Richard, and R. L. Van de Wiele (Eds.), *Sex Differences in Behavior*. New York: Wiley, 1974.

Galenson, E., and Roiphe, H. Some suggested revisions concerning early female development. *J. Am. Psychoanal. Assoc.* 24(5):29–57, 1976.

Galenson, E., and Roiphe, H. The preoedipal development of the boy. Presented to the panel on Gender and Gender Role at the Annual Meeting of the American Psychoanalytic Association, May 2, 1980.

Gay, S. Letter to Ebenezer Gay, March 29, 1809.

Gebhard, P. H. et al. *Sex Offenders: An Analysis of Types*. New York: Harper & Row, 1965.

Glass, L., Kolko, N., and Evans, H. Factors influencing predisposition to serious illness in low birth weight infants. *Pediatrics* 48:368–371, 1971.

Gordon, R. S., and Gordon, K. Social factors in the prediction and treatment of emotional disorders of pregnancy. *Am. J. Obstet. Gynecol.* 77:1074–1083, 1959.

Gorer, G. *The American People*. New York: Norton, 1948.

Gosse, E. *Father and Son* (1907). London: W. Heineman, 1913.

Gouin-Décarie, T. *Intelligence and Affectivity in Early Childhood: An Experimental Study of Jean Piaget's Object Concept and Object Relations*. New York: International Universities Press, 1965.

Gould, R. *Transformations. Growth and Change in Adult Life*. New York: Simon & Schuster, 1978.

Graves, H. A. The Parent's Loss. In H. A. Graves, *The Family Circle*. Boston: 1845.

Green, M., and Beall, P. Paternal deprivation—a disturbance in fathering: A report of nineteen cases. *Pediatrics* 30:91–99, 1962.

Green, R. Sexual identity: Research strategies. *Arch. Sex. Behav.* 4:337–352, 1975.

Greenacre, P. Special Problems of Early Female Sexual Development. In Ruth S. Eissler et al. (Eds.), *The Psychoanalytic Study of the Child*, Vol. 11. New York: International Universities Press, 1950.

Greenacre, P. Certain Relationships Between Fetishism and the Faulty Development of the Body Image. *The Psychoanalytic Study of the Child*, Vol. 8. 1953.

Greenacre, P. Further Considerations Regarding Fetishism. In P. Greenacre, *Emotional Growth: Psychoanalytic Studies of the Gifted and a Great Variety of Other Individuals*, Vol. 1. New York: International Universities Press, 1955.

Greenacre, P. The Childhood of the Artist (1957). *Emotional Growth*, Vol. 2. 1971.

Greenacre, P. Experiences of Awe in Childhood. In Ruth S. Eissler et al. (Eds.), *The Psychoanalytic Study of the Child*, Vol. 11. New York: International Universities Press, 1958.

Greenacre, P. Further Notes on Fetishism (1960). In P. Greenacre, *Emotional Growth: Psychoanalytic Studies of the Gifted and a Great Variety of Other Individuals*, Vol. 1. New York: International Universities Press, 1966.

Greenacre, P. Problems of Overidealization of the Analyst and Analysis: Their Manifestations in the Transference and Countertransference Relationship. *Emotional Growth*, Vol. 1. 1966.

Greenberg, M. First mother rooming-in with their newborns: Its impact on the mother. *Am. J. Orthopsychiatry* 45(5):783–788, 1973.

Greenberg, M., et al. Behavior and cry patterns in the first two hours of life in early and late clamped newborns. *Ann. Paediat. Fenn.* 13:64–70, 1967.

Greenberg, M., et al. *The Father's Relationship to His Newborn in the First Week After Birth.* Unpublished manuscript.

Greenberg, M., and Morris, N. Engrossment: The Newborn's Impact Upon the Father. *Am. J. Orthopsychiatry* 44(4):520–531, 1974.

Greenberg, N. H. The epidemiology of childhood sexual abuse. *Pediatr. Ann.* 8(5):16–28, 1979.

Greenspan, S. I. Intelligence and adaptation: An integration of psychoanalytic and Piagetian developmental psychology. *Psychol. Issues* (Monograph 47/48): 1979.

Greenspan, S. I. Analysis of a five-and-a-half-year-old girl: Implications for a dyadic-phallic phase of development. *J. Am. Psychoanal. Assoc.* 28(3):575–603, 1980.

Greenspan, S. I., Lourie, R. S., and Nover, R. A. A developmental approach to the classification of psychopathology in infancy and early childhood. In J. Noshpitz (Ed.), *The Basic Handbook of Child Psychiatry*, Vol. 2. New York: Basic Books, 1979.

Greven, P. J., Jr. *The Protestant Temperament.* New York: Knopf, 1979.

Grinstein, A. *On Sigmund Freud's Dreams.* Detroit: Wayne State University Press, 1968.

Groddeck, G. *The Book of the It.* New York: Funk & Wagnalls, 1950.

Gunsberg, L. *Father and Child: The Early Years.* New York: Gardner, 1982.

Gurwitt, A. Aspects of Prospective Fatherhood. In Ruth S. Eissler et al. (Eds.), *The Psychoanalytic Study of the Child*, Vol. 31. New York: International Universities Press, 1976.

Gutman, H. G. *The Black Family in Slavery and Freedom, 1750–1929.* New York: Pantheon, 1976.

Hahn, H. H. *The Old Testament in Modern Research* (1954) (expanded ed.). Philadelphia: Fortress Press, 1970.

Handlin, O. *The Uprooted.* Boston: Little, Brown, 1973.

Harlow, H. F. The nature of love. *Am. Psychol.* 13:673–685, 1958.

Harris, L. J. Variances and anomalies. *Science* 206: Oct., 1979.

Hartmann, H. *Ego Psychology and the Problem of Adaptation.* New York: International Universities Press, 1939.

Hartup, W. W. The social world of childhood. *Am. Psychol.* 34:944–950, 1979.

Hays, W. R. *In the Beginning: Early Man and His Gods.* New York: Putnam, 1962.

Heimann, P. A contribution to the re-evaluation of the Oedipus complex: The early stages. *Int. J. Psychoanal.* 23:84–92, 1952.

Herdt, G. H. *Guardians of the Flute.* New York: McGraw-Hill, 1981.

Herzog, E., and Sudia, C. Children in fatherless families. In B. M. Caldwell and H. N. Ricciuti (Eds.), *Review of Child Development Research.* Chicago: Chicago University Press, 1973.

Herzog, J. M. Patterns of parenting. Read to the American Academy of Child Psychiatrists, Houston, Tex., 1977.

Herzog, J. M. Sleep disorder and fatherhunger. Read to The American Academy of Child Psychiatrists, San Diego, Calif., 1978.

Herzog, J. M. Attachment, attunement, and abuse. Read to the Annual Meeting of the American Academy of Child Psychiatrists, Atlanta, 1979.

Herzog, J. M. Macho mania frenzy and despair in 36–60-month-old boys. Unpublished paper.

Herzog, J. M., and Richmond, J. B. From Conception to Delivery. In J. Call (Ed.), *The American Handbook of Child Psychiatry*. New York: Basic Books, 1979.

Hetherington, E. M. Divorce: A child's perspective. *Am. Psychol.* 34:851–858, 1979.

Hoffman, L. W. Early childhood experience and women's achievement motives. *J. Soc. Issues* 28(2): 1972.

Hoffman, L. W. Changes in family roles, socialization and sex differences. *Am. Psychol.* 32:644–658, 1977.

Holmes, P. The etiology of maladjustment in children. *J. Ment. Sci.* 99:654–688, 1959.

Howells, J. Fathering. In J. Howells (Ed.), *Modern Perspectives in International Child Psychiatry*. Edinburgh: Oliver and Boyd, 1969; New York: Brunner-Mazel, 1971.

Hurn, H. T. Synergic relations between the process of fatherhood and psychoanalysis. *J. Am. Psychoanal. Assoc.* 7:324–339, 1969.

Inhelder, B., and Piaget, J. *The Growth of Logical Thinking from Childhood to Adolescence*. New York: Basic Books, 1958.

Ionesco, E. *Victims of Duty*. In E. Ionesco, *Three Plays*. New York: Grove, 1958.

Isaacs, S. An Acute Psychotic Anxiety Occurring in a Boy of Four Years. In S. Isaacs, *Childhood and After*. New York: International Universities Press, 1949a.

Isaacs, S. Fatherless Children. *Childhood and After*. 1949b.

Itani, J. Paternal care in the wild Japanese monkey, macacca fuscata. *J. Primat.* 2(1):61–93, 1959.

Jackson, E. A hospital rooming-in unit for four newborn infants and their mothers. *Pediatrics* 1:28–43, 1948.

Jacobson, E. Development of the Wish for a Child in Boys. In Ruth S. Eissler et al. (Eds.), *The Psychoanalytic Study of the Child*, Vol. 5. New York: International Universities Press, 1950.

Jacobson, E. The Self and the Object World: Vicissitudes of Infantile Cathexis and Their Influence on Ideational and Affective Development. In Ruth S. Eissler et al. (Eds.), *The Psychoanalytic Study of the Child*, Vol. 9. New York: International Universities Press, 1954.

Jacobson, E. On the development of a girl's wishes for a child. *Psychoanal. Q.* 37:523–538, 1968.

Jacques, E. Death and the mid-life crisis. *Int. J. Psychoanal.* 46:502–514, 1965.

Jaffe, D. The masculine envy of woman's procreative functions. *J. Am. Psychoanal. Assoc.* 16:321–548, 1968.

Jarvis, W. Some effects of pregnancy and childbirth on men. *J. Am. Psychoanal. Assoc.* 10:689–700, 1962.

Jessner, L., Weigert, E., and Foy, J. L. The Development of Parental Attitudes during Pregnancy. In E. J. Anthony and T. Benedek (Eds.), *Parenthood*. Boston: Little, Brown, 1970.

Jones, E. Significance of the grandfather for the fate of the individual. In E. Jones, *Papers on Psychoanalysis* (4th ed). Baltimore: William Wood, 1938.

Jones, E. Psychology of childbirth. In E. Jones, *Papers on Psychoanalysis*. Boston: Beacon Press, 1942.

Jones, E. *The Life and Work of Sigmund Freud* (3 vols.). New York: Basic Books, 1953, 1955, 1957.

Jones, E. The early development of female sexuality. In E. Jones, *Papers on Psychoanalysis*. Boston: Beacon Press, 1961a.

Jones, E. The phallic phase. *Papers on Psychoanalysis*. 1961b.

Jung, C. G. Symbols of transformation. In R. F. Hull (Transl.), *Collected Works of Carl G. Jung*, Vol. 5. New York: Pantheon, 1956.

Kafka, F. *Letters to His Father*. Transl. by E. Kaiser and E. Wilkins. New York: Schocken, 1966.

Kahne, M. Personal communication, 1980.

Kakar, S. Aggression in Indian society: An analysis of folk tales. *Indian J. Psychol.* 49(2):119–126, 1974.

Kakar, S. *The Inner World: A Psychoanalytic Study of Childhood and Society in India*. New York: Oxford University Press, 1978.

Kakar, S. *Indian Childhood: Cultural Ideals and Social Reality*. Delhi: Oxford University Press, 1979.

Kalidasa, *Raghuvamsha*. 3.45–46, Transl. by S. Kakar.

Karasic, J. How a child may retain an intact ego despite severe parental abuse (Roche report). *Frontiers of Psychiatry* 9:17, 1979.

Kaufman, I., Peck, A. L., and Taqiuri, C. K. The family constellation and overt incestuous relations between father and daughter. *Am. J. Orthopsychiatry* 24(2):266–279, 1954.

Kaufmann, Y. *The Religion of Israel: From Its Beginning to the Babylonian Exile* (1937–1956). Transl. and abridged by M. Greenberg. Chicago: University of Chicago Press, 1960.

Keller, W., Hildebrandt, K. A., and Richards, M. Effects of extended father-infant contact during the newborn period. Presented to the Society for Research in Child Development, Boston, April, 1981.

Kelly, J., and Wallerstein, J. The effects of parental divorce: Experiences of the child in early latency. *Am. J. Orthopsychiatry* 46(1):20–32, 1976.

Kempe, H., and Helfer, R. *Helping the Battered Child and His Family*. Philadelphia: Lippincott, 1972.

Kennel, J., et al. Maternal behavior one year after early and extended postpartum contact. *Dev. Med. Child Neurol.* 16:172–179, 1974.

Kennel, J., et al. Evidence for a sensitive period in the human mother. Reprinted from *Parent-Infant Interaction* (Ciba Foundation Symposium, no. 33). Amsterdam: Elsevier North-Holland, 1975.

Kernberg, O. *Object Relations Theory and Clinical Psychoanalysis*. New York: Aronson, 1976.

Kessen, W. Human Infancy. In P. Hussen (Ed.), *Carmichael's Manual of Child Psychology*. New York: Wiley, 1970.

Kestenberg, J. On the Development of Maternal Feelings in Early Childhood. In Ruth S. Eissler et al., *The Psychoanalytic Study of the Child*, Vol. 11. New York: International Universities Press, 1956a.

Kestenberg, J. Vicissitudes of female sexuality. *J. Am. Psychoanal. Assoc.* 4:453–476, 1956b.

Kestenberg, J. The role of movement patterns in development: I. Rhythms of movement; II. Flow of tension and effort. *Psychoanal. Q.* 34:1–36; 517–563, 1965.

Kestenberg, J. Outside and inside, male and female. *J. Am. Psychoanal. Assoc.* 16:457–520, 1968.

Kestenberg, J. A developmental approach to disturbances of sex specific identity. *Int. J. Psychoanal.* 52:99–102, 1971.

Kestenberg, J. Notes of parenthood as a developmental phase with special consideration of the roots of fatherhood. Presented at the Spring Meeting of the American Psychiatric Association, Denver, 1974.

Kestenberg, J. *Children and Parents: Psychoanalytic Studies in Development.* New York: Aronson, 1975a.

Kestenberg, J. Parenthood as a developmental phase. *J. Am. Psychoanal. Assoc.* 23:154–166, 1975b.

Kestenberg, J. Regression and reintegration in pregnancy. *J. Am. Psychoanal. Assoc.* 24:213–251, 1976.

Kestenberg, J. Maternity and paternity in the development context: Contribution to integration and differentiation as a procreative person. *Psychiatr. Clin. North Am.* 3(1): 1980a.

Kestenberg, J. The three faces of femininity. *Psychoanal. Rev.* 67(3): 1980b.

Kestenberg, J. Eleven, Twelve, Thirteen: Years of Transition from the Barrenness of Childhood to the Fertility of Adolescence. In S. I. Greenspan and G. H. Pollock (Eds.), *The Course of Life: Psychoanalytic Contributions Toward Understanding Personality Development,* Vol. 2. Washington, D.C.: U.S. Government Printing Office, 1980c.

Kestenberg, J. Parenthood as a Commemorative Phase. In *Volume Commemorating the 25th Anniversary of the Psychoanalytic Division of Downstate University.* New York: Aronson, 1981.

Kestenberg, J., and Marcus, H. Hypothetical Monosex and Bisexuality. In M. C. Nelson and J. Ikenberry (Eds.), *Psychological Imperatives: Their Role in Identity Formation,* Vol. 2. New York: Human Science Press, 1979.

Kestenberg, J., and Sossin, M. *The Role of Movement Patterns in Development II. Epilogue and Glossary.* New York: Dance Notation Bureau.

Kierkegaard, S. *Fear and Trembling* (1843). Transl. by W. Loiorie. Garden City, N.Y.: Doubleday, 1954.

Klaus, M., et al. Maternal attachment: Importance of the first postpartum days. *New Engl. J. Med.* 286:460–463, 1972.

Klaus, M., and Kennell, J. *Maternal-Infant Bonding.* St. Louis: Mosby, 1976.

Kleeman, J. A Boy Discovers His Penis. In Ruth S. Eissler et al. (Eds.), *The Psychoanalytic Study of the Child,* Vol. 20. New York: International Universities Press, 1965.

Kleeman, J. Genital Self-Discovery During a Boy's Second Year. *The Psychoanalytic Studies of the Child,* Vol. 21. 1966.

Klein, M. (1921) The Development of a Child. In M. Klein, *Contributions to Psycho-Analysis.* London: Hogarth, 1948.

Klein, M. Infant Analysis (1923). *Contributions to Psycho-Analysis.* 1948.

Klein, M. Criminal Tendencies in Normal Children (1927). *Contributions to Psycho-Analysis.* 1948.

Klein, M. The Early Development of the Conscience in the Child (1933). *Contributions to Psycho-Analysis.* 1948.

Klein, M. *Envy and Gratitude.* London: Tavistock, 1957.

Kohlberg, L. A Cognitive-Developmental Analysis of Children's Sex-Role Concepts and Attitudes. In E. Maccoby (Ed.), *The Development of Sex Differences.* Palo Alto, Calif.: Stanford University Press, 1966.

Kohut, H. *The Analysis of the Self.* New York: International Universities Press, 1971.

Kohut, H. *The Restoration of the Self.* New York: International Universities Press, 1977.

Kosuke, Y. Unpublished manuscript, 1978.

Kotelchuck, M. The nature of the child's tie to his father. Unpublished Harvard University doctoral dissertation, 1972.

Kotelchuck, M. Father caretaking characteristics and their influence on infant-father interaction. Presented to the American Psychological Association, Chicago, Sept., 1975.

Kotelchuck, M. The Infant's Relationship to the Father: Experimental Evidence. In M. E. Lamb (Ed.), *The Role of the Father in Child Development*. New York: Wiley, 1976.

Kotelchuck, M., and Shaw, L. Inter-reliabilities of Maternal and Paternal Reports of Their Child Care Activities. Unpublished manuscript.

Kouretas, D. The unconscious significance of "Letter to Father" by Kafka. *Med. Ann.* 7(3):251–265, 1967.

Kreitler, H., and Kreitler, S. Children's concept of birth and sexuality. *Child Dev.* 37:363–378, 1966.

Kris, E. *Psychoanalytic Explorations in Art*. New York: International Universities Press, 1952.

Kris, E. Introduction. In Marie Bonaparte et al. (Eds.), *The Origins of Psycho-Analysis: Letters to Wilhelm Fliess, Drafts & Notes, 1887–1902*. New York: Basic Books, 1954.

Kubie, L. The drive to become both sexes. *Psychoanal. Q.* 43:349–426, 1974.

LaBarre, W. *The Ghost Dance*. New York: Doubleday, 1970.

Lacoursiere, R. Fatherhood and mental illness. *Psychiatr. Q.* 46:109–124, 1972a.

Lacoursiere, R. The mental health of the prospective father. *Bull. Menninger Clin.* 36:645–650, 1972b.

Lamb, M. E. Fathers: Forgotten contributors to child development. *Hum. Dev.* 18:245–266, 1975.

Lamb, M. E. *The Role of the Father in Child Development*. New York: Wiley, 1976a.

Lamb, M. E. Effects of stress and cohort on mother-and-father-infant interaction. *Dev. Psychol.* 12:435–443, 1976b.

Lamb, M. E. Interactions Between Eight-Month-Old Children and Their Fathers and Mothers. In M. E. Lamb (Ed.), *The Role of the Father in Child Development*. New York: Wiley, 1976c.

Lamb, M. E. The Role of the Father: An Overview. *The Role of the Father in Child Development*. 1976d.

Lamb, M. E. Twelve-month-olds and their parents: Interaction in a laboratory playroom. *Dev. Psychol.* 12:237–244, 1976e.

Lamb, M. E. Father-infant and mother-infant interaction in the first year of life. *Child Dev.* 48:167–181, 1977a.

Lamb, M. E. The development of mother-infant and father-infant attachment in the second year of life. *Dev. Psychol.* 13:637–648, 1977b.

Lamb, M. E. The development of parental preferences in the first two years of life. *Sex Roles* 3:495–497, 1977c.

Lamb, M. E. The Father's Role in the Infant's Social World. In J. H. Stevens and M. Mathews (Eds.), *Mother/Child, Father/Child Relationships*. Washington, D.C.: National Association for the Education of Young Children, 1978.

Lamb, M. E., and Lamb, J. E. The nature and importance of the father-infant relationship. *Fam. Coordinator* 25:379–385, 1976.

Lampl-de-Groot, J. The Evolution of the Oedipus Complex in Women (1928). In R. Fliess (Ed.), *The Psychoanalytic Reader*. London: Hogarth, 1950.

Lampl-de-Groot, J. The Preoedipal Phase in the Development of the Male Child. In Ruth S. Eissler et al. (Eds.), *The Psychoanalytic Study of the Child*, Vol. 2. New York: International Universities Press, 1947.

Lampl-de-Groot, J. Ego Ideal and Superego. *The Psychoanalytic Study of the Child*, Vol. 17. 1962.

Landis, P. *Making the Most Out of Marriage*. New York: Appleton-Century-Crofts, 1965.

Laye, C. *The Dark Child*. London: Collins, 1955.

Leibowitz, N. *Studies in Bereshit (Genesis): In the Context of Ancient and Modern Jewish Biblical Commentary* (1972). Transl. by A. Newman. 3rd ed. Jerusalem: World Zionist Organization Department for Torah and Culture, 1976.

Leonard, M. Fathers and daughters: The significance of "fathering" in psychosexual development of the girl. *Int. J. Psychoanal.* 47:325–334, 1966.

Lerner, R. M., and Spanier, G. B. (Eds.). *Child Influence on Marital and Family Interaction*. New York: Academic, 1978.

Lerner, S. Grandfathers and other things. Unpublished paper.

Levinson, D. *The Seasons of a Man's Life*. New York: Alfred Knopf, 1978.

Levy, L. D., Stierlin, H., and Savard, R. Fathers and sons: Crisis of integrity and identity. *Psychiatry* 35:48–86, 1972.

Levy, P. Advice and reassurance. *Am. J. Public Health* 44:1113–1118, 1954.

Levy-Strauss, C. *The Savage Mind*. Chicago: University of Chicago Press, 1966.

Lewin, B. D. A type of neurotic hypomanic reaction. *Psychoanal. Rev.* 28:86–91, 1941.

Lewis, D., Shanok, S., and Balla, D. Toward Understanding the Fathers of Juvenile Delinquents: Psychodynamic Medical and Genetic Perspectives. In E. Rexford (Ed.), *A Developmental Approach to Problems of Acting Out*. New York: International Universities Press, 1978.

Lewis, M., and Brooks, J. Infants' Social Perception: A Constructivist View. In L. B. Cohen and P. Salapatek (Eds.), *Infant Perception: From Sensation to Cognition*, Vol. 2. New York: Academic, 1975.

Lewis, M., and Feiring, C. The Child's Social World. In R. M. Lerner and G. D. Spanier (Eds.), *Child Influences on Marital and Family Interaction: A Life-Span Perspective*. New York: Academic, 1978.

Lewis, M., and Rosenblum, L. *The Effect of the Infant on Its Caregiver*. New York: Wiley, 1974.

Lewis, M., and Weinraub, M. The Father's Role in the Child's Social Network. In M. Lamb (Ed.), *The Role of the Father in Child Development*. New York: Wiley, 1976.

Lewis, M., Weinraub, M., and Ban, P. Mothers and fathers, girls and boys: Attachment behavior in the first two years of life. Presented to the Society for Research in Child Development, Philadelphia, March, 1973.

Lichtenberg, J. D. Factors in the development of the sense of object. *J. Am. Psychoanal. Assoc.* 27:375–386, 1979.

Lichtenberg, J. D., and Slap, J. W. Notes on the concept of splitting and the defense mechanism of the splitting of representations. *J. Am. Psychoanal. Assoc.* 21:772–787, 1973.

Lichtenstein, H. *Dilemma of Human Identity*. New York: Aronson, 1977.

Lidz, T. *Birth Without Violence*. New York: Knopf, 1963.

Liebenberg, J. D., and Slap, J. W. Expectant fathers. Presented to the American Orthopsychiatric Association, Washington, D.C., 1967.

Lincoln, Abraham. *The Collected Works of Abraham Lincoln*. Ed. by R. P. Basler. New Brunswick, N.J.: Rutgers University Press, 1953. Vol. 6, pp. 16–17.

Lloyd, D. H. Medical-legal aspects of sexual abuse. *Pediatr. Ann.* 8(5):88–99, 1979.

Loewald, H. W. Ego and reality. *Int. J. Psychoanal.* 32:10–18, 1951.

Loewenstein, R. M. Conflict and Autonomous Ego Development During the Phallic Phase. In Ruth S. Eissler et al. (Eds.), *The Psychoanalytic Study of the Child*, Vol. 5. New York: International Universities Press, 1950.

Loomie, L. S., Rosen, V. H., and Stein, M. H. Ernst Kris and the Gifted Adolescent Project. In Ruth S. Eissler et al. (Eds.), *The Psychoanalytic Study of the Child*, Vol. 13. New York: International Universities Press, 1958.

Lorand, S. Role of the female penis: Fantasy in male character formation. *Int. J. Psychoanal.* 20:171–181, 1939.

Lorenz, K. *On Aggression*. London: Methuen, 1966.

Lourie, R. S. The first three years of life: An overview of a new frontier of psychiatry. *Am. J. Psychiatry* 127:33–39, 1971.

Lucas, Alexander R. Treatment of Depressive States in Psychopharmacology. In J. M. Weiner (Ed.), *Childhood and Adolescence*. New York: Basic Books, 1977.

Lukianowicz, N. Incest: I. Paternal incest. *Br. J. Psychiatry* 120:301–308, 1972.

Luria, Yaacov. The death of a father. *Moment* 4(7):7–8, 1979.

Lusk, S. G. Letter to Sylvester Lusk, Jan. 31, 1840.

Lynn, D. B. *The Father: His Role in Child Development*. Monterey, Calif.: Brooks-Cole, 1974.

MacAlpine, I., and Hunter, R. Observations on the psychoanalytic theory of psychosis. *Br. J. Med. Psychol.* 27:175–192.

Maccoby, E., and Jacklin, C. *The Psychology of Sex Differences*. Stanford, Calif.: Stanford University Press, 1974.

Mahabharata, Vol. 1. Transl. by M. N. Dutta. Calcutta: Oriental Publishing, n.d.

Mahler, M. S. Notes on the development of basic moods: The depressive affect. In R. M. Loewenstein, L. M. Newman, M. Schur, and A. J. Solnit (Eds.), *Psychoanalysis—A General Psychology: Essays in Honor of Heinz Hartmann*. New York: International University Press, 1966.

Mahler, M. S. Discussion of "Healthy Parental Influences in the Earliest Development of Masculinity in Baby Boys." In R. J. Stoller (Ed.), *Psychoanalytic Forum*. New York: International Universities Press, 1975a.

Mahler, M. S. Symbiosis and Individuation: The Psychological Birth of the Human Infant. In Ruth S. Eissler et al. (Eds.), *The Psychoanalytic Study of the Child*, Vol. 29. International Universities Press, 1975b.

Mahler, M. S., and Furer, M. *On Human Symbiosis and the Vicissitudes of Individuation*. New York: International Universities Press, 1968.

Mahler, M. S., and Gosliner, B. On Symbiotic Child Psychosis: Genetic, Dynamic and Restitution Aspects. In Ruth S. Eissler et al. (Eds.), *The Psychoanalytic Study of the Child*, Vol. 10. New York: International Universities Press, 1955.

Mahler, M. S., and Gosliner, M. Discussion of P. Greenacre's problems of over-idealization of the analyst and analysis. *Psychoanal. Q.* 36:637, 1966.

Mahler, M. S., Pine, F., and Bergman, A. *The Psychological Birth of the Human Infant*. New York: Basic Books, 1975.

Main, M. Mother avoiding behaviors: Implications of detachment behavior for social development. Read at the Biannual Meeting of the Society for Research in Child Development, Denver, 1975.

Malmquist, C. *Handbook of Adolescence*. New York: Aronson, 1978.

Marcel, G. *Homo Viator*. New York: Harper & Row, 1962.

Mason, W. Social Development of Monkeys and Apes. In I. Devore (Ed.), *Primate Behavior: Field Studies of Monkeys and Apes*. New York: Holt, Rinehart & Winston, 1965.

Masters, R. E. L. *Patterns of Incest*. New York: Julian Press, 1963.

Mather, C. *Diary of Cotton Mather* (2 vols.). New York: Frederick Ungar, 1969.

McBryde, A. Compulsory rooming-in in the ward and private newborn service at Duke Hospital. *J. Am. Med. Assoc.* 145:625–628, 1951.

McGovern, J. R. *Yankee Family*. New Orleans: Polyanthos, 1975.

McLean, P. D. *A Triune Concept of the Brain and Behavior*. Toronto: University of Toronto Press, 1973.

Mead, M. *Sex and Temperament in Three Primitive Societies*. New York: William & Morrow, 1935.

Mead, M. *Male and Female*. New York: William & Morrow, 1949.

Mead, M. Cultural Determinants of Behavior. In A. Roe and A. Simpson (Eds.), *Behavior and Evolution*. New Haven: Yale University Press, 1958.

Mendes, H. A. Single fathers. *Fam. Coordinator* 25:439–445, 1976.

Meredith, G. *The Ordeal of Richard Feverel* (1859). New York: Holt, Rinehart & Winston, 1964.

Meyer, B. Houdini: The mythmaker. *Psychoanal. Q*. 45:588–611, 1976.

Mill, J. S. *Autobiography*. New York: H. Holt, 1874.

Miller, J. Fathers in the delivery room. *Child Fam*. 3:3–11, 1964.

Miller, J. B. New Issues, New Approaches. In J. B. Miller (Ed.), *Psychoanalysis and Women*. New York: Brunner-Mazel, 1973.

Mitscherlich, A. *Society Without the Father*. London: Tavistock, 1971.

Mohr, J. W., Turner, R. E., and Jerry, M. B. *Pedophilia and Exhibitionism*. Toronto: University of Toronto Press, 1964.

Money, J. Attacking the last taboo. *Time* 115(15):72, 1980.

Money, J., and Ehrhardt, A. *Man and Woman, Boy and Girl*. Baltimore: Johns Hopkins University Press, 1972.

Montgomery, J. Rooming-in of mother and baby in the hospital. *Ill. Med. J*. 102:191–196, 1952.

Morgan, E. *The Puritan Family: Religion and Domestic Relations in Seventeenth-Century New England*. New York: Harper & Row, 1966.

Morris, N. Human relations in obstetrical practice. *Lancet* 1:913–915, 1960.

Moynihan, D. P. The Negro Family: The Case for National Action. In D. P. Moynihan (Ed.), *The Moynihan Report and the Politics of Controversy*. Cambridge, Mass.: Harvard University Press, 1967.

Mussen, P., and Distler, L. Childbearing antecedents of masculine identification in kindergarten boys. *Child Dev*. 31:89–100, 1960.

Nagy, M. Children's birth theories. *J. Genet. Psychol*. 83:217–226, 1953.

Nakashima, I. I., and Zakus, G. Incestuous families. *Pediatr. Ann*. 8(5):29–42, 1979.

Nash, J. The father in contemporary culture and current psychological literature. *Child Dev*. 36:261–297, 1965.

Nelson, J. Anlage of Productiveness in Boys: Womb Envy. In S. Harrison and J. McDermott (Eds.), *Child Psychopathology*. New York: International Universities Press, 1972.

Nemiroff, R., and Colarusso, C. Authenticity and narcissism in the development of the adult self. *Ann. Psychoanal*. 8:74, 1980.

Neubauer, P. The One-Parent Child and His Oedipal Development. In Ruth S. Eissler et al. (Eds.), *The Psychoanalytic Study of the Child*, Vol. 15. New York: International Universities Press, 1960.

Neumann, E. *The Origins and History of Consciousness*. Transl. by R. F. C. Hull. New York: Harper, 1954.

Newton, N., and Mead, M. Cultural Patterning of Perinatal Behavior. In S. Richardson and A. Guttmacher (Eds.), *Childbearing: Its Social and Psychological Aspects*. New York: Williams and Wilkins, 1967.

Niederland, W. The Earliest Dreams of a Young Child. In Ruth S. Eissler et al. (Eds.), *The Psychoanalytic Study of the Child*, Chap. 12. New York: International Universities Press, 1957.

Nunberg, H. *Principles of Psychoanalysis*. New York: International Universities Press, 1932.

Nunberg, H. Circumcision and the problems of bisexuality. *Int. J. Psychoanal.* 28:145–179, 1947.

Offer, D. *The Psychological World of the Teenager*. New York: Basic Books, 1969.

Ostrovsky, E. *Father to the Child*. New York: Putnam, 1959.

Parens, H. Report on workshop: Parenthood as a developmental phase. *J. Am. Psychoanal. Assoc.*

Parens, H. *The Development of Aggression in Early Childhood*. New York: Aronson, 1979.

Parent's Magazine. Family prayer in men of business. May, 1842a. P. 198.

Parent's Magazine. The father. April, 1842b. P. 174.

Parke, R. D. Interactional Design and Experimental Manipulation: The Field-Lab Interface. In R. B. Cairns (Ed.), *Social Interaction: Methods, Analysis and Illustration*. New York: Lawrence Erlbaum, 1978a.

Parke, R. D. Parent-Infant Interaction: Progress, Paradigms and Problems. In G. P. Sackett and H. C. Haywood (Eds.), *Application of Observational-Ethological Methods to the Study of Mental Retardation*. Baltimore: University Press, 1978b.

Parke, R. D. Perspectives on Father-Infant Interaction. In J. D. Osofsky (Ed.), *The Handbook of Infant Development*. New York: Wiley, 1979.

Parke, R. D., and O'Leary, S. E. Father-Mother-Infant Interaction in the Newborn Period: Some Findings, Some Observations and Some Unresolved Issues. In K. Riegel and J. Meacham (Eds.), *The Developing Individual in a Changing World*. Social and Environmental Issues, Vol. 2. The Hague: Mouton, 1976.

Parke, R. D., Power, T. G., Tinsley, B. R., and Hymel, S. The father's role in the family system. *Semin. Perinatol.* 3:25–34, 1979.

Parke, R. D., and Sawin, D. B. The family in early infancy: Social interactional and attitudinal analyses. Presented to the Society for Research in Child Development, New Orleans, March, 1977.

Parsons, T., and Bales, R. F. *Family Socialization and Interaction Process*. Glencoe, Ill.: Free Press, 1954.

Paul, N. Parental Empathy. In E. J. Anthony and T. Benedek (Eds.), *Parenthood*. Boston: Little, Brown, 1970.

Pavenstedt, E. *The Drifters: Children of Disorganized Lower-Class Families*. Boston: Little, Brown, 1967.

Pawson, M., and Morris, N. The role of the father in pregnancy and delivery. Presented at the International Congress of Psychosomatic Medicine in Obstetrics and Gynecology, London, 1971.

Pearson, G. *Adolescence and the Conflict of Generations*. New York: Norton, 1958.

Pedersen, F. A. Mother, father, and infant as an interactive system. Presented to the American Psychological Association, Chicago, 1975.

Pedersen, F. A., Anderson, B. J., and Cain, R. I. An approach to understanding linkages between the parent-infant and spouse relationships. Presented to the Society for Research in Child Development, New Orleans, March, 1977.

Pedersen, F. A., and Robson, K. S. Father participation in infancy. *Am. J. Orthopsychiatry* 39:466–472, 1969.

Pedersen, F. A., Rubenstein, J., and Yarrow, L. J. Father absence in infancy. Presented to the Society for Research in Child Development, Philadelphia, March, 1973.

Pedersen, F. A., Rubenstein, J., and Yarrow, L. J. Infant development in father-absent families. *J. Genet. Psychol.*, 1978.

Pedersen, F. A., Yarrow, L. J., Anderson, B. J., and Cain, R. L. Conceptualization of Father Influences in the Infancy Period. In M. Lewis and L. Rosenblum (Eds.), *The Child and Its Family*. New York: Plenum, 1979.

Piaget, J. *The Child's Conception of the World*. New York: Harcourt, Brace, 1929.

Piaget, J. *The Child's Conception of Physical Causality*. New York: Harcourt, Brace, 1930.

Piaget, J. The Stages of Intellectual Development of the Child (1962). In S. I. Harrison and J. F. McDermott (Eds.), *Childhood Psychopathology*. New York: International Universities Press, 1972.

Piaget, J. *Structuralism* (1968). New York: Basic Books, 1970.

Piaget, J. The Intellectual Development of the Adolescent. In G. Caplan and S. Lebovici (Eds.), *Adolescence: Perspectives*. New York: Basic Books, 1969.

Piaget, J., and Inhelder, R. *The Psychology of the Child*. New York: Basic Books, 1969.

Prall, R. C. The role of the father in the preoedipal years (panel discussion). *J. Am. Psychoanal. Assoc.* 26:143–162, 1978.

Pumpian-Mindlin, E. Omnipotentiality, youth and commitment. *J. Am. Acad. Child Psychiatry* 4:1–19, 1965.

Radin, N. Father-child interaction and the intellectual functioning of four-year-old boys. *Dev. Psychol.* 6:353–361, 1972.

Radin, N. Observed paternal behaviors as antecedents of intellectual functioning. *Dev. Psychol.* 8:369–376, 1973.

Radin, N. The Role of the Father in Cognitive, Academic, and Intellectual Development. In M. E. Lamb (Ed.), *The Role of the Father in Child Development*. New York: Wiley, 1976.

Rado, S. A critical examination of the concept of bisexuality. *Psychosom. Med.* 2:459–467, 1940.

Rangell, L. The interchangeability of phallus and female genital. *J. Am. Psychoanal. Assoc.* 1:504–509, 1953a.

Rangell, L. The role of the parent in the Oedipus complex. *Bull. Menninger Clin.* 19:9–15, 1953b.

Rapid transit and home life. *Harper's Bazaar*. Dec., 1900. P. 200.

Rappaport, E. The grandfather syndrome. *Psychoanal. Q.* 27:518–538, 1958.

Rebelsky, F., and Hanks, C. Father's verbal interaction with infants in the first three months of life. *Child Dev.* 42:63–68, 1971.

Reich, A. Narcissistic object choice in women. *J. Am. Psychoanal. Assoc.* 1:22–44, 1953.

Reik, T. *Ritual*. New York: International Universities Press, 1919.

Reik, T. *The Psychological Problems of Religion*. New York: Farrar, Strauss, 1946.

Rendina, I., and Dickerscheid, J. D. Father involvement with first-born infants. *Fam. Coordinator* 25:373–379, 1976.

Rheingold, H. The modification of social responsiveness in institutional babies. *Society for Research in Child Development* (Monograph): 1956.

Ricketts, H. T. Letter to Myra Tubbs. July, 1896.

Ritvo, S. Late Adolescence. In Ruth S. Eissler et al. (Eds.), *The Psychoanalytic Study of the Child*, Vol. 26. New York: International Universities Press, 1971.

Ringler, N. M., et al. Mother-to-child: Speech at two years. *Behav. Pediat.* 86:141–144, 1975.

Rizzuto, A.-M. *The Birth of the Living God—A Psychoanalytic Study*. Chicago: University of Chicago Press, 1979.

Rodholm, M., and Larsson, K. Father-infant interaction at the first contact after delivery. *Early Hum. Dev.* 3:21–27, 1979.

Roheim, G. *Psychoanalysis and Anthropology*. New York: International Universities Press, 1950.

Rohrer, H., and Edmonson, M. *The Eighth Generation*. New York: Harper, 1960.

Roiphe, H. On an Early Genital Phase. In Ruth S. Eissler et al. (Eds.), *The Psychoanalytic Study of the Child*, Vol. 23. New York: International Universities Press, 1968.

Rose, G. Pregenital aspects of pregnancy fantasies. *Int. J. Psychoanal.* 42:544–549, 1961.

Rose, G. Unconscious birth fantasies and narcissism. *J. Am. Psychoanal. Assoc.* 17:1015–1029, 1962.

Rose, G. Transference birth fantasies and narcissism. *J. Am. Psychoanal. Assoc.*, 1969.

Rose, G., et al. The evidence for a syndrome of mothering disability consequent to threats of survival of neonates: A design for hypothesis testing including prevention in a prospective study. *Am. J. Dis. Child*, 1960.

Rosenberg, J. Torah and interpretation: Literary notes on the Midrashic process. *Response* 9(2):67–94, 1975.

Rosenblatt, J. S. The development of maternal responsiveness in the rat. *Am. J. Orthopsychiatry* 39:36, 1969.

Ross, J. The children's children: A psychoanalytic study of generativity and nurturance in boys. Unpublished New York University Ph.D. Thesis, 1974.

Ross, J. The development of paternal identity: A critical review of the literature on nurturance and generativity in boys and men. *J. Am. Psychoanal. Assoc.* 23:783–817, 1975.

Ross, J. Toward fatherhood: The epigenesis of paternal identity during a boy's first decade. *Int. J. Psychoanal.* 4:327–347, 1977.

Ross, J. Fathering: A review of some psychoanalytic contributions on paternity. *Int. J. Psychoanal.* 60:317–328, 1979.

Ross, J. Notes on paternal identity and its developmental line. Unpublished paper.

Ross, N. Rivalry with the product. *J. Am. Psychoanal. Assoc.* 8:450–463, 1960.

Rossi, A. A biosocial perspective on parenting. *Daedalus* 106:1–32, 1977.

Rossi, A. Life span theories and women's lives. *J. Women Culture Soc.* 6:4–32, 1980.

Rothman, E. K. Intimate acquaintance: Courtship and the transition to marriage in America, 1770–1900. Unpublished Brandeis University Ph.D. Thesis, 1980.

Rotundo, E. A. Manhood in America, 1770–1910. Unpublished Brandeis University Ph.D. Thesis, 1981.

Rubin, L. B. *Women of a Certain Age: The Midlife Search for Self*. New York: Harper & Row, 1979.

Russell, S. Letter to Thomas Russell. Jan. 16, 1845.

Rutter, M. Parent-child separation: Psychological effects on the children. *J. Child Psychol. Psychiatry* 12:233–260, 1971.

Sacher, E. J., et al. Child molesters—Assessment and treatment (Roche Report). *Frontiers on Psychiatry* 9:16, 1979.

Sagan, C. *The Dragons of Eden: Speculations on the Evolution of Human Intelligence*. New York: Random House, 1977.

Samaraweera, S. The need for early intervention in infancy. Presented at the Annual Symposium of the New England Council of Child Psychiatry, Boston, 1974.

Samaraweera, S. A program of primary prevention in infancy. Presented at the 8th International Congress of Child Psychiatry, Philadelphia, 1975.

Samaraweera, S. Issues in Paternity (discussion group, S. Cath chairman). American Psychoanalytic Association, New York, Dec., 1979.

Sander, L. Issues in early mother-child interaction. *J. Am. Acad. Child Psychiatry* 1:141–146, 1962.

Sandler, J., and Sandler, A. M. On the development of object relationships and affects. *Int. J. Psychoanal.* 59:285–296, 1978.

Sandler, L., Julia, H., Stechler, J., Burns, P., and Gould, J. Some Determinants of Temporal Organization in the Ecological Niche of the Newborn. In H. R. Schatter (Ed.), *Studies in Mother-Infant Interaction*. New York: Academic, 1977.

Sarna, N. M. *Understanding Genesis* (1966). New York: Schocken Books, 1970.

Sarnoff, C. A. The Work of Latency. In C. A. Sarnoff, *Latency*. New York: Aronson, 1976.

Sarnoff, C. A. Developmental considerations in the psychotherapy of latency-age children. *Int. J. Psychoanal. Psychother.* 7:283–301, 1979.

Sartre, J.-P. *The Words*. New York: G. Braziller, 1964.

Schaefer, E. S. The ecology of child development: Implications for research and the professions. Presented to the American Psychological Association, New Orleans, Aug., 1974.

Schaefer, R. *Aspects of Internalization*. New York: International Universities Press, 1968.

Schaffer, H. R. Early Interactive Development. In H. R. Schaffer (Ed.), *Studies in Mother-Infant Interaction*. New York: Academic, 1977.

Schaffer, H. R., and Emerson, P. E. A development of social attachments in infancy. *Society for Research in Child Development* (Monograph 29):1964.

Schecter, D. The ideal self and others. *Contemp. Psychoanal.* 10:103–115, 1974.

Schoggen, P. Environmental Forces in the Everyday Lives of Children. In R. G. Barker (Ed.), *The Stream of Behavior: Explorations of the Structure and Content*. New York: Appleton-Century-Crofts, 1963.

Schultz, L. G. Intervention in child sex abuse debated. *Clin. Psychiatr. News* 8(4):12, 1980.

Schur, M. *Freud: Living and Dying*. New York: International Universities Press, 1972.

Schwartzman, M. Fathering: The vicissitudes of the father-child relationship in normal and abnormal development. Yeshiva University Ph.D. Thesis, in progress.

Schreber, D. *Memoirs of My Nervous Illness*. Ed. by I. MacAlpine and R. Hunter. Cambridge, Mass.: Bentley, 1955.

Sears, R. R., Maccoby, E. E., and Levin, H. *Patterns of Child Rearing*. New York: Row, Peterson, 1957.

Sewall, S. *The Diary of Samuel Sewall, 1674–1729*, 2 vols. Ed. by M. H. Thomas. New York: Farrar, Straus, & Giroux, 1973.

Sendak, M. *Where the Wild Things Are*. New York: Harper & Row, 1963.

Seton, P. The psychotemporal adaptation of late adolescence. *J. Am. Psychoanal. Assoc.* 22:795–819.

Sgrol, S. M. Pediatric gonorrhea beyond infancy. *Pediatr. Ann.* 8(5):73–89, 1979.

Shakespeare, W. *King Lear.* Ed. by G. L. Kittredge. Boston: Ginn, 1940.

Shane, M. A rationale for teaching analytic technique based on a developmental orientation and approach. *Int. J. Psychoanal.* 58:95–108, 1977.

Shapin, T., and Perry, R. Latency Revisited. In Ruth S. Eissler et al. (Eds.), *The Psychoanalytic Study of the Child*, Vol. 31. New York: International Universities Press, 1976.

Sherfey, J. J. The evolution and nature of female sexuality in relation to psychoanalytic theory. *J. Am. Psychoanal. Assoc.* 14:28–128, 1966.

Shorter, E. *The Making of the Modern Family.* New York: Basic Books, 1975.

Sigel, I. The Distancing Hypothesis: A Causal Hypothesis for the Acquisition of Representational Thought. In M. Jones (Ed.), *Miami Symposium on the Prediction of Behavior, 1968: Effects of Early Experiences.* Coral Gables, Fla.: University of Miami Press, 1970.

Sigourney, L. The Intemperate. In L. Sigourney, *Sketches.* Amherst, Mass.: 1834.

Simenauer, E. "Pregnancy envy" in Ranier Maria Rilke. *Am. Imago* 11:235–248, 1954.

Siskind, A. A negotiation of the father-son relationship in normal adolescence. Unpublished Smith College School of Social Work Thesis, 1972.

Sitwell, S. *Mozart.* New York: Appleton, 1932.

Snyder, B. R., and Tessman, L. H. Creativity in Gifted Students and Scientists. In H. H. Andersen (Ed.), *Creativity in Childhood and Adolescence.* Palo Alto, Calif.: Science and Behavior Books, 1965.

Socarides, C. W. The development of a fetishist perversion. *J. Am. Psychoanal. Assoc.* 8:281–311, 1960.

Socarides, C. W. *The Overt Homosexual.* New York: Grune & Stratton, 1968; Aronson (reissued), 1970.

Socarides, C. W. A psycho-analytic study of the desire for sexual transformation (transsexualism). *Int. J. Psychoanal.* 45:227–236, 1970.

Socarides, C. W. Discussion of "Healthy" Parental Influences in the Earliest Development of Masculinity in Baby Boys. In R. J. Stoller, *Psychoanalytic Forum.* New York: International Universities Press, 1975.

Socarides, C. W. *Homosexuality.* New York: Aronson, 1978.

Socarides, C. W. Some problems encountered in the psychoanalytic treatment of overt male homosexuality. *Am. J. Psychother.* 33:506–520, 1979.

Solnit, A. Psychosexual Development: Three to Five Years. In J. Noshpitz (Ed.), *Basic Handbook of Child Psychiatry*, Vol. 1. New York: Basic Books, 1979.

Spelke, E., Zelazo, P., Kagan, J., and Kotelchuck, M. Father interaction and separation protest. *Dev. Psychol.* 9:83–90, 1973.

Sperling, M. A case of ophidiophilia. *Int. J. Psychoanal.* 45:227–236, 1964.

Spiegel, S. *The Last Trial: On the Legend and Lore of the Command to Abraham to Offer Isaac as a Sacrifice: The Akedah* (1950). Transl. by J. Goldin, New York: Schocken Books, 1969.

Spitz, R. Hospitalization: An Inquiry into the Genesis of Psychiatric Conditions in Early Childhood. In Ruth S. Eissler et al. (Eds.), *The Psychoanalytic Study of the Child*, Vols. 1 and 2. New York: International Universities Press, 1945, 1946.

Spitz, R. Autoerotism Re-Examined. In Ruth S. Eissler et al. (Eds.), *The Psychoanalytic Study of the Child*, Vol. 17. New York: International Universities Press, 1962.

Spitz, R. *The First Year of Life.* New York: International Universities Press, 1965.

Spitz, R., Emde, R., and Metcalf, D. Further prototypes of ego formation. *Psychoanal. Study Child* 25:417–444, 1970.

Sroufe, L., and Waters, E. Attachment as an organizational construct. *Child Dev.* 48:1184–1199, 1977.

Sroufe, A., Waters, E., and Matas, L. Contextual Determinants of Infant Affective Responses. In M. Lewis and L. Rosenblum (Eds.), *The Origins of Fear.* New York: Wiley, 1974.

Starr, C. *Anthropology To-Day.* Del Mar, Calif.: C. R. M. Books, 1971.

Stender, F. *Fathers in the Delivery Room.* Bellevue, Wash.: International Childbirth Education Association, 1968.

Stephens, J. *The Crock of Gold.* London: MacMillan, 1912.

Stern, D. N. Mother and Infant at Play: The Dyadic Interaction Involving Facial, Vocal and Gaze Behaviors. In M. Lewis and L. Rosenblum (Eds.), *The Effects of the Infant on Its Caregivers.* New York: Wiley, 1974a.

Stern, D. N. The goal and structure of mother-infant play. *J. Am. Acad. Child Psychiatry* 13:402–421, 1974b.

Stern, D. N. Temporal Expectancies of Social Behaviors in Mother-Infant Play. In E. Thoman (Ed.), *The Origins of the Infant's Responsiveness.* New York: Erlbaum, 1977.

Stern, M. M. Fear and death and neurosis. *J. Am. Psychoanal. Assoc.* 16:3–31, 1968.

Stierlin, H. *Separating Parents and Adolescents.* Quadrangle: New York Times Book Co., 1972.

Stone, L. The Family, Sex, and Marriage in England, 1500–1800. New York: Harper & Row, 1977.

Stoller, J. J. *Sex and Gender.* New York: Science House, 1968.

Stoller, R. J. Bisexualité et différences des sexes. *Nouvelle Revue de Psychoanalyse,* 1973.

Stoller, R. J. Healthiest parental influences on the earliest development of masculinity in baby boys. *Psychoanal. Forum* 5:232–262, 1975.

Stoller, R. J. Primary femininity. *J. Am. Psychoanal. Assoc.* 24:59–78, 1976.

Stoller, R. J. Fathers of transexual children. *J. Am. Psychoanal. Assoc.* 27:837–866, 1979.

Stolz, L., et al. *Father Relations of War-Born Children.* Stanford, Calif.: Stanford University Press, 1954.

Stone, L., Smith, H. T., and Murphy, L. B. *The Competent Infant.* New York: Basic Books, 1973.

Sullivan, J., and McDonald, D. Newborn Orientated Paternal Behavior: Implications for Concepts of Parenting. In J. G. Howells (Ed.), *Modern Perspectives in the Psychiatry of Infancy.* New York: Brunner-Mazel, 1979.

Sunley, R. Early Nineteenth-Century American Literature on Child Rearing. In M. Mead and M. Wolfenstein (Eds.), *Childhood and Contemporary Cultures.* Chicago: University of Chicago Press, 1955.

Sutherland, J. The self and personal object relations. Unpublished, 1978.

Tasch, R. J. The role of the father in the family. *J. Exp. Educ.* 20:319–361, 1952.

Teicher, J. The alienated, older isolated male adolescent. *J. Am. Psychother.* 26:401–407, 1972.

Tennes, K., Emde, R., Kisley, A., and Metcalf, D. The Stimulus Barrier in Early Infancy: An Exploration of Some Formations of John Benjamin. In R. Holt and E. Peterfreund (Eds.), *Psychoanalysis and Contemporary Science.* New York: Macmillan, 1972.

Tessman, L. H. *Children of Parting Parents.* New York: Aronson, 1978.

Tessman, L. H., and Kaufman, I. Variations on a Theme of Incest. In O. Pollack and A. Friedman (Eds.), *Family Dynamics and Female Sexual Delinquency.* Palo Alto, Calif.: Science and Behavior Books, 1969.

Tinbergen, N. *Social Behavior in Animals*. London: Methuen, 1953.

Tooley, K. Antisocial behavior and social alienation—post divorce: The man in the house of his mother. *Am. J. Orthopsychiatry* 46:33–43, 1976.

Towne, R. D., and Afterman, J. Psychosis in males related to parenthood. *Bull. Menninger Clin.* 19:19–26, 1955.

Trethowan, W. Sympathy pains. *Discovery* 26:30–34, 1965.

Trethowan, W., and Conlon, M. F. The couvade syndrome. *Br. J. Psychiatry* 111:57–66, 1965.

Trollope, A. *The Warden* (1855). New York: Dumont, Parliament edition, n.d.

Trollope, A. *Framley Parsonage* (1860). New York: Dumont, Parliament edition, n.d.

Trollope, A. *The Last Chronicle of Barset* (1867). New York: Dumont, Parliament edition, n.d.

Tronick, E. An ontogenetic structure of face-to-face interaction and its developmental functions. Presented to the Society for Research in Child Development, New Orleans, 1977.

Trosman, H. The cryptomnesic fragment in the discovery of free association. *J. Am. Psychoanal. Assoc.* 17:489–510, 1969.

Trosman, H. Freud's adolescence and the prolegomena to psychoanalysis. *J. Youth Adolesc.* 7:215–222, 1978.

Tyler, E. Researches into the early history of mankind. In C. S. Ford (Ed.), *Cross Cultural Approaches: Readings in Comparative Research*. New Haven, Conn.: Human Relations Area Files Press, 1967.

Valliant, G. *Adaptation to Life*. Boston: Little, Brown, 1977.

Van der Leeuw, P. J. The Preoedipal Phase of the Male. In Ruth S. Eissler et al. (Eds.), *The Psychoanalytic Study of the Child*, Vol. 13. New York: International University Press, 1958.

Van Leeuwen, K. Pregnancy envy in the male. *Int. J. Psychoanal.* 47:319–324, 1966.

Vellay, P. *Childbirth Without Pain*. New York: Dutton, 1960.

Vygotsky. Quoted in A. R. Luria, *A Cognitive Development: Its Cultural and Social Foundations*. Cambridge, Mass.: Harvard University Press, 1976.

Wallerstein, J. Contributions of studies of divorce: The impact of divorce on children. *Psychiatr. Clin. North Am.* 3(3):1980.

Wallerstein, J., and Kelly, J. The Effects of Parental Divorce: The Adolescent Experience. In J. Anthony and C. Koupernik (Eds.), *The Child in His Family: Children at Psychiatric Risk*. New York: Wiley, 1974. Vol. 3, pp. 479–505.

Wallerstein, J., and Kelly, J. The effects of parental divorce: The experiences of the preschool child. *J. Am. Acad. Child Psychiatry* 14(4):600–616, 1975.

Wallerstein, J., and Kelly, J. The effects of parental divorce: Experiences of the child in later latency. *Am. J. Orthopsychiatry* 46(2):256–269, 1976.

Wallerstein, J., and Kelly, J. *Surviving the Break-up: How Children and Parents Cope with Divorce*. New York: Basic Books, 1980.

Warner, S. B., Jr. *Streetcar Suburbs*. Cambridge, Mass.: Harvard University Press, 1963.

Weil, A. M. The Basic Core. In Ruth S. Eissler et al. (Eds.), *The Psychoanalytic Study of the Child*, Vol. 25. New York: International Universities Press, 1970.

Weinberg, J. Personal communication, 1980.

Weinstein, F., and Platt, G. *The Wish to Be Free: Society, Psyche, and Value Change*. Berkeley: University of California Press, 1969.

Weinraub, M. Fatherhood: The Myth of the Second-Class Parent. In J. H. Stevens and M. Mathews (Eds.), *Mother-Child, Father-Child Relationships*.

Washington, D.C.: National Association for the Education of Young Children, 1978.

Weisman, A. *The Existential Core of Psychoanalysis: Reality Sense and Responsibility*. Boston: Little, Brown, 1972a.

Weisman, A. *On Dying and Denying*. New York: Human Services Press, 1972b.

Weissman, P. The effects of preoedipal paternal attitudes on development and character. *Int. J. Psychoanal.* 44:121–131, 1963.

Wellhausen, J. *Prolegomena to the History of Israel* (1883). Transl. by J. S. Black and A. Menzies. Edinburgh: Adam and Charles Black, 1885.

Welter, B. The cult of true womanhood, 1820–1860. *Am. Q.* 18:151–174, 1966.

Werner, H. *Psychology of Mental Development*. New York: Science Editors, 1948.

White, R. Motivation reconsidered: The concept of competence. *Psychol. Rev.* 66:297–333, 1959.

Wiesel, E. *Messengers of God: Biblical Portraits and Legends*. Trans. by M. Wiesel. New York: Random House, 1976.

Winnicott, D. W. Transitional objects and transitional phenomena. *Int. J. Psychoanal.* 34:89–97, 1953.

Winnicott, D. W. *Mother and Child*. New York: Basic Books, 1957.

Winnicott, D. W. *Collected Papers*. New York: Basic Books, 1958.

Winnicott, D. W. Communicating and Not Communicating Leading to a Study of Certain Opposites. In D. W. Winnicott (Ed.), *The Maturational Processes and the Facilitating Environment*. New York: International Universities Press, 1963.

Winnicott, D. W. *The Child, the Family and the Outside World*. Harmondsworth, Eng.: Penguin, 1964.

Winnicott, D. W. The Mother-Infant Experience of Mutuality. In E. J. Anthony and T. Benedek (Eds.), *Parenthood, its Psychology and Psychopathology*. Boston: Little, Brown, 1970.

Winnicott, D. W. *Playing and Reality*. London: Tavistock, 1971.

Wishy, B. *The Child and the Republic*. Philadelphia: University of Pennsylvania Press, 1968.

Wittig, M. A., and Petersen, A. C. (Eds.), *Sex Related Differences in Cognitive Functioning*. New York: Academic, 1979.

Wolff, P. Observations on the Early Development of Smiling. In B. Foss (Ed.), *Determinants of Infant Behavior*, Vol. 2. New York: Wiley, 1963.

Wolff, P. The Causes, Controls, and Organization of Behavior in the Neonate. *Psychol. Issues* (Monograph 17): 1966.

Wright, F. L. *An Autobiography*. New York: Longmans Green, 1932.

Wright, M. F. *Recording and Analyzing Child Behavior*. New York: Harper & Row, 1967.

Wyllie, I. G. *The Self-Made Man in America. The Myth of Rags to Riches*. New Brunswick, N.J.: Rutgers University Press, 1954.

Yogman, M. W. The goals and structure of face-to-face interaction between infants and fathers. Presented to the Society for Research in Child Development, New Orleans, March, 1977.

Yogman, M. W. Development of the Father-Infant Relationship. In H. Fitzgerald, B. Lester, and M. W. Yogman (Eds.), *Theory and Research in Behavioral Pediatrics*, Vol. 1. New York: Plenum, 1981.

Yogman, M. W., Dixon, S., Tronick, E., Adamson, L., Als, H., and Brazelton, T. B. Father-infant interaction. Presented to the American Pediatric Society; Society for Pediatric Research, St. Louis, April, 1976a.

Yogman, M. W., Dixon, S., Tronick, E., Adamson, L., Als, H., and Brazelton,

T. B. Development of social interaction of infants with fathers. Presented to the Eastern Psychological Association, New York, 1976b.

Yogman, M. W., Dixon, S., Tronick, E., Adamson, L., Als, H., and Brazelton, T. B. Parent-infant interaction under stress: The study of a temperamentally difficult infant. Presented to the American Academy of Child Psychiatrists, Toronto, 1976c.

Yorukoglu, A., and Kemph, J. P. Children not severely damaged by incest with a parent. *J. Am. Acad. Child Psychiatry* 5:111–124, 1966.

Young, J. C., and Hamilton, M. E. Paternal Behavior: Implications for Child-rearing Practice. In J. H. Stevens and M. Mathews (Eds.), *Mother/Child, Father/Child Relationships*. Washington, D.C.: National Association for the Education of Young Children, 1978.

Zetzel, E. (1949) Anxiety and the Capacity to Bear It. In E. Zetzel, *Capacity for Emotional Growth*. New York: International Universities Press, 1970.

Zetzel, E. (1965) On the Capacity to Bear Depression. *The Capacity for Emotional Growth*. 1970.

Zilboorg, G. Depressive reactions related to parenthood. *Am. J. Psychiatry* 10:927–962, 1931.

Zilboorg, G. Masculine and feminine. *Psychiatry* 7:257–296, 1944.

Zinaldin, J. S. The emergence of a modern American family law: Child custody, adoption, and the courts, 1796–1851. *Northwestern University Law Review* 73:1038–1089, 1979.

Indexes

Name Index

Subject Index